LAW AND CRIMINAL JUSTICE: A CRITICAL INQUIRY

Studies Series in association with the Athenian Policy Forum, Inc.

Studies in Law and Public Policy

Law and Criminal Justice: A Critical Inquiry
Edited by L.A. Visano

Studies in Economic Transformation and Public Policy

Exchange Rates, Economic Integration and the International Economy
Edited by Leo Michelis and Mark Lowell (2004)

The State of the Welfare State Anno 1992 and Beyond
Edited by J. Pacolet (2002)

Trade, Competitiveness and Social Protection
Edited by J. Pacolet and E. Claessens (2002)

The Global Economy: Financial Monetary, Trade and Knowledge Asymmetries
Edited by M. Hayford, A. Malliaris and M. Malliaris (2003)

Asymmetries in Financial Globalization
Edited by B. Batavia, N. Lash and A. Malliaris (2002)

Globalization and Economic Growth
Edited by T. Georgakopoulos, C. Paraskevopoulos and J. Smithin (2002)

Money and Finance in the Global Economy
Edited by A. Kintis, P. Koveos, C. Paraskevopoulos and N. Baltas (2002)

Globalization and the Political Economy of Trade Policy
Edited by C. Paraskevopoulos, A. Kintis and A. Kondonassis (2001)

The Asymmetric Global Economy: Growth, Investment and Public Policy
Edited by C. Paraskevopoulos, T. Georgakopoulos and L. Michelis (2001)

An Introduction to Economic Evaluation in Health Care: Methods and Case Studies
M. Marzouk (2001)

LAW AND CRIMINAL JUSTICE: A CRITICAL INQUIRY

Edited by

L.A. Visano

STUDIES IN LAW AND PUBLIC POLICY

APF Press
Toronto, CANADA

Published by APF Press
51 Havenbrook Blvd.
Toronto, Ontario M2J 1A7
CANADA

All remuneration from this book to the editor shall be donated to the *Toronto Youth for Humanity*.

Printed in Canada by Brown Book Company (BBC) Limited

Library and Archives Canada Cataloguing in Publication

Law and criminal justice : a critical inquiry / edited by L.A. Visano.

(Studies in law and public policy)
Includes bibliographical references.

1. Criminal justice, Administration of. 2. Criminal law.
I. Visano, L. A. II. Series.

K5000.L39 2005 364 C2005-906128-6

ISBN 1-894490-17-7

To all those students who have had the courage to speak out,
From whom we have all learned so much

In the eyes of the other, justice punishes the corner drug dealer,
In the eyes of a mother, the dealer, the addict, the criminal is the child she loves;

In the eyes of the other, harsh laws alone will stop the drug epidemic,
In the eye of a mother, the police respect those of "value", wealthy or white;

In the eyes of the other, a judge who is soft on the first time offender reinforces crime,
In the eyes of a mother, a judge's sentence is destruction, and in her heart she cries for peace;

In the eyes of the other, the criminal's mother has absolutely no say,
In the eyes of a mother, does "justice" as love not always learn from the past?

With fallen dreams, I sit alone,
Waiting for all lost children to find their way back home.
(N.M. 2005)

THE ATHENIAN Policy Forum Inc.

"Our constitution...is called a democracy because power is in the hands of not a minority but of the greatest number"

Thucydides II, 37

"We Athenians, in our own persons, take our decisions on policy or submit them to proper discussions: for we do not think that there is an incompatibility between words and deeds; the worst thing is to rush into action before the consequences have been properly debated"

Thucydides II, 40
(Thucydides (460-400 B.C.) Pericles' Funeral Oration)

Contents

CONTRIBUTORS

Claudius Alexander is entering his fourth year of Ph.D. studies in the department of Social & Political Thought at Toronto's York University, where he also earned B.A and M.A. degrees in Political Science. Aside from his more strictly political intellectual interests, Mr. Alexander has over the years given significant time to understanding (European) educational philosophy as developed from the Enlightenment period forward. He is currently working on what he broadly titles the *Politico-Economic [Dis]Incentivesof Higher Education*, a title he uses to constitute the complex of constraints working to exclude certain social/cultural groups from the realm higher education, and an exclusion he sees as in many ways consciously and deliberately maintained by the professoriate itself.

David N. Baker is an Assistant Professor in the Department of Criminal Justice, College of Health and Human Services, University of Toledo. He earned a Ph.D. in Sociology from York University. His research interests include race and crime, critical criminology, white collar crime (predatory lending), community policing, the criminal justice system and the mass media.

Teneeka Barnett, is a Master of Arts candidate in the Department of Interdisciplinary Studies at York University whose work involves the synthesis of three disciplines: Law, Women's Studies and Sociology. Her research centers around critical examinations into the way Black Canadians and Black women in particular are framed within criminal justice. Her research seeks to explore the potential of law to simultaneously institute and combat racism. Prior to full time studies at York, Teneeka studied at Carleton University where she obtained a Bachelor of Arts (Honours) degree in Law.

Paul Baxter is a Doctoral Candidate, Department of Political Studies Queen's University. He has pent six years teaching and developing curriculum for the Justice and Public Safety Institute and the Institute of University Partnerships and Advanced Studies at Georgian College. He is currently, an Assistant Professor (contractually limited appointment) in the Faculty of Arts, Division of Social Sciences, Criminology, at York University.

Glenn Betteridge is a Senior Policy Analyst at the Canadian HIV/AIDS Legal Network. Before joining the Network, he practised law in a clinic serving the legal needs of low income people living with HIV/AIDS. He may be contacted at gbetteridge@aidslaw.ca.

Stephen E. Bosanac received his HBA Sociology and BA Psychology with Minors in Indigenous Learning and Religious Studies in 1998 from Lakehead University in Thunder Bay, Ontario, Canada. Then, after taking seventeen months off from school for health reasons, he resumed his studies at Lakehead in 1999 and received an MA Sociology in 2001. His MA work included an in-depth analysis of Karl Mannheim's sociology of knowledge. He is presently a Ph.D. candidate and fellow in the sociology program at York University where he is currently focusing on the political economy of cyberspace and the potential effects of an overly empirical approach to sociological knowledge.

Paul Brienza is completing his doctoral dissertation in the Department of Sociology at York University. He has previously published on the dilemmas of a humanistic concern with drug addiction treatment and the works of Italian thinker Antonio Gramsci. He is presently working on the relationship between the thought of Giambattista Vico and ancient and present concerns with general issues of justice and community. His research focuses on a critique of knowledge-based accounts and understandings of justice and tries to place such abstract issues within the purview of everyday existence within historically delimited communities.

Claudio Colaguori has a PhD in sociology from York University. He lectures in the Department of Sociology at The University of Toronto and at York University. His current research interests are crime media and the new authoritarianism and the agonistic configurations of culture. He is a recipient of The 'John O'Neill Award for Teaching Excellence' in Sociology at York University

Naomi Couto successfully defended her Ph.D dissertation in April 2005. She is currently teaching Sociological Theory, Political Sociology, and Women in the Criminal Justice System in the Sociology Department at York University, Canada. She has also taught a number of courses at Humber College.

Wesley Crichlow is a tenured Associate Professor in the School of Social Science-University of Ontario Institute for Technology. He holds a Ph.D from the University of Toronto and certificates in Alternative Dispute Resolution and Ontario Civil Justice Review. His research interests are Black youth gang violence; social inequality; theoretical and legal approaches to the study of race; human rights; racial profiling & driving while Black; the racialization of alternative dispute resolution; moral regulation; racialized gay and lesbian rights; critical appraisal of youth restorative justice; new immigrant employment & accreditation training; judicial reform; and section 15 criminal law charter challenges. He is the author of "Buller Men & Batty Bwoys: Hidden Men in Toronto and Halifax's Black Communities"(University of Toronto Press 2003), and has published extensively in refereed journals and in edited volumes.

Peter Della Sciucca , B.A(Hons.), B.Ed, L.L.B, is a member of the Ontario College of Teachers and the Law Society of Upper Canada. His practice, teaching and research are informed by his active involvements in a large number of community based agencies. The utilization of his academic credentials have helped to bridge the gap between theory and methodology in very empowering ways. His position as a teacher has afforded him the unique experience of working not only with vibrant and effervescent students, but also with a number of stakeholders in law and education including. As human rights advocate, his practice seeks to improve the living conditions of vulnerable members of the community and to inspire in the profession a much needed socio-legal metamorphosis.

James Drennan is a Professor with Georgian College's Justice and Public Safety Institute, Police Studies Degree Program in Ontario and a police educator. He served in the PSNI, under the International Oversight process and the Policing Board of Northern Ireland, as Director of the Police College of Northern Ireland between 2002 and 2005.

Andreas Georgiou is a Ph.D. Candidate in Social and Political Thought at York University, and his interests are in the content of the theories of marginalization and the relationships between the marginal status of the theorist and the content in how this relationship contributes to shaping the discourse of marginalization and the nature of engagement between this discourse and it's audiences. His works in progress include: "Towards a Sociology of Praxis" and "Theoretical and Practical Discourse of Law and Punishment from the Margins".

Andrew Graham: has spent four years as Warden, Kingston Penitentiary. He is past President of APEX, the professional association of federal government executives. He has taught at Canadian Police College and continues his involvement in federal government activities through the Leadership Network of Treasury Board. He consults for the Conference Board of Canada and is Adjunct Faculty, the School of Policy Studies at Queen's University.

James F. Hodgson, Ph.D. is an Associate Professor of Criminal Justice and the Director of the Virginia Center for Criminal Justice Studies at Ferrum College in Ferrum, Virginia. His current research interests are policing, juvenile delinquency and social and criminal justice policies and practices. He is the co-editor of *Public Policing in the 21st Century: Comparative Issues and Dilemmas* (Criminal Justice Press) and *Sexual Violence: Policies, Practices and Challenges in the United States and Canada* (Praeger Press), editor of *The Criminal Justice System: Alternative Measures* (Canadian Scholars' Press) and the author of *Games Pimps Play: Pimps, Players and Wives-in-law: A Qualitative Analysis of Street Prostitution* (Canadian Scholars Press), and has published articles, book reviews, and article reviews on policing, juvenile delinquency, social justice, and social consciousness. He also has eleven years of experience as a police officer.

Ralf Jürgens is a consultant working on HIV/AIDS, health, policy and human rights issues in Montreal, Canada. He is the former Executive Director of the Canadian HIV/AIDS Legal Network . From 1992 to 1994, he was the Coordinator of the Expert Committee on AIDS and Prisons of Correctional Service Canada. He may be contacted at r.jurgens@sympatico.ca.

Tamari Kitossa is a Canadian of African Jamaican heritage and holds a PhD in Sociology and Equity Studies Department from the Ontario Institute for Studies in Education. His research interests are the criminalization of African peoples, the psycho-history of the African image in Western civilization, criminology, political economy of education, and equity issues in class, gender, race and the environment

Rick Lines is the Executive Director of the Irish Penal Reform Trust in Dublin. He has worked internationally on HIV/AIDS and harm reduction in prisons since 1993 for several non-governmental organisations. He may be contacted at rlines@iprt.ie. Corresponding Author: Rick Lines, Executive Director, Irish Penal Reform Trust, 53 Parnell Square West, Dublin 1, Ireland. rlines@iprt.ie

Kevin McCormick (PhD) is Dean, Research and Innovation, Georgian College 1999. He is a recipient of several awards for contributions to outstanding teaching: Canadian Professor of the Year; University-Wide Teaching Excellence Award; SUSA Award, York University; Queen's Golden Jubilee Medal; the American Innovative Excellence in Teaching Learning and Technology Award, etc. He has published solo and co- edited books (Carceral Contexts: Readings In Control; Canadian Penology: Advanced Perspectives and Research; Understanding Policing) as well as dozens of articles.

Faisal Mirza B.A., M.A. (U of T.), LL.B. (Osgoode Hall) specializes in criminal defence and constitutional litigation at the trial and appellate levels. Prior to being called to the Ontario bar he was a summer student with Hon. Fred Kaufman (Que. C.A.) and Mark Sandler. He articled at Greenspan Humphrey Lavine. Mr. Mirza has published articles pertaining to section 15(1) of the *Charter* and also mandatory minimum sentencing. Mr. Mirza also successfully challenged subsection 42(5)(a) of the *Youth Criminal Justice Act* as being contrary to section 15(1) of the *Charter* on the grounds that the provision discriminates against young persons on the basis of age.

Catherine Orban is an Assistant Professor of Criminal Justice in the School of Criminal Justice at Grand Valley State University. She has a PhD from York University. While in graduate school she worked as an auxiliary police officer with Durham regional Police Services in Ontario. Her academic interests are in the areas of critical criminology, gender studies, juvenile delinquency, corrections and restorative justice. She is completing her general and family mediation certification.

Currently she is involved in setting up a pilot restorative justice project involving victim/ juvenile offender mediation.

Rai Reece is a Doctoral Candidate in the Faculty of Women's Studies at York University. Her research focuses on the racialized and gendered incarceration of federally sentenced Black women in Canada. In addition, she has coordinated projects and conducted workshops that focus on culturally-conscious approaches to eradicating violence against women and children. She is also a member of the Prisoner's Justice Action Committee.

Heino Stöver, PhD, is a social scientist working at the Bremen Institute for Drug Research in Germany. He may be contacted at heino.stoever@uni-bremen.de

Tammy Turner received an Associate of Science Degree in Computer Technology from Edinboro University of Pennsylvania (1986), a Bachelor of Science in Computer Science from Edinboro University of Pennsylvania (1990), and a Master's degree in Justice Administration from Norwich University, Vermont. (2004). She has held the position of Institutional Business Manager at a State Correction Institution in Pennsylvania, since January of 1995. She is active in Pennsylvania Department of Corrections statewide committees, training, leadership symposiums and the development of institutional character profile policy, all intended to standardize procedures in the Department of Corrections. Tammy is supported in these efforts by her husband Scott and her two sons Travis and Teagan.

Livio Visano (PhD University of Toronto) is a professor and coordinator of the Sociology programme Atkinson, York University. He has published extensively (dozens of articles and books). He has delivered numerous keynote addresses at international and national conferences; he has served as Dean of Atkinson Faculty of Liberal and Professional Studies and as Chair of the Department of Sociology. He has supervised a large number of doctoral dissertations and served as consultant to federal, provincial and local governments and agencies. He is a recipient of several awards for outstanding contributions to teaching.

Christopher J. Williams is a doctoral candidate in the Department of Sociology at York University. His main research interests include "race" and racism, critical criminology, and policing. His published work has appeared in *Race & Class* and his forthcoming work (on racial profiling) will be featured in *Canadian Ethnic Studies.*

Preface

Livio A. Visano

This edited volume takes notice of how law socially constructs inequalities. It is a collection of articles that inquires into the role of law in mediating the relationship between ideologies of inequality and the institutions of education, policing, courts, and corrections. The section on criminological frontiers, in particular, confronts specific criminal formations: the dialectics of crime and the political economy of crime—formations that disfigure a much needed consciousness of justice. Thematically, it is argued that the laws of the criminal justice system dislocate and relocate a multiplicity of insidious dependencies. Laws filter—through a series of complementary and contradictory strategies—the meanings and lived legal experiences of various constituencies profiled on the basis of gender, race, age, sexual orientation and class.

Consistent with critical legal studies and critical criminology, this volume provides a long overdue analysis of the criminal justice system as relationally situated within wider constituting social contexts that hegemonize reproductions of discipline. As such, this critical inquiry defies simplistic etiological interpretations prevalent in conventional criminology by engaging a much needed debate on the intersections of culture, political economy and history. By providing a critical appreciation of the processes and structures of criminal justice, attention is paid to the development of an analytic framework that confronts the phenomenon of regulation. The challenge is levelled on many fronts, interrogating the primacy of ideology, the legitimacy of law and the institutional imperatives that shape the contexts, conditions and consequences of criminal justice.

In deconstructing law, it is clear that the term "criminal justice system" is of dubious value and meaning given that although agencies work together they do so often at cross-purposes when they promote and protect their respective self-serving and specialized interests. The different activities (policing, lawyering, prosecuting, judging and punishing) vary in legal resources, prestige or reputation, and funding. Vitiating any notion of a "system" are not only counterproductive intra-sector and inter-sector conflicts ("turf wars") but also hostile competing initiatives from public (state), private (for-profit), and community-based agencies (not-for-profit, charitable) attempting to secure government funding. This obviously adversarial environment dismantles the basis of a "system" and advances instead both the utility of bureaucratic control and the structural maintenance of an inequitable allocation of resources. Such a Darwinistic epistemology does not and cannot encourage imaginative solutions nor can it challenge the encrusted hierarchies of power as long as so many sector participants are too territorial and too busy tripping over each other to curry state favour. Cheap and groundless slogans ("more with less", "private as efficient") are congruent only with the demands of government and business authorities that frame social control according to the artificial criterion of functional rationality. The legal- punishment industry valorises a market-driven ethos marching to the disciplinary cadence of corporate complicity.

Competition and the contradictions therein are attributable to the interrelated ideologies of modernity, liberalism, and capitalism. Modernism, with its emphasis on the concept of reason and its application in the division of labour, liberalism, with its emphasis on the concept of individual rights (especially property) and its application in contract, and capitalism, with its emphasis on the accumulation of private wealth and its application in the free market, are all central to any understanding of current practices. In addition, these fundamental notions serve as criteria by which to appraise the sustainability or viability of incentives.

Briefly, modernity as an ideology promotes distorted notions of the linearity of progressive economic and administrative rationalizations and differentiations in the social world. The division of labour, consistent with a rationalist methodology, incorporates hierarchy, impersonality, written and informal rules of conduct which set out specialized tasks and highly specialized divisions of technocratic "value-free" knowledge. Concerned with efficiency in this framework, bureaucracies are oriented toward formal rationality and the purposively rational performances of standardized and routine functions.

In classical liberalism and neo liberalism, "individualism" privatizes freedom (Rawls, 1993) and places great value on maximizing one's freedom and right to self-determination, that is, the right to choose and the right to pursue one's own self-interests freely. This distorted sense of social responsibility impairs any moral, communal or collective projects of redistribution and recognition. By privileging individual choice, liberty, and rights, the sanctity of the individual is preserved and upheld as rational, enlightened self-interest.

According to the ideology of capitalism, the economy holds society together. For Adam Smith, the 'invisible hand' guided the universal as it emerged from the actions of self-interested, private citizens. According to Adam Smith (1994 [1776]), individuals are held together by the economic advantages of the division of labour. We associate because, by each playing different parts in the production of economic goods, we produce more goods for consumption. Capitalism interprets socio-economic institutions—including the criminal justice system—in this utilitarian, individualistically materialistic manner. Yet, it is precisely within this framework that the relationships of policing, courts and prisons become controversial.

Despite a rich criminal justice literature, only recently has the discussion shifted to address the connections between institutions and ideologies by exploring the limits of our thinking about traditional criminal justice relationships. Traditionally, criminal justice scholars from relatively similar vantage points have rehearsed and debated the relatively banal benefits of partnerships in familiar and, as always, comfortable contexts. Accordingly, mainstream or normative approaches focus on what are merely the reductivist consequences of the development of particular applied programmes but fail to confront the fundamentally *unjust* character of criminal justice.

Another troubling feature of conventional approaches is the glaring absences of any conceptual grasp of both the *intersections* of identity, institutions and ideologies and the co-joint elements in the ideological-institutional nexus. These absences thwart all promise or prospect of remedy. Typically, contemporary scholarship and administrative policies woefully fail to locate conferred administrative roles within the broader context of ideologies let alone daily institutional practices.

By adopting a dialectical way of thinking of the "criminal justice system", one can more fully appreciate the importance of ideologies in all phases of institutional life. Ideologies are not simply objects that are routinely acted upon; rather, they are "embedded" within each other and play a crucial role in all dimensions of social transformation. The institutional ("real-life experiences") constitute moments in a continuous process of ideological development and change. This alternative perspective offers a fundamentally different way of thinking about the criminal justice system. For instance, the framework encourages a more enlightened reason *rather* than crass instrumental rationalities (modernity); equality *rather* than a mindless predisposition to individualized freedoms governed by self interest (liberalism); and, innovation and measured regulations of market mentalities *rather* than trite declarations of "doing more with less" and other fetishistic approaches to private business self interests (capitalism). Only through such dialectics can we seek to understand and develop authentic partnerships.

This challenging enterprise requires a forthright interrogation of how one interprets simultaneously both the familiar and the foreign—how one transforms the familiar into the foreign and the foreign into the familiar. This volume analyzes the administration of law by considering the impact of layered carceral contexts of culture and political economy on consciousnesses, both individual and institutional. Acknowledging both the intellectual limits of extant thinking, a more prudent approach seeks to make sense of the often-ignored relationship that conditions *a priori* the forms of ideological struggles and identifiable institutional trends.

The aim herein is to provide elements of a toolkit necessary to appreciate critically both the cycle of control and the circle of connectedness. Moving beyond common sense and popular interpretations of crime—fuelled as they are by distorted statistics and biased media accounts—this volume of readings proffers a different set of perspectival and substantive materials. This collection of papers offers a selective critical rendering of the assortment of different "facts". Before one can hope to investigate "criminal justice", it is essential to understand what informs our criminological understanding of law—an understanding that is too often fragmented, distorted and bereft of memory and imagination. It is incumbent upon the reader to move beyond the facile exercise of debunking that which is different and begin instead to interrogate the subtext of one's own credulities, however uncomfortable that may be. One's knowledge of the law is contingent upon the available stock of information and the relevant socialization, differentially rooted cultural contexts, and the interplay of different experiences and resonating problematics. These contingencies become that much more profound in reference to class, gender, sexuality and race.

The reader seeking to move outside of his or her comfort zone, to challenge his or her socialized understandings of "criminal" and "justice" in the search for the authentic, is invited to consider the contributions offered here in light of the following questions. To what extent do structures of dominance define "crimes" and their criminalization? To what extent is the violence of injustice attributable to a criminogenic culture? Might we view the trade in guns, stolen goods, drugs, and sex—commodities with a relatively significant material value—precisely the same as any other commercial activity, fitting perfectly into our culturally framed aspirations for success and wealth? Is it possible that what we consider "criminal" is merely derivative of an enslaving materialism and its sanctity of the marketplace? And to what extent is what we hear or understand shaped by how it is said?

The Message in the Method

Critical inquiry consists of what is said (the message) together with *how* it is being said (the method). It is precisely a concern for the latter that sets this experimental and experiential project apart from other criminological investigations. The strengths of this volume rest not on any one paper but in the collective representation of different voices and the different forms of (re)presentations. Collectively the contributors demonstrate courage to be vulnerable, open and challenging—to move beyond and outside of the self. The strengths of the contributions are in the connections with the subject from so many hitherto neglected vantage points: interdisciplinarity, philosophical, feminist, critical race, legalistic, community-based as well as industry/ professional. The strengths derive equally from the authentic style of presentation—spontaneous, exciting and passionate. In this way, the authors of the papers in this volume offer a very rare, refreshing and empowering set of analytic tools with which to approach law and criminal justice. For every contributor, emancipation is incompatible with consumer capitalism and its overwhelming emphasis on the satisfaction of the desires of individualized economies.

Obviously, one edited volume can hope to do justice neither to the enormous breadth nor to the depth of law nor to its criminal justice relationships nor to the variety of methods available to communicate ideas. Simply to catalogue salient directions is itself an ambitious enterprise that risks trying to do too much and accomplishing relatively little. Nevertheless, this collection does offer a considerable range and variety of treatments of a variety of institutions from a refreshing mix of constituent perspectives.

The message as well as the method of the papers is deliberately oppositional. The authors, each in their own way, each with their own style, challenge disciplinary canons and the totalizing view of traditional "common sense". The uniqueness of this project conceptually and methodologically exists in the different voices (tone and tenor) of the contributors.

Collectively, these voices powerfully highlight the essential elements of critical inquiry, including:

a) a **commitment and conviction** to fundamental social justice, eschewing the convenience of meanings and measurements;
b) a **courage** to comprehend contradictions and dialectics (collusions and collisions) and to attempt to suspend that which has been internalized as "common" sense;
c) a **curiosity** that examines the intersectionality of ideological and institutional, the immanent and transcendent;
d) a series of **connections** to the **community** (praxis) and a relatedness to interdisciplinarity; and,
e) a **strength of character** to be a stranger in questioning that which is presented as knowledge (culturally pervasive erasures) and moving towards an enlightened self/ social interests.

Given our collective commitment to critical pedagogy, the criteria used to evaluate the merits of this project and its constituent contributions were broad, "outside the mainstream box" and intrinsically sensitive to those voices that have traditionally been excluded—especially those students and community activists who act as social justice change agents. Thus, to retain the full essence of the message, editing was kept to an absolute minimum.

Given our collective dissatisfaction with extant texts, these papers individually and in total are intentionally polemical and provocative. By directly (in content) and indirectly (in voice) challenging dominant views, this volume offers the curious reader a refreshing alternative to the mainstream texts. It offers to the marginalized and criminalized a glance into the different ways one might articulate the injustices inherent in our criminal justice systems. For those readers heavily invested in mainstream criminology and dominant scholarly traditions, this book will be uncomfortable to read both in content and in style. It is hoped that it will also be unsettling.

References

Rawls, J. 1993. *Political Liberalism.* New York: Columbia University Press.

Smith, Adam (1994 [1776]) *An Inquiry into the Nature and Causes of the Wealth of Nations.* E. Cannan (Ed.) New York: Random House

Acknowledgements

This project originated with students, graduate and undergraduate, who were quite frustrated with the encyclopaedic "mix and stir" approaches of mainstream texts, written as they are by distant, privileged and 'expert" knowledge brokers. Although students can provide bold and conceptually fertile insights into the competing and converging discourses that implicate law and justice, students are seldom consulted or encouraged to participate in "their" own education. Traditional "banking" approaches to education screen the participation of students and invite commentaries (by "request only") within a framework that expects students to march to the disciplinary cadence of existing pedagogic power structures.

This project emerged from the sentiments expressed by former and current students, a most talented new generation of scholars, whose contributions were far too often marginalized by criminological canons and the self appointed and self-important guardians of the discipline. In this context, this book is importantly a collaborative and collective enterprise. No one paper stands out but all the papers contribute in a unique manner to the whole–a phenomenon foreign to the prevailing ethos of possessive individualism and self-importance.

This project has been long in gestation but quick in delivery. The community of contributors responded immediately and so generously dedicated their energy to this collaborative enterprise. The ideas for it come primarily from my graduate students, current and former, many of whom contributed papers. The contributors, my dear colleagues, responded with incredible energy, support and enthusiasm. They have together shaped the focus of this inquiry and so, importantly, this collection is the product of numerous emotional, spiritual and intellectual connections. The work reflects much of what we have learned from these connections and from our mutual intellectual curiosities.

The contributors represent a fascinating cross section of interests (former police officers, professors, college/university administrators, community activists, human rights lawyers, and graduate students in women's studies, interdisciplinary studies, sociology, social and political thought. For their confidence, pedagogic directions, critical insights and continued personal encouragement I am indebted to them. It has been as much an honour as a delight to collaborate with this team on this project.

Over the years the task of effectively balancing my teaching, service and scholarly responsibilities has been made possible by the always extremely heartening accommodation of members of the administrative and support staff in the School of Social Sciences in the Atkinson Faculty of Liberal and Professional Studies at York University. Paula, Loretta, Joni, Mavis and Rosanna, thank you.

Carole Yawney, a champion of social justice has always been an inspiration to me. From the Mumia event at York University in Canada to our trip to the University of York in the UK; from our CARRP meetings to the Santa Fe conference, Carole's message of harmony prevailed. The memory of Carole's activism and strength will continue to guide us.

To Loraine Brady, words cannot capture my gratitude. Loraine, thank you—many of us were so privileged to have learned so much about life's injustices from you and from the strength of your daily determination. ...for years, never a teaching assistant but always an empowering teacher!

My appreciation of law and criminal justice owes much to those courageous many who have, by personal example, guided my thoughts into necessary but uncomfortable inquiries. These mentors include John Visano, Anthony Lamont, Charlie Roach, Wilson Head, and Ruth Morris.

The enthusiasm of the APF and the APF anonymous reviewers will always be appreciated. I am grateful to Dr. Christos Paraskevopoulos for his ceaseless commitment to critical thought and social justice concerns. APF has always encouraged innovative and progressive projects and Chris guided and encouraged this project every step along the way, from manuscript to book support

I acknowledge with considerable gratitude the direction and counsel of Mavis Griffin. I also thank Mavis for introducing me to the Toronto Youth for Humanity whose work with youth is exceptionally inspirational.

A very special note of thanks goes to Brenda for preparing the articles and for her insightful comments and encouragement. Brenda assisted as well in piecing together some of the more thorny issues by scrutinising carefully more challenging recent conceptual formulations of institutions. Brenda's advice and faith have always been a constant source of strength. I am grateful for this and so much more. To our children Tammi and Anthony, I am always touched by your communion, courage and inspiring loyalties.

L.A. Visano
Toronto, Canada
August 2005

Introduction: The Law - Criminal Justice Nexus as the Locus of Injustice

Livio A. Visano

1. Overview: Symbols, Mythologies and Metaphors

Law and criminal justice are imbricated instruments of regulation. As an interrelationship, this characterization captures social practices that apply control within the realm of cultural (re)production. This intertextuality is a process whereby one text (justice) plays upon other texts endlessly to further legal discourses and open up the possibilities of becoming other texts (control).

The power of the criminal justice system resides in its continual deferral of meaning (Derrida, 1981) to law in order to achieve an unmediated authorial knowledge that explains "justice". The criminal justice system filters trouble, funnels interpretations and marginalizes differences according to convoluted experiences and "inoculated reflexivities" (Giddens, 1992: 3) of a variety of complementary and competing agencies. The criminal justice system as the narrow reading of law is objectified according to a limited range of self-serving organizational criteria. The range of discourses used to construct this system of control consists of ideological practices that typically articulate official formations of truth. To sustain the subtext of legal privilege, there is no integrated text of law therein, only fragmented canons that depict the law as a rational and moral authority. Authority benefits from a multiplicity of signifiers that resist and inscribe narrational discourses. This manipulated corpus of essentializing customs and self serving proscriptions solely respond to "official" meanings of challenge, defined as distance and difference. Moreover, this slippage or elasticity of "deterritorialized" meanings in the justice system "subverts the subject" (Derrida, 1981; Lacan, 1977) by a chain of signifiers -- definitions, written and symbolic. Caught up in the legal labyrinth of images and rituals as *a priori* conditioning, law symbolizes differential identities and experiences (individual and communal) that reflect, enable, and constrain cultural meanings and realities inherent in diverse and dynamic encounters. Meanings and symbols of law penetrate permeable systems of language and individual consciousness, thereby transforming the agent-subject into a self subordinating object. As the law monopolizes the means of mental production, the vulnerability and credulity of the individual are heightened. In this process of deconstructing and reconstructing meaning, discourses are constructed that legitimate conceptions of law in the interests of the criminal justice system.

Accordingly, language becomes both ideological and illusory. The content and morphology of language as well as the attendant scripted vocabularies are anchored in particular histories that circumscribe acceptable expressions. In other words, both the spoken and written languages of law ensure that the "outsider" is "in" but not "of" this privileged juridic community. The exclusionary nature of "law talk" and "law thought", commoditize control by structuring dependency relations. The language of law, as an integral part of a culture of criminal justice, embodies hegemonic relations that transmit the sediments and sentiments of the collective conscience, however contrived. For pubic consumption, the legal lexicon supplies a simplistic taxonomy of an adversarial binary of guilt or innocence. While the grammar of law does not limit individual thoughts and outlook, the lack of an inclusionary vocabulary serves to inhibit communication (Bourdieu, 1977; Habermas, 1976). The structure of legal language or legalese, replete with rules and rituals, inculcates desired norms, socializes into conformity and designates the domination of the groups which impose linguistic reference points on others. Linguistic competence becomes much more than a technical capacity to speak with the right accent, gesture, intonation, and word choices. Rather, as Hall et al. (1992) and de Saussure (1986) note, proficiency invokes a particular framework for analyzing and reproducing established social enterprises. To project one's self as linguistically competent, places one in a set of communicative relationships that recognizes a shared history and a parlance that defines a mutuality of interest. A shared legal linguistic framework, revealed in mythologies, fiction and hyperbolic niceties of a culture conceals the politics of coercion. Lawyers, as technical interlocutors are habituated to "their" professional roles and communicative rules. Their so called technical, efficient and objective language stultifies and disciplines primarily because it presupposes a context of authority whose rules cannot be contradicted. The content and structure of their skills are reflective of and consistent with well established and unquestioned procedures and precedence. The vocational training of lawyers and industry socialization protect and reward this language of legal performance. Given that *relations recognize representations*, levels of one's legal articulation are correlated with professional legitimacy, knowledge and lamentably with importance.The specificity of law is transmitted through language, as Bakhtin (1981, 293) describes, "all words have the taste of a profession, a genre, a tendency, a party, a particular work, a particular person, a generation, an age group".

For Barthes (1973), language contributes to myth making. Language politicizes myths by claiming reference to the seductive illusions of signifying signs, myths and metaphors that facilitate an unchallenged servitude. A mythology, as the source for images of justice and punishment in the contemporary world, elicits a combination of wonder and horror (Arendt, 1994). And yet, despite inexorable proclamations of legal expertise, bureaucratized institutions of law fail to articulate clearly, consistently and logically their goals (mandate, mission, domain) and their corresponding means (procedural regulations),

To fully understand the contradictions and complementarities of law, we turn first to a number of *interlocking myths*. Myths and their accompanying symbolic rituals and ceremonies are designed to shape and solidify favorable impressions of control agencies and the state. These myths are not defects in the law but rather its strengths

(Arnold, 1975: 49) given that every legal authority structure seeks to legitimate itself by referring to fundamental assumptions enshrined in myth (Fuller, 1975: 81). The "imminence of the law" (Boorstin, 1971:87) incorporates the lofty, nostalgic and tantalizing ideal of the "*rule of law.*" According to the Canadian Charter of Rights and Freedoms, "...Canada is founded upon principles that recognize *the supremacy of God and the rule of law*". For centuries the "government of law", neither the rule by divine nor the "rule of men", has become the new truth. The king's palace was replaced by a palace of justice, wherein sits a new kind of monarch. "Judges rules" in case law, jurisprudence and "conventional wisdom" maintain that a judge is an administrator, a functionary applying abstract and universal laws, that is, a judge is required "to interpret and apply general laws to factual disputes" (Becker and Murray, 1971: XIX). Logically, this servant of the law enjoys independence from political pressures (Lloyd, 1974: 257; Moriondo, 1966). But judges are more than mere interpreters of the law; they are monarchs of the courtroom. As Harding (1966: 130) describes "the judge is descended from the [viceroy or governor who] acts in the king's absence ... his glamour is the glamour of the king shining through his alter ego." The judge as monarch enjoys a grandeur that is almost liturgical, while making "interpretations of obscure scriptures" (Quinney, 1972: 34).

The remnant of monarchical power in the judge is dramatically highlighted by the power to convict for "contempt of court," a sort of high treason against the ruler of the court. The judge does not need to have the confidence of the people before the court, As monarch, the judge is not just a mediator but decides *inter alia* what evidence is to be admitted, what witnesses juries may hear, what lawyers the defendants may have, whether media coverage is to be permitted, and so on. The judge's courtroom "rulings" are final and non-negotiable; total deference to the court ruler is demanded; this high priest expects to be addressed as "Your Honor" or "My Lord", persons entering and leaving are expected to bow their heads, no talking is permitted unless allowed by the judge. Challenges to judicial rulings may be made to more powerful palaces of justice, but appeal courts leave the petty monarch much power especially since appeals do not retry the case nor meet the witnesses, nor confirm events described in the transcript As Secretary of Sate Condoleezza Rice noted on March 14th, 2005, "too few in the world know of the value we place on ... the rule of law" (Judt, 2005:15).

This mythical "rule of law" includes a number of "well-articulated corollaries. Law is presented in terms of *consensual*, *monolithic*, and *rational characteristics.* Collectively, these myths mystify the individual's relations with the state and its control agencies; they distract attention from uncomfortable and fundamental questions about the source and distribution of power in society. These myths identify law as a property of the high office of its incumbents; fidelity to law becomes equated with support for established officials. Many citizens see no illogic in arguing that *ipso facto* "it's the law– one has to obey the law" even if the law is clearly based on the bias of a few interests.

A powerful corollary of the rule of law is the myth of "*our law*". This myth holds that law is based on and expresses consensus, "core values" or the common will (Pound, 1942; Goode, 1976: 653). Consensus-based law helps to create social stability by recognizing the yearning in all of us for equal justice, for a forum in which grievances are heard and mended without necessarily disturbing existing power relationships (Arnold, 1975: 50). Many theorists, including Durkheim, Parsons, Pound and Hall, have supported the consensus and integrative models that signify law's capacity to regulate, harmonize, and reconcile conflicting desires or competing claims thereby enhancing the welfare of the larger social order (Hall, 1947: 1). Accordingly, everyone from worker to corporate director—the rich and poor, weak and powerful, can feel secure, knowing that no one is above the law and that all are equal in court (Zinn, 1971: 18).

But, the law consists of diverse sets of laws administered by loosely coupled organizations (Hagan et al., 1979), serving a multiplicity of often inconsistent purposes and conflicting goals (Fuller, 1969: 60; Blumberg, 1967: 19). Interest group conflicts play a critical role in shaping the content and application of laws (Schermerhorn, 1961; Gusfield, 1963; Chambliss, 1964; Lindesmith, 1967; Quinney, 1974; Turk, 1976). Particular interest groups reflect differences in power, that is, criminal justice depends on the "proxemics" of power. The myth of a *monolithic law* succeeds in disguising how laws are aimed by privileged interests at certain target groups.

Equally important is the myth of *legal rationality*. Law is pictured as an orderly system of regulation arising in complex societies where an "objective" frame of reference is used to control behavior. Modernity, as an ideology characterized by the "rational" and its corresponding division of labour with binding obligations and duties, has affected law to such an extent that law today is an instrumental calculation of "social value" and an optimization of "efficiency" (contractual considerations/ exchanges) measured by armies of specialized technicians. For these experts, enlightened thought exists empirically in the data located in the "utility" of crime statistics, forensics, actuarial designs, clearance rates, etc. Law as the formal bond of solidarity displaces and replaces any vestiges of authentic collective consciousness that was previously identified as sacred and traditional. Modernity contributes to the calcification, of legal concepts: classification, methods of induction and deduction, analyses and synthesis of rules, the testing of evidence, etc.

These practices of empiricism are guided by an instrumental rationality, an expertise and an institutionalized discipline which attenuate the promises let alone the prospect of truth. Conditions exist for the law to remain nothing more than an instrumental currency wherein opportunity prevails. Reason, a formidable concept of exigency, is the standard by which law is purportedly measured. Notwithstanding the fundamental antagonisms inherent in extant notions of "justice", the rational preservation of social order claims fairness and equality in the concept and practice of law. Thus, law as a form of domination is shaped by objectivity grounded rationalism, necessity and contingency. The universality of reason, according to the law's logic, ensures the constitution of justice by reconciling conflict. Essentially, an examination of the fundamental elements of modernity is a prerequisite to a more complete understanding of contemporary law. Although modernity is ignored in current mainstream criminology, modernity provides an appreciation of the limitations of law especially in terms of its overwhelming and exclusionary technical knowledge. This distorted idea of the enlightenment remains the backdrop of all legal deliberations, the condition of rationalizing various canonizing ideologies and the consequence of scientizing normativities. By hypostasizing rational-scientific-methodical criteria that neutralize pernicious authorial challenges, the law minimizes the contradictions evident in immutable antagonisms. By appealing to the utilitarian convenience of reason, law seldom appears impervious to both reform impulses and to the rediscovery of new knowledges.

For centuries, reason has always been used to justified inequalities. For example, all theorists of the Enlightenment, including Montesquieu, Voltaire, Hume, Jefferson, and the like, justified slavery on grounds of alleged scientific fact that slaves were sub-humans. This "fact", in turn, became a defense of black servitude. For the "Enlightenment", slavery was consistent with science and rationality. From the congressional abolition of the Slave Trade in 1807 to the 1850 Fugitive Slave Act, laws justified genocide by resorting to "the prevailing reason" which maintained a) the sub-humanity of slaves and b) this sub-humanity was related to the "unreasonableness" of slaves.

Ironically, the idea and practice of reason is so central to law and yet the courts have for centuries failed to define "reasonable", a term so fundamental especially in reference to the celebrated safeguards of *"proof beyond a reasonable doubt"* or the so-called *"reasonable" man's* (sic) *test.* For instance, the Canadian Charter of Rights and Freedoms, the supreme law of the land, guarantees rights and freedoms subject only to such *reasonable limits* prescribed by law as can be demonstrably justified in a free and democratic society". In reference to Legal Rights section 8 maintains that "Everyone has the right to be secure against *unreasonable* search or seizure. By the failure of any judiciary to define "reasonable" is the acknowledgment of the subjectivity and contextual meanings of the term.

Studies of sentencing (Hogarth, 1971), police discretion (Black, 1968) and plea bargaining (Klein, 1976) call into serious question any ethical rationality of legal processes. Notably, "*due-process*", "*one's day in court*" and other claims of legal protection are based on unequal access to power resources. There can be no "due process" when the kind of outcome one gets depends on one's class, gender, race, religion or sexual orientation (Chambliss and Seidman, 1971; Lefcourt, 1971; Friedman, 1977). According to Section 11 of the Charter of Rights and Freedoms: "Any person charged with an offence has the right (d) *to be presumed innocent until proven guilty* according to law in a fair and public hearing by an independent and impartial tribunal". How does the "*the presumption of innocence*" operate when a defendant, denied bail and/or escorted in the courtroom in handcuffs or shackles, is required to sit in a prisoner's box and can only speak through her/ his legal counsel?

How is this dependency on legal counsel consistent with a presumption of innocence? We may sum up the impact of the mythology of law in Blumberg's (1970: 7) words: "The pledges that are embodied in the law and order concepts are almost at once unredeemed, if not denied outright, by our society's institutional arrangements for carrying them out." Much of this biased talk about various presumptions of innocence occurs at the trial but the trial is yet another metaphor, a metaphor that organizes how law conceptualizes justice. The trial is an iconic or symbolic index of communication competence, of linguistic strategies and of skills at gesturing, all of which have little to do with justice and much to say about the spectacle that distracts and stupefies, amuses and abuses. Indeed, the trial is a formidable socio-cultural text of the relationship between law and mythology. Besides, very few cases go to trial and the majority of case outcomes are determined by invisible and at times perniciously self-serving deals among lawyers. Typically, the criminal trial is reserved for the disadvantaged while out of court settlements or plea bargains are custom designed for the more privileged.

All of these images of law predominate as cultural markers designed to mirror a generic deference to the authority. Legal definitions are convenient intrusions into the lives of "those others". Specifically, criminalization is a staged performance that manipulates sanctions by defining disturbances as local accommodations to contests or as totalizing narratives of trouble that warrant closure, containment and coercion. This criminal subject or the so-called "other" is not only essentialized as inferior but remains the consequence of structured inequalities. When layered with colour, class and gender, the "criminalized" other reflects a dramatic threat framed within the logic of challenge and resistance. As Zatz (1987:85) and Balbus (1973) discuss, the legal system serves to represent the interests of a few, to institutionalize bias and to reinforce inequalities.

Historically, "justice" in Canada has been characterized by attractive legal palliatives replete with convenient mythologies. For example, long before the equality sections of the Charter came into effect in 1985, Canada was a signatory of the Universal Declaration of Human Rights in 1948. Article 25 affirmed a number of moral principles which included provisions for a standard of living adequate for the health and well-being of the individual and his or her family, such as food, clothing, housing, medical care and social services, as well as the right to security in the event of disability and/or unemployment. Likewise, the Constitution Act of 1982, notably the Canadian Charter of Rights and Freedoms clearly indicates that within the operation of law, every individual was to be treated without discrimination. Section 15(1) states: *Every individual is equal before and under the* law and the right to the equal protection and *equal* benefit of the law *without discrimination* and, in particular, *without discrimination* based on race, national or ethnic origin, colour, religion, sex, age or mental or physical disability. But this provision alone does not ensure equality. Section 7 of the Charter states that: "Everyone has the right to life, liberty and security of the person and the right not to be deprived thereof *except in accordance with the principles of fundamental justice*". The actual text of section 15 does not grant the right to equal treatment per se; it is not a general norm of non-discrimination (Eberts, 1985:4).

Despite these high-sounding phrases, rights are to be interpreted by the Courts when they are denied by societal institutions. *Procedural* equality, as Eberts (1985:12-14) notes, is not a guarantee of *substantive* equality. Moreover, equality "before" the law has never included the ideal of "equality of opportunity" nor does equality *of* law equate with equality *in* law. The illusory language, convoluted logic, and ambiguous style of legal procedures succeed in creating confidence only among individuals who "know" the law and further succeed in mystifying notions of equality for the majority of citizens. Even a perfunctory glance at history demonstrates that a wide spectrum of groups have been routinely subordinated, despite the benevolent intentions of those who administer legal procedures. Benign and often paternalistic provisions are inadequately designed to consider existing distribution of resources. The elderly, physically and mentally challenged, youth, women, the poor, racial/ ethnic communities, social activists, First Nations, gays and lesbians, are all too familiar with the dubious benefits of legal procedures. Procedures for legal redress simply target or pathologize individual villains while directing attention away from the more oppressive structural inequalities. Note also the overriding contradiction embodied in Section 24(2) "Where, in proceedings under subsection (1), a court concludes that evidence was obtained in a manner that infringed or denied any rights or freedoms guaranteed by this Charter, the evidence shall be excluded if it is established that, having regard to all the circumstances, *the admission of it in the proceedings would bring the administration of justice into disrepute*". All of the above mythologies are not theatrical props in an entertaining fictive drama of justice nor are they weapons of mass distraction; rather, and much more importantly, mythologies are methods that engineer a binding moral consensus (an internalized social discipline) by alluding to the sanctity of legal knowledge within a manageable vocabulary that confirms the consistency of ideals and practice. Missing in the above concatenation of images are the dynamic attributes and dialectical practices of distance, difference and defiance.

2. Criminal Justice: From Trouble Shooting to Trouble Making

The authority of law is layered, that is, power is differentially dispersed among the various elements of the criminal justice "system" from the arresting police officer to the supervising parole officer. All of these agencies or specialized services enjoy inter- and intra- relations, characterized on the one hand by the "independence" of the office, and on the other hand, a deference to each others' discretion. Irrespective of what different public masks are worn on different occasions and irrespective of the antagonistic and/ or affiliative relations of various officials, the "criminal" justice system is designed *fundamentally* to discipline those who "fail to fit" dominant cultural standards.

Despite their obvious differences and relative independence, officials within the criminal justice system are required to be accountable, prospectively and/or retrospectively, to the rule of law. But the legal culture is a complex amalgam of canonical texts - the corpus of substantive and procedural conventions, formal professional training, informal occupational rules, the political economy of the office (pragmatics and politics), administrative or bureaucratic recipes, decisions of other elements "in the system", and the currents of contemporary culture and various historical processes. The activities of the criminal justice system reflect the culture of capitalism and the logic of liberalism that are protected legally and organizationally. To reiterate, the relationship between law and society is mediated by institutions that are structured ideologically, politically and economically to perpetuate inequalities. The criminal justice system is basically an information-processing system. Law provides a ubiquitous framework that governs information about situational roles and identities and grounds criteria which maintain a sense of cultural continuity. This section surveys the institutional practices of legal officials in an effort to demonstrate that at every stage of the criminal justice process one's proximal affiliation with dominant values, rooted in Anglo-centric assumptions, is a determinant of preferential attention.

2.1 Police

The word "police", from the Greek "polis', a city, through the Latin "politia" meaning the condition of a state or government, refers historically to a system of administration and regulation (Radzinowicz, 1956).Public police services as governmental social control (Black, 1976) is the most coercive or repressive apparatus of the state, dealing with actual and perceived challenges to the state. These gatekeepers of the criminal justice system enjoy a legal and legitimate monopoly over physical force. Theoretically, the police officer is an active juridic agent; everything about policing occurs within the context of the legal licence and capability (Shearing and Leon, 1992). Moreover, police officers are independent crown officers or sovereign agents enjoying original delegated legal authority. The police are required *legally* to justify retrospectively and/or prospectively their decision to invoke the criminal justice system and, predictably, police officers interpret their roles according to a legalistic framework. The exaggerated celebration of the law enforcement orientation in "fighting crime" has become a criterion that frames the occupational culture of policing, supplying interpretations from which inferences are drawn and decisions are legitimated. Police approaches, recruitment, training, promotion, and on-the job socialization stress the primacy of law enforcement.

Ideologically, the law enforcement mandate supports the process of producing the "other", that is, the marginalized other who is transformed into a prospective suspect, accused and convict. The nature of the other is determined by the shape of the dominant legal framework. On the one hand, the law grants considerable authority to the front-line or "beat" officer. Under the Police Services Act and the Criminal Code of Canada, officers have a duty to criminalize - to arrest, to discipline and to correct. Case- law interpretations, procedural rules of evidence and ambiguities in law enhance and protect the discretion of the police. On the other hand, the police powers are not arbitrary but restricted legally; statutes and case law limit the state's intrusions or violation of the public and private peace (Skolnick, 1967). Law is ostensibly designed to protect the citizenry from the unwarranted and arbitrary infringements on freedoms and rights. In liberal democratic societies, the institution of private property or peace constrains the collection of reliable information (intelligence gathering) necessary for the investigation of "troublesome" individuals, organizations and communities. Formal police intrusions need to be legally justified given the legal protection of privacy, issues of accountability and specific rights against infringements on liberties such as the Canadian Charter of Rights and Freedoms. Consequently, information may not be as easily attainable for the police; information about suspicious activities is not always forthcoming from the general public where there may not be unequivocal support for the police.

Let us review factors that locate police behaviour and influence police discretion. In general, there are *interpersonal/ interactional*, *institutional / organizational, and structural/ systemic* factors affecting police decisions. *Situational* features include elements of the alleged infraction:

a) the context of the incident: the severity of the "trouble"; previous complaints; socio-political pressures; physical/ environmental factors (the spatial and temporal factors) such as the location of the encounter; the number of the complainants, witnesses, suspects, victims, police officers present; the roles of the complainant, suspect, and victim;
b) the demographic characteristics of the police officers; the experience of the officer; the officer's ideological framework; the officer's perception of the other's sense of belongingness, conflict or distinctiveness;
c) the demographic characteristics of the citizens the race, class, age, and gender of interactants; and,
d) the process and structure of the social interaction: levels of deference exchange and demeanor among interactants, levels of negotiation.

In other words, the nature of the interaction as well as the personality profiles shape outcomes (Bittner, 1970; Manning, 1977). As Sykes and Clark argued (1975), citizen demeanor independently affects police arrest decisions; that is, a non deferential, let alone hostile, demeanor in these exchanges impact negatively on police discretion.

Outcomes are also affected by *organizational or institutional* influences that include styles of policing (legalistic, informal community-based), the nature of the community served (levels of affluence, homogeneity), the social organization of policing including the police hierarchy, the police subculture, jurisdictional considerations, administrative policies, rules, production norms, the unit to which the officer is attached, given priorities to particular investigations, police budget, cost/ benefit analyses, police logistics/ deployment of resources, public pressures from the media and political interests, relations with public and private institutions: the criminal justice system, insurance companies, media, private security, etc.

Systemic factors affecting policing include the law (local and extra local), national and international trends, political economy of policing, historical trends, the culture of capitalism/neo liberalism (the "market" model of governance, the commodification of crime, an actuarial logic of "the bottom line" guided by clearance rates and a market place lexicon.

Regrettably, too much attention on the police has been focused on a "criminal" narrative which limits an appreciation of other equally significant roles notably *crime prevention*, *social services*, and *peace keeping*. Policing is a subject matter that goes beyond expressions of criminal investigations which tend to be reactive or incident- driven. Proactive alternatives are required in order to deal with the more fundamental causes of crime and their concomitant solutions. Effective policing cannot be solely measured by quantitative activities such as arrests, offence tickets, parking tags, clearance rates, and convictions. Officers cannot operate in isolation from the community in solving problems especially since policing exists within wider cultural contexts, political mediations and legal articulations. Theoretically, the police officer within sites of intervention is an active agent situated within wider constituting contexts. This agent of formal social control, as a cultural subject within discourses of power, is engaged in micro-political (local) struggles shaped by more macro-cultural influences (global).The dominant order scripts policing as a commodity that is marketable and profitable for those who have a stake in producing and re-producing existing hegemonic imperatives. Policing, as a political process and a politicized structure, enjoys a plurality of meanings that are displaced and re-constructed in concert with other hegemonic reproductions of discipline. This exercise in control is linked to privilege; Hunt (1993), quoting Althusser, maintains that the law is an instrument of the ruling class. As Ericson describes (1982:7), "their everyday actions are directed at reproducing the existing order (the 'normal and efficient state') and the order (system of rules) by which this is accomplished". In preserving the status quo or "peace", the police historically have been required to engage in intelligence gathering on the individuals, groups or communities designated as "dangerous classes" (Silver, 1992). Not only is policing articulated legally as discussed above, policing is also contextualized culturally and mediated politically.

Moreover, confining discussions of policing to a legal narrative is a meaningless exercise that forecloses any possibility of social justice discourses which presumably must implicate such dynamic features as history and political economy. Likewise, policing is far too serious a subject matter to leave in the hands of self-proclaimed police and legal spokespeople dubiously celebrating sensational criminal investigations. Rather, the study of policing confronts directly the basis of social order, the nature of society and the interpretations of challenges. Policing is a persuasive practice has become an apparatus of social control and a mechanism of moral regulation established within the "carceral network" (Foucault, 1977).

The incredible commitment to law enforcement in policing is disturbing as the following discussion details. In general police officers perceive their responsibility in terms of "catching criminals" and this may not necessarily include complying with debilitating legal and institutional procedures. The job is considered done whenever the person who is guilty anyhow is convicted, *regardless* of how the conviction is obtained (Chevigny, 1969: 150). Colleagues and superiors encourage officers to "play the game" of officially sanctioned deviation. The failure to comply often results in unpleasant and even dangerous assignments, lack of promotion, and other organizational troubles (ibid: 61). But the principal legitimation of this police work is not in terms of personal gain for the officer; it is framed in terms of the *needs of police work*. Without the informally encouraged deviance, wrongdoings or the violation of rules, it is likely that the police, as currently organized, would be "hampered," "hamstrung," and "ineffective" (Chevigny, 1969: 61). An officer in Tifft's study (1970: 185) explains:

> You are forced to lie in some reports because no one respects or can accept the truth." Whether it is traffic law or specialized investigative units, the pressure to produce is not specified as to where and how, but there is informal recognition that "you have to break the law to do the job.... The policeman is being harassed enough by the public that they meet on the street and it is not for the boss to further harass them and break their morale (Tifft, 1970: 193).

An officer in Manning's study (1977: 197) of the British police reported that "if a bloke hasn't got a few investigations in his file [i.e., complaints against him by the public] he's probably not doing his job." The organization and the occupational culture expect its officers to violate formal rules and law to get the work done, and facilitate and protect official deviance through secretiveness and self protection or keeping your mouth shut (Skolnick, 1967; Gardiner, 1969; Bittner, 1967; Cain, 1979; 146; Ramsay, 1978: 92). Since policing requires collective effort, the organization is reciprocally responsible to the individuals who occupy its offices (Wagoner, 1971). Barker and Roebuck (1973: 15ff) conclude that the real organizational task of police administrations (from the staff sergeant level up) is not how to keep the constables honest, but how to manage the level of police deviance so as to get the work done without arousing media or public outrage. Although independent behavior and attitudes are discouraged among police ranks (Grosman, 1980: 31) and although police often pretend that they possess little discretionary power, the operational realities of police work, especially the limits on resources, prevent police from following the law to the letter, (Pugh, 1963; Chevigny, 1969; Bent, 1974: 155; Muir, 1977).

Official deviance questions the mythology that police officers are more obedient to the law than most citizens, that is, the so called "higher" standard of conduct expected of the police as concluded by countless commissions of inquiry into police misconduct. But this duty or mandate is often combined with discretion to act in ways which are illegal, immoral, or at least deceptive, in order to enforce the law. Admittedly, the public may be all too ready to legitimate and even encourage some forms of illegal use of police discretion, simply to "catch criminals" (Chevigny, 1969).

Official police deviance is not only directly encouraged in the police for the sake of production norms; it is also indirectly legitimated by the police culture which separates off and isolates the police and their work from the public (Shearing, 1992). For many in the rank and file, the general public is viewed as ungrateful, ignorant and "helpless" (ibid). Police know when the informal but officially condoned norms expect them to stop, harass, and arrest minorities, Blacks, protesters, picketers, and the like (Brown and Brown, 1973; Penner, 1979; Jamieson, 1971). Random stops, unwarranted strip searches and other convenient forms of humiliation tend to initiate lengthy processes of confrontation. Stopping a motorist often on a flimsy pretext is one of the most frequent ways stops and searches are executed. Once stopped, "suspects" are questioned; a citizen's anger and frustration is often interpreted as a sign of guilt or suspicion. Lies and deception are familiar forms of official deviance. "We have been taught the use of deception," RCMP Inspector Venner reminded the McDonald inquiry into RCMP dirty tricks (Mann and Lee, 1979: 76). "You lie, first to survive ... then ... to serve the image" of the organization, a former RCMP corporal wrote (Ramsay, 1978). Deception of civilians untutored in their legal rights makes police work simpler and gets the job done. In laying charges after an arrest, officers may be asked by superiors to change and even fabricate occurrence reports, at least to delete ambiguous phrases. "Cover your ass" is the informal but binding rule. For example, after assaulting an accused person the officer may add a charge that the suspect assaulted the arresting officer first (Manning, 1977: 185; Van Maanen, 1974: 10). Official deviance offers the police information and arrests not otherwise available, given the absence of a public complaint or insufficient evidence for a search warrant (Marx, 1980˙.436). The arresting officer may be legitimated and even congratulated for deviance from lawful police practice, for example by faking affidavits or communiqués (Mann and Lee, 1979: 59). A Toronto inquiry into police brutality and torture did not only substantiate citizens' complaints, the presiding judge found that police testifying at the inquiry had systematically lied, manufactured evidence, and altered documents to cover up their illegal activities (Morand, 1976). Yet, as in most such cases, very few officers were punished. Westley (1956: 254) found that 73 percent of his sample of police officers would rather perjure themselves than squeal on a fellow officer. Stoddard (1971: 199) found that police officers obeyed a silent "code" to protect fellow officers from prosecution.

The most harmful form of police deviance is the misuse of excessive police force which is often presented as an inevitable aspect of arrest. Kohler (1975) analyzed in detail the circumstances of 1500 situations where a police officer killed a civilian in the course of duty. In many of these situations, the evidence seriously questioned the need for resort to deadly force; for example, young people were shot in the back simply for running away from a policeman who wanted to question them—youth who had not been caught in criminal acts. Kohler found that in only three of the 1500 cases was the police officer eventually subjected to any form of criminal punishment for killing a civilian. Consider the case of six aboriginal men who died in as many years after being arrested by police in Prince George, Williams Lake,

Vancouver and Oak Bay (Hume, 2003: A7). In one case, Ken Munson and Dan Hatchen, two former police officers were convicted in 2001 of unlawful confinement after they drove Darrell Night, an Aboriginal man to the city's outskirts and abandoned him outside on a freezing January night in 2000 (Globe and Mail, 2003: A5). Allegations continue to surface regarding three aboriginal men who were found frozen to death just outside Saskatoon after city police had abandoned them there (Cook, 2003: A8).

A Toronto police constable who holds a sociology degree was handed a rare 30-day jail sentence to be served on weekends after being convicted of assaulting a man. Incarceration is needed to reflect the public's "intolerance for police abuse of power," Justice Peter Wilkie, said ordering Roy Preston to be taken into custody. Not imposing a jail sentence would "send the wrong message to other police officers," the judge added. The maximum sentence for assault under the Criminal Code is five years' imprisonment. The constable was convicted of assaulting Said Jama Jama, 23, in August 2003, outside a Rexdale coffee shop. A key piece of evidence at the spring trial was a videotape showing Preston punching Jama Jama. "Without that video, things wouldn't be the same, everything would be the other way around," he said. Preston initially charged Jama Jama with assaulting police, a charge the Crown withdrew six months later after reviewing the taped encounter. Without the tourist videotape of a brawl outside the Rexdale doughnut shop early on August 4, 2003, that caught Preston punching Jama Jama in the face, an innocent man might have gone to jail, Wilkie said. The justice also said he considered the "unprovoked" nature of the punch followed by Jama Jama being chased across Albion Rd. and attacked by Preston "not once but twice." While the videotape did not record it, Judge Wilkie concluded Jama Jama was beaten during his arrest by Preston and three other officers in what he called "particularly cowardly" and "reprehensible" fashion, similar to an "angry, out-of-control mob." Jama Jama lost a tooth, and his face was bruised and bloodied (Powell: 2005:E2). Outside the courthouse, Jama Jama said he "could live with the sentence," adding his religion "talks about forgiveness ... (so) I'm going to try to forgive the man and move on with life" (Powell: 2005:E2).Compare that response with the reaction from the Toronto Police Association. Association president Dave Wilson blamed the verdict and sentence on Preston's position; he adds:

> If this wasn't a police officer this would not have been…This is over the top and it sends the wrong message back out to the membership…unfair for an officer to end up in custody is devastating (Powell: 2005:E2).

2.2 Judges

Similarly, the judicial process is not self contained; it is embedded in social and political realities with which it routinely interacts, as Peter McCormick notes:

> This rigorous pruning of irrelevant detail is the great methodological achievement of Western legal systems. It also represents a blind side of potentially overwhelming dimensions because it makes lawyers and judges

> the slaves of whatever the previously defined legal categories happen to be (1994:6).

Like the police, judges operate within reactive institutions that demonstrate very little appreciation of how privilege influences their decisions. Judges maintain certain myths, fictions, and illusions about justice. Typically, their legal training is conservative, refusing to make the law more progressive, relevant and accountable (Magee, 1993). For Magee (1993) this "pathological" institution requires a loyalty to traditional texts and the logic of precedence. Spann (1993:2) notes that the discrepancy between the traditional model and actual Supreme Court performance for example is sufficient to preclude any meaningful difference between Supreme Court adjudication and ordinary politics.

Legal rules, the professional peer culture, occupational ideologies (Cohn and White, 1992), bench politics, external political pressures, training (Flemming, Nardulli, and Eisenstein, 1992:4), pragmatic bureaucratic/ administrative exigencies, and personal bias shape the roles, attitudes, discretion, the value of innovation and the behaviour of judges. Justices have a duty to demonstrate judicial virtue in their role as pedagogues. But, like the police, judges operate within institutions that demonstrate relatively little appreciation of how sexism, racism, class elitism influence their decisions (McCormick, 1994:190). For example Mr. Justice Fred Kovach of the Saskatchewan Court of Queen's Bench sentenced Dean Edmondson, a 26 year old white man to a two-year conditional term -- house arrest -- for sexually assaulting a twelve year old native girl. The judge reasoned that the girl was a previous victim of sexual abuse, and sex-abuse victims are known to show "unpredictable sexual behaviour," as a paediatrician testified in the case. (Globe & Mail, September 9, 2003:A22).Seldom do judges have any personal familiarity with the economic cruelties which diminish the lives of the poor (Wright, 1990:12). Law professor Jamie Cameron,

> For the near future, all we can look forward to is a court that is more interested in avoiding controversy than in developing a vision of rights...penchant for unanimous and anonymous decision-making often represents a lapse in -- rather than an example of -- leadership. (Makin, 2002: A11).

Likewise Professor Young notes that the courts have interpreted the Charter to give judges extremely broad powers, and then doing little more than tinkering around the edges of offensive laws and statutes (Makin, 2002: A11).

If police cover for each other, judges "keep the faith" even more so. Of all the major sectors of the legal system to be studied by sociologists, judges have earned the least attention. We have left it to investigative journalists to expose the wheeling and dealing among the "brethren" of the courts (Woodward and Armstrong, 1979). Judges have unparalleled privilege in their protection of official action from the public eye. The structural condition most relevant to the official deviance of judges is the *production norm* of the court system; the caseload in criminal courts continues to escalate more rapidly than courtroom facilities, staff, or judges on the bench. Similar situations have been observed in many jurisdictions, and lead to the inevitable "systematic evasions of the principal norms" of the judge's official duties (Balbus, 1973: 18). On learning that jurors are having difficulty in agreeing on a verdict, it is common practice for judges to summon a sequestered jury to the open courtroom, inform jurors that another jury would have the same problems and remind the jurors of the costs of a new trial. This prompting is sufficient to ensure that that the jury will return with an unanimous verdict. A judge's discussion of organizational factors (costs, delay, the inconvenience of a new trial) is instrumental in expediting and determining the verdict.

The production structure of the legal system also leads judges to appear to address the appeals courts above them rather than the jurors before them. Fully cognizant of organizational command structures, judges may on the one hand instruct jurors not to take notes, while burdening them with complicated and confusing instructions. On the other hand they frame their own statements in a legalistic jargon intended for the ears of appeals court judges. To further lubricate the creaking assembly lines of justice, where the average criminal trial now requires only a few minutes due to the large number of guilty pleas, and judges admit that defendants who insist on going to trial can expect more severe penalties if found guilty (Skolnick, 1967: 13), judges may also prompt the lawyers to "get moving." While meeting the formal requirements of their office by reminding the jurors to keep an open mind, judges may make the direction of their own opinions all too evident through informal cues, interruptions, and promptings.

New judges, irrespective of their well - meaning intentions soon learn the informal rules of the bench. They learn early to avoid emphasizing contradictions in police testimony and to avoid suggesting that the police have lied. At best, the police may be "mistaken." Judicial admissions concerning the extent of policed manipulation of evidence, including police notebooks, are extremely rare (Morand, 1976). Canadian judges have been particularly cooperative with police deviance in obtaining evidence since The Queen v. Wray in which it was held that "if evidence is deemed by the court to be relevant ... a judge cannot reject it, even if it is obtained by the authorities through fraud, deceit or even physical violence." Churning out the sentences is not indicative of "corruption" on the part of judges, but of deviance which goes with the office in an overloaded and increasingly irrational system (Jaros and Mendelsohn, 1967). Former chief justice Antonio Lamer, the: "The investigation of crime and the detection of criminals is not a game to be governed by the Marquess of Queensberry rules." (Globe A14 Saturday, February 3, 2005).

2.3 Juries

Juries in large measure act politically. Using data from mock trials, interviews with numerous jurors, and statistical analyses, Levine (1992) demonstrated that the social, economic, and political values that jurors bring with them to court are important in the way they filter and process information given to them. Moreover, the overall political climate of the times affects the way jurors render decisions. The structured embeddedness of juries in the legal system renders them susceptible to the excessively legalistic jargon, convoluted logic and ambiguous roles (Lee and Visano,

1981). They are often held hostage to the selfish manipulations of courtroom actors who are fundamentally concerned with "winning" the case regardless of ethics and principles of social justice. Deference to the law, however constituted by and for self serving practitioners, violates principles of justice. Ideally, the jury system is premised on notions of impartiality, independence, and representativeness. And yet at all stages, from jury selection to the actual sequestered deliberation of a case, considerable discretion exists. Guided by the judge's charge and the judge's interpretation of the law, the jury is required to assess the facts or evidence. At no point is the jury asked to account for its decision to convict or acquit. Decisions are made *in camera*, and with no public accountability whatsoever. Sentenced to six years, Philip Berrigan (1970:131) wrote that justice is a crass process. That is,

> First, secure a bourgeois jury whose values coincide with those of the Establishment; then narrow the issues to black and white with no grays; exclude discussion of conscience, civil disobedience, national and international illegality; employ contempt of court to intimidate counsel; blind the jury's oath to the judge's assumption of guilt...Justice is a process of rationalizing the irrational.

Likewise, commenting on his trial, Rubin "Hurricane" Carter (1991: 307, emphases added) noted:

> a totally white jury to decide if two black men had killed three white people- with the accusation coming from two white convicts, a white prosecutor, and a white judge who did just about everything but to tell the jury straight out not to believe the black witnesses ... Six whole weeks of legal arguments, crying, pleading, tearing, picking, digging, demanding some mother fucking justice, and these crackers had their shit together within *two hours*...Their verdict was guilty as charged on all three counts, but with a recommendation of mercy, or life imprisonment...

2.4 Lawyers

Criminologists have also paid relatively little attention to lawyers. There are several reasons for this "oversight." One is the fact that lawyering is effectively organized as a profession where infractions of practice are investigated by fellow practitioners; the public and social scientists are effectually excluded (Johnson, 1972). Indeed, it is in the nature of their profession to argue, contest, and sometimes confuse the already vague set of normative "ethics" and rules. They are expected to be bound by a variety of both formal and informal standards of behavior expressed in court practice, Law Society ethics, and their formal training in law. That official, structured deviance exists within lawyers' professional behavior is already well documented (e.g., Nader and Green, 1976; Blumberg, 1970). One structural condition which tends to make lawyers' deviance more prevalent is a significant gap between the formal requirements of a statute and the consensus of informal public and professional opinion about the behavior governed by the statute. The sociology of legal practice has already established that the formal adversarial system is often replaced in fact by an administrative model in which the defense lawyer becomes another cog in the machinery of the court. Lawyers work in a system where ongoing relationships are anticipated with prosecutors and judges, but only a very transient relationship exists with the client (Blumberg, 1967; Casper, 1972). Far from serving as a fearless champion of the client, the defense lawyer is often "more prepared to accept the police version of events ... and the best the solicitor is prepared to do in court is to (present the accused) as a character worthy of clemency, treatment or a second chance" (Carlen, 1976: 91).Not every lawyer looking for a deal in plea bargaining is as forthright as Downie's (1971) example of the lawyer approaching the prosecutor "What can you do for me today?" given that plea bargaining has certainly structured official deviance into legal practice.

Though plea bargaining deviates from what is ideally pretended to be going on in court (Alschuler, 1975: 1210); it is now so pervasive as to be widely accepted as normal (Kadish and Kadish, 1973: 84; Baldwin and McConville, 1977). Any reading of the codes of ethics of Bar Associations would leave a stranger to the courts largely unaware of plea bargaining. But then, as Garbus and Seligman (1976) argue, bar associations may be little more than trade associations, and are certainly not diligent in policing the profession. The following insightful comments from Professor Hutchinson (2001: A15, emphases added) highlight several factors that render the Federation of Law Societies of Canada -- all the law societies governing all of the 81,000 lawyers in the country or the Law Society of Upper Canada -- the governing body for the 31,000 lawyers in Ontario quite ineffective:

> As long as access to justice depends on access to lawyers, society must oblige the legal profession to meet its public responsibilities -- the leading one being that legal services must be genuinely available to all. Or it must relinquish its monopoly; the profession must be subject to anti-trust rules and broken up. After all, we're committed to the Rule of Law, *not the rule of lawyers*. What's good for lawyers is not necessarily good for everyone else... It's a common conceit of lawyers to defend their fees as a function of market economics -- arguing that they're charging what the market can bear and prices will fluctuate with changing market conditions... Lawyers, unlike investment bankers, are not just another sector of the business world. They have sway over a legal system supposedly committed to social justice, and it is one of that system's touted virtues that justice is not for sale to the highest bidder. As long as lawyers are beyond the pocket of most citizens, so is *social justice*... Lawyers hold *a jealously guarded monopoly* on the provision of legal services, controlling entry, education, discipline and regulation ... A more practical, effective intervention would be to let lawyers retain their monopoly, but only on the condition that they truly serve the public. This means that there must be more citizens and clients involved in running the profession, that *lawyers must be answerable to someone other than themselves* ...Courts can play a decisive role. And

> judges already have considerable power to assess lawyers' fees and to discipline prodigal lawyers; they must be prepared to use these powers vigorously and to set appropriate expectations.

In reference to social justice, civil rights lawyer Ruby (2001: A27) similarly adds,

> Lawyers tend to go along with government. Perhaps that is because there are so many of them in government. Perhaps it is because they are inherently conservative... It is the role of lawyers in a free society to defend the rights of the oppressed—and not to be conscripted by government to secretly inform on their clients.

Law school can be an exhilarating intellectual experience and yet students' learning endeavours are upstaged by the professional competition for good jobs (Van Dijk 2001: A15).

For Flemming, Nardulli and Eisenstein (1992), prosecutors are seldom scrutinized in the criminal courts. Researchers maintain that prosecutors purposefully organize their offices and deploy their resources in order to enhance their status *vis-a-vis* judges and other lawyers. Kritzer's (1991:120) analysis of bargaining demonstrated that the negotiation is geared not toward achieving the best outcome possible but toward achieving an appropriate outcome by arriving at some consensus with the opposing party concerning the parameters of the case. Pro forma negotiations also occur where costs are very high relative to probable return, and where there may be little concern about optimal results in individual cases (ibid,125).On the other side of the courtroom, prosecutors or district attorneys know the informal rules necessary to their role in keeping the court system working from day to day. One of these, not written down anywhere and certainly contrary to the ideals of justice, is the overcharging of suspects in order. As Toronto's Judge Vanek observed (Toronto Sun, January 25, 1974), "to serve as a device to force a guilty plea on a minimum charge." The prosecutor gets the conviction, thus legitimating all the prior steps of arrest, detention, and interrogation, and the court system is kept up to production norms-about one criminal case every two minutes (Downie, 1971). In some cases, both defense and prosecuting lawyers collaborate in mutually official deviance from the formal and legal requirements of their offices. For example, in a Toronto burglary trial, defense and prosecution agreed to keep from the judge the fact that it was *armed* burglary. The prosecution thereby gained the dropping of charges of torture by the police to obtain the confession of the accused confession, and the accused pleaded guilty to a lesser charge (Globe and Mail, October 25, 1974). Defense lawyers will deviate from the obligations of their office by advising clients to plead guilty to charges of which they are innocent, and of which the lawyer believes they are innocent, simply because the client cannot afford the lawyer's legal fees.

2.5 Corrections

In institutions to which we send inmates to do penitence for their wrongs, official deviance is endemic (Lieberman, 1972: 121; Hirshkop and Milleman, 1969). "All the crimes committed by all the jailed criminals do not equal in total social damage that of the crimes committed against them," Menninger observed (1969: 28). "The system" would collapse if prison guards went by the book - and if those who insisted on lawful behavior by fellow guards reported those who violated the law. Indeed, attempts to reform guard behavior are as likely to end in a prison riot as in a strike by the guards' union. Guards know how to wreck a reforming warden's plans by tormenting prisoners to rebellion (MacGuigan, 1977).

Prisons are legitimated as places to "re-educate people to law-abiding lives in the community" (Ouimet, 1969: 304). There appears to be a dilemma between the goals of security and corrections; on closer observation one realizes no such contradiction. The two aims in fact serve a single purpose of the state: discipline and control (Foucault, 1977). Prisons have become a "growth industry" expenditures for the "punishment industry" (Friedenberg, 1980: 62) are exorbitant. Within these costly and essentially lawless structures where civilians are largely without civil liberties, guards may punish without the benefit of law, simply by following administrative rules. Inmates may be condemned to solitary confinement for indeterminate periods, without the right to legal counsel or to appeal.

Courts are reluctant to intervene on behalf of prisoners, while top penitentiary officials wash their hands of the action of their underlings. Like Warden Lemarier of Canada's Archambault prison, they may blame the convict subculture for unpunished murders within prison. "We know who is responsible but no one will talk. I don't blame any inmate who won't talk. If he did and somehow he wasn't killed when he came back here, he would eventually be killed on the outside" (Globe and Mail, January 26, 1980). Or the officials may blame a too-powerful guard union, which in turn condemns "convict-coddling" reformers (Globe and Mail, January 31, 1978).

Those who become guards are not necessarily cruel and insensitive as private persons, but they become official cogs in a custodial roulette wheel. The parliamentary inquiry into Canadian penitentiaries in 1977 listed among systematic unlawful behavior by guards: the waking of prisoners at night without necessity, delay and adulterating of meals, locking prisoners up ten minutes before the end of a movie, delaying summoning of inmates when visitors are waiting to see them, and so on. Sidney Katz (Toronto Star, October 5, 1976) described how guards toss inmates into the "hole" for days for just "talking back." The public's need to blame, the court's organizational need to get the work done despite awesome overloading, the police determination to fight so-called lax bail laws, the prison system's reluctance to parole, have all led to a situation where even the Corrections Minister of Ontario can conclude that "there's no reason why a significant number of prisoners could not have been out on bail. Even if one third had been released on bail, that's a phenomenal number of people." His remarks followed a 1979 study of Ontario prisons showing that of 23,369 people remanded in custody for trial, 17,000 of these, when eventually tried, received no prison sentence (Globe and Mail, April 11, 1980).

Parole and probation officers exercise power in a subjective manner through judgments given to the courts, in pre-sentence reports, social enquiry reports and regular supervision reports where custodial recommendations subscribe to a pathology model. Interestingly, racially profiled suspects in general do not receive probation recommendations, that is, although more privileged white offenders who make up a majority of all clients, black offenders are disproportionately represented in the more punitive areas of probation supervision. Probation officers are more inclined to subscribe to rehabilitative models for white probationaries while adopting a punitive/ social control perspective for black adult offenders (Klein, 1979). Unlike their white counterparts, black offenders are routinely assessed according to their mental state, their nationality and place of birth, (Denney, 1992: 24). Race was often related to blameworthiness. On the basis of his review of a large number of empirical studies, Denney concludes that probation officers perceive black offenders in a manner incorporating varying degrees of prejudice and racism; probation officers include irrelevant material in their respective social enquiry reports; and, there are different styles in report writing (ibid, 38-39). According to probation officers white offending is attributable to alcoholism, dysfunctional families while anti-authority attitudes, a tendency to rebel, accounted for black offending (ibid,41, 62). These officers cite irresponsibility, peer pressure, depression as contributing to white crimes, whereas provocation, pragmatics, anger, lifestyle are emphasized in their talk about black offenders (ibid, 61-77).

The above overview demonstrates that the police officers, judges or jurors, and correctional staff are loyal to the their respective offices which are replete with its legal duties, informal norms, organizational pressures, professional customs, codes of collegiality, symbols of official institutional membership, etc. that defer to the legitimacy and authority of the criminal justice system. In the phenomenal realm, as a lived medium of meaning and value, the work of these agents is not simply conspiratorial but rather it is the project of legal, political and economic rationalizations that maintains relations of domination that define the status quo.

3. Conclusions: The Logic of Necessity as Deviance Denial

As noted above, the concept of law exists as a discoursal practice that is socially or relationally situated. In addition to the law's ideological affiliation with liberalism, capitalism and modernity, law is simultaneously institutionally linked to situationally relevant contextual codes that frame decision points or procedural judgements. The *occupational/ institutional culture* is one of the most significant influences on socio-legal conditioning that translates the spirit and letter of law. Criminal justice exists in the "office" of various agencies or as often put by incumbents, "it's part of the job description but it's never written down anywhere." Admittedly, it is officials who act, not organizations per se, but officials act out of perception of organizational needs and goals" (Gouldner, 1961: 87).

To cope with the contradictions in both the law and organizational regulations, all agents of the criminal justice system rely on the informal rules of the work culture. This occupational culture refers to an organized and recognized constellation of values that are specific to the required activities. First, the collegium exerts influence in perpetuating a sense of professionalism replete with norms, roles and attitudes. This culture as a historically transmitted pattern of symbolic meanings communicates, perpetuates, and develops "useful" knowledge about and attitudes towards work and their "clients". As argued above, it is important to know how these agents, as representatives of an occupational culture, make sense of contradictions and controversy, the inscription of dominant ideologies (narratives), and, their 'preferred", "oppositional" and "negotiated" styles.

The structure of the criminal justice system is a contingency that shapes the neophyte's self-image, as well as his or her understanding of situational difficulties. This culture or opportunity structure awaits the arrival of prospective members. The respective professions offer both limitations to, and possibilities for, effective, critically responsive approaches. The self-identities that they construct for themselves are congruent with the possible identities that are afforded them within the professional/occupational culture. This culture provides a coherent narrative of identities, ensures social recognition of these identities and a sense of "we-ness" that stress the similarities or shared attributes around which group members coalesce. A collective wisdom emerges that serves to guide and validate perspectives and activities; normative self serving and self important attributes and images emerge to essentialize identity. Acculturation, that is, the process of learning the "ways and means" (coping strategies: accommodation and resistance) from collegial involvement, offers a collective solution to actual and perceived strains and values a symbolic framework for the development and maintenance of a collective identity as well as individual self esteem.

When officials violate the normative expectations of their offices, it is "only natural" that they will make excuses. But explanations based in "human nature" are rarely satisfying to the social scientist, who wonders why a certain social order is more "natural" to one population than to another, or to one era and not another. Noble and patriotic motives may excuse FBI dirty tricks in the eyes of citizens who would not accept the same excuse from those who challenge state authorities.

As noted, much of the groundwork of legitimating official deviance in the legal system is accomplished by myths which do not have to be argued. But from time to time, the extent of official deviance exposed by the media is so deep and pervasive that officials feel called upon to provide "explanations." At such times, "bureaucratic propaganda" is manufactured to disarm critics and defuse investigations (Altheide and Johnson, 1980). A common theme in modern bureaucratic propaganda is the "*logic of necessity*." The logic of necessity may be offered wholesale or retail. The Hoover Commission in 1954 offered wholesale argument for official deviance from lawful methods in controlling "subversion": "Hitherto accepted norms of human conduct no longer apply.... We must learn to subvert, sabotage and destroy our enemies by more effective methods than those used against us" (Stockwell, 1978: 252). Likewise, Henry Kissinger argued that if democratic elections in Chile put Allende in power, there was no need to "stand by because of the irresponsibility of the voters" (Barnet, 1975).

The logic of necessity appears more commonly in retail amounts. For example, official transgressions of the law is seen by many as justified because it was "only technically illegal", "because you didn't ask me the right question" or it was "an exception" during a crisis or urgency. Another way of stating the logic of necessity is to argue quite simply that present practice works. For example, a brief by the Toronto police to the Krever commission investigating police violation of the privacy of medical documents argued: the fact that it is illegal is irrelevant; the very fact that it happens proves that it is necessary. If the present laws were rigidly enforced, the police would be hampered in their work (Krever Commission, Briefs, 1980). The argument that illegal behaviour of official agents is necessary and that it works is more than a rationalization. It is a reserve of organizational power to be tapped when other resources fail to get the day's work done. "Necessity" may ultimately provide officials with more power than the formal rules of office. Yet the logic and rules of such necessity are rarely written into any "guidelines" of official behavior, a fact which helps to preserve the myths of rationality and "rule of law, not of men" in our legal system. Gouldner (1961) argues correctly that it is possible to structure organizations so as to "necessitate" positive and democratic effects. However, what Mills (1959: 341) called the "higher immorality" of modern society makes the call for the structured necessity of openness in organizations seem "naive."

There is a popular "new sophistication" (in the worst meaning of the root of sophistry) which argues that we must be "realistic" about organizations. This new sophistication may combine with a certain sociological laissez-faire of the functionalist sort, which finds social meaning and usefulness in whatever organization actually exists. The new sophistication assumes that the FBI, CIA, CSIS, RCMP and the like "must have good reasons" for their dirty tricks or else they wouldn't have done them. The new sophistication proposes to legalize what is already done by the organization, making it no longer deviant. Legitimation becomes a routine matter (Vidich, 1975). For example, if the police have been profiling Muslims illegally and claim that this is "necessary" to "catch terrorists" or subversives, then the new sophistication responds by changing the law to make it legal. It is worth reiterating that neither the logic of necessity nor the new sophistication has ever been extended by officials to the powerless and the dissident.

Disavowal of organizational deviance ranges from outright denial that it exists to assertion that the actions are only exceptions, or only *technically* illegal, to outright moral justification of the acts as examples of "noble purpose" in the organization, that is, as "the overzealous pursuit of duty." Disavowal may also take the form of language manipulation - unlawful acts become "wrongdoings" or "indiscretions." If these forms of disavowal and neutralization fail, the organization may revert to demonology, invoking a variety of stigmatized "enemies" against which deviant methods may appear legitimate; the targets are labeled "subversives," "foreign agitators," and "terrorists." Organizations have structural advantages in disavowing deviance: large and diverse bureaucracies may divert attention from an exposed sector to one where some legitimacy and even honor can be claimed for current official activities. Failing all other efforts to disavow deviance, the organization whose continued survival relies heavily on a covert pattern of official deviance will attempt to prevent full public disclosure of such deviance by throwing one or more guilty officials to the wolves. A public sacrifice of one or more officials as "bad apples" not the barrel nor the orchard, highlights the individual not the *systemic* nature of abuse. Scotland Yard has undergone three purges of a total of more than 400 detectives in a decade Barry Cox et al. (1977). The legal system refuses to recognize the organizational structuring of the "bent bobby," and instead castigates guilty individuals. Thus Judge Melford Stevenson lectured certain convicted detectives:

> You poisoned the wells of criminal justice and set about it deliberately. What is equally bad is that you have betrayed your comrades in the Metropolitan police force, which enjoys the respect of the civilized world-what is left of it-and not the least grave aspect of what you have done is to provide material for the crooks, cranks and do-gooders who unite to attack the police whenever opportunity occurs [Cox et al., 1977: 127].

For the official interacting with the organization as everyday experience, the socially constructed organization becomes externalized and real (Berger and Luckmann, 1966). What was originally intended or sought after now becomes "necessary." Thus, the logic of necessity—the grammar of needs and goals of an organization—serves as a link between individual experience and organizational structure, between micro and macro worlds.

The most pervasive form of official deviance is plain and simple *lying* (Chevigny, 1969; Mann and Lee, 1979; Altheide and Johnson, 1980). Official secrecy is the means to cover up and protect lying. As Simmel foresaw, the extent of modern bureaucratic official lying has created a secret world alongside the manifest world (Wolff, 1950). It is a system where a lie told by one side - the police and prosecution - is much more likely to gain credence, simply because of the official status of the liar. There are many opportunities to lie in the legal system. A large proportion of cases are settled in plea bargaining, which is neither public nor recorded. Discretionary power hidden from public view provides countless opportunities for lying. Given that officials use techniques of stonewalling, secrecy and conflict of interest they should never be allowed the luxury of investigating themselves. Professionalization, as Johnson (1972) points out, is simply a way of staking out exclusive control over an occupation, and repelling any suggestion of "outside" interference. More bureaucracy, more official status and professional control, more opportunities for secrecy and bureaucratic propaganda, simply extend the powers of state discipline and control. The ultimate neutralization for official deviance comes from the average citizen's willingness to legitimate the system. Just as the images of kings must topple before their thrones, the images of official deviance must be challenged before the structure can be reformed. Remedies which avoid criminalizing behavior by passing new laws are more hopeful. Douglas and Johnson (1977: 407) are correct in their paradox that "the more rules [we make to control deviance] the more official deviance there will be." Remedies based on assuring a greater flow of accurate information about bureaucracies are remedies in the right direction. The secrecy and the interminable simultaneity of necessity which covers up so much official deviance must be penetrated and exposed as modalities of cultural pathologies and contradictions in social fracture. The confluence of contradictions, ambiguities and metaphors provides a much-needed contingent sense of institutional relations that evades thinking. The dangerous contradictions advanced with impunity by institutions of law must be exposed. Compare and contrast both the quality and quantity of responses of legal authorities to the tragedies of 9/11 in New York City and Katrina on New Orleans in August 2005.

As Audrey Lorde and Albert Einstein respectively observed "the master's tools will not dismantle the master's house" and "no problem can be solved from the same consciousness that created it". Instead, as Fanon reminded us, the solution to this inherent cycle of violence in criminal justice rests in a phenomenon that has become so foreign to everyday life—consciousness of transcendence, a commitment to the humanity of interconnectedness. Regrettably, a frighteningly fetishistic delirium shifts attention away from the injustices of everyday to the comfortable conceit of cherished illusions of freedom.

References

Alschuler, A. 1975 "The Defense Attorney's Role in Plea Bargaining." *Yale Law Review* 84, 6: 1179- 1314.

Altheide, D. and J. Johnson 1980 *Bureaucratic Propaganda*. Toronto: Allyn & Bacon.

Arnold, T. 1975 "Law as Symbolism," In V. Aubert (ed.) *Sociology of Law*. London: Penguin.

Arendt, H. 1994 "Some Questions of Moral Philosophy *Social Research*; 1994, 61, 4, Winter, 739-764.

Bakhtin, M. 1981 *The Dialogic Imagination*. Austin: University of Texas Press.

Balbus, I. 1973 *The Dialectic of Legal Repression*. New York: Russell Sage Foundation.

Baldwin, J. and M. McConville 1977 Negotiated Justice. London: Robertson.

Barker, T. and J. Roebuck 1973 *Typology of Police Corruption*. Springfield, IL: Charles C Thomas.

Barnet, R. J. 1975 "Dirty Tricks and the Intelligence Underworld." *Society* 12, 3: 52-63

Barthes, R. 1973. *Mythologies*. London: Cape.

Becker, T. L. and V. G. Murray 1971 *Government Lawlessness in America*. New York: Oxford.

Bent, A. 1974 *The Politics of Law Enforcement*. Toronto: Lexington.

Berger, P. and T. Luckmann 1966 *The Social Construction of Reality*. New York: Doubleday.

Berrigan, P. 1970. *Prison Journal of a Priest Revolutionary* NY: Ballantine

Berkeley, George 1969 *The Democratic Policeman*. Boston: Beacon.

Bittner, E. 1967 "The Police on Skid Row" *American Sociological Review* 32, 5: 699-715

Black, D. 1976 *The Behavior of Law*. New York: Academic Press.

Blumberg, A. 1970 *The Scales of Justice*. New York: Aldine.

Blumberg, A. 1967. "The Practice of Law as a Confidence Game." *Law and Society Review* 1: 15-39.

Boorstin, D.l971. "The Perils of Indwelling Law" In R. Wolff (ed.) *The Rule of Law* New York: Simon and Shuster.

Bourdieu, Pierre *Outline of a Theory of Practice*. New York: Cambridge University Press, 1977.

Brown, L. and C. Brown 1973An Unauthorized History of the RCMP. Toronto: Lewis and Samuel.

Cain, M. 1979 "Trends in the Sociology of Police Work." *International Journal of the Sociology of Law* 7: 143-167.

Carlen , P. 1976 *Magistrates' Justice*. London: Robertson.

Carter, R. H. 1991. *The 16th Round* NY: Penguin.

Casper, J.1972 *American Criminal Justice: The Defendant's Perspective*. Englewood Cliffs, Prentice-Hall.

Chambliss, W.1964 "A Sociological Analysis of the Law of Vagrancy." *Social Problems* 12: 61-77.

Chambliss, W. and R. Seidman 1971 *Law, Order and Power*. Reading, MA: Addison Wesley

Chapman B. 1970. *Police State*. New York: Praeger.

Chevigny, P. 1969.*Police Power*. New York: Pantheon.

Cohn, E.S.and S.0.White. 1992. *Legal Socialization: A Study of Norms and Rules*. New York: Springer-Verlag.

Cook T. 2003 *Globe and Mail* September 9, P A8

Cox, B., J. Shirley, and M. Short. 1977.*The Fall of Scotland Yard*. London: Penguin.Addison-Wesley.

Denney, D. 1992. *Racism and Anti-Racism in Probation* London: Routledge

Derrida, J. (1981). *Positions*. Chicago: The University of Chicago Press.

Derrida, J. 1990; " Force of Law, The Mystical Foundation of Authority trans M. Quarntance. In *Cordozo Law Review* p925

de Saussure, F. 1986. *Course in General Linguistics* (translation R. Harris), Illinois: Open Court.

Douglas, J. and J.Johnson. 1977 *Official Deviance*. Philadelphia: J. B. Lippincott.

Downie, Leonard 1971 *Justice Denied*. New York: Praeger.

Eberts, M. 1985. "Sex and Equality Rights" In A. Bayefsky and M. Eberts (eds.) *Equality Rights and the Canadian Charter of Rights and* Freedoms Toronto: Carswell.

Ericson, R. 1982. *Reproducing Order* Toronto: University of Toronto Press

Flemming, R.B., P. F. Nardulli, and J. Eisenstein. 1992 *The Craft of Justice: Politics and Work in Criminal Court Communities* Philadelphia: University of Pennsylvania Press.

Foucault, M. 1977 *Discipline and Punish*. New York: Pantheon.

Friedenberg, E.1980. *Deference to Authority: the Case of Canada*. New York: M. E. Sharpe.

Friedman, L. M. 1977 *The Legal System*. New York: Russell Sage Foundation.

Fuller, L. 1969 *Anatomy of Law*. New York: Mentor.

Fuller, L. 1975 *The Morality of Law*. New Haven, CT: Yale University Press.

Garbus, M. and J. Seligman 1976. "Sanctions and Disbarment," in R. Nader and M. Green (eds.) *Verdicts on Lawyers*. New York: Harper & Row.

Giddens, A. 1991. *Modernity and Self-Identity* Stanford: Stanford University Press.

Giddens, A. 1992. *Transformation of Intimacy* Stanford Stanford University Press

Globe and Mail, January 26, 1980.

Globe and Mail, January 31, 1978.

Globe and Mail, April 11, 1980.

Globe and Mail, October 25, 1974

Globe and Mail Tuesday, September 9, 2003 - Page A22

Globe and Mail A14 Saturday, February 3, 2005

Globe and Mail , Wednesday, May 7, 2003 - Page A5

Gardiner, J. 1969 *Traffic and the Police: Varieties of Law Enforcement Policy*. Cambridge, MA: Harvard University Press.

Goode, M. R. 1976 "The Law Reform Commission of Canada; Political Ideology of the Criminal Reform Process." *Canadian Bar Review*: 53 (September).

Gouldner, A. W. 1961"Metaphysical Pathos and the Theory of Bureaucracy," in S. M. Lipsett and N. J. Smelser (eds.) *Sociology: Progress of a Decade*. Englewood Cliffs, NJ: PrenticeHall.

Grosman, B. 1975. *Police Command*. Toronto: Macmillan.

Grosman, B. 1980. *New Directions in Sentencing*. Toronto: Butterworth.

Gusfield, Joseph 1963 *Symbolic Crusade: Status Politics and the American Temperance Movement*. Urbana: University of Illinois Press.

Habermas, J. 1976. *Legitimation Crisis*. London: Heinemann Educational Books.

Hagan, J., J. Hewitt, and D. Alwin 1979 "Ceremonial Justice: Crime and Punishment in a Loosely Coupled System." *Social Forces* 58 2: 506-527.

Hall, J. 1947 *General Principles of Criminal Law*. Indianapolis: Bobbs-Merrill.

Hall, S. et al. (1992). *Culture, Media, Language*. London: Routledge

Harding, A.1966 *A Social History of English Law*. London: Pelican.

Hirshkop, P. and M. Milleman 1969 "The Unconstitutionality of Prison Life." *Virginia Law Review* 55: 795-839. I

Hogarth, J.1971. *Sentencing as a Human Process*. University of Toronto Press.

Hume, M , 2003, "B.C. urged to probe deaths of natives in police custody" *Globe and Mail* , September 17 p A7.

Hunt, A. 1993. *Explorations In Law and Society: Toward Constitutive Theory of Law*. New York: Routledge.

Hutchinson , A. 2001 "Justice is greedy: The real cost of high lawyers' fees is a legal system that's unjust, argues Osgoode Hall law professor" *Globe and Mail* Tuesday, February 6, A15

Jamieson, S. 1971 Times of Trouble, Study 22. *Task Force on Labour Relations*. Ottawa: Queen's Printer.

Jaros, D. and R. Mendelsohn 1967 "The Judicial Role and Sentencing Behavior." *Midwest Journal of Political Science* 11: 471-475.

Johnson, Terence 1972 Professions and Power. London: Macmillan.

Judt, T. 2005. "The New World Order" New *York Review of Books* (July 14), p14.

Kadish, M. R. and S. H. Kadish 1973 *Discretion to Disobey: A Study of Lawful Departure from Legal Rules*. Stanford, CA: Stanford University Press.

Klein, J. 1976 *Let's Make a Deal: Negotiated Justice*. Lexington, MA: Lexington Books.

Klein, M. 1979. "Deinstitutionalizationand Diversion of Juvenile Offenders: A Litany of Impediments" In N. Morris and M. Tonrey (eds.) *Crime and Justice* Chicago: University of Chicago Press.

Kohler, A.1975. "Police Homicide in a Democracy." *Journal of Social Issues* 31: 163-170.

Krever, Judge H. 1980 *Commission on Police Access to Medical Records*. Toronto: Queen's Printer.

Kritzer, H. K. 1991. *Let's Make a Deal: Understandinq the Negotiation in Ordinary Litigation*. Madison, WI: University of Wisconsin Press, 1991.

Lacan, J.1977 *Ecrits: A Selection*. trans. Alan Sheridan. New York: W.W. Norton.

Lee, J. and L. A. Visano. 1981. "Official Deviance in the Legal System" In H. Ross (ed.) *Law and Deviance* Beverly Hills: Sage

Lefcourt, R.1971 *Law Against the People*. New York: Vintage.

Levine.J.P. 1992. *Juries and Politics* Pacific Grove, California: Brooks/Cole.

Lieberman, J. K. 1972 *How the Government Breaks the Law*. New York: Stein and Day.

Lindesmith, A. 1967 *The Addict and the Law*. New York: Random House

Lloyd, D. 1974 *The Idea of Law*. London: Pelican.

Lloyd, R. P. 1972 "Toward a Sociology of Secrecy and Security Systems." *Social Problems* 19: 439- 450.

MacGuigan, M 1977 *Report of the Subcommittee on the Penitentiary System in Canada*. Ottawa: Supply and Services Canada.

Magee, J. 1993. "Managing with a Pathological Institution: Judicial Review in American Democracy". Annual Meeting of the American Political Science Association, Copyright by the American Political Science Association Washington, D.C., September 2-5.

Makin, K. 2002 Supreme Court cowed and confused, speakers say *Globe and Mail*, April 13, p A11

Mann, Edward and John Alan Lee [eds.] 1979 *The RCMP versus the People*. Don Mills: General.
Manning, P. 1977 *Police Work: the Social Organization of Policing*. Cambridge: MIT Press.
Marx, G. 1980 "Police Undercover Work." *Urban Life* 8, 4 (January): 399-446.
McCormick, P. 1994. *Canada's Courts* Toronto: James Lorimer & Co.
Menninger, K 1969. *The Crime of Punishment*. New York: Viking.
Mills, C. W.1959 *The Power Elite*. Oxford University Press.
Morand, Justice D. 1976 *Commission into Metropolitan Toronto Police Practices*. Toronto: Queen's Printer.
Moriondo, E. 1966 "The Value System of Italian Judges." Papers, Sixth World Congress of Sociology, Evian.
Muir, W. 1977 *Police: Streetcorner Politicians*. Los Angeles: University of California Press.
Nader, R. and M. Green. 1976 *Verdicts of Lawyers*. New York: Harper & Row.
Niederhoffer, A. 1969.*Behind the Shield: The Police in Urban Society*. New York: Doubleday.
Ontario Commission of Inquiry into the Ontario Provincial Police. 1974.*Report* to the Solicitor General of Ontario.
Ontario Police Commission Inquiry into Police Practices in the Waterloo Regional Police Force. *Report* to the Solicitor General of Ontario.
Ouimet, R. 1969 *Report* of the Canadian Committee on Corrections. Ottawa: Information Canada.
Penner, N. 1979 "How the RCMP Got Where It Is," in E. Mann and J. A. Lee (eds.) *The RCMP versus the People*. Don Mills: General.
Pepinsky, H. 1975 "Reliance on Formal Written Law." *British Journal of Sociology* 26: 330-341
Powell, B. 2005. "Officer jailed in `cowardly' assault" . Toronto Star. E2. Sept 24.
Pound, R. 1942. *Social Control Through Law*. New Haven, CT: Yale University Press.
Pugh, D. S. 1963 "A Conceptual Scheme for Organizational Analysis." *Administrative Science Quarterly* 8: 296-300.
Quinney, R. 1969 *The Social Reality of Law*. Boston: Little, Brown.
Quinney, R. 1972 "The Ideology of Law." *Issues in Criminology* 7, l.
Quinney, R. 1974 *Critique of the Legal Order*, Boston: Little, Brown.
Radzinowicz, L. 1956. *A History of English Criminal Law and its Administration from 1750*, Vol 3, London: Sweet and Maxwell.
Ramsay, J. 1978 "My Case Against the RCMP," in J. Haas and B. Shaffir (eds.) *Decency and Deviance*. Toronto: McClelland and Stewart.
Rawls, J. 1993 *Political Liberalism*. New York: Columbia University Press.
Ruby, C. 2001 When lawyers should fight the law *Globe and Mail* , December 11, A27
Schermerhorn, R. 1961 *Society and Power*. New York: Random House.

Shearing, C. and J. Leon. 1992. "Reconsidering the Police Role: A Challenge to a Challenge of a Popular Conception" In *Understanding Policing* (eds.) K. McCormick and L. Visano Toronto: Canadian Scholars.

Silver, A. 1992. "The Demand for Order in Civil Society". In *Understanding Policing* (eds.) K. McCormick and L. Visano Toronto: Canadian Scholars Scholars

Skolnick, J. 1967. *Justice Without Trial*. New York: John Wiley.

Spann, G. 1993. *Race Against the Court: the Supreme Court and Minorities in Contemporary America* NY: NY University Press.

Steadman, R. 1972 *The Police and the Community*. Baltimore: Johns Hopkins University Press.

Stockwell, J. 1978 *In Search of Enemies*. New York: Norton.

Stoddart , E. 1971 "Blue Collar Crime," in L. Radzinowicz and M. Wolfgang (eds.) Crime and Justice, volume 2. New York: Basic Books.

Sykes, R. and J. Clark. 1975 "A Theory of Deference - Exchange in Police-Civilain encounters" Understanding Policing McCormick and Visano Torornto Canadian Scholars

Tifft, T. 1970 *Comparative Police Supervision Systems, and Organizational Analysis* Ph.D. dissertation, University of Illinois.

Toronto Sun, January 25, 1974

Toronto Star, October 5, 1976

Turk , A. 1976 *"Law as a Weapon in Social Conflict." Social Problems* 23, 3: 276-291.

Van Dijk, B. 2001 "Training for law—or learning to lie?" A15 Globe and Mail , February 22, A15

Van Maanen, J. 1974 "Working the Street; a Developmental View of Police Behavior," in H. Jacobs (ed.) The Potential for Reform of Criminal Justice. Beverly Hills: Sage.

Vidich, Arthur 1975 "Political Legitimacy in Bureaucratic Society." Social Research 42, 4: 778-811.

Wagoner, C. 1971 *"Organizational Structure and Police Alienation."* Ph.D. dissertation: Indiana University.

Washnis, George 1976 Citizen Involvement in Crime Prevention. Toronto: Lexington.

Westley W. 1956 "Secrecy and the Police" Social Forces 34(3)254-7

Wilson, J. 1968 Varieties of Police Behavior. Cambridge, MA: Harvard University Press

Wright, B. 1990 Black Robes, White Justice New York: Carol Publishing.

Wolff, Kurt 1950 The Sociology of Georg Simmel. New York: Free Press.

Wolff, R. P. [ed.] 1971 The Rule of Law. New York: Simon and Schuster.

Woodward, Bob and Scott Armstrong 1979 The Brethren. New York: Simon and Schuster.

Zatz, M. 1987. "The Changing Forms of Racial and Ethnic Biases in Sentencing" Journal of Research in Crime and Delinquency 24(1): 69-92.

Zinn, H. 1971 "The Conspiracy of Law," In R. P. Wolff (ed.) The Rule of Law. New York: Simon and Schuster

PART A

CRIMINAL JUSTICE EDUCATION

1. On Justice and Education

Naomi Couto

1. Introduction

The origins of this essay started with my own teaching and learning experiences at York University. Over these last eight years, as both tutorial assistant and course director, I have recognized that today's students are, irrespective of class, extremely anxious about their postsecondary education; they arrive at the University but are not "there". This condition is a consequence of an inability to *articulate* who they are and what they want (hence they cloak themselves in airs of boredom). These 'new types of knowers' have no or limited language – many students have not been provided with the requisite literary tools or skills in a high school system, but more importantly, they have not developed the academic self-confidence to make their "own" decisions. Essentially, they have not learned *how to* learn.

Further exacerbating this condition is the insidious attraction to post-modernism. This concept is far too often invoked around the University, with little or no effort to unpack the social consequences of postmodernism on everyday living, let alone thinking. Post-modernism, commonly described as *reproducibility* or an age of mass consumerism, *hyper-reality* as replacing reality, and questions around *legitimation* ('whose' power), came to be the thread that informed my research in the area of education. I sought to discover whether this *ethos* could sustain the classroom environment of teaching and learning. For our purposes here, it is imperative to determine how *justice* itself comes to be discussed in a post-modern climate. The question that integrates and sustains my research is, 'how does one teach *integrity* (virtue and good will) in a post-modern world and culture-less society?'

My preliminary work was informed by Aristotle's writings on rhetoric, notably his three appeals to pathos (emotional), logos (rational), and ethos (credibility, trust-worthiness). It is the third appeal, *ethos*, which I use in order to try and understand the 'mood of energetic emptiness that pervades today's University life'. If ethos is a disposition/character peculiar to a specific culture or people, how does post-modernism inform our own experiences and dilemmas in the process of educating and becoming educated? I locate my work by viewing this "post" in post-modernism as a woefully artificial construct – an 'ideal type' of the many rationalities that go into thinking about our (western) modernity. Primarily using the writings and ideas of Aristotle, Friedrich Nietzsche, and Zygmunt Bauman, my aim is to illustrate that students today are not challenged, that is, not encouraged to cultivate a character of virtue and integrity. If custom or everyday action is pulled out from under them, *prudence* (wisdom, judgment, considerateness, judiciousness), that is, the ability to participate in the political or legal community becomes groundless. One must go beyond the perniciously weak and yet seductive attraction of post-modern teachings, which leave students believing that 'all is relative' especially in *grounding* their knowledge.

Education is not simply a formulaic application of instrumental knowledge. The fundamental problem concerns a priori thinking. Our students constitute "education" – the consequences of that which the dominant culture/ethos passes onto the University. These 'new types of knowers' have heard that knowledge is "all relative": before they have learned how to think, they have learned how to challenge. Teaching and learning communities, must use the *ethos of integrity* to illustrate that the training of minds cannot become obsolete. Integrity, as an ethos that respects plurality and the attendant narrative for its knowledge base, are rooted in critical intelligence. This ethos provides 'a kinder and more decent humanity. If language permits thinking, as I believe it does, all areas accessible to teaching and learning, including how one teaches and learns about "justice", can be explored thoughtfully through an ethos of integrity.

2. Education as Social Justice and Social Justice as Education

Mindful of the proverb that states 'the teacher appears when the student is ready' and accepting this fundamental premise to be true, my primary undertaking as an educator is guided by an interest in making my students ready. This is no easy task in a modern world shaped by the mass media, capitalistic values, and a host of many other ideological distractions, distractions from knowledge, not simply as a commodity, but as a way of being in the world. Our method here must be Socratic. Just as in Plato's *Republic*, where Socrates approaches the topic of justice by considering it from a multiplicity of perspectives, so too we must reflect on how justice gets interpreted in and by our society: namely in connection to the alacrity to treat all knowledge (the state of our education system) as a marketing tool (acquisition).

Let us now turn to a brief and general sketch of the word *justice*. How does a society measure *right* and *wrong*, *good* and *bad*? Webster's dictionary offers justice as "a being righteous, fairness, rightfulness, reward or penalty as deserved, the use of authority to uphold what is just, the administration of law" and so on. What are we as teachers and students of this concept to do with such an interpretation? Is there a code of conduct that can guide how we come to think about and discuss the application of justice? Are all interpretations of justice equally valid? How is our view of 'what is just' reflecting the technological, economic, and political anxieties of the day. After all, we claim that our society is a democracy. Is it a democracy of consumers and not of citizens? That is, the education of consumers who cannot engage in a critical social and self-understanding of what it means to be free and active members in a political community?

Here then is the basic tenet for the work ahead. Justice as an abstract but enduring concept has been addressed by societies everywhere and anywhere. As a *universal* ideal, however, it stands apart from its everyday *application* (or "playing out" from one society to another). Meaning, that we must be educated culturally and historically to understand that justice is not an absolute way of looking at and interpreting the world. Justice must be applied through a sense of integrity, constituted by (as far as humanly possible) a complete and sincere understanding of the particular situations at hand. Herein lies the invaluable importance of how we educate ourselves. An awareness of our pluralistic communities must be coupled with an educational system that underscores the empowerment of reading and writing with a view to active and reflective membership. Society weakens the role of its citizens when it allows its educational systems (whether consciously or not) to encourage a disdain for reading, revolt at lengthy writing assignments, and insist on the speed of completing one's education as superior to the content of what one receives and puts into it. This denial of responsibility is truly an injustice to society as a whole that will reverberate for generations.

This now brings us to the ethos of post-modernity. If all knowledge is relative hence the need to deconstruct all grand narratives including 'Truth', 'Beauty', and 'Justice' – how do we teachers of "justice" begin our task? How do students prepare themselves for learning in a social atmosphere that claims "all knowledge is relative?" Admittedly, this seems to be the very essence of our problem – that we have learned that knowledge is relative, or that truth is different for each individual, social group or historic period, before and without having learned anything substantial about those individuals, groups or historic periods. How can declaring that this frame exists (i.e. justice is relative), tell us anything about the content and circumstances within it (i.e. the awareness of social, political, and other motivations for their sense of what is just). For this reason, trying to discuss justice within a weak post-modern condition can make us uncertain and hesitant in articulating how and what we believe – but only if we let it. In *Postmodern Ethics*, Zygmunt Bauman writes:

> And so now we miss what we resented before: an authority stronger than us, one which we can trust or must obey, one which can vouch for the propriety of our choices and thus, at least, share some of our 'excessive' responsibility. Without it, we may feel lonely, abandoned, helpless. And then 'in our effort to escape from aloneness and powerlessness, we are ready to get rid of our individual self either by submission to new forms of authority or by a compulsive conforming to accepted patterns' (Bauman 1993: 20).

Note specifically how Bauman attends to a type of human nature that must understand its own thinking process in order to understand the frames of knowledge that claim authority over it. Here is where we, as students and teachers in the studies of justice, must pay special attention. Can we honestly go around claiming that all knowledge is relative when everyday we make choices on how to apply this knowledge (capital punishment, euthanasia, genetic engineering etc…) and morally justify its application to ourselves and the community as a whole? How is responsibility to be had (both failure and success) if we have no grounds to root our reasoning and actions in? For Bauman, without these grounds, our capacity to think in terms of common interests and fates diminishes.

Our concern over 'what is justice' and how it can be taught within the confines of the classroom continues from here. Noting that I take education itself to be a *just* act towards humanity as a whole – whether learning to sign one's name, reading the Bible or Koran for oneself, or the right to vote, education enables one not only to successfully function in a society but to also engage in the goals and aspirations for the betterment of that society. This means that individualization and privatization of education can only feed into the disinterest in politics and the 'just life' becomes an academic pursuit that we occasionally hear about. As Bauman (2000: 51) relates,

> (t)he truth is that the consumer's skills, indeed, rise at the same time as the citizen's ineptitude and, ultimately, the citizen's impotence. The 'consumer's skill' consist in seeking biographical solutions to socially-produced afflictions; to use a metaphor – it consists in fighting a nuclear threat by purchasing family nuclear shelter, or pollutions of drinking-water supplies by finding a reliable brand of bottled water. Consumer skills emphatically do not include the art of translating private troubles into public issues and public interests into individual rights and duties – the art that constitutes the citizen and holds together the polity as the congregation of citizens.

3. Education and the Justice System

Grounding ourselves well within the above general outline, we now turn to a practical application of teaching through an *ethos of integrity*. University courses in the broad area of criminology (including issues in policing, crime, punishment, and the justice system itself) have proliferated in both numbers and popularity. Many authors in this field consider the mass media as playing a role in this; namely, "the media serve to stimulate our interest in crime. Newspapers, for example, detail the exploits of criminals, while television news and crime drama focus on crimes" (Cavender and Bond-Maupin 1993: 308). Note the saturation of "hit" crime television shows like *C.S.I., NYPD, Law & Order* etc…

The incredible interest in criminology and criminal justice says much about a culture ridden with anxiety and uncertainty (the post-modern condition). How is it that the majority of our students reconcile their absolutist perceptions of *right* and *wrong, good* and *bad* with their firm beliefs about knowledge as relative? Many have gathered their sense of "the criminal" or "the victim" from distorted and fragmented media treatments of these types and the like. *Perception* seems to be the key term. That is, *how* they have come to think about these topics seems to be couched in the *style* or presentation of the material, rather than in the content and analysis of the *substance*. After all, *C.S.I.* has one hour (including commercials) to label, catch, and moralize "the criminal". *CNN* spends about three minutes on each new breaking story – five minutes if they interview an 'expert' on the matter. Is there room for any reflection? And even prior to this, where is the process of reasoning and the accountability of that reasoning, that allows for debate, dialogue, and any voices left unaccounted? In other words, how do we address the ontological complexities of these issues when Hollywood has succeeded so well in simplifying "good and evil" within a culture aching for security and quick solutions?

For Cavender and Bond-Maupin (1993: 315), "crime is a metaphor for a world gone berserk, for life out of control". Hence the swelling numbers in our criminology courses. 'If only we could order, rationalize and perfect the criminal justice system'... they seem to cry, 'then we would all be safe and happy'. This seems to be the covert attraction (at least initially) for many criminology students – (the glamorization of it on television, I'm sure, also plays its role). This sensibility is akin to the anxiety that Friedrich Nietzsche (1893: aphorism 16) discusses in relation to his own day and time:

> (t)hat which we now call the world is the outcome of a host of errors and fantasies which have gradually arisen and grown entwined with another in the course of the overall evolution of the organic being [...] Rigorous science is capable of detaching us from this ideational world only to a limited extent – and more is certainly not desirable – inasmuch as it is incapable of making any essential inroad into the power of habits of feeling acquired in primeval times.

Yet still today, it is to the so called 'rigorous science' (DNA, genetic profiling, etc) that we turn for answers. How is it that we still desire certainty and absolute types – "just the facts" – from our *social* surroundings? Much of this can be traced to that primordial animal in human nature that still fills us with fear of the unknown – of ourselves. Nietzsche alludes to this above; that monster, that thing that today still murders, rapes – that is, still exists in us. Maybe our "wannabee" criminologist longs to figure out "what makes the serial killer tick" but at a deeper level of the psyche is, "am I capable of that?" This fear and anxiety leads into declaring that this is not possible since we are "good" and the criminal is "bad" or in a more affirmative light, that we will cut this gene out of us (once science has discovered it). Fact and fiction become so blurred that the fallible thinking process behind such reasoning goes unnoticed.

So how does an ethos of integrity aid in the classrooms of our criminology courses? Clearly, this exercise asks us to recall the grounding of all knowledge as necessary places to construct "how" society engages in custom, religion and/or science. Yes, knowledge as constructed is acknowledged but never left at that. We cannot claim that all criminological theories are relative and move on. From this awareness of knowledge as multiple, we must then decide on which theories and perspectives best illuminate the study of criminology in the *advancement of group life*. Namely, that education is not in the service of a happier individual but in the direction of a happier citizenship. This is the "beyond" post/modernity that both Bauman and Nietzsche discuss (my own aim is a consideration of criminology that first asks the students involved to account for their interest and desire in studying the discipline). Below, Nietzsche seems to foreshadow our own failings in a market-oriented education system. It is up to us, teachers and students alike, to hear his warning of the 'hedonistic, strolling spectator' who readily consumes but does not understand. This I believe is a double-edged concern that allows students to think not only about what they are learning, but why.

> men have to be adjusted to the purposes of the age in order to be ready for employment as soon as possible; they must labour in the factories of the general good before they are mature, indeed so that they shall not become mature – for this would be a luxury which would deprive the 'labour market' of a great deal of its workforce [...] The young man is harried through all the millennia: youths who understand nothing of war, diplomacy, commerce are thought fit to be introduced to political history. But just as the young man races through history, so do we moderns race through art galleries and listen to concerts. (Nietzsche 1983 [1873]: aphorism 7)

References

Bauman, Zygmunt. 2000. *Liquid Modernity*. Cambridge: Polity Press.

Bauman, Zygmunt. 1993. *Postmodern Ethics*. Oxford: Blackwell Publishers .

Cavender, Gray and Lisa Bond-Maupin. 1993. "Fear and Loathing on Reality Television: An Analysis of America's Most Wanted and Unsolved Mysteries" in *Sociological Inquiry*, pp. 305-317. (August).

Nietzsche, Friedrich. (1984 [1893]). *Human, All Too Human: A Book For Free Spirits*. Translated by Marion Faber, with Stephan Lehmann. Lincoln: University of Nebraska Press, 1984.

Nietzsche, Friedrich. (1983[1873]). Untimely Meditations II. Translated by R. J. Hollingdale. Cambridge: Cambridge University Press, 1983.

Webster's New World Dictionary. 1983. New York: Warner Books, Inc.

2. Crises in the Classroom: A Critical Analysis of the Legal Duty and Authority of Teachers

Peter Della Sciucca

There is no greater or more honourable a profession than teaching. There is enormous effervescence and change in education. One important debate relates to the legal paradigm that governs the interaction of teachers and students. It is therefore important to discuss the following issues as they relate to our topic of inquiry: the history of teachers' duties and authority; the physical health and safety of students; the legal bases of liability and the concept of negligence; matters of defence; the duty to report child abuse; the enforcement of discipline and implications of the Canadian Charter of Rights and Freedom; the recent Supreme Court decision concerning search and seizure in schools and finally a personal reflection as an educator and lawyer regarding discipline and authority in schools today.

This paper examines a plethora of thorny issues surrounding the duty, authority and discipline of teachers. The examination is conducted within a legal / educational framework of inquiry. It is argued that the relationship between various stakeholders in the legal and educational arena remains in a constant state of flux and vacillation. Court decisions, statute and legislation continue to impact the classroom in dynamic, effervescent and metamorphic ways. This paper will inquire into the interactions between teachers and students and analyze their attendant legal relationships. Particular attention will be devoted to the examination of the duties and authorities of teachers in their profession and within a legal classroom paradigm.

It does indeed take a village to raise a child. Educating children is and has been the responsibility of the community. In the past, a teacher was invested with the parental responsibility of not only educating children, but also to protect children from harm while in the care of a teacher. Thus, teachers have stood "*in loco parentis*" (in the place of a parent) and given parental custodial responsibilities and authority. The teacher became a surrogate parent by virtue of their status. Early precedent decision in, *Williams* v. *Eady,* 1894, helped to give birth to this notion. Lord Esher developed what has been known as the "careful parent test". This meant that teachers were to take all necessary steps to assure that the same kind of care was taken as would that which would be taken by the parent of a student.

Over the years, the status of "*in loco parentis*" has been transformed through diverse social metamorphoses. Currently, there is an understanding that a parental decision is not always in the best interest of a child. Laws have extended themselves into the homes and educational institutions where children and students stay. The decrease in parental authority has consequently affected the concept of the "*in loco parentis*" adherence. Governmental and political involvement into the domain of parental authority over children and students gathered great momentum under the impetus of a strong children's law reform movement in the late nineteenth century. Furthermore, the courts often reserved the right to act as the guardian of the interests of those who could not take care of themselves where there were no parents or inadequate parenting. Now, legal obligations to and authority over children involve the direction of the state to enact and enforce child welfare legislation. The courts have assumed parental authority in many cases. They are responsible for balancing diverging interests and rights that comprise the realm of obligations concerning children. The teachers' role has also become complex and problematic, attributable chiefly to the transformation of the *"in loco parentis"* doctrine. Teachers must now look beyond the delegated parental powers and duties in order to re-examine their legal rights and obligations. Indeed, child welfare legislation, under the *Child and Family Services Act* has redefined and imposed responsibilities on educators that may place parents and teachers in an adversarial relationship.

The physical health and safety of students are sites of risk that remain of paramount juridic concern. Given that children have been and will always be adventurous, careless and care-free, their status does not reduce the standard of care required of teachers. Mr. Justice McIntyre in a 1981 Supreme Court decision held a teacher negligent in having allowed a 17 year old boy to go unsupervised to practice on the flying rings. He states: The respondent (teacher) should have anticipated reckless behaviour from at least some of the young boys sent off by themselves to work on gymnastics equipment... and **the proclivity of young boys of high school age to act recklessly** in disregard, if not in actual defiance of authority is...well known. *(Myers* v. *Peel County Board of Education,* 1981, p.238; emphases added).

The tendencies of children and students to engage in risk taking behaviour remains constant, but there is also a growing perception that today's educational environment and modern life provide more opportunities for accidents. An important and early Canadian study has shown that in 212 schools in the 1981-82 school year, there were 5.8 reported injuries per 100 elementary children, about 25 percent of which were serious (Feldman et al, 1983). The numbers could have even been higher since not all injuries are reported. Today, the numbers are even more alarming. Added to these statistics is a willingness among students and parents to enforce accountability for these accidents and injuries through civil suits for damages. Given a modern school environment built with potential dangers, a readiness among them to sue has become a preoccupation by educators, school boards and ministries of education.

This brings us to the concept of liability. The law provides that employers and school boards are responsible for the torts and civil wrongdoings of their teachers that are committed during the ordinary course of their employment (Fleming, 1983). This is the doctrine of *vicarious liability*. This doctrine however does not completely absolve teachers from legal liability; it simply means that their employers will also be legally responsible for the payment of any damages awarded. In all practicality, it will mean that the teacher is insulated from the monetary shock of the awarded damages. If, however, the teacher's negligence occurred outside the ordinary scope of employment, then the board would be entitled to deny its vicarious liability and the teacher is left facing a civil action and must absorb the legal costs associated with its defence. Boards (in reality their insurers, who have the right to defend the lawsuit on behalf of the boards) may make such denials in certain situations. For example, in a precedent decision in *Beauparlant v. Board of Trustees of Appleby* (1955), two teachers had arranged for students to attend a concert in a nearby town and had obtained a truck to transport the children. After some of the children tumbled out of the overloaded and unsafe truck and were injured, a lawsuit for negligence was brought against the teachers' school board. The court found that the teachers had been negligent in failing to ensure that the method of transportation was safe, but upheld the board's denial of liability on the basis that there was not "*any express or implied authority*" from the board for this excursion and that the accident therefore had occurred outside the scope of the ordinary course of the teachers' employment. Had the teachers been sued, they would have been left to their own personal financial resources to satisfy any judgment against them.

The responsibility of teachers to protect the health and welfare of the students under their care obliges them to neither intentionally commit acts nor omissions that result in physical harm to their pupils. Provincial education statutes and regulations commonly provide that the teacher's duties include seeing to the safety of their pupils (Education Act of Ontario, s. 265) and (Ontario regulations 298, s. 20[g]).The standard of care of teachers is derived from the "in loco parentis" doctrine, although it continues to face an onslaught of criticism. The careful parent test derived from *Willians v. Eady* (1894) is often, though not exclusively applied by the courts in determining whether teachers have been negligent. Many cases have suggested the courts dilemma in adhering to this doctrine including: *McKay v. Board of Govan*, (1968), *Thornton v. Board of School Trustees* (1975), *Myers v. Peel County Board of Education*, (1981) and many more cases currently in the court system.

While teachers have a duty to supervise their students, this duty does not mean constant supervision (*Board of Education v. Higgs*, 1959). In determining whether a teacher has breached her/his duty of care will depend upon consideration of whether the teacher's conduct was "reasonable" under the circumstances. This will inevitably take into account the type of accident, the approved general practice and the forseeability (probability) of the accident. The interpretation of "inherently" versus "potentially" dangerous activities ahs been and remains a thorny issue for the courts to decide (*Gard v. Board of School Trustees of Duncan*, 1946) and (*Hall v. Thompson*, 1952).

With respect to matters of defence, even if a teacher is found by a court to have been negligent and thereby to have caused injury to a student, it cannot be assumed that there will be a finding of complete liability. The doctrines of a voluntary assumption of risk and a contributory negligence have assisted teachers in the apportionment of blameworthiness. Some cases that have sheltered teachers' negligence include *Petersen v. Board of School Trustees*, 1991) and *McEllistrum v. Etches*, 1956). The "shelter doctrine" continues to face a litany of punctures by policy makers and lobbyists.

Teachers have a duty to report child abuse under the Child and Family Services Act. This duty is one based not on the finding of reasonable grounds of belief, but rather, merely the "suspicion" of child abuse. (Child and Family Services Act, s. 85). The suspicion must be one where the following question is answered in the affirmative; "would a reasonable person in a teacher's position give cause or be alerted to a ground of suspicion to report". The responsibility of educators to provide a learning environment that is both physically safe and academically sound carries a necessary corollary – the responsibility to enforce rules of discipline within the school context. It has been said that without discipline there can be little assurance of learning (*R. v Dimmell*, 1980). Discipline in schools is undoubtedly a high societal priority (*Livingstone & Hart*, 1980). The survival of education will depend most notably on securing a safe environment for learning.

The legal bases of teachers' authority over students' behaviour are based both in statutes and the common law. Most provincial education legislation determines the general responsibilities and powers of educators concerning the maintenance of order and discipline within schools. For example, the Education Act (1990) of Ontario requires principals "to maintain proper order and discipline in the school" (s.265[a]) and teachers "to maintain under the direction of the principal, proper order and discipline in her/his classroom and while on duty in the school and on the school ground" (s. 264[1][e]). What is considered "proper" order and discipline is provided in the Ontario Regulation stating that it is the duty of a student to "accept such discipline as would be exercised by a *kind, firm and judicious parent*" (Reg. 298, s.23[1][c]).

Legal theory of discipline over school children that rests exclusively upon an implied delegation of parental authority will indeed be vulnerable when parents seek to withdraw their delegated authority. Because of the potential administrative chaos that would ensue if school authority and discipline depended solely on authority delegated from parents, the courts have preferred to ground educators' disciplinary authority in the social utilitarian need to maintain order and discipline in the schools in order to foster an environment where learning will take place (*Murdock v. Richards*, 1954). Teachers may therefore reasonably discipline pupils without the permission of their parents, however within certain guidelines. Moreover, the Supreme Court's ruling in *Ogg-Moss v. R* (1984) casts much doubt on the viability of the doctrine of in loco parentis, per se, as a legal rationale for teachers' disciplinary authority.

The strongest and most recent examination of the limits on teachers' disciplinary authority is found in the Supreme Court decision in *Re: M* . Portions of the judgment are included herein given its significant impact on the issue of search and seizure in a school context. In this case, a junior high school vice-principal was given reasonably reliable information from students that the accused, a student, was intending to sell drugs at a school function on school property. He asked the accused and his companion to come to his office where he asked each if they were in possession of drugs and advised them that he was going to search them. A plain-clothed RCMP constable, called by the vice-principal pursuant to school policy, was present but said nothing while the vice-principal spoke to the students and searched them. The vice-principal seized a hidden cellophane bag of marijuana and gave it to the constable who advised the accused that he was under arrest for possession of a narcotic. The constable read to him the police caution and his right to counsel, and advised him that he had the right to contact a parent or adult. The accused attempted unsuccessfully to reach his mother by phone and stated that he did not wish to contact anyone else. The constable and the accused then went to the locker of the accused and searched it but nothing was found there.

The trial judge found that the vice-principal was acting as an agent of the police and held that the search violated the rights of the accused rights under the Canadian Charter of Rights and Freedoms. He excluded the evidence found in the search. The Crown did not offer any further evidence, and the charge against the accused was dismissed. The Court of Appeal allowed the Crown's appeal and ordered a new trial. At issue here is when and in what circumstances a search by an elementary or secondary school official should be considered unreasonable and therefore in violation of the student's rights under the *Charter*.

The appeal was later dismissed. The majority of the Supreme Court held that the *Charter* guarantee against unreasonable search and seizure (s. 8) is engaged because schools constitute part of government. The mere fact that there was cooperation between the vice-principal and the police and that a police officer was present during the search was not sufficient to suggest that the vice-principal was acting as an agent of the police. The search would have taken place without the presence of the police officer and was not materially different than it would have been had there been no police involvement. To establish a violation of s. 8 of the *Charter*, the accused must first establish a reasonable expectation of privacy with respect to the relevant place. Given that the search was of the accused's person, the existence of a subjective expectation of privacy and the objective reasonableness of that expectation are important. A subjective expectation of privacy with respect to one's person has been historically recognized and is reasonable and is not rendered unreasonable merely by the student's presence at school. A reasonable expectation of privacy, however, may be diminished in some circumstances. It is lower for a student attending school than it would be in other circumstances because students know that teachers and school authorities are responsible for providing a safe school environment and maintaining order and discipline in the school. Students know that this may sometimes require searches of students and their personal effects and the seizure of prohibited items.

A different standard should be applied to searches by school authorities. Teachers and principals are placed in a position of trust that carries the onerous responsibilities of teaching and of caring for the children's safety and well-being. In order to teach, school officials must provide an atmosphere that encourages learning. The possession of illicit drugs and dangerous weapons at school challenges the ability of school officials to fulfill their responsibility. Current conditions require that teachers and school administrators be provided with the flexibility needed to deal with discipline problems in schools and to be able to act quickly and effectively. One of the ways in which school authorities may be required to react reasonably is by conducting searches of students and seizing prohibited items. Where the criminal law is involved, evidence found by a teacher or principal should not be excluded because the search would have been unreasonable if conducted by the police.

Under the general rule established by this Court, a search to be reasonable requires prior authorization (usually a warrant) and reasonable and probable grounds for the search. A search conducted without prior authorization is *prima facie* unreasonable. To require that a warrant or any other prior authorization be obtained for the search would clearly be impractical and unworkable in the school environment. Teachers and principals must be able to react quickly and effectively to problems that arise in school, to protect their students and to provide the orderly atmosphere required for learning. Their role is such that they must have the power to search. Further, students' expectation of privacy will be lessened while they attend school or a school function. This reduced expectation of privacy coupled with the need to protect students and provide a positive atmosphere for learning clearly indicate that a more lenient and flexible approach should be taken to searches conducted by teachers and principals than would apply to searches conducted by the police. A search by school officials of a student under their authority need not be based upon reasonable and probable grounds. Rather, in these circumstances, a search may be undertaken if there are reasonable grounds to believe that a school rule has been or is being violated, and that evidence of the violation will be found in the location or on the person of the student searched. Searches undertaken in situations where the health and safety of students is involved may well require different considerations. All the circumstances surrounding a search must be taken into account in determining if the search is reasonable.

A teacher or principal should not be required to obtain a warrant to search a student and thus the absence of a warrant in these circumstances will not create a presumption that the search was unreasonable. A search of a student will be properly instituted in those circumstances where the teacher or principal conducting the search has reasonable grounds to believe that a school rule has been violated and the evidence of the breach will be found on the student. These grounds may well be provided by information received from just one student that the school authority considers credible. Alternatively the reasonable grounds may be based upon information from more than one student or from observations of teachers or principals, or from a combination of these pieces of information which considered

together the relevant authority believes to be credible. The approach to be taken in considering searches by teachers may be summarized in this manner:
(1) A warrant is not essential in order to conduct a search of a student by a school authority.
(2) The school authority must have reasonable grounds to believe that there has been a breach of school regulations or discipline and that a search of a student would reveal evidence of that breach.
(3) School authorities will be in the best position to assess information given to them and relate it to the situation existing in their school. Courts should recognize the preferred position of school authorities to determine if reasonable grounds existed for the search.
(4) The following may constitute reasonable grounds in this context: information received from one student considered to be credible, information received from more than one student, a teacher's or principal's own observations, or any combination of these pieces of information which the relevant authority considers to be credible. The compelling nature of the information and the credibility of these or other sources must be assessed by the school authority in the context of the circumstances existing at the particular school.

The search conducted by school authorities must be reasonable, authorized by statute, and appropriate in light of the circumstances presented and the nature of the suspected breach of school regulations. The permissible extent of the search will vary with the gravity of the infraction that is suspected. The reasonableness of a search by teachers or principals in response to information received must be reviewed and considered in the context of all the circumstances presented including their responsibility for students' safety. The circumstances to be considered should also include the age and gender of the student. The factors to be considered in determining whether a search conducted by a teacher or principal in the school environment was reasonable can be summarized in this manner:
1. The first step is to determine whether it can be inferred from the provisions of the relevant *Education Act* that teachers and principals are authorized to conduct searches of their students in appropriate circumstances. In the school environment such a statutory authorization would be reasonable.
2. The search itself must be carried out in a reasonable manner. It should be conducted in a sensitive manner and be minimally intrusive.
3. In order to determine whether a search was reasonable, all the surrounding circumstances will have to be considered.

This modified standard for reasonable searches should apply to searches of students on school property conducted by teachers or school officials within the scope of their responsibility and authority to maintain order, discipline and safety within the school. This standard will not apply to any actions taken which are beyond the scope of the authority of teachers or principals. Further, a different situation arises if the school authorities are acting as agents of the police where the normal standards will apply. In the case at bar, the vice-principal was not acting as an agent of the police and the police officer himself did not carry out the search. The mere presence of the police officer was not sufficient to conclude that the officer was in fact the authority carrying out the search. The officer was at all times completely passive. The test applicable to searches conducted by teachers therefore applied. The search was by inference authorized by the provisions of the Nova Scotia Education *Act*. As a student the accused would have a reduced expectation of privacy. The vice-principal had reasonable grounds to believe that the accused was in breach of school regulations and that a search would reveal evidence of that breach. The search was conducted in a reasonable and sensitive manner. Taking into account all the circumstances, the search was not unreasonable and did not violate the s. 8 rights of the accused. This case dealt only with a search of students in an elementary or secondary school. No consideration has been given to searches made in a college or university setting.

The compelled attendance of a student at a principal's office or some other form of restraint by a school authority, even if it could be understood as falling within the strict terms of the definition of "detention", should not be considered as "detention" for the purposes of s. 10(*b*). This section was meant to apply to relations between individuals and the state, usually focused upon the investigation of a criminal offence, and not to relations between students and teachers. Its application in the school context is inappropriate and would lead to absurd results. In a dissenting opinion, Justice Major in his dissent postulated: The actions of school officials as an extension of government are subject to the *Charter*. A student on school property has an expectation of privacy sufficient to engage s. 8 but that expectation is and should be lower than a member of the general public.

A warrantless search is *prima facie* unreasonable. To prove reasonableness, the Crown must demonstrate that the search was authorized by a reasonable law and carried out in a reasonable manner. A warrantless search can be justified if:
(1) the information predicting the crime was compelling;
(2) the source was credible; and
(3) the information was corroborated. These factors should not be applied as strictly to searches conducted by school officials acting *qua* school officials. Here, the vice-principal, because of the school policy requiring the school authorities to contact the police when a student was found in possession of drugs, was acting as a *de facto* agent of the police. The search as conducted therefore required that the accused be given his *Charter* protections. Further, the circumstances of the search breached s. 8 as they failed to meet the standards necessary for a valid search. The vice-principal, as a police agent, did not investigate to corroborate the information that he received; he acted solely on the word of the informants. Had the vice-principal been acting as vice-principal, he could have lawfully conducted the search because of the modified standard of reasonableness governing searches by school officials.

In determining whether evidence obtained in breach of the *Charter* should be admitted under s. 24(2) of the *Charter*, trial fairness, the seriousness of the breach and the effect that excluding the evidence would have on the repute of the administration of justice must be considered. Given that the accused was detained by the vice-principal and felt that he had to comply with the requests of the vice-principal and police officer, the evidence was conscriptive. Its admission would adversely affect trial fairness and accordingly it should be excluded under s. 24(2) of the *Charter*.

The Parliament of Canada has legislated limits on the use of physical punishment by parents, teachers and others acting in loco parentis. These limits are set out in section 43 of the Criminal Code of Canada: Every school teacher, parent or person standing in the place of a parent is justified in using force by way of correction toward a pupil or child, as the case may be, who is under his / (her) care, if the force does not exceed what is reasonable under the circumstances. The statutory defence available to teachers charged with assault is based upon the imprecise test of whether the force applied was "reasonable under the circumstances". Reasonableness must be decided on a case by case basis in light of each case's particular facts (*R. v. Haberstock,* 1970). This proves to be a matter of much judicial interpretation and assessment.

The legal paradigm of teachers' duty and authority to discipline involves a plethora of thorny issues. The concerned stakeholders continue to grapple endlessly with the changing tide of case law and legislation. The bell has rung, class is out and still we await a final determination on the scope of authority and discipline within the classroom.

References

Attis v. Board of School Trustees. District 15. 1990. 15 C.H.R.R. D/339 (N.B. Bd.Inq.).

Beauparlant v. Board of Trustees of Appleby. 1955. 4 D.L.R. 558 (Ont.HC).

Board of Education for City of Toronto and Hunt v. Higgs. 1959. 22 D.L.R. (2d) 46 (SCC).

Child and Family Services Act, R.S.O. 1990. c. C-11.

Constitution Act, 1982 (en. By the Canada Act, 1982 [U.K.] c. 11, Sched. B.) (Charter of Rights and Freedoms, ss. 1-34).

Criminal Code, R.S.C. 1985. c. C-46.

Dickinson, G.M. 1993. Exploding the Myth..One More Time. *Education & Law Journal,* 4, 226-30.

Education Act, R.S.O. 1990, C. E. 2.

Farry, M. 1996. *Education and the Constitution*. Dublin: Round Hall Sweet and Maxwell.

Feldman, W., Woodward, C.A., Hodgson, C., Harsany,Z., Milner, R., & Feldman, E. 1983. Prospective Study of School Injuries: Incidence, types, related factors and initial management. *Canadian Medical Association Journal*, 129, 1279-83.

Fleming, J.G. 1983. *The Law of Torts* (6th edn.). Toronto: Carswell.

Goss v. Lopez, 419 U.s. 565. 1975.

Hurlbert, E.L., & Hurlbert, M.A. 1992. *School Law under the Charter of Rights and Freedom* (2nd ed.n). Calgary: University of Calgary Press.

Hull v. Thompson, [1952] O.W.N. 133 (H.C).

Hicks v. Board of Eduaton for the City of Etobicoke et al. 1988. School Law Commentary 3-8-3.

Ingraham v. Wright, 430 U.S. 651. 1977.

MacKay, A.W. 1985. *Making and Enforcing School Rules in the Wake of the Charter of Rights*. Paper presented at a meeting of the British Columbia School Trustee Association, Vancouver: British Columbia School Trustees Association.

MacKay, A.W. 1984. *Education law in Canada*. Toronto: Emond Montgomery.

Murdock v. Richards, [1954] 1 D.L.R. 766 (NSSC).

Myers v. Peel County Board of Education. 1981. 37 N.R. 227 (SCC).

Ogg-Moss v. R.. 1984. 11 D.L.R (4th) 549 (S.C.C).

Ontario Human Rights Commission v. Peel Board of Education. 1990. 12 C.H.R.R.. D/364.

Ontario Ministry of Education. 1981. *Corporal Punishment in the Schools* (Review and Evaluation Bulletins. Vol.2, No.1). Toronto: Ontario Ministry of Education.

R v. Zundel. 1992. 1 S.C.R. 731 (SCC).

Suneet Singh Tuli v. St. Albert Protestant Board of Education. 1987. School Law Commentary 1-6-3.

Thornton v. Board of School Trustees of School District no. 57, [1975] 3 W.W.R. 622 (BCCA). 2

Williams v. Eddy. 1894. 10 T.L.R. 41 (CA).

3. Criminal Justice Education: From the Paradigms of Professionalism to the Pedagogy of Praxis

Kevin R.E. McCormick

1. Introduction

The study of crime, law and justice in the university has changed remarkably over the years. The internet and other technologies as well as a system of higher education that is more responsive to concerns regarding inequalities of the criminal justice system are challenging not only traditional pedagogies but foundational structures of colleges and universities. Competing forces ranging from market demands to social justice concerns are shaping the relationship between the criminal justice educator, student and the nature of the teaching and learning process. Specifically, the techniques attendant with criminology/criminal justice education have been affected profoundly by factors such as the virtual classroom, distance education, continuing education and law enforcement officers as students. Further, crucial issues in the administration of both the university and the criminal justice system, include racism, sexism, classism, ageism and ableism which have all become fundamental concerns for both students and educators. Clearly, the structural and substantive challenges to traditional university education have redefined the trajectory of criminological higher education and called on educators, administrators and policy makers to develop strategies that are responsive to the changing nature of the university.

The aims of this paper are two fold. First, this inquiry provides a critical examination of the current state of criminology/criminal justice higher education in the university setting. Specifically, this paper will compare the attitudes of university students and faculty with respect to the future of criminology programmes and the role of higher education in addressing these challenges through innovations in curricula, administration, technology and pedagogy. This research is informed by intensive interviews conducted with educators and students in criminology/criminal justice courses, with respect to their opinions on the changing nature of criminal justice higher education. This section concludes with recommendations for changes to the criminological higher education system that will influence all sectors of the university criminal justice programme including: administrators, educators, students and policy makers.

The second interrelated aim of the paper is to analyze from a comparative perspective the contributions of critical pedagogy to criminological teaching and learning. Specifically, this research provides a comprehensive review of both theoretical paradigms and highlights their applications to criminal justice education. Further, this section is also informed by intensive interviews conducted with educators and students in criminology / criminal justice courses in both Canada and the United States. An 'inclusive' pedagogic model is developed within the critical criminological tradition that establishes a more empowering learning environment for both teachers and students. The paper concludes with recommendations based on comparative findings for an inclusion of the critical pedagogic tradition directly into the criminological teaching and learning process.

2. Higher Education as Criminal Justice Education: An Outline of Research and Programmes

The practices and policies attendant with criminology/criminal justice education in the university have recently been transformed by and through various administrative, financial and pedagogic influences. The criminology classroom now constitutes a dynamic forum in which numerous students are interacting, each with personal experiences that shape their definitions of 'crime and justice'. Criminal justice education that occurred a decade ago has been radically altered by numerous factors which impact directly on the nature of Canadian higher education, including: computers, a changing justice system and increased linkages between the university and law enforcement agencies. These determinants are crucial for university educators and administrators, because they constitute the "criminological filters in the teaching and learning process" through which students interpret criminal justice - curricula, texts, lectures and other related educational practices and policies.

Research focusing on criminological higher education at the university level is expansive and highly diverse with respect to its applications in various contexts of the teaching and learning process. Clearly, the impact of issues such as: distance education, multi-media technologies and combined programmes with other post secondary institutions including community colleges (Levin, 1994) have lead the university to re-examine its position within the larger frame work of higher education. Empirical studies and pedagogic discussions that address the intersections between the criminal justice system and the Canadian higher education system can be divided into four ideal type categories: *Professional, Research Oriented, Applied, and Critical.*

The first area of research into criminology/criminal justice education at the university level is the *Professional.* This body of work focuses on the educational needs of students with backgrounds in various areas of the criminal justice system including: police, corrections, probation and parole. Specifically, this module examines the formal training requirements of criminal justice institutions and the role of higher education in facilitating such agendas. *Professional* education in the university attempts to draw direct correlations between the needs of criminal justice institutions and the ongoing training of its employees. This area emerged partly in response to the fact that many criminal justice officers attending university receive their education free of charge, as a condition of their ongoing "professional training" (Blair and Jones 1993). The increased emphasis on life time learning is clearly illustrated in the increased number of police officers attending university, pursing an undergraduate or graduate degree, or a specialized certificate programme in areas such as race relations or labour studies. research in this area while extensive, focuses predominantly on the evaluation of programmes and policies and does not necessarily explore the complex processes associated with criminological teaching and learning. Thus, contributions in Professional criminology/criminal justice education envision university education as inextricably linked to law enforcement training and the role of innovations in higher education in responding to the needs of the criminal justice professional.

The second category of research examining the linkages between higher education and the criminal justice system is *Research Oriented*, which focuses on the university and the specific programme as a site of analysis. This work explores the history and the current state of the university and how issues surrounding criminal justice education are situated within discussions of higher education. Specifically, this area of higher education utilizes general research on both Canadian and international perspectives on the university and draws inferences that impact on the administration and pedagogy associated with criminology/criminal justice higher education. Issues covered include, demographics of the criminology classroom, distance learning models and co-operative programme development with other higher education institutions such as the community college. Therefore, while the specific topic of research is not always related directly to criminological models of higher education, in many instances these works serve as the foundation upon which many policies and practices in the Canadian university are formulated and implemented.

The *Applied* area of criminology/criminal justice education in the Canadian university focuses on the techniques employed by educators at various levels of the system. While the *Professional* focused predominantly on the education of criminal justice professionals, the *Applied* examines the teaching and learning that is occurring in institutions of higher education as they relate to the needs of all students, whether they be currently employed by or merely interested in some aspect of the criminal justice system. Research in this area examines techniques that can be employed by educators to establish a more effective teaching environment, through innovative pedagogic devices and techniques (Pollock 1993; Wonders and Caulfield, 1993; Koser, 1991; Ryan, 1993; DeKeseredy and MacLean, 1993; Wright, 1987). Contributions in this field of higher education include teaching manuals (Murphy, 1994) annotated bibliographical resources and comprehensive/critical reviews of texts (Wright, 1995; Wright, 1995; Wright, 1994; Tunnel, 1993) and criminological studies as they relate directly to classroom teaching. While criminal justice education has been explored by numerous scholars representing diverse disciplinary, theoretical and methodological orientations, there remained a void in the research that incorporated a critical analysis directly into the process. This area of higher education research encompassed all areas of criminal justice and criminological university education, including: Professional, Research Oriented and Applied, with a critical examination of educational issues such as curricula, programme design/administration, technology and pedagogy. In *Critical* criminal justice educational studies (DeKeseredy, and MacLean, 1993; Michalowski, 1977) issues of social equality are incorporated (Daly, 1994; Visano, 1998; MacLean, 1996; O'Reilly-Fleming, 1996; MacLean, and Milovanovic, 1991; Taylor, Walton, and Young, 1974) Issues such as sexism, racism, classism, ableism and ageism are situated within the university setting. Critical criminologists have clearly identified that while criminal justice education has made advancements, further recognition of the difficulties inherent in criminological higher education is required. Much of the research in this tradition utilizes the contributions of critical pedagogy. As Juliani et al. (1983) note:

> The failure of universities to prepare students to design and implement the social change that is necessary is an accusation that is justly laid against them. Programs of applied studies must do more than prepare students to get into occupational slots. They must, while providing students with the basic skills for job performance, endow them with the sensitivity for detecting the need for change and equip them with the ability to effect that change.

Criminological university higher education must not only equip students with the technical skills to obtain positions in the criminal justice system, but instil in them a critical appreciation of the policies and practices attendant with "crime and justice" if a truly equal and empowering environment will be constituted for criminology/criminal justice students.

3. Transforming the Criminology Classroom: Pedagogies and Practices

The criminology teaching - learning nexus constitutes multi-faceted processes, comprised not only of curricula, administrative and pedagogic philosophy, but also of competing interests among teachers, students and criminal justice institutions. Comparative educational research on the university (Hayhoe, 1995; Hughes, 1994; Jallade, 1992.) is therefore the most instructive perspective to ascertain the changing nature between all parties in the educational process. Further a comparative approach to the study of criminal justice higher education in the university illustrates clearly the intersections between the teacher and student, as contextualized by and through the dynamic nature of the teaching and learning process. Respondents were selected from criminology/criminal justice related programmes and courses at various Canadian universities (York University, University of Toronto, Guelph University, Ryerson University, Laurentian University, University of Windsor). This research utilized open-ended questions and an emerging interview format to allow for respondents to identify key issues and practices associated with university based criminal justice education. Upon a critical understanding of the complexities associated with university based criminological education, strategies can be generated that provide recommendations for changes in higher education based criminal justice curricula, programme design, administration and pedagogy.

A critical examination of the teaching and learning processes of university criminology/criminal justice courses and programmes indicate clearly that traditional foci are not consistent with the changing dynamic of the classroom. Specifically, issues such as: racism, sexism, classism, ableism and ageism are topics that students do not want merely addressed in a lecture, but in many instances feel that an entire course is required to properly address the complexities of the issue. As one student (A1) noted in a senior level seminar on Racism and the Legal Order:

> When I started at this university, I only heard of racism and policing when I discussed current events in my 'intro' course. The course that I am in now allows me to get into the substantive issues that the criminal justice system is facing in light of an increased attention on issues like racism. We use books, guest speakers and other resources that directly address race relations and policing, exactly what many of us hoping to work in the area wanted from our university education.

This shift in the trajectory of criminology/criminal justice higher education is consistent with other changes in the nature of university education in Canada. As Schuetze (1995) adds, Canadian higher education has changed quite dramatically over the last four decades. This is most visible with respect to the growth in student numbers and new types of institutions that have emerged, partly in response to the growing demand. Students pursuing a criminology degree expect a more interdisciplinary approach to the study of crime and criminal justice, which incorporates perspectives not typically associated with criminological discourse. A critical and specialized emphasis in Canadian higher education is consistent with the establishment of anti-racist and feminist studies programmes throughout Canadian universities that emerged out of a call for the higher education to directly confront systemic barriers to social justice. This shift calls on educators for dynamic responses in the higher education process that address issues of criminal justice within the larger rubric of social justice, a call that criminology programmes cannot continue to ignore.

The linkage of criminal justice departments with other higher education programmes is evident in the large number of students who are pursuing a criminology or criminal justice focused degree in conjunction with another degree or specialized certificate. Many of the students pursuing criminal justice studies in conjunction with another university programme note that a double major allows them to focus their interests in criminological issues with other programmes that are consistent with the student's professional and personal interests. As one student (A2) pursuing a degree with a criminal justice focus in conjunction with a certificate in race relations notes:

> The reason that I am doing both my degree and the certificate is because by combing my studies I make myself more marketable. I will be knowledgeable in the criminal justice system, but I will also have a speciality, in race relations. Also, I am very committed to combating racism in the justice system and this way I understand the way the police and prison operate. Though I also understand the way racism is manifested in the system and hopefully can make a difference once I am part of the system.

Whether it be women's studies, race relations or labour studies, combining a university degree with another programme or certificate is a growing phenomenon in the Canadian university and specifically among students pursuing criminal justice studies.

Currently, many criminal justice students are not only linking their studies with other programmes in the university, but are combining their education with other higher education institutions. Community college programmes, such as law enforcement, police studies, and justice studies offer students with the applied knowledge in a specific area, while the university provides a more analytic understanding of the processes of criminal justice (Visano, 2004). While some students pursue a community college certificate in law enforcement while attending university, a majority of those combining their higher education opportunities choose to complete the community college and then attend university. These students represent two groups, current criminal justice workers and those aspiring officers. The current criminal justice professionals return to university after completing their formal training at the police college and gaining a position in some area of the criminal justice system. Their attendance at university is to ensure career advancement within the system. As a police officer (K07) who recently returned to university after a seven year hiatus commented:

> When I got on the force all you really needed was a college certificate in law enforcement, but now with all the university educated recruits coming on the force, you are stuck as a constable for life unless you get a university degree.

Other students find their career opportunities limited with only a community college certificate in law enforcement and enrol in university as a way of increasing their chances to be hired by a police force or other criminal justice institution. One such student (A04) reflected:

> I came to university to add to my community college education. I figure that the only way to get on a good force and move up the ladder is to have a degree. The university degree will look very good on my resume and that combined with my practical training from the college will show a force that I can 'think' but also 'do' the job of a police officer. That should increase my chances greatly.

Higher education as it relates to criminal justice has become a multi-disciplinary exercise in many institutions and others are beginning to follow in the wake of curricula, administrative and pedagogic change. Further, criminology and criminal justice programmes are quickly becoming transformed not only by substantive course topics but by the changing demographics of the classroom. No longer are students all directly from a secondary institution, but rather are from diverse backgrounds including: criminal justice professionals pursuing a degree in criminological related areas. The changing composite of the university student and their attendant academic and professional needs have become extremely important issues for universities as they seek to develop specialized programmes and respond to a changing demography.

Criminal justice/criminology programmes and courses with a professional orientation have called on university educators to develop strategies that incorporate both the concerns of the criminal justice professionals and the impacted constituencies within the frame work of higher education (Visano, 2004).The specialization of university programmes and recognition of the unique requirements of criminal justice professionals presents a challenge for university educators and administrators, because the traditional homogeneity of the classroom has been transformed by a myriad of personal and professional student based experiences and expectations. As a professor of criminology commented (T04):

> The university is changing dramatically, in both the ways that we teach and students learn. I remember when students learned about the police from lectures, texts and ride - a - longs, if they were available. Now, in the majority of my classes there is a very good chance that I have police officers directly in the class. This presents me with a great opportunity to bring her/his experiences into the class so that the topic becomes real for everyone in the class.

The university criminology classroom has a diverse membership, which in most cases consists partly of police officers, correctional officers, social workers and others involved in some area of the criminal justice system. The changing demography of the criminal justice classroom was reflected in the comments of a police officer (M04) who returned to university to complete her undergraduate degree:

> During a lecture the professor made reference to changes that she said had been implemented in a specific police force. It was the force that I was a member of and a few of the points that she mentioned were inaccurate, so I addressed my concerns. The professor asked 'What informs your opinion on the issue' to which I responded eight years of law enforcement. The professor said we could discuss the details after lecture, my question was why not let me discuss what I knew in the class for the other students to learn about? It was as if the professor did not want my practical experience messing up the lecture material.

These and other responses indicate that the changing nature of the university criminology/criminal justice classroom is a great opportunity to expand the traditional pedagogies associated with higher education and develop dynamic and empowering teaching and learning techniques. Research indicates clearly that students from a criminal justice background want the university to do more than merely educate them in the theories, methodologies and histories associated with traditional criminology; they want the teaching and learning process to relate to their experiences as criminal justice professionals and as members of society. These sentiments are echoed by law enforcement officers enrolled in continuing university studies, as one officer/student (K09) noted:

> Unfortunately, many of the teachers seem to think that no one knows anything about policing but them and that is not the case, as I know of three officers from different forces in this very course. When was the last time this professor was in a cruiser [police car] or in a station seeing what we really do day-to-day?

Also, many criminal justice professionals attending university are not doing so out of a desire to expand their minds intellectually, but as many other students are attempting to utilize their education for careerist interests. A sergeant (K10) in a mid-sized police force expressed the following reason for attending university:

> While I have had my formal training at the college, [police college] if I want to

> increase my chance within the system I need a university degree. This stage in my career requires me to go back to school, and since I have a community college certificate in police studies the next step is a university degree and of course the most useful programme is criminology. I am not sure if I will use a lot of want I learn on the job, but they see it as a requirement for senior positions and they pay for it, so I will do the degree and see how it really helps me move within the force.

Post secondary education has become a discriminating variable in career movement.

Another area that was identified by numerous students, faculty and administrators was the role of technology in changing the nature of criminal justice higher education. According to Sirotkin (1987), technology is transforming the way higher education goes about its business - that is, its missions of teaching, research and public service. Rapid advances in information and communication technologies have meant profound changes in how we learn and what we learn. Clearly, students and- faculty engaged in criminological higher education have identified computers and other multi-media technologies as dramatically impacting on the nature of the teaching and learning process. A faculty member (N14) who has been teaching for over twenty years reflects: Criminal justice related material has become instantaneous for students to acquire. They can sit at home and find things that would have taken the student ten years ago a week at least. Why, the Internet has allowed students to link up with world wide information servers and interact with other students, in other courses at universities around the globe. The question is though, how are we [educators] going to incorporate these devices into our work and not students and the get lost in an information overload?

Further, many students employed in the criminal justice system are shift workers and hope that computers and the super information highway will offer them alternative methods for completing their university education. One student (A15) who is currently a constable in a large metropolitan police force notes:

> I understand that many courses in the States are offered completely on the 'Net' [Internet]. Why that makes perfect sense when you think that a lot of officers don't work 9 to 5 and cannot make every course. If [name of university] started something like this, more officers would take degree programmes because education was made available.

Only through identifying the changes that technology causes in the higher education process can the university respond in effective fashions that address, administrative, curricula and pedagogic imperatives.

4. From Criminal Justice to Social Justice

Currently, both critical criminology and critical pedagogy are redefining for researchers and teachers the trajectory of social justice practice and pedagogy. Clearly, the works of critical criminologists (Visano, 1998; MacLean 1996; O'Reilly-Fleming, 1996; MacLean, and Milovanovic, 1991; Taylor, Walton, and Young, 1974) have challenged the boundaries of traditional criminological discourse, resulting in a redefinition of 'crime' and 'criminal justice'. This "new criminology" (Fleming, 1989; Taylor et al.,

1973) is responsive to the exclusionary practices of the state, as defined by capital and contexualized within the political economy. Furthermore, the contributions of the critical pedagogy (Freire 1995; McLaren, 1995; Giroux, 1988; Freire, 1985; Giroux, 1983; Freire, 1976; Freire, 1972) articulate dynamic and empowering strategies to address the inequities of conservative educational philosophies and programmes. This approach to teaching and learning has developed a pedagogical model that is dynamic, inclusive and empowering for both teachers and students. Therefore both critical pedagogy and criminology when explored through a comparative analytic paradigm demonstrate a complementarity both conceptually and ideologically as they relate to critically examining struggles for social justice in both the criminal justice and education system.

Interestingly, while both the traditions of critical criminology and critical pedagogy articulate strategies of social change, a synthesing dialogue between these two perspectives has not been explored from either a conceptual or praxis oriented position. In both paradigms, strategies addressing systemic impediments to social justice—including classism, racism, sexism, ableism—are contextualized within the politically articulated and economically determined discriminatory practices of the state. By explicit design, the "hegemonic" (Gramsci, 1971) control of the teaching and learning process ensures that society's members are immersed in precepts of the state and subsequently defend the perceived 'integrity' of institutions, such as education and criminal justice. Explicitly, this challenge to the power of the state, is at the epicentre of both the research and teaching strategies of critical criminology and critical pedagogy.

The purpose of this section is to examine the theoretical and educational praxis based relationship between critical criminology and critical pedagogy. Interestingly, a comparative examination of the ways in which the liberation strategies of the critical pedagogic tradition (Freire, 1972, 1973, 1985, 1995) are analogous with the dynamic approaches presented by critical criminologists (O'Reilly-Fleming, 1996; Visano, 1996; Ratner, 1984: Taylor, et al., 1974) remains a very under-investigated topic. This critical investigation incorporates both the contributions of comparative criminology (Burnhan, 1993; Heiland, 1991; Beirne, 1983; Meyer, 1972) and comparative higher educational studies (Hayhoe, 1995) in the critical examination of the changing nature of criminology/criminal justice higher education in the university setting (Morn, 1995). This comparative analysis while guided by a comprehensive review of theoretical traditions is also informed by interviews conducted with both teachers and students in criminology/criminal justice courses and programmes, with respect to the changing nature of the criminology classroom. Clearly, through exploring the linkages between these two paradigms, strategies can be developed that empower criminology teachers and students with the analytic skills to interrogate the structures of privilege, which rooted in the political economy legitimate and perpetuate the oppressive practices and policies of the criminal justice system. Thus, this section will provide a comparative examination of theoretical and praxis oriented contributions of both critical pedagogy and critical criminology to establishing a dynamic and empowering higher educational context in which to examine the definition and administration of criminal justice in a myriad of environments.

5. Critical Criminology as Critical Pedagogy

Throughout critical criminology research the underlying assumption is that the definition of 'crime' and the administration of criminal justice are firmly founded on the exploitation of countless subjugated constituencies. As research has indicated, the police, corrections, courts and other attendant institutions of the criminal justice system have a long history of preferential persecution and discrimination. The commodification of the "juridic actor" (Visano, 1997) through various criminal justice sites is premised on systemically established exclusionary criteria, including: classist, racist and sexist interests. Since the inception of the term "critical criminology" (Taylor, et al., 1974), the challenge to those committed educators has been to respond to the structures which oppress in the name of 'justice' and articulate dynamic strategies of change throughout all aspects of the criminal justice system. Fundamentally, the role of the critical criminology in the classroom is to instil in students the analytic, conceptual and research skills which will enable them to raise their consciousness to a critical level. As one professor (K12) noted:

> The criminology student today wants to understand not only how the criminal justice system operates, but the ways in which social factors like race relations affects the system and how they can effect change themselves. They [criminology students] want the lectures and readings to go beyond benign discussions pertaining to criminal justice administrative procedures and jurisdictional boundaries. The students want their education to explain to them strategies that they can adopt to change what in many cases the students believe to be an unjust criminal justice system.

It is this commitment to the development of critical skills which is the foundation for the address of the commonalities between critical criminology and Freire's (1972) pedagogy of social change. As Shor (1993: 25) notes: Freire's social pedagogy defines education as one place where the individual and society are constructed, a social action which can either empower or domesticate students.

Clearly, critical criminology has sought to challenge the precepts of 'law and order' embodied in the institutional practices and policies of the criminal justice system. While criminological research began to reach beyond the traditional bulwarks associated with the study of crime and incorporate paradigms that critically addressed issues of exclusion and oppression, the classroom remained ignored as a site of social change. Systematically, the study of crime and associated institutions is becoming situated with the larger cultural context and a more dynamic definition of 'crime' and 'social justice' was emerging. Though extremely challenging on the level of scholarship, critical criminology is examining the role of criminological and criminal justice education in replicating the structures and processes of oppression.

Criminological pedagogy at this time constituted a monologue, premised on accepted theoretical perspectives, empirically verifiable indicators and the assumption that the student was present to "learn and listen" and the faculty member to "profess" her/his knowledge. A retired faculty member (F12) noted:

> When I was a student, many years ago, we [the class] listened to what the professor had to say. The course was on what he [the professor] was interested in, lectures, assignments and readings. I would have never dared introduce a topic into the context of the class, because that would have been a challenge to the authority of the professor. It was only in graduate school that I experienced some freedom, but even then the limits of freedom where extremely narrow.

This educational process transforms students into "docile bodies" (Foucault, 1977: 135) controlled by the disciplinary cadence dictated and enforced by conservative educational philosophy and curricula. Unquestionably, this period in criminology/criminal justice higher education was firmly entrenched in a philosophy known as "banking education" (Freire, 1972), which did not facilitate the critical exchange of ideas, but rather subscribed to Socratic and monolithic educational model. This traditional banking approach is contrary to the professed critical orientation of this new school of criminological thought given:

> Banking education is invaluable for maintaining an oppressive social order, for the more the students put their efforts into receiving and storing information deposited in them, the less they can attain the critical consciousness that comes from intervening as makers and transformers of the world. (Lankshear, 1993: 90)

Subsequently, the call for a critical examination of the criminal justice system echoed by countless criminologists must be responded to not only in their written research, but rather incorporated directly into their classrooms and interactions with students, community groups and other educators.

While many rejected a reformulation of the classroom, from a podium upon which to espouse views in a Socratic and distant manner, to a dynamic forum in which the exchange of ideas between the teacher and her/his students is of paramount importance for understanding the fundamental nature of 'law and order' and generating effective solutions. For these reasons critical pedagogy provides both the teaching tools to make the criminological learning experience (Unnithan, 1994) more participatory (Norman, 1991) and establishes the basis upon which fundamental problems with the criminal justice system can be critically addressed and actions to remedy these inequities generated and acted upon. Unquestionably, Freire in his reformulation of the teaching and learning process creates a challenging and dynamic environment for critical criminology students and educators. That is, Freire's:

> ... pedagogy challenges teachers and students to empower themselves for social change, to advance democracy and equality as they advance their literacy and knowledge. His critical methods ask teachers and students to question existing knowledge as part of the questioning habits appropriate for citizens in a democracy (Shor, 1993: 25).

Therefore if critical criminology is to achieve a consciousness that will address the state's control over definitions of "crime" and the exclusionary practices inculcated in criminal justice policy and practice, the lessons inherent in critical pedagogy must not be ignored. This recognition is consistent with critical pedagogy, where as McLaren observes "educators must examine the development of pedagogical discourses and practices that demonize "Others" who are different through transforming them into absence or deviance" (1994: 213). For many years, the "other" had either been relegated to a variable in an empirically substantiated study or ignored by obedience to static theoretical paradigms, void of any praxis orientation.

If critical criminology is to effectively create a consciousness that results in a recognition and change in the exclusionary practices of the criminal justice system, the classroom must be an integral part of the process. Many students entering a criminal justice course bring with them diverse life histories that are inextricably linked with their learning needs and expectations. An emphasis on life experience relevant models of higher criminology/criminal justice education is clearly illustrated in the comments of one student (A17) in a large university course on Policing noted:

> What I want to learn is how things in the justice system go this way and how they can be changed. I live in an area that they [police] have defined as a 'bad area' and I want to know why they think this way and what can my community do to change our future.

Sentiments such as these have been responded to by some educators in innovative ways that establish the classroom as a dynamic place for teaching and learning. Courses presently offered in some universities and colleges incorporate directly into the learning process, texts and community liaisons that empower students with the insights and confidence to challenge the prevailing order that oppresses countless groups in the criminal justice system. As McLaren (1994: 213) notes: "A solidarity has to be struggled for that is not centred around market imperatives but develops out of the imperatives of freedom, liberation, democracy, and critical citizenship." Establishing a pedagogical setting in which teachers and students can exchange ideas and life experiences (Unnithan, 1994) on the changing nature of the criminal justice system is a challenge for the traditional higher educational institution. Mohanty, (1994: 162) notes:

> Creating such cultures in the liberal academy is a challenge in itself, because liberalism allows and even welcomes" plural" or even "alternative" perspectives. However, a public culture of dissent entails creating spaces for epistemological standpoints that are grounded in the interests of people and which recognize the *materiality* of conflict, of privilege, and domination.

For teachers of critical criminology the structural impediments presented by the traditional learning environment can be responded to in active and emancipatory fashions. Whether through the introduction of challenging texts or through the inclusion of guest speakers from impacted communities, students and teachers can begin to situate the voices of the oppressed in the criminal justice system within the larger context of domination.

Currently, criminology courses have emerged that seek to overcome impediments to critical learning, through inclusive and empowering pedagogical innovations. While some courses claim a critical orientation merely through including in its reading list texts that have been defined as 'cannons' of the critical criminological tradition, other classes have become transformed into sites of critical exchange between committed teachers and students. Courses that reach beyond the traditional precepts inculcated in criminological research and pedagogy, succeed in constituting the classroom as a forum for the expression and development of critical thought. As one student (K19) in a senior level seminar course commented:

> In this course we are able to discuss issues in a way that made me feel part of the process, not standing by the side and watching what was going on. I am able to present the way I see things in the C.J.S. [criminal justice system] to my class, including the professor, and hear how they received my opinions. For the first time in a course I feel like I am really understanding the subject matter, because it is made to fell applicable to my situation, and that makes learning far more interesting.

Further, criminologists have begun to challenge the normative assumptions underlying criminal justice education and present paradigms that are responsive and challenging for both teacher and students. Criminologists who question the traditional foundations of teaching and learning and seek to overcome these practices and policies through innovative pedagogic techniques which are consistent with the precepts inculcated in: The Freireian pedagogy which tries to develop this critical consciousness is a student-centred dialogue which problematizes generative themes from everyday life as well as topical issues from society and academic subject matter from specific disciplines. (Shor, 1993: 33)

Critical criminologists by opening up the learning experience to include and validate the life histories of the student, empower the confidence to learn and the respect for other opinions. It is upon this emancipatory foundation that criminal justice system can be critically examined and strategies for social change articulated and acted upon.

The process of establishing an educational context which challenges both teachers and students and generates strategies of social change is constituted by and through a pedagogy that is clearly premised on a critical appreciation of the inequities of both the criminal justice and educational systems. These aims are consistent with the concerns echoed by countless critical criminological texts (Visano, 1997; MacLean, 1996; O'Reilly-Fleming, 1996; Ratner and McMullan, 1985; Hinch, 1994; Maclean and Milovanovic, 1991; Taylor et al. 1974) texts, which seek by deliberate design be to challenge the unequal conditions which under the name of "law and order" imprison the working class, while exonerating those "privileged" classes. The "caceral contexts" (McCormick, 1994) in which individuals finds him/herself are replete with contradictions premised on the unequal distribution of wealth and the power embodied in the law and controlled institution with a vested interest in maintaining the state's hegemonic control, such as: police, corrections, rehabilitative services, courts and the legal system.

6. Conclusion

The university in North America has undergone a dramatic reconfiguration in both pedagogic and administrative agenda. This change is evident when examining the transformations that many criminology/criminal justice programmes have experienced as a result of factors such as: distance education, continuing education, specialized certificate programmes and law enforcement officers as university students. Overall, criminal justice higher education has become a multi-faceted process shaped by and through the changing nature of the Canadian university. Currently, issues such as: criminal justice professionals as university students, collaborative programmes with other higher education and criminal justice institutions and alternative teaching and learning methods, have created a dynamic environment for higher education researchers and educators to consider.

Through a comprehensive comparison between critical criminology and critical pedagogy, it is clear that the fundamental concern for social justice is at the foundation of both perspectives. Through interrogating the structures of privilege that criminalize some and ignore others, critical criminology must by deliberate design be "counter hegemonic" to the traditional perspectives which mediate societal definitions of 'law and order'. This concern for issues of social justice is also evident with critical pedagogy, which:

> ...is engaged in assisting students to interrogate the formation of their subjectivities in the context of advanced capitalist formations with the intention of generating pedagogical practices that are non-racist, non-sexist, non-homophobic and directed towards the transformation of the larger social order in the interests of greater racial, gender, and economic justice. (McLaren, 1995:232).

The definition of social justice called for by critical educators is consistent with the transformation of the social order echoed in the works of critical criminologists who also desire a reconfiguration of the economic order in the name of social justice.

The control that critical criminological pedagogy must be challenged to respond to the oppressive nature of the traditional criminal justice teaching and learning. As critical educators, the classroom must be transformed by and through learning that is dynamic, experiential and responsive to the needs and concerns of the individuals that comprise the class. Through synthesising critical criminological concerns with a liberating critical pedagogy or even an "engaged pedagogy" (hooks, 1994: 13) criminal justice education can truly become transformative, changing the oppressive conditions that continue to imprison in the name of profit and punish according to market imperatives. Criminology must not only be critical of the institutions that oppress in the name of "law and order", but interrogate the nature of the learning experience, because: Critical teaching is one of many politicizing and polarizing forces in the culture as a whole. It plays a contributory and non measurable role in the process of social change. In a time of insurgent movements, the impact of critical classrooms is visible and immediate (Shor, 1980: 270).

Recognition of the complex composite of the learning experience in relation to the advancement of critical criminological concerns will connect powerfully issues of oppression with the lived experiences of the students. The "banking education" (Freire, 1972) model which continues to control the trajectory of criminological research and pedagogy, imprisons the learner in a system of assertions that compartmentalizes knowledge, a pedagogic "discipline organizes an analytical space" (Foucualt, 1977: 143; Deacon and Parker, 1995). For many teachers and students the classroom and the learning experience has become prison like in the sense that actions and opinions are regulated and filtered through existing perspectives and cannons of knowledge, unapproachable within the confines of traditional criminological education.

The traditional criminology classroom establishes a "panoptic" (Ryan, 1991; Foucault, 1977: 195) gaze over the student whose vision is limited by and through the limitations and assumptions of "accepted" traditional criminological cannons and pedagogic practices. As Visano (1994: 208) notes: "By removing certain institutional blinders which hinder social inquiry, we are witnessing the embrace of a critical imagination. Subsequently, this exercise includes the more innovative elaboration of conventional sets of instruments, techniques of analysis as well as levels of empirical applications."

What is required in order to transform the nature of criminological pedagogy is a multi-dimensional approach to the critical teaching and learning experience, "An agenda of values for that pedagogy could describe it as: Participatory, Situated, Critical, Democratic, Dialogic, Desocialization, Multicultural, Research-Oriented, Activist and Affective " (Shor, 1993: 34). Educators must transcend the boundaries of the classroom and the mandates of conventional learning and establish a dynamic foundation upon social justice is not relegated to the text book, which in many instances is fraught with contradictions (Wright, 1995a, 1995b, 1994; Tunnel, 1993) and liberal chatter in a lecture, a fundamental concern both within the class and within the larger societal setting.

The implementation of innovative teaching techniques and the development of a pedagogic environment which is sharing, experiential and firmly grounded in larger issues of social justice will transform not only the criminal justice system, but the entire social context in which it exists. Teachers must not isolate the classroom from the 'outside' realizing that oppression is not manifested in the criminal justice system, but also within the structures which seek to understand it, namely education. It is therefore imperative that educators develop in themselves and their classrooms a dynamic environment that reaches beyond the limitations of traditional educational practices and policies and challenges both the teacher and student to become critical participants in various facets of the criminal justice system.

References

Beirne, P, 1983. "Cultural Relativism and Comparative Criminology", *Contemporary Crises,* (7) 4: 371-391.

Blair, R. and Jones, W. 1993. *Corrections and Higher Education Monograph*, Eastern Kentucky University, College of Law Enforcement.

Burnham, R. W. 1993. "The Promise and Perils of Comparative Criminology", *Howard Journal of Criminal Justice,* (32) 1: 67-72.

Daly, K. 1994. *Gender, Crime and Punishment,* New Haven: Yale University Press.

DeKeseredy, W. and MacLean, B. 1993. "Critical Criminology Pedagogy in Canada: Strengths,

Limitations, and Recommendations for Improvements", *Journal of Criminal Justice Education*, 4(2) 361-376.

Fleming, T. 1985. *The New Criminologies,* Toronto: Oxford University Press.

Freire, P. 1995. *Pedagogy of Hope: Reliving Pedagogy of the Oppressed,* New York: Continuum Publishing.

Freire, P. 1985. *The Politics of Education: Culture, Power, and Liberation,* Boston: Bergin Garvey.

Freire, P. 1972. *Pedagogy of the Oppressed,* Harmondsworth: Penguin.

Freire, P. 1973. *Cultural Action for Freedom,* Harmondsworth: Penguin.

Freire, P. 1976. *Education: The Practice of Freedom,* London: Writers and Readers.

Foucault, M. 1977. *Discipline and Punish: The Birth of the Prison,* New York: Vintage Books.

Giroux, H. 1983. *Theory and Resistance: A Pedagogy for the Opposition,* New York: Bergin and Garvey.

Giroux, H. 1988a. *Teachers as Intellectuals,* Minneapolis: University of Minnesota Press.

Giroux, H. 1988b. *Schooling and the Struggle for Public Life: Critical Pedagogy in the Modern Age,* Minneapolis: University of Minnesota Press.

Gramsci, A. 1971. *Prison Notebooks: Selections,* Hoare and Smith (Trans.) New York: International Publishers.

Hayhoe, R. 1995. "An Asian Multiversity? Comparative Reflections on the Transition to Mass Higher Education in East Asia", *Comparative Education Review*, 39 (3).

Heiland, L., I. S. and Katoh, H. 1991. *Crime and Control in Comparative Perspectives*. Berlin: De Gruyter.

hooks, b. 1994. *Teaching to Transgress: Education as the Practice of Freedom*. London: Routledge.

Hughes, R. 1994. "Legitimation, Higher Education and the Post-Colonial State: A Comparative Study of India and Kenya." *Comparative Education*, 30 (3).

Jallade, J.P. 1992. "Undergraduate Higher Education in Europe: Towards a Comparative Perspective" *European Journal of Education,* 27.

Juliani, T., Jayewardene, C. and Talbot, C. 1983. *'Teaching Applied Criminology in Canada'*, in Deviant Designations: Crime, Law and Deviance in Canada, Fleming, T. and Visano. L. (eds.), Toronto, Butterworths.

Koser, W. 1991. "Feminist Pedagogy in Criminology". *Journal of Criminal Justice Education*, 2(2) 81-93.

Lankshear, C. 1993. "Functional Literacy From a Freirean Point of View". In P. McLaren and P. Leonard (eds.) *Paulo Freire: A Critical Encounter*. London: Routledge.

Leonard, P. 1993. "Critical Pedagogy and State Welfare: Intellectual Encounters with Freire and Gramsci, 1974 - 86". In P. McLaren and P. Leonard (eds.) *Paulo Freire: A Critical Encounter*. London: Routledge.

Levin, J. 1994. "Change and Influence in the Community Colleges of British Columbia''. *Canadian Journal of Higher Education*, 24 (2).

MacLean, B. 1996. *Crime and Society: Readings In Critical Criminology*. Toronto: Copp Clark.

MacLean, B. and Milovanovic, D. 1991. *New Directions in Critical Criminology*. Vancouver: Collective Press.

McCormick, K. 1996. "Prison of Impulses: Punishment and the Electrified Correctional System' In T. Fleming (Ed.) *Post-Critical Criminology*. Toronto: Prentice Hall.

McCormick, K. 1994. "Carceral Contexts and Political Contests: Challenging the Boundaries". In K. McCormick (ed.) *Carceral Contexts: Readings In Control*. Toronto: Canadian

Scholars' Press.

McCormick, K. 1994. *Carceral Contexts: Readings In Control*. Toronto: Canadian Scholars' Press.

McCormick, K. and Visano, L. 1992a. *Canadian Penology: Advanced Perspectives and Research*. Toronto: Canadian Scholars, Press

McCormick, K. and Visano, L. 1992b. *Understanding Policing*. Toronto: Canadian Scholars' Press.

McLaren, P. 1995. *Critical Pedagogy and Predatory Culture: Oppositional Politics in a Postmodern Era*. London: Routledge.

McLaren, P. 1994. "Multiculturalism and the Postmodern Critique: Toward a Pedagogy of Resistance and Transformation". In H. Giroux and P. McLaren (eds.) *Between Borders: Pedagogy and the Politics of Cultural Studies*. London: Routledge.

McLaren, P. (ed.) 1992. *Postmodernism, Post-Colonialism, and Pedagogy*. Australia: James Nicholas Publishers.

McLaren, P. 1989. *Life in Schools: An Introduction to Critical Pedagogy in the Foundations of Education*. New York: Longman.

Michalowski, R. 1977. "A Gentle Pedagogy: Teaching Critical Criminology in the South". *Crime and Social Justice*, 7:69-73.

Mohanty, C. 1994. "On Race and Voice: Challenges for Liberal Education in the 1990s" In H. Giroux and P. McLaren (eds.) *Between Borders: Pedagogy and the Politics of Cultural Studies*. London: Routledge.

Morn, F. 1995. *Academic Politics and the History of Criminal Justice Education*, Hartford: Greenwood Press.

Murphy, C. 1994. *Problem Oriented Policing: A Manual for the Development and Implementation of Problem Oriented Policing*, Ministry of the Solicitor General and Correctional Services of Ontario and the Solicitor General of Canada.

Norman, W. 1991. "Students as Theorists in a Criminology Course". *Teaching Sociology*, (19)2: 249-254.

O'Reilly-Fleming, T. 1996. *Post-Critical Criminology*. Scarborough: Prentice Hall.

Pollock, J. 1993. "Ethics and the Criminal Justice Curriculum". In *Journal of Criminal Justice Education*, 4(2) 377-390.

Ratner, R. 1984 ."Inside the Liberal Boot: The Criminological Enterprise in Canada". *Studies in Political Economy*, 13: 145-164.

Ratner, R. and McMullan, J. 1987. *State Control: Criminal Justice Politics in Canada*. Vancouver: University of British Columbia Press.

Ryan, J. 1991. "Observing and Normalizing: Foucault, Discipline, and Inequality in Schooling". *Journal of Educational Thought*, (25)2: 104-119.

Ryan, J. 1993. "Teaching About Crime and Punishment". *Focus on Law Studies*, (8) 2: 1-12.

Schuetz, H. 1995. 'Funding, Access and Teaching: The Canadian Experience of a Mass System of Education'. In *The Changing University*, Schuller, T. (ed.) Great Britain, Open University Press and The Society for Research into Higher Education.

Shor, I. 1987. *Critical Teaching for Everyday Life*. Chicago: University of Chicago Press.

Shor, I. 1993 . "Education is Politics: Paulo Freire's Critical Pedagogy". In P. McLaren and P. Leonard (eds.) *Paulo Freire: A Critical Encounter*. London: Routledge.

Shor, I. and Freire, P. 1987. *A Pedagogy for Liberation*. Hartford: Bergin and Harvey.

Sirotkin, P. 1987. "Foreword". In *State Higher Education Policies in the Information Age*, McGill, Mollie and Jonsen, Richard, (eds.), Boulder Colorado, Western Interstate

Commission for Higher Education.

Taylor, I. 1981. *Law and Order: Arguments for Socialism*. London: Macmillian.

Taylor, I. Walton, P. and Young , J. 1973. *The New Criminology: For A Social Theory of Deviance*. London: Routledge and Kegan Paul.

Taylor, I. Walton, P. and Young, J. 1974. *Critical Criminology*. London: Routledge and Kegan Paul.

Tunnel, K. D. 1993. "Political Crime and Pedagogy: A Content Analysis of Criminology and Criminal Justice Texts". *Journal of Criminal Justice Education*, 4: 101-114.

Unnithan, P. 1994. "Using Students' Familiarity and Knowledge to Enliven Large Sociology Classes". *Teaching Sociology*, (22)4: 333-336.

Visano, L. 1994. "The Culture of Capital as Carceral: Conditions and Contradictions". In K. McCormick (ed.) *Carceral Contexts: Readings In Control*. Toronto: Canadian Scholars' Press.

Visano, L. 1998. *Crime and Culture*. Toronto: Canadian Scholars' Press.

Visano, L. 2004. "Degrees of Freedom" The Institute of Applied Research and Innovation, Georgian College, Barrie.

Wonders, N. A. and Caulfield, S. 1993. "Women's Work? The Contradictory Implications of Courses on Women and the Criminal Justice System". *Journal of Criminal Justice Education*, 4: 79-100.

Wright, R 1987. "Incorporating Women and Crime into Criminology Classes: Assignments, Exercises and Projects". *Teaching Sociology*, (15)1: 95-98.

Wright, R. 1994. "Twenty Recent Criminology Textbooks: Continued Diversity Without Currency or Quality". *Teaching Sociology*, (22)1: 87-104.

Wright, R. 1995a. "Women as 'Victims' and as Resisters': Depictions of the Oppression of Women in Criminology Textbooks". *Teaching Sociology*, (23)2: 111-121.

Wright, R. 1995a. "Where There's a Will There's a No Way: The Treatment of the Choice Debate in Criminology Textbooks, 1956 to 1965 and 1983 to 1992". *Teaching Sociology*, (23)1: 8-15.

Young, T. 1985. "Social Justice vs Criminal Justice: An Agenda for Critical Criminology". *Journal of Sociology and Social Welfare*, 12: 552-575.

4. The Challenges of Leadership in a Divided Society—A Problem-Solving Solution that Works: The Leadership Grid Contribution to Policing in Northern Ireland

James Drennan

1. Introduction

On November 1st 2001, the long-standing and historically well-known 'Royal Ulster Constabulary' became the Police Service of Northern Ireland. Why? The Independent Commission on Policing (the Patten Report) which had its origins in the 'Good Friday' Peace Agreement, provided a vision that spelled out an approach to a 'new beginning for policing' in Northern Ireland. The Government of Northern Ireland accepted the terms of the agreement and the set the new vision:

> "It is essential that policing structures and arrangements are such that the police service is professional, effective and efficient, fair and impartial, free from partisan control : accountable, both under the law for its actions and to the community it serves; representative of the society it polices, and operates within a coherent and cooperative criminal justice system, which conforms with the human rights norms." (Patten Commission)

The 'Patten' report recommended a change programme unprecedented for any Police service in the democratic world. Some of the features were far reaching and included measures that would ensure that the predominantly protestant police service hired and maintained an equal proportion of Catholic members. This transition, as painful as it may have been to many members of the RUC both new and old, was viewed as essential to ensure a balance of religious background in all members of the police service. In addition, and without going into the detail of the many contentious issues such as; the release of offenders from Northern Ireland prisons under the 'Good Friday Peace Agreement' and the elimination of any association to the Crown and Monarchy of the United Kingdom, which now had to be removed from all visible police objects, change was going to happen. Police buildings, uniforms, markings, policies, practices and structures, had changed within hours and along with that came the abandonment of many police traditions within the old RUC. Many members of the service have struggled with the loss of their historic identity while others simply refused to accept what had happened.

Some 302 police officers have been murdered, on and off duty, under the name of the Royal Ulster Constabulary. To support the transition, a master severance plan was launched in which hundreds of members elected to retire. This retirement plan transition has had both a positive and negative impact on the police and the community of Northern Ireland. The PSNI presently consists of about 10,000 police and civilian members policing throughout twenty-nine district commands in Northern Ireland. This is a down from its original 13,500 total membership with a target of some 7,500 total employees.

The history of conflict in Northern Ireland, much of it historically directed at the police, had created a culture of division and a tremendous challenge for the new police service, a challenge where a new vision of leadership change would be critical. Moreover, the new Police Service suffered a planned exodus of over 1500 seasoned senior officers, replaced in many cases by less experience officers and civilians. The leadership change would have to focus on behavioural issues rather than structural or process issues. As the Director of Training, Education and Development, I was tasked with examining traditional approaches to organisational change models connected to a new leadership approach and, when attempting to ensure that the focus of the new service would be more on behavioural changes rather than process changes, the 'Leadership Grid' by Blake and Mouton was the obvious best solution.

2. A Backdrop for Change in Policing Northern Ireland

It seemed clear from the outset that the police service would require, and benefit from, a strategic approach to leadership development that was different than what had been in place in the past. The dominant style of strong 'Command and Control' would now have to change. A real team focus on the elimination of blame-finding, the integration of other opinions and thoughts, and a clear action plan on improving leader conceptual ability, critical thinking, business administration skill and community awareness and acceptance, would all be required. One of the most critical skill areas that needed to be addressed was the lack of member problem-solving ability at all levels through constructive team development. The ongoing 'Oversight Commission' reports had already addressed this kind of need in leader development. This was supported by the organisational assessment of leadership and management competencies identified by the Occupational Psychologists for the PSNI. The inability to 'develop others' (by the new cadre of managers) was a serious concern identified through the data collected. All of the above contributed to the clear need for a strategic approach or model for 'leadership learning' across the PSNI.

Other well known leadership programs did not offer the experiential component that the 'Grid' could offer. Nor could they offer the critical feedback sessions that would help identify how people really behaved when the stakes were high. The 'Grid' offered these added characteristics to the learning and that was confirmed by all the participants. Every participant also agreed, this was observed from the evaluation and feedback on completion of the learning, that they had never worked so hard in any similar course or program. There seemed to be a positive correlation between the appreciation of the 'Grid' learning experience and the heavy workload required to complete the course. Sound practical exposure built on a sound theoretical foundation had led to the success of the 'Grid' across the PSNI.

It is about this one particular strategy of success that this article focuses on, and it is one which is a great lesson in leadership that should be considered by many services facing such change, yet albeit, less drastic transition initiatives. It really is all about leadership and learning that can help with even the most significant transition in policing. This article is not about the differences between policing in Canada and Northern Ireland, but the similarities. To begin, we will have to accept that police core functions are the same in any democracy. This particular article is about how one leadership-learning programme has provided hope and understanding to both police and community members alike and one that illustrates the importance of providing a balance of task completion without sacrificing the opinions and involvement of all members in decision-making.

Through the attainment of improved problem-solving, critical thinking and team decision-making, the overall behavioural change needed in the PSNI, no doubt, will be achieved. The acceptance of this leadership learning change approach that the Oversight Commission, Policing Board and Command teams have promoted, will now contribute to years of increased confidence and competence in PSNI members. These 'skills' improvements and leadership development have already resulted in a corresponding improvements to community based policing.

It is important however, to first provide the context and some background of the struggle in Northern Ireland that has brought us to a model of 'leadership in action' that has been developed, delivered and assessed relating to a transition in police leadership in the Police Service of Northern Ireland. The program is truly viewed as a transformational approach to leadership development.

The brief description in my opening paragraphs was of course, a price that had to be paid for peace and reconciliation within this divided society, a province of Great Britain but still a geographic part of one island. To the south, west and northwest is the Republic of Ireland, a much larger area of land that surrounds Northern Ireland with its own beauty, its own currency, economic system, justice system and independent government, all part of the European Union. The struggle to bring Northern Ireland into the Republic homeland (the south) by the Nationalist community, with the intent of creating a one-island country, has been faced by an equally resistant and determined Unionist movement to keep Northern Ireland part of Great Britain. The often-viewed perception from outside Northern Ireland is that the turmoil, which has continued for years, has been viewed as having roots in a religious divide between Catholics and Protestants. Although this may be partially the case in my opinion, the division is far more complex than mere religious differences would indicate.

In any understanding of policing in Northern Ireland, one must first attempt to understand the complex nature of the political landscape, in itself no easy task! The Policing Board representation includes all factions of the conflicting political and social makeup of Northern Ireland. In addition, community factions of all kinds, with differing religious and philosophical perspectives, all want to drive the policing agenda. The result is a confusing reflection of the society of Northern Ireland. Such complexities only detract from the police being able to do their jobs independently of the state or of such political influence.

Regardless of the opinions on either side and irrespective of the different factions within these respective sides, the fact remains today that even with the Good Friday Agreement, the police service has been seen as serving neither the interests of the Nationalists (Republicans) nor Unionists (Loyalists).The PSNI as it is now known, is not responsible for (selecting) hiring new recruit members, that is done by an external private sector provider. This approach is intended to ensure a balance of new student officers at '50% Catholic and 50% Other' denominational, ethnic and/or community reflective backgrounds.

Oversight and governance of the police service is massive with no less than seven government and non-governmental agencies monitoring, questioning, advising and directing the police service. Could we imagine for a moment, a Chief of Police in Canada facing so many oversight bodies and, at the same time, attempting to lead a massive change programme with ongoing significant challenges from so many political, community and special interest authorities?

What had to happen and happen quickly was to enlist support for a transition in thinking for both communities to be served and for the police themselves. There had to be an integrated programme of not just process in solving difficult issues in Northern Ireland society (an ENDS strategy), but a programme that actually worked and was successful at changing the fundamental behaviour of both groups (a MEANS strategy). Process models of leadership would be ineffective alone, systems for solving community and police problems in a partnership approach through real behavioural change, had to be found.

Members of this new service had to be prepared to deal with a community with whom they had seldom interacted because they policed in groups and did so from behind fortress walls and in armoured vehicles, and escorted by the military in many areas of Northern Ireland. This was essential for the preservation of their lives, a very serious business with tremendous security demands required for mere survival. Everything would hinge on the ability of the members of the new police service and the divided, yet somewhat accepting of change, communities they served. In order to make a successful transition from crime control policing to one of community centred and community-driven action, more than physical structures had to change. Think of just how difficult achieving 'policing with the community' is within a normal society, never mind for a police service that was separate from, and not a part of, society for so long. A police service hated by so many community elements on both sides yet expected to suddenly overnight, become a caring and compassionate institution of peace and reconciliation that could apply a 'community interest approach' to policing.

Real behavioural changes had to take place for both police and community. Increasing everyone's problem-solving ability, expressions of candour without being offensive, increasing team effectiveness (police/community teamwork was unheard of in many respects), increasing the quality of the decisions that had to be made, integration of everyone's thoughts and contributions, abandoning personal prejudices and increasing understanding and application of ethical decision-making and human rights. The ability to learn to do 'What is Right' as opposed to the daily pressure of doing 'Who is Right' in day-to-day policing, would demand a significant ethical requirement. This all seemed to be too much to expect of the new service that had such a history of 'Command and Control', a model of crime control and the (bunker) fortress approach to policing communities that had been used for so long. The Royal Ulster Constabulary was a police service that worked directly with military armed patrols, collectively they merely attempted to keep public order, never mind solve crime. In much of the collective thinking in the RUC, reflecting a belief that the police were at war, and therefore, unique strategy and questionable practices may have been acceptable tactics. A leadership and member development plan that promoted improvements in all of the above aspects of human and organizational effectiveness had to be put in place.

3. Leadership Grid

Clearly, one of the best models identified, a model that could achieve such wholesale and lasting change through practical learning, was the 'Leadership Grid' programme established in the 60's by Blake and Mouton, two social scientists whose research identified the benefits and means to achieve a balance between the tasks needing to be done and the consideration of the thoughts and ideas of the people who had to carry out those tasks. Surely the 'Leadership Grid' would be a strategic approach to overcoming such barriers to change and organisational effectiveness. The only way to really find out was to try the programme out and examine the Grid's effectiveness against such complex challenges in human behaviour.

In the spring of 2003, a proposal to hold police and community joint seminars was accepted and a pilot approach to a year-long scheme was put in motion. The Canadian affiliated firm with Grid International (Robinsonleadership.com), was brought to Belfast and a plan for ongoing sessions over the next two years, was established. The four day, intensive workload of learning from the 'Leadership Grid' was launched and the plan called for extensive evaluation and assessment of the programme. Reviews on every seminar were held and participants from all areas of the service were identified, police and civilian. Community members and experts were invited in to the seminars to ensure openness and transparency was achieved. External police services including: the Republic Police known as the Garda Siochana, the Royal Canadian Mounted Police, the Swedish Police Service and Latvian National Police, all joined the PSNI members in the seminars. Government officials and community members, other public sector employees and even members of England's well-known 'Centrex Police College' (formerly Bramshill) attended with PSNI members. The Chief Constable and his entire senior command team, both police and civilian, completed the entire seminar after hearing one consistent message from their members, "the Chief Constable and his team must complete this program if it is going to have any lasting effect on our organization!" The senior command team then did complete the entire program in June of 2004.

Along with the 'Grid' model came a system of evaluation and assessment that would prove to be of great importance in promoting the quality and impact of this program of change. The Grid session results were consistently assessed and reviewed by both the program provider and by the service command structure. Long term impact was also being developed to measure the 'organisational wide' overall impact on the police members and their communities. Additionally, the PSNI ensured that all of their own Occupational Psychologists attended the extensive program to ensure that a fundamental quality control element was applied to the entire program review.

The results were simply amazing. In short, the top team stated, through the Chief Constable, that the Grid 'would be' the change model for leadership development through problem-solving and decision-making improvements for the future. A new five year plan for developing a critical mass of the total membership was put into place just recently and the benefits across the service, resulting from the now 700 plus members having done it already, has simply been excellent. Members of the Department of Education, the University of Ulster top management team and others, have all now determined that the need for similar development through the 'Leadership Grid' would be of great benefit to their own organisations. One of the most consistent statements of support has been that the programme in 'Grid' development has not only been the best learning members have ever undertaken, but it has really changed their lives. It was not only liked but also learned, not only was it unanimously seen as improving the member's own behaviour and ability to solve problems in teams, it has done the same for the organisation. Most commented that it would forever, change the way they approached decision-making and problem-solving in their daily work and home lives. The program offers so many valuable lessons for all levels of the police service, both police and civilian members alike.

I have now been in policing and education for thirty-two years and I have never seen a more beneficial and pragmatic programme approach to real change management. The 'Grid' provides a functional, hands-on and total individual involvement 'learning experience'. Remember what the significant change barriers were in Northern Ireland policing. Remember the challenges and the changes everyone had to endure and more importantly, remember how significant the demands have been on the PSNI police service in moving from a crime control focus to a 'policing with the community' culture. The 'Leadership Grid' programme has already proven to be a significantly important aid to this transition and it does this through one of the most valuable learning events we have witnessed. In short, everyone who has taken it has liked it, learned it, stated they could all use it and felt it would make a real difference in their human interaction, problem-solving, communications, decision-making and conflict resolution, to name but a few aspects of the learning that has been achieved. In addition to all of the above, the Policing Board and the Police College, through a new learning advisory council system, have created a series of long-term 'Key Performance Indicators'. One of these indicators involves the measurement of the impact of this leadership development model.

PART B

POLICING

5. Role and Nature of Law Enforcement Agency Activities: Specific Responsibilities of Police

Andrew Graham and Paul Baxter

1. Structure of Policing in Canada

The structure and regulation of policing in Canada may be characterized as a complex network of overlapping jurisdictions and responsibilities that mirrors Canadian federalism. The *Constitution Act 1867-1982* sets out of the framework for the levels of police services in Canada; thus, it is also the cause of the confusion of contesting jurisdictions in Canadian law enforcement. The essence of the problem is that section 91 (27 and 28) of the Constitution Act clearly states that responsibility for criminal law and the maintenance and administration of federal penitentiaries is in the hands of the federal government. Section 91 also grants the federal government the power to take such actions as may be deemed necessary to preserve the "peace, order, and good government"[1] of the nation. While this "residual power" seems sweeping, in fact it has fallen into disuse since Confederation, but the intent of the framers of Confederation is clear: they intended to create a strong central government with the power to enforce its laws across the entire territory of Canada. Centralized control over the police services, as the coercive branch of the young Dominion of Canada, seemed a necessary but not sufficient step toward the consolidation of Canada as a sovereign nation-state.

Section 92 of the Constitution Act, however, bestows upon the provinces jurisdiction over provincial prisons and reformatories, protection of property and civil rights, the administration of justice, enforcement of provincial offences such as the Ontario Highway and Traffic Act, and all other matters of a purely local nature. In addition to these two constitutionally recognized levels of government[2], there are municipal governments which also take up policing responsibilities by funding and managing their own police services, contracting with larger units to police their communities, and by creating local by-laws (such as parking offences, licensing of pets and bicycles and so forth) that must be enforced by the police services. In another article, we will discuss the consequences of this kind of division of labour in policing, but our purpose in this article is to introduce the reader to the structure of policing in Canada, and to provide a brief description of how these over-lapping jurisdictions have gained a semblance of coherence in the Canadian justice system. It is worthwhile to begin with a discussion of the federal, provincial, and municipal police services.

2. The Federal Police Service: The Royal Canadian Mounted Police (RCMP)

The Royal Canadian Mounted Police (RCMP), established by the federal government, is a federal police force and is authorized to enforce federal laws anywhere in Canada. However, as a federal police force, the RCMP cannot enforce provincial or municipal laws unless clearly authorized to do so by provincial legislation. This is because the provinces are responsible for the enforcement of all laws of general application within their territorial limits, as noted above. However, the provinces may and do contract with the RCMP to provide their police services, which serves to further complicate the role of the RCMP.[3] The three territories and all of the provinces, except Ontario and Quebec (which have established their own provincial police forces), have entered into contractual arrangements with the federal government whereby the RCMP acts as the provincial, and in some instances, municipal police force. In this role, the RCMP enforces provincial law, some municipal by-laws and the *Criminal Code*.[4]

However, it is important to note that, as a matter of constitutional law, no provincial authority can intrude into the internal management of the RCMP. This remains the responsibility of the RCMP Commissioner, who is in turn responsible to the federal Solicitor General, now called the Minister of Public Safety and Emergency Preparedness Canada. This means that the disciplining of RCMP members, whether they are acting in a federal or provincial policing capacity, is an exclusively federal responsibility. This can limit the extent of control that provinces that contract with the RCMP can control its activities as a provincial police service. It also affects the impact of provincial legislation governing the civilian oversight of police services, usually only applied to municipal police services. The RCMP is a federal police force. It is governed by the *RCMP Act* and has a number of responsibilities, which may be described in terms of four levels of activity. Figure 1.1 gives a graphic illustration of these four levels of activity. They are:

1. Community, Contract, and Aboriginal Police Services, which is that branch of the service that delivers services to local communities.
2. Provincial and Territorial Police Services, which delivers police services to eight provinces and all three territories.
3. National Policing Services, which is probably the most unique of the roles of the RCMP. This level of service delivers highly specialized programs such as "Threat Assessment" and the "Protective Security Program" (the Canadian equivalent of the American Secret Service Agency that guards dignitaries and important politicians. Perhaps the most important national service the RCMP provides are the national crime data-bases CPIC (Canadian Police Information Centre), and ViCLAS (Violent Crime Linkage System). All operating police services in Canada have access to these systems, and others are coming on-line (this will be discussed in a separate article).
4. International Crime and Customs Enforcement, includes the maintenance of border integrity, anti-smuggling operations, drug enforcement, anti-terrorism activities, and a number of different intelligence operations. The RCMP works closely with other organizations from around the word,

including other law enforcement agencies and Non-Governmental Organizations in this role.[5]

As of January 01, 2004 the RCMP had an operational strength of 22, 239 members. Of this number, 14,384 are constables, corporals, or sergeants (i.e, front-line police officers). The command staff for this large force is rather small, consisting of only 86 members from the Commissioner down to the Chief Superintendents.[6]

Figure 1.1: The Four Roles of the RCMP

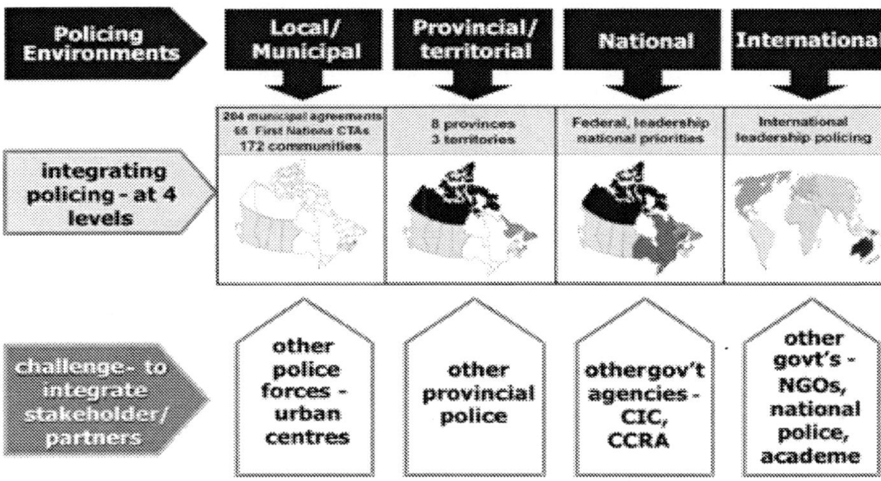

Source: *Royal Canadian Mounted Police Performance Report, 2002-2003*, p. 20.[7]

3. Provincial and Local Police Services

Provincial police acts set out the terms by which police are governed. In Ontario and Quebec, there is legislation in place that regulated policing in the province. At the first level, these acts (The Police Services in Ontario[8] and the Police Act[9] in Quebec) regulate the provincial police services (the Ontario Provincial Police and Surete du Quebec). However, these acts also set out how the provincial and municipal polices services will work together, and the conditions under which a municipality may or may not have their own police service.

In terms of the structure of policing, the division of labour for law enforcement varies from province to province. Provincial police services (whether independent or contracted with the RCMP) police the major highways of the provinces and they provide police services to rural areas and small towns. In most provinces, municipalities are required to provide their own police services once they reach a certain size. In British Columbia, Manitoba, Ontario, and Quebec, municipalities must provide their own police services once they reach a size of 5000. In Alberta, municipalities take responsibility for policing once they reach a size of 2500, and in Saskatchewan municipalities take responsibility for policing once their populations reach a paltry 500 people. To the east, New Brunswick and Nova Scotia require that every municipality provide or contract for police services, while Newfoundland and Prince Edward Island seem silent on this issue.[10]

Municipalities have three options when they reach a size that requires them to take responsibility for their own policing under provincial legislation: they may create their own police service, join an existing municipal service (consolidate), or they may enter into contracts with the provincial police service or the RCMP. In 2002-2003, there were 562 municipal police services in Canada.[11] This includes 201 RCMP municipal contracts and 97 OPP municipal contracts.[12] Municipal policing accounted for 65% of all police officers and 56% of all policing costs in 2002.[13] The 264 municipal services that were not contracted by the RCMP or OPP constitute over 33,090 officers, or 86% of all the municipal police officers in Canada.[14]

Federal and provincial police services have also been involved the creation and support of First Nations Police Services. The RCMP has "tri-partite agreements" with 65 aboriginal communities.[15] This permits the aboriginal community to have its own police service, which generally acts like a municipal service with its own governance, staff and accountabilities. The application of federal laws, e.g. drug enforcement, would still be in the hands of the RCMP. Clearly, these First Nations Policing services are not fully autonomous from the RCMP. In fact, in terms of law enforcement for serious crimes, they are often completely on the RCMP for support. In Ontario, the OPP has administrative responsibility for 36 First Nations, which constitutes a dramatic reduction of its responsibilities since the mid-1990's.[16] The reason for this is that the goal of the First Nations in Ontario, and lately of the OPP as well, has been to create fully autonomous "stand-alone" police services for First Nations that could bare the cost. Like many municipalities, Ontario's First Nations Peoples have managed to create their own police services by consolidating into larger administrative or regional units such as the Nishnawbe-Aski Police Service[17] and the Anishinabek Police Service.[18] The development of self-directed police services on First Nations is regarded by many First Nations leaders as a necessary first step on the road to aboriginal self-government in Canada.

4. Regionalization and Restructuring

For many police forces, regionalization has come to be seen the most cost-effective and efficient way of doing business. Owing to budget cuts and downsizing, creative solutions, like regionalization, have been adopted. For example, at the local level, municipal police forces have joined together with other municipalities and rural areas to create a regional police service. This regional police force offers reduced costs, improved service and centralized administrative services. In many instances, this has also reflected the reorganization of municipal governments into larger units by the Province. In other instances, the police regionalization has been independent of this.

Similarly, the RCMP, while it remains the national police service, has become highly decentralized and regionalized. This is for several reasons. As pointed out above, it serves as the provincial police service in all but two of the provinces. As such, its regional senior officers must maintain a close liaison with provincial authorities. Second, policing priorities, even for a national service, will vary across the country. In order to ensure that the RCMP is responsive to these differences, regional senior staff (Assistant Commissioners of the RCMP) have considerable latitude in setting priorities.

The process of regionalism is most pronounced in the densely populated region of Southern Ontario, and in the Greater Toronto Area (GTA) in particular. The twelve municipalities in the immediate vicinity of the city of Toronto coalesced into Metropolitan Toronto Police Department in 1957.[19] Since that time, the outlying communities of the GTA have either contracted with the OPP, or they have formed their own regional police services. Today, the GTA is ringed by four massive regional police services: York Region to the north, Peel Region to the west, Durham Region to east, and Niagara Region to the south. There has been a debate over the efficacy of regionalizing, and while regionalizing may be a *fait accompli* in the GTA, it is by no means accepted everywhere in Canada. Critics have attacked regionalism for several reasons. They claim that regionalizing causes a loss of local control over the police service, creates high start-up costs, causes a loss of local identity, detracts from the task of embedding good community relations as the best practice of a police service, and causes a shift in resources from suburban areas to urban core (or other "high crime") areas. It is unlikely that any of these normative arguments will have much affect on the process of regionalization. This dynamic is driven by the high cost of policing (see below), and many municipalities that are holding off the regionalizing pressures are being squeezed financially to the point where citizens are beginning to feel unsafe. In the last analysis, police services will regionalize when the citizens in their community have reached their tax threshold.[20]

5. Key Government Players in Policing

In Canada, there has been an historical separation of the minister responsible for justice, i.e. the creation of the law and the minister responsible for its administration, i.e. police, security and correctional services. The exception to that has been in provinces that contract for their police services. Depending on the province, attorneys general, solicitors general or ministers of justice develop policy for the direction of policing. They are also responsible for correctional institutions for inmates serving sentences of less than two years, provincial parole systems, and the court system. With respect to the provinces which maintain their own provincial police service, the organizational structure is similar to the RCMP, with a Commissioner of Police responsible to a Minister in the government.

Federally, the Minister of Public Safety and Emergency Preparedness Canada, who is responsible for the Canadian Border Services Agency, Canada Firearms Centre, Canadian Security Intelligence Service, Correctional Services of Canada, the National Parole Board, and the RCMP. The reporting structure in most provinces is remarkably similar. In those provinces under the RCMP, the Deputy-Commissioner in command of the region reports to the relevant minister on provincial matters, but to the federal minister on federal matters. In practice, the two sides coordinate their efforts. Similarly, provincial police commissioners report directly to a provincial cabinet minister. Municipal police services work differently in so far as most municipal police chiefs report to a civilian police services board. These boards are usually comprised of at least four members, two of whom are appointed by the province, one by the police service, and one civilian member from the community. Municipal police services are also under the jurisdiction of the municipal council of their community, so they are a only obliquely tied to the provincial government, although their service is governed by an act of the provincial legislature.

6. Police Powers

Federal police powers:

The Royal Canadian Mounted Police enforces federal statues and all laws made by, or under, the authority of the Canadian Parliament.

Provincial police powers:

Provincial police forces enforce the *Criminal Code* and provincial statues within each province or areas that are not served by a municipal police force (i.e. small towns or rural areas).

Municipal Police powers:

Municipal police forces enforce the *Criminal Code*, provincial statues, and municipal by-laws within the specific boundaries of a municipality or within several adjoining municipalities which make up a region (e.g. Durham Regional Police). Where a municipal policing contract is granted to a provincial force or to the RCMP, these police agencies automatically assume municipal police powers. As well, where a provincial policing contract is granted to the RCMP, the RCMP automatically assumes provincial policing powers. Increasingly, municipal governments are employing "by-law enforcement" services to ease the pressure on police services to enforce local by-laws such as parking infractions. Police forces usually follow a specific rank and promotion system. The RCMP and Ontario Provincial Police differ slightly from municipal police agencies. The rank system in Quebec is different again. Generally, however, there are three rank categories: front-line officer, middle ranking (sergeant, staff sergeant) and senior or Deputy and Chief ranks. More significantly in the past three decades has been the increase in number of inspector level positions with high degrees of specialization, e.g. drug enforcement, computer crimes, hate crimes and discrimination. This has reflected the changing nature of crime and criminal organizations as well as the realized benefits of specialization in the long-term concentration of expert resources on a specific problem.

7. The Cost of Policing

The following provides a few quick facts about the cost of policing:

- Policing expenditures totaled $7.8 billion in 2002, or $249 per capita[21]
- Municipal policing continues to account for approximately 56% of policing expenditures, provincial policing 23%, and federal and other RCMP costs account for the remaining 21% of the total expenditures [22]

Where there are municipal and provincial contracts, the municipal and provincial government is responsible for funding their respective police forces. Where RCMP is granted a policing contract to police a municipality, under the billing agreement, municipalities with a population under 15,000 are billed 70% of total expenditures, and municipalities of 15,000 and over are billed 90% of total costs. In the provinces and territories where the RCMP are contracted to provide provincial level policing, the provinces are billed 70% of the total contract costs in most cases. The remaining funds come from the federal government.[23]

Provinces allocate funds for their policing budgets from the general budget of the provinces. The situation in municipalities varies, but generally funds come from the municipal budget voted by the municipal council from general revenues. Generally, however, municipal councils may not vote on specific budgetary items for the police service, but only approve or deny the overall budget as recommended by the police service board, a citizen oversight board. In areas of dispute between the board and the municipal council, the province must intervene.

8. Canadian Policing Statistics

Canada ranks 24th in the world in terms of police per capita at 182 police officers per 100,000 citizens (tied with Japan and New Zealand). Canada's police services are approximately 25% of the size of their counterparts in the United States (244 per 100,000) and the United Kingdom (233 per 100,000).[24] Further, Canada's police services are only about one third of the proportion of much more heavily policed countries. For example, Italy ranks first in the world with a ratio of 559 per 100,000, followed by Portugal (459 per 100,000) and the Czech Republic (445 per 100,000). The peak ratio of police to citizen population occurred in 1975, when the ratio was 206 per 100,000.[25] This decline may seem to make sense of commensurable declines in the crime rates in Canada since the 1970's; however, the complexity of the law and the crimes being investigated more than make for the shortfall in personnel. Debates are beginning to break out throughout Canadian communities over whether or not we are under-policed, and whether or not regionalizing or consolidating police services will solve the problem. Table 1.1 below summarizes the personnel numbers in Canadian police services. One of the most promising signs of increased equality in Canada's police services is the successful advancement of women in policing. Between 1965 and 2003, women have moved from constituting less than 1% of the police officers in Canada to constituting approximately 16% of the police officers in Canada.[26] The greatest increases in the representation of women has occurred between 1995 and 2003, when the numbers jumped from just under 10% to 16%. This makes Canada the seventh highest ranking nation in world for female participation in policing. Moreover, the number of women at the non-commissioned (sergeants and corporals) and commissioned officers (staff-sergeants and above) have increased to 8% and 5% respectively.[27]

Table 1.1: Trends in Police Personnel in Canada 1999-2003

	1999	2000	2001	2002	2003
			Number		
Police Personnel (Total)	75,489	75,863	77,074	79,177	81,210
Police Officers	55,321	55,954	57,076	58,422	59,494
Civilian Personnel	20,168	19,909	19,998	20,755	21,716
Police-Civilian Ratio	2.74	2.81	2.85	2.81	2.74
			Rate		
Population per Police Officer	549.6	548.5	543.5	536.8	531.6
Criminal Code Incidents per Police Officer	42.6	42.0	41.6	40.8	NA

Source: Statistics Canada, CANSIM, table 254-0002 and Catalogue Number 85-225-XIE

Questions have been raised in Canada regarding the extent of representation of First Nations Peoples and visible minorities in the police organizations. One of the first principles of community policing is that the police service should reflect the community it polices; thus, one would expect to find at least proportional representation of marginalized, ethnic, or cultural minorities serving on the police services. Recent statistics are hard to come by, but a Statistics Canada study done in 1996, but not released until 2002, provides some insight on this problem in the Canadian context.[28]

This study found that in 1996 aboriginal people represented 2.3% of all justice workers in the Canadian system. This amounts to 6,965 people. Of that number, 31% were females, 35% worked as private security guards, and 27% worked as police officers.[29] There are several noteworthy aspects of these numbers. First, it is clear that a disproportionate number of aboriginal people are participating in the criminal justice system at the lowest-paying and least significant level (i.e., private security). Very few First Nations Peoples make it to positions of real influence or power in the criminal justice system. Second, even though some people may argue that aboriginal representation in the criminal justice is consistent with their representation in the working population, and that this number is proportional to the aboriginal population in Canada as a whole[30], it still demonstrates a failing a of the system when one considers the fact that in provinces such as Alberta, Manitoba, and Saskatchewan First Nations Peoples make up as much as 60% of the inmates in provincial jails.[31] Given the over-representation of Canada's First Nations Peoples in the criminal justice system as clients, one would naturally suspect that over-representing them in agencies that are tasked with solving and preventing those problems might be a good first step towards a solution. To date, there is no evidence that this problem has been solved. Police services still engage in targeted hiring to entice aboriginals to join their services, but they cannot seem to convince many to become recruits.[32] We find a very similar set of circumstances for non-aboriginal visible minorities. The 20, 570 visible minorities working in the justice system constitute 6.8% of the total number of justice workers in Canada. This is substantially lower than the 10.7% of the population that is comprised of visible minorities. Of those workers, 37% were women, 45% were working in other protective services (primarily as security guards), and another 14% were working as legal secretaries. Only 13% of these workers were lawyers or notaries, and only 8.9% of them were police officers.[33] As in the case of aboriginal people, the police services have been trying entice members of visible minority communities to join their services, but so far they have met with little success.

Notes

[1] See the introduction to Section 91 of the *Constitution Act* 1867, available at http://laws.justice.gc.ca/en/const/index.html.

[2] Municipal governments are explicitly recognized in the formal division of powers between levels of government in Canada. This is not to suggest that they are not relevant, but it is important to note that local governments at the municipal level are completely dependent on the federal, and, more importantly, the provincial governments for their existence. This information can be found at http://laws.justice.gc.ca/en/const/index.html on the Department of Justice Website. Please note that I will refer to publicly available sources, usually accessible from the internet, as much as possible. This should give readers some avenues for further investigation.

[3] *Police Resources in Canada, 2003*. Ottawa: Canadian Centre for Justice Statistics, Catalogue no. 85-225-XIE, released December 2003, pg. 5.

[4] Frank Schmalleger, David Maclister, and Paul F. McKenna, *Canadian Criminal Justice Today*. Toronto: Pearson-Prentice Hall, 2004, pp. 110-111.

[5] The organizational of the RCMP is explained on webpage entitled "The Organization of the RCMP", at, http://www.rcmp.ca/html/resources_e.htm.

[6] *Ibid.*

[7] This document is freely available at the RCMP website at, http://www.rcmp.ca/html/resources_e.htm.
[8] *Police Services Act*, R.S.O. 1990 C. P 15.
[9] Quebec Police Act, R.S. Q. 2003 Q. P-13.1.
[10] This issue is described well in Frank Schmalleger, David Maclister, and Paul F. McKenna, *Candian Criminal Justice Today*, pp. 114-115.
[11] *Police Resources in Canada, 2003*, Canadian Centre for Justice Statistics, pg. 18.
[12] *Ibid.*
[13] *Ibid.*
[14] *Ibid.*
[15] *Royal Canadian Mounted Police Performance Report, 2003-2003*, retrieved electronically at http://www.rcmp.ca, pg. 32.
[16] See, the *Ontario Provincial Police Business Plan* 2004, at http://www.gov.on.ca/opp/bplan/english/oppplanen2004.htm.
[17] This is a massive police service across Ontario's extreme north. More information can be found on their website at, http://www.naps-net.org/, and to get a sense for the sheer magnitude of the area covered by this police service, examine their maps of their regions at, http://www.naps-net.org/detach_map.htm. There are very few good resources on First Nations Policing in Canada. One of the best sources of information is First Nations Chiefs of Police Association website, which can be found at, http://www.fncpa.ca/. The only comprehensive study of First Nations Policing so far has been done in a coordinated effort between the First Nations Chiefs of Police Association and Human Resources Development Canada. The study is now a few years old, but it offers a wealth of information on First Nations Policing. The report may be downloaded for free at, http://www.fncpa.ca/hrstudies.htm.
[18] See, Bryan D. Cummins and John L. Steckley, *Aboriginal Policing: A Canadian Perspective*. Toronto: Prentice Hall, 2002, pp. 94-95. Note that both of these First Nations Police services cover land-areas of thousands of square kilometers in Ontario's north.
[19] C.K. Talbot, T.J. Juliani, and C.H.S. Jayewardene, "Policing in Canada: A Developmental Perspective", *Canadian Police College Journal*, Vol. 8, No. 3, 1984, pg. 320.
[20] For more on this debate see, J. Seagrave, *Introduction to Policing in Canada*. Scarborough: Prentice-Hall, 1997, and *Closing the Gap: Policing and the Community, The Report, Section D, Regionalization of Police Services, Victoria B.C.*. Attorney General of Canada.
[21] *Police Resources in Canada, 2003*, Canadian Centre for Justice Statistics, pg. 16.
[22] *Ibid.*
[23] *Ibid*, pp. 18-19.
[24] *Ibid*, pg. 25.
[25] *Ibid.*

[26] *Ibid*, pp. 13-14.
[27] *Ibid*, pg. 15.
[28] *A Statistical Profile of Persons Working in Justice-Related Professions in Canada, 1996*. Ottawa: Canadian Centre for Justice Statistics, Catalogue no. 85-555-XIE, 2002.
[29] *Ibid*, pp. 24-25.
[30] The 2001 Census shows that First Nations Peoples constitute 4.4% of the Canadian population. *2001 Census Analysis Series: Aboriginal Peoples of Canada: A Demographic Profile*. Ottawa: Statistics Canada, Catalogue no. 96F0030XIE2001007, released Jan. 21, 2003, pg. 5.
[31] *Aboriginal Peoples in Canada*. Ottawa: Canadian Centre for Justice Statistics Profile Series, Catalogue no. 85F0033MIE, released June 2001, pp.8-10. Much has been written about Restorative Justice initiatives, but there is little with critical merit on aboriginal policing. Aside from the sources cited above, see, Wendy Chan and Kiran Mirchandani, *Crimes of Colour: Racialization and the Criminal Justice System in Canada*. Peterborough Ontario: Broadview Press, 2002, Chapters 8-9 *passim*.
[32] See, for example, the "OPP Bound" program, which was directed toward enticing aboriginal recruits in 2004 and women in 2003: http://www.gov.on.ca/opp/recruit/english/oppbound04.htm.
[33] *A Statistical Profile of Persons Working in Justice-Related Professions in Canada, 1996*. pp. 23-24.

References

Canadian Legal Information Institute: http://www.canlii.org/

Canadian Police Link: http://www.policelink.ca

Census Analysis Series: Aboriginal Peoples of Canada: A Demographic Profile. 2001 Ottawa: Statistics Canada, Catalogue no. 96F0030XIE2001007

Chan, W. and Mirchandani, K. 2002 *Crimes of Colour: Racialization and the Criminal Justice System in Canada*. Peterborough Ontario: Broadview Press.

Cryderman, B.K., O'Toole, C. and Fleras, A. 1998 *Police, Race and Ethnicity: A Guide for Law Enforcement Officers*. Toronto: Butterworths.

Cummins, B.D. and Steckley, J.L. 2002 *Aboriginal Policing: A Canadian Perspective*. Toronto: Prentice Hall.

First Nations Chiefs of Police Association: http://www.fncpa.ca/

Ontario Provincial Police: http://www.gov.on.ca/opp/

Royal Canadian Mounted Police: http://www.rcmp.ca

Schmalleger, F., Maclister, D. and McKenna, P.F. 2004 *Canadian Criminal Justice Today*. Toronto: Pearson-Prentice Hall.

Seagrave, J. 1997 *Introduction to Policing in Canada*. Scarborough: Prentice-Hall.

A Statistical Profile of Persons Working in Justice-Related Professions in Canada, 1996. Ottawa: Canadian Centre for Justice Statistics, Catalogue no. 85-555-XIE, 2002.

Talbot, C.K., T.J. Juliani, and C.H.S. Jayewardene, 1984 "Policing in Canada: A Developmental Perspective", *Canadian Police College Journal*, Vol. 8, No. 3.

6. Cyber Crime and Policing: A Comparative Analysis

David Baker

1. Setting the Stage

The principal framework that shapes predictions of the future directions of policing remains Herbert Packer's model of the U.S. criminal justice process. Packer's model for the past 30 years has had considerable explanatory power, and it appears that its explanatory power will continue to be dominant in mainstream criminology. However, in making predictions, this chapter will not limit itself to Parker's vision of possible futures for criminal justice but attempt to gaze in the future, to venture some predictions in an area where Parker's model is completely silent – *Cyber crime: The issue of jurisdiction in Cyber space.*

Herbert Parker's (1968) *The Limits of the Criminal Sanction* claims that the criminal justice process in the United States is the outcome of competition between two value systems, two value systems that represent two model of the operation of criminal justice – the "crime control" model and the "due process" model. From a political standpoint, the crime control model reflects traditional conservative values, while the due process model embodies traditional liberal values (Miller, 1973). Accordingly, when political conservative values are dominant in society, as they are currently, the principles and policies of the crime control model seem to determine the operations of criminal justice (Bohm and Haley 2002). During more politically liberal periods, such as the 1960s through the 1970s, the principles and policies of the due process model dominated criminal justice discourses and practices (ibid).The two models are ideal types, but do not correspond precisely to the actual day-to-day practice of criminal justice. However, they both provide appropriate ways of appreciating current and future applications of criminal law. This paper is concerned with the following set of interrelated questions related to these competing frames of reference. What are the fundamental challenges posed by the crime control model especially in reference to cyber crime? What is the impact of cyber policing on the future of law enforcement? What are the contradictions inherent in the due process model in reference to cyber crime? To what extent does the traditional notion of jurisdiction still apply to cyber space? Lastly, what are the benefits of a comparative analysis?

2. Issue of jurisdiction in Cyber space

The new paradigm of communications, cyber space that has been developing rapidly over the years cuts across territorial borders. Indeed, in cyber space, geo-political boundaries have become meaningless. But in relation to criminal justice the issue of jurisdictional space is significant. Jurisdiction, as Cherl Conner (1998) reminds us, is a problematic concern given that traditionally courts could only exercise authority over persons and/ or property present in the political domain in which an action is brought. What then are the implications of jurisdiction when the concept of sovereignty within a geo-political space is challenged by "cyber" activities? The Internet has ushered forms of interaction in which the traditional notions of criminal justice –from enforcement to adjudication are increasingly inapplicable (Visano, 2004). The proliferation of cyber engagements has created a need to reexamine traditional paradigms in an effort to examine the creation of new laws and legal institutions that are not restricted territorially. This challenge poses incredible problems that impact on rights and sovereignty for which the local national jurisdictional laws are ill equipped. As Visano (2004) argues, the socio-political contexts of control are contests shaped by cultural imperatives that ensure values promoting privilege. Moreover, Cinotti and Visano (2005:2) elaborate:

> The current normative emphasis on the primacy of the procedural as currently manifested in this new war on techno -mediated crime subverts a more meaningful awareness of the implicated ideology - institution nexus, an analysis of which is fundamentally necessary in order to appreciate contemporary reductive and reactive measures that opportunistically exploits the credulities of the misinformed in an effort to muster support, mobilize resources and justify contagion. Equally, efforts to understand the impact of the internet on policing must move beyond a convenient police accommodation to either a supply-side (increased intelligence gathering, satellite intrusions, enhanced technical capabilities accompanied with law enforcement/ military options) or a demand-side (awareness campaigns, race training, public relations, community development) set of interventions.

3. The Absence of Territorially based Borders on the Internet

Cyber space has no territorial boundaries; the transmission of information (digital data) is almost entirely independent of physical location. Furthermore, the development of the global network is destroying the link between geographical location and the *power* of local governments to take control over online behaviors. The Internet is available to transact communication between people who do not know nor will ever know the physical location of the other party. Network system is indifferent to the geographical location of those servers, even if there is no relation between domain name and a physical jurisdiction. For example, a server with a ".com" domain name may not necessarily be located in the United States; it can be anywhere. Users easily disregard the physical location of their server. Thus, the traditional notion of physical jurisdiction may no longer exist in cyber space. Furthermore, there are no universal standards defining Internet jurisdiction. This phenomenon not only renders local courts ineffectual but is also exacerbated by the absence of international enforcement.

4. The domain name conflict

Present trademark law is definitely based on geographical divisions. Its rights typically arise within a given country, usually on the grounds for the use of a mark on physical goods or in connection with the condition of services in specific sites within that country. All countries have different trademark laws, with important differences on matters such as whether the same name can be used in different lines of business. As David Johnson (1996) points out, in the United States, the same trademark can be used for the same line of business if there is adequate geographic separation of use to avert confusion. In fact, there are many local businesses with indistinguishable names that do not interfere with each other because customers do not overlap. However, in cyber space there is a problem regarding identical trademarks. Domain name systems, like www.yahoo.com are actual conversions of Internet protocol addresses like "211.248.254.XXX". In any country, people who wish to construct their own web site can use a domain name system. For example, if someone wants to use the name "www.nike.com", that individual can register the name on cyber space. Likewise, corporations doing businesses in foreign countries appropriate local popular names to advance their corporate commodities. In this laissez faire, frontier mentality where everything goes not all have equal access to corporate or individual resources to engage in trademark theft. So called global entities can easily use local names of other jurisdictions with impunity.

5. Illegal activity on the Internet - USA

The ineffectiveness of courts are illustrated in the following examples of jurisdictional trespasses – from gambling to name/ identity theft. Gambling is an attractive activity on the Internet. For instance, there are a number of services outside of Minnesota that offer Minnesota residents the opportunity to access the web site and bet on sporting events or join a virtual casino games. These services are illegal in the state of Minnesota. According the Minnesota Statute Section 609.05, Subdivision 1 (1994), "Minnesota's accomplice statute provides that one who intentionally aids, advises, counsels, or conspires with another to commit a crime is equally liable for that crime." Therefore, persons who knowingly help Internet gambling company in any unlawful activity may themselves be held liable for that unlawful activity. Internet access providers and credit card companies that continue to provide a "pay gate services" to gambling company after knowing that the activities of the company is illegal would be subject to accomplice liability. Further, under Minnesota law, the gambling company appears to violate provision of the federal law, 18 United States Code Section 1084 that prohibits the foreign or interstate transmission of bets or information on bets through the wire communication. As "The Attorney General of Minnesota has asserted the right to regulate gambling that occurs on a foreign web page that was accessed and "brought into" the state by a local resident." Further, " Persons outside of Minnesota who transmit information via the Internet knowing that information will be disseminated in Minnesota are subject to jurisdiction in Minnesota courts for violations of state criminal and civil laws" (Statement of

Minnesota Attorney General On Internet Jurisdiction 1994). In this case, the defendant claimed that Minnesota court did not have jurisdiction because his activity was outside of Minnesota. However, the Minnesota Attorney General asserted that the Minnesota Supreme Court hold that "the intentional impact within Minnesota land created jurisdiction" (ibid).

In another case (*Bensusan Restaurant Corp. v. King),* the plaintiff corporation owned the internationally famous "Blue Note" nightclub in New York City. The defendant was the owner of a nightclub in Missouri also called "The Blue Note," which provided a popular entertainment source to college students at the nearby university. The plaintiff sued in New York for trademark infringement on the basis of the defendant's homepage. And he asked the court to order the defendant to change the name of the club and to shut down the homepage, which contained a hyperlink to the New York Blue Note site. According to Ogilvy Renault (1998) "the U.S. Court of Appeals upheld the trial decision dismissing the lawsuit for lack of jurisdiction". The court asserted that, "Under New York's long-arm statute, a court has jurisdiction if a tort is committed in the state or damages are suffered there" (ibid).

In the U.K. a court ruled that a web-site owner may be brought to court if the content of a website is available for viewing in UK. A judge dismissed a defendant's argument that since his servers where located in the U.S. therefore, the UK court has no jurisdiction to render a ruling. However, the court ruled that since the U.K. the British police have been able to view the content of the site the publication occurred in Britain, and thus, the British courts have jurisdiction over the matter (news.bbc.co.uk/hi/English/sci/tech/newsid). In this case the U.K. court reasoned that if the defendant enters into contracts with residents of a foreign jurisdiction that belong to repeated transmission of digital data, such as, files over the internet, personal jurisdiction is appropriate.

The United States began to use a new concept of copyright, and cyber crime legislation that would be applied to both the U.S. and other countries. The most obvious example of this extra-territorial approach originates in the U.S. Anti-cyber squatting Consumer Protection Act (ACPA), a law enacted in 1999 to deal with cases of domain name cyber squatting (Geist, 1999). From 1999, U.S. courts have dealt with numerous cases involving the application of the ACPA. But this law has its limits. The ACPA resolves and protect trademark holders who have dot com, dot net, dot org domains that root servers located in Virginia. The U.S courts, regardless of the defendant's country, can apply the ACPA equally to the foreign trademarks. The ACPA now covers every dot-com domain, regardless of where it was registered (ibid). However, Ogilvy Renault (1998) pointed out "Defendants sued in foreign courts more and more frequently attempt to bring the case back to their own domestic forum. Under the forum non convenience principle, a court may stay or dismiss a suit if it is persuaded that there is another forum that is more closely connected to the events giving rise to the suit, or otherwise better suited to adjudicate the issues." As an above principal, Canadian court holds that if another country's authorities are in a better position to decide, jurisdiction may be declined.

6. The current status of cyber crimes in Korea

Cyber crimes in Korea have multiplied approximately 21 times over the past five years. The perpetrators of these crimes are below the age of 30 that account for nearly 58 percent of the statistics. In 1998, there were approximately 355 cases of cyber-crime. By 2002 an explosive growth resulted in 7,487 cases of cyber-crimes. A total of 1,007 people were detained in 2002 on related charges, comparable to figure for 1998 where only 83 people were detained on related charges (Korean Ministry of Information, 2003). According to the Korean National Police Agency report (2003) computer crimes have increased 80 percent since 2001, reporting 60,068 cases. The number of arrests have also soared 85 percent from 22,693 in 2001 to 41,900 in 2002. Reported cases of invasion of privacy had a 125-percent increase, rating the highest jump. Cases of online communication and game fraud rated second with a 120-percent increase. Online communication and game fraud cases made up 51 percent of all computer crimes with 31,109 cases. Some 14,159 cases were reported for hacking and virus infringement, 3,155 for libel and sexual harassment, 2,496 for invasion of privacy, 1,889 for distribution of computer virus. Further, according to Korean ministry of information and communication's report for Korean Parliamentary audit, June 2003, KT Corp., Hanaro Telecom Inc. and other broadband carriers are providing the so-called ADSL (asymmetric digital subscriber line) services to more than 11 million households and about sixty-four percents of Korean people are regularly surfing the Web. According to a recent survey done by the Korea information security agency (Korea Ministry of information and communication, June. 2003), 50.8 percent of those in their 40s surf the Web at least once a month, up 11.9 percent from 2002. The portion of Internet users among thirty-year-olds reached 78.5 percent, up 11.8 percent from a year ago, while the Internet usage rate for teens and those in 20s reached a saturation point. A majority of Internet users, or 71.6 percent, said they surf the Web to find information, followed by reading e-mail at 54.9 percent and gaming at 50 percent.

7. Cyber crimes and Juvenile Delinquents

Traditional juvenile delinquents offences have been steadily decreasing in Korea. Interestingly, cyber offenses committed by younger teenagers are drastically rising, according to statistics from the Korean National Police Agency (2003). Further, the number of criminals aged 12-19 declined by 12.1 percent from a year ago to 115,210 in 2002, accounting for 5.9 percent of the total. The number of teenage offenders dropped steadily since setting a new benchmark at 153,380 in 1997. The police figures, however, show criminal offenders under the age of 14 jumped by 21 percent from 2001 to more than 1,660 in 2002. The number of students committing crimes amounted to 60,702 in 2002, down 7.2 percent from the previous year. But the number of offenders attending elementary and middle schools rose by 8.7 percent and 0.4 percent, respectively. Criminal offenses committed by high school and college students in 2001 declined by 10.7 percent and 5.5 percent from a year earlier. Of the juvenile delinquencies tallied in 2002, felonies including murder, burglary, rape and arson decreased by 16.8 percent from the previous year to 2,041 cases. But intellectual theft jumped by 43.3 percent over the cited period to 8,564, showing that teenagers are vulnerable to the temptation of cyber crime. While these numbers may seem conservative for Korea, it offers an example as to what opportunities exist in cyber space. As Kit Burden, Creole Palmer, Lyde Barlow and Gilbert Barlow (2003) points out "The Internet offers criminals unparalleled opportunities. This is not surprising when one considers the anonymity it can provide, the speed with which it operates, the ease with which cyber criminals can get on line, and the size of the market into which to tap".

8. Implications

In the United States, the issue of jurisdictions between states has been under scrutiny, while those between other countries and the U.S. this issue of sovereignty has avoided much attention. In cases that involved foreign jurisdiction, the approach of U.S. courts have been inadequate. Increasingly U.S courts are applying ACPA without exception to protect trademark holders given that dot com and dot. org servers under investigation have been located in Virginia. Thus, the courts claim that they have complete jurisdiction against domain name dispute between dot com holders. But the domain holder may not necessarily be a resident of the US. If this principle is applied in all cases, then an American who lives in the US and has a dot kr domain, sued in Korean court over domain dispute, would that individual be punished by Korean law? For these disputes, the forum non-convenience principle, which has been applied in Canadian courts, appears more reasonable. Cyber space is not an homogeneous space making traditional standards inappropriate. This new paradigm with the unique character of "no physical boundary" has created confusion of jurisdiction in criminal justice system. Moreover, without developing technology, governments cannot control transmission of information in the cyberspace. Thus, a traditional law enforcement approach cannot resolve this problem of Internet jurisdiction.

If the future of law enforcement reflects the principles and policies of the crime control model then society might expect fewer limitations on how the government agencies should deal with crimes. For example, the practice of detaining and arresting suspects for investigation without probable cause is likely to increase as in the length of time a suspect may be held before being charged. Again, what if that suspect server is in another country? If the due process model were to determine future law enforcement practices, electronic surveillance will be suspect and strictly limited to a few types of crimes - crimes that threaten national security, such as treason and espionage.

9. Conclusion

Advances in law enforcement technology are inevitable. That technology must be employed according to due process principles – to protect citizens. The future of law enforcement in the U.S. is likely to be very different from law enforcement today; new styles of policing, such as Internet policing (Cyber policing), will be embraced wholeheartedly. The form that change ultimately takes will depend largely on whether there is a dramatic shift towards the principles and policies of the crime control model or towards the principles and policies of its due process counterpart. Given that technology is an unregulated and seemingly democratic forum for criminal and non criminal activities that has become incredibly privatized especially for profit, cyber space has become a "lawless" frontier protected ironically by law itself.

References

Bohm, R.M., & Haley, K.N. 2002 *Introduction to Criminal Justice* (3rd ed.). McGraw-Hill

Burden, K. & Palmer, C. 2003 Cyber Crime- A new breed of criminal? *Computer Law & Security Report,* 19 (3), 222-227.

Corb-Cinotti, A. and Visano, L. 2005 "The Social Organization of Internet Policing: From Pornography to Terrorism." In C. Orban and J. Hodgson (Eds.) *Public Policing in the 21st Century: Comparative Issues and Dilemmas* Monsey, NY: Criminal Justice Press .

Conner, C. L. 1998 Creating Jurisdiction Through Internet Contacts. *The Richmond Journal of Law and Technology,* 4.

Geist, M. (1999). *In Web Disputes, U.S. Law Rules the World* Online HTTP: www.michaelgeist.ca/resc/html_bkup/feb242003.html (accessed August 2005).

Johnson, D. R. and Post, D.G. 1996 Law And Borders—The Rise of Law in Cyberspace. *Standford Law Review* 48 (1367).

Korean Ministry of Information and Communication. 2003 *Report for Korean Parliamentary Audit.*

Korea Ministry of Information and Communication. 2003 *Survey of Internet Users.*

Korea National Police Agency. 2003 *Crime Data: The Present Status of Juvenile Delinquency.*

McCormick, K. and Visano, L. 1992 *Understanding Policing* Toronto: Canadian Scholars' Press. Toronto.

Miller, W.B. 1973 Ideology and Criminal Justice Policy: Some Current Issues. *Journal of Criminal Law and Criminology,* 64, 141-62

Packer, H. 1968 *The Limits of Criminal Sanction.* Stanford: Stanford University Press

Renault, O. 1998 Jurisdiction and the Internet: Are Traditional Rules Enough? *Uniform Law Conference of Canada.* Online HTTP

http://www.law.ualberta.ca/alri/ulc/current/ejurisd.htm (accessed August 2005)

Statement of Minnesota Attorney General on Internet jurisdiction. (1994) Minnesota Statute Section 609.05, Subdivision 1

The Internet Court Jurisdiction. Online HTTP:
news.bbc.co.uk/hi/English/sci/tech/newsid_s82000/382152.stm (accessed August 2005)

Visano, L. A. 2004 "A Critique of the Cultures of Control: A Case Study of Cyber Rape". In J. Hodgson and D. Kelly (Eds.) *Sexual Violence NY Criminal Justice Press* NY

7. To Unnerve and Detect: Policing Black Activists in Toronto

Christopher J. Williams

1. Introduction

Conventional thinking about policing is largely undergirded by the following chain of equivalence: policing = law enforcement = crime control. Effectively captured by seemingly omnipresent ideas and images of police officers as bulwarks against destructive chaos, the serviceability of such thought becomes evident when one considers how the reification of the law, and the concomitant universalization of particular (elite) interests, enables the performance of important ideological sleights of hand. More specifically, the fetishization of the law (i.e. the mantra that a given country is one of "laws not men") makes a direct contribution to the valorization of law enforcement, notwithstanding marginal(ized) concerns about the propriety of specific enforcement tactics. The third term of the equation, crime control, is significant insofar as its apparent synonymity with policing elevates the latter to the status of a practice that produces unimpeachable outcomes. As one prominent police studies scholar observes, "Their 'product' of crime control is conveniently elastic, carries a virtuous ring, and cannot be easily assailed: who can deny a people's desire for peace and security, or at least for a *feeling* of security (Ericson 1982:4, emphasis in original)? All of this explains, in part, why the tripartite equation has become hegemonic.

If, on the other hand, one moves beyond this formulation, a more veridical understanding of policing comes to the fore. Policing, as carried out by police officers, is essentially a mode of micro-governance concerned with the macroscopic aim of ordering the body politic in such a way that extant social, political, and economic arrangements remain stable. This is a key reason why police almost invariably side with the more established and influential party when important conflicts arise: they tend to favour capital over labour, whites over people of colour, property owners over tenants, university administrators over students, and so on, all of which accords with the logic of order maintenance. In this context there are any number of instances when effective policing is compatible with criminal activity (rather than law enforcement), as was demonstrated in 1972 when the RCMP burned down a barn in Quebec on the grounds that they sought to prevent a meeting between members of the FLQ and the Black Panthers; the "minor evil" (arson) was committed to serve the "greater good" (maintaining order). Furthermore, the "policing is crime control" assertion cannot explain why, for example, the FBI fomented violent conflicts between certain leftist groups in the 1960s and early 1970s (O'Reilly 1989:293-324), or why

> Members of various African American and Latino groups, such as the Young Lords, the Black Panthers, Brown Berets, Black Men Against Crack,

> and the Cripps [*sic*]and Bloods (after these gangs became politicized), can testify that when they were involved in crime they had less trouble from the police than when they became politically mobilized against drugs, police brutality, and exploitative social relations within the inner-city communities (Parenti 1996:38).

As grim as it may sound, the fundamentally conservative character of policing dictates that intra-subaltern violence is considered less problematic than incipient or mature radicalism.

Though concrete instantiations of police aversion to radicalism can take the form of police violence against protestors on the streets, the repressive returns on investments in ostentatious displays of force are in some ways less than those of a more "soft," subtle, and sophisticated approach to the task of neutralizing oppositional organizations and movements. Here we are referring to police intelligence, the core features of which have been outlined by Frank Donner, a US based civil liberties attorney, writing on the basis of decades of observation:

> In its traditional configuration, intelligence consists of (1) physical surveillance of a 'subject,' usually conducted in secret and frequently termed 'information gathering' or 'data collection,' benign usages characteristic of this system of repression; (2) a body of techniques that, in addition to informer infiltration, ranged from observation and mail opening to wiretapping and photography; (3) the compilation and dissemination of files and dossiers about individuals and organizational 'subjects'; (4) the assessment of file data; and (5) the aggressive use of such data to do injury to the subject (Donner 1990:3).

This essay presents a critical case study of how this system of repression was directed toward Black activists in Toronto from the end of the 1960s to the mid-1990s, an operational posture on the part of police that had everything to do with policing–and nothing to do with law enforcement or crime control.

2. Conflictual Contexts: Police Power versus Black Power

According to Alan Wolfe, author of *The Seamy Side of Democracy* ,"repression is a mechanism designed to prevent people from exercising control over the institutions that affect their lives" (1978:200). If this is indeed the case, some would argue, repression is either non-existent or infinitesimal in liberal democracies, such as Canada and the United States, for the major institutions of these countries are considered legitimate–and therefore able to exist–only insofar as they are responsive to the demands of their citizens. This essential responsiveness is actuated by an elaborate ensemble of pluralistic participatory practices, culminating in the formation of institutional policies that reflect the interests of those directly and indirectly engaged in pressure group politics, a reasonably wide swath of the population, or so the argument goes.

Against this picture of substantive political inclusiveness stand critical perspectives on liberal democracies that expose the extent to which hallowed notions of popular participation are far from popular in elite circles (Chomsky 1992:351-401), and explicate how large segments of civil society tend to embrace a conception of democracy bounded by the narrow parameters of conventional electoral politics. Accordingly, historian Howard Zinn, in his characteristically non-euphemistic manner, offers this view of democracy in the US: "Our most cherished moment of democratic citizenship comes when we leave the house once in four years to choose between two mediocre white Anglo-Saxon males who have been trundled out by political caucuses, million dollar primaries and managed conventions for the rigged multiple choice test we call an election" (1997:637). The combination of elite antipathy toward meaningful public participation in public affairs, mass acceptance of electoral politics and modest reformism as *the* cornerstones of democracy, and, a third element, the presence of groups whose political views and aspirations transcend the bounds of reformism, fosters a mode of statecraft whereby reform and repression are dialectically linked in such a way that they

> are tried simultaneously. These are not alternative options but complementary ones. However, as reform reveals itself incapable of subduing pressure and protest, so does the emphasis shift towards repression, coercion, police power, law and order, the struggle against subversion, etc. Faced as they are with intractable problems, those who control the levers of power find it increasingly necessary further to erode those features of 'bourgeois democracy' through which popular pressure is exercised....The state must arm itself with more extensive and more efficient means of repression, seek to define more stringently the area of 'legitimate' dissent and opposition, and strike fear in those who seek to go beyond it (Miliband [1969]1973:242-43).

The coercive component of this reform-repression concatenation becomes especially salient when one considers the extent to which the repressive arm of the state has come to establish and maintain an undemocratic posture: "The police more than any institution exhibit an antagonism, both in concept and in practice, to some of the basic precepts of a democratic society. In many respects, the phrase 'democratic police force' is a contradiction in terms" (Berkeley, 1969:1-2 as quoted in McLaughlin 1991:109). Police opposition to democratic precepts manifests itself in numerous ways–hostility toward civilian review boards, claims of professionalism designed to buttress the idea that policing is specialized to the point where critiques put forth by "outsiders" are basically useless, ringing endorsements of right-wing politicians who promise to fight crime by "taking the handcuffs [read: democratic constraints] off police"–and, not surprisingly, groups who seek to democratize policing (in addition to other key institutions) are normally regarded as profoundly problematic. Bearing this in mind, Aboriginal peoples and radical organized labour qualify as groups who have been subjected to repression, given their engagements in movements for substantive institutional-level change. Another group, as history has consistently shown, are Blacks.

Conflicts between police and Blacks are best understood from a structural perspective, one that entails foci on extant distributions of power and competing material interests. In large measure the relationship between police power and Black power[1] tends to be construed in zero-sum terms, a view captured by a declaration put forth by LAPD Chief William H. Parker following the 1965 Watts uprising: "Now we're on the top and they're on the bottom" (Donner 1990:253); those on the top were police while those on the bottom were the residents of predominantly Black Watts. An obvious caveat that should be applied to this zero-sum perspective is that it neglects the ways in which a host of mediating factors (i.e. public opinion, legislation, various forms of coalition building) shape the nature of the relationship between police and Blacks; such a blind-spot results in the imagining of a one-dimensional drama where the two parties battle in a hermetically sealed realm devoid of third-party interference or influence. Nonetheless, to the extent that police and Blacks regard a gain for one side as a loss for the other, this mutual perception has a non-negligible affect on how the two "sides" interact. Furthermore, it would be wrong to contend that this zero-sum take on power constitutes a total departure from material reality (i.e. "It's all in their heads"), for evidence exists to suggest that it is somewhat accurate.

On one hand, since "there is in most police actions someone who is being policed *against*" (Reiner 1992:4, emphasis in original)–someone who is often a member of a marginalized group–it is not unreasonable to argue that the "empowerment of the police always has drastic implications for the powerless" (McLaughlin 1991:111). In the US during the 1960s and 1970s, for example, local, state, and federal police worked vigorously, with varying degrees of coordination, to undermine the efforts of Blacks to bolster their aggregate power and thereby defend themselves against racism in its individual, institutional, and structural forms. Since the 1980s the highly selective "war on drugs" has provided police with the resources, rationalizations, and racial discourses necessary to conduct ongoing quasi-low-intensity warfare against Black communities across the US (Chambliss 1994; Parenti 1999:111-138), one key factor in the development of a political milieu in which concerns regarding astronomical rates of Black imprisonment often elicit little more than shrugs. Undoubtedly, numerous other examples could be cited which lend support to the idea that if there is an iron law of policing it is this: the effects of increased police power–far from being uniform–have a disproportionate and detrimental impact on those who are relatively powerless. On the other hand, as Pamela Irving Jackson observes, throughout the 1970s Black power increased in some large industrial cities, resulting in attenuations of police power:

> As blacks grew in relative population size in these cites, achieving or approaching numerical majority, citizen demands for police accountability and fiscal cutbacks constrained the municipal police agenda. Citizens assumed greater control over police policymaking. Curbs were placed on police use of deadly force and new codes of ethics specified severe sanctions for excessive use of force by police officers. Public expectations for policing scaled back permissible violence and emphasized police

accountability (1992:98).

These sharp oppositions between police power and Black power take on special importance given the different structural positions of the two groups. For Cleaver (1974:28):

> The police are the armed guardians of the social order. The blacks are the chief domestic victims of the American social order. A conflict of interests exists, therefore, between blacks and the police.

A key advantage of apprehending police–Black community conflict in structural terms is that such an approach enables one to move beyond facile notions about "negative attitudes on both sides," "conflicting subcultures," "mutual antagonism," and so on, all of which do little in the way of explanation and much in the way of deflecting attention from a fundamental question–that of power.

3. Battleground: Toronto

Within the field of mainstream Canadian public discourse, the relationship between Canada and the US is commonly described in familial terms. From high ranking public officials to corporate power brokers to the wo/man on the street, Canada's geographical, economical, and cultural closeness to the world's sole superpower is frequently hailed as a genuine source of (inter)national pride. Consequently, notwithstanding the issue of health care, Canadians who put forth strident critiques of the US run the risk of being disparaged and dismissed as "anti-American," not especially by Americans who are largely oblivious to the vicissitudes of Canadian public opinion, but by fellow Canadians who feel compelled to attack those who are critical of their "family members" south of the border.

At the level of policing similar expressions of quasi-familial attachment manifest themselves in numerous ways. With respect to the fabled Mounties, for example, S.T. Wood, a fierce anti-radical who became RCMP commissioner in 1938, was a personal friend of J. Edgar Hoover (Brown and Brown 1978:78), and since the 1950s the RCMP has had a working relationship with the CIA (Taylor 1986:67). Such processes of US-Canadian cross-fertilization became more pronounced when the Law Enforcement Intelligence Unit, a private organization operating beyond the purview of government control, was founded in 1956; within twenty-five years over 200 police intelligence units in US and Canadian cities were members (Institute for the Study of Labor and Economic Crisis 1982:116). Not surprisingly, the authors of *An Unauthorized History of the RCMP* conclude, following their examination of police repression of various dissident groups, that the "opinions of police officials in Canada on law and order and political protest did not differ basically from their American counterparts" (Brown and Brown 1978:98). When other affinities are taken into account (i.e. information sharing at bi-national police conferences, mutual attendance at police funerals, etc.) it becomes clear that despite operating in different countries, US and Canadian police are strikingly similar in terms of ideology, culture, and politics.

The politically conservative ties that bind Canadian and US police have special implications for Blacks. From Edmund Burke to the present, a key aspect of conservative thought has been the supposition that social hierarchies–as logical outcomes of human differences in wisdom, intelligence, and moral rectitude–are sacrosanct. It follows that those who seek to alter the prevailing order in significant ways must be regarded as, at best, very misguided. When this brand of ideology collided with the social upheavals of the 1960s, one result was widespread police efforts (primarily undergirded by anti-communism, conspiratorial interpretations of radical activism, and fears of Black empowerment) to restore stability by imposing their version of law and order on those challenging the status quo. In Canada, therefore, at the end of the 1960s, conflict between police and Blacks became salient.

> An awareness within the Toronto Black community of police bias against Blacks was in part born with the widespread publicization of the Sir George Williams affair in Montreal. The incipient Black power movement in Canada, catalysed by the clash between students and police in 1969, provoked police surveillance of Black organizations by both municipal and federal forces. That same year, a film entitled, 'Revolution Underway', linking Black Power movements in the United States to an international communist conspiracy aimed at overthrowing the government, was used in Toronto for training in police work. After meeting with protests from citizen groups, which branded it as racist propaganda, the film was publicly destroyed by then Police Chief, Judge C.O. Bick (Stasiulis 1989:66).

The extent to which Bick's ostentatious gesture was more symbolic than substantive was revealed when his intelligence unit staff increased from forty-four to sixty-four in direct response to a 1971 Black People's conference featuring well-known Black power advocates from abroad (Stasiulis 1989:81-82, 11n). So whereas some segments of the population, such as "ethnic Europeans," were able to further their interests by engaging in various types of empowering politico-economic activity, similar aspirations on the part of Blacks were met with pre-emptive measures by police who have rarely expressed concern about Black powerlessness and the poor life chances that go along with it. Black power, however, *is* cause for concern, hence the institutionalization of practices informed by ominous visions of Toronto being overrun by Blacks.

"Police officers will be reluctant to act and to arrest black people and they'll just take over the city and you'll be back to Detroit"–this warning by former Toronto Police Association President Art Lymer was issued in response to the levying of manslaughter charges against Constable David Deviney for his role in the killing of Lester Donaldson, a Black man (Jackson 1994:220).[2] The year was 1989, two decades after the "Revolution Underway" incident, and, as key observers (Jackson 1994:217; Forcese 1992:74) note, tension between police and Blacks reached new levels of intensity following a series of controversial police shootings. While it would be hyperbolic to suggest that a full blown legitimation crisis was underway, the tenor of the times was not exactly in tune with the notion that police live and die "to serve and protect." Police critics argued that, among other things, police racism (individual and institutional), a deeply entrenched tradition of non-accountability, and government indifference, resulted in situations where Blacks–often unarmed and/ or fleeing–were unnecessarily killed by police. Some US based research lends support to the proposition that certain contextual factors, especially those of a political sort, may contribute to the probability of gratuitous uses of force. In their discussion of police shootings in Philadelphia (1972-1979, inclusive) when former police commissioner Frank Rizzo served as mayor,[3] Jerome Skolnick and James Fyfe report that the Philadelphia Police Department (PPD) was remarkably unrestrained in its use of firepower:

> During Rizzo's eight years as Philadelphia's mayor, fatal shootings by PPD officers increased by about 20 percent annually. In a study conducted for the U.S. Justice Department, one of us reported that, while individual Philadelphia cops were no more likely than New York cops to make arrests or to come face to face with armed people, they were *thirty-seven times* as likely as New York cops to shoot unarmed people who had threatened nobody and who were fleeing from suspected non-violent crimes (1993:140, emphasis in original).

In this case a link was established between signals from the suites and police activity in the streets, a finding at odds with the common exculpatory claim that police shootings are simply direct and inevitable responses to life-threatening situations. Still, studies of this sort had yet to be conducted in Canada, so criticisms of Toronto police were generally dismissed on the grounds that they were simplistic, impressionistic, anecdotal, and hopelessly biased.

Nonetheless, critics remained steadfast in their opposition to questionable police practices. At the forefront of this activism stood the Black Action Defence Committee (BADC), a grassroots organization formed in 1988 following the aforementioned killing of Lester Donaldson. The formation of BADC was in some ways a good indication of how the gulf between police and Blacks had failed to narrow over the course of several years. In 1979, following the high profile police killing of Albert Johnson, a Black man, members of the Black community formed alliances with numerous groups (gays, Sikhs, Arab Canadians, leftists, and others) to engage in activities–such as an eight-hour, eight-mile, 3000 person protest march–intended to bring public attention to abusive modes of policing (Stasiulis 1989:68-69). And throughout the 1980s, various Toronto based groups continued the tradition of working to make police reform a reality. In one sense, then, BADC was an instance of historical continuity, the latest incarnation of the will to ensure that public policy is informed by the input of those on the margins. In another sense, however, BADC represented a departure from previous police critics insofar as their collective voice featured a tone more strident than most.

In the course of issuing a series of critical statements regarding the state of policing in Toronto, BADC members developed a reputation for speaking in very forthright terms, a communicative style that runs the risk of being met with derision in Canada, a society that has been popularly described as deferential. As Metis scholar-activist Howard Adams, author of *Prison of Grass: Canada from a Native Point of View,* explains, "my language is too political, confrontational and rhetorical. I do not apologize. My language is in harmony with my race, class and colonization. Behind my back, I hear the whites whisper in mockery, 'He's nothing but a Red Power radical.' My credibility is destroyed and I am reduced to a politicized Halfbreed" (1999:1). Similarly, as members of a historically oppressed group, BADC activists spoke in a manner concordant with their experiential base–the practice of mincing words in the name of "tact" and "diplomacy" is a generally a luxury that only the privileged can afford. So, for example, one BADC representative, Dari Meade, suggested that unless the issue of police brutality was properly addressed, Blacks would begin "meeting force with force," while prominent spokesperson Dudley Laws characterized Toronto police as "the most brutal, murderous force in North America" (Jackson 1994:220). Though some observers responded by studying the concrete conditions that inspired these statements, others chose to focus on the statements themselves (as though they sprung forth from a vacuum) and, predictably, derided BADC as a band of lunatics with no legitimate grievances or credibility whatsoever.

Equally predictable was the determination on the part of Toronto police that BADC qualified as a serious enemy. Accordingly, police drew upon various resources (media access, political backing, "moral authority," etc.) in their mission to undermine the counter-narratives and, more generally, credibility of BADC. As Howard Becker explains, political conflicts between super ordinate and subordinate groups are such that the credibility of the latter is especially crucial:

> The [subordinate] group engages in political activity designed to change existing hierarchical relationships and the credibility of its spokesmen directly affects its political fortunes. Credibility is not the only influence, but the group can ill-afford having the definition of reality proposed by its spokesmen discredited, for the immediate consequence will be some loss of political power (1967: 243-44).

Hence one strategy employed by police in their campaign against BADC was the invocation of a "good Blacks/ bad Blacks" dichotomy designed to promote the idea that BADC did not represent the respectable, law-abiding majority of the Black community who were (supposedly) highly supportive of police. While it was obvious that BADC could not claim the entire Black community as its constituency, a considerable degree of police presumptiveness was evinced by the suggestion that only the most uncivil members of the community were represented by BADC. One might add, parenthetically, that although some consider the marking of a distinction between "good" and "bad" Blacks–as opposed to placing all Blacks in the "bad" category–as rough proof of (differentiating) non-racist thought, the practice of dichotomizing the Black community in accordance with dominant normalizing judgements has been a feature of anti-Black racist ideology for over a century. In fact, even the most reactionary elements of North American society have been known to embrace some concept of "good n-----s" (harmless, humble, docile) and "bad n-----s" (dangerous, uppity, obstinate).

Somewhat similarly, the first two months of 1989 featured the issuance of police statements that dovetailed with reactionary academic work dedicating to establishing the allegedly innate criminality of Blacks. In January, J. Philippe Rushton, a University of Western Ontario psychology professor, presented a paper at the American Association for the Advancement of Science conference in San Francisco which, among other things, claimed that due to their particular genetic make-up, Blacks were more criminally inclined than whites or Asians (Roberts and Gabor 1990:292). In February, as debates raged over the validity of Rushton's research, Julian Fantino, a police staff inspector, released statistics purporting to prove that Blacks were responsible for a disproportionate amount of street crime in Toronto's Jane-Finch corridor (Roberts and Gabor 1990:294), a low-income area with a fairly sizable Black population.

According to some observers, Fantino's strategy was designed to undercut allegations of police racism by presenting his staff as rational, objective, and unbiased law enforcers whose actions (arrests, beatings, shootings) were logical and predictable by-products of their active engagement in ongoing conflicts with dangerous Black criminals. Insofar as this reading of the situation is accurate (at the very least it offers the most plausible answer to the question of why the statistics were released at that particular time) police practices in the Jane-Finch corridor–informed by the dubious goal of "proving" Black dominance in the field of street crime–lead to the emergence of a rather paradoxical picture: police targeted Blacks in order to refute the charge that they targeted Blacks. Considering the content and timing of the race-based statistical report, it undoubtedly added fuel to the fires of anti-Black racism, but failed to render BADC criticism of police null and void.

In addition to the "good Blacks/ bad Blacks" and "rampant Black criminality" strategies, police employed a more direct method of attacking BADC's standing in the court of public opinion, one grounded in the realization that within the context of political conflict it is often more effective to present a prominent individual as the living embodiment of all that is odious about the opposition rather than focus on more diffuse targets such as an organization, a movement, or an ideology. So concentrating on, say, Farrakhan, Leonard Peltier, or Castro is strategically better than focusing on the Nation of Islam, the American Indian Movement, or statist socialism, respectively. For some observers, therefore, it was less than surprising when in 1994, six years after the establishment of BADC, spokesman Dudley Laws–described by a popular local magazine as "Toronto's most infamous radical black activist" (Jackson 1994:220)–was convicted of conspiring to smuggle illegal immigrants into the US and Canada.

Given that the foundation of the case against Dudley Laws consisted of evidence provided by an undercover police officer who convinced Laws to help smuggle a "cousin" from the US into Canada, some commentators argued that the sixty year-old activist was a victim of entrapment (Foster 1994; McTair 1994). Clarence Munford, a history professor at Guelph University, went further by situating Laws' conviction in the context of officially orchestrated attacks against Black dissidents throughout North America:

> Frame-ups are an essential feature of the criminal justice system. They have been occurring with increasing regularity since the Civil Rights-strained 1960s....The main focus...has been on railroading an entire generation of Black political dissidents from H. Rap Brown to Dhoruba Bin Wadah to Assata Shakur. In Canada too, smashing Black critics of white racism sits at the top of the agenda. Ontario's Dudley Laws, leader of the Black Action Defense Committee, has felt the crackdown. He was entrapped, jailed, tried, and in February 1994 convicted (1996:355).

This view is in close accord with the observation that "over the last several decades just about every African American protest leader who achieved any local or national prominence eventually ended up either under indictment, in jail, on appeal, in hiding, in exile, or murdered by the forces of 'law and order'" (Parenti 1996:35). In sharp contrast, however, others put forth two main counterclaims: (1) the fact that Laws was convicted proved that he was not entrapped, and (2) the entire incident demonstrated that Toronto police had accurately gauged the nature of BADC. Despite the importance of weighing the validity of these competing claims, the legalistic task of ascertaining whether Laws was a victim of entrapment is beyond the scope of this essay. Instead, we turn our attention to a confidential intelligence report that surfaced during Laws' trial, a document which revealed that since the founding of BADC, Toronto police regarded the organization, its political activities, and its allies as worthy of intense scrutiny.

4. Police Backstage: The Intelligence Report

The report, dated April 25, 1989 and prepared by two police officers, was concerned with 13 organizations (BADC, described as the "most active," was the primary target) and 18 individuals. The "narrative" portion of the report includes the following observations:

> The majority of persons mentioned in this report are self-appointed spoke persons [*sic*] or so called leaders within the Black Community.
>
> Over the years their basic objectives have been to struggle for status, fighting for equal education and aspiring to the future devoid of judgements based on skin color.
>
> These groups became quite vocal at various demonstrations but posed no threat due to their lack of organization and financial resources, and as a result mellowed out. Within the past year, several police related shootings involving black persons have rejuvenated these groups and seen the formation of new ones. Continous [*sic*] Media coverage has increased attendance at their demonstrations and as a result, organization has improved as well as their financial resources.
>
> The main objectives of these new groups are to stamp out racism within the Police Force, Mandatory Affirmative Action and the

> establishment of an Independent civilian police review board to restore confidence in the public.

While this passage could be interrogated and deconstructed in a various ways, here, in the interests of brevity and focus, we will concentrate on the topic of power by noting that police cognizance of the positive relationship between resources and power, combined with their general adherence to the notion that an inverse relationship exists between police power and Black power, results in virtually obsessive concerns with determining the relative strength of Blacks who are perceived as adversaries. Accordingly, the extent to which BADC and other targeted organizations were deemed to pose a collective threat was inferred with reference to their ability to secure additional resources, all of which, not incidentally, are enjoyed in abundance by police themselves: money, media access, and public support. Indeed, the perceived status shift of these organizations (from "mellowed out" to "rejuvenated") would likely have intensified police hostility toward them: "repression has often increased markedly following some clear display of increasing influence or some major success by dissenting groups" (Goldstein 1978:567). Again, Black powerlessness is unproblematic; obversely, Black power is anathema.

Community control of local institutions is a central theme in Black power praxis.[4] When applied to policing this may include calls for residency requirements, meaningful community input regarding hiring and firing, and other measures designed to increase the likelihood of police being accountable to the communities within which they work. As an engine of social change, Black power, despite its generally radical orientation, is not necessarily incompatible with incrementalism. Consequently, its adherents have been known to support patently liberal measures, such as affirmative action or civilian review boards, designed to bolster police accountability, even while acknowledging that these policies do not go far enough. For many police, however, these policies go too far: affirmative action dilutes the quality of policing by excluding fully qualified white males in favour of members of "special interest groups," and civilian review boards are one weapon in a broader strategy to undermine police authority, legitimacy, and efficacy. Although dated, the following statement from a publication by the National Fraternal Order of Police speaks to these concerns:

> No matter what names are used by the sponsors of the so-called Police Review Boards' they exude the obnoxious odor of communism. This scheme is a page right out of the Communist handbook which says in part, '...the police are the enemies of communism, if we are to succeed we must do anything to weaken their work, to incapacitate them or make them a subject of ridicule' (Skolnick and Fyfe 1993:222).

Paranoid visions aside, the relevant point is that police tend to perceive accountability-enhancing measures as harmful to their interests and act in accordance with such a perception. In this context, therefore, the intelligence report reflects typical police concerns about Blacks who deploy resources to pursue agendas that are, among other things, anti-racist, pro-affirmative action, and pro-civilian review board. As Richard Ericson states, "power mediates between actors' intentions and the realization of outcomes. In use, power involves the mobilization of resources to effect outcomes which serve particular interests" (1982:12), and, as we have seen, Blacks in some US cities attained enough power to produce outcomes stemming from their desire to democratize policing. Insofar as "so called leaders within the Black Community" of Toronto aimed for similar results, the fact that police viewed them as threatening is a less than astounding outcome stemming from standard police logic.

Aside from power, though, what about the question of criminal activity? Is it not the case that the intelligence report contains *some* references to wrongdoing on the part of those targeted? The answer is that aside from standard intelligence information such as organizational affiliations, birth dates, addresses, telephone numbers, vehicles, occupations, and aliases, the subjects–some of whom are described as "Very Radical" and "Very Outspoken"–are cited for acting and being acted upon in a number of ways: subject #2 for "Being groomed by Father to be a Spokesperson," subject #4 for "Active involvement in most demonstration [*sic*]," subject #5 for "Newspaper Article" and for being "photographed at Rally," subject #6 for being a "Rally Organizer," subject #12 for being "Very Radical during a phone in talk show February 22, 1989 with subject #7," subject #13 for being an "Advocate of Mandatory Affirmative Action Hiring Practices in Police Forces," subject #15 for "Newspaper Articles Re: Strong Opinions," subject #18 for "Newspaper article–sent a letter to the United Nations asking them to investigate shooting of Wade Lawson,"[5] and so on. At this point an observation made by Frank Donner is especially germane:

> Sheer accumulation of entries–signature on a peace petition, presence at a demonstration protesting welfare cuts, receipt of left-wing literature, a speech at a panel on police brutality, each innocuous in itself–leads the intelligence mind to the conclusion that the subject is subversive. Quantity is transformed into quality; the end result is greater than the sum of its parts (1990:70).

So while the report contains numerous references to activities that constitute wrongdoing from the perspective of police subculture, none of the subjects are cited for probable or actual criminal activity. This is all the more interesting considering (1) the report presumably reflects core police concerns, and (2) one of the four individuals on the report's restricted dissemination list is staff inspector Julian Fantino, an official with a reputation for having a keen interest in crimes committed by Blacks. But perhaps the report was not prepared with Fantino in mind. And perhaps the possibility that the subjects were involved in criminal activity was so obvious to all concerned that to even make mention of it would have been superfluous–possible but hardly plausible. Speculation aside, police made no mention of crime until public exposure of the intelligence report compelled them to explain their actions.

5. Police Front Stage: Justifying The Intelligence Report

When the intelligence report entered the public arena in February 1994, parties ranging from the intelligence subjects to journalists to civil liberties attorneys to local public officials were astonished that dissidents in *Canada* could be subjected to modes of repression more commonly associated with police states. For example, Alan Borovoy (1994), general council of the Canadian Civil Liberties Association, asked "why in the world should such reports be done on lawful dissent and dissenters?" Kamala-Jean Gopie, a high school teacher cited in the report, declared "to suggest that the organizations listed in that report are radical is incredible. Frightening really. They obviously don't understand the nature of those organizations" (English 1994). Metro councillor Roger Hollander stated, "from my point of view, it's lawless activity" (Wright 1994). In sum, the report, a document that illuminated a minute section of the shadowy intelligence world, generated a good amount of consternation.

Virtually any reader who is familiar with crime-centred images of North American policing will not be surprised by how Toronto police justified the intelligence operation. Here is a representative sample of statements put forth in the wake of the controversy:

> *Ron Sandelli, head of intelligence services:* "How do you know whether a group is involved in criminal activity unless you investigate them?" (Brent 1994).
>
> *Police Chief William McCormack:* "In all groups there are people capable of causing very serious things to occur. And it is our duty to prevent crime" (Lakey 1994).
>
> *Constable Denny Dias (co-author of the report):* "These groups were unknown to police and we had a look to see the formation of the groups and whether or not they were supported by criminal activity. Were they a threat to the community? Were these terrorist groups?" (English 1994).
>
> *Dias:* "As a matter of procedure, we would look at each subject to see if they have any criminal activity" (English 1994).

Invocation of potential criminal/ terrorist activity, interpellation of "the people" ("the community"), utilization of bureaucratic language which strips intelligence of its political character ("a matter of procedure")–all of this is standard justificatory police discourse. More implicit, but no less significant, is the presentation of police as purely reactive beings who must respond in a predetermined manner to those segments of the population who might cause "very serious things to occur." Just as police (allegedly) have no choice but to use lethal force when confronted by (allegedly) dangerous suspects, the advent of organizations such as BADC (allegedly) *forces* them to launch intelligence operations. Hence, in the face of what seems to be an inexorable law of nature, police are faultless. What we have here, then, is an expedient image of law enforcement agents as men and women who lack agency.

Additionally, police attempted to counter charges of discrimination by invoking the discourse of universality. As quoted above, Chief McCormack made reference to the notion that "*all* groups" feature sub-populations that may engage in criminal activity. Furthermore, approximately one week later, he claimed that police routinely directed intelligence at *any* groups who held demonstrations; ergo it was erroneous to suggest that the Black community was targeted in a discriminatory manner (Wright 1994). In his effort to drape intelligence in the garb of fairness and and universality, however, McCormack inadvertently revealed the ways in which class biases are embedded in the practice of intelligence.

In theory any group is capable of organizing and carrying out a demonstration, but in practice this form of protest is the tactic of those who do not fall within the purview of the privileged classes. Quite simply "political opposition to the Establishment encounters monetary as well as legal impediments, and so demonstrations (meetings and processions) are particularly important forms of challenge, for they are relatively cheap to organize" (Bowes 1966:76). In contrast, of course, wealthy and powerful segments of society enjoy the luxury of staging their own special "protests" in the context of high-level, closed-door meetings with influential public officials–and without police interference. It is in this sense that McCormack's universalistic claims amounted to little more than cant.

Having taken account of how police justified the intelligence operation, a rather important question ought to be addressed, however cursorily: why are police responses to criticisms of such uses of intelligence characterized by such a high degree of uniformity? One can begin by noting that at a general level "opinions and attitudes are not acquired, structured or used arbitrarily. As social and cultural beliefs they must be functional, that is, they must in principle serve the goals or interests of the group or institution" (Dijk 1993:42). Sustaining legitimacy is, for example, a fundamental police goal that is partially met by the practices of giving obligatory nods to democratic ideals and presenting policing as an ensemble of benevolent, apolitical activities, both of which are captured in the familiar (and highly functional) refrain that intelligence exists for the sole purpose of controlling crime. Departing from this refrain would open up the possibility of police presenting a more accurate picture of the uses and abuses of intelligence, but insofar as this option departs from the path of expediency, and the rules of police discourse, the police officer who resorts to it would be a very anomalous figure indeed.

Dennis Forcese, who combines the insights of social psychology with a consideration of secondary socialization in the form of specialized training regimes, makes a point that further explains uniformity within police culture:

> Subgroups within a society develop a repertoire of shared meaning or definitions of their reality, a bag of familiar stimuli, and learn to respond in certain ways to these environmental features. Occupational training is intended to sensitize the novice to the group's definitions and responses. It is not remarkable, therefore, to find that police respond in patterned and predictable ways to environmental cues or stimuli (1992:64).

A benefit of this perspective is that it enables one to transcend the caricatural image of police as bands of pathological liars who will, in the name of self-interest, do everything in their power to deceive the public. But even if we were to concede that police lie more frequently than others, this would not necessarily entail a resort to individual level explanations: the police officer and the janitor may both have the same propensity to lie, but the former, given the very nature of her position, may feel compelled to lie more often for reasons that have little to do with idiosyncratic personality quirks. In sum, police invoke crime control in the face of critical comments about intelligence because this response is functional in terms of prevailing institutional imperatives.

Police officers are not automatons, however, which explain why Constable Dias, in the course of outlining reasons for the intelligence operation, made the following comment: "When we see new groups, we regard them as radical groups. They were radical in their thinking at that time, and my word reflected that" (English 1994). Although this statement is somewhat confusing (there is no logical reason to regard all new groups as radical unless some mysterious X factor disables police in such a way that they see nothing but radical groups), and contains a naive claim of objectivity (the notion that the targeted groups were radical, far from constituting an unproblematic fact, was a product of Dias' interpretation–his word reflected *this*), it comes closest to explaining why the intelligence report was produced. Given that individuals such as the late Wilson Head (a sociology professor at York University, born in 1914, who is regarded as the "grandfather of the Canadian race relations movement") were targeted, it seems clear that the intelligence operation, as Dias suggests, was motivated by the desire to repress those guilty of "radical thinking" rather than genuine concerns about preventing criminal activity. Indeed, the intelligence report itself reveals as much.

6. Discussion and Conclusion

Having come to this point, it would be a mistake to construe police repression as a series of unfortunate excesses that are grave departures from salubrious liberal democratic practices. Far from being aberrational, intelligence of the sort directed at BADC is one of the means by which the social order is stabilized in accordance with elitist models of what one might call truncated democracy. What is the main thrust of such models? Ralph Miliband, a scholar critical of the establishment, gives some indication when he states, "it is certainly in the interests of dominant classes in advanced capitalist societies that very large masses of the population *should* be politically apathetic and inert, at least in regard to issues which are, from the point of view of these classes, politically dangerous" ([1969]1973:212, emphasis in original). Lest one dismiss this contention as the product of paranoiac conspiracy-based leftist thought, Samuel Huntington of Harvard University, a scholar firmly ensconced within the establishment, argues, in his contribution to the Trilateral Commission report *Crisis of Democracy*, that

> the effective operation of a democratic political system usually requires some measure of apathy and non-involvement on the part of some

> individuals and groups. In the past, every democratic society has had a marginal population, of greater of lesser size, which has not actively participated in politics. In itself, this marginality on the part of some groups is inherently undemocratic, but it has also been one of the factors which has enabled democracy to function effectively (Crozier et al. 1975:114).

The "crisis of democracy" stemmed from the efforts, during the 1960s, of groups such as African-Americans, Native Americans, and others, to move from marginality to empowerment, a project that would entail a commitment on the part of dominant groups to substantially modify their exercises of power.

One key aspect of the repressive counter-project was the ensemble of intensive, overlapping, well-coordinated intelligence operations spearheaded by the FBI in order to prevent democracy from becoming "excessive," that is, extended so that major institutions, such as police, would be formally *and* substantively responsive to the concerns of those most affected by them. Indeed, the "Revolution Underway" police training film evinced the high degree of concordance between police ideology and elite perspectives that frame certain demands articulated from the margins of society as dangerously subversive. It is in this sense that intelligence should not be apprehended as a shocking and unusual blemish on an otherwise pristine democratic montage.

Although this essay is primarily explicative by design, such an approach does not, of course, preclude the inclusion of prescriptive comments. Police have been described as a shield of the status quo, but this description, however critical it may sound, implicitly re-inscribes the conventional notion that the police role is fundamentally *defensive*. Against this, a more accurate understanding rests upon a recognition of how police also act as a sword, with an extensive history of conducting preemptive attacks on individuals, organizations, and movements regarded as "radical in their thinking." Under these conditions the task of effecting progressive change is far more daunting than it would otherwise be. The key to altering this state of affairs will almost certainly not hinge on the presentation of moralistic appeals for police to abandon their determination to repress groups such as BADC. Rather, the very ability of police to engage in such repression would have to be sharply diminished, if not eliminated.

Notes

[1] In their pioneering explication of Black power, Kwame Ture and Charles V. Hamilton state, "The goal of black self-determination and black self-identity–Black Power–is full participation in the decision-making processes affecting the lives of black people, and recognition of the virtues in themselves as black people" (1992 [1967]:47).

[2] Deviney was later acquitted. Years later, during a January 1997 phone conversation with another officer, Deviney referred to Blacks as "apes" and "niggers." Deviney was, however, unaware that Andy Eastmond, the officer with whom he was

speaking, is Black. In response, Eastmond launched a complaint, resulting in Deviney being convicted of discreditable conduct by a police tribunal. The sentence was a loss of 15 days' pay (Duncanson 1998).

[3] For a vivid account of Rizzo's tenures as police commissioner and mayor see Donner (1990:197-244).

[4] Notwithstanding claims regarding the supposedly untenable nature of the idea of community control, Sandra Harding puts for the following argument: "Just how democratic social control will best be achieved will and should vary in different circumstances....Nevertheless, we can call on John Dewey's very general principle to guide the design of institutions, practices, and cultures of democracy: those who bear the consequences of decisions should have a proportionate share in the making of them" (1996:160, 5n).

[5] Lawson, a Black teenager, was shot in the back of the head and killed by police in 1988 while joyriding in a stolen car. His mother and aunt were subjects of the intelligence report.

References

Adams, H. 1999 *Tortured People: The Politics of Colonization*. Penticton: Theytus Books.

Becker, H. 1967 "Whose Side Are We On?" *Social Problems* 14: 239-247.

Berkeley, G.E. 1969 *The Democratic Policeman*. Boston: Beacon Press.

Borovoy, A. 1994 "How to make the police accountable." *The Toronto Star*, March 2.

Bowes, S. 1966 *The Police and Civil Liberties*. London: Lawrence & Wishart.

Brent, B. 1994 "Borovoy urges new monitors for police investigation of black activists." *The Toronto Star*, April 29.

Brown, L. and Brown, C. 1978 *An Unauthorized History of the RCMP*. Toronto: James Lorimer & Company.

Chambliss, W.J. 1994 "Policing the Ghetto Underclass: The Politics of Law and Law Enforcement." *Social Problems* 41: 177-194.

Chomsky, N. 1992 *Deterring Democracy*. New York: Hill and Wang.

Cleaver, E. 1974 "Domestic Law and International Order." In A. Platt and L. Cooper (Eds.) *Policing America*,. Englewood Cliffs: Prentice Hall.

Crozier, M., Huntington, S.P. and Watanuki, J. 1975 *The Crisis of Democracy: Report on the Governability of Democracies to the Trilateral Commission*. New York: New York University Press.

Dijk, T.A. van. 1993 *Elite Discourse and Racism*. Newbury Park: Sage.

Donner, F. 1990 *Protectors of Privilege: Red Squads and Police Repression in Urban America*. Berkeley: University of California Press.

Duncanson, J. 1998 "Deviney loses 15 days' pay." *The Toronto Star*, February 5.

English, K. 1994 "Metro police probed black 'activists.'" *The Toronto Star*, February 11.

Ericson, R.V. 1982 *Reproducing Order: A Study of Police Patrol Work*. Toronto:

University of Toronto Press.

Forcese, D. 1992. *Policing Canadian Society*. Scarborough: Prentice-Hall Canada.

Foster, C. 1994 "One group's criminal is another's hero." *The Toronto Star*, March 21.

Goldstein, R.J. 1978 *Political Repression in Modern America: From 1870 to the Present*. Cambridge: Schenkman Publishing Company.

Harding, S.1996 "Standpoint Epistemology (a Feminist Version): How Social Disadvantage Creates Epistemic Advantage." In S.P. Turner (Ed.) *Social Theory and Sociology: The Classics and Beyond*. Cambridge: Blackwell.

Institute for the Study of Labor and Economic Crisis. 1982 *The Iron Fist and the Velvet Glove: An Analysis of the U.S. Police*. San Francisco: Crime and Social Justice Associates.

Jackson, P.I. 1992 "Minority Group Threat, Social Context, and Policing." In A.E. Liska (Ed.) *Social Threat and Social Control*,. Albany: SUNY Press.

Jackson, P. 1994 "Constructions of Criminality: Police-Community Relations in Toronto." *Antipode* 26: 216-235.

Lakey, J. 1994 "Eng queries secret study on Blacks." *The Toronto Star*, February 12.

McLaughlin, E. 1991 "Police Accountability and Black People: Into the 1990s." In E. Cashmore and E. McLaughlin *Out of Order?: Policing Black People*. London: Routledge.

McTair, R. 1994 "Police target: An individual or a community?" *The Toronto Star*, April 18.

Metropolitan Toronto Police Force. 1989 Confidential Intelligence Report (1989-04-25).

Miliband, R. [1969] 1973 *The State in Capitalist Society*. London: Quartet.

Munford, C.J. 1996 *Race and Reparations: A Black Perspective for the 21st Century*. Trenton: Africa World Press.

O'Reilly, K. 1989 *"Racial Matters": The FBI's Secret File on Black America, 1960-1972*. New York: The Free Press.

Parenti, C. 1999 *Lockdown America: Police and Prisons in the Age of Crisis*. New York:Verso.

Parenti, M. 1996 *Dirty Truths: Reflections on Politics, Media, Ideology, Conspiracy,Ethnic Life and Class Power*. San Francisco: City Lights.

Reiner, R. 1992 *The Politics of the Police* (2nd edition). Toronto: University of Toronto Press.

Roberts J.V. and Gabor, T. 1990 "Lombrosian Wine in a New Bottle: Research on Crime and Race." *Canadian Journal of Criminology* 32: 291-313.

Skolnick, J.H. and Fyfe, J.J. 1993 *Above the Law: Police and the Excessive Use of Force*. New York: The Free Press.

Stasiulis, D.K. 1989. "Minority Resistance in the Local State: Toronto in the 1970s and 1980s."*Ethnic and Racial Studies* 12: 63-83.

Taylor, I. 1986 "Martyrdom and Surveillance: Ideological and Social Practices of Police in Canada in the 1980s." *Crime and Social Justice* 26: 60-78.

Ture, K. and Hamilton, C.V. 1992[1967] *Black Power: The Politics of Liberation.* New York: Vintage.

Wolfe, A. 1978 *The Seamy Side of Democracy: Repression in America* (2nd edition). New York: Longman.

Wright, L. 1994 "Police report on blacks under attack." *The Toronto Star*, February 18.

Zinn, H. 1997 *The Zinn Reader: Writings on Disobedience and Democracy.* New York: Seven Stories Press.

8. Police Response to Rural Sexual Violence: A Qualitative Analysis

James F. Hodgson

1. Introduction

Increasing requests for diverse and specialized police services in the 21st Century continue to challenge urban and rural police agencies to develop and design policies and practices that meet consumer needs and demands. Social, economic, technological, and political demands and expectations have encumbered many police agencies to re-evaluate their service delivery systems (Cavanagh 2004; Bayley and Shearing 2001). The police accountability and professionalism agenda has encumbered many police agencies to attempt significant reformations in order to meet consumer service expectations (Conser and Russell. 2000; Dantzker 2000). Many of these reformations have argued for the development of policies and practices in an attempt to effectively respond to the needs of "special populations" (Palmiotto 2003; Birzer 1999; Cavanagh 2004).

Some urban and rural police agencies have indeed met the challenge of r reform and are attempting to respond to the needs of special populations (Carter and Radelet 1999; Shusta et. al. 1995). Other police agencies steadfastly embrace traditional response methodologies, which often result in less than satisfactory service delivery to community members in need of police services. Most police agencies have not adopted service-oriented ideology despite much rhetoric regarding community-based policing principles (Oliver 2001; Palmiotto 2000). Much of the community-based policing emphasis purports to foster partnerships with the community to provide a service and problem-solving oriented policing environment (Goldstein 1990; Oliver 2001). A complete service oriented ideology would mandate significant assessment and evaluation of consumer satisfaction. Although some police institutions have developed instruments to evaluate service, most of these efforts only provide a cursory amount of information and are devoid of any type of empirical methodological context (Alpert and Moore 1993; Bayley 1994).

Performance measurement is at the heart of the evaluation of the police response to calls for service (Maguire 2002; Deakin 1988; Decker 1981). Traditional measures of police agency performance include crime rates, arrest rates, clearance rates, and response time. Traditional measures do not adequately measure police-community relations, public confidence, corruption, brutality, responses to calls for social service or order maintenance or any other police work that may not be related to crime (Maguire 2003; Eck and Rosenbaum 1994). Specifically, the evaluations of the police response to special populations, such as survivors of sexual violence, are inadequate. Therefore, very little data exists that evaluates or assesses the police response to community requests for services (Hatry 1999; Mastrofski 1999; Maguire 2003; Walker 1998). Subsequently, we are often left with individual complaints or in some cases, community outrage as an indicator as to whether or not the police are meeting the needs of the community.

This void in assessment and evaluation data reflecting urban or rural police responses to survivors of sexual violence is extremely problematic when consideration is given to the frequency of requests for police to respond to this violent exchange. We understand that sexual violence is a significant social and cultural problem in our communities. In 1999 in the United States, 89,107 rapes were reported to the police resulting in a rate of 32.7 rapes per 100,000 persons (FBI 2000). Statistics from the National Crime Victimization Survey (NCVS) revel that 141,000 rapes and 60,000 attempted rapes occurred in 1999 for a total of 201,000 rape cases (BJS 2000). Data from the National Violence Against Women Survey (NVAW) supports that 1 in every 6 women within the United States has experienced either a rape or attempted rape at some point in their lifetime (Tjaden and Thoennes 1998). Sexual violence constitutes an experience that affects the lives of many individuals, at some point during a lifetime, although very few of these violent acts are reported to the police. Despite the prevalence of sexual violence in our communities and the frequency in which the police are called upon to provide services to the survivors of sexual violence, very little data has been collected to evaluate police responses. It is the purpose of this exploratory research to provide a qualitative analysis of rural police responses to survivors of sexual violence in order to reveal systemic and cultural barriers that may prohibit the delivery of effective police services.

Over the last 30 years, reforms in legislation that addresses sexual violence have been established in all 50 States in order that sexual violence offenses would receive more attention from the judicial system and the community (Lord and Rassel 2002). The objectives of these legislative changes were to recognize the crime of rape as a crime of violence, more effective administration of the criminal justice system for survivors of sexual violence, and increased capability of the law to act as a deterrent (Bourque 1989; LaFree 1989; Searles and Berger 1987). Lord and Rassel (2002) point out that these changes include:

> (1) reform of rape laws to include all types of sexual penetration, the elimination of requirements for physical resistance, and protection of the victim's sexual history; (2) development of medical protocols that meet legal requirements for evidence collection; (3) emergence of rape crisis centers to provide emotional support to the victims and educational programs for the public; and (4) the creation of special prosecution units (p. 155).

There is little evidence that these changes in rape law have affected the disposition of rape cases (Bourgue 1989; Horney and Spohn 1991). The rape law reform appears to have had little effect on reports of sexual violence to the police or the processing of sexual violence cases (Lord and Rassel 2002).

Police officers are not only the "gate keepers" to the criminal justice system, but also the first contact that most survivors of sexual violence have with the criminal justice system (Lyman 2002; Cavanagh 2004; Moriarty 2002). Law enforcement officers are obviously the most important criminal justice officials involved in sexual assault cases (Frazer and Haney 1996; LaFree 1989). Police officers usually determine the "legitimacy" of the complaint, determine the arrest of any potential offender, and often determine the severity of the charge. Subsequently assessing the police response to survivors of sexual violence becomes tantamount to fully understanding the dimensions of this pervasive social phenomenon in our communities.

2. Methodology

The methodology utilized in this assessment and evaluation of rural police responses to sexual violence includes an exploratory qualitative approach to understanding the dynamics and dimensions of this social exchange. Qualitative methodology as operationalized within a "Natural" or "Practical" context provides significant opportunities for understanding complex social phenomena (Lofland and Lofland 1984; Glassner and Hertz 1999). The "naturalism" or "naturalistic research" concepts of Qualitative methodology speak to the practical application of knowledge. "Learning by doing" is fostered within qualitative methodology as it provides researchers with the experience of applying such research skills as participant observation and intensive interviewing (Flaherty 1996; Lofland 1976; Prus 1996). This exploratory methodology allow researchers and readers to "make sense of the non-sense" as social meanings and typologies unfold before their eyes (Beck and Geer 1970; Hodgson, 1993). The promise of qualitative analysis of discovering the nature of things such as the "what, where, how, and when" of social phenomena permits the meaning of social interaction and exchange to be revealed (Lofland 1976; Prus 1996; Visano 1987). Specifically, this methodology facilitates an inquiry into the systemic and cultural barriers that survivors of sexual violence in rural areas experience in their interactions with police agencies. The practical application of participant observation and intensive interview methodology enables the researcher to "get access to" and "make sense" of elements and structures of police responses to rural sexual violence from the "insiders view" (Flaherty 1996; Lofland 1976; Prus 1996; Visano 1987). This methodology offers the promise of discovering the viewpoint of the "social actors" involved in this unfolding social phenomenon and their relationships with the responding police agencies (Websdale 1998; Bachman 2001).

The application of satisfactory intensive interviews and field observational methodology places the researcher in the position of facilitating the methodological charge of interactionism by permitting the researcher to obtain first hand experience and knowledge about the everyday lives of the survivors of sexual violence and the inter-relatedness with police agencies (Beck and Geer 1970; Hodgson 1993; Schutt 2004). The immersion of the researcher into the social world of the survivors of sexual violence enables the researcher to document the social reality of the survivors and to develop conceptual apportionments from the observational and interview data.

The participant observer and intensive interview model moves social research beyond the "keyhole observer" (Garfincle 1967) methodology and immerses the researcher into the social world of the survivors of sexual violence. Qualitative methodology allows the field worker to "immerse himself {herself} into the native scene", "steps into another society", or become "physically and morally a part of the community" (Lofland and Lofland 1984). Participant observation and intensive interviewing facilitates the lowering, or in some cases removal, of the informational barriers that are often in place when observing a research site from a distance or from the "outside looking in" (Flaherty 1996; Lofland 1976; Prus 1996; Visano 1987).

This exploratory qualitative approach facilitates intensive interviews with thirty-two survivors of sexual violence. The survivors of sexual violence were originally contacted by staff members of rape crisis centers and safe houses to determine their willingness to participate in the study. Thirty-two of the survivors of sexual violence who were selected were located in Central Virginia and reported to police agencies in rural Virginia localities that they were victims of sexual violence. The criterion used to determine "rural" was based on town or county population of 15,000 or less. The interview schedule was also established by rape crisis centers and safe house staff. The survivors of sexual violence were introduced to the researcher by staff of the centers and they were provided information regarding the intent and purpose of the study. Significant care was taken to ensure that the survivors of sexual violence were indeed completely informed and providing consent without duress or promise from the researcher or the center staff. The thirty-two women consented to full participation as "conversational partners" in "giving voice" to their experiences with rural police agencies. The conversational partners responded to open-ended questions that were prepared in advance in order to facilitate an accurate depiction of the survivors' of sexual violence experiences. A time frame of January, February, March, and April of 2002 was utilized to facilitate the conversational partners' schedules, and to ensure sufficient time to facilitate the intensive interviews, reviews, and offer feedback.

Issues of confidentiality are critical here as all participants were assured anonymity and confidentiality in the release of any information that might reveal their identity or specific geographic location. Confidentiality of the survivors of sexual violence is of the utmost importance therefore the identity of the conversational partners or their associates will not be revealed. In keeping with the social science practice of guaranteeing anonymity, pseudonyms are utilized throughout the study to protect the dignity of the survivors of sexual violence. Although many of the names of the survivors of sexual violence are available on the public records of the criminal and civil courts, it serves no purpose to further stigmatize survivors of sexual violence who, in most cases, have moved on with their lives.

This exploratory qualitative assessment provides an opportunity to reveal systemic barriers as inherent within practices and policies of rural police institutions. The intensive interviews with the conversational partners in this study reveal many typologies and themes that emerged with alarming regularity. These typologies and themes included the survivors' of sexual violence not being satisfied with the services received from the responding rural police institutions; feeling they had to convince the police officers that a sexual assault took place, having to convince the police officers that they did not consent to the sexual assault, feeling the police response seemed focused on the sexual aspects of the crime, and the police focused much of their investigation on the activities and background of the victim. This assessment discloses much needed policy assessment and reformation of rural police institutions to develop strategies to provide effective responses to sexual violence intervention process and investigation.

3. Sexual Violence in a Rural Context: A Qualitative Examination

Many of the intensive interviews revealed that rural police institutions, as an expression and representative of dominant cultural ideologies and practices, are often sexist in nature. Traditionally the state apparatus has not treated gender issues and gender crimes with an equitable or appropriate level of importance, until such a time as public or political pressure or litigation induced policy and procedural change (Johnson 1996; Kilpatrick et al. 1992; Hodgson 2002). The intensive interviews clearly highlighted many problematic features regarding the methods by which rural police institutions delivered services to survivors of sexual violence. Two recipients of police services, Amanda and Wendy respectively, report their encounters with two different rural law enforcement agencies in noting that:

> When I called the sheriff's office to report that I had been raped, they were rude and condescending on the phone. The woman on the phone kept asking me a bunch of stupid questions before she said she would send out a deputy. I didn't really want to answer the questions on the phone but she refused to send an officer unless, in her words "I became more cooperative". When the deputy finally arrived, it got even worse. The deputy seemed annoyed that I had bothered him with my complaint. Their overall attitude stunk. They obviously didn't want to deal with my rape. They for the most part accused me of making up a story about my rape... (Interview: 21 year old female: March 2002)

> The first police officer that arrived seemed okay and really seemed to care about what happened to me. He was asking questions about the suspect and was getting a description and things. The second officer arrived a few minutes later. He acted like a complete asshole. I don't know if it was the good cop bad cop thing but he immediately began to insist that I knew who attacked me and that what I really wanted to report was a domestic dispute. I tried to explain that the guy grabbed me from behind as I was getting into my car. The one officer just didn't want to believe me and kept asking me questions about my background. His attitude was just pathetic. He was

> obviously one of the good old boys and I had interrupted his good old boy evening. (Interview: 28 year old female: April 2002)

Several themes and typologies immediately began to emerge from the intensive interviews that supported that many survivors of sexual violence believed that the police did not effectively respond to the sexual violence investigation. Arlene, Karen, and Beth report, respectively, similar experiences of not being satisfied with the delivery of police services by revealing:

> As soon as the sheriff showed up, I knew that there was going to be a problem. His demeanor and attitude showed me that he did not want to have to deal with me. He was rude and kept asking questions in such a way that it seemed like I was keeping him from something more important, like some sort of real crime. He really made me feel cheap and dirty, I will never respect the police again because of this...(Interview:32 year old female: February 2002)

> My mother insisted that we call the police. When the officer showed up it was like he was really pissed off to be there. He did not want to take a report. When another officer showed up a few minutes later, they began arguing about who should take the report. They didn't give a shit about my condition or what happened to me. Their questions to me were even worse as they accused me of leading the guy on because I had a drink with him and let him walk me to my car. They were more concerned that I was drinking under age than the fact that I was raped. I finally got fed up and drove myself to the hospital. (Interview: 20 year old female: March 2002)

> The officer who showed up actually told me that he was going to charge me with giving false information to the police. They didn't believe that I was raped. They didn't really believe me until the same guy raped another girl two nights later. Suddenly then they became interested in what happened to me. They were originally so dammed rude and ignorant about the whole thing. You know they never ever did apologize to me for not believing me. (Interview:24 year old female: February 2002)

It is important to recognize that although policies and procedures may have been altered within some police institutions, many of the prevailing or traditional ideologies, norms, and values, and beliefs continue to be produced and reproduced by and within the occupational subculture of policing (Hodgson 2002; Bernat 2002; Kelley 2002; Gregory and Lees 1999).

The intensive interviews revealed that police investigations are often riddled with the facade of assessing the complainant's believability and creditability. Sheri and Debra, respectively, disclose their experiences with two different rural police departments in which their complaints were not taken seriously until the police officers were convinced that a sexual assault had occurred:

> When the police arrived, they made me feel as though I was a suspect or something. They made me tell them what happened about 4 times over and over, and keep picking on little things and trying to get me confused. I really don't think they believed me until the Doctor reported to them that I had a lot of bruising and other problems from the assault. I really don't know what their problem was but they really pissed me off. I can tell you this, I will have second thoughts about ever calling the police again. (Interview: 22 Year old female: April 2002)

> I called the police because my girlfriend said that I needed to. When the officers arrived they acted like I had done something wrong. I didn't call them right after the attack and they made a big deal about that and I called my girlfriend first and they made a big deal of that too. I guess that got them all upset because the officers were not really very supportive. They seemed annoyed with me or something. (Interview: 19 year old female: May 2002)

The interviews highlight that sexual violence pervades a "sexual mystique" which is rooted in traditional, historical, cultural, and legislative responses. Nancy and Megan respectively report their experience with the police who seemed to embrace elements of the sexual mystique:

> The police didn't believe a dammed thing that I told them. They kept insisting that it was not rape because I had lived with Todd three years ago. I had not seen him for three years and he shows up at my house drunk and rapes me and the police think that I consented to that. I couldn't do anything to convince them that I was raped. They kept asking about witnesses and things. Of course there was no witnesses, it happened in my house. (Interview: 33 year old female: March 2002)

> The deputy kept focusing on the sexual aspects of what happened. He was making me uncomfortable because he seemed to be getting off on my answers. He was creepy. Of course because I was married to Cliff two years ago, they said that it was not really rape and it wouldn't go anywhere in court. I really don't think they would have believed me or done anything if Cliff hadn't blackened my eye and put a big bruise on my wrist. (Interview: 28 year old female: April 2002)

Within a historical context, a male could not be charged with raping his wife as long as they were legally married. Within the patriarchal apparatus, women are usually relegated as the property of the husband (Bernat 2002; Denike 2002; Clark and Lewis 1977; Wallace and Roberson 2001). Carol and Lisa, respectively, disclosed their experience in reporting sexual violence to the police:

> David and I had been legally separated for eight months when he came over to my place in a drunken stupor and raped me. When I called the police, one of the first things the deputy asked me was whether or not I knew who

> attacked me. When I told them that it was my x [former husband] they seemed to lose their interest in investigating the case any further. They said that they had to talk to the Commonwealth Attorney and that I really needed to think long and hard as to whether or not I wanted to go through with laying charges. They kept making a big deal about the consent thing because I let David into the house. Like I was consenting to be raped because I let him into my house? I finally gave up on the issue and told them to forget it. (Interview: 41 year old female: May 2002)
>
> When I told the police that the guy who raped me used to be my boyfriend, things changed quickly. Suddenly the police changed their attitudes and started suggesting that Ken and I were on a date or something. Like I gave consent for Ken to rape me. I hadn't seen the guy in 7 years. I ran into him that night at the bar and he followed me out to my car. I don't think the police ever believed me that I was raped that night. (Interview: 29 year old Female: April 2002)

Traditionally, in order to secure a conviction for the charge of rape, legislation required the survivors of sexual violence must be of previously "chaste" character and much of a victim's testimony had to be corroborated by other independent evidence Wallace and Clifford 2001; Hodgson 2002; Schwendinger 1983). Both Karen and Monica's reports of their experiences with the police, suggest that the police continue to embrace traditional norms and values by disclosing that:

> The police were asking a lot of questions about my past boyfriends and things. I didn't understand what the issue was. One of the deputies then told me that I had quite a "reputation" in the community, and I said what the hell does that mean and what does that have to do with being raped. They kept saying that these were issues that had to be dealt with in court. I asked them what not being a virgin has to do with catching the asshole that raped me. They even asked me what type of outfit I was wearing. They kept saying that they need other evidence; obviously my word was not good enough. (Interview: 25 year old female: February 2002)
>
> Once they [the police] found out that I worked 8 years ago as a stripper, their attitudes changed. They started treating me like I was lying to them or something. They treated me like I was trash or something. They started accusing me of being with one of my former customers or something. It didn't make any sense to me. They even asked me which church I went to as if that would establish that I was telling the truth. They really didn't want information about the guy who raped me; they wanted information all about me. They didn't believe anything I told them. (Interview: 31 year old female: March 2002)

These interviews certainly highlight the traditional legal response, which clearly suggests that women cannot be trusted to tell the truth without other evidence to corroborate their complaint. This "sexual mystique" presents a shroud of "rape myths" that are expressed within social, moral, and cultural notions. These rape myths portray that women secretly "like to be raped" and therefore they provoked the act, or that the victim was indirectly "asking for it" by her choice of attire or location, or that "no really means yes" (Hodgson 2002; Clark and Lewis 1977; Johnson 1996).

The intensive interviews revealed time after time that the police embraced the historical perspective that the victim could not be trusted to be telling the truth. There is no other crime, property or personal in which the police will continuously question the authenticity of the victim's complaint (Hodgson 2002; Bernat, 2002; Clark and Lewis 1977; Gregory and Lees 1999). Stacey and Rosa, respectively, provide further examples of the reluctance of the police to believe survivors of sexual violence:

> I spent the whole time trying to convince the police that I was not somehow asking for it or wanted to be raped. They just didn't get it at all. One of the officers suggested to me that what happened was "accidental intercourse" and that I was not raped at all. They were really disturbed that I didn't call them for about two hours after I was raped. I called my girlfriend first and talked to her about what happened first. I just didn't know what to do. (Interview: 19 year old female: April 2002)

> I didn't want to call the police but my sister called them anyway. It turned out that one of the deputies was friends with the guy who raped me. They were suggesting that I was making the whole thing up to get back at Greg or something. It was a waste of time calling the police. They said that I needed witness or some type of physical evidence for court. Next time I will look after it my own way. (Interview: 20 year old female: February 2002)

There is no other crime in which the police will spend so much time trying to assess the credibility or chasteness of the victim. The police often respond to the level of physical injury to the victim, or the lack thereof, as an indicator of consent (Bart and OBrien 1985; Hodgson 2002; Kelley 2002; Gregory and Lees 1999). Carla and Mary, respectively, provide further examples of the police response to calls for service:

> The police kept asking if I consented to the rape. I said "why would I consent to such a thing". They said that they needed evidence that I did not give consent. Obviously my word was not good enough. I didn't know what else to say or give them. They kept asking about all the details about the sex part of the attack. (Interview: 25 year old female: March 2002)

> The police seemed to keep focusing on the sex stuff, and how much I had to drink, and what I was wearing. The officer even asked me if there was anything that I did or said that would have given the suspect the impression

> that I wanted to have sex with him or something. I told them that it was not sex, the guy raped me and he was an animal. They also asked me about my background. They directed all of their questions about me. They didn't seem concerned with asking about information about the rapist. (Interview: 21 year old female: April 2002)

It becomes most apparent as articulated in the intensive interviews that the police continue to investigate sexual violence as a crime of sex as opposed to a crime of violence.

The intensive interviews reveal that the police appear to often operate within a "criterion of victim believability" in that victims who have received significant physical injury are perceived as not having consented to the sexual violence. The police often use this criterion or stereotype to assess the believability of the victims' complaints. The interviews support that the police also use other factors to assess believability such as the victim's appearance, that is, dressing in a provocative manner; the victim's age; marital status; occupation; alcohol use; the victim's "mental state" before and after the assault; the victim's sexual history and practices; the location of the attack; and time of first report. (See Figure 1) Cathy and Sandy, respectively, provide other examples of the police response to sexual violence:

> The sheriff's office did not take my complaint seriously. They seemed to be trying to prove that my rape did not even occur. It seemed like they were trying to build a case against me. I had to tell them at one point, hey I'm the victim here not the suspect. Did they think I raped myself or something? They asked me about my drinking habits, what medication I was taking, if I had ever been to see a shrink before and those types of questions. (Interview: 22 year old female: March 2002)

> The police officer was obviously uncomfortable asking me questions about the rape, but his questions were directed toward my activities and not the guy who raped me. I felt like I was a suspect or something. They asked me a bunch of questions about my personal circumstances that seemed for some reason to be relevant to them. When they found out that I had broke off with my boyfriend only three nights ago, suddenly they suggested that my claim of rape was to get attention to myself. Figure that one out. I will never forgive those officers for making me feel like I was lying about what happened. I will never trust the police again.
> (Interview: 27 year old female: April 2002)

The criterion of victim believability is utilized by the police to assess "founded" and "unfounded" cases of sexual assault. These criteria set up a model of "women who cannot be raped," in that victims who do not meet the believability criteria as set out by the police often cannot be and often are not classified by the police as victims (Gregory and Lees 1999; Clark and Lewis 1977; Holmstrom and Burgess 1983; Burt 1991).

4. Systemic Institutional Discrimination

It is important to recognize that although legislation, police policies, and practices may have been altered, many of the prevailing ideologies, norms, values, and beliefs continue to be produced and reproduced by practitioners within the criminal justice system. Often the change in police policies and procedures amounts to little more than "impression management," masking the public face of the police institution while the internal operations, for the most part, go unchanged and unchallenged (Hodgson 2002, Hodgson and Kelley 2002). Impression management strategies within police institutions allow for systemic discriminatory policies and practices to be operationalized with much anonymity.

Systemic institutional discrimination occurs when the frequently inherent social, economic, political, or customs of an organization or culture have an impact on a historically disadvantaged group that prohibits or denies full societal participation and consideration. Systemic discrimination results in inequality of condition and opportunity that affects current societal groups and is reproduced through successive generations (Schwendinger 1983; Clark and Lewis 1977). Systemic discrimination is often difficult to detect because of its latent application and practice within our social, economic, and political apparatus. Often an individual does not even know that he or she has been the victim of systemic discrimination. Systemic discrimination is very difficult to detect until the trained observer steps back to observe the macro picture, which often reveals the social, economic, and political barriers that may be in place to affect the macro social conditions or circumstances (Hodgson and Kelley 2002; Denike 2002).

Systemic discrimination is the differential and unequal treatment of a group, deeply embedded in social, economic, and political institutions. This is discrimination that occurs as a result of the structure and functioning of public institutions and their policies. Institutional, systemic discrimination includes the systemic exclusion of people from equal access to and participation in a particular institution because of their race, religion, class, ethnicity, or gender. Systemic exclusion can lead to another type of discrimination, which can be described as the interaction of the various spheres of social life to maintain an overall pattern of oppression (Hodgson 2002; Hodgson and Kelley 2002).

The police response to sexual violence provides for an unfortunate example of systemic discrimination against women both in policy and practice (Gregory and Lees 1999; Hodgson 2002). The historical legal analysis discloses, for example, as indicated earlier, that a male could not be charged with raping his wife as long as they were legally married, that a survivor of sexual violence had to be of pervious chaste character in order for a rape charge to be sustained, and that a survivor of sexual violence had to present testimony that could be corroborated by other independent evidence. The merging of these historical considerations with the shroud of sexual mystique, that is expressed within a systemic discriminatory context, can construct the social, moral, and legal notions that women secretly like to be raped and that they often provoked the act, or that women are indirectly "asking for it" by their choice of attire or location, or that "no really means yes." Some of these values and beliefs were obviously present in the police institutional systemic responses to the survivors of sexual violence as disclosed in the intensive interviews. Many of these same ideologies continue to be expressed as systemic discriminatory practice in the service delivery systems of the police institutions that responded to the survivors of sexual violence in this study. These systemic discriminatory expressions can be exposed by assessing the police response to sexual violence, the priority given to crimes of sexual violence, and the allocation of human and technical resources assigned to respond to sexual violence.

5. Conclusion

This exploratory study has facilitated the evaluation of rural police service delivery to survivors of sexual violence by disclosing the systemic discriminatory process and practices as operationalized by the police and sheriff departments that responded to the survivors of sexual violence. The rural survivors of sexual violence revealed in the interviews the consequences when police departments are informed and guided by rape myths and historical legal notions about sexual violence. The police responses to the sexual violence, as disclosed in this study, were tainted from the onset because of the discriminatory views and assumptions that the various officers held about sexual violence. The intensive interviews disclose that the police officers that responded to the calls for service compromised the investigations, strained community relations, and lost the trust of the survivors of the violence as a result of the police officers' obsession with assessing the believability of the survivors of sexual violence. As the interviews revealed, many of the police officers embraced traditional legal historical values and attitudes about sexual violence. Subsequently, the survivors of sexual violence in this study received police services that were discriminatory and unprofessional. The discriminatory and unprofessional actions of the police generated an inappropriate tainted police service delivery response and investigation that obviously affected subsequent police decisions regarding protecting the community and apprehending offenders.

Figure 1. Factors used by police institutions to assess the validity and credibility of survivors of sexual violence

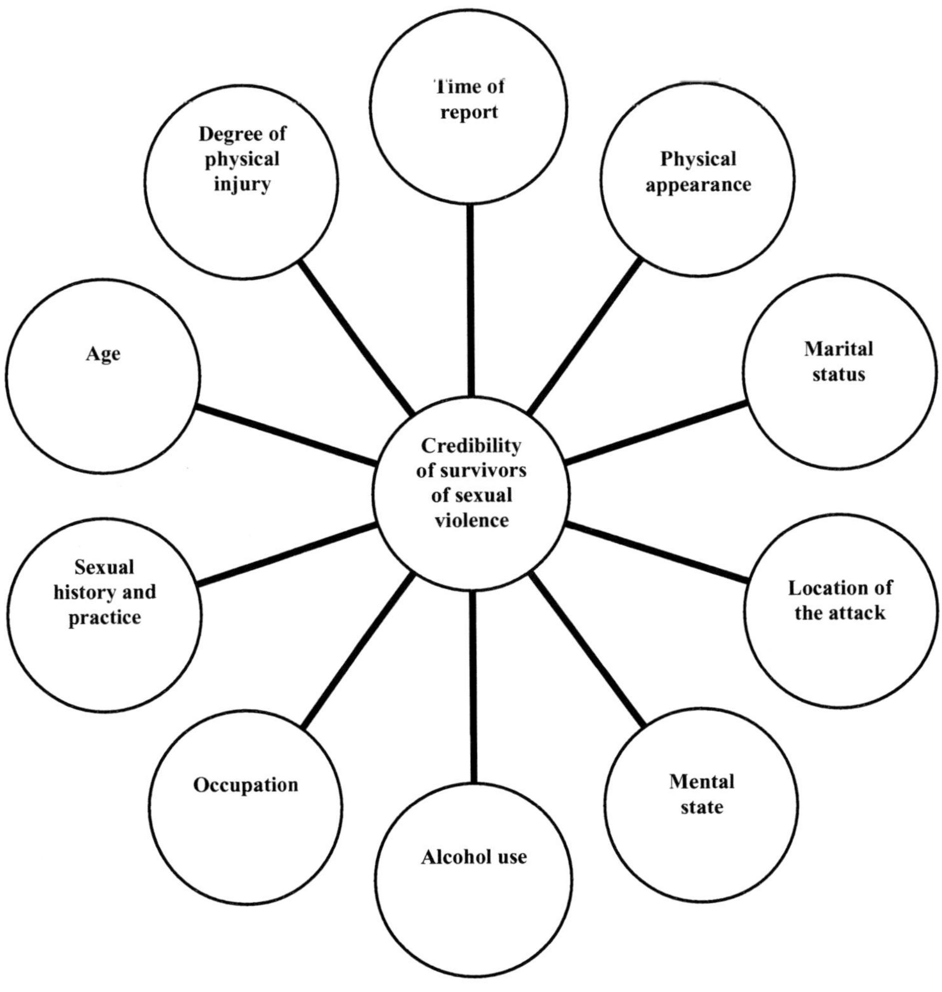

References

Alpert, G.P., and Moore, M. H. 1993 Measuring police performance in the new paradigm of policing. In U.S. Department of Justice, Bureau of Justice Statistics, *Performance Measures for the Criminal Justice System.* Washington, D.C.: U.S. Government Printing Office.

Bachman, R. and Schutt, R.K. 2001 *The Practice of Research in Criminology and Criminal Justice.* California: Pine Forge Press.

Bart, P.B. and O'Brien, P.H. 1985 *Stopping Rape: Successful Survival Strategies.* New York: Pergamon Press.

Bayley, D.H. 1994 *Police for the Future.* New York: Oxford University Press

Bayley, D.H. and Shearing, C.D. 2001 *The New Structure of Policing.* (NCJ187083). Washington, DC: U.S. Department of Justice.

Beck, H and Geer, B 1970 Participant observation and interviewing: A comparison, in Filstead, W. (ed)., *Qualitative Methodology.* Chicago: Rand McNally.

Bernat, F.P. 2002 Rape law reform. In J.F. Hodgson and D.S. Kelley (Eds.) *Sexual Violence: Policies, Practices, and Challenges in the United States and Canada.* Westport, CT: Praeger Publishers

Birzer, B. 1999 Police training in the twenty-first century. *FBI Law Enforcement Bulletin, 68,* 16-20

Bourque, L.B. 1989 *Defining Rape.* Durham, NC: Duke University Press.

Bureau of Justice Statistics. 2000 *Criminal Victimization, 1999.* Washington, DC: U.S. Department of Justice, Bureau of Justice Statistics.

Burt, M. 1991 Rape myths and acquaintance rape. In A. Parrot and L. Bechhofer (Eds.) *Acquaintance Rape: The Hidden Crime,* New York: John Wiley and Sons.

Cavanagh, M.E. 2004 *Policing Within a Professional Framework.* New Jersey: Pearson, Prentice Hall.

Clark, L. and Lewis, D. 1977 *Rape: The Price of Coercive Sexuality.* Toronto: The Women's Press.

Conser, J.A. and Russell, G.D. 2000 *Law Enforcement in the United States.* Gaithersburg, MD: Aspen Publishers.

Dantzker, M.L. 2000. *Understanding Today's Police* (2nd edn.). Upper Saddle River, New Jersey: Prentice Hall.

Deakin, T. 1988 *Police Professionalism: The Renaissance of American Law Enforcement.* Springfield, IL: Charles C. Thomas.

Decker, S.H. 1981 Alternate measures of police output. *American Journal Police.* 1 (1), 23-35.

Denike, M.A. 2002. Myths of women and the rights of man: The politics of credibility in Canadian rape law. In J.F. Hodgson and D.S. Kelley (Eds.) *Sexual Violence: Policies, Practices, and Challenges in the United States and Canada.* Westport, CT: Praeger Publishers

Eck, J.E. and Rosenbaum, D.P. 1994 The new police order: Effectiveness, equity, and efficiency in community policing. In D. Rosenbaum, (Ed.) *The*

Challenge of Community Policing: Testing the Promises. Thousand Oaks: Sage Publications.

Federal Bureau of Investigation. 2000 *Crime in the United States, 1999.* Washington DC: U.S. Government Printing Office.

Flaherty, M. 1996 Some methodological principles from research in practice: Validity, truth, and method in the study of lived time. *Qualitative Inquiry,* 2(3), 285-299.

Frazier, P., and Haney, B. 1996 Sexual assault cases in the legal system: Police, prosecutor, and victim perspectives. *Law and Human Behavior* 20: 607-628.

Garfincle, H. 1967 *Studies in Ethnomethodology.* New Jersey: Prentice Hall.

Glassner, B. and Hertz, R. 1999. *Qualitative Sociology as Everyday Life.* California: Sage Publications.

Goldstein, H. 1990 *Problem-Oriented Policing.* New York: McGraw-Hill.

Gregory, J. and Lees, S. 1999 *Policing Sexual Violence.* London: Routledge.

Hatry, H.P. 1999 *Performance Measurement.* Washington, DC: Urban Institute.

Hodgson, J. F. and Kelley, D. (Eds.) 2002 *Sexual Violence: Policies, Practices, and Challenges in the United States and Canada.* Wesport: Praeger Press.

Hodgson, J.F. 1993 *Police Community Relations: Analysis of the Organizational and Structural Barriers Inhibiting Effective Police-Community Exchanges.* Toronto: Unpublished PhD Dissertation York University

Hodgson, J.F. 2002 Policing sexual violence: A case study of Jane Doe v. the Metropolitan Toronto Police. In J.F. Hodgson, and D. Kelley (Eds.) *Sexual Violence: Policies, Practices, and Challenges in the United States and Canada.* Wesport: Praeger Press.

Holmstrom, L. and Burgess, A. 1983 *The Victim of rape: Institutional Reactions.* New Brunswick, New Jersey: Transaction Books.

Horney, J. and Spohn, C. 1991 Rape law reform and instrumental change in six jurisdictions. *Law and Society Review* 25:117-53.

Johnson, H. 1996 *Dangerous Domains: Violence Against Women in Canada.* Toronto: Nelson Canada.

Kelley, D.S. 2002 The measurement of rape. In J.F. Hodgson and D.S. Kelley (Eds.) *Sexual Violence: Policies, Practices, and Challenges in the United States and Canada.* Westport, CT: Praeger Publishers.

Kilpatrick, D.G., Edmunds, C. and Seymour, A. 1992 *Rape in America: A Report to the Nation.* Arlington, VA: National Center for Victims of Crime: Charleston, SC: Medical University of South Carolina, Crime Victims Research and Treatment Center.

LaFree, G.D. 1989 *Rape and Criminal Justice: The Social Construction of Sexual Assault.* Belmont, CA: Wadsworth Publishing Co.

Lofland, J. 1976 *Doing Social Life.* New York: John Wiley.

Lofland, J. and Lofland, L. 1984 *Analyzing Social Settings: A Guide to Qualitative Observations and Analysis.* California: Wadsworth Publishing.

Lord, V. and Rassel, G. 2002. Law enforcement's response to sexual assault: A comparative study of nine counties in North Carolina. In J.F. Hodgson and D. Kelley (Eds), *Sexual Violence: Policies, Practices, and Challenges in the United States and Canada*. Westport: Praeger Press.

Maguire, E.R. 2002 Multiwave Establishment Surveys of Police Organizations. *Justice Research and Policy,* 4 (Fall Issue): 39-60.

Maguire, E.R. 2003 Measuring the Performance of law Enforcement Agencies, in *CALEA Update*. February 2003.

Mastrofski, S.D. 1999 Policing for People. *Ideas in American Policing.* Washington, DC.:U.S. Department of Justice, Police Foundation (March)

Moriarty, L.J. 2002 *Policing and Victims.* New Jersey: Prentice Hall.

Oliver, W.M. 2001 *Community-Oriented Policing: A Systemic Approach to Policing.* (2nd edn.). New Jersry: Prentice Hall.

Palmiotto, M.J. 2000 *Community Policing: A Policing Strategy for the 21st Century.* Gaithersburg, MD: Aspen Publishers.

Palmiotto, M.J. 2003 *Policing and Training Issues*. New Jersey: Prentice Hall.

Prus, R. 1996 *Symbolic Interaction and Ethnographic Research.* Albany: State University of New York Press.

Schutt, R.K. 2004 *Investigating the Social World.* (4thedn.). California: Sage Publications.

Schwendinger, J.R. and Schwendinger, H. 1983 *Rape and Inequality.* London: Sage.

Searles, P., and Berger, R. 1987 The current status of rape reform legislation: An examination of state statutes. In *Women's Rights Law Reporter* 10:25-43.

Shusta, Robert M. et al. 1995 *Multicultural Law Enforcement: Strategies for Peacekeeping in a Diverse Society.* New Jersey: Prentice Hall.

Tjaden, P. and Thoennes, N. 1998 *Prevalence, Incidence, and Consequences of Violence Against Women: Findings from the National Violence Against Women Survey.* Washington, DC: National Institute of Justice and U.S. Department of Health and Human Services, Centers for Disease Control and Prevention.

Visano, L. 1987 *This Idle Trade.* Concord: VitsSanna Books.

Walker, S. 1988 *Achieving Police Accountability.* Research Brief, The Center on Crime, Communities and Culture, 3 (September), 1-16.

Wallace, H. and Roberson, C. 2001 *Principles of Criminal Law.* (2ndedn.) Massachusetts: Allyn and Bacon.

Websdale, N. 1998 *Rural Women Battering and the Justice System: An Ethnography.* California: Sage.

9. Women Policing or the Policing of Women: Exclusionary Practices of an Occupational Culture

Catherine Orban

1. Introduction

Women who work in an occupational culture based on a paramilitary structure are required to assimilate to a code of behaviour that denies their authentic selves. In general, these women suffer extreme difficulties and share with other women a struggle of self-identity working in male-dominated occupations. Feminist or lesbian women working in traditional male occupations are threatened with verbal slurs as they attempt to prove to others that they can do "male" work. Even in the absence of admittance to the political and/or the social, women in male dominated occupations are confronted with accusations that quickly label them 'Bitches', 'Dykes', or 'Whores'. The challenge that confronts the career of policewomen is fundamentally related to a prevailing misogyny, replete with male myths about the appropriateness of women "doing" police work.

This paper studies the interactional or situational experiences of women in one traditional male occupation - policing. The meaning of non-traditional work is captured by examining women's interpretation of occupational expectations within their social setting. An examination of the occupational journeys of women as they move through their career reveals the nature of gender control. The general aim of this paper is to provide a discussion of the concept "proving oneself" in the occupation of policing. This paper addresses the research questions: to what are police women loyal? To what extent do they lose their self-identity? What is the differential impact of self respect on social acceptance?

2. Theoretical Perspective

To fully appreciate the obstacles women encounter in the occupation of policing, it is appropriate to outline the structural and cultural process to which women negotiate their identities and relations to the dominant structure. According to McCall (1992:837), "how to theorize the relationship between structures of male domination and the intersubjective experience of women can be termed a central problem in feminist theory." As we approach the beginning of the twentieth century, we can assert that feminists have not fully conceptualized the relationship between gender, social structure and interaction. An attempt at understanding women's subjugation is riddled in complex social relations between women, culture, and the state. Clearly, there is no single conceptual umbrella that integrates social process and structure. In this context, I would like to employ a feminist-symbolic interaction approach as a framework for interpreting women's work in the traditional male occupation of policing.

2.1 Feminist Symbolic Interaction Framework

A radical feminist perspective views women's subjectivity through discourses of state mechanisms. The issues raised under this perspective are pornography; violence against women; the worth of women's work in the home; sexual discrimination in employment, salaries and promotions; sexual harassment in the workplace; and women's access to non-traditional occupations, and so on. The focus of this study is on the obstacles women confront in non-traditional occupations.

Within a radical feminist perspective, patriarchy is at the root of the oppression of all women. Patriarchy is defined as "the totality of male domination and its pervasiveness in women's lives (Smith, 1983: 314). Control and power are the foundation of patriarchal values; they are the key elements that legitimize the existence of a patriarchal culture. Hierarchical division or power relations exist between the dominant and the dominated within all structures of society. Both men and women will experience patriarchy. However, the patriarchal forces will have a detrimental impact on women. Historically, gender has been treated as a hierarchy of social relations. Gender is not only categorized as a "master status" but it " . . . is so socially significant that the perceptions, expectations and reactions of others are likely to be organized around this aspect of the person rather than any other"(Laws, 1979: 1). For Mackinnon (1987: 8), gender is not defined by difference but is identified by "the inequality of power, a social status based on who is permitted to do what to whom." Patriarchy functions to reproduce inequality and the division of labour (Mackinnon, 1982; Maroney and Luxton, 1987). Its features are structural and situationally experienced. Patriarchy is an ideology that is ubiquitous. Its manipulative process can be examined in the social institution of the family, the educational system, the legal system and in the occupational structure of work sites.

According to a radical feminist perspective, traditional occupation and status is socially constructed by institutions that are rooted in male domination. The relationship between patriarchal occupational structure and interaction is gender control. This in turn produces gendered forms of social control that identifies "men's" work and "women's" work. Alternatively, for the Marxist feminist perspectives, occupation is the division of labour that positions women as the lowest class. Occupation is sex segregated, that is, there are social conceptions of women's roles in a capitalist society. In comparison to men, women work in a narrow range of occupations. Few women have "top" jobs, and on average earn less than men. This unequal distribution between the sexes is attributable to the gender control of the means of production. The substantive position taken by many feminist scholars is that the examination of gender power relations is needed to critically evaluate past and more importantly present day power relations. It is with this point of reference that I would like to discuss the concept of power and its correlation with the social reality of women working in traditional male occupations using a feminist symbolic interaction perspective.

Feminism acknowledges the oppressive nature of patriarchal institutions that subjugate women. Women's social role in the community is defined by the normative features of patriarchy. Traditional social definition of women's behaviour emphasizes that women are less capable human beings than men. The male myth is carried on in patriarchal institutions insofar as men are viewed as individuals and leaders whereas women are followers and are to be dominated. For women in policing there are structural barriers that limit women to non-managerial positions. The low representation of white women and women of colour are blatant in the extant statistical reports.

Women's inferior status is embedded in a bureaucratic process which perpetuates male superiority by promoting men in positions of authority and power. In the occupation of policing, men occupy positions of authority in which they can institutionalize official policies and influence rank promotion procedures that control women. As an outcome, women remain in positions of lower rank within the hierarchical structure and continue to justify their capability of "doing police work" to male co-workers. Kanter (1977) observed that organizations in which one group make up 85 percent of the employee's population and another group constitutes the remaining 15 percent display specific sets of interpersonal behaviour. She identifies those in the minority group as "tokens" and those in the majority group as "dominants." Simply stated, tokens are identified by the majority in occupations that adhere to Affirmative Action Policy or Equal Opportunity Employment initiatives. The term token is defined as: "people identified by ascribed characteristics or other characteristics that carry with them a set of assumptions about culture, status, and behaviour highly salient for majority category members"(ibid, 165). Although, we can generalize that more women are working in non-traditional jobs, these women must still deal with the ascribed token label.

The concept of power is central to Kanter's study (1977, 1979) on "Occupational Sex Segregation." Kanter (1977: 166) defined power as:

> . . .the ability to do, in the classic physical usage of power as energy, and thus it means having access to whatever is neededfor the doing. The problems with absolute power, a total monopoly on power, lie in the fact that it renders everyone else powerless. On the other hand, empowering more people through generating more autonomy, more participation in decisions, and more access to resources increases the total capacity for effective action rather than increases domination. The powerful ones who have access to tools for action.

As Kanter claims, the social inequality of power relations ". . . thus is critical to the effective behaviour of people in organizations" (ibid, 205).

New employees typically enter into an occupation with a set of motivation and expectations that will help them create a sense of meaningfulness of work in their lives (Mayer, 1993: 16-19). For Kanter (ibid, 249) these processes which constitute,

> [t]he feedback between structure and behaviour can produce upward cycles

> of advantage, or downward cycles of disadvantage. And it is hard for a person to break out of the cycle once begun. To some extent, low opportunity, powerlessness, and tokenism constitute self-perpetuating, self-sealing systems, with links that can be broken only from outside.

Kanter describes the concept of power as either immobilizing or empowering. Yet, what needs to be acknowledged is that power is embedded in culture and remains an invisible factor that continues to control the minority. For the individual, power can be enabling when it is shared by all groups. However, if these mechanisms of control continue to exist in occupational structures, then power cannot be empowering but can only act as an agent that reproduces emissaries and challengers. Furthermore, if the ideology of the institutional structure still upholds the male culture and if the opportunity structure only permits emissaries of that ideology, then power, even though it is shared can limit women's mobility within the hierarchical structure.

For Foucault (1979: 187), disciplinary power is exercised through its invisibility; at the same time it imposes on those whom it subjects a principle of compulsory visibility. In discipline, the subjects have to be seen. Their visibility assures the hold of the power that is exercised over them. It is the fact of being constantly seen, that maintains the disciplined individual in her subjugation. And the examination is the technique by which power, instead of emitting the signs of potency, instead of imposing a mark on its subjects, hold them in a mechanism of objectification. In this space of domination, disciplinary power manifests potency, essentially, by arranging objects. The examination is, as it was, the ceremony of this objectification.

"Symbolic interaction" refers to the peculiar and distinctive character of interaction as it takes place between human beings. The peculiarity of symbolic interactionism (SI) claims those human beings interpret or define rather than merely react to each other's actions. These actions are based on their concomitant meanings. Thus, symbols mediate human interaction. SI highlights the process and dynamic nature of definitions of self, others and situations. Humans act in a world that is interactively defined. Interaction, therefore, is the primary organizing unit of analysis.

According to the SI perspective, occupation is culturally constructed by social institutions (actors). Likewise, the role of gender is culturally mediated in ongoing socializing interactions between actors and institutions. Consequently, the symbolic labelling of "men's work" and "women's work" is linked to culturally ascribed sex (gender) roles. Stereotyping in occupations is culturally manufactured in gendered institutions. Stereotypical notions of male work and female work identify clerical, household labour occupations as traditional female occupied roles; for the most part, the military, corporate business, and policing are identified as male occupied roles. In other words, women who perform male roles are typically perceived as pursuing non-traditional work.

SI provides a link between the structures of male domination and the marginalization of women by locating gender inequality in cultural norms. The socialization process throughout the course of one's life being male or female involves learning sex roles. Socially constructed institutions replicate sex roles. Levels of appropriate and inappropriate behaviour are regulated by cultural norms that are constructed in gendered institutions. Occupational requirements form the structure of male domination; occupational expectations control human behaviour. The relationship between male domination and women's place in the occupation of policing is that women are the marginalized social group, an occupational status that is inferior to men.

The conceptual juxtaposition of SI and feminism as well as an analysis of the empirical findings of this study will further contribute to an understanding of a quintessential sociological problematic articulated in terms of a specific site: Why do policewomen subject themselves to gendering practices that reinforce male domination?

3. Method

The nature of this study was based on exploratory research. The sociological method employed in this research was a feminist qualitative praxis. The motivation for conducting this research is inspired by a lack of Canadian research material on policewomen (Linden and Minch, 1982; Linden, 1984; Martin, 1993). The primary objective in this exploratory study was to record women's experiences in a traditional male occupation and to draw upon those experiences by addressing recurring themes that the women were concerned with. It became clear after a short period in the interview process that policewomen in some regimental form, adhere to occupational expectations because it is the only way to obtain the approval of male co-workers. The concept of "proving oneself" will be examined in the remainder of this discussion paper. Between 1995 and 1996, I undertook a study of 25 female officers, whose rank ranged from 4th class Constable to Superintendent of a police service. The length of service or "on the job" service ranged from one to twenty-one years. There were three types of police services that the researcher examined: municipal, provincial and federal agencies.

4. The Occupation of Policing

The social organization of policing consists of patriarchal rules and regulations that demand full compliance from its male and female police officers. From the moment new members enter the police force they are subjected to not only occupational norms but also organizational values which socially controls its members. Both men and women learn the "do's" and "don't's" of police officer behaviour through various socialization sites.

The police college is one location site where new recruits learn appropriate police behaviour. The academy or police training college also offer a wide spectrum of bonding activities that introduces the new members/recruits to the ideology of the organization-- the "Esprit De Corp." The Esprit De Corps, a feeling of shared pride and honour, is experienced by all police officers. It is an ideology which reflects the *status quo* of the paramilitary structure. The Esprit De Corps, an emotional and spiritual connection between police officers and the organization, indoctrinates recruit's to embrace the structural features of the organization . After the new recruits have completed their training time in the police college, they are assigned a platoon or sector in which they will work. The recruit is then assigned a coach officer, usually a senior police officer, who will train him or her in the "reality" of doing police work. At this point, the new recruit will learn the importance of the "Esprit De Corps" and additional appropriate police officer behaviour from the experienced police officer; male recruits will be introduced to the "brotherhood." On the other hand, female recruits learn their place in the male police culture.

For six weeks the new recruit trains with the coach officer to learn the in and out's of doing police work. However, the difference between male and female police officers is the length of time that it takes male co-workers to approve of the new female recruit. Women's past and present experience of gender oppression and subordination within patriarchal structures will define their place in the dominant male police culture. Because women are a minority in the police department, they become highly visible to other members. Women's visibility will place them under the inspection of male co-workers. On the other hand, there is less pressure on male officers not to make mistakes because of their majority group status.

The point made here, is that male officers do not fear as much of the social evaluation from administrators or peers because they share a common sex-role status; male bonding or male celebration occurs in order to unite the male subculture. Men's "master status" endows them with a privileged status and acceptance into the police culture. Policewomen's location in the hierarchical structure on the other hand, will bequeath them with a lesser status then their male colleagues. As a result, women struggle to be accepted in the male police culture.

From the findings of this study, most participants reported difficulties in achieving the approval of their male co-workers. Some of the participants acknowledged the difficulty of getting along with their coach officer; in all instances of reported conflict, the coach officer was male. The argument proposed by this researcher is that a male recruit or male police officer will be taken under the wings of the "brotherhood" more expediently than a female recruit or female police officer.

The "Esprit De Corps" and the "brotherhood" co-exist as a celebration of the male culture. The "Esprit De Corps" reinforces the ideology of patriarchy, obedience to power, authority, homophobia and the subjugation of women. The brotherhood reinforces male collegiality and trust among male members. To gain the trust of male co-workers, women will struggle with the process of being accepted throughout the course of their career in policing. Because women today still remain the minority in police departments, they will continue to be marginalized until those mechanisms of social control are replaced with more impartial techniques of administration.

While in the transition stage between police college training and on-the-road training, the new recruits will have completed their battery of tests at the police academy and they will have received a work performance evaluation from their coach officer. At this stage, the male recruits will be under the protection of the brotherhood, while the female recruits will be sent out into the trenches to either sink or swim under the scrutiny of the organization. These women will adopt a code of behaviour that will prove loyalty to the patriarchal culture and at the cost of minimizing their identity.

4.1 Expectations

The social organization of control remains an underlying principle of the police institution. The organization's expectations of its police officers require obedience, loyalty to power, authority and the solidarity of its members as a police culture. The police culture serves as a self-regulating agency that surveillance undisciplined members.

One policewoman (PO5) commented on her initial experience with the discipline process that had taken place in the interview stage:

> I had a personal interview, walked in there all suited up with a nice suit and a long leather coat, and my five man panel did not ask me to take off my coat. I was sweating buckets sitting under the pressure cooker of this five man panel and the winter quilted lining.

The interview process can be considered an introduction to obedience and respect of authority figures; conformity to regimental rules and regulations of the paramilitary police structure.

There are occupational expectations that direct police officers with information on doing police work and police officer behaviour. These expectations include: the officer's ability to be independent, and to use logical reasoning when doing police work; to be able to respond in a professional manner in a crisis situation. The police organization, as stated by Blumberg and Niederhoffer (1985), produces common characteristics among its members; the occupational culture reflects the values of the police organization. All disciplined members will experience the following characteristics: kinship and solidarity, common hazards and dangers, respect for power and authority, secrecy, loyalty, a sense of minority-group (public) status, political conservatism, cynicism, suspiciousness, social isolation and pressure to produce. Policewomen will experience these characteristics plus the following: pressure not to make mistakes (to combat cultural stereotypes), minority-group visibility (public and private) status, suspicion (not trusted by male co-workers), limited kinship and solidarity, respect for male power and authority. Women will experience these additional characteristics as outsiders within the police culture.

Overall, the participants in the study knew the organization expected its police officers *to be professional* in their police duties and responsibilities. For the policewomen, to be professional meant to do the best job that they could do and this philosophy coincided with their self-concept of "to be the best that you can be".

The women's interpretation of appropriate police officer behaviour is illustrated in the following comments:

> You were able to do the job as a generalist Constable. You were able to go out there and arrest criminals and to serve and protect the community; to be impartial in dealing with people; to remain calm in difficult situations. To pull my weight and to know what I was doing. Basically just to do a good job, meet the needs of the community. Be conscience. You work as a team with your squad. Nobody wants you to be booking off sick. Just cohesiveness (PO 06).

The expectation to "be the best" and to "be professional" invokes pressure on the individual's self concept to be accepted by male co-workers and administrators. As one police woman suggested, it is the personality of the individual not the sexes that creates "good" workers and poor workers. She may be correct in saying it's the individual's behaviour that invokes positive or negative judgement of the police officer. However, primarily the individual's minority group status have been discussed to be determinant factors in administrators and co-workers response to the individual before they can properly be evaluated on their work performance. There are cultural stereotypes embedded in the patriarchal institution on minority groups. In the occupation of policing, policewomen are judged by their co-workers before they are given an equal chance of performing their job function. Personalities can attribute to an accepting or non-accepting peer/administration response, however, women as a minority group are judged with suspicion based on their gender and not their competence in doing police work.

5. The Concept of Proving Oneself

There are additional social codes of conduct that are aimed at female police officers. By "proving oneself" to others that they deserve to be there will lead to work performance pressures on women which will cause policewomen to go above and beyond occupational expectations. And in return for complying to occupational expectations women will seek acceptance from their male co-workers. However, there is no guarantee of women not ever having to prove themselves; this socially organized process is temporarily limited. In comparison, male police officers will simply step into the police culture with minimal work towards gaining the trust and approval of their peers and without having extreme work performance pressures placed on them by the organization. In other words, male officers do not have to continuously prove to others that they deserve to be there. Men's sex-role identification privileges them with a "free" life time membership status to the brotherhood. It would be okay for policemen to be dominated by the administrators of "the rank and file", but to be controlled by policewomen would be a catastrophe!

Policewomen in the study were concerned with "proving themselves" to the police organization, administration, and to male peers. For the policewomen "to prove oneself" meant to demonstrate: capability, competency and loyalty to the organization and male peers. The women believed that if they could prove oneself to others, then they would be accepted by the organization, administration and male co-workers. One woman (PO 07) noted that proving oneself was a test by male peers:

> No I still don't know if I'm accepted and that's just because they're so two faced that you never know. As far as my ability to do the job, I have been accepted, but I'm not the other person--who knows. I think the first challenge every female officer faces is the challenge of being accepted. And the type of thing that would accomplish that would be a situation that arises at work where you're handling it well the situation goes through, all the dust has settled—the guys look at the situation and go alright she's okay. And it sickens me that it is that way. But the fact is-- that's how it is for a woman. It takes proving yourself before being accepted. So, that is the first challenge every woman faces and if that doesn't happen or something happens that you can't prove yourself, then you're in for a rough ride.

However, proving ones self does not always guarantee male peer acceptance, even when a woman has "handled the situation well". She is uncertain of being accepted by her peers, despite her time on-the-job. A Police Constable of 8 years comments that the organization perpetuates a patriarchal image:

> I think [the department] is very concerned with image and its been reinforced with a number of things that I have seen and there's a lot of old boys club going on. If you're not in the old boys club, they don't give a shit about you, and they'll treat you very badly and it perpetuates the old boys club. The chosen few get promoted and get to go where they want and when they want--they walk on water. No matter what employment equity says or anyone says, [the department] is run by white men who have been around for ages. And they have their image of what a policeman should be and they perpetuate that image. And when they see a young officer with those qualities than they fast track that officer. That officer will have every opportunity and that officer will perpetuate that line—that G pool. Male or female. If she's married to a cop which would then obviously make her competent enough, if a cop thinks she's alright to marry, then she must be okay (PO10).

She noted that the "old boys club" will promote police officers who meet the white male image. Also, she believes that a woman, who is married to a member of the brotherhood, will be judged by the old boys club as being okay, that she must be competent and trustworthy, "if a cop thinks she's alright to marry". Also, if a woman shows dedication to her work by choosing "not to take time off" to have a family, then she is trustworthy and loyal to the organization and police culture. One woman, a Constable of six years, elaborates on her experience on the department's requirement of career dedication and "informal networking":

> Getting into the pecking order was difficult for me because I didn't want to be in the competition of the pecking order. And it was expected and I'm going--wait a minute, sorry can't buy you a beer tonight and become part of the group because I have to go home and relieve my babysitter and feed my

> kids. I was quite disillusioned by the extent of politicking. When I first entered with the support of my support group outside of policing, I promised I would never compromise my femalehood or my personhood. And I found that to some of my co-workers, superiors and supervisors, I had to play the airhead and that discouraged me very much. I've got an I.Q. in the 93rd percentile. So, when you put that up against somebody that got out of grade 12 and got on the police force to carry a big gun and fight in bars...I was quite discouraged that there was so much informal networking--and just give me my pay cheque, I want to go home. If you don't take the opportunity to network that's it or if you network with the wrong individual's, then that's it. I was never part of that 'in crowd'. You can't be when you have to run home to babies. I was the first single mom they hired. (PO12)

She also states that for this reason, she believes that she is not accepted by her male co-workers. To compromise her femalehood or personhood meant obliterating her responsibilities as a single parent in the replacement of career dedication and "becoming one of the boys".

This woman also explains that, she did not want to be identified by the department as a "token female" or as "one of the boys. For this woman and many others, proving oneself to others that they can do the job professionally is important for their self-integrity. As one police officer states:

> I wanted to prove to them only in a professional way. I wasn't going to do it by tokenizing myself. I wasn't going to it by compromising my personhood...Anybody who would say--oh who did you sleep with to get on the job, well excuse me. That came with tokenism. This is why I was offended [with being called a single mom]. Some women will sit and if a comment comes out what I might find offending, they haven't a clue, they weren't offended. I think because I had been doing some studies in the women's area, women's study...I had a heightened awareness that made me go--now wait a minute, what do you mean I make your wife nervous. I want my pay cheque, not your body. I wanted to prove to them in a professional way by knowing my stuff. (PO 02)

A few of the women talked about their experiences of not posing a threat as female officers to male co-workers. It was believed by the women, that if they challenged the system, then they would be viewed as a threat to organization and police culture. A Police Officer of 8 years contends to this fact. She states:

> The organization will accept women so long as they're not a threat to the regime. And if they are a threat to the regime, they will be singled out and their lives will be made miserable. (PO10)

One form of threat in the view of these women is to not challenge the organization and administration on employment equity issues. A Sergeant with twenty years on elaborates:

> A new year approaches when in February, we will be back in the same crap

> again with women in the promotion process. They have done nothing to make it different, no matter how they promise each year when it goes bad. Equity training for persons nominating people for promotion should be mandatory. About 4 days after info was in our newsletter about the committee on harassment policy, a colleague of mine (a Staff Sergeant) came to see me. He is our legal advisor and backs me 100%. He told me that there are a lot of rumblings in the Superintendent level about this harassment thing and that if I want my career to continue in a nice straight line, I should be very careful how I approach the committee. He didn't advise me to quit, just be very positive. For example, never insinuate there have been cases of gender inequality or harassment; we are just trying to prevent any from ever happening. Never say we have a hostile work environment, it is healthy and we want to keep it that way. This was his advice to me.
> (SO 02)

This woman is viewed as a threat by the organization for her views on equity issues. She continues:

> People respect my abilities as a cop. But people who, like my boss, every time I get a new boss he respects my decision making abilities and my abilities as a cop. But don't trust me one bit because they're afraid of what I'm going to say about women's issues. That's the only thing that I'm not trusted about. They think I'm carrying a torch and this tight rope and they're on it, and if they make a waddle or move, then I'm going to kick them off. (SO 02)

Both women were advised by a superior to respect authority which meant to "not rock the boat". One police officer (PO11) expresses her experience with what might be seen by her peers as "challenging the system":

> ...I met the Chief, and this one particular day he came to our platoon and was talking about his mission statement. Shoving it down our throats...So he went on about 20 minutes on this mission statement. I put up my hand and said--I've studied strategic policy...I understand what your saying, but what seems to be missing here is, you have this mission statement but in order to achieve that mission statement everything in the organization has to be consistent with that mission statement and I don't see that as being the case here.
>
> For example, you talk about the community-based policing...and my evaluation is still based on how many tickets I give in a month. That is not consistent; you're not rewarding the type of behaviour you want in order to obtain your mission statement. So what steps are you going to be taking so that everything in the organization is consistent with that? He just about choked. And everyone is staring at me—how dare you stump the Chief. I thought it was a valid question and I wasn't trying to stumble him. I figured he probably would say—well we're revising the evaluation,

> he choked a bit and came off with some comment...I was the only person out of all those platoons that asked a question on a topic he was speaking on. All the others said—when are we getting our 9mm guns, when are we going to get shorts? ... So it turned out that he was quite impressed and pulled my file. Subsequent to that, I ended up having a conversation with him. And I've talked to him about some W's, a volunteer organization, to come to our functions. The evaluation since then has been revamped.

In this police woman's situation, she may be viewed by male peers as not respecting authority figures, like the Chief of police. By asking the Chief an accountability question, she is seen as "rocking the boat". She is not playing the passive, conformist role that is expected of her by the patriarchal organization. Although her question to the Chief of Police embraces the critical pedagogy found in the concept of accountability, her behaviour crosses the line of police conduct and conformity. The patriarchal structure embraces discipline and the "Esprit De Corps", while discouraging individuality. Other police officers in that meeting were concerned with the "tools" to help them in their performance on the job, rather than the "mission statement" that guided their actions in the community.

A Sergeant with twenty years on the job (SO 02) , expresses her experience of being viewed as a threat because she was performing better than her male co-workers. Proving to the organization that one is not a threat to the organization and male culture will demonstrate that women are trustworthy and loyal to the institution of patriarchy. This woman emphasizes:

> The treatment I got when I worked in the Vice unit was unbelievably stressful. I spent over two years going to a psychologist twice a month to help work off the stress I was feeling. (I had become depressed and was having trouble functioning at work.) There was an everyday atmosphere there of taunting and put downs. Talk about a poisoned work environment. Things like:
>
> I was working with a married fellow and everyday the others in the squad would call her[his wife] and tell her where we went for lunch. He would come home to "How come you never take me there?" The jokers in the office thought I would be moved out of the unit. What happened was the member had to retire to prove to his wife that he was not seeing me anymore. He messed around all the time on her anyway, but that was okay with the guys. As a matter of fact, I knew he had been seeing hookers after work, but that too was "A" okay. When he told our boss that he had to change partners, his boss called me in and said that his (the boss's) wife would never let him work with a woman, so he understood perfectly and would reassign me.
>
> I worked my butt off and developed informants in the massage clinic industry. I was eventually able to obtain the only at-trial conviction on a massage clinic bawdy house in the history of the department. No one from the police said--good for you or anything, they just dumped

> complaints about clinics on my desk and told the boss to assign them to the "fucking expert". I came to work one day and found a photo of me with a gunshot between the eyes hanging over my desk. That one, the boss made them take down. I was getting really successful in prosecuting pimps. It drove them crazy that the women on the street would talk to me freely. No wonder, the guys spent more time looking down their blouses and up their skirts to have a conversation.
>
> The guys decided I needed to be discredited, so they began telling lies about me to the women--such as that I couldn't be trusted, that I was just using them to make myself look better, referring to me as "that fucking bitch who can't get laid, and the Queen". Before long, many of them quit talking to me. I confronted the Inspector, and was advised that the whole problem with me not getting along with the guys was my fault. That I was a "libber" and was egging them on. I was told that if I was a guy, I could punch them out, but since I was a woman, I would have to take it. . . .I was told that I treated the women on the street as if they were worth something, and then they thought they could just call for help whenever they liked. I was spending too much time talking to people. I thought this was the whole point of my job. Ratings during my 5 years there were consistently poor, even though I had become recognized as the leading expert on prostitution. The courts, the press, social agencies etc..., called on me for advice, but not a single police officer in my rank or immediately above would consult me at all. Lower ranks came to me all the time, so did the chief/deputies, but I never got credit.

Women were concerned with making mistakes and not fitting into the expectations of the organization; more importantly the failure of not proving oneself to others that "women" can do police work in what has been traditionally described as a male occupation. Throughout the interviews women spoke about the need to be prove themselves as competent police officers. Along with this need to prove themselves, women communicated the need to be accepted by their male co-workers. The participants defined their situational roles as proving oneself to others in order to acquire the trust--acceptance of their male colleagues. Proving oneself, however, is an occupational expectation that is also temporarily limited for policewomen. To be accepted is temporary depending on the level of women's conformity and resistance to the male police culture. As stated by one police officer: "because women are in the minority in the occupation of policing, they do not have a track record", and for this reason women must continually prove oneself throughout their career. The occupational expectation of "proving oneself" meant not being labelled a "token" female. For each policewoman "proving oneself" meant demonstrating her loyalty to the organization and male police culture. Loyalty included respecting organizational values and authority figures which meant that she not challenge the patriarchal structure. Loyalty also meant showing her male co-workers that she is trustworthy and that she will cover-up male co-workers mistakes. For each policewoman "proving oneself" meant the demonstration of her physical and mental competence in doing "male" work to her male colleagues and the organization.

6. Conclusion

Throughout their career of policing, women will try to prove to others that they can be part of the occupational culture and show allegiance to the "Esprit De Corps". Feminist symbolic interactionism identifies those mechanisms that keep women in the lower power relations, that is, the control mechanisms that keep women in the margins of the male culture. The institutional agenda of policing demands that female police officers conform to the male ideology. The institution of policing thrives on a paramilitary structure that disciplines it "soldiers", police officers as men who are assigned by the sovereign to maintain order, protect the weak, and "focus on criminal law enforcement" (Forcese, 1992: 14). When female police officers comply to the shared social codes, they tend to mask the patriarchal tradition that is embedded in policing.

Foucault's surveillance model (1979) is perhaps the most compelling conceptual framework that facilitates comparisons with other disciplinary institutions. His analogy of the prison system as a "carceral network" is replicated in the institution of policing. The male police culture can be described as a carceral agency that marginalizes women's status among male rank-and-file in the institution of policing. Patriarchal values are produced and reproduced in this carceral form; conformity to institutional codes of conduct is mandatory for the reproduction of patriarchal policing.

The institution of policing produces and reproduces resistance by "the male police establishment" to women on patrol (Linn and Price in Blumberg and Niederoffer, 1976: 75). Administrators and patrolmen are seen as culprits in this process because there is little ideological and cultural change that they encourage to welcome policewomen. Empirical evidence, scarce as it is, can be seen in studies that look at hiring and promotional practices in the police force (Adler, 1990; Balkin, 1988; Fletcher, 1995; Hunt, 1990; Martin, 1980, 1996). These studies are reported proof of the negative attitudes that exist toward policewomen. Increasing the hiring numbers for policewomen, paradoxically, will not completely promote change because male behaviour has not changed toward women. Policemen "fear that if too many women enter policing, police service might 'drift into its having a soft social therapy image, blurring right and wrong'" (Linn and Price: 75). Male attitude towards women is a central organization contingency that makes it a struggle for women "getting in" and "staying in" a police career.

Policewomen's struggle for approval from both police "brass" (administrators) and policemen is historically traced to women's first inception into police work. Empirically speaking, this struggle for acceptance has only been documented in a few qualitative studies addressing the experiences of policewomen (Friedman, 1989; Martin, 1980; Mayer, 1993). The nature of the institution of policing embraces a para-militaristic model that "emphasiz[es] discipline and hierarchical control" (Auten in Blumberg and Niederhoffer, 1976: 123). Those individuals recruited to this institution are governed by historically created patriarchal norms and values that are designed to shape "[t]he policeman's 'working personality'...in his constabulary role of the man on the beat"(Skolnick in Blumberg and Niederhoffer, 1976: 81). The social organization of the occupational culture for policing is based on an ideology that upholds the status quo of the "brotherhood". Thus, acceptance is differentially experienced by individuals that differ in race, culture, sexual orientation, and gender characteristics because they are not part of the white male heterosexual group that make up institutional structure. Policewomen can be described as being "in" but not "of" the organization.

Women's self-policing behaviour constantly conforms to male standards. A macho image revolves around male police officers. Slowly the inception of women into patrol duty is transforming this image. However, women are still searching for the respect, of difference in doing police work, by their male peers. Women's bodies and minds are not only under constant scrutiny but have also adapted to male patriarchal beliefs and practices in the occupation of policing. Women's self-policing behaviour is driven by the need to be accepted by the male police culture. To prove ones self is an institutional exercise in gender control. Proving ones self becomes normative among the minority group.

So imagine, if you will, a woman who self proclaims her individuality or personhood? In a male occupational culture that demands conformity of its subjects, a woman to self identify as feminist or lesbian would be suicidal to her career in policing.

The women who enter the occupation of policing carry with them a "personal baggage" that is socially constructed in past and present conditions of gender relations. These women entered policing well versed with the knowledge that policewomen were viewed by male co-workers as tokens in the system. Women have entered policing with the knowledge that police work is a non-traditional occupation for women, in which they must prove to male co-workers and the organization that they are competent in doing "male work." According to Williams (1989:66), the incorporation of women into a male domain has threatened men's "raison d'etre." Women "doing" men's work, and successfully at that, threatens not only men's masculinity but also the significance of the "brotherhood." If the brotherhood is a celebration of male culture, then women's entrance is a violation of that sanctity. In this study, women reported the experience of having to continuously "prove oneself" of their capabilities in doing police work to their colleagues.

One woman discusses her perspective on wearing the uniform:

> When I put on the blue uniform I am a police officer. I'm not a female police officer or a male officer, I am a police officer. When I have that uniform on I represent everyone in uniform. And I go out and help people and sometimes catch the bad guys and that makes me feel good (PO 12)

Women intentionally downplay their gender because of the underlying threat of being labelled a "token" female. A police Constable of 10 years discusses her concern with being labelled a "token female":

> The first step of getting hired, I wanted to be accepted. I wanted to be considered, you know, I didn't want to be a token female who is hired just because she was female. I wanted all my co-workers, the guys to know that I was hired because I deserve to be hired and because I can do the job well. I don't want to be considered some dumb broad, or dumb Barbie doll who became a police officer because she was female. And I don't want to be seen as some female who became a police officer because she wanted to marry a policeman. (PO 15)

Several women expressed that they did not want to be degraded by insults or slander propagated by male police officers. Another woman comments:

> "...policewomen are described by the men as **'Dykes'** or **'Sluts'**. I just laugh it off; very few women can do that. Men are sexist and crude and that won't change" (PO 02).

In the first few years of building their reputation, women are cautious of telling policemen about their personal life. As one police officer of 8 years on notes, "you say as little as possible".

Policewomen under pressure are compelled to accept institutional core perspectives "incorporating values, attitudes, and views" (Salaman, 1974: 15) of the patriarchal culture. From the position of "marginalized status" (Smith, 1990) or "outsider" (Becker, 1963), women are monopolized by male authority that is institutionalized in the structures of: the recruitment process, officer training, on-road training with a coach officer, and through the promotion process. Women are expected to learn a set of core values, beliefs, and ways of acting. Recognition and approval are acquired rewards that are achieved by the ongoing development and application of knowledge. Women's access to this information is gained through their interaction with "informed" others. Policewomen learn appropriate skills in the anticipation of gaining the approval of male co-workers. Favourable reactions or approval of others "validate" (Lemert, 1972: 81) the woman's self conduct, as a police officer. Throughout a woman's career in policing, she will establish and sustain meaningful identities for herself and other women. Wearing the blue uniform and the badge is what many officers refer to as "earned" but not without individual harm. Women have proven their loyalty to an occupation that continues to deny them equal access to opportunities within the rank and file, at the cost of minimizing self-identity.

References

Abella, R. 1984 Equality in Employment Ottawa: Canadian Government.

Adler, Z. 1990 Hill Street Clues: The US Police Record on Promoting Women. *Personnel Management*, 28-33.

Auten, J. 1976 Paramilitary Model of Police and Police Professionalism'. In A. Blumberg and E. Niederhoffer, (Eds.) *The Ambivalent Force: Perspectives on the Police* New York: CBS.

Baker, D., Hodgson, J. and Orban, C. 1991 The Brotherhood: Badge before Race and/or Gender, Unpublished manuscript.

Balkin, J. 1988 Why Policeman Don't Like Policewomen'. *Journal of Police Science and Administration* 16 (1): 29-37.

Ball, S. 1990 *Foucault and Knowledge* London: Routledge.

Bartky, S. 1990 *Femininity and Domination* New York: Routledge.

Becker, H. 1963 *Outsiders N*ew York: Free Press.

Bell, D. 1973 Policewomen: Myths and Reality'. *Journal of Police Science and Administration* 10(1): 112-120.

Berg, B. and Budnick, K. 1986 Defeminization of Women in Law Enforcement: A New Twist in the Traditional Police Personality. *Journal of Police Science and Administration* 14 (4): 314-319.

Blumer, H. 1969 *Symbolic Interactionism*, Englewood Cliffs: Prentice-Hall.

Blumer, H. 1970 What is Wrong With Social Theory. In Filstead, W. (Ed.), *Qualitative Methodology*, Chicago: Rand McNally.

Brewer, J. 1991 Hercules, Hippolyte and the Amazons—or policewomen in the RUC. *British Journal of Sociology* 42 (2): 231-247.

Brown, J. and Campbell, E. 1991 Less Than Equal. *Police Review*, 7 (Winter): 325-333.

Brownmiller, S. 1984 *Femininity*, London: Paladin.

Crawford, B. and Stark-Adamec, C. (1992) Women in Canadian Urban Policing: Why Are they Leaving?. *The Police Chief*, (October): 121-128.

Curtis, J. 1981 *Essentials of Sociology*, Toronto: Rinehart and Winston.

Diamond, I. and Quinby, L. (Eds.) 1988 *Feminism and Foucault.* Boston: Northeastern University Press, 1988.

Enloe, C. 1980 *Police Military and Ethnicity: The Foundation of State Power.* New Brunswick, N.J.: Transaction Books.

Fletcher, C. 1995 *Breaking and Entering.* New York: Harper Collins.

Forcese, D. 1992 *Policing Canadian Society* Scarborough: Prentice-Hall.

Foucault, M. 1979 *Discipline and Punish*, New York: Vintage Books.

Foucault, M. (Ed.) 1980 *Power/Knowledge*, Great Britain: Harvester Press.

French, M. 1985 *Beyond Power*, New York: Ballantine Books.

Friedman, T. 1989 *The Experience of Being A Female Police Officer*, Ann Arbor: Bell and Howell Company.

Gelsthorpe, L. and Morris, A. 1990 *Feminist Perspectives in Criminology*, Philadelphia: Open University Press, 1990.

Glaser, B. and Strauss, A. 1967 *The Discovery of Grounded Theory*, Chicago: Aldine.

Goffman, E. 1959 *The Presentation of Self in Everyday Life*, New York: Double Day Anchor.

Griffiths, C., Klein, J. and Verdun-Jones, S. 1990 *Criminal Justice in Canada: An Introductory Text*, Toronto: Butterworths.

Griffiths, C. and Verdun-Jones, S. 1989 *Canadian Criminal Justice*, Toronto:

Butterworths.

Krause, E. 1971 *The Sociology of Occupations*, Boston: Little Brown and Company.

Hall, S., Critcher, C., Jefferson, T., Clarke, J. and Roberts, B. 1978 *Policing the Crisis*, London: the Macmillan Press.

Hagen, J. 1985 Toward a Structural Theory of Crime, Race, and Gender: The Canadian Case, *Crime and Delinquency*, 31(1): 129-146.

Heidensohn, F. 1992 *Women in Control* New York: Oxford University Press.

Heyl, B. 1977 The Madam As Teacher: The Training of House Prostitutes. *Social Problems*, 24 (June): 545:555.

Hodgson, J. 1993 *Police-Community Relations*, Unpublished PhD Dissertation, Toronto: York University.

Hopper, M. 1977 Becoming a Policeman. *Urban Life* 6 (July) 2: 149-169.

Hunt, J. 1990 The Logic of Sexism Among Police *Women and Criminal Justice*, 1 (2):3-30.

Hughes, E. 1958 *Men and Their Work* Glencoe: Free Press.

Kanter, R. 1977 *Men and Women of the Corporation*, New York: Basic Books.

Kanter, R. (1979) Some Effects of proportions on group life: Skewed sex rations and responses to token women *American Journal of Sociology*, 82 (5): 965-990.

Lemert, E. 1972 *Human Deviance Social Problems and Social Control*, Englewood Cliffs: Prentice-Hall.

Linden, R. 1984 *Women in Policing: A Study of the Vancouver Police Department*, Ottawa: Ministry of the Solicitor General.

Linden, R. 1984 *Women in Policing: A Study of Lower Mainland R.C.M.P. Detachments*, Ottawa: Ministry of the Solicitor General.

Linden, R. and Minch, C. 1982 *Women in Policing: A Review*, Winnipeg: Institution of Social Research.

Lofland, J. and Loffland, L. 1984 *Analyzing Social Settings: A Guide to Qualitative Observations and Analysis*, California: Wadsworth.

Low, P. 1991 Are Women that Different? *Police Review*, 7 (Spring): 15-19.

Lunneborg, P. 1989 *Women Police Officers: Current Career Profile*, Springfield: Thomas.

Mackie, M. 1991 *Gender Relations in Canada: Further Explorations*, Toronto: Butterworths.

Martin, L. 1993 Women Workers in a Masculine Domain: Jobs and Gender in a Yukon Mine. *Work in the Canadian Context* Canada.

Martin, S. 1989 Women on the Move?: A Report on the Status of Women in Policing, *Women and Criminal Justice*, 1 (1): 21-40.

Martin, S. 1980 *Breaking and Entering: Policewomen on Patrol*, California: University of California Press, 1980.

Martin, S., 1978 Sexual Politics in the Workplace: The Interactional World of Policewomen. *Symbolic Interaction* 1 (2):4-60.

Martin, S. and Jurik, N. 1996 *Doing Justice, Doing Gender*, California: Sage Publications.

Mayer, C. 1993 *Changes in the Role-Definition of Female Police Officers*, Ann Arbor: Bell and Howell Company.

Mackinnon, C. 1987 *Feminism Unmodified*, Cambridge: Harvard University Press.

McCall, L. 1992 Does Gender Fit? Bourdieu, feminism, and conceptions of social order. *Theory and Society*, 21 (6): 837-867.

Milgram, S. 1969 *Obedience to Authority: An Experimental View*, New York: Harper and Row.

Miller, P. 1987 *Domination and Power*, New York: Routledge.

Nicholson, L. (Ed.) 1990 *Feminism and Postmodernism* New York: Routledge.

Rhodes, C. 1969 *Authority in a Changing Society*, London: Anchor Press.

Salaman, G. 1974 *Community and Occupation*, London: Cambridge University Press.

Schaef, A. 1985 *Women's Reality*, New York: Harper and Row.

Schur, E. 1984 *Labelling Women Deviant*, Philadelphia: Temple University Press.

Skolnick, J. 1976 A Sketch of the Policeman's Working Personality. In A. Blumberg and E. Niederhoffer (Eds.) *The Ambivalent Force: Perspectives on the Police*, New York: Holt, Rinehart and Winston.

Smith, D. 1990 *The Conceptual Practices of Power*, Toronto: University of Toronto Press, 1990.

Smith, D. 1987 *The Everyday World as Problematic: A Feminist Sociology*, Toronto: University of Toronto Press.

Spradley, J. 1980 *Participant Observation*, New York: Holt, Rinehart and Winston.

Strauss, A. 1987 *Qualitative Analysis for Social Scientists*, New York: Cambridge University.

Van Maanen, J. 1976 Observations on the Making of Policemen. In A. Blumberg and E. Niederhoffer (Eds.) *The Ambivalent Force: Perspectives on the Police*, New York: Holt, Rinehart and Winston.

Visano, L. 1987 *This Idle Trade*, Concord: VitaSana Books.

Walker, G. 1995 Social Mobilization in the City's Countryside: Rural Toronto Fights Waste Dump. *Journal of Rural Studies*, 11(3): 243-254.

Walker, S. 1993 *The Status of Women in Canadian Policing:1993*, Ottawa: Solicitor General.

Wasquant, L. 1993 From Ideology to Symbolic Violence Culture, Class, and Consciousness in Marx and Bourdieu. *International Journal of Contemporary Sociology*, 30 (2): 125-141.

Williams, C., 1989 *Gender Differences at Work: Women and Men in Nontraditional Occupations*, California: University of California Press.

Zimbardo, P. 1970 The Human Choice: Individuation, Reason and Order Versus Deindividuation, Impulse, and Chaos. In W. Arnold and D. Levine (Eds.), *Nebraska Symposium on Motivation*, Lincoln: University of Nebraska Press.

PART C

COURTS

10. *Malleus Maleficarum Africanus:* The Criminalization of African Canadians and "Due Process" as a Property of Whiteness

Tamari Kitossa

1. Introduction

Virtually every text which concerns itself with questions of race, crime and justice includes a disclaimer that: "…at some times some 'black' young people appear to be disproportionately involved in particular types of crime, there is little hard evidence to indicate that, in general, 'black' young people are more prone to involvement in persistent and serious offending than white young people." Though broadly correct, rather than explaining why the author is about to ignore the subject, this disclaimer almost invariably serves as the springboard from which s/he dives head-first into it…Given the paucity of empirical evidence we might well ask why, since the early 1980's, so many criminologists, journalists and politicians have concerned themselves with these issues at all. But, of course, the debate is not, first and foremost, about criminological 'facts', but about political anxieties (Pitts, 1993, 96-7).

Construct an internal enemy, as both focus and diversion. Pathologize the enemy in scholarly and popular mediums; recycle, for example, scientific racism and the mythos of racial superiority in order to naturalize the pathology. Criminalize the enemy. Then prepare, budget for and rationalize the building of holding arenas for the enemy – especially its males and absolutely its children (Morrison, 1995, 238).

In my encounters with European Canadian men that became confrontational, I have been threatened and actually had the police called on me. These were not problems that could not have been resolved easily; but I suspect their impatience with my refusal to demonstrate the appropriate reflexes of subordination reinforced their *a priori* belief that, a) I was in the wrong and b) the State would protect their presumed superior rights by ruling in their favour. These interactions indicate that my blackness connotes guilt, their whiteness innocence and that a symbiosis exists between the criminal justice system and the "court of public opinion" in which the centrality of whiteness is assumed. Consequently hereafter in the following discussion of race and crime, the "court of public opinion" will be referred to as the *court of "White" public opinion*, because it is a locus for deeply held beliefs that are articulated, retrieved and practiced by operatives of the criminal justice system.

I am aware of the vast sociological distinction between the criminal justice system and the *court of "White" public opinion*, but there is a point of connection that is so obvious it has not received adequate attention for its implications on the social construction of criminal identities and the mal/distribution of justice relative to the criminalization of people of African descent and "due process" as a property of whiteness. Edwin Sutherland's observation that "behind the behavior of the courts is public opinion" (Sutherland, 1955, 4) can be extrapolated to assert that since the operatives of the criminal justice system are members of society, and are themselves subject to the orienting ideologies of capitalist reality, their reactions and rulings are sensitive to "public opinion". Now in a society in which racism and other forms of exclusion are embedded and encoded into its ideological fabric, daily consciousness and institutional practices will reproduce racism in public and private life. In the arena of the social construction of crime, that the operatives of the criminal justice system are overwhelmingly of European descent, their consciousness of crime is shaped by Eurocentric Canadian cultures prevailing assumption and appropriation of specific rights as the property of whiteness. In the racial articulation of crime and "due process", these facts of cultural, private and public life play prominent roles in constituting the criminal justice system and the civic *court of "White" public opinion* as a unified panoptic fortress that envisions blackness as evil intentioned and whiteness as doubtfully associated with criminality. This has implications for how race informs conceptions of criminal identities and shapes the administration of justice.

2. Whiteness and "Due Process"

When Paul Bernardo was arrested and later convicted for killing Justin French and Leslie Mahafie, as an African Canadian man, I wondered why the expression of the public's 'moral indignation' was absent a 'panic' that culminated in an irrational fear and suspicion of *all* "White" men? And, related to this, why didn't the "denunciation" of Bernardo in the "court of public opinion" result in a 'ritual destruction' of the collective 'virtual' "White" male image? What was the connection between the absence of panic and the respect for "due process" given this "White" man and others like him? The police in fact suspected Bernardo was the famed "Scarborough rapist" who raped at least 14 women between 1987 and 1991. They had his DNA in cold storage for two years and refused to release his police sketch for as long a time. There was of course the danger posed to women who were neither "served or protected" by the suppression of Bernardo's police sketch, but also, because Bernardo remained at large for so long a period of time, I wondered whether "White" men, particularly those with blond hair, felt and lived with the nagging sensation that based on shared phenotypical traits with Bernardo they were implicated in his crimes. During the time the "Scarborough rapist" was at large, were "White" men insecure in the knowledge that they were under suspicion and could be reported or apprehended by "mistaken identity"? Compared to the 'panic' and "numerous" sightings of the assailants at the Just Desserts restaurant who killed Georgina Leimonis, was there ever a reported case of "mistaken identity" in Bernardo's case? We know now that in the Just Desserts case O'neil Grant was wrongfully implicated in Leimonis's murder.

The relationship to "due process", the absence of collective character assassinations through ritual destruction and racial preference is evident, *a priori*, in *all* cases of comparative analysis between so-called "Black" and "White" crime. When Kevin McVeigh, the Oklahoma City bombing suspect was charged with domestic terrorism, one Toronto newspaper asked: "Is this the face of a killer?" Similarly, when Michael Briere, a software programmer, was arrested for killing ten year old Holly Jones, the press belatedly posted his picture at the behest of Police Chief Julian Fantino, one paper queried: "could he be Holly Jones's killer?" In 2002, Toronto's Mayor, Mel Lastman, helped to scuttle Toronto's hopes for hosting the 2008 Olympic summer games with the "off the cuff" remark that as a member of that city's Olympic delegation that was to visit Africa he feared being boiled for dinner by the "natives". This image could be invoked as a credible reaction/joke because it has an *a priori* history in the "White" collective imagination. The myth of Tarzan rescuing hapless European explorers from the kettles of the cannibalistic/criminal natives is clearly evident here. Certainly, cannibalism in the "White" psyche does not conjure an image of Jeffrey Dahmer, a "White" blond hair blue eyed male, selectively dining on his cornucopia of harvested "Black" and "Brown" flesh: after all, is not Jesus depicted as a "White" blond hair blue male? Against what prior realm of self-implicating knowledge in the European psyche and court of "public opinion" is such a cannibalistic act to be judged? Eurocentric culture in Canada contains no condition in which "White" collective and individual identity and symbols of whiteness can carry stigmatic connotations. Regardless of ethnic and linguistic distinctions, as the supra ordinate social group, whose shared pan-cultural dynamics establish and depend on an Other-oriented racial ontology, whiteness establishes a threshold for a host of assumptions and property rights that are exclusive (Harris, 1993, 1707). Individualism, the assumption of non-criminality and "due process" are three such *de facto* rights that are appropriated as the cultural property of European Canadians. These racially specific appropriations shape differential racial outcomes in the criminal justice system and the *court of "White" public opinion*.

3. *Malleus Malificarum Africanus*

In the criminal justice system and the *court of "White" public opinion*, the treatment accorded European Canadian males who commit crime differs markedly from that meted out when African Canadian males are implicated in a criminal act (Lee, 1995, 61). For historical reasons relevant to European manichean racial ontology, European enslavement of Africans and the normative foundations of the legal system that ensured the racial distinctiveness of the slave condition and bequeathed us its legacy, there is an *a priori* assumption that African males accused of crime are guilty and those who have not are criminals in waiting. In addition to the historicity of law and race, the racially articulated assumption of criminality and guilt fall within the sociological framework of a publicly announced curse: "degradation ceremonies" whose "affective behavioural paradigm" are the aversion, social distancing and "ritual destruction" of the persons(s) being denounced (Garfinkel, 1975). The assumed *a priori* criminogenicity* and resulting denial of "due process" relative to African Canadians and other world majority people, is a racial expectancy embedded in whiteness that shapes the criminal justice system and *court of "White" public opinion's* ideal image of the "criminal".

In *The Rich Get Richer and the Poor Get Prison*, Jeffrey Reiman asks his readers to "Think of a crime, any crime. Picture the first 'crime' that comes to your mind. What do you see?" Reiman suggests that if you are like him, violent interpersonal crime: murder, physical and sexual assault and robberies come to mind. Structurally excluded from thought are the violent outcome from the premeditated decisions of business executives to make and sell products known to be dangerous or shoddy (ie., Ford Pinto), dump toxic waste or ignore occupational health and safety regulations. Since, public images of crime also carry explicit images of perpetrators, imagine what the perpetrator of "street crime" as opposed to "suite crime" looks like. Reiman suggests that "my hunch is that you – like me, like almost anyone in America – picture a young, tough, lower-class male when the thought of crime first pops into your head" (Reiman, 1990, 50).

Although Reiman is a sharp witted criminologist who does address race, he problematically subsumes race to class. As a result, his central statement does note connote the implications of the racism in the in the criminal justice system and the *court of "White" public opinion's* construction of crime. Ray Surette however recognizes the dialogic relation between racism, images of criminality and the denial of "due process":

> Many crimes are reported without any description of the perpetrator and the public is left to fill in the image...Since most crime news is about violent interpersonal crime, the image that is filled in is that of the faceless predator...[T]he public's image of criminals reflected the stereotypical street criminal – a young, unemployed, black male. (Surette, 1992, 64)

Given that we live in a society that itself generates anxiety and fear from the violence of capitalist social relations, anxiety and fear of violence at the hands of strangers play important roles in generating consensus and social solidarity without challenging the social order that our lives and livelihoods depend. But, if you are a reader of European descent, reflect for a moment on the most heinous mass murderers and rapists in contemporary memory and you may uncomfortably arrive at an image of Sam Berkowitz, Paul Bernardo, Michael Brier, Ted Bundy, Jeffrey Dahmer, John Wayne Gacy Jr., Clifford Olson, Marc Lepine, Robert Pickton and more recently Dennis Rader (suspected BTK). Your discomfort may rise further if you lived in a world where, because of the colour of your skin, you or your brothers or fathers were held accountable and suspect for the behaviour of these men only because like you, they are "White". In fact, excluding this hypothetical situation I

---

* By culture or genetics, inherently predisposed to commit crime.

just described, you may be uncomfortable with whiteness being associated with criminality because this image is not part of the White psychological lexicon.

Where "White" males are the perpetrators of heinous crimes, where is the chorus of "who commits more crime" from the character assassins such as conservatice criminologists, the news media, police chiefs (ie., Julian Fantino), police union representatives (ie., Art Lymer[1] and Gregg Bromell) and an assortment of politicians? Along with the deafening silence that will surely answer this question, to what can we attribute the fear of young men of African descent who, unlike some of their White peers who have gleefully gunned down their teachers and classmates? We can of course implicate the news media, police and politicians for the misplaced assocation between crime and men of African descent. Racism of any form however is not simply the product of indoctrination: audiences, society's managers and voters are not *tabula rasae*. The image of the Black criminal is an important feature of "White" popular culture and it does important work there in the resolution of everyday/everynight contradictions and problematics. In what may be called the *empirics of belief*, a situation in which *a priori* unsubstantiatable belief constitutes its own veracity, the image of African Canadian men as criminals strikes a note of resonance because it is part of a worldview, a set of assumptions and beliefs that are held to be true by both the ruling elites and subordinate classes of Eurocentric Canadian culture.

The relationship to anxieties about crime and the racial articulations of "due process" appear to reflect existential anxieties of anomic social conditions mapped onto racially articulated social relations. Indeed, in a white supremacist society that tacitly discourages White-on-White violence, and, as part of the 'wage of whiteness' sanctions passive aggressive behaviour toward people of African descent, the cultural denial of "due process" inherent in the public 'denunciation' of so-called "Black" crime articulates itself through an impassioned public outcry. Whereas the crimes of "White" men symbolize the general ills of social violation and inspire approbation that is directed at no social group in particular, like Edvard Munch's haunting image of a primal existential cry, so-called "Black" crime becomes a lightening rod for the release of pent-up reflexes of hatred and psychic aggression equal to acceptance of the status quo and its rules of order.

4. The expectation of African criminality

The foregoing discussion asserts that the application of "due process" and related racist images of criminality in the criminal justice system and the *court of "White" public opinion* are an everyday feature of Canadian and US popular cultural landscape. The consequence of this everyday racism has a significant impact on the *belief* that men of African descent are criminogenic and are therefore expected to commit crime. This criminalizing *empiric of belief* in African criminality has profound implications for all levels of the criminal justice system: policing, jury selection/verdicts and sentencing and the way the public perceives criminal identities. For example, the expectation that men of African descent are likely perpetrators of violent crime lent credibility to false accusations laid by Susan Smith and Charles Stuart: both of whom were European Americans who killed their loved ones. The credibility of these false accusations fall within the scope of "racial profiling": a process in which police and others act on the (institutionally validated) belief that men of African descent are "reasonably suspect" and members of civil society believe the imputation of criminality toward men of African descent is justifiable. In essence, the *court of "White" public opinion* and the operatives of the criminal justice system expect that African people are likely to commit crime.

The dependency and mutually referencing relationship between law-and-order politicians and the news media play a prominent role in shaping this expectancy. On the front pages of newspapers and at the top of newscasts in urban Canada and the US, one can expect reports of "Black" crime and disproportionate incarceration. This quality of expectedness lead Michael Moore to comment in *Stupid White Men*, that

> When I turn on the news each night, what do I see again and again? Black men alleged to be killing, mugging, stabbing, gangbanging, looting, rioting selling drugs, pimping, ho-ing, having too many babies, fatherless, motherless, Godless, penniless. "the suspect is described as a black male. The suspect is described as a black male...THE SUSPECT IS DESCRIBED AS A BLACK MALE..." No matter what city I'm in, the news is always the same, the suspect is always the same unidentified black male. I'm in Atlantic tonight, and I swear the police sketch of the black male suspect on TV looks just like the black maloe suspect I saw on the news last night in Denver and the night before in L.A. In every sketch he's frowning, he's menacing – and he's wearing the same knit cap! Is it possible that it's the same guy committing every crime in America?

Susan Smith and Charles Stuart believed that the rest of "White" America would believe them. Here in Canada, when the Metro Toronto Police force issued a public alert for Mohammed Kassim on May 14 2004 for killing his wife and kidnapping their three year old son, the laws of physics were bent as Kassim was reportedly *seen* between Windsor and Toronto – simultaneously! Fortunately Kassim was apprehended on the 16th, thus disabling the frenzy of a 'panic' that could have jeopardized the lives of many innocent African Canadian men between Windsor and Toronto who could have been 'mistakenly' apprehended and possibly abused. That 'mistaken identity' regularly occurs as a feature of African Canadian and American life, Dorothy Roberts comments that it "is a concrete manifestation of the deeply ingrained racial identification of crime in the white psyche. The unconscious association between blacks and crime is so powerful that it supersedes reality: it predisposes whites to literally see black people as criminals" (Roberts, 1954, 1992-1993).

Irrespective of the idea championed by politicians and police officials that African Canadian men *commit more crime* than say European Canadian men is more fantasy than fact, it is nonetheless expected and experienced as real in the *court of*

"White" public opinion. As a result, the salience of fear of crime equates to expectedness and fear of men of African descent as violent criminals. For example, a 1993 University of Pennsylvania study found that many European Americans are likely to associate pictures of African Americans with violent crimes, and even in cases where reported crimes were not committed by African Americans, they believed the perpetrator to be an African American male. So influential is this fear and expectedness that people of European descent even invert reality. As was the case with Rodney King being pummelled by four LAPD officers, Sheri Lynn Johnson found that "[W]hite witnesses expect to see black as criminals. This expectation is so strong that whites may observe an interracial scene in which a white person is the aggressor, yet remember the black person as the aggressor" (Johnson, 1984, 950-951; Butler, 1993).

The criminalization of African Canadians and Americans, particularly the males, constitute the *Malleus Maleficarum Africanus*: a process in which state and civil society are unified in a panoptic management and surveillance of African existence. This process has vast implications for racial bias in the mis/administration of justice. For example, studies in the US have shown that "White" people, as police and civilians, are more likely to misidentify a perpetrator who does not share their racial characteristics (Ibid; Johnson, 1985, 1611). Racial difference is a material factor in police decisions to make stops and searches, the sentencing decisions of judges, and the decision-making of "White" juries to pronounce guilty verdicts for African Americans that in similar cases they exonerate European Americans defendants.[2] As a result of this culturally engrained cultural bias, Sherri Lynn Johnson found that in mock jury studies the race of the defendant "significantly and directly affects the determination of guilt" (Johnson, 1984, 1626). Of course, the determination of guilt is strongly correlated to whether a Black defendant has victimized a White plaintiff. In the US, the death penalty is disproportionately handed down to African Americans, most frequently in former slave holding states and most often when the victim is European American (Baker, 1987). And, although Canada abolished its death penalty in 1979, indicating that racial expectancy played a part in the normative foundation of the criminal justice system here, as early as 1868 Sir John A. Macdonald wrote in a personal correspondence that Canada retained the death penalty because African Canadian men were "prone to felonious assaults on White women" (as cited in Backhouse, 1991, 98).

In 1996, I participated in a televised community cable program in which the role of the news media in perpetuating anti-African racism was discussed. I asked one of the co-panelists, a "White" male professor of media studies, if he had any personal fears for his safety and liberty during the time the "Scarborough" rapist was at large. He admitted he did not give any thought to his safety as a consequence of being implicated by mistaken identity. What a luxury! It seemed that as a "White" man he was immune from the insecurity and uneasy feelings created by the white supremacist panoptic gaze that criminalizes *all* African men for the actions of a few. This is a gaze that projects criminality onto African men and holds African people in subjection and subject to a "White" "punishing and punishable universality" of "'White" normalizing judgment: the *Malleus Malificarum Africanus*. Through these media/ted events whiteness forms a panoptic fortress, an "uninterrupted play of calculated gazes" that discipline and punish "Black" bodies, while reasserting without direct consciousness the privileged location of whiteness (see Foucault, *Discipline and Punish*, 178). In this sense, there is an irrational transposition from judging an individual to judging a collective on the basis of what their public image is made to represent. The crime of one African male when it becomes widely known in the *court of "White" public opinion* becomes the basis for mass character assassinations in the public domain. It subjects individual African men to collective punishment and censure that ranges from social distance, denial of employment and housing, police harassment and questionable killings.

The relationship between the ideas of *race* and *crime*, are not simply abstractions, but articulations of what is conceived as *crime*, who and what groups are perceived as *criminal*, what treatment is experienced by those who are stigmatized, and what opportunities are made unavailable to those who are imagined to be racially *criminogenic* (Dee Cook, 1993; Pitts, 1993). The implications for the entire society are vast, for it shapes collective mood and social solidarity, public policy, personal behaviour, and attitudes towards entire communities whose "virtual identities" become signs of criminality. Race, thus, plays a central role in the social construction of crime and informs social responses to those racial groups that are criminalized.

5. Racial expectancy and law as a Eurocentric enterprise

In spite of evidence to the contrary, it is commonly believed that inasmuch as the criminal justice is above the influence of phenomenon of racial expectancy, so too is law. In that law in a context of European domination is an institution and part of an ideological framework that sustains whiteness, it is "part of a broader cultural endeavor that attempts to promote European values and interests at the expense of all others" (Nunn, 1997, 328). The neutrality of law therefore is an ideology, a fiction in a culture deeply committed to racism (and class, gender, homophobia and other exclusions) that is deeply implicated in the manufacture of racial expectancy as a feature of its normative foundation. To appreciate this fact, one must recognize that in large measure, the vast majority of Africans that were part of the "New World" adventure were enslaved by Europeans. Whether economics or racism were the essential motivating factors in the forced patriation of African people is debatable; but what is not, is that slavery was a socio-cultural and economic enterprise in which law was the principal instrument that constructed the African person as chattel and the European as deserving of "due process" as property right.

As a system of total control, slavery established in law and reinforced the cultural a priori belief in Eurocentric culture that African people were inherently criminal. On one hand slavery was a criminalizing institution that existentially determined that any existence outside the domains of legally determined servitude was abnormal; and on the other hand, slavery was a criminogenic institution because it imposed conditions of material destitution and promoted moral depravity through the destruction of self-regulating institutions such as families and kin relations. The former and latter are related but not synonymous. In the case of the latter slavery led to non-political acts of crimes – some enslaved Africans committed crime for not for gain, but for survival. Frederick Douglass, one of the great American Abolitionists, who himself had committed one of the cardinal sins of slavery – running away – wrote:

> I suffered much from hunger, but much more from cold. In hottest summer and coldest winter, I was kept almost naked – no shoes, no stockings, no jacket, no trousers, nothing on but a course tow linen shirt, reaching only to my knees. I had no bed. I must have perished with cold, but that, the coldest nights, I used to steal a bag which was used for carrying corn meal. I would crawl into this bag, and there sleep on the cold, damp, clay floor, with my head in and feet out. My feet have been so cracked with the frost that the pen with which I am writing might be laid in the gashes. (Frederick, 1995, 26).

Based on Douglass's account, it is likely that in spite of censure, necessity drove countless other men, women and children to steal for survival. Slavery as well, in promoting drinking and carousing at Christmas as a way of tension release and in undermining moral socialization in family life, undermined the articulation of community standards (Frederick, 1968, 86).

While slavery created material conditions for the violation of property that contributed to the myth of "Black" crime, the more important elements of this myth were generated by the legal philosophy of chattel slavery itself. In this regard, what should be understood as important about slavery was that the resistance of African people brought the material and legal philosophy of a system of brutal exploitation into stark relief. In other words, because resistance to slavery and its precepts were illegal and required policing and control, therein lies one aspect of the criminalization of African existence itself. In this context there were a multitude of acts motivated by the politicization of resistance that constituted criminality under the Slave and later Black codes. For instance, reading and the pursuit of knowledge were regarded as dangerous criminal offences because they threatened to undermine the slave order through the power of knowledge. Feigning ignorance, stupidity, working slowly and damaging other *property* besides themselves were political, but also criminalized acts of resistance.

Under slavery, Africans did not have a *selfhood* that was recognized in law as such. Injuring themselves as acts of resistance was punishable because it was considered damaging *property*. Suicide and infanticide were to be counted in this latter example. Africans, either too proud to be enslaved or too unwilling to face a life-time of brutality, used suicide and infanticide as powerful political and psychological acts that rejected "White" domination. Such actions sought to impose a burdensome cost on the master by asserting both self-determination and destroying his, or in some cases her, investment in their property. For those Africans, who were unsuccessful in killing themselves or their children, or were discovered in planning suicide and infanticide, brutal beatings often to death were the consequences for such law breaking. To make it clear to slaves that their lives were only worth living when in service to their masters, they were killed to show their fellows that the power over their own lives did not belong to them. The ambiguity and paradox of property, maiming, killing or damaging property were mental contortions of the "White" mind in which the slave codes saw no contradiction. Since any act of self-defiance and self-determination of chattel property were ideologically precluded, one could no more imagine or permit a horse or mule exercising self-determination than a chattel slave.

Under these brutal conditions, running away, a greater act of theft than stealing food or clothing, was a crime of the highest magnitude punishable by maiming, whippings, and in some instances death. The work of Winthrop Jordan clearly indicates that the response to runaways was clearly gendered:

> The lines between public and private punishment of offending slaves was of course by no means distinct. Until 1722, slaveholders in South Carolina were required, under penalty of law, to have any of their female slaves running away for the fourth time "severely whipped...branded on the left cheek with the letter R, and her left ear cut off." In that colony in 1732 a man named Charles Jones met resistance from a runaway Negro [male] and killed him on the spot; Jones thereupon dutifully went to inform a justice of the peace what he had one and was instructed to cut off the Negro's head and stick it up on a pole at the crossroads. (Jordan, 1977, 112-13)

"Running away" was considered particularly egregious not merely because it represented "stealing one's self" (McIntyre, 1993, 168), thereby depriving one's master of their property, but more importantly, it was associated with rebellions and plots to incite freedom through acts of violence. Slave societies everywhere in the Americas lived schizophrenically: exultant at the multiform benefits of violent exploitation of African (and Aboriginal) peoples, yet living in thinly disguised fear of mass annihilation at the hands of their slaves. (James, 1985; Jordan, 1977, 111)

"Freedom," as Winthrop Jordan put it, "wore the red cap of bloody rebellion, and the colonists [in early America] never doubted for a moment that their slaves might suddenly clap it on their heads" (Jordan, 1977, 111). Certainly, Thomas Jefferson did not take this reality for granted. Anticipating Abraham Lincoln, Jefferson states:

> Deep rooted prejudices entertained by the whites; ten thousand recollections, by the blacks, of the injuries they sustained; new provocations; the real distinctions which nature has made; and many other circumstances, will divide us into parties, and produce convulsions which will probably never end but in the extermination of the one or the other race. (Martinot, 2003, 4)

Since clearly the "White" population had to ensure its survival and continued domination, under these conditions life brought forward the criminalization of African people and an atmosphere of panoptic surveillance, which today we call "racial profiling". Curiously, in spite of its long history and diffusion throughout "White" society, "racial profiling" is denied by the police and the bulk of a "White" society who benefit from its practice. Just as it was during slavery, today there is an equal hold-over of "White" suspicion that arises when more than one African male is congregating in public places. Such a presence of undesirable congregation not only signals that African bodies can be 'out of place', but is embedded in a prior history of fear and anxiety that is, at this point, merely an unconscious "White" reflex. It was, however, during slavery and just as prominently after it, a profound moment of compressed anxiety channeled through the "White" panoptic gaze: "white policing of black populations became an integral component of each stage of white racial dominance of blacks. As we would expect, the stage of slavery necessitated the first system of white policing of black populations" (Hawkins and Thomas, 1991). This criminalizing gaze solidified whiteness and the object status of African men and women as criminal by the very nature of slavery as a social system. It was at once political and psychological in nature: it modified class conflict among Europeans, empowered the "White" poor, and established a basis for "White" mental security in the face of the anxieties generated by the realities of African resistance, (Martinot, 2003).

In the contemporary context of crime committed by African males in particular, the law responds as though such violations are "part of an ongoing insurrection" (Hacker, 1997, 242). The heavy-handedness of the so-called war on drugs is but one example of how the law in Canada and the US is used to differentially and disproportionately punish men and women of African descent, (Berndt, 2003; *Report of the Commission on Systemic Racism in the Ontario Criminal Justice System* 1995). This distinctiveness and disproportionality, essentially entitlements that are appropriated as white property, draws from prior racial preferential treatments. Most notable of which was until 1834 in Canada and 1865 in the US, free and manumitted Africans could be resold into slavery for even miniscule violations such as being out past curfew without permission (McIntyre, 1993; Roberts, *supra* note 9, at 1955). Very troubling in the US, given the dramatic overrepresentation of African Americans, is that not only was slavery conditionally abolished, the 13th amendment establishes the basis for the continuity of slavery through incarceration:

> Neither slavery nor involuntary servitude, *except as a punishment for crime whereof the party shall have been duly convicted*, shall exist within the United States, or any place subject to their jurisdiction" [italics added][3]

Law then as a Eurocentric enterprise reflects bourgeois society's ideological assumptions about *who* is criminal, and therefore dangerous, presents a hegemonic and stereotyped image of *the* "criminal": poor, "Black", "Brown", and "Red", rather than "White", male, and wealthy (Reiman, 1990; Visano, 2001; Visano 1998).

Visano points out that with respect to racial inequality, the unequal character of bourgeois legal framework is self-deceptively cloaked to those who believe and benefit from it, because in the "institutional practices and discourses" that "allows particular understandings of whiteness to materialize":

> A commonsense nature of whiteness saturates discourses of law. Consequently, in everyday law talk, the whiteness of ones skin is equated with the naturalness of authority. As law legitimates whiteness, "the public" is led to believe in the suspicious propensities of "non-whites". Once the connections of criminality and colour are "naturally" made, then it seems to follow that whites should criminalize "others" (Visano, 2001, 3).

Law does not simply stand as an abstraction that mysteriously shapes the public image of the criminal as usually an African male; it achieves this end within the framework of culture, history, race, political economy, and media/ted reality. Thus,

> Not only is race used in identifying criminals, it is also used in defining crime. In other words, race does more than predict a person's propensity for committing neutrally-defined offenses. Race is built into the normative foundation of the criminal law. Race becomes part of society's determination of which conduct to define as criminal. Crime is actually constructed according to race. (Roberts, 1993, as cited in Nunn, 1997, fn 195).

To the construction of crime according to race, one must add class and gender, because it is in their intersection within the frameworks I have just mentioned that the image of the "typical" criminal – "Black", young, and male – arises.

Critical to the contemporary reality of law is that it shapes what constitutes crime in the popular imagination and at the same shapes as much as it responds to the publics ideal image of the criminal. While crime is ubiquitous in society and will take the form of the contravention of any law, the popular conception of "crime" is by definition interpersonal, violent, and thus violating of individual liberty and security (Boskin, 1980, 144; Hall et al., 1979, 68). This definition of crime rests on a discourse that vividly articulates the alluring supposition of an imagined community of "insiders/normals" who are threatened by the ubiquitous presence of dangerous "outsiders/deviants" who exist in their very midst. This definition of crime focuses less on the social costs of crime, but more on the benefits of generating a shared belief in a common threat to a common existence (Mead, 1918, 591). In short a Folk Devil (Hall et al., 1979, 161). Law, as Visano suggests, in addition to its taken-for-granted and powerful coercive component, is "construed as a set of spectacular and performative moments that display a contrived consensus" (Visano, 2001, 1). But, as to whether law consecrates or fails to consecrate consensus is contingent on the representation and meaning of the nature of certain crimes and the attendant display of punishment (Garfinkel, 1975). Certainly, the image of white collar criminals such as Ivan Boesky, Michael Milken, Nick Leeson, or the masterminds of the Savings and Loan scandal in the USA, hardly plays on emotional sentiments and feelings of in/security. Rather, violent interpersonal crimes, like those in the O.J. Simpson trial/circus, the Central Park jogger case (who like the Scotsboro Nine have now been exonerated), or even the trial of the Just Desserts suspects in Toronto, are spectacles around which the publicity of law promotes consensus and social solidarity against violent crime. O.J. Simpson notwithstanding, the crimes of the rich are too far removed from visibility, too protected by the bourgeois legal apparatus, and are granted too much deference by a society that acquiesces far too easily to status to be legitimate spectacles for the generation of consensus. Importantly, the suggestion here is that the capacity of law to generate consensus does not exist on its own. Along with class, race plays a vital role in determining the public's perception of crimes and offenders deemed most dangerous.

6. Blackness/Whiteness, Crime and African Males as Folk Devils

Capitalist Eurocentric societies demand the production of enemies upon whom can be projected the effects of class tension and "social closures" that arise from the gap between unequal conditions and opportunity and limited achievement. In the context of European culture, the selection of Folk Devils are not arbitrary. They cannot be arbitrary, because given that the Folk Devils are a functional necessity toward the maintenance of consensus and solidarity among antagonistic and competing elements of the supraordinate European Canadian and American group. In short, Folk Devils are able to function in 'moral panics' because they have specific and unique histories pertinent to their axiological, cognitive and psychological function.

If social danger is to be seen and felt, and so produce the effect of social solidarity, that danger must be brought into existence against an embodied force whose negative image communicates the stigma of negation. In Western culture, from the image of the Devil as an African male to Ham as a cursed deviant, African males have come to denote a unique ontological threat to whiteness and the Eurocentric socio-cultural order. It is not the case that African men are committed to the destruction of the Eurocentric, patriarchal and capitalist society, they too wish to share in the bounty of a capitalist imperialist society. Yet, whether they are upper middle class or underclass, the fact is that "White" racism dehumanizes their image and *being* at every turn. In essence, the "virtual" and "actual" identities of African men are conflated and reduced to the totality of the sign of blackness. It is the outsiderness of African men, enforced by the image of danger and pollution that they represent to white supremacist society that constructs them as dangerous. African men, therefore, enter an *a priori* framework of objectification and "thingification" that is a fact of European historicization: the fact of blackness (Fanon, 1967, 109). But in addition to this historical fact of transhistoriocity, the "thingification" of African men is systematized and institutionalized in the thought and behaviour of Europeans. It is by these means, latent and manifest, historical and temporal, that African men are accorded the "virtual" and assumed "actual" identity of the archetypical criminal.

It is important to understand in white supremacist societies that the African male is imagined as embodying the negative connotation of blackness denoted in the

European imagination. Noel Manganyi points that in this ontological pathology, the "Black" body is invented in a deformed manner to exist for the glory of the "White" body:

> In the colonial and following situations of black-white interaction, the black body has become the repository of and target for all the bad objects in the collective psyche of the West – the stereotype for everything from dirt to evil. The sociological schema of the victim of racism has been made available for the adaptive resolution of the alienation of the racist from his own body (Manganyi, 1977, 76).

This convergence between blackness and "Black" men, and the related process of the transference of the *primary symbol* (abstract) of blackness into a *secondary* (concrete) and animate symbolic representation, converges and transfers the meaning of blackness. Implicating these processes, Dubois commenting on the criminalization of Jack Johnson, explained that "It all comes down, then, after all to this unforgiveable blackness" (Dubois, 1914). Because of what blackness denotes, and because this connotation determines the public image of African men, deviance and criminality are presumed to be a essential aspects of his *being*. The implication is that his presence animates the construct of "street" crime, thereby signalling a mutual and associated danger in which men of African descent are imagined to criminalize whatever space their bodies inhabit. By such means, men of African descent are constituted as "phobogenic" (Fanon, 1967, 154) objects that threaten and endanger from the vantage point of the "White" ontological field of racial visibility. From this, it can be said that blackness exists on a negative continuum, and at each terminus the representation of African men is either negative-negative (i.e., the criminal) or positive-negative (i.e., athletes and entertainers):

Offenders	*Non-offenders*
---	+
BLACKNESS =	NEGATIVE CONTINUUM

The image of "street" crime, a "black" place of "black" deeds, thus carries with it an *a priori* interpretive framework taken from European culture that locates the "black" body as the penultimate locus of social endangerment. *The* image of the archetypal offender, implicit in *the* archetype of "crime" is imagined as a thuggish feral African Canadian and American male. In Canada and the UK, most principally, those that are Jamaican born, who, hiding in the shadows of the "concrete jungle", prey on unwitting European suburbanites who risk life and limb to work and play in the city – the concrete jungle. There is an unshakable convergence in the social and cultural consciousness of a Eurocentric and white supremacist societies between "crime" typified by violence, and "race" typified by "non-whiteness" that is located in and on the bodies of African men.

This convergence and transference of blackness is reproduced in the tangible evidence of racist assumptions held by law enforcement officers and the legal apparatus. Visano provides data which indicate that there exists "A policing strategy that regards Blacks as intrinsically criminal and a potential threat to law and order paves the way for even greater police over-reaction" (Visano, 2001, 8). The consequences are not infrequently deadly. Not only are African people more routinely shot and killed by law enforcers, but, compared to Europeans, they are disproportionately targeted for search and seizures and arrests by police (often accompanying the excuse of mistaken identity). This accounts for higher arrest rates that are a function of what is now referred to as "racial profiling". Visano points to studies in Canada, the United Kingdom and the United States that detail both the grave disparities in the entire structure of the criminal justice/legal system with respect to the racial implications of crime and punishment as well as the disproportionate incarceration rates of men of African descent in Canada and the United States (Visano, 2001, 13-14). Ironically, what these studies and others either explicitly state or suggest is that the crimes for which African men are disproportionately punished are paradoxically crimes disproportionately committed by European Americans and Canadians. The drug trade for instance, largely associated with young males of African descent is, in terms of its political economy, a "White" male dominated industry. This indicates that in fact and fiction, the image and bodies of African men are a property that is subsidizing the income, freedoms, and self-image of "White" people. Because "crime" is 'blackened up', it is hard to see that "The majority of violent crime against whites are committed by other whites, and in most cases not on media dubbed 'crime-scarred' ghetto streets but out in pristine suburbia" (Hutchinson, 1996, 14). This points to the unforgivableness of blackness and the awesome power of "White" self-delusion and political expediency in maintaining the myth of "Black" criminality. Now, this all does not suggest that some "Black" men are not involved in crime. Some are, and in fact, like "White" offenders whose propinquity to other "Whites" increases the likelihood of "White-on-White crime", factually, men of African descent men are more likely to be the victims of crimes, as well as disproportionate offenders in such interpersonal crime: they in essence tend, by virtue of networks and social propinquity to be each others victims. This contextualization of race and crime suggests the popular image of the "Black" predator hunting "White" people is not only mythological, but that its perpetuation owes its psychology to the production of demons that moderate the anxieties of capitalism and "White" inter-tribal class conflicts.

In order to explain how "crime" equals the presence of blackness and the absence of whiteness, and to explain how by definition "race" is synonymous with Africans and not Europeans, it is essential to articulate and examine the component parts of white supremacist capitalist culture and its mechanics. To this end, I have focused on the negative image construction of African men as an *a priori* latent and *trans-historical* negative force in European psycho-history. My contention is that where, when, and how African males enter the field of European visibility it is a field of visibility that is "racially saturated" with *a priori* codifications (Butler, 1993, 15). Like Ralph Ellisons *invisible man*, he enters as a psychic force that is disfigured and disfiguring by "the fact of blackness". Against the best wishes of African men, their "virtual" bodies swim in an unforgiving and unforgivable sea of anti-blackness deep in the recesses of the European cultural imagination, and are not to be forgiven for what they have been made to represent – blackness itself.

As blackness is not to be forgiven, by extension, where, when, and how European males enter, they do so in a world of their culture's making and in which whiteness exonerates the collective identity of those who are European from any collective stigmatization. The convergence and transference of the *primary symbol* of whiteness into its *secondary animation* of "White" identity, "due process" and the myth of non-criminality, constitutes an eternal realm of "forgivableness" in the presentation of the "White" public image. Counter to blackness, whiteness exists on a positive continuum along which the terminus of each point is marked by negative (ie., criminal) or positive (ie., scientist, capitalist) representations:

Offenders *Non-offenders*
--- +

WHITENESS = POSITIVE
CONTINUUM

Paradoxical though it may be to those who are not part of the European cultural dynamic, unsavoury characters such as Al Capone, Bugsy Siegel, Bonnie and Clyde, Jesse James and Butch Cassidy and the Sundance Kid are regaled in "White" folklore as heroes of sorts. In essence, because of the positive construction of whiteness, its associated property rights (*de facto* and *de jure*), and active strategies that protect the image of Europeans, European men may commit crimes, but "White" men are not collectively criminalized. Anything else would be self-negating since whiteness does not represent danger to itself. I argue that no matter the demonization of individual "White" offenders in the news media, the white supremacist context that protects the "White" collective image and militates against extrapolating this degradation to the "White" collective. Further, because one of the central aspects to the power of whiteness is that the collective image of Europeans must not be subject to public "ceremonies of degradation," (Garfinkel, 1975, 187) media exposure must never reduce the totality of the "White" racial subject to the sign of degradation. As Farmanfarmaian points out, "White" rules of representation prohibit the collective depiction of "White" men "in a state of degradation" (Farmanfarmaian, 1992, 122).

[1] Art Lymer commented that: ...some of the people that have come over here from Jamaica...are prone to violence, they are very violent. They have very little respect, you know, for life...It's the infiltration of drugs and the one main drug is crack and the people that were pushing that in the communities, 98 per cent of them were Blacks. And of the Blacks, I think 90 per cent were from Jamaica. Cited in Jackson, 1992.

[2]Ibid; Steffensmeier, and Herbert, 1999; Steffensmeier, and Demuth, 2000; *Report of the Commission on Systemic Racism in the Ontario Criminal Justice System*, 1995.

[3] US 13th Amendment.

References

Backhouse, Constance. 1991.*Petticoats and Prejudice: Women and law in the nineteenth century*. Toronto: Published for the Osgoode Society by Women's Press.

Baker, David Victor.1987.*Race, Racism and the Death Penalty in the United States: An Historical, Theoretical and Empirical Analysis*. PhD dissertation, Department of Sociology at the University of California at Riverside.

Berndt, Brooks. 2003. "Ritual and Racism: A social-historical analysis of the crack sentencing guidelines," *Crime, Law and Social Change*, 39.

Boskin, Joseph. 1980. "Denials: The Media View of Dark Skins and the City," in B. Rubin,ed., *Small Voices and Great Trumpets: Minorities and the Media*. New York: Praeger.

Butler, Judith.1993.Endangered/Endangering: Schematic racism and White paranoia," *Reading Rodney King, Reading Urban Uprising*, edited by Robert Gooding-Williams. London: Routledge.

Cook, Dee.1993. "Racism, Citizenship and Exclusion," in Dee Cook and Barbara Hudson, eds., *Racism and Criminology*. London: SAGE Publications.

Daniels, Lee A.1995."The American Way: Blame a Black man," *Emerge*, (February), 61.

Douglass, Frederick. 1968. *My Bondage and My Freedom*. New York: Arno Press and The New York Times.

Dubois, W. E. B. 1914. "The Prize Fighter," *Crisis*.

Fanon, Frantz. 1967. *Black Skin, White Masks*. New York: Grove Press, Inc.

Farmanfarmaian, Abouali. 1992. "Did you measure up? The role of race and sexuality in the Gulf War," in Cynthia Enloe, ed., *Colleteral Damage: The New World Order at Home and Abroad*. Boston: South End Press.

Foucault, Michel. 1979. *Discipline and Punish: Birth of the Prison*. Translated by Alan Sheridan. New York: Vintage Books.

Garfinkel, Harold. 1975. "The Conditions of Successful Degradation Ceremonies," in Ronald A. Farrell and Victoria Lynn Swigert, eds., *Social Deviance*. Philadelphia, New York, Toronto: J. B. Lippincott Company.

Hacker, Andrew. 1995. "Malign neglect: The crackdown on African-Americans," *The Nation*, 26 (1) 2.

Hall, Stuart and Chas Critcher, Tony Jefferson, John Clarke, and Brian Roberts. 1979. *Policing the Crisis: Mugging, the State, and Law and Order*. London: MacMillan Press.

Harris, Cheryl, 1993 "Whiteness as Property," *Harvard Law Review* Vol. 106: 1707.

Haymes, Stephen Nathan. 1997. "Race, Repression, and the Politics of Crime and Punishment in Joe L. Kinchloe, Shirley R. Steinberg and Aaron D. Gresson III, eds., *Measured Lies: The Bell Curve examined.* New York: St. Martin's Press.

Hawkins, Homer and Richard Thomas. 1991. "Policing Black Populations: a history of race and social control in America," in Ellis Cashmore and Eugene McLaughlin, eds. *Out of Order: Policing Black People*. London: Routledge.

Hutchinson, 1996.*Assassination of the Black Male Image*. New York: Simon and Schuster.

Jackson, Peter.1992. "Policing difference: 'race' and crime in metropolitan Toronto," in Peter Jackson and Jan Penrose, eds., *Constructions of Race, Place and Nation*. San Diego, CA: Association of American Geographers.

James, C.L.R. 1985. *A History of Negro Revolt*. London: Race Today Publications.

Johnson, Sherri Lynn. 1985. "Black Innocence and the White Jury," 83 *Michigan Law Review*, 1611.

Johnson, Sherri Lynn. 1984. "Cross-Racial Identification Errors in Criminal Cases," *Cornell Law Review*, 69, 934.

Jordan, Winthrop. 1977. *White Over Black: American attitudes toward the Negro, 1550-1812*. New York: W. W. Norton and Company.

Lemelle Jr., Anthony. 1995. *Black Male Deviance*. Westport, Conn: Praeger.

Manganyi, Noel.1977.*Alienation and the Body in A Racist Society: A study of the society that invented Soweto*. New York: Nok Publishers.

Martinot, Steve. 2003. *The Rule of Racialization: Class, Identity, Governance.* Philadelphia: Temple University Press.

Mead, George H. 1918."The Psychology of Punitive Justice," *The American Journal of Sociology*, 23, no. 5.

McIntyre, Charshee. 1993. *Criminalizing A Race: Free Blacks During Slavery.* New York: Kayode Publications.

Morrison, Toni. 1995. "The Marketing of Power: Racism and Fascism," *The Nation*, #260, 21 cited in Stephen Nathan Haymes, "Race, Repression, and the Politics of Crime and Punishment in The Bell Curve," in Joe L. Kinchloe, Shirley R. Steinberg and Aaron D. Gresson III, eds. 1997. *Measured Lies: The Bell Curve examined* (New York: St. Martin's Press), 238.

Nunn, Kenneth B. 1997."Law as a Eurocentric Enterprise," *Law and Inequality: A Journal of Theory and Practice*, Vol. XV, no. 2.

Pitts, John. 1993."Thereotyping: Anti-racism, Criminology and Black Young People," in Dee Cook and Barbara Hudson, eds. *Racism and Criminology*. London: Sage.

Reiman, Jeffrey. 1990.*The Rich Get Richer and the Poor Get Prison: Ideology, class and criminal justice*. New York: Macmillan Publishing Company.

Report of the Commission on Systemic Racism in the Ontario Criminal Justice System. 1995. Queen's Printer of Ontario.

Roberts, Dorothy E. 1993. "Crime, Race and Reproduction," *Tulane Law Review*, 67,[1954].

Steffensmeier, Darrell and Stephen Demuth. 2000."Ethnicity and Sentencing Outcomes in U. S. Federal Courts: Who is sentenced more harshly?" *American Sociological Review*, Vol. 65, no. 5.

Steffensmeier, Darrell and Chris Herbert. 1999. "Women and men Policymakers: Does the Judge's gender affect the sentencing of criminal defendants," *Social Forces*, Vol. 77, no. 3.

Surette, Ray. 1992. *Media Crime and Criminal Justice: Images and realities*. Pacific Grove, Calif: Brooks/Cole Publishing Company.

Sutherland, Edwin H.1955.*Principles of Criminology* (5th edition). Revised by Donald R. Cressey. Chicago, Philadelphia, New York: J. B. Lippincott Company.

Visano, Livy. 2001. "Crime, Culture and Criticality – Risks and Resistance: The impact of whiteness on the culture of Law," (Unpublished).

Visano, Livy A. 1998.*Crime and Culture: Refining the Traditions*. Toronto: Canadian Scholars' Press.

11. Laying it on the Table—Black Women and the Criminal Justice System: Some Initial Thoughts

Teneeka Barnett

1. Introduction

This paper is born of a wider concern with Black women's engagement with the Canadian criminal justice system, and the study of the law as a dual mechanism with the potential to simultaneously institute as well as combat racial inequality. Serving as the introductory chapter to such an exploration, this paper lays the conceptual groundwork in outlining a rationale for the study of Black women's criminality as separate from Black men's. In so doing, this paper locates such a discussion within feminist legal theories as developed by theorists such as Carol Aylward, Kimberle Crenshaw and Patricia Hill-Collins amongst others and examines the more practical manifestations of how issues of race/ gender/class unfold in the sentencing process via the examination of three recent Ontario decisions. Concluding phases of the assessment outline the sorts of questions which would of necessity be addressed, en route to the broader question of whether the Canadian criminal justice system is equipped to negotiate a place for the Black woman and her experiences and the burning implications which arise from such a consideration.

To understand the apprehension with which one engages in a critical, analytic approach to issues surrounding Black women's criminality within a Canadian context is hardly in itself an arduous task. By virtue of the necessity to at once engage in controversial discourse around race as well as gender, a number of apprehensions are immediately mobilized. Undoubtedly, one stands on precarious ground when such sensitive issues are addressed, particularly when this is done in an environment which heralds itself as discrimination free – where ideologies of the absence of racist and sexist notions prevail. Indeed, as it becomes more and more obvious that the time has come to pen out my initial thoughts on this dissertation I am perturbed; I am perplexed by the sheer complexity of the task being undertaken; by the daunting task of how to convey on a theoretical, analytic level the 'onion like' predisposition of the topic under scrutiny – how to revel its many layers and whether I will even be able to devise a reasonably constituted paradigm within which to address these issues.

Yet I am perplexed not only by the complexity of this task, but also by the radical way in which it may simultaneously be drastically understated or oversimplified; 'the void in literature concerning Black women exists because there is simply nothing there to discuss'; 'but there have been countless studies done on racism in Canada - the problem is that you are not sufficiently engaged in the literature'; or 'what is a Black women's experience? People are so diverse that in this day, you can hardly speak of a unitary existence- have you never heard of post structuralism?' Equally troubling are other conceptions which would underlie the issue of racism as it pertains to the criminal justice system; 'the law is supposed to be colour blind - what do you want? A box of tissues because you happen to be "doubly burdened?"' What is that anyway?' and last but certainly not least – 'what makes you think Black women are so special? There have been numerous attempts to decipher women's relationship with the Canadian criminal justice system; race is an issue because you people make it an issue; after all, are you not a woman?'

It is with these thoughts in mind that I embrace the task of mapping out a rationale for what has become, over the past year, a phrase imbued with a deeper meaning- a rationale for a critical interdisciplinary exploration of Black women's engagement with the criminal justice system.

2. On the Issue of Racism

That I stand among many who have made attempts to 'stick a pin' or debunk the ideology of Canada as an idyllic and altogether harmonious, racism free country is blaringly obvious. Theorists such as Mosher (1998), Aylward (1999), Walker (1997), government appointed bodies such as the Commission on Systemic Racism (1995) and others such as Henry and Tator (2002) have all gone to great lengths to delineate a framework within which racism as it stands in Canadian society may be understood. This section of the analysis draws from the findings of these authors, in an attempt to once again provide the basis of understanding of 'where we are' in Canada on the issue of racism. More succinctly, the question as is stands explores the extent to which the issue of racism exists in Canadian society. Are we really making a big deal out of nothing?

In underscoring a more general tone of racism, Mosher (1998) suggests that discrimination was rampant in all facets of Canadian society in the years spanning 1892 – 1961; furthermore, this discrimination took the form of a strong Anti-Asian as well as Anti-Black sentiment. As he states, '...Asians and Blacks were subjected to considerable discrimination in virtually all spheres of the Canadian social, legal and criminal justice systems in the period from 1892-1961' (Mosher 1998: 196). Mosher's findings reveal that negative sentiments and stereotypes frequented the Canadian media accounts with the pervasive effect of these stereotypes being manifested in the groups' access to resources such as housing, employment, social services. Within the realm of criminal justice in particular, the experiences of the group in question reflected the influence of systemic racism. (Mosher 1998:196-97)

In more recent times, Mosher and Aylward point to the Court of Appeal decision in *R v* Parks (1993, 84 C.C.C. [3d] 353 [Ont. CA]) where it was held that 'racism... is a part of our community's psyche. A significant segment of our community holds overly racist views. A much larger segment subconsciously operates on the basis of negative racial stereotypes. Furthermore, our institutions, including the criminal justice system, reflect and perpetuate those negative stereotypes. These elements combine to infect our society as a whole with the evil or racism.' (Mosher, 1998 quoting R v Parks 1993, Canadian Criminal Cases 84:368)

As documented by the Report of the Commission on Systemic Racism in the Ontario Criminal Justice System (1995), discriminatory practices as they occur within a Canadian setting usually take on a systemic form. That is, as practical manifestations within society, these practices take on more subtle undertones; finding a hiding place in the systems, practices and laws that seem neutral on the surface but which are ridden underneath with implications that are at best detrimental for people of colour. Other authors such as Rosenthal seemingly espouse a similar sentiment, which is evident in his view that '[m]any ethnic and racial groups in Canada have been victims of direct and explicit discrimination in the past. Today, discrimination persists in forms more difficult to discern such as stereotypes, assumptions and singular viewpoints. It manifests itself as systems, practices, policies and laws that appear neutral, but that, under close inspection, have serious detrimental consequences for members of ethnic and racial communities' (Aylward 1999: 39).

James Walker, in his analysis of racism within the Canadian contemporary context points out that data based on a ten year span of time runs along a similar vein of thought, highlighting the fact that:

> Visible minorities" and especially African Canadians had consistently lower – than – average incomes and higher levels of unemployment. Even when qualifications, experiences and regional factors were considered, Canadians of African and Asian origin earned less than White Canadians in comparable circumstances... Racial discrimination was widely reported in housing as well, and in one 1986 test of apartment rentals in Toronto, more than 40% of applications were denied on apparently racial grounds. Perhaps most insidious of all, studies by the Toronto Board of Education showed that Black school children were streamed into "basic" courses at a rate more than double for White children (Walker 1997: 339).

Yet the threads of racism are seemingly woven deeper within the Canadian fabric, going beyond issues such as education, housing and employment. In returning to the findings of the Commission on Systemic Racism (1995), it has been suggested that incarceration rates within the province on a one year time line from 1992-1993 was five times that for White adult males, proportionate to their representation in the population. Furthermore, it has been reported that Black admissions to prisons in the metropolitan area increased by several thousand percent in the seven year period spanning 1986- 1993 (Commission on Systemic Racism 1995).

It would be entirely superficial to consider only the more palpable forms of racist practices. As one author framed the dilemma with such an exercise; racism exists not merely in the streets (van Dijk 1993). Undoubtedly, the character of racism is at times difficult to discern because it is a phenomenon so deeply embedded within the institutionalized practices of elite institutions such as the media, politics and business corporations and because of its transmission through influential talk and text (Henry and Tator 2002; van Dijk 1993). As indicated by van Dijk, "...the elites largely define and constrain the major life chances of minority groups, especially in or through education, employment, economic affairs, social affairs, the media and culture. Spontaneous popular racism can be effective only when it is spread throughout the population at large by the mass media and similar forms of public discourse controlled by the elites." (van Dijk 1993:11).

Clearly then, any serious attempt to uncover racism as a phenomenon which is deeply entrenched with the framework of the society in question must also devote some segment of the analysis to the ways in which elitist institutions create as well as perpetuate incidences of racism for 'much of the motivation and many prejudiced arguments that seem to inspire popular racism are "prepared" by elites' (van Dijk 1993:10). One such attempt was undertaken by Henry and Tator (2002) who embark upon a critical analysis of the media and its influence in shaping racist attitudes within society.

In particular, the study seeks to illustrate how members of the Canadian press 'give voice' to racism and more broadly, 'how the media marginalize, denigrate and silence ethno racial minorities' (Henry and Tator 2002: 4).

Among Henry and Tator's findings was evidence to suggest that there was a tendency to over report those crimes perpetuated by ethnic minorities, especially Blacks, who were portrayed as having criminal propensities (Henry and Tator 2002: 64). The authors contend that these findings confirm earlier studies by Entman and Rojecki (2000) which suggest that Black suspects are four times more likely to be shown in mug shots and handcuffs. Furthermore, the media search for the newsworthy victim results in over representation of 'Black crime' which is sensationalized. The media then, for the most part, report crime through 'the narrow lens of law and order'(Henry and Tator 2002: 165). From this assessment, the authors concluded that three themes permeated the literature. There was firstly, the misrepresentation and invisibility of people of colour, the preservation of cultural hegemony on the part of the mainstream media despite its commitment to equality and fairness, and the concentration of media ownership in the hands of the White elite who often espoused conservative values (Henry and Tator 2002). This perceivable 'whiteness' manifests itself not only within institutions, but also stands at the very core of the criminal law system. As suggested by one author, "... the criminal law and the culture of liberalism reproduce an insidious hegemony of white privilege" (Visano 2002: 209). Elaborating further on this, the author, suggests that 'the whiteness of one's skin is equated with the naturalness of authority' (Visano 2002: 209).

It would be remiss then to embark upon any attempt to deny the existence of racism within Canadian society; despite its commitment to equality. Henry and Tator (2002) in their works develop the concept of *democratic racism* where race is presented as a phenomenon that permeates society despite ideological foundations of liberalism and the institution of legislative frameworks geared towards minimizing the prevalence of racism. They suggest that the ideal of democratic racism represents the fundamental tension between a commitment to ideals of justice and equality and negative feelings about minority groups and discrimination (Henry et al 2000). The question then becomes the extent to which the law as a hallmark of society is able to recognize the prevalence of race as a phenomenon with very real implications. In an attempt to formulate an initial look into the ways Canadian criminal courts have dealt with the issue of systemic discrimination in recent times, it would perhaps be best to turn to the case of *R v Borde.*

3. R v Borde (2003) O.J. No. 354

R v Borde concerns an appeal from a young Black male, aged 19 at the time of sentencing, with a substantial youth record. The accused pleaded guilty to numerous offenses including possession of a loaded restricted weapon, aggravated assault and the use of a firearm in the commission of an indictable offense (para. 1) and was on probation at the time at which the offenses were committed. The plea resulted in a sentence of five years and two months less 31 months which amounted to credit served for time spent under 'particularly barbaric conditions'. The appellant sought to have this sentence reduced in light of the systemic and background factors facing young Black males in the Toronto community; a consideration had not been submitted to the trial judge. Justice Rosenberg, in assessing the background of the accused noted that:

- The appellant was one of seven children and had no stable father figure. He had a chaotic upbringing and in stages of his childhood had been placed in foster homes (Para 11). The appellant was involved in a common law relationship with a woman with whom he had a child. Despite a bail order prohibiting the accused from being in the Regeant Park area, he visited his spouse and child on a daily basis. It was suggested that his spouse and her mother encouraged these visits despite the fact that some of the appellant's assault convictions related to the physical abuse of the spouse (Para 12).
- The appellant had a substance abuse problem (alcohol) that started at the age of 15 and claimed, despite his spouse's denial of the fact, that he had been intoxicated at the time at which the offenses were committed (Para 13).
- The appellant had no marketable skills and was 'chronically truant from school'. Furthermore, his response to probation was poor, though he did well in custody (para 14).

The judge reviewed the sentencing decision as outlined by the trial judge, noting his insistence that the sentence relay the message that 'violent assaults… especially with handguns will result in serious penalties' (para 15) in conjunction with literature put before him reflective of the incidence of systemic racism in Canada. Such literature included the Report of the Commission on Systemic Racism that highlighted the dramatic increase in the number of Black offenders who were sentenced to prison in recent years and the strong correlation between drug offences and high rates of incarceration. It was also suggested that circumstances which were unique to the Black community such as the absence of positive role models and the surmountable problems faced such as unemployment, harassment and few career opportunities (para 21), all of which fell under the general umbrella of the effects of systemic discrimination were among those considerations that should be taken in formulating a sentencing decision. The incorporation of such considerations, it was argued, would fall very much in line with the Court's direction in *R v Gladue* ([1999] 133 C.C.C. [3d] 385) where it was ordered that such factors be taken into consideration for Aboriginal Canadians.

Though conceding that there were similarities between the plight of Aboriginals and African Americans, and conceding further that these factors might be brought in as mitigating factors to the extent that they are relevant, it was decided that such factors should be introduced at trial where its evidence and relevance may be appropriately explored (Rosenberg at para 30). In further extrapolating from the decision handed down in *Gladue*, it was determined that section 718.2(e) was applied with the aim of providing a framework more true to Aboriginal tradition with restoration as its aim; a 'link' which was missing in the case of the African American community (para. 32). By the dictates of section 718.2 (e), all available sanctions other than imprisonment that are reasonable in the circumstances should be considered for all offenders, with particular attention to the circumstances of aboriginal offenders.

Justice Rosenberg conceded that while he would not fail to admit the fresh evidence concerning systemic discrimination based on the above factors, he deemed it inappropriate to admit the evidence because it 'would not affect the result' (para. 33). Making reference to *Gladue* and *Wells*, the judge determined that the more serious and violent the crime, the less likely it was that the sentence handed down even to the Aboriginal offender would differ from that handed down on any other offender. The background factors then were relevant, but only to the extent that consideration of these factors allows for individualized sentencing (para. 35). The trial judge did err, however, in appropriating a sentence of five years and two months in light of the fact that this was the first penitentiary sentence to be served by the appellant. By virtue of this, the sentencing decision should not have been determined solely by the objectives of general deterrence and denunciation (para. 36). Upon review of the length of the sentence then, the overall length of sentence was reduced by one year, to a total of four years and two months.

An assessment of this case is crucial to the extent that it provides some insight into how systemic racism fairs in acting as a mitigating factor in sentencing in the event that the accused is a Black male; and in a more general sense, to highlight the criminal court's treatment systemic discrimination on the basis of race. What is perhaps most interesting is the fact that the judge, despite recognizing the importance of systemic racism, was unable to accord enough weight to the factors to allow them to mitigate, because of the seriousness of the offenses committed. The question which arises is whether a mere recognition on the part of the judge there are disadvantages which accrue from systemic racism is tantamount to providing an effective framework within which Black men's criminality may be addressed.

Should there be a more proactive stance taken with regard to eliminating or at least making an attempt to curb the effects of systemic discrimination and if so, what would such an endeavour look like? This case then could seemingly substantiate the idea that race is more than an abstract theory; but is rather, a concept which when taken beyond the borders of conceptualization and into the realm of practicality has very real implications for those who find themselves in a disadvantaged position in relation to the dominant power; in so far as it may be legitimately claimed that there is a dichotomy of dominant and subordinate powers._Authors such as Collins (2004) have expressed this sentiment

The case on a whole then, is useful as a guide for pointing out the sorts of issues that may typify the Black man's experience in the sentencing process. The question that arises is whether Black women would have similar experiences especially with overrepresentation in correctional facilities and whether adding another dimension such as gender allows systemic racism to successfully mitigate a sentence. Put another way, how is the law equipped to deal with a scenario in which the Black woman stands in the place typically held by the Black male?

4. On the Issue of Black Women

Deborah King (1993), for one, speaks to the special circumstances which typify Black women's lives by virtue of the commonalities shared with all women as well as by virtue of the bonds to men of race; expanding on this, the author suggests that 'the interactive oppressions that circumscribe our lives provide a distinctive context for Black womanhood' (King 1993: 220). In advocating the notion that Black women constitute a unique group, King speaks to the theoretical invisibility of the Black woman, stating that 'the experience of Black women is apparently assumed, though never explicitly stated, to be synonymous with that of either black males or white females; and since the experience of both are equivalent, a discussion of Black women in particular is superfluous' (King, 1993: 221). Iyer (1993: 90) seemingly echoes the same sentiment in her suggestion that:

> (t)he law requires the racial minority woman to establish that she is just like a white woman or just like a racial minority man because that is what establishing a sex/race discrimination claim means. In order to succeed... the racial minority woman must decide whether her experience was more like what a white woman would have encountered (in which case it was sex discrimination) or more like what a racial minority man would have encountered (race discrimination), even though she is neither a white woman nor a racial minority man and it is very possible that the discrimination occurred precisely because she was not those other people.

In elaborating on this sentiment, King adds that 'it is mistakenly granted that either there is no difference in being Black and female from being generically black (i.e. male) or generically female (i.e. White). The analogy obfuscates or denies what Chafe refers to as 'the profound substantive differences between Blacks and women' (King 1993: 221). It does indeed seem then that there would be some merit in interrogating the standing of the subject group in relation to the law, if only to avoid at a most intrinsic level the sort of essentialism warned against above.

The general trend of thought then seems to revolve around the idea of exclusion on the part of mainstream academia and perhaps society on a whole to acknowledge the uniqueness of a Black woman's experience. On the origins of the birth of critical race feminism, for example, Aylward (1999) suggests that the birth of this doctrine lay in the realization on the part of American Black feminists and other feminists of colour, that mainstream feminism had, to a large extent, overlooked the fact that White supremacy and dominance affects women of colour; and to highlight the inability of mainstream feminist theory to negotiate a place for the Black woman who is oppressed not only by virtue of race but also gender. Following this line of reasoning, Aylward (1999) further postulates that gender discrimination is but one of the barriers faced by women of colour. In addition to this, there exist barriers that are predicated on race and class that must be overcome by the Black woman, (as is the case with the Black man) if full participation is the aim. Aylward (1999: 36) further points to the explanation as provided by Cleaver, where it is stated that:

> Eliminating gender discrimination in itself does not remove the contortion blighting the lives of women whose colour, race, national origin, or economic marginalization causes them such pain... Until White feminists discover how to see the insidious way that racism constricts the lives of millions of women, they cannot oppose it. Worse, they may blindly fail to perceive how their ancestry positions them to benefit passively from racism's perpetuation, and remain oblivious to the racialized nature of gender.

Similarly, Kimberle Crenshaw (2003: 29) argues that courts, as well as feminist and civil rights leaders,

> have treated Black women in ways that deny both the unique compoundedness of their situation and the centrality of their experiences to the larger classes of women or Blacks, and the compounded nature of their experiences absorbed into the collective experiences of either group, or as too different, in which case Black women's Blackness or femaleness has sometimes placed their needs and perspectives at the margin of the feminist and Black liberationist agendas.

This exclusion, according to Crenshaw, stems from an uncritical and disturbing acceptance of dominant lines of thought concerning discrimination. In elaborating on this, Crenshaw suggests that the definition of discrimination as it stands in anti-discrimination law remains problematic. Here, the term is described as the wrongful proceeds from the identification of a specific class or category; either a discriminator intentionally identifies this category or a process is adopted which somehow disadvantages all members of the same race equally, with the effect that 'any significant experiential or statistical variation within this group suggests either that the group is not being discriminated against or that conflicting interests exist which defeat any attempts to bring a common claim' (Crenshaw 2003: 29). The net result of all this is that one generally is unable to reconcile the two variables with each other and cannot combine the categories, and the variables of race and sex become significant only to the extent that they disadvantage the victims (Crenshaw 2003). Furthermore, 'the paradigm of sex discrimination tends to be based on the experiences of white women; the model of race discrimination tends to be based in the experiences of the most privileged Blacks. Notions of what constitutes race and sex discrimination, are, as a result, narrowly tailored to embrace only a small set of circumstances, none of which include discrimination against Black women' (Crenshaw 2003: 29-30). The assessments as provided by Aylward, Iyer and King do much to illustrate exactly how it is that mainstream feminist theory, whether intentionally or not, has perpetuated the exclusion of a true assessment of the intersectionality of Black women's identity, and how the failure to do so 'has manifested in the almost complete absence of analyses which go beyond gender and patriarchy to consider the impacts of racism, sexism and classism on women of colour' (Aylward 1999: 36). Through Aylward's work, an assessment is provided of the arguments of Louis Kushnik who argues that by its very nature, institutional racism determines resource allocation, and opportunities for advancement through education and employment and it is the members of the majority race who are privy to such resources.

The effect of all this, according to Kushnik, is that the class system is maintained by 'reinforcing a race consciousness rather than a class consciousness among the white working class… One has only to look at the history of "race riots" – programs- against people of colour in times of economic and political crisis, for example the race riots … and the current escalation of racial violence among unemployed and alienated whites' (Aylward 1999: 47). To this extent then, socialist feminists, while able to apply critical theory to the situation as it affects White women, fail to examine the intersection of race and class on women and men of colour (Aylward 1999). Aylward points further to Kushnik's assertion that the ruling class engages in a valiant effort to separate issues of race and class, but in this, it can hardly be denied that White working class racism incorporates and maintains the racist ideology of the ruling class.

Iyer (1993) too speaks of the theoretical invisibility of the Black woman in human rights cases within a Canadian context; examining in particular the Canadian human rights' law's response to instances of discrimination faced by minority women over a ten year span. In contrasting her findings with the general trend as it unfolds in the USA, Iyer points out that while in the USA distinctiveness is portrayed negatively, in Canadian cases, there was little realization that racial minority women existed as a group. Iyer found it difficult to locate racial minority women when the CHHR categorized sex and gender separately. Secondly, in the event that there was a successful attempt to locate the subject group, these minority women were depicted as raceless and or genderless; as '… some sort of "generic" person whose racial and gender identity, especially in relation to the racial and gender identity of the complainant was quite irrelevant' (Iyer 1993: 81).

In pinpointing exactly how it is that Black women are legitimized as an entity within themselves, Collins examines the doctrine of 'standpoint theory' whereby group allocation in hierarchical power relations produces shared challenges for individuals in these groups. These common challenges can foster similar angles of vision leading to a group knowledge or standpoint that in turn can influence the group's political action' (Collins 2004: 66). Collins examines this theory in light of the current academic environment where post structuralism reigns rampantly, examining in particular, the extent to which standpoint theory becomes nullified by 'postmodern rubrics of decentering, deconstruction and difference.' (2004: 67) In reconciling the two (post structuralism and standpoint theory) Collins suggests that recognition of the 'intersectionality' of women's identity could perhaps be a worthwhile compromise.

This notion of intersectionality acts as a bridge then; allowing for group difference while recognizing that shared oppressions mean similar experiences (Collins 2004). Intersectionality, then, 'as a heuristic device... references the ability of social phenomenon such as race, class and gender to mutually construct one another' (Collins 2004: 68). In adding context to this for the Black woman, Collins suggest that this group 'can be seen both as a group that occupies a distinctive social location within power relations of intersectionality and as one wherein intersectional processes characterize Black women's collective self definitions...whereas race-only or gender-only perspectives classify African American women as a subgroup of either African American or women, intersections of race, class and gender, among others, create more fluid and malleable boundaries around the category of "African American women"' (2004: 68). In elaborating on this, Collins points to Crenshaw's analysis, whereby 'intersectionality captures the way in which the particular location of Black women in dominant American social relations is unique and in some instances unassimilable into the discursive paradigms of gender and race domination' (Collins 2004: 68; Crenshaw 1992: 404).

Black women's experience then will by default be different from white women's according to Collins' analysis, for 'although African American women and white American women participate in the same system of institutionalized racism and sexism, each group assigns a different salience to race and gender. Race and class and gender may all be present in all social settings in the United States, yet groups will experience and "see" them differently (Collins 2004: 70). The question that remains upon consideration of Collins' analysis is whether the same would be true of Black women in Canada, in light of the shared history of racism and sexism, yet in spite of the differences in other features such as demographics and social policy.

The purpose of presenting Collins' work is not to embark upon a thorough analysis of Black women's identity- for such an analysis is beyond the scope of this paper – rather – the purpose in presenting her theory on the juncture between post structuralism and standpoint theory serves to sufficiently expel the notion that there can never be a body of literature presented as a general representation of the experience of a particular subject group. Suffice to say, one must be cognizant of the fact that differences do exist within the group perhaps in light of the intricacies associated with the particular ways in which issues of class/ race/gender intersect to form an individual, unitary experience (Collins 2004). That being said, there is room left to suggest that there will be a set of experiences – common to a particular group (in this case Black women) which are wrought by virtue of the fact that this group faces similar experiences or find that they stand at a similar point because of the fact that they occupy multiply oppressive categories and the fact that these categories are experienced simultaneously. The point of this exploration then, would be to interrogate the extent to which the Canadian criminal justice system indeed other elitist institutions such as the media enforce such oppression.

On a secondary level, Collins' work does much to express a more practical way of speaking of race as a category- going beyond discourse which speaks of race as an entity which is nothing but a mere social construction- an ideological myth that has no practical accomplishment but to exist as an oppressive category within which people place themselves or embellish against reason. As Collins states, 'despite well intentioned gestures (eg. placing "race" in quotation marks to signal the socially constructed notion of race as a category of analysis), declaring a moratorium on using the word *race* does not make housing segregation, under funded inner city schools, and employment discrimination any less real' (Collins 2004: 77).

Certainly, it is not difficult to add to this canvas the idea that it would not make any inequality as it exists in the criminal justice system any less real. The purpose of this inquiry then, is to explore whether there is a legitimate basis for a claim of incompatibility of Black women and the mechanisms of the Canadian criminal justice system. Before it is even possible to envision what a politicized effort to address any oppression/ disharmony/ incompatibility would look like, or even to suggest that there ought to be some consideration of the extent to which Black woman's experience is appropriately placed in the law- for admittedly this would be a more humble approach- what must first exist is a practical attempt to decipher the relationship between the two. As a practical example of how this scenario unfolds, it would perhaps be useful at this point to incorporate into this discourse a discussion of the cases *R v Hamilton* and *R v Spencer*.

5. R v Hamilton (2003) O.J. No. 532

"...there is something unique when it comes to women about cocaine importing, and I'm trying to figure out what it is, and I'm trying to figure out when I see black women before me, day in, day out, assignment court after assignment court, what it means in terms of the crime of cocaine importing, and what it should mean to me, if anything, as a sentencing judge obliged to apply equality principles, and constitutional principles in the exercise of a discretion, which sentencing is."
(Para 102)

The case *R v Hamilton* concerns two women, Marsha Hamilton and Donna Mason, who were charged with and plead guilty to the act of illegal cocaine importation. Both women were Black, single mothers on welfare; Donna Mason's conflict with the law was perhaps more precarious because she faced the additional risk of deportation upon conviction. The Ontario Superior Court of Justice was asked to impose a sanction on the two women. Both were first time offenders.

En route to sentencing the women, Judge Hill embarked upon a thorough assessment of the instance of 'drug muling', and a number of factors were taken into consideration. Such factors included:

- The negative social impact of narcotics such as cocaine including the costs to health care (para 18).
- The incidence of drug muling in Canada including the notion that there was a target group chosen specifically for trafficking drugs into Canada. (It was noted that this group often comprised individuals with no criminal record living at the poverty level who often participated in the act for a 'one time payment') (para 24) along with the steady increase in the numbers of federally sentenced women in prison (para 71).
- The difference in the cost of incarcerating men and women and the lower incidence of criminality among women (para 72-74), the unlikelihood that the convicted woman would reoffend (para 76) and the unique set of circumstances surrounding women's criminality including the greater chance that the woman would be a single parent and the likelihood that these women would have been physically abused. Also pointed out was the low percentage of women who would have had formal qualifications beyond basic education and steady employment (para 79).
- A detailed assessment of the incidence of criminality among Blacks and in particular among Black women. Information was pulled from cases such as *Golden v The Queen* (2001), 159 C.C.C. (3d) 449 (S.C.C) and the Report of the Commission on Systemic Racism along with data published by Corrections Service Canada suggesting that Black women and men were "massively over-represented" in Canadian prisons.
- The relationship between the practice of drug muling and the over incarceration of Black women. Judge Hill stated 'African American women, in actual numbers, represent the single largest group of persons appearing before the court charged with cocaine importation' (para 104).
- Evidence as presented to suggest that though criminalization in itself provided visible crime control benefits, there was 'no conclusive evidence that supports the conclusion that harsh sentences would reduce crime through the mechanism of general deterrence' (Dr. Doob para 120 - 22). Also assessed was the importance of taking into account sections 718.1 and 718.2(e) of the Criminal Code (para. 186). The terms of this provision mandate that 'a sentence must be proportionate to the gravity of the offense and the degree of responsibility of the offender' As previously stated, this

clause mandates that 'all available sanctions other than imprisonment that are reasonable in the circumstances should be considered for all offenders, with particular attention to the circumstances of aboriginal offenders.

In analyzing the information put before him, Judge Hill also took into consideration the social context of the sentencing decision to be made, which was seen as crucial within multicultural society (para 179). Furthermore, the essence of equity and individualized sentencing meant that systemic factors were of necessity taken into consideration. Reference was made to the case of *Wells v The Queen* ([2000], 141 C.C.C. (3d) 368 [S.C.C.]) where it was noted that in considering cases concerning Aboriginal offenders, a sentencing judge must consider the unique systemic factors faced by this particular offenders (para 187). It was further determined that those effects of systemic racism which were applicable to Aboriginal Canadians (for example high unemployment, lack of opportunities and lack of education) were equally applicable to African Canadians (para 187). In addition to this, it was noted that incidences of cocaine importation in Brampton were not the result of greed, but were the result of attempts to maintain 'subsistence level existence' (para 191).

In turning to the unique circumstances of the women awaiting sentencing, Judge Hill highlighted the fact that both were single mothers of three with no financial contributions from the fathers of the children; placing this within the broader framework of the feminization of poverty as a social phenomenon particularly relevant in the Canadian context. There was also some consideration of the fact that six children would be left parentless should the women be imprisoned; and was deemed to be an important factor to be taken into consideration (para 197). Upon review of these factors, Marsha Hamilton was sentenced to 20 months imprisonment to be served on a conditional basis; Donna Mason was sentenced to 24 months served on a conditional basis the risk of her deportation was given due consideration in light of cases such as *R. v Critton* (2002) O.J. No. 2549.

In August of 2004, the Ontario Court of Appeal rendered a decision on the Hamilton case. Though the sentence as appropriated by Justice Hill was not overturned, Justice Doherty, speaking on behalf of the Court held that 'the trial judge stepped outside of the proper role of a judge on sentencing and ultimately imposed sentences that were inconsistent with the statutory principles of sentencing and binding authorities from this Court' (R v. Hamilton 2003, 172 C.C.C. [3d] 114, at para 3).

Justice Doherty conceded that the nature of the proceedings had changed because of the trial judge's tendency to assume 'the combined role of advocate, witness and judge' (para 65). According to Doherty, though trial judges may, of necessity, play an active role in the sentencing proceedings, there is nothing to state that the trial judge's power is unconditional or without limits. The adversarial nature of court proceedings means that the judge's role is primarily to listen and evaluate the merits of competing cases. It was articulated then that judges must be extremely cautious upon deciding to introduce issues into the sentencing proceedings. Furthermore, Justice Doherty suggested that the manner in which the proceedings were conducted raised four major problems:

- By assuming the role of advocate, witness and judge, the trial judge risked his impartiality, even if he did not fall susceptible to abandoning it (para 71). The Crown had challenged the manner of the sentencing proceeding arguing that the trial judge raised issues not brought before him, instructing the Crown to produce evidence on these issues, and in other instances produced his own evidence of the issues in question; the sentences imposed were based on these findings and on his own personal experience. In so doing, the trial judge lost his appearance of impartiality (Para 33).
- The judge's approach produced a 'fundamental disconnect between the case on sentencing presented by counsel for the respondents and the case of the paradigmatic cocaine courier constructed by the trial judge' (para 73). Evidence suggests that the trial judge based his sentences on the circumstances of the typical drug courier as opposed to the women before him.
- The proceedings created the risk of inaccurate fact finding for example on the unverified statistical data relating to black women's over representation in prisons, despite evidence to suggest the contrary (para 75-81).
- The judge's introduction of the 'certainty of detection' issues consumed a great deal of time and effort, and in the end played no role in appropriating a fit sentence (para 82).

With regard to the fitness of the sentences imposed, it was concluded that the trial judge's imposition of a conditional sentence 'amounted to reversible error' (para 84). Furthermore, a court will only vary a sentence if it reflects an error in principle, demonstrates failure to consider a relevant factor, or is somehow demonstrably unfit. In declaring a sentence, there must be adequate attention given to the principles of proportionality, parity, totality and restraint and in addition to this, 'conditional sentences for those who import dangerous drugs like cocaine into Canada will usually be a viable sentencing option only where, in addition to the usual mitigating factors, there are one or more extraordinary mitigating factors such as cooperation with the authorities in their attempts to identify and arrest those behind the drug trade' (Justice Doherty para. 113).

On the relevance of systemic factors, Justice Doherty concluded that there was no attempt on the part of the respondents to introduce any fact of institutional racial and gender inequality or any attempt to refer to the sorts of generalizations made by the trial judge. Under these circumstances, it was inappropriate for the trial judge to correlate the respondents' economic circumstances with systemic discrimination. Furthermore, as to the weight to be given to the economic considerations, the trial judge stated,

> (t)he crime of importing cocaine is no less serious because the importer did it for reasons which attract empathy and mitigate personal culpability. Because factors which go to explain the reason for the offender's commission of the crime do not reduce the seriousness of the crime, those

> factors must be given les weight in cases like these where the seriousness of the offence is the pre-eminent consideration on sentencing. The same factors could be given more weight in cases involving less serious crimes where the personal responsibility of the offender takes on more significance (para 139).

For these reasons, the trial judge erred in the finding that systemic racial and gender bias justified conditional sentences. With respect to the appropriateness then of the conditional sentences, the judge found that:

- The conditional sentences did nothing to advance the restorative objectives that usually fuel conditional sentences (para 146).
- The imposition of conditional sentences feeds into the philosophy of drug overseers and makes the group more susceptible to targeting (para 147).
- Routine conditional sentences for such an offense 'undermines significantly the possibility of gaining the cooperation of these persons in the investigation and arrest of higher-ups on the drug-distribution chain' (para 149).

On the issue of there being an inordinate delay in the proceedings, the appellate court concluded that in light of the numbers of issues brought into the hearing, the time taken to complete the proceedings was far from inordinate. Though the judge considered imprisonment time of twenty months to be an appropriate sentence for Ms. Hamilton and two years less a day imprisonment time would be an appropriate sentence for Ms Mason, it was decided that credit should be given for the amount of time already served conditionally. Furthermore, it was decided that there would be no justice in incarcerating the women for a few months after having served as much time as they had conditionally; the conclusion was made that "(t)he administration of justice is best served by allowing the respondents to complete their conditional sentences" (para 167).

Perhaps what most is interesting about the trial level decision is the fact that Judge Hill makes an attempt to create a framework within which Black women's criminality may be assessed, rather than trying to assess the case through the lens of already established frameworks for the Black man or the White woman; the judge is able to engage in discourse then on the layers of a Black women's identity where she is marginalized not only b y virtue of race but also gender and socio-economic status.

The fact that the judge too, is able to recognize that the legal system alone cannot be expected to solve 'deeply rooted and profoundly complex social problems, and that the criminal justice system cannot be expected to eliminate criminal wrong doing' (para 150) is commendable. As one author states, such an exercise of judicial humility can only be welcomed (Kaiser 2003), but it begs the further question of the extent to which the criminal justice system is able at all to address complex questions concerning race and gender.

At the appellate level, there is room for the argument that the decision effectively extinguishes the development of a concrete framework which seeks to address the Black woman as an entity in her own right as formulated by the trial court, the question of whether the law is at all able to adequately address the concerns of individuals who are at once 'doubly burdened' or twice or perhaps even thrice marginalized becomes more of a burning consideration.

Important questions are also raised surrounding the question of the appropriateness of using race and gender as mitigating factors in sentencing decisions as an attempt to reflect the injustices incurred because of the influences of these factors (that is, race and gender). Perhaps the most immediate question which stems from this is the role of such an undertaking in generating stereotypes about the group in question. Seemingly it is this friction that concerns Justice Doherty; this is evident in his caution in appropriating a correlation between economic circumstances and systemic discrimination on the basis of race and or gender. Yet if it is not appropriate to address questions of race and gender within the sentencing realm, then the question stands as to where it should be placed in the law. Is there an inherent difficulty in suggesting that race and gender should find some place in the sentencing process and how much credence is to be given to the claim that introducing these concepts in the realm of sentencing allows for the perpetuation of negative stereotypes?

6. R v Spencer (ONSC 5914-02)

The case *R v Spencer* concerns 25 year- old Tracey-Ann Spencer (aged 23 at the time of offence) who was caught importing cocaine at Toronto Pearson International Airport. It would be remiss to deny the impact of the decision rendered in *R v Hamilton* ([2003] O.J. No. 532) on the sentencing decision handed down in Spencer. To all extents and purposes, it may be confidently asserted that Justice Mossip relied heavily on the reasoning put forward by Justice Hill (at the trial division) in sentencing each of Marsha Hamilton and Donna Mason. Ms. Spencer, like each of the accused in Hamilton, was a Black single mother with three children (para 7); and at the time of the offence had been the recipient of social welfare (para 9). Though at the time of the offence the accused was not working, at the time of sentencing she was fully employed, earning a gross income of approximately $23, 500.00 (para 11); in addition to this, there were monthly child support payments of $1000.00 (para 15). Ms. Spencer had no previous criminal record at the time of the offence, though she did have a charge related to the possession of stolen property for which she had received a suspended sentence and year's probation (para 15). In addition to this, there was a year's probation being served in relation to theft and threats uttered with regards to two pairs of jeans (para 15).

Justice Mossip suggested that it would be inappropriate to 'make different "findings" on the issues of systemic racism, the overrepresentation of single black mothers as couriers, and general deterrence issues, given the evidence... on this hearing... I both accept and rely on those parts of the Mason and Hamilton judgement which deal with the above issues as I find them necessary for the determination of a fit sentence' (para. 28-30).

In sentencing Ms. Spencer, then, Justice Mossip followed the pattern as devised in Hamilton; determining that the accused in this case too, should have imposed 'a term of imprisonment in the reformatory range and having so determined... (this) sentence should be served on a conditional basis' (para 31). En route to such a decision, Mossip found it to be relevant that:

- Richard Langlay, another accused apprehended at the same time had plead guilty and received a sentence of two and a half years. It was held that though the two were not co-accused, they were engaged in the act of importation together. The issue of parity was compelling in this case, and was particularly relevant when one co-accused introduces a guilty plea. (para 34); it was important that Ms. Spencer was not punished for not having joint Mr. Langlay in submitting a guilty plea (para 35).
- There was a 31 month lapse in time from the instance of offence to the time of sentencing; of this time, three months was attributable to the defence, with the remaining time attributable to institutional delay, including a significant waiting period in which the case *R v Hamilton* was being determined (para 38).

Justice Mossip seemed to be equally compelled to consider evidence associated with the accused's status as a single Black mother. Within this sphere of consideration was the concern that imprisonment for the accused would render inevitable her children becoming wards of the State (para 41). The judge also considered testimony from witnesses suggestive of the strong mother- child bond between the accused and her children, concluding that:

> at paragraphs 196 to 198 of the Hamilton and Mason judgement, Justice Hill succinctly outlines both the case law and policy reasons that I rely on in considering the best interests of Ms Spencer's children in determining a fit and just sentence. I accept the findings and reasoning set out in those paragraphs and consider the fact that the three children of Ms Spencer will not have someone to care for them in their home or have any one who can provide the loving care Ms Spencer does, as a mitigating factor with respect to my sentencing disposition (para 44- 45).

The trial judge also considered Ms. Spencer's additional risk of deportation to be of sufficient weight to mitigate the sentence handed down (para 50). Making reference again to Justice Hill's reasoning in Hamilton, Justice Mossip was keen to the existing social context in determining a fit and just sentence, including the assertion that 'offenders like those before the Court are subject to both the systemic economic inequality of women caring on their own for young children' (Hamilton, para. 198 Hamilton) who are further preyed upon by the 'drug distribution hierarchy', resulting in further disadvantage. Though conceding that the intricate web of factors inclusive of race, crime and imprisonment is difficult to decipher, 'adopting too rigorous a standard of proof of such matters threatens not only to ignore the nature of racism itself but also to perpetrate its insidious effects' (para 55).

In addition to this, Justice Mossip held that it would be absurd to ignore the 'clear evidentiary link between the systemic and background factors affecting Ms.

Spencer which played a role in the commission of the offence of importing' (para 56). Justice Mossip concurred with Justice Hill's determination of a 'purity adjusted weight' and applied a similar approach in determining the amount of cocaine being imported and hence the appropriate range of sentence to be applied; Ms Spencer was found to be outside the range set out in Madden and Cunningham (para. 74); furthermore, 'the imposition of a conditional sentence is punitive and can have both denunciating and general deterrence effect as has been enunciated in numerous decisions starting with *R v Proulx* (2000 140 C.C.C.[3d] S.C.C.' (para 77). The accused was sentenced to two years less a day to be served on a conditional basis (para 84) with additional punitive conditions. Included herein are: a 10 year weapons prohibition and the mandate that the accused remain within the residence except when necessary for 20 months and a daily curfew; maintenance of dependent children and enrolment in a community program in order to obtain personal counseling (para 86).

On appeal, Justice Doherty (who incidentally also delivered the appellate decision in R v Hamilton) made reference to the heavily reliance on the part of the trial judge on the decisions as they unfolded in *Hamilton*). Upon consideration of the decision as formulated by Mossip, Doherty held that:

- There was an error in principle in deciding that Ms Spencer fell outside the range as stipulated by Madden (para 22).
- 'None of the factors described by the trial judge as mitigating justified any departure from the Madden range, much less a conditional sentence of two years less a day' (para 24).
- With regard to issues of systemic discrimination on the basis of race and gender, Doherty, in continuing the stream of thought unveiled in the appeal decision to the Hamilton case, highlighted the fact that the seriousness of cocaine importation curtailed the extent to which a mitigated sentence would be appropriate. The seriousness of the offence played a role in explaining the personal circumstances of the offender that may mitigate personal culpability, but could not justify conditional sentences. Furthermore, Ms. Spencer's circumstances were very different from those the each of the accused in *Hamilton*. As he suggested, 'Ms. Spencer cannot be equated with Ms. Hamilton just because, like them, she is a single mother. A sentencing judge must look at the specific circumstances of each case' (para 26). In addition to this, there was no evidence that the accused was in such dire need that perhaps there was some desperation on her part. As he states, 'I do not think that the receipt of government assistance means that she was impoverished, or more to the point, that her financial circumstances had anything to do with race or gender' (para 28). In continuing this line of reasoning, Justice Doherty concluded that the analysis of Ms. Spencer's situation as provided by the trial judge was largely inaccurate. In particular, the finding that the accused had no marketable skills after high school 'is a description that would fit the vast

majority of high school graduates in Canada' (para 31).

On the issue of the accused being sentenced as a drug courier and nothing but, Justice Doherty suggested that 'the trial judge erred in diminishing Ms. Spencer's personal culpability based on speculation as to how and why she came to be involved in this crime' (para 34). As to the appropriateness of the sentence delivered at trial, it was held that though the trial judge appropriately considered the two and a half year sentence imposed on Mr. Langlay, this is no way however justified a sentence of less than two years; nor did it justify a conditional sentence.

With regard to the claim that there was an inordinate delay in proceedings which should mitigate the sentence meted down, Justice Doherty reviewed *R v Bosley* (1992) 18 C.R. (4th) 347 (Ont. C.A.), inferring from this decision, that the seven month delay in proceedings was not long enough to warrant mitigation of the sentence. As he suggests, 'Ms. Spencer was on bail throughout the trial proceedings. The terms of her bail imposed virtually no restraint on her liberty. Neither her bail terms standing alone nor those terms considered in combination with the length of time needed to complete the process warranted any mitigation of the sentence' (Justice Doherty, para 43). Furthermore, with regards to the likelihood of deportation, the fact that a sentence of two years or more would put her in a 'worse' position with respect to the likelihood of deportation was insufficient to justify a sentence that does not fit the offence (para 45).

With regard to the impact of the personal circumstances of the appellant, it was held that the fact of having three children does not diminish the severity of the crime committed. 'It is a grim reality that the young children of parents who choose to commit serious crimes necessitating imprisonment suffer for the crimes committed by their parents' (para 46). In addition to this, the accused was not entitled to the substantial mitigation that flows from a guilty plea; and hence the appropriate sentence at trial would have been 40 months of incarceration time – though the appellate judge did concede that the accused should be given a 16 month credit for time already served. In deciding the appropriate course of action, Justice Doherty indicated that 'the sentence imposed on Ms Spencer at trial was so manifestly inadequate that this is not a case where it can be said that the administration of justice would not be served by incarcerating Ms Spencer at this time' (para 50). The accused was further sentenced to 20 months of incarceration time.

As a concluding note, perhaps what would be most useful is a thorough outline of the sorts of questions to be explored in the course of this thesis; most of which have been derived from an examination of the interplay between issues of race, gender and class in each of the decisions in *Borde*, *Hamilton* and *Spencer*. What will be explored is the extent to which there really is merit to Hill's claim that there is some sort of correlation between Black womanhood and the incidence of drug muling. As was stated by Justice Hill in Hamilton, "...there is something unique when it comes to women about cocaine importing, and I'm trying to figure out what it is, and I'm trying to figure out when I see black women before me, day in, day out, assignment court after assignment court, what it means in terms of the crime of cocaine importing, and what it should mean to me, if anything, as a sentencing judge obliged to apply equality principles, and constitutional principles in the exercise of a discretion, which sentencing is."(para 102). As a means of doing so, what will unravel is a socio-legal deconstruction of the term 'drug muling' to uncover the intricacies associated with the term; and to tease the question of the extent to which the law serves as a dual mechanism with the potential to simultaneously institute and combat racism. This is done following in the footsteps of Hall's (1978) deconstruction of the crisis of 'mugging' in his pioneer work, Policing the Crisis: Mugging, the State and Law and Order.

Subsidiary questions expected to arise include:

- To the extent that there is differential treatment of women within the criminal justice system, how is this tension heightened by adding another variable such as race and or class? Similarly, to the extent that systemic racism is a factor which is given credence in the sentencing of Black males, does this recognition take on a different form in the instance that the perpetrator is female instead of male; and to what extent? The aim here is to interrogate the assumption of double oppression and differential treatment under the law... Do the Courts recognize this double oppression? And is this evinced in differential treatment or added or lessened weight given to instances in which systemic racism is deemed to have played a role in commission of the offence? Undoubtedly, an examination of Hamilton, Spencer and Borde would be useful as starting point for such a discussion.
- To what extent may it be legitimately asserted that the law, through influence from the media and judiciary institutes racism and or sexism? How does the image of the Black woman play into this assertion?
- To what extent may it be legitimately asserted that attempts such as those which endorse the use of systemic discrimination as a mitigating factor represent attempts to curb further discrimination or to combat existing discrimination on the basis of race, class or sex? Do the trial decisions in each of Spencer and Hamilton reflect attempts on the part of the Criminal Courts to curb or at least recognise the incidence of systemic discrimination? How do the appellate decisions interfere with this dynamic?

Conclusively then, the major question which stands is how the law negotiates a place for the Black woman and what does it means if there is no place for her experiences in the law? Where it has been advanced through the works of King, Iyer, Crenshaw and Aylward that theory is ill equipped, is the construct of the law similarly ill equipped? To the extent that the law is White, what does it mean if there is no place for issues of systemic discrimination in the event that the law has some place in generating race as an oppressive category through its agents?

References

Aylward, C. 1999 *Canadian Critical Race Theory: Racism and the Law*. Nova Scotia: Fernwood.

Collins, P. 2004 "Some Group Matters: Intersectionality, Situated Standpoints and Black Feminist Thought." In V. Taylor and N. Whittier (Eds.) *Feminist Frontiers VI*. New York: McGraw Hill.

Commission on Systemic Racism in the Ontario Criminal Justice System. 1995 Report. Ontario: Queen's Printer.

Crenshaw, K. 2003 "Demarginalising the Intersection of Race & Sex: A Black Feminist Theory and Antiracist Politics." In A. Wing (Ed.) *Critical Race Feminism: A Reader. 2nd edition,* New York: NYU Press.

Hall, Stuart. et al 1978. *Policing the Crisis: Mugging, the State and Law and Order*. London: Macmillan Education.

Henry, F. and Tator, C. 2002 *Discourses of Domination: Racial Bias in the Canadian English- Language Press*. Toronto: University of Toronto Press.

Iyer, N. 1993 "Disappearing Women: Racial Minority Women in Human Rights Cases" *Canadian Journal of Women and the Law* 6 (1): 25-44.

Kaiser, H.A. 2003 "Borde and Hamilton; Facing the Uncomfortable Truth About Inequality, Discrimination and General Deterrence". *Criminal Reports* 8(6): 289-298.

King, D. 1993 "Multiple Jeopardy: The Context of a Black Feminist Ideology." In A. Jaggar and P. Rosenberg (Eds.) *Feminist Frameworks: Alternative Theoretical Accounts of the Relations between Women and Men 3rd ed.*, USA: McGraw Hill, Inc.

Mosher, C. 1998 *Discrimination and Denial: Systemic Racism in Ontario's Legal and Criminal Justice Systems 1892-1961*. Toronto: University of Toronto Press.

R v Borde 2003 O.J. No. 354.

R v Hamilton 2003 O.J. No. 532, (2003) 172 C.C.C. (3d) 114.

R v Spencer 2003 ONSC 5914-02.

Walker, J. 1997 *"Race" Rights and the Law in the Supreme Court of Canada: Historical Case Studies*. Toronto: Osgoode Society for Canadian Legal History & Wilfred Laurier University Press.

van Dijk, T.A. 1993 *Elite Discourse and Racism (volume 6)*. California: Sage Publications, Inc.

Visano, L.A. 2002 "The Impact of Whiteness on the Culture of Law: From Theory to Practice." In C. Levine-Rasky (Ed.) *Working Through Whiteness: International Perspectives,* Albany: State University of New York Press.

12. How Far Have Our Courts Come and How Far Will They Go? Racializing Courts and Racializing Judgements

Wesley Crichlow

"Judges shall discharge their duties objectively and impartially so that they may earn the trust and affection of the people".
(From The Arthashastra, a Hindu political treatise written over two thousand years ago.)

1. Introduction

Traditional and contemporary white reactions to both racism and anti-racism are rooted deeply within seemingly innocuous traditions of liberal conscience. This conscience informs, in turn, the rhetoric of convenient juridic chatter (Visano, 2001). Judges in Canada are aware that Canada's legal system and its attendant jurisprudence both reflect convenient juridic chatter and operate in the context of racial privilege that is historically rooted and institutionally protected. This paper sets out first a brief summary of Canada's 1996 and 2001 statistical count on the changing multi-racial make up of the country. It then proceeds with an analysis of the impact of R.v. R.D.S.,(S.C.N.S. SH No. 112404, Heard by Chief Justice Constance Glube of the Supreme Court of Nova Scotia on April, 18th 1995, applying the guidelines as set out by the Supreme Court of Canada in Law v. Canada (Minister of Employment and Immigration) [1999] S. C. J. No. 12, (1999) 170 D.L.R. 4th) and informed by Critical Race Theory. Specifically, both the historical and hermeneutics of law are considered in terms of significance of race and the RDS case. I consider what new racialized judiciary gains have been made in the judicial pronouncements by our Canadian judges. In addition, particular attention will be paid to the substantive positions expressed by justices L'Hereux Dube and Beverly McLachlin, as expressed in the Supreme Court's ruling on R.D.S. The judicial pronouncement of these two judges will be the driving tool to further advance my article's main claim.

2. Demographic Racial Make Up From 1996 to 2001Canadian Census Statistics

Judges must understand, in broad terms, the racial and ethnic mix of the people they see in our/their courts. They must begin to learn to unlearn some of the negative stereotypes they hold about racialized individuals and begin to apply bias free legal logic and while learning a little more about racialized persons, refugees, new immigrants, the disabled, and their communities demographic make up. The composition of the population of Canada has changed drastically over the last several decades. In fact, the 1996 census reveals that nearly one in six persons in Canada is an immigrant.

Moreover, the face of immigration has changed with the passage of time. For example, prior to 1961, approximately 3 per cent of immigrants were persons of colour. In the period from 1991 to 1996, nearly 74 per cent of immigrants were persons of colour. The 1996 census also reveals that 44 per cent of the Canadian population reported at least one ethnic origin other than British, French, or Canadian, and 17.4 per cent of the population had at least one mother tongue that was neither English nor French. And 20,921,770 or 73.4 per cent of Canada's total population of 28,528,125 are English-speaking, while 6,890,880 or 24.6 per cent are French-speaking. Today racial minorities make up 20 per cent of the island of Montreal, 12 per cent of the metropolitan region of Montreal, and 6 per cent of the provincial population. One Quebecker in ten is a member of an ethnic community that is not French, English, or Aboriginal.

There has been a three-fold increase according to Statistics Canada in relations to visible minorities since 1981. Canada was home to almost four million individuals who identified themselves as visible minorities in 2001, accounting for 13.4 per cent of the total population. Visible minorities are defined by the Employment Equity Act as "persons, other than Aboriginal peoples, who are non-Caucasian in race or non-white in colour". Proportions of Canadian-born visible minorities varied widely from group to group, in large measure a reflection of historical immigration patterns. About 65 per cent of the Japanese were born in Canada, the highest proportion of all visible minority groups, followed by 45 per cent of Blacks, 29 per cent of South Asians, 25 per cent of Chinese, 21 per cent of Arabs and West Asians, 20 per cent of Latin Americans and 17 per cent of Koreans (Statistics Canada, 2001). As of May 15, 2001 5.4 million people or 18.4 per cent of Canada's total population of 31,499,560 were born outside the country. This was the highest proportion since 1931, when foreign-born people made up 22.2 per cent of the population. In 1996, as mentioned earlier that proportion was 17.4 per cent (Ibid) Of the 1.8million immigrants who arrived between 1991 and 2001, 58 per cent came from Asia, including the Middle East; 20 per cent from Europe; 11 per cent from the Caribbean, Central and South America; 8 per cent from Africa; and 3 per cent from the United States (ibid). If recent immigrant trends continue according to Statistics Canada, the visible minority population will continue to grow rapidly over the next couple of decades. Projections show that by 2017, visible minorities will account for one-fifth of Canada's population (ibid). What's more, by Canada's 150th birthday, almost 95 per cent of visible minorities would live in metropolitan areas, with three-quarters living in Toronto, Vancouver or Montreal. And about one-half of the people living in Toronto and Vancouver would belong to a visible minority by 2017 (ibid). Chinese and South Asians were the largest visibly minority groups in Canada according to the 2001 census, and the projection does not see that changing. Roughly one-half of all visible minorities would belong to those groups by 2017 (ibid). Blacks would remain Canada's third-largest minority group, reaching a population of about one million (ibid). In Montreal, blacks and Arabs would remain the largest visible minority groups, representing 27 per cent and 19 per cent of the minority population, respectively (ibid). The Aboriginal population like many others are also growing. Aboriginals now account for 3.3 per cent of the total population, compared to 2.8 per cent five years ago. Further, Aboriginal and visible minority youth now make up the two largest sectors in Canada's growing racialized populations (ibid). Utilizing visible minority and some Aboriginal statistics we can begin to identify future concerns and issues for the judiciary in the area of critical legal race reasoning, to debunk stereotypes in criminal law.

As with most changes, this shift in the dynamic of the population has led to increased tensions and stresses. For some years now in this country the police, other criminal justice administrative departments, and commissions have also been collecting, in a systematic but not public or legally official way, statistics on the over-representation of Black, Aboriginal, and other racial minorities in the criminal justice system. This data collection also highlights for us that racial disparities in the treatment of some minority groups has not changed over time, which is very important to remember.

3. The Defining Struggle

To define racism is both easy and difficult. Easy if one already has the conviction that the phenomenon exists, experiences it daily, and one consequently acknowledges racism's various forms/components. Difficult if one expects and demands that any proposed definition be so complete as to encompass all of its possible manifestations, and conditions upon which it operates, a task sometimes asked of racialized minorities in order to substantiate claims of racial discrimination. However, one irrefutable fact remains, a vast difference exists between the victim's perspective and that of the un-informed or directly affected individuals. Victims who understand the many manifestations of racism and the racist expressions have an uninterrupted and continuous perspective on and expressive body language of the dynamics or workings of racism which permit them to put each isolated incident into the proper perspective. Victims are already wearing, living and seeing through the eyeglasses that allow them to make intelligible their experiences and to see accurately. The concept of racism is not limited simply to easily discernible forms of antagonism or hostility. Rather, racism consists also of psychic failings such as the failure to act, without any consciousness of differential treatment based on colour. This is better known as "subconscious" or "unconscious" racism. This practice we can label "normative" or "everyday" racism: daily experiences and acts of racism as "normal" experiences for minority groups of racialized peoples. Succinctly, as Calmore (1982: 203) notes:

> Racism is more easily recognized than explained and is best viewed as an "ideology," or a social belief system diffused through the public mind. . . . The ideology of racism supports a socio political program that victimizes a group of people on the basis of race and skin colour for the concrete or psychological benefit of the dominant group. . . . Racism is not a neat

> concept, but, rather, one composed of an assembly of diverse fragments, held together by an exceptionally strong strand of white superiority. Racism is an ideological collage that pastes together exploitation, subjugation, domination, oppression, and suppression. . . . In terms of black–white relations, for example, racism's root manifestation was, of course, chattel slavery.

Many Canadians, including Quebeckers, fail to realize that slavery existed in Quebec. They proudly proclaim that "at least it's not as bad here as in the United States." This syndrome sets up a justified hierarchy of oppression in which it is seen that oppression in Canada is better than oppression in the United States. Further, one is left with what appears to be a logical explanation (although racist but not able to see it) as Canada having good racist while the US has bad racist Or in the words of Statzewich, "one of our most enduring national myths is that there is less racism here than in the United States (1998:11). To this end, a historical perspective is an essential component for judicial decision making in order to understand the social situations/contexts of Blacks and other racial minorities. Many Canadians are equally unaware that in Quebec a slave woman by the name of Marie-Josée Angelique was hanged, in what is today Old Montreal, for burning down her master's and sixteen other homes—one of the biggest revolts in Canadian slavery. In addition, Blacks were not allowed to sit anywhere in theatres (Frederick Johnson case, 1898) or to be served in public establishments in Montreal until the 1950s. Judicial support for racial segregation in Montreal is evident in *Loew's Montreal Theatres Ltd. v. Reynolds* (1919), 30 Q.B.R. 459.As late as 1940, the Supreme Court of Canada held that it was legal to refuse to serve Black people in places like the Montreal Forum (King case, 1940).

In 1919, the Quebec Appeal Court declared it legal for Loew's Theatre in Montreal to continue its practice of restricting Blacks to balcony seats. Indeed, few Quebeckers know that it was only in 1963 that Quebec adopted a law banning racial discrimination in public accommodation and, in 1964, a law banning racial discrimination in employment. During the period 1891 - 1965 the Separate Schools Act was designed to segregate Black and white students. The extent to which it affected different cities and Provinces varied across Canada: In Chatham until 1891; Harrow until 1907; Amberstburg until 1917; North Colchester and Essex until 1965; Alberta until the 1960s (Winks, 1969: 2). While these examples informs us that racism is an unpalatable subject, it must be dealt with.

The prevailing attitude that Canadian racism is somewhat more benign than in the U.S. has served to suppress and sanitize, rather than sensitize themselves and others through dialogue, patience and understanding on the damages of racism. Consequently, it is imperative that the task of "social context education" for judges be an enlightened dialogue: dialogic relationships must involve ongoing education of the judiciary about the historical context of unsettling relations, processes of denial regarding racism, and the role played by the judiciary in maintaining exclusionary practices. To achieve effective critical race and legal consciousness, it is necessary to uncover subjugated knowledges and confront an organized analysis of differing cultural spaces, appositional legal practices of race and gender, and their impact on accepted traditional legal norms. This approach to education leads to long-term changes and enhances the equitable adjudication of particular claims. Given that law was used in the past to violate people's human rights in Canada, can we use law today to liberate these very groups and how can this be achieved?

It is possible the person who has not experienced racism will merely see some isolated incidents which are themselves reprehensible but this uninformed individual will not necessarily spontaneously perceive or grasp the cumulative, sum total or fluid and dehumanizing effects and nature of racism which tends to generate it's own energy. It becomes therefore imperative to validate or valorize the victims reality, by being particularly attentive, sensitive, patient, and caring to their feelings and perspective by hearing the victims voice. In general, racism is an ideological expression of the manner in which the dominant majority relate to other cultures. It is a pejorative distinction based on skin colour and the "racial social construction" of other as "different" or "alien". Race is used here as a social construct, all social constructions can also be socially resisted. In 1903, W. E. DuBois (1989) commented that "the problem of the 20th century is the problem of the colour-line" (1989: 29). When we examine academic and other professional bodies of literature, political debates, 9/11 security debates, Bill C-36, immigration concerns, employment equity, poverty and high school push outs, we see his prediction uttered under divine inspiration extends well into the 22nd century. Toni Morrison for example, argues that despite the scientific refutation of race as legitimate, race continues to be a powerful "social" construct and "signifier": Race has become metaphorical — a way of referring to and disguising forces, events, classes, and expressions of social decay and economic division far more threatening to the body politic than biological "race" ever was. Expensively kept, economically unsound, a spurious and useless political asset in election campaigns, racism is as healthy today as it was during the enlightenment. It seems that it has a utility far beyond economy, beyond the sequestering of classes from one another, and has assumed a metaphorical life so completely embedded in daily discourse that it is perhaps more necessary and more on display than ever before (1992: 63).

An essential feature of racism is the power of a dominant group to make "naturalized" or subconscious assumptions of inferiorized differences thereby imposing burdens or obligations of deference from the designated "inferior other" group. The historical and contemporary treatment of Aboriginal/First Nation's, Blacks, Chinese, Japanese, Jews just to list a few in Canada's past demonstrates the consequences, conditions and contexts of racism. Likewise, the relationship between French Canadians and British/English Canadians highlight the vagaries of discrimination. Despite the abundance of evidence to support Canada's racist past against the above mentioned groups, the only successful claim compensated without litigation is the redress claim for the internment of Japanese Canadians during and after the Second World War (1991). Clearly from these examples, operating at the level of culture, racism seeks to deny racialized people their own voices, histories and struggles. This we can argue in part is due to the fact that the master narrative is woven into the Canadian national hierarchy of white prejudice, privilege and power representing white voices as the only legal and legitimate claim or experience worth knowing.

4. Racism and the Justice System

In order to develop a more shared understanding of the problem, it is crucial to begin a dialogue about how to understand racism and racial inequality in the judicial system. Canadian race theorist Professor Joanne St. Lewis, in her article "Racism and the Judicial Decision-Making Process," defines racism in the judicial context as:

an attitude in the judicial decision-making process which assumes the inherent superiority of the values of the dominant cultural/racial group and the concomitant inferiority of another cultural/racial group. The issue is fundamentally about power of the mass and the shared belief system; the power to shape reality in accordance with one's values; the power to give voice to or to silence the diversity of others; the power to rewrite history and develop legislation which meets the socioeconomic imperatives of the majority (1994: 15).

We may want to consider whether the judiciary should ultimately focus on the eradication of racism, that is, protection of the liberal democratic entitlements of those who appear before judges, especially those from the most disadvantaged social situations. Alternatively, should the role of the courts or judges be to animate the process, to act as catalysts for social change? Finally, what will happen to social justice anti-racist movements and affected racialized individuals when the courts do not rule in their favour? Where would they turn, what will happen to the movements and the people affected and doing the work? This is sometimes referred to as the "sword versus shield" dichotomy. That is, should the law be used as a protective measure against race discrimination in the criminal justice system, with the aim of creating a more equitable society? Another, perhaps more useful way of articulating the overall challenge is to focus on the notions of white supremacy and social closure. However, it is equally important to talk about the limitations of using law alone as a tool for social justice and social change.

"White supremacy" in this context does not refer to the philosophy or actions of extreme right-wing organizations. More appropriately, the concept of white supremacy refers to the privileging of whiteness as an invisible norm and societal organizing tool principle & tool, that is, when white is implicitly deemed to be "right." In her article "Whiteness as Property," Cheryl Harris explains how the concept of whiteness is built on both exclusion and racial subjugation:

[A]s it emerged, the concept of whiteness was premised on white supremacy rather than mere difference. White was defined and constructed in ways that increased its value by reinforcing its exclusivity. Indeed, just as whiteness as property embraced the right to exclude, whiteness as a theoretical construct evolved for the very purpose of racial exclusion [1992:23].

In developing effective social context education for judges, one of the problems we face is understanding the ways in which different groups are racialized — experience racism — and each is unique, based on its historical, contemporary, political, social, and economic experiences. It is important for each affected group to articulate its own experiences in order to be able to properly remedy that particular exercise of racial oppression and stereotyping. For example, in Quebec, a stereotype commonly held by many people is the assumption that every Black person in Montreal is a Haitian or a recently arrived immigrant. Likewise, Toronto went through a period in which every Black person was wrongly identified as a Jamaican, or every Black person arrested by the police for criminal wrong doing or gang and gun activity was supposedly believed to be Jamaican.

What this stereotyping leads us to is a simplistic formula of using the Haitian or new immigrant experience or perspective to generalize the experiences of all those who are socially constructed as "other," "different," or "alien," rendering their life experiences invalid. It also has the effect of reducing Blacks whose ancestors were in Canada or Quebec for many generations to the marginal status of "immigrant", "alien", "outsider" and "burden" on the "system", or worse, dismissing the identity of Canadian Blacks. This also raises a fundamental question that many Blacks and other racialized people often ask themselves: When do they stop being labelled "different", "immigrant," "alien," "other," or "outsider", "boat people", and when does the question "where are you from" stop been asked and gain Canadian status? But it appears because white power is an unquestioned "normative" white power privilege, racialized individuals will always be seen as belonging somewhere else and never fully gain the status and privileges accorded to white Canadian citizens. Ben Johnson's in the 1988 Olympics after testing positive for illegal performance enhancement substances, illustrates how in twenty four hours or less how one can be constructed as Canadian sprinter for winning the gold and become Jamaican or immigrant born for illegal substance use and shame on the country, only after it was discovered.

But in order to help avoid generalizations, and stripping people of Canadian status overnight, one must start with the premise that each Black person, Arab or new immigrant has individual and unique needs and experiences. Therefore, judges are and should be encouraged to ask questions about and around race, culture and identity that will or might be interpreted by the accused or the defence as having racial overtones. To avoid using sweeping generalizations and stereotypes, judges need to ask the following questions: "Is race an issue in this case? Do the particular circumstances of this case have anything to do with the fact that the person charged before me is Black?" If the answer is yes, the next step is to find a strategy for invoking legal reasoning, by asking oneself what alternatives there are, if any, to the existing legal rule or practice. Another question is "What harm might be done or caused to the racialized accused if race is an issue and it is not addressed?" How has past racial wrongs affected the individual and the community to which they belong? What are the social political and economic conditions under which the accused lived/lives daily that shapes/shaped their present condition? How do judicial institutions function to maintain racism? How do judicial law schools or educational judicial discourses function to maintain racism? Equally, important is how do judges "normative" and "common sense" understanding of racism shape their judicial pronouncements? Finally, how does everyday racism affect the accused lively hood of been successful and their view of the world?

In addition, if race appears to be a factor but neither the defence nor the Crown has opted to raise it, the following question is warranted: "Do I have a legal and ethical obligation to raise it in order to ensure equal protection and benefit of the law for the racialized accused or victim before me?" Are some members of the practising legal profession ready to ask themselves the pressing question, what training did I lack throughout legal and non-legal education in the area of race base jurisprudence, that I must now seek out? Finally, what role should judges play if they are aware of government commissions, social science research, and other studies documenting unfair treatment and racist stereotyping of racial minorities, especially when defence and the Crown are not or refuse to be knowledgeable about racism?

Given the explosive nature of the above questions, the issues of racism and the social construction of race as real are likely to subject a trial judge to considerable controversy and allegations of bias. But failing to attend to these questions invites injustice. And can lead to calling the justice system into disrepute. For this reason courts must adopt a cautious approach when examining a trial judgement to determine if it gives rise to "a reasonable apprehension of bias." Judges must adopt an approach of scrupulously identifying the relevance and significance of any reference to race, because, as Cornell West (1994) reminds us, "race does matter." Hence, an explanation to defence and the accused as to where the trial judge is going with the questions about race will clearly reduce any perceptions of bias and will be more consistent with a fair inquiry. To not allow judges to take race into account without formal evidence, where it may be a factor, would not only be unreasonable, it would be discriminatory, or even unconstitutional. Substantively, prohibiting the taking of race into account without such formal evidence would be to deny the accused the right to equal treatment under subsection 15(1) of the *Charter of Rights and Freedoms*. In identifying race as a relevant factor for one racial group or accused, you have the equal responsibility to draw upon the commonality of experience among different racialized or racial minority groups.

5. Building the Case of Unfair Treatment in the Justice System

Law and order exist for the purpose of establishing Justice . . . when they fail in this purpose they become the dangerously structured dams that block the flow of social justice and progress. (Martin Luther King Jr., 1963)

Law professor Allan Hutchinson argues that, despite the rhetoric of fairness in Canadian society, Black Jamaicans, First Nations and other racial minorities remain a distinct underclass in Canada. It is the race of the accused that is determinative.

Stephen Lewis, in his report to the then-Premier of Ontario, Bob Rae, labels the over-policing of Blacks and their unfair or unequal treatment in the criminal justice system as anti-Black racism fuelled by an anti-Jamaican sentiment. For more on the case that coined the term "anti-black racism," see *R. v. Parks* (84 C.C.C. [3d] 353 [O.C.A.]) wherein the Ontario Court of Appeal held that the accused Black man, who was charged with the murder of a White victim, should be allowed to challenge jurors for racial prejudice because of the overwhelming evidence of anti-Black racism in Toronto and Canada.

The Report by the Commission on Systemic Racism in the Ontario Criminal Justice System also labels it anti-Black racism and anti-Jamaican sentiment. The various inquiries into police–Black Relations after shootings and killings by the Montreal, Toronto, Ottawa, York Region, and Nepean police forces have all documented heavy over-policing of racialized people, and Blacks in particular. For example, the following people were shot by police without benefit of any adjudication of guilt, and many without even being charged with an offence.

Most of these Black people died or were injured as a result of a police shooting targeted at them, with little or no accountability by the police for the killings: Andrew "Buddy" Evans on August 9, 1978; Albert Johnson, August 26, 1979; Michael Sargeant, November 20, 1979; Leander Savoury, January 30, 1985; Anthony Griffin, November 11, 1987; Lester Donaldson, August 9, 1988; Earl Edwards, November 7, 1988; Michael Wade Lawson, December 8, 1988; Sophia Cook, October 27, 1989; Marlon Neal, May 4, 1990; T. T. (a young offender), September 20, 1991; Marcellus Francois, July 3, 1991; Vincent Gardner, September 26, 1991; Royan Bagnaut, November 3, 1991; Jonathan Howell, November 9, 1991; Raymond Lawrence, May 2, 1992; Ian Coley, April 20, 1993; Albert Moses, September 29, 1994; Tommy Barnett, January 10, 1996; Andrew Bramwell, March 15, 1996; Wayne Williams, June 11, 1996; Faraz Suleman, June 19, 1996; Douglas James Payne, 1996; John Braithewaite, 1996; Francis Nicholls, January 1, 1997; Edmund Yu, February 6, 1997; and Hugh Dawson, March 30, 1997. These shootings reveal deep-rooted anti-Black prejudice in the criminal justice system of Canada (Visano, 2003) and Quebec.

The overwhelming data in the past was well documented by the Commission on Systemic Racism in the Ontario Criminal Justice System, which released its findings from a three-year ethnographic study in 1995. The Commission found that, although there is no evidence that Black people are more likely to use drugs than others or that they are over-represented among those who profit most from drug use, Blacks are the most likely to wind up in jail. More recently the Toronto Star also ran a series of articles highlighting and reinforcing the practice known as racial profiling and anti-Black racism in Toronto.

Intensive policing of low-income areas in which Black people live produces arrests of a larger and disproportionate number of Black male street-dealers. The Commission's report said that once the police have done their work, the practices and decisions of Crown prosecutors, justices of the peace, and judges operate as a conveyor belt to prison. The report also informs us that, of those convicted of similar drug charges, for example, 55 per cent of Blacks and only 36 per cent of Whites go to jail. About 66 per cent of the Blacks convicted of drug trafficking were imprisoned, compared with 36 per cent of Whites. Simple possession of drugs reflected the same statistics: 49 per cent of Black offenders were sent to prison, compared to 18 per cent of White offenders.

The Commission noted that, while in prison, Blacks are subjected to the racist language, culture, and attitude that plague the environments of many Ontario prisons. The disregard, silence, and the failure of managers to take preventive action contribute to the maintenance of racially poisoned environments. Racism is tolerated as the assumed price that must be paid in order to maintain peace and order: some prisons tolerate and encourage racial segregation in the allocation of prisoners among living units, and the rehabilitation services available to black and other racial-minority prisoners are inadequate. The Ontario prison system caters principally to White Euro-Canadian norms, and many of the service needs of Black and other racial-minority prisoners remain unacknowledged or dismissed. Many institutions fail to recognize the "inherent dignity and worth" of prisoners or to "treat prisoners as individuals" (Commission Report, 1995).

The Quebec situation is unquestionably similar. A 1990 study done by the Comité de protection de la jeunesse showed that Black, Latino, and Aboriginal youths were three times more present in the youth protection system than they were in the population at large. All these examples involve a reverse triangle. In provinces and courts across this county, it is common to see a White judge, police officer, Crown attorney, and defence lawyer, with a Black or Aboriginal suspect or accused in the middle — an experience that is not unique to Quebec, Toronto, or Halifax.

Ontario criminal lawyer Clayton Ruby, Professor Francis Henry, Carole Tator, Evelyn Kallen, and others have written extensively about the unfair treatment of Blacks in the criminal justice system and in Canada in general. More recently, a Canada Customs study (1998) brought to light an old form of racist policing of Black and racialized people at border-crossings and in customs across this country. It serves as a perfect illustration of the types of challenges facing judges who are presiding over cases involving racism in either explicit or hidden fashion. The practice in question is known as racial profiling, and it has been documented in Canadian, American, British, European Airports, by state officials after 9/11 and at the U.S.– Canada border. The following excerpts capture official responses that connect crime to colour, thereby perpetuating and "naturalizing" the whiteness of the law and racial profiling of Blacks and other stigmatized minorities. It is often difficult for most victims of racial profiling to proof that they were victims of the draconian practice. Often, a racial profiling claim can rarely be proven by direct evidence since a police officer is not likely to admit that they have been influenced by racial stereotypes in the exercise of their discretion or execution of their job. Therefore, racial profiling must be proven by inference drawn from circumstantial evidence. This is where the victim's testimony must be leaning towards persuasive evidence. Where the evidence shows that (a) the circumstances surrounding a police detention correspond to the phenomenon of racial profiling and (b) provide a basis to infer that the police officer is lying about the reason for singling out the accused; then the record is then capable of supporting a finding that the stop was based on racial profiling.[Lawyers Weekly] . The following cases are a few Canadian examples of racial profiling where our courts have given notice to law enforcement and Crown Attorneys that the practice of racial profiling must end. In Ontario R.v. Parks, (1993) C.C.C. (3d) 353 (Ont. Ca.). Parks was charged with second-degree murder and convicted of manslaughter. He appealed the conviction and sentence . Parks was a drug dealer and the victim a cocaine user. Parks argued that the trial judge should have allowed defence counsel to ask prospective jurors whether the fact that the accused was a black man and the victim a white woman would adversely affect their ability to impartially perform their duties (ibid). In Parks, Justice Doherty of the Ontario Court of Appeal concluded that "our institutions, including the criminal justice system, reflect and perpetuate negative stereotypes. These elements combine to infect our society as a whole with the evil of racism. Blacks are among the primary victims of that evil"(ibid, 371-372). In R.v. Hamilton, (2000) O.J. No. 2722 (Gen Div.). Mr. Hamilton was charged with the possession of marijuana assaulting a peace officer with intent to resist arrest and escape from lawful custody.(ibid). A compelling piece of evidence came from an off-duty security officer who was walking with his family through the park, where the incident occurred and testified in court that he heard the two officers call Mr. Hamilton "nigger". Justice Reinhardt found that, based on the evidence, the police had conducted themselves improper and violated the rights of the accused under section 10 of the Charter of Rights & Freedoms and dismissed the charges (ibid). In a more recent case reported in the lawyers Weekly [May 23, 2003], on April 16, 2003, the Ontario Court of Appeal released its decision in R v. Brown, [2003] O.J. No. 1251, which deals with the occurrence of racial profiling by the police during investigation, detention and arrest. It also addresses the trial judge's handling of the Charter application based on the allegation of racial profiling raised by the accused. On November 1, 1999, Constable Olson, a Metro Toronto police officer, stopped Decovan "Dee" Brown, a young man of African-American descent and a former professional basketball player for the Toronto Raptors, as he was driving down the Don Valley Parkway. The officer's reason was that Mr. Brown was driving in excess of the speed limit and, on two occasions, his car had crossed out of and back into the lane in which he was traveling (ibid). Brown was administered a roadside screening device test, which he failed. As a result, he was taken to the police station and administered a breath test. Brown's blood-alcohol concentration registered at 140 mg per 100 ml of blood. He was charged with driving over the legal limit (more that 80 mg of alcohol in 100 ml of blood) (ibid). At trial, it was argued that the only reason Mr. Brown was stopped was because he was a young black man driving an expensive car (i.e., racial profiling). As a result, said the defence, the arrest was contrary to section 9 of the Charter and the results of the breath tests should be excluded. The trial judge dismissed the defendant's application and convicted him. Brown was fined $2000. Brown appealed to the Superior Court of Justice. The conviction was overturned and a new trial ordered. The appeal judge, Justice Brian Trafford, ruled that there was a reasonable apprehension of bias created by the trial judge's handling of the racial profiling issue and ordered a new trial. The Crown appealed to the Ontario Court of Appeal. The court of appeal concluded that, indeed, there was a reasonable apprehension of bias. It came to this conclusion based on comments by the trial judge made during (a) the cross-examination of the arresting officer, (b) during defence counsel's submissions on the Charter application and, (c) during the sentencing process. At one point the trial judge characterized the Charter application as "serious allegations, really quite nasty, malicious, potentially, accusations based on, it seems to me, nothing..." During the sentencing process, the trial judge suggested that Mr. Brown apologize to the officer for raising the racial profiling issue, which he characterized as "distasteful". The Ontario Court of Appeal confirmed that the test for determining a reasonable apprehension of bias was whether an informed person, viewing the matter realistically and practically – and having thought the matter through – would conclude that it was more likely than not that the decision maker, whether consciously or unconsciously, would not decide fairly. In relation to a racial profiling case, it confirmed that the reasonable person must be taken to be aware of the history of discrimination faced by disadvantaged groups in Canadian society protected by the Charter's equality provisions and that these were matters of which judicial notice could be taken. On the issue of racial profiling, the Ontario Court of Appeal made the following pronouncements: In the present case, the Ontario Court of Appeal found that there was evidence capable of supporting a claim of racial profiling. This included evidence that 1) the accused was a young black man wearing a baseball hat and jogging clothes driving an expensive car; 2) evidence that the officer looked into the car of the accused car before stopping him; 3) evidence of a second set of notes prepared by the officer to firm up his reasons to justify the stop once he realized that the accused was a person of considerable means capable of defending the charge; 4) evidence of a licence check that the officer made before the stop; 5) evidence of discrepancies between the times recorded in the officer's notebook and those, which he gave to the breathalyser technician (ibid). In Montreal according to the CBC news Judge Juanita Westmoreland-Traore-Judge cites racial profiling, throws out charges [Wed, 02 Feb 2005, CBC News] Judge Westmoreland-Traore threw out drug charges against a black man, saying he was a victim of racial profiling. Two Montreal police officers acted unlawfully last April when they detained and searched 24-year-old Alexander Campbell, Quebec Court Judge Juanita Westmoreland-Traore ruled. Police said they thought Campbell was acting suspiciously when they saw him leaning forward in a taxi. One of the officers testified he and his partner began following Campbell as he left the taxi. They asked him to stop but he began running. They chased him, tackled him and forced him into handcuffs. Police searched him on the spot, lowering his pants nearly to his knees. They found a cellular phone, $175, a scale and a gram of marijuana. Westmoreland-Traore dismissed two charges of drug possession against Campbell, ruling that his arrest was illegal and the search excessive. The judge said she did not believe the testimony of one of the officers, who said that after the arrest, Campbell tossed a 26-gram package of crack cocaine under the back seat of the patrol car. She also said the fact that Campbell ran didn't mean he was guilty of anything. "The accumulation of these factors... constitute a preponderance of proof that the accused was the object of racial profiling," wrote the judge. "In the context of a minority person, his reflex to move away from the police does not necessarily infer that he has committed an offence," she continued. Westmoreland-Traore's judgment came down days after Montreal police admitted they have a problem with racial profiling and are bringing in a number of measures to fight it.[ibid]. Likewise we saw the Supreme Court of Canada adopting a race base litigation approach with Canada's First Nations people, in the case of R. v. Gladue, (1997) a move to remedy the overrepresentation of Aboriginal people in prisons and the Criminal Courts, employing a critical race analysis to section 718.2 (e) of the Canadian Criminal Code. To elaborate, on her 19th birthday Jamie Tanis Gladue of Nanaimo, British Columbia, murdered her common-law husband, whom she suspected of romancing her sister. She plead guilty to manslaughter for killing her common-law husband, and was sentenced to three years imprisonment for manslaughter, but received full parole after serving less than a year. Her argument was simple: as an Aboriginal woman, she should qualify for a lesser sentence that would allow her to serve her time at home. The Supreme Court's April 23rd decision urged judges to remember section 717 and 718 of the Criminal Code.

6. Applying the R.D.S Framework: *R. v. R.D.S* — Facts and Case History

On trial before Judge Corrine Sparks — Nova Scotia's (and Canada's) only Black female judge at the time — on December 2, 1994, was R.D.S. A fifteen-year-old Black Nova Scotian youth, R.D.S. was charged with unlawfully assaulting a police officer, unlawfully assaulting a police officer with the intention of preventing arrest, and unlawfully resisting a police officer in the lawful execution of his duty, contrary to the Criminal Code of Canada (R.S.C. 1985, c. C- 46.R. *v. R.D.S.*, N.S. YO93-168). In court, in addition to R.D.S., was Constable Steinberg, the arresting officer, who is White.

At the trial, R.D.S. testified that he was riding his bike from his grandmother's house to his mother's house when he noticed that his cousin, N.R., had been detained by a police officer on the sidewalk. R.D.S. approached and asked N.R. if he was all right and if he would like him to inform his mother of what was happening. R.D.S. further testified that the police officer told him to shut up his mouth; otherwise he too would be placed under arrest. The police officer testified that R.D.S. ran his bike into him, yelled at him, and pushed him. What also makes this case interesting is that R.D.S. and the police officer were the only two witnesses at the trial, and the trial judge acquitted R.D.S. on a finding of credibility. In her deliberations, Judge Sparks wrote

> In my view, in accepting the evidence, and I don't say that I accept everything that Mr. S. has said in Court today, but certainly he has raised a doubt in my mind and, therefore, based upon the evidentiary burden which is squarely placed upon the Crown, that they must prove all the elements of the offence beyond a reasonable doubt, I have queries in my mind with respect to what actually transpired on the afternoon of October the 17th (67–68).

The Crown appealed the acquittal on the basis that some of the trial judge's comments reflected a reasonable apprehension of bias. The Crown argued that Judge Sparks's finding of credibility, which ran in favour of the Black youth's discharge, was questionable and biased. The Crown further argued that there was no reason for Judge Sparks to attack the credibility of the police. Judge Sparks responded with the following remarks:

> The Crown says, well, why would the officer say that events occurred the way in which he relayed them to the Court this morning? I'm not saying that the constable has misled the Court, although police officers have been known to do that in the past. And I'm not saying that the officer overreacted, but certainly police officers do overreact, particularly when they are dealing with non-white groups. That, to me, indicates a state of mind right there that is questionable. I believe that probably the situation in this particular case is the case of a young police officer who overreacted. And I do accept the evidence of Mr. S. that he was told to shut up or he would be under arrest. That seems to be in keeping with the prevalent attitude of the day. (68–69).

At issue here is the credibility of the Black judge in question asserting bias — and racial bias — against the police. The Nova Scotia Supreme Court (*R.v. R.D.S.*, S.C.N.S.; SH No. 112404), heard by Chief Justice Constance Glube of the Supreme Court of Nova Scotia on April 18, 1995 held that there was nothing in the trial transcript itself that would give rise to the impression that the trial judge was biased or inciting racism against the police. However, they argued that her comments were without foundation, and this is what in their opinion had led to the charge of bias.

In this case, the claim of racial discrimination is, contrary to subsection 15(1) of the Charter, based on a variety of contextual factors. To begin with, there is the fact that the incident took place in an area of Nova Scotia that has historically been known to be racially charged, and in which relations between the police and the African-Canadian community are toxic. The incident involves an altercation between an African-Canadian youth and a White police officer. The trial judge, Judge Sparks, was an African-Canadian woman. The race of the trial judge and the allegation of reasonable apprehension of bias against her immediately raise the issue of the extent to which judges may incorporate their life experiences and lived reality into their decision-making. Also at issue are the judge's ability to take judicial notice of the history of racial tension within a particular community and the characterization of the relationship between the police and members of a particular community as reflecting this historical tension. Judicial notice is commonly understood to be the acceptance of a fact without proof. It applies to two kinds of facts: (1) facts that are so well-known as not to be the subject of dispute among reasonable persons; and (2) facts that are capable of immediate and accurate demonstration by resorting to readily accessible sources of indisputable accuracy.

Examination of these contextual factors leads to the conclusion that the alleged violation of equality as guaranteed under subsection 15(1) is not aimed at a particular legislative provision, its application, or its non-application. In this case, the claim of racial discrimination is based on the determination of the Nova Scotia Supreme Court and the Court of Appeal that a reasonable apprehension of bias existed where the trial judge's consideration of the historically tense relationship between the police and members of the African-Canadian community resulted in deeming a member of that community to be more credible than a police officer. The real equality violation in this case is the failure of the appellate courts to appreciate the considerations that ought to be made by the judiciary in order to secure equality.

7. Integrative Case Analysis: Application of the Law Guidelines

The approach outlined in the Law case requires that attention be paid to the following three central issues:

1. whether a law imposes treatment that is different between the claimant and others, in purpose or effect: Determination of differential treatment can be made only upon consideration of whether a different result would have occurred had any of the contextual factors outlined above not been present. The equality challenge here is not based on a particular law, but on the Crown's allegation and the appellate court's determination that the comments made by Judge Sparks reflected a reasonable apprehension of bias. In theory, the claimant in this appeal could have been Judge Sparks, alleging violation of her right to equality on the basis of race, in that her impartiality was questioned because of the combination of her race and the perspective that her racial background provided in her assessment of credibility. But, practically speaking, the appellant, R.D.S, is the claimant who alleges a violation of his equality rights on the basis of race, in that the appeal of his acquittal was motivated by questions relating to comments made by the trial judge, which were informed by the experience of a racial heritage that she shared with R.D.S. His claim of a violation of equality rights is based on the argument that the acquittal would not have been challenged or overturned had she, the trial judge, or both of them not been members of a racialized community. This reasoning clearly establishes differential treatment on the basis of race.

Law v. Canada (Minister of Employment and Immigration) establishes a new set of guidelines to be applied by the courts in determining a violation of equality rights under subsection 15(1) of the Charter. The case dealt with the issue of age discrimination brought by Ms. Law against the Canada Pension Plan for delaying her receipt of survivor's benefits until she had reached 65. Ms. Law was 30 at the time of her husband's death. She applied for the survivor's benefit under the CPP and was denied, on the grounds that she was under 35, not disabled, and did not have any dependent children.

The challenge of Judge Sparks's comments raises suspicions as to whether it is fully accepted that judicial members of racialized or equality-seeking communities can be truly objective in adjudicating matters involving members of their own communities. This begs the further question as to whether the impartiality of judicial members from non-racialized groups is similarly challenged when they adjudicate over matters involving members of their own communities. This case does not simply raise the issue of differential treatment between witnesses, or between this particular accused and another from a non-racialized community, but also raises the issue of the level of judicial scrutiny that is applied to judges from racialized communities, a scrutiny to which "most white Judges" are not subjected . This is so too because the test for the "reasonable" person is still based on a White model, and more so on a White male model. When you raise these questions positively, many Blacks and other racial minorities tend to see an appearance of fairness and impartiality on the surface, and they approach the system with much more positive energy and also see you as on their side. Hence, a deconstruction of the "reasonable person" and legal rules needs to challenge the so-called neutrality and objectivity of judges and laws. When the impartiality of a judge is questioned as it was in this case, within this particular context, then the effect of society's deeply entrenched racial prejudice and bias is seen to impair the operation of the judicial system.

- whether one or more enumerated or analogous grounds of discrimination are the basis for the differential treatment: The enumerated ground of race is the basis for the differential treatment.
- whether the law in question has a purpose or effect that is discriminatory within the meaning of the equality guarantee.

As previously stated, what is at issue in the *R.D.S.* case is not a particular law or legislative provision, but that the allegation of bias against Judge Sparks and the application of the test to determine reasonable apprehension of bias are challenged as being discriminatory on the basis of race.

A determination of discrimination requires that a court make the following three broad inquiries:

1(i). Does the impugned law draw a formal distinction between the claimant and others on the basis of one or more personal characteristics?

The determination that a formal distinction has been drawn is based on the conclusion that Judge Sparks's comments would not have been challenged had she not been a member of the same racialized community as the accused. The formal distinction drawn is that, had the accused and the trial judge not been members of the same racialized community, and had the trial judge not uttered comments that made reference to her personal understanding of the contextual factors at play within that community, then those comments would not have raised the suspicion of bias or partiality. This establishes that the basis for the distinction is the enumerated ground of race.

1(ii). Does the impugned law fail to take into account the claimant's already disadvantaged position within Canadian society, resulting in substantively differential treatment between the claimant and others on the basis of one or more personal characteristics?

The reaction to the trial judge's consideration of the already disadvantaged position that people from racialized communities face vis-à-vis the police is the basis for the claim of discrimination. The accusation of bias against Judge Sparks represents a clear failure to consider the context of the already disadvantaged position that R.D.S held in Canadian society by virtue of his membership in a racialized community. Judge Sparks had properly considered the contextual factors that established the background against which the facts of the case played out. The allegation of bias sought to discount this consideration. And it is this failure to take into account R.D.S's already disadvantaged position within Canadian society, which resulted in substantively differential treatment between R.D.S and another individual who might not have been a member of a racialized community.

2. Is the claimant subject to differential treatment based on one or more enumerated and analogous grounds?

The allegation of bias against Judge Sparks, if proven, would have had the effect of overturning R.D.S.'s acquittal and causing his credibility to be assessed without the benefit of contextualization, clearly subjecting him to differential treatment on the enumerated ground of race.

3. Does the differential treatment discriminate by imposing a burden upon or withholding a benefit from the claimant in a manner that reflects the stereotypical application of presumed group or personal characteristics, or that otherwise has the effect of perpetuating or promoting the view that the individual is less capable or worthy of recognition or value as a human being or as a member of Canadian society, equally deserving of concern, respect, and consideration?

The differential treatment discriminates by withholding a benefit, namely the benefit of assessing credibility within the context of all relevant factors. The mere fact that Judge Sparks's comments were challenged for reasonable apprehension of bias suggests that race was clearly a factor in this case. Not only did Judge Sparks take proper consideration of race and other contextual factors, but it was her duty to take this into account in making a fair assessment of the credibility of the youth R.D.S. vis-à-vis the police officer.[R.v.R.D.S]

8. R.D.S. and Challenges for an Adoption of Critical Race Theory in the Courts

According to Richard Delgado and Derrick Bell (1995), critical race theory sprang up in the mid-1970s as a response to the slow pace of racial reform in the United States. In Canada, critical race theory came to light legally in the mid-1980s, along similar lines of racial reform as in the United States. It is also a critique of critical legal studies, which deciphers legal doctrine to expose both its internal and external inconsistencies and reveal the ways that "legal ideology has helped to create, support and legitimate America's present class structure" (Crenshaw, 1988). More importantly for a critical race theorist, critical legal studies fail to provide pragmatic strategies for material social transformation. Here Cornell West argues,

Critical legal theorists fundamentally question the dominant liberal paradigms prevalent and pervasive in American culture and society. This thorough questioning is not primarily a constructive attempt to put forward a conception of a new legal and social order. Rather, it is a pronounced disclosure of inconsistencies, incoherences, silences, and blindness of legal formalists, legal positivists, and legal realists in the liberal tradition. Critical legal studies is more a concerted attack and assault on the legitimacy and authority of pedagogical strategies in law school than a comprehensive announcement of what a credible and realizable new society and legal system would look like (West, 1993: 196).

On the other hand, critical race theory begins with the notion that racism is "normal, not aberrant, in North American Society" (Delgado, 1995) and, because it is so enmeshed in the fabric of our social order, it appears both normal and natural to people in this culture. Hence critical race theory departs from mainstream legal scholarship, and it sometimes employs narratives of storytelling to give voice, to name one's reality, and to analyze social conditions and situations, as in the case of R.D.S. (Delgado, 1995; Aylward, 1999). Storytelling allows lawyers to debunk the myths of "neutrality" and "objectivity" by placing the encounter between the Black youth and the White police officer, who represents the state, in its social and historical context of racial discrimination. Storytelling is fundamental for healthy social relationships. To feel connected and respected we need to tell our own stories and have others listen. For others to feel respected and connected to us, they need to tell their stories and have us listen. Having others listen to your story is a function of power in our culture. The more power you have, the more people will listen respectfully to your story. Consequently, listening to someone's story is a way of empowering them, of validating their intrinsic

Delgado suggests (1989) that there are at least three reasons why it is important to name one's reality in legal discourse:

1. much of "reality" is socially constructed,
2. stories provide to members of outgroups a vehicle for psychic self preservation, and
3. the exchange of stories from teller to listener can help overcome ethnocentrism and the dysconscious (King, 1992) drive or need to view the world one way.

In the case of R.D.S., the Black community's reality was constructed and told by lawyers representing R.D.S.

Law professor Carol Aylward argues that in the context of *R.D.S.* case, the critical race theory method of deconstruction took the form of challenging and deconstructing the doctrine of reasonable apprehension of bias, the reasonable person test, the myth of "neutrality" and "objectivity" in the context of judicial decision-making, the concept of formal equality, and the concept of legal reasoning as ahistorical. More important for judges is the issue of social context and the "reasonable person." She further argues that, from a critical race perspective, the majority decision has expanded the "reasonable person" to include an awareness of the social context of a case, such as societal awareness and knowledge of the prevalence of racism or gender bias in a particular community (Aylward, 1999).

In a recent compilation of critical race theory key writings, Crenshaw (1995), like Aylward (1999), pointed out that there is no "canonical set of doctrines or methodologies to which critical race scholars all subscribe. But these scholars are unified by two common desires: to understand how a "regime of white supremacy and its subordination of people of colour have been created and maintained in America" (xiii) and to change the bond that exists between law and racial power.

In order for critical race theory to go very far in social context education, it must not be seen as a tool of "radical" lawyers. Rather, it must be seen as a framework for judicial equity, and that means exposing racism in the judiciary at every level and proposing changes to those horrendous situations that people experience in the system. Even more importantly, we must not reproduce workshops — a movement of the late '80s aimed at educating and conscientizing racist individuals and institutions by sensitizing judicial gatekeepers and criminal justice officials on race and ethnicity — that can be seen as "professionalization" of prejudice reduction. They are limited in their efficacy of language and the constructs used, with no mention of colonialism, domination, or exploitation, for example. Any change resulting is limited to one personal insight: cosmetic surgery that does not auger well for social change in a judiciary that needs operative surgery. Critical Race Theory in judicial education allows us to recreate legal knowledge and language informed by a body of literature that empowers judges to move into that thorny area call race based litigation by providing a framework to challenge judicial racism in all its forms, by analysing, defining it.

9. The Reasonable Person Test: Analysis of the Judgement

Justice Cory, writing for himself and Justice Iacobucci on whether Judge Sparks gave rise to a reasonable apprehension of bias, argues that one must be mindful of the appropriate test. The traditional test, as articulated by Justice de Grandpré in *Committee for Justice and Liberty v. National Energy Board*, [1978] 1 S.C.R 369 at 394 is as follows:

> the apprehension of bias must be a reasonable one, held by reasonable and right-minded persons, applying themselves to the question and obtaining thereon the required information. . . . [The] test is "what would an informed person, viewing the matter realistically and practically — and having thought through the matter — conclude?"

The key considerations in this test are the concept of the "reasonable person," who she is, and what experiences and background factors inform her assessment of the situation. Applying the standard of reasonableness to the facts of the *R.D.S.* case, it could realistically be said that the reasonable person would be aware of the relevant contextual factors characterizing the community in which the incident occurred and, in particular, the context of the relationship between the police and members of the African-Canadian community.

Justice Cory properly reasoned that if a system of justice is to have the respect and confidence of its society, then trials must appear fair to the reasonable and informed juror. In the context of a multicultural and racially diverse society, fairness includes considerations of racial aspects where appropriate. It is therefore essential that judges be able to know when and to what extent to include racial considerations of fairness. Fairness and impartiality may at times require that irrelevant complicating factors be disregarded. At other times, the attainment of these ideals may necessitate proper and thorough consideration of relevant and even pivotal circumstances and characteristics. The challenge is to determine what is required in each individual instance.

Justice Cory was alert to this need; he expresses in paragraph 95 that, by virtue of Canada's status as a multicultural society, "Judges must be particularly sensitive to the need not only to be fair but also to appear to all reasonable observers to be fair to all Canadians of every race, religion, nationality and ethnic origin." This indicates that recognition of the reality of Canada as a multicultural, heterogeneous society should be factored into judicial reasoning. In his reasons, Justice Cory discusses at length the notions of judicial integrity, judicial impartiality, and the requirement that judges be seen to make every effort to adjudicate from a position of neutrality. Justice Cory refers to the fact that judges, like anyone else, are members of Canadian society, with a history of lived experiences. He states that the requirement for neutrality does not require judges to discount the very life experiences that may so well qualify them to preside over disputes. This recognition may be at the root of determining the impropriety of the allegation of bias against Judge Sparks.

Judge Sparks was challenged for doing the very thing that Justice Cory acknowledges is often necessary for judges to do, that is, to take into account their own life experiences where appropriate to their adjudication. Support for this is found in the Canadian Judicial Council's *Commentaries of Judicial Conduct* (1991: 12), as quoted in paragraph 119 of Justice Cory's reasons:

[The duty to be impartial] does not mean that a judge does not or cannot bring to the bench many existing sympathies, antipathies or attitudes. There is no human being who is not the product of every social experience, every process of education, and every human contact with those with whom we share the planet. Indeed, even if it were possible, a judge free of heritage of past experience would probably lack the very qualities of humanity required of a judge.

Judges are not required, nor certainly can they be expected to rid themselves of their personal realities and lived experiences when they perform their judicial function.

Justice Cory emphasizes in paragraph 152 that, although some elements of Judge Sparks's impugned comments may be troubling, the comments must be read in the context of the whole proceeding, with an awareness of all the circumstances that a reasonable observer would be deemed to know. Such a reading would not result in a determination of a reasonable apprehension of bias.

Judge Sparks's comments had the effect of rebutting the presumption that a police officer, by virtue of her occupation, could be more readily believed than an accused. The existence of this presumption in and of itself creates a reasonable apprehension of bias. Viewed in this way, then, Judge Sparks's comments functioned to remove the bias that had been so deeply embedded within the fabric of the criminal justice system that it had often mistaken to reflect a fair and proper determination.

With regards to Judge Sparks's reasonable apprehension of bias, Justices L'Heureux-Dubé and McLachlin arrived at the same reasoning as Justice Iacobucci. In paragraph 41 of their reasons, in recognizing the value of judicial inquiry into the factual, social, and psychological context within which litigation arises, they argue that: [t]here is more to a case than who did what to whom, and the questions of fact and law to be determined in any given case do not arise in a vacuum. Rather, they are the consequence of numerous actors, influenced by the innumerable forces which impact on them in a particular context. Judges, acting as finders of fact, must inquire into those forces. In short, they must be aware of the context in which the alleged crime occurred. This is a strong argument for the importance of contextualization in judicial decision-making. In fact, it seems to apply that fair adjudication requires consideration of relevant factors.

Justices L'Heureux-Dubé and McLachlin did not find that Judge Sparks's comments were inappropriate or came close to the line of acceptability, as Justice Cory did. Justices L'Heureux-Dubé and McLachlin put forth a strong argument for contextualization. This argument takes into consideration the reality that ordinary Canadians do not live in a vacuum, nor should judges be expected to carry out their judicial function in a vacuum, oblivious to the contextual realities that shape and affect all aspects of daily life.

Justices Gonthier and La Forest adopted the joint reasons of L'Heureux-Dubé and McLachlin. The dissenting Justices Major, Lamer, and Sopinka frame the issue as being not whether racism exists in our society, but whether there was evidence before Judge Sparks to base her finding that the police officer's actions were motivated by racism. This clearly was not the issue. Judge Sparks did not suggest that the officer's action was motivated by racism. The framing of the issue in these narrow terms reflects a failure on the part of the dissenting justices to fully appreciate the nature and characteristics of a multicultural society.

The minority justices' reasoning states that Judge Sparks failed to limit the basis of her decision-making to the evidence before her. The minority further state that there was no evidence presented to Judge Sparks on the issue of the prevalence of racism, or even that the actions of the police officer were motivated by racism, so as to enable her to factor this evidence into her assessment of credibility.

But what the minority judges failed to consider is that it was within the discretion of Judge Sparks, as the trial judge, to take judicial notice of the historically undisputed fact of the existence of racial tension between the African-Canadian community and the police in Nova Scotia, and to use this judicially noted fact as a backdrop against which to assess the credibility of the two witnesses. Yet, in a very strange contradictory or ironic way, the minority judges had the following to say:

[t]he life experiences of this trial judge, as with all trial judges, is an important ingredient in the ability to understand human behaviour, to weigh the evidence, and to determine credibility. It helps in making a myriad of decisions arising during the course of most trials.

10. Conclusion

We now live in a time when legal racial discrimination no longer exists, or so we are made to believe. Perhaps it is not surprising that a growing number of racialized people are not as conscious as they should be about their racialized marked positions in society. What is even more disturbing is that although they are the prime beneficiaries of the rights and freedom struggle, they distance themselves from it. They have come to the false conclusion that what they have accomplished was by their own individual talents and effort. And they actively attack the thesis that racialized complain too much and expect too much without working for it. Many of them Black argue that blackness, in and of itself, has any cultural value, outside of the uplifting affects of whiteness. Not too many of them are aware that Audrey Kobayashi, in her article "Do Minority Women Make a Difference?" (1989), highlights another barrier that has to do with racism in the justice system. She writes:

Not only do we need to recognize that systemic racism is just that — systemic — and that it involves the entire system completely, we also need to look outside the system for a new rationale for judgement. The rationality of current legal language is unequal to the task. Racism is more powerful . . . . I do not want only to see discrimination removed from judicial appointments, I want to see the judiciary turned into a force against racism. I want to show just how culpable the law is in the perpetuation of racism in our society [199].

Racism in the judicial system is no surprise, given that persons of colour are chronically under-represented in the legal system in terms of profession, and over-represented in other areas, such as prisons. Although persons of colour are not a homogenous group, their diversity in Canadian society is not even close to being proportionally represented in the judicial system. For example, in the 1996 census of Canada, of 2,315 judges, 70 were visible minorities (3 per cent) and of 58,820 lawyers and Quebec notaries, 2,755 were visible minorities (less than 5 per cent). Of the 60,265 police officers in the labour force, 1,835 were visible minorities (3 per cent). For comparison, it should be noted that visible minorities constitute 17 per cent of the Canadian population and 19 per cent of the labour force. Currently, according to law professor Carol Alyward of Dalhousie Law School, there are only five Black judges at the Superior Court level and approximately twelve in the provincial courts across the country.

Under-representation in the judiciary renders the system alienating and distrustful to members of an increasingly multicultural and multiracial society. One commonly known fact about racial minorities, however, especially those with little formal education, is that they tend to see the courts as oppressive and a cause for fear (Commission on Systemic Racism, 1995). They do not like police or immigration officials and, by extension, they also do not trust judges. These feelings can now only be heightened as a result of 9/11. The language of the courts is scary, and these people lack the facility to function. Many racialized accused persons feel that their chances of winning a case are best served by representation from White defence attorneys.

These feelings can be strengthened if the judgements rendered by members of the judiciary that involve members of racialized communities continue to be interpreted by the latter as being insensitive to their life experiences or their cultural sensibilities. There is no doubt that alienation and distrust can eventually beget disrespect for the law and the legal institutions that judges have come to embody. In essence, how judges and other active members of civil society confront, prevent, and strive to reduce judicial conduct or decisions that contribute to these feelings is what social context training is all about. The issue goes beyond making cosmetic changes in the form of more minority or Aboriginal representation in the judiciary. It has to do also, if not first of all, with how the values, aspirations, and interests of the many sectors of our pluralist society can find a legitimate daily place in the hearts and minds of judges. That will help breathe life and social justice into the notion of the law's being of the people, by the people, and for the people.

The lack of diversity in the legal profession has meant that equality jurisprudence has developed without different perspectives, which in turn explains the Court's sluggishness or reluctance in addressing racial discrimination in law — hence the retarding of racial reform.

All judges need as a matter of course to take race into account in their legal deliberations. Adjudication based on fairness, social justice, and equality for all persons enhances a more consistent enforcement of equality jurisprudence. Socially, moreover, judges in so doing indicate that race must not get consigned to an inferior status or place in the courtrooms. Finally, learning to unlearn the traditional ways of doing things must be recognized as a lifelong and demanding process wherein patience and institutional support will be instrumental in recognizing the challenges facing the courts. Fortunately, in 1997 the Supreme Court provided a helpful clarification of judicial criteria and rules governing race and judicial notice, in *R.D.S. v. The Queen*.

Judges are more aware of the level of judicial scrutiny applied to their behaviour by official language communities and women justices. But because there have been too few judges from racialized communities, and because those few on the bench feel less confident about speaking out because of perceived reprisals, social context education provides in part a remedy. This strategy is contingent upon the willingness and ability of those with the most power and influence to ask the "race" question and create a support mechanism for racialized judges to validate their deliberations. Social context education will create a more just, humane, and honest collegial relationship in the judiciary, a more socially responsive judiciary, and a more just application of the law.

References

Abella, I and Troper, H. 1991 *None Is Too Many: Canada and the Jews of Europe, 1938-1948.* University of Toronto Press.

Adachi, K. 1976 *The Enemy That Never Was: A History of Japanese Canadians.* Toronto: McClelland & Stewart.

Aylward, C. 1999 *Canadian Critical Race Theory: Racism and the Law.* Halifax: Fernwood Publishing.

Bell, D. 1987 *And We Are Not Saved: The Elusive Quest for Racial Justice.* New York: Basic Books.

Bell, D. 1992 *Faces at the Bottom of the Well.* New York: Basic Books.

Bell, D. 1995 Who's Afraid of Critical Race Theory? *University of Illinois Law Review.* 893-910.

Calliste, A. 1993 Race, Gender and Canadian Immigration Policy: Blacks from the Caribbean 1900-1932. *Journal of Canadian Studies* 28:131-94.

Calmore, J. 1982 Exploring the Significance of Race and Class in Representing the Black Poor. *Oregon Law Review* 61: 201–3.

Commission on Systemic Racism in the Ontario Criminal Justice System 1995 Report. Ontario: Queen's Printer.

Crenshaw, K. 1988 Race, Reform, and Retrenchment: Transformation and Legitimation in Anti-discrimination Law. *Harvard Law Review* 101 (7): 1331–87.

Crenshaw, K., Gotanda, N., Peller, G. and Thomas, K. (eds.) 1995 *Critical Race Theory: The Key Writings That Formed the Movement.* New York: Free Press.

Delgado, R. 1990 When a Story Is Just a Story: Does Voice Really Matter? *Virginia Law Review* 76: 95–111.

Delgado, R. 1995 *Critical Race Theory: The Cutting Edge.* Philadelphia: Temple University Press.

DuBois, W.E.B. 1989 *The Soul of Black Folks.* New York: Bantam Double Day.

Furniss, E. 1994 *Victims of Benevolence: Discipline and Death at the Williams Lake Indian Residential School, 1891-1920.* Vancouver: Arsenal Pulp Press.

Halkow, Y. 1996 Personal Impact of Residential Experiences on First Nations People. University of Alberta, Unpublished Thesis.

Harris, C. 1993 Whiteness as Property. *Harvard Law Review* 106: 1707–91.

Hayes, Paul. 1989 The Myth of Race In Political Ideologies and Political

Philosophies. In McCullough, H.B. (Ed.) 187-192.

Jakubowski., L. and Visano, L. 2002 *Teaching Controversy.* Halifax: Fernwood Press.

King, J. 1992 Diaspora Literacy and Consciousness in the Struggle against Miseducation in the Black Community. *Journal of Negro Education*, 61: 317–40.

Kobayasi, A. 1998 Do Minority Women Judges Make a Difference? *Canadian Journal of Women and the Law* 10: 199 - 212.

Law v. Canada (Minister of Employment and Immigration) [1999] S.C.J. No. 12 (1999) 170 D.L.R. (4th): 1 (Iacobucci, J., for the Court).

Milloy, J. 1999 *A National Crime: The Canadian Government and the Residential School System, 1879-1986.* Winnipeg: University of Manitoba Press,.

Morrison, T. 1992 *Playing in the Dark: Whiteness and the Literary Imagination.* Cambridge, MA: Harvard University Press.

Nuu-Chah-Nulth Tribal Council. 1996 *Indian Residential Schools: The Nuu-Chah-Nulth Experience.* Nuu-Chah-Nulth Tribal Council.

R.D.S. v. The Queen, [1997] 151 D.L.R. (4th) 193 (S.C.C.).

Visano, L. 2002 The Impact of Whiteness on the Culture of Law: From Theory to Practice in Levine-Rasky, C. (Ed.) *Working Through Whiteness: International Perspectives.* Albany: State University of New York Press.

Visano, L. 1998 *Crime and Culture: Refining the Traditions.* Toronto: Canadian Scholars' Press.

Walker, J. 1985 *Racial Discrimination in Canada: The Black Experience.* Ottawa: Canadian Historical Association, Historical Booklet No. 41.

Winks, R. Negro School Segregation in Ontario and Nova Scotia. *Canadian Historical Review* 50, 2.

[1997] 3 S.C.R. 484, (1997) 151 D.L.R. (4th) 193.

13. Developing a Framework of Factors that Accentuate the Likelihood of Racial Profiling

Faizal Mirza

1. Introduction

Although the existence of racial profiling in policing is now a judicially noted fact, the ability to prove the existence of racist policing in a particular trial continues to be an unduly difficult legal hurdle. In theory, judges are open to make findings of racial profiling based on their review of the factual circumstances of a particular case. However, there currently is no legal framework or evidentiary compass to guide justices in deciphering whether certain police conduct is consistent with racial profiling or racist policing. It is trite to state that police officers will not admit that they detained or searched an individual primarily on the basis of their racial or ethnic background. Given the absence of such direct evidence in cases involving the issue of racial profiling, it is necessary that a non-exhaustive list of indicators that accentuate the likelihood of racist policing be established that will assist justices in determining the validity of a racial policing defence. This article will focus on the need to devise a common law framework to assess claims of racial profiling. It is argued that it is imperative that members of the judiciary develop a non-exhaustive list of indicators that may be relied upon and applied by their colleagues to properly assess the merits of a racist policing defence.

2. Development of Case Law

Case Law: the gift and the curse

There are a small number of significant cases such as *R v. Parks R v. Parks [(*1993), 84 C.C.C. (3d) 353 (Ont. C.A.)] and *R v. Brown R v. Brown* [(2003), 64 O.R. (3d) 161 (C.A.)] that have recognized the existence of racism in the criminal justice system. These cases have also astutely noted that the existence of racism within institutions and on the part of specific individuals in the criminal justice system is immensely difficult to prove in the course of formal legal proceedings. Although the widespread and prevalent nature of racial profiling was judicially noted in *Brown*, in the course of a criminal proceeding, it remains unduly difficult for an African Canadian person to demonstrate that he or she was racially profiled. Racially motivated police stops will rarely be proved through direct evidence. Even through the assistance of the most able cross-examinations by defence counsel, it is unreasonable to expect that police officers will concede that they stopped an individual because of the individual's race. It is even less likely that an accused will possess sufficient resources to demonstrate that a particular officer disproportionately stops black persons (Tanovich 2002: 162).

In 1993 the Ontario Court of Appeal in the case of *R. v. Parks*, acknowledged that racism exists in our institutions, including the criminal justice system and used this finding to expand challenges for cause to potential jurists. However the court also took note that it is difficult to prove that an individual or institution is discriminating against an accused on the basis of race. Speaking for the Court in *Parks*, Justice Doherty stated that "the existence and extent of racial bias are not issues which can be established in a manner normally associated with the proof of adjudicative facts." Justice Doherty further wisely noted that racism operates on the subconscious and systemic levels:

> There are those who expressly espouse racist views as part of a personal credo. There are others who subconsciously hold negative attitudes towards black persons based on stereotypical assumptions concerning persons of colour. Finally, and perhaps most pervasively, racism exists within the interstices of our institutions. This systemic racism is a product of individual attitudes and beliefs concerning blacks and it fosters and legitimizes those assumptions and stereotypes.

In 2003 the Ontario Court of Appeal in the case of *R v. Brown* acknowledged the existence of racial profiling in policing. The Court noted that the reality of the invidious phenomenon is supported by significant social science research. The Court also held that racial profiling by police officers may be based on sub-conscious racial stereotyping: "The attitude underlying racial profiling is one that may be consciously or unconsciously held. That is, the police officer need not be an overt racist. His or her conduct may be based on subconscious racial stereotyping."

In *Brown*, the Court of Appeal endorsed a broad and unspecific approach for proving racial profiling. In particular, in non-descriptive terms, the Court of Appeal stated that one way racial profiling can be proven is by circumstantial evidence where: the circumstances relating to the detention correspond to the phenomenon of racial profiling; and the circumstances provide a basis for the court to infer that the police officer is lying about why the police officer singled out the accused person for attention (ibid, para 44 -45). The Court offered no substantive guidance with respect to which factual circumstances are frequently consistent with racial profiling.

The recent decision of *R v. Khan* [(2004) O.J. No. 3819 (Sup. Ct.)] is another example of the gift and the curse in the jurisprudence relating to racial profiling. In *Khan*, Superior Court Justice Molloy found that the two Toronto police officers stopped and searched the accused "because he was a black man with an expensive car." (ibid at para. 68). The police claimed that the accused had been driving erratically and appeared distracted with something inside of his Mercedes, so they decided to pull him over. The police further alleged that after they directed the accused to pull over, as they approached they observed him fumbling further inside the vehicle. When the police got to the vehicle one of the officers pulled the accused out of the vehicle at which time the officer claims to have smelled a strong odour of cocaine emanating from the car. Inside the vehicle the police located a bag containing approximately one kilogram of cocaine. The accused claimed no knowledge of the cocaine and testified that he had loaned his vehicle recently to his brother.

Although this decision is remarkable to the extent that it provides a powerful statement that the police officers racially profiled the accused, it also supports the contention that it is necessary that a common law framework be developed to assist triers of fact to properly assess racial profiling arguments. Ultimately, in *Khan*, it appears that Justice Molloy ruled in favour of the accused because based on her sophisticated evaluation of the testimony and factual circumstances, she decided that the evidence of the accused was more credible than that of the police (ibid at para. 66 and 71). In a rare finding, Justice Molloy rejected much of the evidence of the police officers and notably their position that race played no role in their decision to stop the vehicles of the accused. This decision demonstrates that members of the judiciary with the right circumstances are open to making findings of racial profiling. However, the exceptional nature of this decision implicitly reminds counsel that many justices confronted with similar circumstances, operating without a framework to guide their interpretation of the facts, more frequently reject the evidence of the accused and endorse the evidence of the police that race played no role in their investigation.

In deciding the merits of the racial profiling defence, Justice Molloy added (referring to a previous motion ruling in this case--[2004] O.J. No. 3811 (Sup. Ct.) that in addition to the approach stated in *Brown*, another way racial profiling could be proved is that an accused could also rely on evidence that the officer in question had acted in a similar manner in the past or on evidence of bias. Justice Molloy's additional method of proving racial profiling theoretically may be a step forward but as demonstrated by her own application of this new approach in *Khan*, the success of this approach is likely to be in very limited. First, it is extremely difficult to locate witnesses that could provide similar fact evidence. Second, even if counsel or the accused is able to obtain such witnesses, the admissibility of their evidence is in doubt.

In *Khan*, some of the significant problems with the effectiveness of this further approach of proving racial profiling were revealed. Defence counsel was uniquely situated in that he had another client that had been apparently profiled by the same police officers in a similar manner. As a result, counsel's other client testified for the defence that he had been subject to a stop and search under similar suspect circumstances by the same officers. Despite the apparent advent by Justice Molloy of this additional method of proving racial profiling, she concluded in large part because of the criminal history of the witness, that the similar fact evidence could not be admitted because it was too frail. Ultimately, because of this finding, Justice Molloy relied upon the general approach stated in *Brown* to assess the profiling argument (ibid at para. 58).

Although *Parks, Brown, and Khan* represent significant developments in the law of equality rights and criminal procedure, the decisions intimate that it is easier for the court to recognize that racism exists in the criminal justice system and more specifically in policing, but it is dramatically more complex and infrequent for the courts to find that racism played a part in the decision making of a particular police officer.

There is currently a profound void in the criminal common law with respect to proving and properly adjudicating claims of racial profiling. The Court of Appeal's recognition of the fact that a police officer may discriminate against visible minorities, especially African-Canadians, on the basis of ideas, thoughts, or beliefs embedded at the subconscious level that cannot be easily exposed even under the most scrupulous cross examination, supports the contention that the next logical step in the development of equality rights is for the courts to respond to this evidentiary void by explicitly addressing the obstacles associated with proving racial profiling.

3. The Legal Basis for Developing the Framework

A contextual analysis of the impact of systemic racism in the criminal justice system on African Canadians ensures the proper reform of the administration of criminal justice. For instance, in *R v. Golden* (2001) S.C.C. 83, [2001] S.C.J. No. 81, the Supreme Court of Canada gave special consideration to the over-representation of African Canadians in the criminal justice system in the reformation of the procedural law of strip searches. As a direct result of over-representation of African-Canadians in the system, the Court developed a framework explicitly designed to "prevent unnecessary and unjustified strip searches before they occur." (ibid at para. 83).

Similar to the reasoning in *Golden*, the optimal way for the courts to address the difficulty of proving racial profiling by the police in criminal cases is to use the current understanding of racism in policing and the broader criminal justice system as a basis to respond to the needs of those adversely affected. Specifically the courts should take the knowledge of the existence of sub-conscious racism in policing and use it as a foundation to develop a set of flexible evidentiary guidelines that can be relied upon by triers of fact to determine the merits of racial profiling arguments. An express and flexible evidentiary framework to deal with racial profiling is mandated by the reality that African Canadians are over-represented in the criminal justice system and are therefore more likely to experience involuntary interactions with the police, making them more likely to be subjected to investigative detentions and searches. In addition, to the extent that the power to detain and search a suspect resides largely within the discretionary authority of individual police officers, it can be expected that this discretion will be exercised disproportionately against African Canadians.

The recent decision by the Ontario Court of Appeal in *R v. Calderon* ([2004] O.J. No. 3474 C.A.) is of assistance in developing a non-exhaustive list of indicators that accentuate the likelihood of racial profiling. In *Calderon*, in the context of a highway traffic stop, the Court of Appeal examined police reliance on profiles to establish articulable cause. The Court properly dismantled the use of certain "indicators" relied upon by the police to infer that the accused were drug. By determining that many of the alleged "indicators" of drug smuggling relied upon by the police as a basis to detain and search the accused were actually "neutral facts", the court found that the section 8 and 9 Charter rights of the accused were breached.

Specifically, the police stopped the accused after allegedly observing his car exceed the speed limit by ten kilometres. Upon stopping the vehicle the police testified that they observed in the car what they believed to be "indicators" of drug smuggling: pagers, cell phones, road map, some fast food wrappers and two duffel bags. One of the police officer's conducting the stop also stated that he thought the Lincoln vehicle the accused were travelling in seemed too expensive "for what the driver and the passenger looked like to me" (ibid at para 71). The officers then searched the vehicle and found marijuana.

The majority decision of the Court delivered by Justice Laskin found that the police did not possess reasonable grounds to detain the accused and that the factors they relied upon objectively viewed, were not indicators of drug smuggling. In finding a section 9 breach, Justice Laskin found that the "indicators" of a smugglers profile cited by the police to justify the stop and subsequent search were nothing more than speculation and guess work and could not establish the requisite "objectively discernible facts" needed to establish articulable cause pursuant to *R v. Simpson* [(1993), 79 C.C.C. (3d) 482 (Ont. C.A.)]:

> However, on cross-examination Osborne admitted that these "indicators" were neutral, that they might be found in any car. In the world we now live in, that is not a surprising admission - fast food, duffel bags, a road map, cell phones, even pagers now form part of many people's lives. Moreover, Osborne conceded that since he had taken the training course he had stopped between ten and twenty cars relying on these indicators and had made no arrests. Rome also took the training course, and relying on these same indicators, he had stopped between fifty and one hundred cars. He, too, had made no arrests. Given the neutrality and apparent unreliability of these indicators, I fail to see how their presence could amount to reasonable grounds for detention.
>
> I give no credence at all to Osborne's observation about the appellants' driving an expensive car. This type of stereotyping recalls the words of Doherty J.A. in Simpson, supra at 202:
>
> Such subjectively based assessments can too easily mask discriminatory conduct based on such irrelevant factors as the detainee's sex, colour, age, ethnic origin or sexual orientation. Equally, without objective criteria detentions could be based on mere speculation. A guess which proves accurate becomes in hindsight a "hunch". [Calderon, at paras. 71 to 75]

Similarly, in cases in which racial profiling is in issue, the judiciary can and should use reliance by the police on "neutral facts" and stereotypical assumptions to support the likelihood that the accused was racially profiled. The decision in *R v. Peck*, is a useful example of the how reliance by the police on neutral facts and stereotypical assumptions to detain and search an African Canadian can support a judicial finding of racial profiling. In *Peck*, the accused, described as a well-dressed black man, was walking near Dundas and Yonge Street with two women in the early evening, while plain clothes officers were executing a drug bust in the vicinity. The accused passed by the police who claimed that because of the reputation of the area for drugs and the fact that his hands were in the area of his pant pockets they formed the belief that the accused may be a drug dealer. Subsequently, one of the officer's said "Police" but did not produce a badge and then asked the accused what he had in his pocket. The police officer reached to detain the accused who fled on foot but was later tackled by the police officer. A subsequent search revealed that the accused had a bag of crack cocaine in his pocket.

Justice Trafford determined that the police had detained and searched the accused on the basis of stereotypical assumptions. The factors relied upon by the police in *Peck* were also consistent with concept of neutral facts as discussed in *Calderon* (ibid at para. 18).

> The presence of a reasonably well-dressed young black man, Mr. Peck, with two female friends who are similarly well-dressed, Ms. Prince and Ms. Henry, in an area notorious for street level drug activity around 5:00 p.m. on November 18, 1998 does not meet such criteria. The random movement of the arm of Mr. Peck in the vicinity of the pocket as he walked past Constable Murphy does not, in itself or contextually, provide such grounds. The reputation of the area in itself is not sufficient to do so. The overall area around O'Keefe Lane was, in any event, a diverse commercial area characterized by the racial and cultural diversity of downtown Toronto. Nor, I say most emphatically, does the race of a person and, in particular, a young black male person, provide such a basis by itself or in the context of the other circumstances as found by the court. Stereotypical assumptions linking young black men and the illegal use of narcotics do not provide a lawful basis to detain or arrest them.

The Supreme Court of Canada's recent decision with respect to investigative detentions of pedestrians in *R v. Mann* is also of some assistance in the development of a starting list of neutral facts that may establish racial profiling. Similar to Justice Trafford's comments in *Peck*, in *Mann*, ([2004] S.C.J. No. 49) Justice Iacobucci speaking for the majority of the Court also found that the presence of the accused in a "high crime area" on it's own, is insufficient to establish reasonable grounds to suspect in all the circumstances that the individual is connected to a particular crime and that such a detention is necessary from an objective point of view. (ibid at para. 47).

4. Possible Indicators of Racial Profiling

Based on a common sense approach and the jurisprudence examined, it appears that there are certain factors that assist a trier of fact in determining whether an individual accused was racially profiled. The following is a suggested starting point of a non-exhaustive list of factors that assist a trier of fact in determining whether racial profiling was an ingredient in the decision by an officer to investigate, detain and or search an African Canadian for criminality:

i Overemphasis on stereotypical factors, including but not limited to:
   a) reliance on overly general descriptions: "black male/ female";
   b) over-emphasis on the dress of the target: casual attire, sports jerseys, baggy hip-hop style clothing;
   c) explicit or implicit emphasis on the target driving an expensive vehicle;
   d) presence of the accused at the time of investigation in a "high crime area;" or
   e) any other assumption objectively viewed that could be properly perceived to be stereotypical

ii Reliance on neutral facts or factors: facts or factors that objectively viewed would not consistently cause the police officer to detain, search, or arrest a person;

iii Based on objective analysis of the overall circumstances and each fact viewed. Individually, it appears that the dominant reason for the detention is because the individual is black.

iv Police use the "detain the black person first investigation approach": singling out African Canadians for investigative detentions where there are other persons or sources of investigation in the area;

v Nature of Questioning by the police: questions that appear to assume involvement in criminal activity;

vi Failure to interview civilian witnesses when available rather than merely singling out individual police claim is suspicious.

5. Conclusion

Although racism has had a profound adverse impact on our social institutions for centuries, it is only over the past eleven years that criminal law jurisprudence has genuinely taken notice of the existence and the impact of racism in the criminal justice system. Any of the disproportionate number of African Canadians brought into criminal the justice system that have been the victim of racial profiling deserve to have their experience with racist law enforcement effectively reviewed by the courts. However, presently there is no interpretive aid established in the common law to assist justices to properly assess evidence that is potentially probative of racial profiling. An established legal framework of factors that accentuate the likelihood of racial profiling will assist triers of fact to properly assess the merits of racial profiling arguments and will also fill the significant void in the jurisprudence.

References

Tanovich, D. 2002 Using the *Charter* to Stop Racial Profiling: The Development of an Equality-based Conception of Arbitrary Detention. *Osgoode Hall Law Journal* 40(2)145, at 162

Cases:
R v. Brown 2003, 64 O.R. (3d) 161 (C.A.)
R v. Calderon 2004 O.J. No. 3474 (C.A.)
R v. Golden 2001 S.C.C. 83, [2001] S.C.J. No. 81,
R v. Khan 2004 O.J. No. 3819 (Sup. Ct.)
R v Mann, 2004 S.C.J. No. 49
R v. Parks 1993, 84 C.C.C. (3d) 353 (Ont. C.A.)
R v Peck 2001 O.J. No. 4581 (Sup. Ct.)
R v. Simpson 1993, 79 C.C.C. (3d) 482 (Ont. C.A.)]

PART D

CORRECTIONS

14. Outside Women Inside: Defining Deviance, Incarcerating 'Race' and Sexuality[1]

Rai Reece

1. Introduction

The female body in many ways serves as a contextual 'site' upon which various tropes and discourses of "hatred" are mapped out. Historically the Canadian State has had a precarious and more often that not, insidious relationship with the exertion and coercion of hegemonic power over women's bodies. This relationship is explicitly illuminated when exploring the discursive and ideological imprisonment of women. Prisons, then, are 'sites' that demonstratively open up spaces for engaging in the dialectics of sexuality, race, gender and law. Specifically in terms of law, crime and justice, the Canadian Criminal Justice System has failed to take into account the racial and gendered implications that are implicitly connected to incarceration measures for women of colour. The exigent need to stabilize, regulate and subjugate women's sexuality is implicitly and explicably connected to the gendered-incarceration of women. Theoretically the framework from which I will situate this discourse focuses on how the Canadian state, specifically the Ministry.of Corrections and the Canadian Judicial System uses prisons as a form of social control dependent on State configurations of power, ideology, sexuality, gender, 'race' and class. By examining the hegemonic politics associated with engendered incarceration this paper examine how the Canadian state, particularly the Ministry of Corrections under the guise of 'rehabilitation' re/produces racialized and sexualized docile bodies. The regulation and continual medicalization of women's bodies is literally and metaphorically connected to ideological colonial, imperial and patriarchal discourse specifically linked to the incarceration of Black and Aboriginal Federally incarcerated women.

This paper is meant to explore the dynamics of penal incarceration for female inmates in Canada while providing a general discussion of incarcerated female inmates of colour. For theoretical and ideological purposes, the intent of this paper is not to address the specific "crimes" that were committed by women in prison, since definitions of "criminal" behaviour under Canadian law is problematic. My intention is not to negate the fact that socio-political and economic structures are embedded in divergent discursive frameworks of penal incarceration' in light of this I recognize that the scope of that discussion is too large to address in the context of this paper.

---

[1] A summary of this paper was presented at the *Race, Gender, Class, and Sexuality Symposium* on February 27, 2004.

2. Historical Overview: Social Control and Deviance

Prison is the only place where power is manifested in its naked state, in its most excessive form, and where it is justified as moral force....What is fascinating about prisons is that, for once, power doesn't hide or mask itself; it reveals itself as tyranny pursued into the tiniest details; it is cynical and at the same time pure and entirely "justified," because its practice can be totally formulated within the framework of morality. Its brutal tyranny consequently appears as the serene domination of Good over Evil, of order over disorder (Foucault, 1975).

In order to understand *how* prisons work, it is important to question *why* they are viewed as a necessary apparatus for social control and reformation discourse that negotiates the intricacies of state power. Michel Foucault's (1975) work *Discipline and Punish*, perhaps provides one of the most salient theoretical frameworks in which to situate discussions concerning penal punishment. Although Foucault never explicitly wrote concerning women's bodies, his work involving power, knowledge, and discourse fundamentally provides a solid framework for understanding the ideological constructions of punishment and penal incarceration. Penal punishment is historically rooted in methods of social control, torture, and reform. I postulate then, that justice - the very premise law is supposed to uphold - is expressly linked to the notion of dehumanization and spectacle for the human body that has been condemned to invisibility, coercion, and depravity. In this sense the contemporary understanding that the correctional system in Canada takes toward punishment is based on a historical colonial ideology constituted in and from class, 'race' and gender social paradigms. As such, Foucault (1975) argues punishment is the most hidden part of the penal process and penal punishment is historically rooted in methods of social control and reform depravity. In this sense the correctional system in Canada takes its cues for punishment from the Canadian judicial system – a system whereby women are re-criminalized *and* re-victimized and placed in prisons – the majority for drug related, prostitution or property/poverty crimes. The prison becomes engendered in the sense that the patriarchal associations and ideologies of the prison become the umbrella *for* which and *from* which incarceration is understood; incarceration then, is based on an interpretation of, and the perspective of maleness.

Historically and contemporarily, crime and criminality are seen to be characteristic of the poor and/or working class. Associations with social conditions (living environments, education or race) are bound up with the idea that persons who commit crimes exist in situations "generated by deplorable social conditions which necessarily [produce] human beings deformed or deficient in certain ways (Gamberg 1984: 27). This notion of crime and criminality has been expressly linked to the concept of deviance and as such is the concept of deviance is understood in a particular context:

> The concept of deviance, then, underwent some modification while a dominant, if not general, societal consensus was still assumed. The adoption

> of a pluralistic perspective, however, made the concept more relativistic: behaviour which was normative for one group may violate the prescriptions of a second group and be considered by them to be deviant...(Gamberg, 1984: 27)

Gamberg presents his analysis of deviance as defined by 'North American' standards at the beginning of the twentieth century. He argues that the defining parameters of deviance were later challenged, but it was 'class' strata that was linked to crime. Consequently, historical connotations that exploring the dynamics of torture elucidate that the purpose of torture was to deter crime.

Public executions were displays of spectacle in the early eighteenth and nineteenth century France where punishment was understood as that which explicitly invoked physical pain and suffering (Foucault, 1975). The body, then, (read: male body) was the site upon which torture, dismemberment, and amputation was played out (Foucault, 1975). By placing the body in the public sphere, the very visual display of pain was equated with deviant persons who stood apart from the more virtuous members of Victorian society. The body served as a central symbol of torture during the eighteenth century in England, France and Russia (Foucault, 1975). Hence, torturing the condemned body can be viewed as an allegorical symbol of power, control, and judiciary politics. The argument can be made that the body, (particularly women's bodies) is a political 'site' where discourses and ideologies of "hatred", fear, and punishment are mapped out. The infliction of pain as deemed necessary by a governing judiciary sends a very clear message about state power and human rights – as well as the loss of human rights for the condemned criminal. In retrospect, much of the discourse concerning twentieth century penology measures can be attributed to ideological formations of punishment that surfaced during the eighteenth century in France. This period illustrates a time when judicial governance was interconnected with the idea that legally the state could deter crime by presenting a visual display of the consequences of crime. The affirmation of state power, law, and societal control was just as important as was the idea that "torture and execution be ever-present in the heart of the weak man [*sic*] and dominate the feeling that drives him to crime (Beccaria 1764 cited in Foucault, 1975: 104). Consequently, the public display of condemnation for the criminally deviant via the infliction of physical pain was embedded in the socially accepted definitions of morality.

Although the public exhibition and execution of prisoners was maintained in France as of 1831, an ideological and discursive shift would take place where by the end of the eighteenth and nineteenth century, punishment as spectacle began to disappear (Foucault, 1975). The body as a signified object and the ideology of punishment would become intertwined with the idea that the spectacle of punishment was inhumane:

> [In some way] this rite that concluded the crime was suspected of being in some undesirable way linked with it. It was as if the punishment was thought to equal, if not exceed, in savagery the crime itself, to accustom the

> spectators to a ferocity from which one wished to divert them, to show them the frequency of crime, to make the executioner resemble a criminal...to make the tortured criminal an object of pity or admiration...(Foucault, 1975: 9).

Much of this 'intolerability' of punishment helped establish key meanings and definitions of imprisonment. The 'discourse' of representing the prison must be seen in a more sophisticated way than the traditional definition of the term. In terms of the production of knowledge about prisons, discourses operate on many different levels. In one way, the 'language' of prisons supports the 'meaning' of deviance. For example, we use terms such as 'criminal', 'deviant', or 'insane' in conjunction with imprisonment or institutionalization, hence we construct a discourse of incarceration that produces a particular kind of knowledge about the inmates inside the prison. Furthermore, this language of incarceration allows "good citizens" to formulate an ideology of what and who they are, as opposed to who they are not. On another level, it can be argued that a discourse is not a closed system; it can draw on other discourses in order to "bind a network of meaning" where relations and differences among and between discourses operate systematically (Hall, 1996: 202). In this sense, the meaning of the execution, called for the audience to take up the subject position of the criminal – in essence to become the criminal, and to feel the pain of punishment. This realization that torture was akin to inhumanity would create a discursive shift whereby physical punishment processes would become hidden and new ways in which to 'humanize' incarceration were designed.

The period of enlightenment, then, created a diagnostic distance and a socio-political "ideology" of incarceration. This diagnostic distance meant that upper caste virtuous Europeans of the Victorian era - those who were generally not seen to be criminals – could be spared the cruel and exacting visual display of punishment. An ideological distance was created whereby criminals were "distanced" from the more "civilized" members of society; hence building an infrastructure (prison) that would physically and ideologically confine deviance, was understood to be of the utmost importance. Physical distance would be created between the "criminal" and the "civilized", and the power of surveillance by an organized State faction could secure an ideology of punishment.

Hall (1996) further argues that according to Foucault, ideology is based on delineating the difference between truths and falsehoods. In this sense political, social, and moral facts are presented as truth, and this production of knowledge is rarely challenged (Hall, 1996). Since the presentation of 'facts' does not ask for us to decide what is true or false, we take substantive 'truths' as those ideas that are necessary for the maintenance of societal good. Therefore, it becomes a 'fact' that in order to maintain societal good through incarceration, persons deemed criminally deviant must be punished. And because we take this 'fact' as 'truth', the ideology of punishment remains unchallenged. Moreover, the tenets of punishment – pain, suffering, and/or death - are coupled with the idea that societal good, social control and order can be maintained by exercising state power. The ideology of the state, then, was promulgated on the idea that the moral superiority of 'mankind' [*sic*] could be demonstrated via the overt wielding of power by the state, and the necessity to protect societal good and the moral fabric of society. Furthermore, the ideological and diagnostic-distance that prisons create are strategic elements for organizing societal "good":

> [A]n examination of the institutional and cultural practices involved in the production of citizens is crucial. While penal governance can be seen as a representation of juridical power and repressive forms of disciplinary power, it can also be analyzed as a form of productive power that has the intention of producing individuals who meet certain normative expectations (Hannah-Moffat, 2001: 7).

Hannah-Moffat's argument here is useful for feminist/womanist analysis of power relations and female incarceration and in terms of hegemonic power relations, Karlene Faith (1993) argues that "the punitive nature of prisons [are] a measure and expression of power relations in society" (Faith, 126). Prison incarceration, then, purports a paradigmatic framework whereby "good" citizens (read: White European women) are seen apart from "bad" people (read: women of colour).

3. Sick Bodies: The Process of Becoming a 'Good Person'

Power, control, and political efficacy would become central points of conjecture for much of the medical theory behind prison construction. Consequently, the notion that the Canadian state could reform the criminally minded was an idea that took shape during the period of Enlightenment whereby the construction of a prison also meant the rehabilitation of a criminal. Rehabilitation processes would allow the state to wield its power by fundamentally structuring punishment as more 'humane'. Gone were the days of overt physical torture – this was now being replaced by a 'new' ideology of punishment that included reformation practices. State relations of power operate strategically and operationally in regard to punishment and penal incarceration for women. These overt power relations are supported by the fact that discursively and ideologically, prisons can be seen as site for supporting and controlling the constraint of ones physical and mental faculties. By building a prison or a penitentiary – a large scale structure representative of institutional power - the condemned female body can serve as an intermediary instrument upon which the state can deny individual liberty and human rights (Foucault, 1975). This system of deprivation is central to the idea of rehabilitation because it is promulgated on the discursive notion that criminal retribution can be reinforced by state power (Duffee, 1989: 10). In retrospect, the idea of torture as a deterrence was popular concept, but by the nineteenth century the ideology around punishment shifted to one in which the prisoner could be institutionally 'reformed' having paid their debt to society:

> The traditional rationale for the use of prisons is the glaring imposition of punishment as the just desserts means of paying one's debt to a centralized state, which must be compensated for harm done to an impersonal society as opposed to the needs of the forgotten individual victim, if there is one,

who becomes subordinate to the adjudication process (Faith, 1993: 125). As Faith has pointed, out rehabilitation can be argued to be one of the most debated and problematic arguments coinciding with incarceration processes. In fact, the fluidity of the term introduces numerous discursive frameworks in which to discuss how it relates to penal incarceration for women, and state power.

Much discussion around incarceration and reformation involves the ideas of retribution and hard labour. The notion that confinement and solitude would provide the inmate an opportunity for them to change their behaviour, was part and parcel of the discursive apparatus of penology in early nineteenth century Canada. Most importantly, the concept of rehabilitation stems from the idea that those who have committed crimes, particularly women, are socially flawed (Faith, 1993). Hence, women who deviated from dominant ideological normative standards set by the 'moral' members of society were seen to be inherently criminal. Faith argues that rehabilitation discourse "shifts from the event of the crime to the woman who "falls" from grace due to sin or sickness, or who, in deviating from consensual behavioural norms, violates an abstract social contract..." (1993: 125). Intrinsic to this notion of rehabilitation, is the perception that the State can 'correct' those who have violated their state privileged citizenship rights. Parenthetically, it is outside the scope of this essay to discuss the many incidences past and present where the Canadian State has perpetrated violence towards its "citizens." In order to do this discussion justice, it is important to note that the Canadian State carries with it a sordid history of racism, classism, heterosexism and sexism, to name a few of the salient issues that are alluded to in this paper

Imbued in this concept, is the view that federal penitentiaries can provide adequate and necessary vocational and educational training for inmates. Traditionally, for male inmates, therapeutic interventional strategies and techniques such as group counselling, federal prisons designed programs sought to "treat" the criminally deviant (Ekstedt and Griffiths, 1988). For example in the 1956 report from a Committee of Inquiry, chaired by Mr. Justice Fauteux, it was stated that "persons who violate the criminal law are persons who have been damaged in the process of growing up" (Ekstedt and Griffiths, 1988: 53). Because the model for the first female prison in Canada was based on Kingston Penitentiary - a prison built exclusively for men - this discourse paved the way for medical personnel (psychiatrists and psychologists), and medical models of treatment to be introduced in the realm of penal punishment for women. MacNamara (1977) cited in Ekstedt and Griffiths underscores this point:

> The medical model....assumed the offender to be "sick" (physically, medically and/or socially; his [*sic*] offense to be a manifestation or symptom of his illness, a cry for help....Early and accurate diagnosis, followed by prompt and effective therapeutic interventional, assured an affirmative prognosis – rehabilitation (1988: 53).

Clearly, a shift had taken place in regard to the punishment ideology of the past. Historically punishment focused on torturing the (male) body in the public sphere, and the physical pain associated with this act was inherently connected to social control, crime deterrence and societal good. These philosophies are still disseminated regarding penology discourse about women, as modern penitentiary practices has shifted its gaze from the infliction of corporal pain on the body, to attempting to cleanse the mind and soul of incarcerated women. In essence this is process of subjugating and 'medicalizing' the female body.

4. (Re)Constructing Colonial Spaces for Women

Having 'disgraced' their sex/gender, women who were imprisoned presented a challenge to the ideological dimensions of womanhood and nation building. During the early nineteenth and twentieth century, the politics of colonial rule were unequivocally connected to the politics of gender. Women (read white: women) played many divergent roles in the building and sustaining of empire for British colonial states. In many cases European women were seen to set the normative standards for virtue, prosperity, and motherhood (Davin, 1978) thus these were the 'good' women in Victorian society. This same ideology was prevalent in Canada, and consequently, women who were poor, prostitutes, or of colour were not considered favourable in the construction of nationhood. Furthermore, "African", "Asian", "First Nations", and poor white women were seen to be detrimental to imperial and colonial rule. These women, sometimes labeled criminal "lunatics" would come to wear the badge of deviance - they would provide the foundations for racist and ideological discourse that would position incarcerated women in a contested 'space' in which their bodies were pathologized and criminalized.

The work of gender in the discourse of nation building solidified an ideology of who and what the virtuous woman was. Canada's 'good' women were those willing to work towards nationalism, not those who committed crimes. Criminal women, who contravened the ideological and nationalistic tenets of the Canadian State, were not seen as 'good' mothers, or 'good' women, therefore they should be punished accordingly. Similarly, Clarice Feinman (1994) explains how the virgin/whore duality is explicitly connected to definitions of defining and punishing female criminal behaviour:

> Implicit in the Madonna / whore duality is women's subservience to men, who assumed the role of protectors of the madonna and punishers of the whore...The evil women...destroys man and brings pain and ruin...[t]he evil women manipulates and ruins man with lies and sex, [thus], [t]he evil women [can] be redeemed only by painfully bearing children and being controlled by her husband (1994: 4).

The connection here, between power, patriarchy, and gender, is especially formidable in any attempt to contextualize why penal discourse concerning women has historically been erased from more formal discussions regarding incarceration. In retrospect, punishment was centered on the male body, and since the numbers of women in conflict with the law were few, there did not seem to be much interest in having debates about female inmates. This form of paternalistic discourse has commandeered much of the scholarship and research about the experiences of women in prison. This spectrum of thought is entrenched in the notion that power marks 'spaces,' and defines what and who is important. In relation to paternalistic ideology, prisons are patriarchal colonial spaces. In other words, the confinement of women's bodies is also the 'conquering' of deviance and difference, and the silencing of women's voice. The prison, then, represents a 'site' where colonial processes illuminate the fact that patriarchy was/is a central facet of penal punishment for women. Moreover, this depravity is explicitly connected to 'race', sexuality, and medicalization processes.

Disturbing notions about women in prison, particularly Black and Aboriginal women are caught up in a dialectic that positions the female offender "as 'poor and unfortunate' on the one hand, and 'lazy and worthless' on the other" (Cooper, 1993: 33). In Canada, during the early nineteenth century, in order to rehabilitate these 'types' of women, it was argued that a separate prison for women needed to be constructed. Criticism of female punishment was deliberated along side discussions of how to 'fittingly' punish female offenders as they did not make up the majority of 'criminals' during this time period. Traditionally, prisons in Canada were built for men, by men, and women who had committed crimes were housed in the cramped quarters of male prisons (Faith, 1993). Most women who were incarcerated were convicted for non-violent crimes: petty theft, prostitution, or drunkenness. Faith (1993) describes how imprisoned women were locked away, and kept in the attic of Canada's Kingston penitentiary:

> [T]hey were literally hidden away, under cold, abominable conditions including infestations of insects and rodents, filth, inadequate nutrition, disease, total idleness or meaningless labour, [and subject to] harsh punishments for prison infractions, and sexual abuses by male guards (129).

Punishing women by means of flogging, then confining them in male prisons, with male guards in unsuitable conditions, led to a public outcry (Cooper, 1993). In order to address this issue, in 1848 the Brown Commission was appointed to investigate a range of abuses specifically related to female inmates being housed at Kingston Penitentiary (Cooper, 1993). Although the conditions and abuses of female inmates were disturbing, this was not the central focus of the Brown Commission. Since labour was to be an integral element to penal punishment and reformation, the Commission was concerned with the fact that Kingston Penitentiary did not provide ideal conditions for women's labour. According to the Warden of Kingston Penitentiary, women were,

> [p]oor unfortunate creatures...generally of the unfortunate classes. They are taught the usefulness of labour, and those well disposed are allowed to learn the working of the sewing machine, so that on their release, they may obtain a livelihood (quoted in Cooper, 1993: 36).

Even though sewing was not considered 'hard' labour, whereas doing laundry was, clearly the emphasis on traditional sex-gender roles for women was determined to be necessary for the reformation of 'bad' women. This "inconvenience" of women's work coupled with poor living conditions, led to the creation of a separate unit for women in Kingston Penitentiary. Established in 1913, this unit did little to improve the living conditions for women (Cooper, 1993); rather it reinforced the misguided beliefs that female inmates were 'oversexed parasites.' In order to combat this 'deviant sexual' desire, an attempt was made to 'cure' the female inmate. In this sense, what better way to 'save' the wayward woman, than to train her to serve a family as a proper wife and mother (Faith, 1993)? The point herein is to focus on the irony of the comment. I unequivocally am not making the assumption that women should be confined to the home (private sphere). Women of colour historically have not been grated the "luxury" of having definitions of motherhood equated with their race or ethnicity. Karlene Faith (1993) makes and excellent point that native women and, I would add Black women have not traditionally be confined to *their* own homes, but rather the homes of white European women as domestic workers

Women offenders would eventually 'achieve' a prison of their own. Construction of the Prison for Women (P4W) would begin in May 1925, and be completed in January 1934 (Cooper 1993). Four years later in 1938, it would be recommended by the Archambault Commission that the prison be closed, and 66 years later, amidst much controversy surrounding allegations of rape and abuse, it would eventually close its doors.

5. Engendered Incarceration: The Intersectionality of 'Race', Class, Gender and Sexuality

Historically the Canadian State has had a highly racialized and class-influenced coercive relationship over women's bodies. For example in 1919, the Canadian eugenics movement was flourishing whereby the elimination of "degenerate" members of society (women of colour, or disabled persons) were subject to sterilization processes. The colonial history that is played out on the bodies of women of colour has is roots entrenched in processes past and present that are descriptive of the fluid nature of racism, sexism, and classism. For centuries women's bodies, particularly Black bodies and other bodies of colour have been subjugated and pathologized via the discourse of science and technology. For our purposes the term 'black women' describes African/Caribbean women of that ancestry. In no way is this term meant to essentialize the bodies of black women or their voice. For the purposes of this paper the term 'black' is used to make the articulation and understanding of the dialogue more cohesive for the reader.

However, in terms of penology discourse surrounding Black and Aboriginal women, there has been little dialogue that explores the politics and interconnectedness of incarceration, 'race' and gender in the Canadian context. Research in the area of 'race' and the Canadian Criminal Justice System, notably, the work of Kelly Hannah-Moffat (2001), Margaret Shaw (1994) and Sherene Razack (1991, 1998, 2002) has been influential to the development of feminist penology. For example, Hannah-Moffat (2001) has argued that the focusing of gender-only discussions runs the risk of negating other important issues.

Consequently, the differential impact of racism that incarcerated women experience, forces us to look at how systems of patriarchy, colonialism, and imperialism are interconnected. As such, Razack (1998) challenges us to locate and `name' racism within the Canadian Criminal Justice System.

It can be argued that generally, Canada is (re)presented as a peace keeping country, void of overt incidences of racism. This cloak of "multiculturalism" is a fallacy. More accurate is the argument that the insidious nature of systemic racism is embedded in many immigration, refugee, employment, and economic policies. These policies are entrenched in a colonial history that delineates "Canadians" (read: white people of European descent) from "immigrants" (read: people of colour). Clearly, immigrants are not always people of colour, and people of colour should not always be stereotypically referred to as immigrants. My point here is to emphasize the discursive ideological framework in which "Canadian" is understood and idealized. Like many other social and ideological constructs, the definition of who and what a "Canadian" is has been created and normalized. More often than not, this construction does not include people of colour. In regard to penal punishment, troubling race relations between the Canadian State and people of colour are illuminated via the politics of incarceration for women. The historical confinement of female bodies of colour deemed criminal and unfit to aid in the project of empire building, represents a contemporary discursive continuum of racism perpetuated through power and coercion tactics. Strategically, this renders women of colour in Canada, invisible.

There has been much documentation about the disproportionate numbers of Native women in conflict with Canadian Law (Kline 1990; Fiske 1991, 2000). This disturbing and convoluted history between First Nations women and the Canadian state, describes numerous situations whereby race has played a major factor in the application of unfair justice. Stereotypical derogatory images of Native women have historically been wound up in the judicial discourse of imprisonment. The "squaw" woman or "savage Indian" are colonial terms which have been used to silence and perpetuate a vicious cycle of racism. Moreover, the Canadian State can be criticized for inherent racist practices when it comes to statutory obligations. For example, the 1876 Indian Act defined "Indian" through paternalistic means. A First Nations women could only remain "Indian" is she married a registered Indian man (Stevenson, 1999: 67). The Act eroded traditional rights that Native women had, and rendered them invisible. Such an example is demonstrative of the kind of racist discourse that subjugates Native women. If Native women had no status under Canadian law as citizens, how then were they to receive judicial impartiality? Patricia Monture-Angus (2000) has argued that although Native women are overrepresented in the criminal justice system they are also underrepresented. She explains that

> the solution to the overrepresentation of Aboriginal peoples in the criminal justice system and the systemic discrimination in that system requires the re-creation of Aboriginal justice systems...and to suggest that the problem

> Aboriginal people have with the justice system is one of overrepresentation alone is a drastic simplification of the situation. Understanding the full scope of the difficulties in representing this foreign system of justice further substantiates the need for the re-creation and legitimization of Aboriginal social control mechanisms (238).

Her point is well taken; the systemic exclusion of Aboriginal representation, whether that is lawyers, judges, correctional workers or police officers, is systematic of instances of institutional racism and practice. According to one Aboriginal parolee,

> The critical difference is racism. We are born to it and spend our lives facing it. Racism lies at the root of our life experiences. The effect is violence, violence against us, and in turn our own violence. The solution is healing: healing through traditional ceremonies, support, understanding and the compassion that will empower Aboriginal women to the betterment of ourselves, our families and our communities." (Aboriginal Parolee, quoted in Creating Choices, 2002).

Patricia Monture-Angus (1992) has argued for Aboriginal justice to be a central part of the Canadian Justice system. With the exception of the *Okimaw Ochi Aboriginal Healing Lodge*, in Saskatchewan, the Canadian justice system has failed Aboriginal women. Monture-Angus' argument must be acknowledged not only because there are disproportionate numbers of Native women incarcerated, but also because the Canadian justice system has historically denied, subverted, and de-legitimized the tenets of Aboriginal justice. The very narrow construction of "justice" for Native women needs to be expanded and reworked. There needs to be an accepted understanding that in terms of punishment and justice, the Canadian state has a responsibility to accept and acknowledge the multi-vocality of Native voice, and thus, the plurality of different forms of punishment.

Interestingly, there has been little documentation about Black women incarcerated in Canadian prisons. In one study focusing on "the disjuncture between an individualized conception of dependency and women's lived experience," Shoshana Pollack (2000) conducted five interviews with Black Caribbean-Canadian women federally incarcerated in Ontario. In another instance, Karlene Faith (1993) has argued that in the province of Nova Scotia, Black women make up the majority of the approximately twenty women in the provincial prison. Although, these works reference an often forgotten segment of the female prison population, there is still an exigent need for critical analysis and representation of the voices of Black women who are incarcerated in Canada.

In the United States, the imprisonment of Black and Hispanic women has reached disproportionate numbers. In her book Partial Justice, Nicole Hahn Rafter (1990) outlines distinctively how race and racism were salient factors in the judiciary process:

> Racism continued to influence prisoner populations powerfully after the Civil War. The proportion of blacks, including black women, continuously swelled in the prisons of the Northeast and Midwest, while the previously

white prisons of the South become engorged with newly freed blacks (133-134).

Similarly, Anne M. Butler (1997) argues that the discourse of "deviance" was crucial to the imprisonment of black women. She explains that "[w]omen of color, with their identities falsely titled toward sensuality, deviance and criminality by whites, found a clash with Anglo law further pushed them beyond the dominant society" (27). It has become evident that 'hatreds' are played out on the bodies of women of colour. For incarcerated women, these bodies do not "fit" into the dominant Eurocentric ideals of virtue implicit in the ideological construction of morality.

6. "Race" Politics and the "Politics" of Race: Towards a Black Feminist/Womanist Criminological Framework

The plurality of feminist/womanist theory and voices are central to understanding the complexities of female incarceration. This final section explores how feminist/womanist discourse can constitute and contribute to multi-vocal approaches of reformation for women in prison. In order to explore why prison incarceration is particularly detrimental to women, one needs to examine the socio-economic, racial, and class dynamics that are often very present for women in prison. According to Margaret Shaw (1994), incarcerated of women have been housed in accommodations that reinforce societal sex-gender roles of domesticity, while providing little infrastructure for programs and training that will benefit women upon release. The point here is not to reinforce the notion that women are in conflict with the law; rather the infra/structure of the judicial system, with a its lack of analysis on systemic and social racism and oppression is on conflict with the very real lived experiences of women. The Canadian Criminal Justice system, with its consistent emphasis on enacting a 'law and order' agenda, The explicit politics of female confinement directly connects to historical sex-gender stereotypes that attempt to reinforce paternalist ideals in an effort to reform the "bad" woman. Thus, the gendered nature of prisons subsumes the historical ideologies of sexism and patriarchy that are entrenched in the social reformation and regulation processes reinforced by the Canadian state.

Historically and contemporarily, as women's prisons have been built, the ideological and administrative philosophies of punishment procedures for men have been the model for female institutions. In many aspects this model has failed. Due to the oppressive nature of historical penal practices, incarcerated women have been pigeon-holed into deplorable spaces that further institutionalize them. Educational, counselling, or social development programs are under funded; many female inmates have been raped, assaulted, and are heavily sedated into a state of unconsciousness; women's labour is highly exploited; and incidents of HIV/AIDS is on the rise. By refusing to adequately provide safe and humane incarceration measures, the Canadian state contributes to, and reinforces the gendered nature of incarceration. While Kelly Hannah-Moffat (1990) reminds us that in the 1970s feminists began to challenge the sexist assumptions that examined the deplorable living conditions for women in prison, critical to this analysis is the fact that often these same feminists negated the politics of 'race in favour of gender-only discussions. Male and female prisoners do not have the same needs in prison; as such it is wise not to essentialize this notion of "women" by placing gender as the primary concern. The focusing of gender-only discussions runs the risk of negating other important issues. Accordingly, "[a]n emphasis on the commonalities of women results in an insensitivity to the differences among women; as a result, the experiences of women prisoners are trivialized" (Hannah-Moffat, 2001: 191). Subsequently, penal punishment for women cannot be looked upon in the same way as it is for men. Moreover, the intersectionality of race, class, and sexuality are interconstituted in the politics of gendered incarceration. Although this essay does not discuss the socio-economic or political implications of incarceration, it is important to remember that these too are factors that differentiate women's experience.

The voices and experiences of women of colour are valuable to feminist frameworks of punishment theory. In terms of critical legal theory, the intersectionality of Black and Aboriginal women's differential experiences should not be "slotted" into penology theory as a means addressing "special interest" issues. In many cases a single–axis framework is produced whereby white women's experiences become the pillar upon which to measure all women's experience and this contributes to the marginalization of Black and Native women's experience (Crenshaw, 1989). Working towards anti-racist feminist criminological theory should seek to implore an application of anti-racist theory and practice in relation to the epistemological paradigms and activist ideology that concerns the racialized nature of incarceration.

The law acts discursively, hence the legality of the law operates in conjunction with racial, political, social, and gendered systems. In many divergent ways, the voices of women of colour are recast into debates around the legitimization of their claims (Crenshaw, 1989), and the ways in which those claims are understood under the eyes of the law. The knowledge(s) produced about what "law" is, and does is entrenched in historical ideological discourse – law, then, is not neutral. Evidently, the politics of race and racism also works discursively in the area of criminality. Researching the confluence of race and the criminal justice system has long been studied. However, Black feminist discussions of race in the context of the Canadian justice system have hardly been mentioned. This is an area in which much work needs to be done. Karlene Faith notes there "are increasing numbers of women of African heritage, from the U.S. and the Caribbean...serving time at P4W on importing and trafficking convictions" (1993:184). Although the disproportionate number of Black women in US prisons has been greatly documented, in Canada and the US there still needs to be a womanist analysis that focuses on the intersectionality and spatiality of race and gender.

Daly and Stephens (1995: 195) state that "legal scholars taking feminist and critical race perspectives argue that relations of inequality are structured and reproduced in law and legal process". Consequently, it has been a trend for feminists to focus on either race *or* gender, as opposed to race *and* gender. This sameness-difference dilemma often confronts feminists, and it is a slippery terrain to have to navigate. For the vindication of judicial impartiality, Black women aim for race-conscious particularism to have their differences recognized, however when these differences are an instrument of oppression, the dilemma posed for critical race theory and politics is challenging (Cook, 1992 cited in Daly and Stephens, 1995: 195). Crenshaw (1989) argues when feminist theories evolve form a white racial context, the value of these theories serve unproductive to discussions concerning women of colour. When white women speak for all women, their voices become authoritative, and when a single-standpoint feminist theory attempts to describe women's experience by analyzing patriarchy, sexuality or separate spheres ideology from this context, this overlooks the role of 'race'. It is essential then, that other ways of knowing, learning and doing, are recognized as key elements in critical 'race' and legal theory. Working towards Black feminist criminological perspectives means placing Black women and other women of colour at the center of any and all discussions regarding the discourse of female confinement.

7. Intersectional Strategies: Transforming Justice, Transforming Lives

Feminist/Womanist criminology should seek to explore how should feminism negotiate this spatial difference between and among women in regards to incarceration? A good place to begin is by including and legitimizing multi-vocal and multi-dimensional feminist frameworks. These frameworks needn't only include the voices of academics, but also the necessary narratives of previously or currently incarcerated women. Organizations such as the Canadian Association of Elizabeth Fry Societies (CAEFS), the Aboriginal Women's Council of Saskatchewan, and the Manitoba Action Committee on the Status of Women have argued that there is some correlation between crimes committed by women and the conditions of these women's lives. Socio-economic factors, domestic violence, rape, and racism can all contribute in some way to women committing crimes. While this is an essential argument, I am not arguing that all women are victims, because that discredits women's agency and self-imbued power (Hannah-Moffat, 2001; Bosworth, 1999).

The politics of incarceration, then, asks 1) how do we punish perpetrators of crimes against women and girls (particularly sexual assaults, domestic violence, and child abuse) when that same state sanctioning of punishment and incarceration is used against women? 2) How do we negotiate between and among judicial and social systems that advocate for societal-safety when women in prison are themselves not safe? And 3) is prison in itself, another reformulation of violence and oppression whereby the system of corrections fundamentally defines incarcerated women as deviant and in need for social and moral regulation?

In an attempt to answer some of these questions, abolitionist and reformation discussions abound. The use of these two terms interchangeably is problematic. For one, reformations of the penal system do not call for the abolishment for prisons. A reformationist standpoint focuses more on querying the multiple ways in which punishment is exacted – making prisons more humane. In contrast an abolitionist standpoint critiques the prison as an isolated institution (Davis 2003). In order to work towards changing our current hegemonic social order, penal abolitionists such as Angela Davis (2003) argue that "[w]e would recognize that punishment does not follow from "crime" in the neat an logical sequence offered by discourses that insist on the justice of imprisonment, but rather punishment…is linked to the agendas of politicians, the profit drive of corporations, and media representations of crime" (112).

Any attempt to move towards answering some of the above questions calls for the re-articulation and deconstruction of "woman" as a social and political construct. Part of this pedagogical and ideological deconstruction further involves de-essentializing the theoretical and practical epistemological ways in which this construct is understood and utilized. In regards to the Canadian Criminal Justice System, a move towards eradicating the subjugation of women includes the utilization of anti-racist theory and practice at all levels of judicial legislation and administration, and by extension also to various political, personal, and institutional echelons of society including but not limited to educational institutions, social welfare agencies, and healthcare facilities/hospitals. Particularly, in regard to incarceration, it is essential that women in prison feel some sense of security. They should not be at risk for rape, assault, or any other inhumane atrocity. Women should not be used as guinea pigs for drug experiments, nor should their labour be exploited via the big business economic enterprise of the Prison Industrial Complex. The super-max private owned prisons have become big business. The Prison Industrial Complex (PIC) refers to the ways in which governments allow for private companies to purchase prisons and "rent" out inmate labour at a cheap cost to other companies. For example, the airline Company TWA, lingerie company Victoria's Secret and technology company Motorola, all use prison labour to subsidize their work. This highly exploitative and unregulated "ownership" of labour allows for "legitimate" companies to choose the conditions upon which they treat their "employees.

The stigma surrounding women in prison is attached to definitions of deviance. In order for incarcerated women to reintegrate back into communities and for healing to take place, the erasure of social stigma for current and ex-prisoners is essential. If we are bombarded everyday with paternalist hegemonic ideals of who and what constitutes the "good" woman, how do protect against those ideologies that claim women who don't fit the norm, are expendable and worthless?

This paper has attempted to highlight some of the constant dilemmas that are pertinent to penology discussions for incarcerated women in an effort to realize that these dialogues are ongoing contestations that illuminate the explicit need for an intersectional analysis of punishment procedures to be at the forefront of all penology discussions. It is essential that Canada's judicial and correctional system deconstruct indices of power and coercive tactics that subjugate the bodies of female inmates.

This paper specifically argues for womanist intersections of critical race and legal theory to be included in any and all discussions of incarcerated women. Consequently, it serves to remember that any form of social phenomena (race, class, gender, sexuality), defines and constructs many of the ideas and representations that we have about criminality. In retrospect, the bodies of female inmates are represented as sexually deviant, undervalued and "different" from the prescribed norm. Furthermore, my argument rests on the notion that the politics of incarceration for women of colour by the Canadian Judicial System lacks insight into the intersectionality of 'race', gender, class and colonial history.

References

Butler, Anne M. 1997. *Gendered Justice in the American West: Women Prisoners in the Men's Penitentiaries*. Urbana and Chicago: University of Illinois Press.

Cooper, Sheelagh. 1993. "The Evolution of The Federal Woman's Prison" in Ellen Adelberg and Claudia Currie (eds) *In Conflict with the Law: Women and the Canadian Justice System*. Vancouver: Press Gang Publishers.

Creating Choices: Report of the Task Force on Federally Sentenced Women (Ottawa: Correctional Service of Canada, 1990). [Online] available: <http://www.csc-scc.gc/text/prgm/fsw/choices/choic2e_e.shtml>, (Retrieved 11/29/2002)

Crenshaw, Kimberle. 1989. "Demarginalizing the Intersection of Race and Sex: A Black Feminist Critique of Antidiscrimination Doctrine, Feminist Theory and Anti Racist Politics," *The University of Chicago Forum*, pp. 139-167.

Daly, Kathleen and Deborah J. Stephens. 1995 The 'dark figure' of criminology: towards a black and multi-ethnic feminist agenda for theory and research," in Nicole Hahn Rafter (ed) *International Feminist Perspectives in Criminology: Engendering A Discipline*. Buckingham, Philadelphia: Open University Press, pp. 189-215.

Davin Anna 1978. "Motherhood and Imperialism" in *History Workshop Journal* 5: 9-57

Davis, Angela Yvonne 1971. *If They Come in the Morning: Voices of Resistance*. New York, Third Press,

Davis, Angela Y. [afterward], Silliman, Jael and Anannya Bhattacharjee 2002. *Policing the national body: sex, race and criminalization ; a project of the committee on women, population, and the environment* Cambridge, Massachusetts: South End Press.

Davis, Angela Y. 2003. *Are Prisons Obsolete*? New York: Seven Stories Press.

Duffee, David E. 1989.Corrections: Practice and Policy. New York: Random House.

Ekstedt, J. W. and Curt T. Griffiths. 1988. Corrections in Canada: Policy and Practice. Canada: Butterworths Canada Ltd.

Faith, Karlene, 1993. *Unruly Women: The Politics of Confinement and Resistance*. Vancouver: Press Gang Publishers.

Feinman, Clarice. 1994. Women in the Criminal Justice System. Westport, Connecticut: Praeger.

Fiske, Jo-Anne, 1991. "Native Women in Reserve Politics Strategies and Struggles," *Journal of Legal Pluralism and Unofficial Law* 30-31.pp.121-137.

Fiske, Jo-Anne and Betty Patrick. 2000..*Cis dideen kat (When the Plumes Rise): The Way of the Lake Babine Nation*. Vancouver: University of British Columbia Press.

Foucault, M. 1963. *The Birth of the Clinic: The Archaeology of Medical Perception*. NY: Random.

Foucault, M. 1976.*The History of Sexuality; Volume 1 – Introduction*. NY: Random.

Foucault, M. 1975.*Discipline and Punish: The Birth of the Prison*, trans. Alan Sheridan. New York: Vintage.

Gamberg, H. *The Illusion of Prison Reform*. New York: Peter Lang Publishing, 1984

Grosz, Elizabeth. 1995. .*Space, Time and Perversion*. Routledge: London.

Hall, Stuart. et al. 1996. *Modernity: An Introduction to Modern Studies*. NY: Blackwell Publishing.

Hannah-Moffat, K. 2001. *Punishment in Disguise*. Toronto: University of Toronto Press.

Kendall, Kathleen. 2000. "Psy-ence Fiction: Governign Female Prisons Through the psychological Sciences," in Kelly Hannah-Moffat and Margaret Shaw (eds) *An Ideal Prison?* Halifax, Nova Scotia: Fernwood Publishing, pp. 82-93.

Kline, Marlee. 1990. *Child welfare law, ideology, and the First Nations*. Thesis (LL.M.) -- York University.

Monture-Angus, Patricia. 2000. "The Roles and Responsibilities of Aboriginal Women: Reclaiming Justice," in Robynne Neugebauer (ed) *Criminal Injustice: Racism in the Criminal Justice System*. Toronto: Canadian Scholars' Press.

Pollack, Shoshana. 2000. "Dependency Discourse as Social Control" in Kelly Hannah-Moffat and Margaret Shaw (eds) *An Ideal Prison?* Halifax, Nova Scotia: Fernwood Publishing, pp. 72-81.

Rafter, Nicole Hahn. 1990. *Partial Justice: Women, Prisons, and Social Control*. New Brunswick (USA): Transaction Publishers.

Razack, Sherene H. 1991.*Canadian feminism and the law: the Women's Legal Education and Action Fund and the pursuit of equality*. Toronto: Second Story Press.

Razack, Sherene H. 1998. *Looking White People in the Eye: Gender, Race, and Culture in Courtrooms and Classrooms*. Toronto: University of Toronto Press.

Razack, Sherene H. 2002. *Race, space, and the law: Unmapping a White Settler Society*. Toronto: Between the Lines.

Shaw, M. 1994. "Women in prison: A literature Review," In *Forum*, January Volume 6, Number 1 [Online] available; retrieved, 11/07/2002. <http://198.103.98.138/text/pblct/forum/e06/e061d.shtml,

Stevenson, Winona. 1999. "Colonialism and First Nations Women in Canada." In Enakshi Dua, and Angela Robertson (eds) *Scratching the Surface*. Toronto: Women's Press

15. Taking Action to Reduce Injecting Drug-Related Harms in Prisons: The Evidence of Effectiveness of Prison Needle Exchange in Six Countries*

Rick Lincs, Ralf Jürgens, Glenn Betteridge, Heino Stöver

1. Introduction

The need for an effective response to HIV, hepatitis C (HCV), and injection drug use in prisons is a significant international concern. In many countries, including Canada, rates of HIV and HCV infection in prisons are much higher than those found in the general population. Community syringe exchange programs have proven to be an effective harm reduction measure to reduce the sharing of syringes, and therefore the risk of HIV and HCV transmission among injection drug users.. Since 1992, syringe exchange/distribution programs have been implemented in prisons in six different countries – Switzerland, Germany, Spain, Moldova, Kyrgyzstan, and Belarus. This article examines the evidentiary basis for prison needle exchange programs, based on international experience and evidence (current to 31 March 2004), including site visits to prisons in four countries. The authors conclude that prison needle exchange programs are effective in preventing the transmission of HIV, can be implemented without jeopardizing institutional safety and security, and that governments have a moral and ethical obligation to provide sterile injecting equipment to injecting drug using prisoners without delay based upon the numerous international guidelines and covenants supporting the provision of HIV prevention measures to prisoners,

---

* This article was originally published in the International Journal of Prisoner Health (vol. 1, no. 1, 2005). (Sections have been renumbered to render the presentation consistent with this volume.) It is summarised from the report, *Prison Needle Exchange: Lessons from a Comprehensive Review of International Evidence and Experience* (R Lines, R Jürgens, G Betteridge, H Stöver, D Laticevschi, J Nelles), published in October 2004 by the Canadian HIV/AIDS Legal Network. We would like to acknowledge the contributions of our co-authors on that report: Dr. Dumitru Laticevschi (Moldova) and Dr. Joachim Nelles (Switzerland). The full report provides a comprehensive review of the evidentiary and legal basis for prison needle exchange programs. Its goal is to encourage prison systems with HIV and hepatitis C (HCV) epidemics driven by injection drug use to implement needle exchange programs. The full report, *Prison Needle Exchange: Lessons from a Comprehensive Review of International Evidence and Experience*, is available online at http://www.aidslaw.ca/Maincontent/issues/prisons.htm in English, French, and Russian.

2. Harm Reduction Programmes are a Pragmatic Response to HIV, HCV and Injecting Drug Use in Prisons

Harm reduction programmes have been implemented in the prison systems of many countries since the early 1990s (Lines, 2002; MacDonald, 2004; Stöver, 2002). These programmes include the provision of condoms and other safer sex measures, disinfectants and bleach, substitution treatments such as methadone, buprenorphine and even heroin, and initiatives to reduce the risk of disease transmission via unsafe tattooing (Correctional Service Canada, 2004; Lines, 2002; MacDonald, 2004, Roca Tutusaus, 2004; Stöver, et al., 2004; Lines/Stöver 2005). In these countries, harm reduction initiatives have been implemented as a pragmatic public health response to the risk of HIV and/or HCV transmission in prisons via unprotected sex and the sharing of injecting equipment.

a) The evidence supporting the need for prison health interventions based in a harm reduction philosophy is significant.
b) High rates of HIV and HCV seroprevalence are evident in many prison systems internationally. It is often the case that rates of HIV and/or HCV infection are many times higher among prison populations than in the population outside of prisons (Lines et al., 2004, with numerous references).
c) High-risk behaviours for the transmission of HIV and HCV – such as injecting drug use and unprotected sex – are prevalent in prisons across the world. It has also been found that the incidence of syringe sharing by people who inject drugs increases when those same people are incarcerated (Lines et al., 2004, with numerous references; UNAIDS 2004, p. 81f).
d) Evidence of HIV and HCV transmission within prisons has been documented in various countries. This includes cases of individual transmission and instances of larger outbreaks of infection among networks of prisoners who inject drugs (Lines et al., 2004, with numerous references).
e) Harm reduction initiatives, and especially needle exchange programmes – both inside and outside prisons – have proven effective in reducing high-risk behaviour and HIV/HCV transmission (WHO 2004; UN 2001).
f) The failure to provide access to essential HIV and HCV prevention measures to people in prison is a violation of prisoners' right to the highest attainable standard of physical and mental health under international law, and is inconsistent with numerous international instruments dealing with the health of prisoners, and HIV/AIDS (Lines et al., 2004, with numerous references).

While many prison systems have implemented some if not all of the above measures, prison syringe exchange remains under-utilised internationally. In countries with HIV epidemics driven by injecting drug use, needle exchange has proven to be the most controversial – and therefore least commonly implemented – of prison harm reduction interventions. Opposition to PNEP is often based upon the belief that such programmes are incompatible with the prison environment, in which drug possession and consumption are illegal and point to a failing of the prison system to stop drugs from entering the prison or rehabilitate drug addicted prisoners. Additionally, many of those involved in prison systems fear that providing sterile syringes to prisoners would result in an increase in drug use and drug injecting, present an undue safety risks to prison officers by placing a potential weapon in the hands of prisoners, and compromise the "drug free" ethos of the prison system thereby undermining other abstinence-based and drug treatment programmes.

However, the evidence and experience of prison needle exchange is clear that none of these fears has been realised. It is also clear that these programmes have resulted in significant improvements in prisoner health and in institutional safety and security.

3. Background

This article examines the issue of prison needle exchange programmes (PNEP) based upon the international experience and evidence in six countries. The term "needle exchange" is used to refer to the one-for-one exchange of a used needle for a sterile needle, as well as to the distribution of sterile needles without exchange. Unless otherwise indicated explicitly or by context, the terms "needle" and "syringe" mean a device used to inject fluids into the body, and are used interchangeably throughout the article.

4. Methodology

The evidence for the report on which this article is based was gathered over an 18-month period beginning in October 2002.A review of the existing international literature was undertaken. This included extensive research on prisons and

- HIV
- HCV
- injecting drug use
- harm-reduction measures
- needle exchange programs

Sources referenced include international published reports, journal articles, conference presentations, government publications, and prison service reports. These materials include previous work and research on these topics published by the authors. In addition, original research was conducted during site visits to prison needle exchange programmes in the four countries operating such initiatives in October 2002. Site visits were made to the following prisons:

- Moldova: Prison Colony 18 (Branesti), November 2002
- Spain: Soto de Real (Madrid), May 2003
- Switzerland: Hindelbank (Berne), Saxerriet (Salez), Obershöngrün (Berne), June 2003
- Germany: Lichtenberg (Berlin), Vechta (Lower Saxony), June 2003

During these site visits, the needle exchange programmes were observed and unstructured interviews were held with prison medical staff, prison management, external professionals working in drug policy and/or harm reduction, and prisoners.

In some cases government officials and/or representatives of non-governmental organisations were also interviewed. During the course of the research, prison needle exchange programmes were initiated in two other countries – Kyrgyzstan and Belarus. Since these programmes were not in operation at the time the research plan was developed in October 2002, site visits to prisons in these countries were not possible. Therefore, research was conducted via

- personal communications with the staff involved in coordinating the needle exchange programmes
- personal communications with the organisations funding the programmes
- written documentation provided to the authors by the above sources, including funding proposals, project reports, conference presentations, and other documents

Because site visits were not possible in these cases, the information provided in the Kyrgyzstan and Belarus sections of the report is less detailed than that for the other countries. In March 2004 and January 2005, the authors followed up with contacts in a number of the countries to verify and clarify information previously obtained and/or to obtain updates on the situation in a particular country's prison system.

5. Overview of Countries that Provide Prison Needle Exchange Programmes

At the time of writing, prison needle exchange programmes are operating in over 50 prisons in six countries – Switzerland, Germany, Spain, Moldova, Kyrgzstan and Belarus. At least three other countries – Kazakhstan, Tajikistan and Poland – are seriously considering the implementation of pilot programmes in 2005 (M Curtis, personal communication, 20 October 2004; Ksel, 2004). A programme to provide people detained in some Scottish police stations will also be initiated in 2005 (Edwards, 2005). In Ukraine, two prisons in which pilot programmes will be started, most likely in early 2006, have been selected (R Jürgens, personal communication, 21 April 2005). Recommendations supporting the introduction of prison needle exchange pilot projects have also been made in publications and scientific work from other countries (e.g. Black/Dolan/Wodak for Australia 2004; Allwright et al. 1999 for Ireland).

This section provides a brief overview of the history and current availability of PNEPs internationally.

5.1 Switzerland

In 1992 Switzerland became the first country to introduce a prison needle exchange programme. This programme was started on an informal basis by a physician at the Oberschöngrün men's prison who, ignoring prison regulations, began distributing sterile syringes to patients he knew to be injecting drugs and sharing needles. In 1994 the first formal needle exchange pilot project was established in the Hindelbank women's prison. After a successful trial and evaluation at Hindelbank, needle exchange programmes were expanded to a total of seven Swiss prisons.

The Swiss prisons utilise two models of syringe distribution: automated syringe dispensing machines and hand-to-hand exchange through prison medical and counselling staff. Some prisons utilise both methods. Prisoners participating in the programmes are mandated to store their syringe in a hard plastic safety case to reduce the risk of accidental needle-stick injuries. Improperly stored syringes, or syringes that are not part of the official programmes, are considered contraband and seized with the prisoner in question being punished by the institution.

In the years since the initial implementation of PNEPs, some prisons have adapted their programmes based upon experience. Hindelbank, for example, will now provide prisoners participating in the programme with up to five additional "points" (needles) to attach to the main body of the syringe. This is to accommodate people who inject drugs and who may have trouble injecting due to difficulty finding veins. In such cases, the user may need to make several attempts to inject. With additional "points," the prisoner need not reuse a needle that gets duller with each attempted injection. Oberschöngrün also follows a flexible approach to its syringe exchange programme, and does not adhere to a strict one-for-one policy.

5.2 Germany

In 1996, pilot needle exchange programmes were established in three German prisons. In the women's prison in Vechta, exchanges were done using one-for-one syringe dispensing machines based upon the Hindelbank model. In the men's prison in Lingen 1 Dept Groß-Hesepe, exchanges were made by staff from the medical unit and the drug counselling service. In the open prison Vierlande in Hamburg, syringes were distributed by an external organisation, which also provided counselling as well as vocational training for prison personnel. Following a successful two-year pilot phase and evaluation, the programmes were continued in these three institutions and were expanded to four others. However, over the last two years these programmes have come under increasing attack from German political leaders elected to office on a "zero-tolerance to drugs" platform, and who have used the issue of PNEP to advance their political interests. Despite the encouraging results of scientific evaluations, and positive practical experiences of the prisons and prison staff involved, six of the programmes have been cancelled.

The one remaining German PNEP (in Lichtenberg women's prison in Berlin) utilises a syringe dispensing machine (see overview Stöver 2003).

5.3 Spain

The first prison needle exchange programme was introduced in July 1997 in Basauri prison, Bilbao, in the Basque region (Menoyo et al., 2000). This was followed by pilot programmes in Pamplona prison (1998) and the Orense and Tenerif prisons (1999) (Grupo De Trabajo Sobre Programas De Intercambio De Jeringuillas En Prisones, 2000). In June 2001 the Directorate General for Prisons ordered that needle exchange programmes be implemented in all prisons, and the mandate to institute needle exchange programmes exists for all 69 prisons under the jurisdiction of

Spain's Ministry of the Interior, with the exception of psychiatric prisons and one high-security-level prison. By the end of 2001, syringe exchange was provided in 11 Spanish prisons. By the end of 2002 the number of prisons providing needle exchange had grown to 27, and by the end of 2003 to 30 (Sanz Sanz et al, 2003a).

There are also pilot needle exchange programmes operating in 2 of the eleven prisons under the jurisdiction of the autonomous government of Cataluña. In 2005, the government of Cataluña plans to expand the availability of PNEP, with the ultimate goal of having needle exchange available in all prisons (Roca Tutusaus, 2004). All of the Spanish and Cataluñan programmes practice hand-to-hand exchange by health-care staff (nurses, physicians), or health-care staff in collaboration with external non-governmental organisations (Sanz Sanz et al, 2003b). Harm-reduction kits – which include a syringe in a hard plastic transparent safety case (in which prisoners must store theor syringe), distilled water, and an alcohol swab – are provided rather than single needles alone. Some institutions also provide a sterile cooker and filters in their kits. Two different gauges of syringes are available to people who inject drugs, depending upon whether the person is injecting heroin or cocaine. One of the pilot projects in Cataluña is testing the distibution of one-use-only retractible syringes (Roca Tutusaus, 2004).

The Spanish guidelines do not mandate strict adherence to one-for-one exchange. While they advise that "the rule should be exchange, i.e., the previous syringe must be returned before a new kit is handed out," they also recognise that "a flexible attitude should be maintained towards [the one-for-one rule's] application keeping in mind that the primary objective of the programme is to prevent shared use of syringes." (Ministerio Del Interior & Ministerio De Sanidad y Consumo, 2002) Neither prisoners participating in methadone maintenance nor those living in drug-free units or involved in abstinence-based programmes are denied access sterile needles (Ministerio Del Interior & Ministerio De Sanidad y Consumo, 2002; Prisión Soto de Real, undated).

5.4 Moldova

The first prison needle exchange programme in Moldova was initiated in May 1999 in Prison Colony 18 (PC18) in Branesti, a medium/maximum-security prison with a population of approximately 1000 men. Originally, sterile syringes were provided to prisoners through the prison health unit. However, after four to five months, the distribution method was changed to a peer model, which continues to the present.

Under the supervison of the prison physcian, eight peer volunteers are trained to provide harm-reduction services in four different sites in the prison. Two peer volunteers are assigned to work at each site and they are available on a 24-hour basis, as the sites are based within the prison living units. In addition to one-for-one syringe exchange, peer volunteers also distribute condoms, disinfectants, antiseptic pads and razors for shaving. They also provide harm-reduction and HIV-prevention information, including information on safer injecting and post-injection problems (Bodrug, 2002).

Based upon the success of the pilot project in PC18, a second syringe exchange programme was initiated in May 2002 in Prison Colony 4 (PC4) in Cricova. A third project, in the women's prison in Rusca, was opened in August 2003. As of December 2004, there are four prisons in Moldova providing needle exchange (Pintelli, 2004). All utilise the peer-based model of syringe distribution.

5.5 Kyrgyzstan

In October 2002 a pilot needle exchange project was introduced in Prison IK-47, a maximum security institution. The project provideed services for approximately 50 prisoners who exchanged needles on a daily basis, and exchanges were made my prison health staff in the medical ward. The pilot also provided secondary exchange using prisoners as peer volunteers, using the Moldovan model, as the project coordinators found that both options were necessary.

In early 2003 an order was issued approving the provision of sterile needles in all Kyrgyz prisons. As of September 2003 needle exchange programmes were operating in six of the 11 prisons in Kyrgyzstan (five men's prisons and one women's prison). In February 2004 funding was obtained to expand the programmes to all 11 prisons and by April 2004 sterile needles were available in all prisons. In all 11 institutions, needle exchange is done using prisoners trained as peer outreach workers who work with the medical unit (all information provided by R Abdyldaeyva & E Muratalieva, personal communications 2003 & 2004).

5.6 Belarus

In April 2003 a pilot PNEP was initiatied at the Reformatory School 15/1 in Minsk, a prison with a population of 2000. This site was selected based on the availability of scientific and medical specialists and because the prison also houses the National Hospital, which provides primary HIV care for all known HIV-positive Belarussian prisoners. The programme follows the Moldovan model, and uses 20 volunteers from the prisoner population to distribute needles to their peers. The pilot was originally scheduled to run until January 2004. This term was extended until June 2004. Concurrently, the needle exchange programme was extended to two other prisons. The Ministry of Internal Affairs is prepared to expand prison syringe exchange throughout the country, although securing funding for such an initiative is a major barrier to realising this goal. (all information provided by L Savischeva, personal communications 2003 & 2004).

6. Analysis of the Evidence of PNEPs

Based upon the evidence and experience of PNEPs six countries, a number of conclusions can be drawn.

6.1 Increased institutional safety

Implementing prison needle exchange programmes does not necessitate a trade-off between health and security. There was not one report of a syringe from a PNEP being used as a weapon against either a prisoner or a staff member in any of the countries investigated. There were no reported problems with safe disposal of used syringes, and some prisons reported syringe return rates of over 98% (Stöver & Nelles, 2003). In addition, many prisons – as well as prison staff interviewed for this study – reported an *increase* in staff safety. This is because prisoners participating in the PNEP is some countries were made to store their syringe in a hard plastic safety case and in a safe (i.e. visible) location. Overall, the PNEPs meant that there was no longer a need for prisoners to hide or conceal syringes, and indeed there were often punitive sanctions for doing so rather than taking part in the official exchange programme. As a result, accidental needle stick injuries to staff from hidden syringes during cell searches have been significantly reduced.

6.2 No increase in drug consumption or injecting

With one exception, the scientific evaluations undertaken of prison syringe exchange programmes (while limited in number) have consistently found that the availability of sterile syringes *does not* result in an increased number of drug injectors, an increase in overall drug use, or an increase in the amount of drugs seized in the institutions. In a recent review of 11 evaluated prison needle exchange programmes in Switzerland, Germany, and Spain it was found that in no case did levels of drug use or drug injecting increase, and that in two prisons levels of drug use actually decreased (for one prison no data was available on this question) (Stöver & Nelles, 2003).

The one exception is a qualitative study carried out at the same time as the epidemiological study of the prison needle exchange in Hamburg/Vierlande in Germany (1998). In that evaluation, it was found that some prisoners (the report does not specify how many) who had stopped using drugs started to use them again in prison, and that some went from inhaling drugs to injecting. It was suggested in the study that the presence of anonymous syringe dispensing machines in the prison served as a temptation for prisoners and therefore encouraged relapse (Gross 1998). This suggestion has been the subject of much debate. In particular, the suggestion – which has not been confirmed by any of the other studies evaluating PNEPs – came from focus groups, and critics have pointed out that it is unclear to what degree statements by prisoners identifying the syringe dispensing machines as a temptation for relapse were in fact simply an attempt on their part to rationalise and "legitimise" their re-initiation of drug use. The results of this qualitative study are also at odds with the results of the epidemiological study done in the same prison at the same time, which found no increase in drug use or drug injecting (Heinemann & Gross, 2001).

It is also debatable to what extent the existence of syringe exchange machines can be held responsible for some prisoners switching from inhaling or smoking to injecting as this has also been observed in prison systems without syringe exchange programmes. For example, Long (2004) reported this behaviour in her study in the Irish prison system but concluded that it was the low availability of heroin that encouraged the change from smoking to injecting. Initiation to drug injecting in prisons has in fact been identified in many countries, most of which do not have prison needle exchange programmes. For example, a 2002 report prepared for the European Union found that 0.4% to 21% of people who inject drugs started injecting in prison (European Monitoring Centre for Drugs and Drug Addiction, 2002).

6.3 PNEP is part of a continuum of drug-related programming

The provision of sterile needles has not meant condoning the use of illegal drugs in prisons, and the provision of sterile needles in prisons in the six countries examined in this report has not resulted in prison officials condoning or otherwise permitting the use, possession, or sale of drugs. In all cases, drugs remain prohibited within institutions where needles exchange is in place, and security staff is instructed to locate and confiscate all such contraband (including needles that are not part of the exchange programme).

Fears that PNEPs would undermine abstinence-based approaches have not been realised. Rather, the evidence shows that PNEP can actually *increase* the uptake of ongoing drug treatment services. This was the conclusion of the German pilot programmes, and has also been the experience in Spain, where officials concluded not only that "It is feasible for a NEP and other drug addiction prevention or intervention programmes to coexist," but also that "NEPs in prison facilitate referral of users to drug addiction treatment programmes" (Ministerio Del Interior & Ministerio De Sanidad y Consumo, 2002).

Ideally, needle exchange programmes should be one component of a comprehensive drug service within prisons that includes abstinence-based programmes, drug treatment, drug-free units, and harm-reduction measures. In the prisons in all six countries studied, PNEP is part of larger harm-reduction initiatives which includes HIV/HCV education, substitution therapy for drug treatment, condom distribution, distribution of bleach or other disinfectants, antiseptic wipes, razors for shaving, and/or confidential HIV and HCV testing.

6.4 PNEPs reduce risk behaviour and prevent disease transmission

The most important lesson emerging from the international evidence on prison needle exchange is that these programmes are very effective in reducing needle sharing and therefore in preventing the transmission of HIV and HCV.

A recent review of eleven evaluated PNEPs found that the programmes strongly reduced syringe sharing in seven of nine prisons for which data was collected (of the other two prisons, one exhibited no change in sharing and in the other sharing was observed in "single cases" only). In five of these prisons, blood testing was performed as part of the programme evaluation and no seroconversions were observed (Stöver & Nelles, 2003; Keppler 2003).

6.5 Other positive outcomes on prison health

Some prisons reported a dramatic decrease in fatal and non-fatal heroin overdoses among incarcerated people who inject drugs.* For example, the Swiss prison of Hindelbank averaged between one and three fatal heroin overdoses annually during the years before the needle exchange programme was implemented. Since the programme has been in place, Hindelbank has experienced only one fatal heroin overdose in the past nine years (D DeSantis, interview with R Lines 2 June 2003). This experience was also reported in the Swiss prison of Oberschöngrün, which has a heroin maintenance programme in addition to a syringe exchange (H Stutz & U Weibel, interviews with R Lines 4 June 2003). Both Hindelbank and Oberschöngrün also reported a near disappearance in abscesses.

6.6 Effective in a wide range of institutions

PNEPs have been successfully implemented in a wide variety of prison settings.
Researchers for this report visited PNEPs in men's and women's prisons, military and civilian prison regimes, prisons of all security levels, small prisons (Oberschongrun prison in Bern, population 70) and large prisons (Soto de Real prison in Madrid, population 1,600), and prisons with radically different physical environments (living units of individual cells as well as barracks-style facilities that have 70 or more prisoners living and sleeping in a single room). The cases examined also demonstrate that needle exchange projects can be successfully implemented in jurisdictions that are relatively well resourced and financed (Switzerland, Germany, Spain), as well as in countries in economic transition that operate with significantly less funding and infrastructural supports (Moldova, Kyrgyzstan, Belarus).*

---

* Prison staff interviewed offered two reasons for this outcome. 1) Providing each injection drug user with his/her own personal needle enables the individual to consume a smaller amount of drug with each injection. In the past, when a syringe was shared among many prisoners, a person who injected drugs would only have limited access to it and would be more likely to inject large doses on those rare occasions when he/she was in possession of the syringe. 2) The implementation of needle exchange and the adoption of a harm-reduction philosophy within the institution fundamentally changed the way that prison health and social work staff were able to engage in counselling with prisoners. Because injection drug use was recognised as a reality by all concerned, counsellors and health workers and prisoners were able to be much more open and frank in discussions about drug use and harm reduction. The need for prisoners to pretend to be "drug free" was therefore removed, and honest discussions about risk behaviour and overdose prevention were able to take place in an atmosphere where prisoners did not fear sanctions for admitting their drug use.

* It bears mentioning that some of the countries in transition studied for this report have been able to take advantage of resources from international donors to implement needle exchange programs. Therefore, access to funding and resources in

6.7 Different methods of needle distribution have been effective

Different countries (and different prisons within a given country) have adopted different methods to distribute (or exchange) needles. The different methods used for needle distribution by the countries studied were:

- distribution by prison nurses or physicians based in a medical unit or other areas(s) of the prison
- distribution by prisoners trained as peer outreach workers
- distribution by external non-governmental organisations or other health professionals who come into the prison for this purpose
- distribution by one-for-one automated needle-dispensing machines.

The distinct features and outcomes associated with each method of distribution is reviewed in turn.*

Hand-to-hand distribution by prison nurse and/or physician

- Provides personal contact with prisoners and an opportunity for counselling
- Can facilitate outreach to and contact with previously unknown drug users
- Prison maintains high degree of control over access to syringes
- One-for-one exchange or multiple syringe distribution possible (as necessary, and as reflects individual prison policy)
- Lower degree of anonymity and confidentiality, which may reduce the participation rate (although high acceptance by prisoners is possible if confidentiality is maintained)
- Access more limited, as syringes are available only during the established hours of the health service (this is particularly true if the prison follows a strict one-for-one exchange policy)
- Creates possibility of proxy exchanges by prisoners obtaining syringes on behalf of those who do not want to participate in person due to lack of trust with staff

Hand-to-hand distribution by peer outreach workers

- High acceptance by prisoners
- High degree of anonymity and trust
- High degree of accessibility (peer outreach workers live in the prison units, and are available at all hours)
- No direct staff control over distribution, which can lead to increased fears of workplace safety among staff

---

domestic budgets in and of itself is not a determinant of the ability of a jurisdiction to provide needle exchange to prisoners.

* This analysis is adapted and expanded from that found in Stöver & Nelles, 2003.

- One-for-one exchange more difficult to ensure

Hand-to-hand distribution by external non-governmental organisations or health professionals

- Provides personal contact with prisoners and an opportunity for counselling
- Facilitates outreach to and contact with previously unknown drug users
- Prison has opportunity to maintain high degree of control over access to syringes
- One-for-one exchange or multiple syringe distribution possible (as necessary, and as reflects individual prison policy)
- Provides a higher degree of anonymity and confidentiality, as there is no interaction with prison staff
- Access limited. Syringes available during set hours or set times of the week (this is particularly true if the programme follows a strict one-for-one exchange policy)
- Anonymity and confidentiality may be compromised by policies that require the external agency to provide information on participation to the prison
- There can be mistrust by prison staff of the external services providing syringes
- External workers may experience more barriers in dealing with the prison bureaucracy than internal prison health staff
- Turnover in staff of non-governmental organisation may result in a lack of programme continuity and lack of a consistent "face" for the programme for prisoners and prison staff

Automated dispensing machines

- High degree of accessibility (often multiple machines are in various places in the institution, which can be accessed outside the established hours of the medical service)
- High degree of anonymity, as there is no involvement with staff
- High acceptance by prisoners
- Strict one-for-one exchange
- Machines are vulnerable to vandalism and damage by prisoners and staff who are not in favour of this programme
- Technical problems with functioning of the dispensing machines can mean syringes are unavailable for periods of time, which can decrease prisoner confidence in the programme
- Some prisons are not architecturally suited for the use of dispensing machines (i.e., lack of discreet areas freely accessible to prisoners in which machines may be placed)

- Because the machines must be individually designed and constructed, the expense of providing them in sufficient numbers in multiple prisons can be prohibitive for some prison systems.

7. Common factors in effective prison needle exchange programmes

The evidence from the prison needle exchange programmes shows that the actual method of syringe distribution is less important than ensuring that the programme responds to the needs of the institution, the prisoner population, and the prison staff. As detailed in 6.7 (above) PNEPs have adopted various methods of syringe exchange/distribution. Each of these methods has proved successful, and has been implemented without jeopardising the safety or security of the institution. Despite the differences in the various needle exchange programmes examined for this report, the combined evidence of the programmes indicates a number of common factors characterising effective prison needle exchange programmes. These common factors are reviewed in this section.

7.1 Leadership of prison administration and support of prison staff

As with other controversial measures, or those measures that apparently run counter to accepted orthodoxy within a system, it is crucial to have supportive leaders at the highest level to successfully create and implement prison needle exchange programmes. Practically, this may mean leadership by key senior officials responsible for prison health-care services, or prisons generally, and support by the head of the prison in which the needle exchange is being established. The support of prison staff has also been shown to be an integral part of successful programmes, and educational workshops and consultations with prison staff have been a key component in the development of prison needle exchange in all jurisdictions visited for this report.

This is not to say, however, that staff in these institutions have been universally supportive from the start. In several cases, as is evidenced in the evaluations, staff members were reluctant at the start, yet grew to support the programme over time as its benefits were experienced first-hand. The initial reluctance of staff makes the need for committed, informed, inclusive leaders supporting the implementation of prison needle exchange programmes all the more important.

7.2 Need for confidentiality and trust

The issue of confidentiality has been a key factor in the creation of successful needle exchange programmes. From the perspective of many prisoners, confidentiality is the most important factor in establishing trust in the needle exchange programme. Inside any prison, absolute confidentiality of prisoners' personal information may be impossible. However, in the context of prison needle exchange programmes, it is crucial to preserve the confidentiality of prisoners who use drugs and access sterile needles to the greatest extent possible. The successful programmes examined in this report have all striven to identify needle distribution methods that would gain the trust of the prisoner population and thereby maximise participation in the programme.

7.3 Adequate access to needles

In addition to maximising confidentiality, providing adequate access to the needle exchange programme has also been a key factor in ensuring that programmes meet prisoner needs. In some cases, this is has been accomplished by the placement of multiple dispensing machines within a single institution, as was the case in the Hindelbank pilot. When hand-to-hand methods of distribution have been chosen, staff sought to identify areas (sometimes multiple) in the prison that were both discreet *and* easily accessible to prisoners. In the Moldovan and Kyrgyz experience, the decision to use a peer-based structure allowed for 24-hour access, since the peer outreach workers lived in the prison units where they distributed needles.

7.4 Needle exchange as part of a comprehensive harm-reduction programme

It has also been shown that the goal of reducing HIV and HCV transmission is best accomplished when prison needle exchange is one component of a broader, comprehensive harm-reduction strategy. In prisons in all six countries studied for this report, prison needle exchange programmes are part of larger harm-reduction initiatives. Although the issue has not been scientifically evaluated, from the primary evidence and experience presented in this report it appears that prison needle exchange programmes and other harm-reduction measures are mutually reinforcing, and that the (prior) existence of other harm-reduction measures has contributed to the successful implementation of needle exchange programmes.

7.5 Importance of evidenced-based decision-making: evaluating pilot projects

One final common aspect is the use of a well-evaluated pilot project as a first step to broader expansion. In some countries a single pilot has been used, while others such as Germany implemented several pilots running in parallel. The outcomes of the pilot programme evaluations have then been used to guide future planning. In some instances the prisons selected for the initial pilot programmes were relatively small institutions and/or open or half-open institutions with lower security levels. In these cases, programmes were tested and evaluated in these prison environments before expanding the programmes into larger, closed prisons with higher security levels. However, in Moldova the pilot project was done in a medium/maximum-security prison with a population of approximately 1,000 prisoners. In Belarus, the institution selected for the pilot had a population of 2,000 prisoners.

The experience of the six countries studied for this report demonstrates that pilot projects do not have to take prolonged periods of time to emerge, nor delay broader implementation of needle exchange programmes. For example, in Kyrgyzstan a pilot needle exchange was opened in October 2002, in early 2003 approval was given to expand the programme, as of September 2003 programmes were operating in six of 11 prisons, and by April 2004 programmes were operating in all 11 prisons. Nor do evaluations have to be fully completed before programmes are expanded to other prisons. For example, in Belarus a programme was piloted in one prison beginning in April 2003, scheduled to run until January of 2004. Although the term of the pilot was extended to June of 2004, it was also extended to two other prisons, and the Ministry of Internal Affairs signalled its willingness to expand needle exchange to prisons throughout the country. It is important to note that in the prison systems presented in this article, pilot projects have not been relied on as a tactic to delay the broader implementation of needle exchange programmes.

8. Conclusion: A Call for Leadership on Prison Needle Exchange Programmes

Although the number of countries that have implemented prison syringe exchange is relatively small, programmes have been successfully implemented in a wide range of prison settings. Prison needle exchange programmes can be found in countries of Western Europe, Eastern Europe, and Central Asia. They are operating in well-funded prison systems and severely underfunded prison systems. They are operating in civilian prison systems and military prison systems, and in institutions with drastically different physical arrangements for the housing of prisoners. They are operating in men's and women's institutions, and in prisons of all security classifications and all sizes. They are operating as individual pilot projects, and as integrated components of overall prison policy. They utilise various methods for distributing syringes.

While these prison syringe exchange programmes have been implemented in diverse environments and under differing circumstances, the results of the programmes have been remarkably consistent. Improved prisoner health and reduction of needle sharing have been achieved. Fears of violence, increased drug consumption, and other negative consequences have not materialised. Based on the evidence and experience, it can be concluded unequivocally that prison needle exchange programmes effectively address the health-related harms associated with needle sharing in prisons and do not undermine institutional safety or security. In fact, the evidence and experience demonstrate that PNEPs make prisons safer environments in which to live and work.

However, when it comes to the issue of needle exchange in prison, objective evidence has often proved secondary to political and ideological considerations, and public apathy toward issues faced by prisoners, prison staff, and prison systems. Many countries that exhibit significant rates of HIV, HCV, and injection drug use in prisons refuse to consider needle exchange programmes despite the evidence of their effectiveness and safety. This has even been the case in countries that have acted to implement other harm-reduction measures to address injection drug use, HIV, and HCV in prisons. Yet a harm-reduction strategy that does not include sterile needle exchange is not only a suboptimal public health measure; it is in contravention of international norms related to prison health, and fails to meet best practice.

Among the lessons learned from the research conducted for this article, two stand out in encouraging prison systems with HIV and HCV epidemics driven by injection drug use to implement needle exchange programmes.

The first lesson is that prison needle exchange is a pragmatic and necessary health response to the problems of HIV, HCV, and injection drug use that has been proven to be effective and safe. Needle exchange has been available in some prisons for as long as 10 years, and it is an approach that has been rigorously evaluated everywhere it has been enacted. Prison systems and governments can no longer avoid their responsibilities to provide for the health of prisoners by dismissing prison needle exchange programmes as something new or untested. They are neither.

The second lesson that emerges is that no matter how effective in practice, prison harm-reduction initiatives remain controversial. Decisions about prison conditions, or the failure to make decisions, are often unrelated to the evidence, to the detriment of the health of prisoners, prison staff, and the general public. For some people, prisons become a focal point for expressions of political ideology, with little regard for the evidence about measures that in fact promote the health and safety of prisoners, prison staff, and the general public. This was demonstrated in the case of Germany, where long-term successful needle exchange programmes were groundlessly terminated by newly elected governments.

These two lessons point to the need for leadership from elected officials and prison authorities on the issue of prison needle exchange programmes. Leadership is also required from individual prison staff (both security staff and health service staff) and from outside physicians who work in prisons. In the context of needle exchange programmes in prisons, leadership implies a number of attributes. First, leadership implies an understanding of the legal obligations of prison systems to respect, protect, and fulfil prisoners' right to health. Second, leadership implies knowledge of the experience of and evidence from existing prison needle exchange programmes. Third, leadership implies a willingness and commitment to make prison needle exchange programmes responsive to the needs of prisoners and prison staff (both health care and correctional). This means involving prisoners and prison staff in the design and implementation of programmes.

References

Allwright, S., Barry, J., Bradley, F., Long, J., Thornton, L. 1999. Hepatitis B, hepatitis C and HIV in Irish Prisoners: Prevalence and Risk. Report prepared for the Minister for Justice, Equality and law Reform by the Department of Community Health and General practice, Trinity College, Dublin/Ireland

Black, E., Dolan, K., Wodak, A 2004. Supply, demand and harm reduction strategies in Australian prisons. Implementation, cost and evaluation. NDARC-Research paper, July 2004

Bodrug, N. 2002. A pilot project breaks down resistance. In Harm Reduction News: Newsletter of the International Harm Reduction Development Program of the Open Society Institute 2002; 3(2).

Correctional Service of Canada. Memorandum: CSC Safer Tattooing Practices Initiative Pilot Implementation dated 24 December 2004. Copy on file.

Edwards, G. 2005. "Police station prisoners to be handed free needles". In Edinburgh Evening News. 14 January.

European Monitoring Centre for Drugs and Drug Addiction 2002. Annual report on the state of the drugs problem in the European Union and Norway. Luxembourg: Office for Official Publications of the European Communities.

Gross,U.2003.Wissenschaftliche Begleitung und Beurteilung des Spritzentauschprogramms im Rahmen eines Modellversuchs der Justizbehörde der Freien und Hansestadt Hamburg Evaluationsbericht eines empiri-schen Forschungsprojekts. *Kriminologisches Forschungsinstitut Niedersachsen,* November 1998. (Forschungsbericht No 73.)

Grupo De Trabajo Sobre Programas De Intercambio De Jeringuillas En Prisones April 2000. Elementos Clave para la Implantación de Programas de Intercambio de Jeringuillas en Prisión. Spain: Secretaría del Plan Nacional Sobre el SIDA/Dirección General de Instituciones Penitenciarias. Translated from the original Spanish.

Heinemann A & Gross U. Prevention of blood-borne virus infections among drug users in an open prison by vending machines. *Sucht* 2001; 47(1): 57-65.

Keppler, J. 2003. AIDS- und Hepatitis-Viren: Infektionserfassung und Prävalenz bei Frauen im Strafvollzug. Oldenburg/Germany

Ksel, M., 2004. Presentation at the WHO-Europe 10th annual conference on Prison and Health, De Leeuwenhorst, The Netherlands, 21 October 2004.

Lines, R. 2002. Action on HIV/AIDS in Prisons: Too Little, Too Late – A Report Card. Montréal, Canada: Canadian HIV/AIDS Legal Network.

Lines, R., Jürgens, R., Betteridge, G., Stöver, H., Laticevschi, D., & Nelles, J.2004. Prison Needle Exchange: Lessons from a Comprehensive Review of International Evidence and Experience. Montréal, Canada: Canadian HIV/AIDS Legal Network.

Lines, R., Stöver, H. 2005. HIV/AIDS Prevention, Care, Treatment and Support in Prison Settings. Background notes. Paper prepared for the United Nations Office on Drugs and Crime, Vienna/Austria, 17 March.

Long, J. 2004. Prisoners' views of injecting drug use and harm reduction in Irish prisons. In: The International Journal of Drug Policy 15, pp139-149

MacDonald, M. 2004. A Study of Existing Drug Services and Strategies Operating in Prisons in Ten Countries from Central and Eastern Europe. Birmingham, UK: University of Central England. (July).

Menoyo, C., Zulaica, D., & Parras., F. 2000. Needle exchange programs in prisons in Spain. In Canadian HIV/AIDS Policy & Law Review 5(4): 20-21.

Meyenberg, R.; Stöver, H.; Jacob, J.; Pospeschill 1999 Infektionsprophylaxe im Niedersächsisches Justizvollzug. Oldenburg/Germany

Ministerio Del Interior & Ministerio De Sanidad y Consumo October 2002. Needle Exchange in Prison: Framework Program. Madrid, Spain: Ministerio Del Interior/Ministerio De Sanidad y Consumo.

Pintelli, L., 2004. Presentation at the WHO-Europe 10th annual conference on Prison and Health, De Leeuwenhorst, The Netherlands, 21 October.

Prisión Soto de Real (undated). Recomendaciones sobre los Programas de Intercombio de Jeringuillas (PIJ). Obtained from the Prisión Soto de Real, Madrid. Copy on file.

Roca Tutusaus, X. 2004. Presentation at the WHO-Europe 10th annual conference on Prison and Health, De Leeuwenhorst, The Netherlands, 21 October.

Sanz Sanz, J., Hernando Briongos, P., López Blanco, J.A., 2003. Syringes Exchange Programs in Spanish Prisons. Presentation at the conference of the European Network of Drug Services in Prison, Rome, 22-24 May.

Sanz Sanz, J., Hernando Briongos, P., López Blanco, J.A., 2003. Syringe-exchange programmes in Spanish prisons. In Connections: The Newsletter of the European Network Drug Services in Prison & Central and Eastern European Network of Drug Services in Prison 13: 9-12.

Stöver, H. (2002). Drug and HIV/AIDS Services in European Prisons. Oldenburg, Germany: Bibliotheks- und Informationssystem der Universität Oldenburg.

Stöver, H., Hennebel, L., & Casselman, J. 2004. Substitution treatment in European Prisons. A study of policies and practices of substitution treatment in prisons in 18 European countries. London, UK: Cranstoun Drug Services.

Stöver, H. & Nelles, J., 2003. Ten years of experience with needle and syringe exchange programmes in European prisons. In International Journal of Drug Policy 14(5/6).

Stöver, H. 2003: 10 years of syringe provision to intravenous drug users in prisons – an end to the projects in Germany. In: Connections Newsletter, June.

UNAIDS 2004. 2004 Report on the global AIDS epidemic. 4th global report. Geneva.

UN 2001. Preventing the Transmission of HIV Among Drug Abusers: A Position Paper of the United Nations System (Approved on behalf of ACC by the High-Level Committee on programme at its first regular session of 2001, Vienna, 26-27 February). Paragraph 37.

World Health Organisation 2004. Effectiveness of sterile needle and syringe programming in reducing HIV/AIDS among injecting drug users. Evidence for Action Technical papers. Geneva.

16. A Consideration of Sexuality, Stereotypes and Gender Issues in Correctional Facilities: How These Elements Affect Professional Relationships between Staff and Inmates

Stephen E. Bosanac and Tammy Turner

1. Introduction

Changing times, cultures and economics have brought sexuality to the forefront in the workplace. The steadily rising numbers of women in the workforce and the corresponding increase in nuances surrounding sexuality in the workplace have had a significant effect on traditional ideals surrounding male dominated conceptions of work. This is especially true within the criminal justice professions. Issues concerning sexuality have been found to be problematic in both criminal justice work and living environments, particularly because management prefers to deny that these issues exist (Pollard and Sorbello 2000). Issues surrounding sexuality are more prevalent when the primary function of the business is caring for people as is the case in a correctional, or total institutional, environment (2000). Further, the dramatic increase in female correctional staff in conjunction with the even more notable increase in the size of the female inmate population in recent years exacerbates the need to examine these issues more closely.

The purpose of this chapter is to examine the myriad ways that sexuality affects communication and interactions in a gendered prison environment. It will examine some of the processes involved in stereotyping, the development of gender roles and the evolution of sexuality. It will also consider some of the socialization processes that are unique within the work experiences of correctional staff. This will allow for a comprehensive understanding of the problematic relational issues including sexualized work environments, staff misconduct and employee fraternization that can occur within the correctional work environment. It will also note some of the effects these processes might have on incarcerated persons, and the role prisoners might play in the development and/or resolution of these phenomena. These themes will add depth to the forthcoming presentation of legal issues surrounding each of these elements.

2. Stereotypes, Gender, Sexuality and the "Missing Link" in Professional Relationships

Stereotypes and gender roles have persisted over time and appear to dominate much of recorded history in one form or another with some exceptions, particularly among the First Nations people of Canada. These social constructs have been, and are, adhered to on a continuum ranging from a strict, legally sanctionable division of gender roles, to a casual separation of 'gender-appropriate' responsibilities.

From generation to generation, these ideas have been 'unconsciously' passed down, to the extent that corresponding definitions of 'men' and 'women' have become tacit knowledge, or taken as 'fact'. Stereotypes and gender roles <u>may</u> have had their purpose for maintaining social and/or economic order at one time. However, in recent history many cultures and peoples have demonstrated opposition towards the long-standing divisions brought about by the maintenance of traditional gender roles and stereotypes. This breakdown between traditional social roles and the expectations of contemporary men and women may be a significant contributing factor to the social and professional role conflicts experienced by many correctional staff (Turner and Bosanac 2005).

Stereotypes are exaggerated generalizations utilized in the assessment of a particular group of people. They define inappropriate/inapplicable standards of measurement and identification for individuals within a group. It is important to note that these 'standards' are not consistent among all members of the group. In fact, these generalizations may not apply to ANY member of the group. Stereotypes for women include weak, subservient, passive, nurturing, friendly, amiable, confidant, peacemaker, gullible or naïve, rescuer-savior, liberal, and sympathizer (Etheridge, Hale and Hambrick 1984). Stereotypes for men generally reflect the opposite of those listed for women and include ideas of strength, aggression and emotional coldness/detachment (Turner and Bosanac 2005). Because of these stereotypes, greater demands and expectations are generally placed upon women in a work environment shaped by beliefs founded in sex and gender role stereotypes (Lerner 1988). For example, an enthusiastic female manager might be described as frenzied, whereas an equally ardent male manager might be described as passionate. On the other hand, when comparing a proactive, assertive female manager to a similarly composed male manager, the female might be described using negative terms such as 'bitchy' or 'uncooperative'. The male however might be positively described as professional or motivated (Blodget 1986). These stereotypical perceptions have the ability to sway opinions and decisions, and may very well undermine the female manager's credibility and professional status (1986).

A gender role is an assignment, determined by social definitions and presumed responsibilities, bestowed upon a person perceived as belonging to a particular gender group. This is also known as an ascribed status. Gender roles are established using norms and values that are socially constructed as 'normal' for each respective gender. While sex is determined biologically, gender is a social and cultural development – a social construction (Turner and Bosanac 2005).

Male gender roles include father, provider, protector and disciplinarian. Female gender roles include homemaker, mother, caregiver, girlfriend and daughter. Stereotypical professional gender roles for women include nurse, teacher and librarian, while men are deemed 'better suited' for professional roles including doctor, policeman, fireman and lawyer (Jurik and Martin 2001).

Essential to each of the previous gender roles is the concept of sexuality. Sexuality is defined in so many different ways that it is difficult to find any aspect of life that is excluded from such a powerful force...[D]efinitions include various aspects of sexuality including gender, historical, private, attractiveness, activity, romance, threatening, stereotyping, biological, physiological, psychological, fantasy, power and political...Sexuality is diverse and can mean sexual orientation, sexual intercourse, sexual behaviour, sexual activity, sexual desires, sexual identities, sexual practices, sexual violence, sexual harassment, sexual fantasies, sexual experience(s), sexual domination, sexual abuse, sexual dynamics, sexual politics, sexual games and sexual discrimination (Civil 1998: 33 – 34).

Simply stated, sexuality can be defined as the boundaries that demarcate a person according to perceived biological indicators in combination with culturally established and accepted norms and values relating to sexual desires and behaviours. However, it is more important to note that sexuality also represents a significant element of a person's core identity (Burrell and Hearn 1989). Female sexuality in Western culture is measured against 'wholesome', maternal attitudes and images including girlfriend, wife and mother. Women who cannot be easily categorized in these terms are often perceived negatively and stereotyped as promiscuous, whores, teases, lesbians, and/or man-haters (Pollard and Sorbello 2000). Male sexuality is not measured on this same continuum. Rather, 'family men' are noted as loyal, noble, virile and strong, while promiscuous men are described as 'players' and/or less emotionally invested (Turner and Bosanac 2005). In other words, while a promiscuous man is generally described as 'sowing his wild oats' until he meets the woman of his dreams, an equally, or even less, promiscuous woman is considerably more likely to face negative social consequences and is much more likely to be categorized as a social problem or concern.

The combination of stereotypes (cultural and sexual) and gender roles (general and professional) can be complex, and feature myriad points of interaction that are manifested socially. People tend to act in accordance, however subconsciously, with these culturally established norms and behaviours. Through the tacit acceptance of gendered patterns of interaction, these behaviours and attitudes are reinforced continuously throughout the lifecycle of each member of a society. Consequently, traditional patterns of development from adolescent to adult to professional do not typically provide for female-male interactions beyond interactions related to socially acceptable gender roles. For example, interpersonal interactions with the 'opposite sex' include the traditional binary pairs of father-daughter, mother-son, boyfriend-girlfriend, and rescuer-victim. These relationships are generally rooted in cultural standards of patriarchy and paternalism, and do not include a model of 'ideal' professional interaction between genders. That is to say, during their developmental years, children are not consistently socialized to novel and/or alternative interaction patterns with members of the opposite sex. In particular, they are not taught how to interact in a gender-neutral, professional manner with those not in their sex category in a professional/work setting (Lindsey 1994).

Little girls are taught to play with dolls. They are instructed to sit still and be quiet. They are encouraged to be involved in care-taking activities. They are taught to wear dresses, to look pretty, to keep their bodies covered and to be modest. During adolescence, young women are taught that the body is sacred and should not be 'shared' until marriage. They are 'protected' by parents/families/society. They are socialized to enjoy non-competitive passive activities, subservience, weakness, and the 'need' to be protected. They are taught to share information in order to make connections and gain emotional contacts. They are taught to value/desire closeness and find physical contact acceptable (Debell 2001).

Little boys are taught to be rough, tough and loud, and to play with toy guns and plastic 'tool sets'. They are encouraged to play physical team sports and are not generally sheltered from the risks that these types of activities provide. Adolescent males are taught to be sexual and to 'sew their wild oats'. They are taught that sexual experimentation (with girls) is natural. They are encouraged to be aggressive, competitive, and physical. They are socialized to believe that men are supposed to be less emotional, less communicative and less open to emotional intimacy (McCampbell and Lyman 2000).

Very early in the socialization process, interaction patterns between males and females are encouraged primarily, if not exclusively, within the boundaries of these divergent socializing processes. The father-daughter and mother-son binaries are generally the earliest gender interactions. These relationships eventually come to include the boyfriend-girlfriend, husband-wife and rescuer-victim binaries. However, in time, men and women move into the workforce and are not prepared for mature, gender-neutral, non-sexual working/professional relationships (Lindsey 1994).

In particular, two social phenomena complicate interaction patterns between the genders in correctional professions. First, the 'defining/constructing' of conceptions of male and female is problematic. Second, the lack of professional and gender-neutral interactions before entering correctional professions presents a substantial obstacle to open, equitable relationships in the professional environment. Both of these elements contribute to a clearly and inappropriately gendered workforce, with the latter representing the 'missing link' in the effective development of gender-neutral work environments.

3. The History of the Gendered Correctional Workforce and Population

In the early 19th century, female volunteers known as prison matrons were utilized to assist in reforming female offenders. Their initial purpose was to educate female prisoners in the ways of womanhood and to encourage the development of 'the proper lady'. Later, the initiatives turned to improving morals and providing life skills. Eventually, these prison matrons improved conditions for female offenders as well as female criminal justice professionals.

Simultaneously, feminist advocates for prison reform were active in the development of the juvenile justice system. The involvement of women in the regulation of the welfare of children was deemed acceptable, as women were believed to be the most capable of providing nurturing and care. Women in this field were seen as 'natural' caretakers and mothers (Platt 1977). Other perceived 'female' skills held by these workers included patience, the ability to communicate with children, and the ability to teach. The new juvenile justice system brought about by this movement offered reputable and honourable opportunities for women who wanted to extend their housekeeping functions into community service (1977).

During the mid-19th century, prisons for men employed mostly men. The few women who did work in male facilities did so in traditional female occupations including nursing or clerical work (McMahon 1999). In 1972, Title VII of the Civil Rights Act of 1964 extended equal employment opportunities to women in the United States. This opened the door to non-traditional criminal justice positions as a career choice for women. The introduction of women into these male-dominated professions was complicated by confusion surrounding, and the clash between, 'normal' and novel gender, sexual and professional roles. This led to hostile work environments caused largely by co-workers for co-workers. Additionally, sexual harassment, gender harassment, flagrant discrimination and alienation were ritualized in order to dissuade women from entering into careers in the criminal justice professions generally, and correctional facilities in particular. Male Correctional Officers (CO's) were accustomed to using tough and aggressive language and behaviour with inmates as well as co-workers. The presence of women threatened their masculinity by threatening traditional organizational/workplace culture that was secured by, and rooted in, physicality and aggression (Farnworth 1992).

Many assumptions about women working in a correctional environment have remained in place since the introduction of women into the correctional field. There are three primary assumptions that must be specifically noted. One, in order to maintain control over inmates a person must be able to use physical force and be stronger than the inmate. Two, women must be protected from the many hazards found in the correctional environment. Three, female CO's are <u>always</u> at risk for a sexual attack in the correctional environment (Jurado 1999). The stereotype holds that if a woman is weak she may not be able to apprehend an inmate who is out of control, or adequately support other CO's in crisis situations. Many male officers envision themselves as being forced to decide between protecting a woman, assisting another officer, and/or controlling inmates. Many still believe that permitting female CO's to work in male correctional facilities places all staff members at additional risk for unnecessary harm.

Unfortunately, many practitioners and laypersons are not aware that much recent research demonstrates that physical strength is no longer especially necessary to the performance of care, custody and control duties. New self-defense techniques in combination with improvements in security technology have alleviated much of the dependence on raw, physical strength for the smooth operation of a facility. Perhaps more importantly, research shows that the introduction and refinement of interpersonal communications skills coupled with increasingly sophisticated training in conflict management and resolution have essentially eliminated the concern that women have to be protected from inmates in the correctional workplace. In fact, substantial research has demonstrated that an increase in female staff in correctional facilities seems to correspond to diminished assault levels and improved behaviour on behalf of male inmates as well as male staff members (Pollard and Sorbello 2000; Rowan 1996; Zimmer 1986; Jurado 1999).

4. Transference of Roles and Stereotypes

We may now move into a discussion of how professional relations develop within correctional professions. Given that most of us are ill-equipped to easily develop gender-neutral relationships at the workplace, this process appears to follow a path that was chosen by 'default'. Without a model of professional relations between genders, men and women are left to perceive one another in roles with which they are comfortable and familiar. The resultant process is known as gender role displacement/transference. In this process, a person confronted with an unfamiliar form of gender interaction applies patterns of gender interactions they are familiar with to the novel interaction (Turner and Bosanac 2005):

> Perhaps the male [Correctional Officer] will apply the brother/sister binary to his relationship with a female partner. Perhaps the female [Correctional Officer] will apply the mother/son binary to their relationship. This would create a dissonant situation wherein each partner has differing expectations of the other based on divergent values and needs. In the end, none of these expectations are associated with the professional relationship that should stand as the primary influence on their patterns of interaction (Turner and Bosanac 2005: forthcoming).

The misapplication of these binaries serves to confound professional expectations and inhibit clear communications between the coworkers. Simply stated, this situation can be compared to watching two people playing a board game. For example, Monopoly, but each player is playing by their own set of rules from another, not necessarily related, game, and each player is oblivious to the rules the other is following: The male may envision his role when interacting with a sister as that of protector. The female might see herself as a caregiver, nurturer [or perhaps even authoritarian]. These perceptions assume certain elements in their relationship and set potentially dysfunctional boundaries. Perhaps the male partner would expect less professional assistance from the female than he would from a male officer. If the male officer feels compelled to protect his female partner, will the female officer become dependant upon that protection? The expectations developed due to gendered perceptions, rather than professional expectations create a multitude of problematic situations for consideration (Turner and Bosanac 2005: forthcoming). In this scenario, participants tacitly accept the idea that the other understands them and their motivations, goals and objectives. As we can see in the examples given, that is not the case.

5. Convolution of Gender Roles among Staff and Inmates

Prisons feature a distinctive social structure that is significantly shaped by two unique elements – forced confinement and very limited exposure to members of the opposite sex. It is important to note that socialization of incarcerated females is distinctly different from socialization of incarcerated males. Further, corrections professionals are socialized in yet another way, although this process is more congruent with traditional, free society. However, convolution of gender roles occurs for both inmates and staff when they are required to navigate the atypical social structures and interactions that prevail in total institutions. Four examples follow which will allow the reader to consider some of the numerous combinations of stereotypes, gender roles, and binaries that are possible within interpersonal relationships in a correctional setting among, and between, both staff and inmates.

Convoluted Interaction #1

Incarceration creates a condition of 'forced' celibacy. In a prison housing male inmates, the presence of females is minimal given staff to inmate ratios and the fact that the majority of employees in almost all correctional facilities are male (Turner and Bosanac 2005). Consequently, the few women present become the focus of the heterosexual male inmate's sexuality (Pollard and Sorbello 2000). This phenomenon, however, is not limited to inmates. Male staff members project their attitudes regarding gender roles and sexuality on female staff members as well. These projections are based on both personal experience and commonly known stereotypes and binaries as previously discussed. Even as female staff members reasonably expect to find themselves in a professional, work-based relationship, the males they work with frequently seem to view them in accordance with the previously mentioned binaries of father-daughter, mother-son or boyfriend-girlfriend (2000). When this projection occurs in the workplace, some female employees might feel uncertain and confused as to why they are viewed in this light (2000). Because of this incongruity, communications break down, job performance falters and morale suffers.

Convoluted Interaction #2

It is common to see latent and manifest social sanctions placed upon an employee who is perceived to have acted inappropriately regarding sexual codes of conduct both written and unwritten. These sanctions are often imposed before and/or without awareness of the actual events that led to the perception of wrongdoing. In many cases, the facts of the situation are not shared with co-workers, or they become distorted as they pass through the 'rumor mill' (Bosanac 2005). For example: A [female] therapist's session with a particular prisoner ran well over an hour, after which the prisoner emerged from the session red faced. Prison staff were concerned that the prisoner and the therapist had sex. In reality, the prisoner had been in tears for most of his session and did not want to return to the wing until it was less obvious he had been crying (Pollard and Sorbello 2000: 6).

In this scenario, suspicions regarding the therapist's actions might remain in the minds of co-workers. Consequently, unfounded negative perceptions of the 'accused' may never be corrected.

Convoluted Interaction #3

In a female correctional facility, male staff are often targets for the 'affection' of female inmates. This affection can be genuine or manipulative in nature. Incarcerated females who feel genuine affection for a male staff member might find value and comfort in a traditional family structure. Perhaps they are trying to establish a level of 'normalcy' within a social and hierarchical structure that diverges notably from the norms to which they are accustomed (Owen 1988). Others might only be seeking sexual gratification. The quest by some female inmates to create family structures may create inappropriate binaries with staff. For example, a female inmate may project the father-daughter or husband-wife binary on a male staff member or a more sexualized interaction schema such as boyfriend-girlfriend. Initially, the male staff member might remain unaware of the feelings/intentions of the inmate. However, a great deal of problems can result from these types of non-professional interaction patterns whether or not they are reciprocated. The consequences of these projections and the wide range of potential reactions range from personal inconvenience to legally punishable violations (Bosanac 2005).

Convoluted Interaction #4

Dangerous sexual interactions are possible in situations where a staff member or inmate's core identity relies predominantly on a gender stereotype. Consider a male who's identity is rooted in the idea that he must be powerful and in control, or a female who's identity is rooted in ideas of subservience. Both of these personality types are subject to weakened professional relationships, and both of these scenarios can lead to fraternization, especially in combination. A subservient female may submit to a sexualized role as a result of her socialization and her understanding that sexual subservience is expected, even though inappropriate in a prison setting. Conversely, a male might respond sympathetically to a woman's 'need' to be rescued. Even if fraternization never reaches the point of physicality, the interaction creates a sexualized, non-professional environment with the potential for many problematic outcomes.

Some of these perceptions and behaviours are the earliest forms of a sexualized workplace environment. Others represent the convolution of gender and professional roles among staff and inmates. People tend to interact with others in ways that validate their perceptions. For example, when staff members define a female co-worker as the sexual stereotype of 'tease', or a male co-worker as a possibility for a sexual relationship, the perception is often played out. At some point, these behaviours can affect the quality of work, or escalate negatively into sexual harassment, or positively into long-term loving relationships.

Owen indicates that the culture of female correctional facilities is shaped by the developmental and pre-prison experiences of inmates, the role of women in modern society and the manner in which women depend upon personal relationships to survive prison terms (1998). Owen's fieldwork shows that patterns of female inmate interpersonal relationships consist of emotional, practical, and material connections as well as sexual and familial ties (1998). In other words, while incarcerated females tend to develop deep attachments that may or may not be sexual in nature. This results in a social structure that in many ways resembles that of the traditional familial relationships found in free society. In short, the socialization of incarcerated females tends to mirror that of free society with the exception that some women take on masculine roles including father, husband or brother in the absence of biological males (1998).

Male prisoners view long-term confinement and the loss of liberties as a loss of manhood. Their perceived losses are dominance, independence, autonomy and sexual access to women (Miller 2000). With involuntary confinement, male inmates develop an informal hierarchy that reconstructs masculinity and redistributes power on a relatively simple basis. "Sexual dominance and subordination is the principal hierarchy that has emerged among male prisoners" (Miller 2000: 10). Consequently, sexual dominance and subordination define the social status of inmates. The hierarchical structure is based on 'Men', 'Queens' and 'Punks'. Men hold power and control within the facility. Queens represent female roles, are 'voluntarily' submissive to Men, and are excluded from positions of power. Punks are those who are raped or forced into sexual submission and treated as slaves (Miller 2000).

6. Sexuality, Privacy and the Law in Total Institutions

Jordan v. Gardner, No. C89-339TB (W.D. Wash. Feb. 28, 1990) demonstrates that physical, emotional and psychological differences between men and women with respect to privacy and bodily searches may very well cause women, and more particularly physically and sexually abused women, to react differently to bodily searches than would male inmates subjected to similar searches by women. The *Jordan* case presented expert testimony on how differences in gendered socialization processes generally lead to differences in the sexuality of men and women. That is, women experience touching as intimate and appropriate, or as abusive based on individual life experiences, while men find touching either unnecessary or motivated by the desire to display/assert power over another (Lindsey 1994). Entwined in these findings are society's normalized expectations that women are more emotionally open, more delicate, require more privacy and are more modest than men (Taslitz 1996).

Many female inmates have taken the position that cross-gender surveillance, body searches, and strip searches are violations of their privacy. *Lee v.*

Downs recognizes that cross-gender searches may be humiliating even though privacy is surrendered upon incarceration (Ingram 2000). The limited rights to privacy maintained by inmates are substantiated in a number of cases. These cases include *Lee v. Downs, 470 F. Supp. 188, 192 (E.D. Va. 1979), Hudson v. Palmer, 468 U.S. 517, 525-26 (1984)* and *Bowling v. Enomoto, 514 F. Supp. 201, 203 (N.D. Cal. 1981)*. The loss of privacy is substantiated in these cases by the necessity of privileging facility security over the privacy of inmates. Cases that further support the privileging of security needs over inmate privacy include, *Johnson v. Phelan, 69 F.3d 144, 147 (7th Cir. 1995*), *Grummett v. Rushen, 779 F.2d 491 (9th Cir. 1985)*, and *Johnson v. Pennsylvania Bureau of Corrections, 661 F. Supp. 425, 435 (W.D. Pa. 1987)*.

However, *Forts v. Ward, 621 F.2d 1210, 1216 (2d Cir. 1980)*, tempered these rulings by deciding in favour of an additional, limited amount of privacy for female inmates as opposed to male inmates. Privacy rights granted to female inmates by *Forts* include providing sleep wear and allowing them to cover their cell windows for 15 minutes while attending to personal hygiene. Miller suggests that *Forts* and *Hudson* were decided on the premise that women are sexually vulnerable, and need to be protected (2001). That is to say, many believe that incarcerated women need additional protection from the State and additional privacy in order to deter inappropriate intrusions upon their bodies by male correctional staff (2001).

Advocates of increased levels of privacy for female inmates argue that cross-gender searches and observation constitute cruel and unusual punishment for women who have suffered abuse at the hands of men. The ruling in the *Jordan* case reinforced the idea that female inmates suffer when subjected to cross-gender body searches. The case of *Ellison v. Brady, 924 F.2d 872, 879 (9th Cir. 1991)* further demonstrated that cross-gender searches either caused pain or were unreasonable and therefore unconstitutional after finding that the majority of victims of sexual assault and abuse are women. In *Bagley v. Watson, 579 F. Supp. 1099, 1105 (D. Or. 1983)* the court stated that the indignity of women being searched by men is less tolerable to society, when compared to the employment rights of male correctional staff. Further, the district court residing over *Torres v. Wisconsin Dep't of Health and Soc. Servs., 838 F.2d 944 (7th Cir.), rev'd in part 859 F.2d 1523 (7th Cir. 1988)* ruled that increased privacy for women was appropriate as the court is capable of ascertaining what society will tolerate regarding acceptable cross-gender supervision. Finally, in order to ensure maximum levels of privacy for female inmates AND rigorous security standards, the *Hudson* decision asserts that cross-gender searches of female inmates may only occur in emergency situations. In summary, while female inmates are afforded additional levels of privacy, male inmates have not received the same allowances.

Until the 1970's, the privacy rights of inmates were not considered. Ironically, with the passage of Title VII and the subsequent employment of female correctional staff, it was initially MALE inmates who expressed concern regarding privacy. But, as noted, WOMEN are the sole recipients of additional levels of privacy in correctional facilities. The *Bagley* ruling addressed the concerns of male inmates by noting that although society does recognize male inmate's concerns regarding privacy issues, these concerns are minimal and minor indignities should be well tolerated by men. Consequently, *Bagley* supposes that privacy is of little concern to men and that being viewed or touched by women is not disturbing for a male inmate.

This perspective stems from cultural expectations that men are socialized to be strong, less modest, participate in activities in close proximity to peers and dress, undress, shower and attend to personal hygiene in the company of others (Lindsey 1994; Jurado 1999). *Michenfelder V. Sumner, 860 F. 2d 328 (9th Cir. 1988)* affirms that there is no violation of inmate privacy rights if female CO's observe strip searches of male inmates. From 1973 to 1986, the courts agreed that privacy rights for male prisoners were secondary to employment and security concerns (Jurado 1999). Specifically, "the privacy rights of male prisoners prohibited neither the assignment of female guards to conduct extensive clothed body searches, nor their assignment to surveillance posts within the prison living units" (1999: ¶ 2). Example after example demonstrates that society does not view the male need for privacy and protection from members of the opposite sex as commensurate with a woman's need for these same protections.

7. Sexual Harassment

Generally, sexuality in prisons is 'managed' by denial or default (Pollard and Sorbello 2000). Consequently, while the presence of a female in a predominately male work environment can represent a series of challenges for all employees in the workplace, many of these challenges often go unrecognized. However, correctional administrators face two specific challenges that have been reified. The first of these challenges is eliminating sexual harassment and misconduct. Title VII prohibited employment discrimination due to sex in 1967 (Zupan 1992). This established ideals surrounding affirmative action, equal access to employment/promotion opportunities for all groups, and the recognition of sexual harassment as deviant, unacceptable behaviour.

There are at least four models of sexual harassment. The first is based on sexual attraction and is basically a quid pro quo arrangement – something for something (U.S. Department of Justice, Office of Justice Programs [OJP] 1998). The second model of sexual harassment is the hostile work environment, which is described as "sexual jokes, suggestive comments, suggestive pictures, obscene gestures, unwanted physical contact and other situations that interfere with an employee's work performance" (1998: 70). A third type is the sociocultural model that is a reflection of society valuing men over women. This concept bestows power and status to men at the expense of women and states that sexual harassment occurs when men try to maintain dominance over women (Summers 1996).

However, the most common model of sexual harassment is the sex-role *spillover* model. This type of sexual harassment stems from the failure to separate a woman's role as co-worker from her sexual role (1996). This spillover may occur for a variety of reasons. However, the primary reason for spillover is the unbalanced male-female ratio in many work environments, especially within correctional fields (Gutek and Morasch 1982). When the ratio favours men, men have less opportunity to interact with women as co-workers, and it is more likely that female colleagues will be treated in accordance with traditional stereotypes (Summers 1996).

Thomas describes sexual harassment as unwelcome sexual advances, requests for sexual favours, and/or other verbal or physical conduct of a sexual nature, when submitted as a condition of employment. Sexual harassment is also noted as an incremental process wherein the conduct eventually interferes with the victim and/or the victimizer's work performance, and/or creates an intimidating, hostile or offensive work environment (Thomas 1982).

Neugarten and Shafritz explain that sexual harassment evolves, in part, from traditional experiences of men exerting power over women, and women being viewed as subordinate and/or submissive (1980). This pattern is a result of women's historical dependence on men for their survival. Consequently, women are assessed based on their desirability to men. Men offer protection and resources, while women offer their objectified selves in return. As these concepts are perpetuated and consequently reinforced over time, the dominance of men in society is legitimized (1980). Accordingly, sexual harassment in the workplace might be viewed as a mechanism that preserves the status quo, and reflects more than sexuality – issues of social power and cultural control.

Surveys show that anywhere from 42 to 90 percent of working women encounter some form of sexual harassment on the job (Summers 1996). A 1991 survey found that women were overrepresented in the group of sexual harassment victims relative to men (1996). Conversely, male co-workers represented the clear majority of defendants in these claims (OJP 1998).

Sexual harassment must be eliminated from the workplace because of the detrimental affect it has on both victims and the workplace environment generally. Sexual harassment creates a sexually-charged atmosphere that is both intimidating and inhospitable to women. The detrimental effects of negative emotional reactions flow over into the work place and are observed by all. In the end, harassed staff may take legal action against the employer (Civil 1998). Morton clearly states that "the presence of sexual harassment in the workplace generates as much, or more, liability for the employer and the offending employee as any inmate civil rights suit" (1991: 51).

8. Bona Fide Occupational Qualification

The second challenge faced by correctional facility administrators is ensuring appropriate employment of bona fide occupational qualifications (BFOQ). The Civil Rights Act in the United States and the Charter of Rights in Canada ban discrimination based on race, colour, religion, sex or national origin in voting, public accommodations, education, employment and government spending among other things (Valdivia et al 2003). However, exceptions are permitted in some circumstances. This phenomenon is known as a bona fide occupational qualification (BFOQ). Simply stated, religion, sex or national origin may be considered a BFOQ if any of these are considered 'reasonably necessary' to the operation of a business or institution. Situations that do not qualify as a BFOQ include refusing to hire women on the assumption that their turnover rate is higher, refusing to hire based on the preferences of clients and refusing to hire because it would require the employer to provide separate facilities, for example, change rooms or restrooms (2003).

Dothard, 433 U.S. at 346, Griffin v. Michigan Dep't of Corrections, 654 F. Supp. 690, 703 (E.D. Mich. 1982,) and *Torres,* claimed BFOQ for their hiring practices. *Dothard* was successful in claiming that it was necessary to hire only men due to the unconstitutionally overcrowded Alabama maximum-security prison for men. However, the height and weight requirements that excluded women from contact positions were identified as based solely on gender, and thus discriminatory. The state failed to show how height and weight requirements were job related. They also failed to demonstrate what amount of strength was necessary for a Correctional Officer to effectively perform their duties. Nevertheless, language from *Dothard* indicates that while the viewing of male prisoners by female guards does amount to an invasion of privacy, it is no more a violation of personal privacy than an examination by a female doctor.

Griffin and *Torres* were unsuccessful in proving BFOQ. *Griffin* argued for the privacy rights of prisoners, the safety of female CO's and effective institutional security. The court cited the limited right to privacy in prisons and the professional behaviour of female staff when viewing male prisoners as primary reasons for disallowing BFOQ in this situation. *Torres* argued that BFOQ was necessary in female prisons as the assignment of male CO's to female housing units would undermine the rehabilitation process because many incarcerated women had suffered physical or sexual abuse at the hands of men. Again, no objective evidence was submitted to support these claims.

For the most part, the claims of correctional facilities aimed at mandating gender-exclusive staffing practices have been unsuccessful. However, when these cases are successful, they are generally related to a scenario wherein female inmates are deemed as needing 'protection' from male correctional staff. As the reader can see in these examples, gender stereotypes have significant influence on how women, both inmates and staff, are treated and perceived in the correctional setting (Martell 1996). Most of these rulings seem to state that male correctional staff members lack the professional tools to deal appropriately with female staff and inmates, while female staff members are well-equipped for dealing effectively and professionally with both male co-workers and inmates.

However, none of these cases provide any discernible degree of objective evidence for these rulings and attitudes. Consequently, the reader can see how peer, subordinate and managerial behaviours and attitudes are clearly affected by unsubstantiated, socially constructed gender or sexual roles including daughter, wife, mother, whore, or father, son, husband, 'player'. These stereotypes are utilized because these roles are easily understood and quickly employed (Etheridge et al 1984).

9. Inappropriate Sexual Behaviour and Misconduct

Let us expand upon the previously outlined definitions of sexuality in a manner that is contextualized within the realms of familiar human senses and interactions. Sexuality is no single thing. It refers to the body, the sense of touch, emotionality and desire, thought and fantasy, image and appearance (Civil 1998). Perceptions of sexuality are equally wide-ranging and unwieldy. A person's attire and sense of style provide an entry point into ascertaining their personal sexuality. A person's preferred style and manner of communicating can also be utilized to situate their sexuality. This includes a person's demeanor, composure and/or comportment – the manner in which they carry themselves and how they hold their body and maintain personal space. Sometimes indicators of sexuality are blatantly obvious. For example, messages and photos posted in local personal ads or on-line dating services can be extremely open or even pornographic Other indicators of sexuality can include jewelry and accessories, hair style, nails, and makeup (McCampbell and Lyman 2000). As we can see, many indicators are socially constructed cultural artifacts that have developed from over-arching patriarchal notions of appropriate, gendered sexuality, and comprise a broad scope of behaviours, many of which have clear and common social repercussions.

Despite appearances and all of the previously mentioned elements that are entrenched in cultural ideals of beauty, sex and gender, human sexuality is mostly imagined or fantasized. In other words, people construct what is desirable to them within the boundaries of their own minds and cultural limitations which are determined by the combination of socialization, enculturation and socially constructed physical desire. But, what is sexuality without physicality? Any consideration of sexuality must consider physical interactions – both consensual and unwelcome.

Inappropriate sexual behaviour ranges from mild flirtation and light 'touching' to overt sexual acts, whether consensual or forced (Stone 1977). It is imperative to understand that ALL sexual contact and/or sexualized communications between correctional staff and incarcerated persons are illegal, and perhaps more importantly, a severe breach of the inmate's rights to safety, security and rehabilitation. As such, any sexualized act, regardless of consent, is inappropriate and considered sexual misconduct. This also holds true in the case of sexual contact between co-workers at the workplace, regardless of consent. Sexual misconduct with inmates often begins with a sexualized work environment and inappropriate sexual behaviour among staff (McMahon 1999). This unprofessional, sexualized atmosphere contributes to sexualized communications and interaction patterns between staff, inmates, AND staff and inmates.

A sexualized work environment also sets up an atmosphere of permissive behaviour for inmates wherein they might feel that they can violate institutional codes of conduct and/or disobey correctional personnel more easily. Sexually inappropriate discussions, emails, jokes, demeanors, and/or unprofessional dress that are visible to inmates, or specifically presented to inmates by staff members, are clear signs of a sexually charged atmosphere. A sexualized correctional environment can cause staff-inmate dynamics and interaction patterns to deteriorate dramatically, and to the detriment of both professionalism and rehabilitation (1999). The off-duty behaviours of correctional staff, for example, dating habits, marital relations and lifestyle choices can influence the work environment as well. It is imperative that correctional staff 'leave their personal lives at the gate' upon arriving at work. Professionalism and objectivity are compromised when relationships with supervisors, subordinates, co-workers and inmates become inappropriate, especially as this information becomes public knowledge at the facility (1999).

Factors contributing to inappropriate sexual behaviour and misconduct are numerous. For example, men most frequently interact with women in other than work roles and feel most comfortable interacting with women by relying on the traditional gender role binaries previously listed, especially in novel or unfamiliar situations. "Perhaps men are more likely than women to project sexuality into ambiguous behaviour between sexes at work, and to feel that such sexuality is appropriate in the work environment" (Farnworth 1992: 25). Sometimes, institutional culture may also condone inappropriate behaviour, however inadvertently (LIS Inc. 2000). Personal characteristics might also contribute to inappropriate behaviour. Female inmates, particularly victims of abuse, may have a distorted sense of appropriate gender interaction patterns. For victims of abuse, abuse or sexual contact might equate to love and/or affection. In other words, abusive relationships might provide an inappropriate sense of 'normalcy' and 'comfort' for these people (McMahon 1999).

Further, correctional staff may simply opt to disregard policy and training regarding fraternization with co-workers and/or inmates. Knowledge and training regarding inappropriate behaviour might be overcome by the imbalance of power that exists in a custodial setting (1999). The authority of correctional staff members leaves great potential for abuse of legitimate access to incarcerated person's bodies (Miller 2001). The effects of staff sexual misconduct are copious. Misconduct serves to victimize the vulnerable, weaken facility security, create stress, undermine professionalism, expose the institution to liability, create hostile work environments, violate the law and create an environment of mistrust (McCampbell and Lyman 2000).

Prison administrators are obligated to eliminate sexually charged work environments. Case law, for example, *City of Canton, Ohio v. Harris 489 U.S. 378 (1989)* specifies that failure to train employees to recognize the harm surrounding a sexualized environment, could be interpreted as contrary to governmental policy and result in civil liability. Further, *Farmer v. Brennan 114 S. Ct. 1970 (1994)* indicates that prison officials have the responsibility of keeping prisoners from harm.

The growing population of females working in correctional environments at all levels, and the rapidly rising number of incarcerated women require administrators to be more active in managing issues of sexuality in correctional facilities. The isolated nature of living and working in a correctional environment coupled with the forced state of dependency in which incarcerated persons live situates these institutions as 'natural' environments for the development of intimate relationships (Quinn 1984). Understanding this and appropriately managing for these circumstances is essential. Otherwise, rehabilitation will suffer, and liabilities will continue to grow.

10. Conclusion

Sexuality is a difficult and unwieldy topic that has the potential to wreak havoc in an environment where the primary responsibility is to care for and rehabilitate people. The origins and development of sexuality affect almost every aspect of human life. The affects of sexuality in correctional facilities for incarcerated individuals as well as their caretakers are amplified due to isolation and dependency issues. Reconciling diverse socialization models as well as varied institutional cultures is a difficult process. It is essential to recognize that even the smallest sexual overture can progress from a relatively innocent call for affection or attention to a violation of federal law.

Maintaining 'professional distance' can be challenging while attempting to stay committed to the stated rehabilitation and resocialization goals and objectives of most correctional facilities. However, constitutional law and case law has attempted to set forth doctrines that are both ethically and morally appropriate within the scope of existing law and security requirements. Most correctional facilities provide a code of ethics and training to guide the correctional professional through interpersonal relations. Staff members must take ownership of their actions and interactions by realizing and considering the potential effects of ideologically-based stereotypes and biases. They must also be receptive to setting aside traditional stereotypes and gender roles in order to contribute to the development of the female professional-male professional binary. Administrators must recognize the complexity of these gender and sexuality issues and facilitate the development of this relatively new binary.

References

Bagley v. Watson, 579 F. Supp. 1099,1101- 1105 (D. Or. 1983).

Blodget, N. 1986. "I Don't Think that Ladies Should be Lawyers." *American Bar Association Journal,* December 72: 48 – 53.

Bosanac, Stephen E. February 2005. Personal Communication.

Bowling v. Enomoto, 514 F. Supp. 201, 203 (N.D. Cal. 1981).

Burrell, G. and J. Hearn. 1989. "The Sexuality of Organization." Pp. 1-28 in *The Sexuality of Organization*, edited by J. Hearn, D. Sheppard, P. Tancred-Sheriff, and G. Burrell. Newbury Park: Sage.

City of Canton, Ohio v. Harris 489 U.S. 378 (1989).

Civil, J. 1998. *Sexuality at Work: How does It Affect You?* London: B.T. Batsford Limited.

Debell, J. February 2001. "The Female Offender: Different...not Difficult." *Corrections Today.*

Dothard, 433 U.S. at 346 (Marshall, J., dissenting).

Ellison v. Brady, 924 F.2d 872, 879 (9th Cir. 1991).

Etheridge, R. C. Hale, and M. Hambrick. 1984. "Female Employees in All-Male Correctional Facilities." *Federal Probation* 48, 4: 54 – 65.

Farmer v. Brennan 114 S. Ct. 1970 (1994).

Farnworth, L. 1992. "Women Doing a Man's Job: Female Prison Officers Working in a Male Prison." *The Australian and New Zealand Society of Criminology* 25, 278-295.

Forts v. Ward, 621 F.2d 1210- 1217 (2d Cir. 1980).

Griffin v. Michigan Dep't of Corrections, 654 F. Supp. 694-703 (E.D. Mich. 1982).

Grummett v. Rushen, 779 F.2d 49-492. (9th Cir. 1985).

Gutek, B. A. and B. Morasch. 1982. "Sex-Ratios, Sex-Role-Spillover, and Sexual Harassment of Women at Work." *Journal of Social Issues* 38:55 – 74.

Hudson v. Palmer, 468 U.S. 517, 525-26 (1984).

Ingram, J. D. 2000. "Prison Guards and Inmates of Opposite Genders: Equal Employment Opportunity Versus Right of Privacy." *Duke Journal of Gender Law and Policy* 7, 3-28. Retrieved May 17, 2005 (http://www.law.duke.edu/journals/djglp/index.htm).

Johnson v Phelan, 69 F.3d 144, 147 (7th Cir 1995).

Johnson v. Pennsylvania Bureau of Corrections, 661 F. Supp. 425, 435 (W.D. Pa. 1987).

Jordan v. Gardner, 986 F.2d 1521-1537 (9th Cir. 1993).

Jurado, Rebecca. 1999. "The Essence of Her Womanhood: Defining the Privacy Rights of Women Prisoners and the Employment Rights of Women Guards." American University Journal of Gender, Social Policy & the Law. Distinguishing Societal Expectations of Privacy Section ¶ 2. 7, 1.

Jurik, Nancy C. and Susan E. Martin. 2001. "Femininities, Masculinities, and Organizational Conflict: Women in Criminal Justice Occupations." Pp. 264-

281 in *Women, Crime and Criminal Justice*, edited by C. M. Renzetti and L. Goodstein. Los Angeles: Roxbury Publishing Co.

Lerner, Harriet Goldhor. 1988. *Women in Therapy: Devaluation, Anger, Aggression, Depression, Self-sacrifice, Mothering, Mother Blaming, Self-betrayal, Sex-role Stereotypes, Dependency, Work and Success Inhibitions.* Northvale: J. Aronson.

Lee v. Downs, 470 F. Supp. 188, 192 (E.D. Va. 1979).

Lindsey. L. L. 1994. *Gender Roles: A Sociological Perspective.* (2nd edition). Prentice Hall.

LIS Inc. 2000. "Sexual Misconduct in Prisons: Law, Remedies, and Incidence." *Special Issues in Corrections.* May, Retrieved May 17, 2005 (http://www.nicic.org/pubs/2000/016112.pdf).

Martell, R. 1996. "Sex Discrimination at Work." Pp. 329-331 in *Women and Work: A Handbook*, edited by P. Dubeck and K. Borman. New York: Garland Publishing.

McCampbell, S., and Lyman, E. P. October 2000. "Training Curriculum for Investigating Allegations of Staff Sexual Misconduct with Inmates." Tamarac, Florida: Center for Innovative Public Policies, Inc. Retrieved May 17, 2005 from (http://nicic.org/Library/016804).

McMahon, M.W. 1999. *Women on Guard: Discrimination and Harassment in Corrections.* Toronto: University of Toronto Press.

Michenfelder V. Sumner, 860 F. 2d 328 (9th Cir. 1988).

Miller, T.A. 2000. "Surveillance: Gender, Privacy, & the Sexualization of Power in Prison." *George Mason University Civil Rights Law Journal* 10, 291.

Miller, T.A. 2001. "Keeping the Government's Hands off our Bodies: Mapping a Feminist Legal Theory Approach to Privacy in Cross-gender Prison Searches." *Buffalo Criminal Law Review* 4, 861.

Morton, J.B, ed. 1991. *Change, Challenge, and Choices: Women's Role in Modern Corrections.* American Correctional Association.

Neugarten, D. A. and Shafritz, J. M. eds. 1980. *Sexuality in Organizations: Romantic and Coercive Behaviors at work.* Oak Park, Illinois: Moore Publishing Company, Inc.

Owen, B.A. 1998. *In the Mix.* Albany: State University of New York.

Platt, A. M. 1977. *The Child Savers, The Invention of Delinquency* (2nd edition). Chicago: The University of Chicago Press.

Pollard, Jacinta and Laura Sorbello. October 2000. "*Whore to Madonna and Back: The Challenge of Being a Female Therapist in a Male Prison.*" Presented at WIC: Staff and Clients Conference, Adelaide, Australia.

Quinn, R. E. 1984. *Managing Organization Transition.* Homewood.

Rowan, J.R. 1996. "Female Correctional Officers Said to Reduce Prison Violence." *Criminal Justice Newsletter, 7,* 2-3, April 27.

Stone, L. 1977. *The Family, Sex and Marriage in England 1500-1800.* Weiderfield & Nicolson.

Summers, R. 1996. "Sexual Harassment." Pp. 260-263 in *Women and Work: A Handbook*, edited by P. Dubeck, and K. Borman. New York: Garland Publishing.

Taslitz. A. E. 1996. *Patriarchal Stories I: Cultural Rape Narratives in the Courtroom.* S. Cal. Rev. L. & Women's Stud. 5, 387-500.

Thomas, C. 1982. *Sex Discrimination*. St. Paul: West Publishing Company.

Torres v. Wisconsin Dep't of Health and Soc. Servs., 838 F.2d 944 (7th Cir.), rev'd in part 859 F.2d 1523 (7th Cir. 1988).

Turner, T. and Stephen E. Bosanac. (2005). Women in the Criminal Justice Professions: Stereotypes, Challenges and Systemic Barriers to Entry and Advancement. Pp. forthcoming in *The Professionalization of Work*, edited by Merle Jacobs and Stephen E. Bosanac. Toronto: de Sitter Publications.

U.S. Department of Justice, Office of Justice Programs [OJP]. 1998. *Women in Criminal Justice: a Twenty Year Update*. Pp. 70 NCJ 173416. Retrieved April 22, 2005. (http://www.ojp.usdoj.gov/reports/98Guides/wcjs98/wcjspdf.pdf).

Valdivia, Anderson, Weinzierl, Ostrove, Stohr, and Vinnitsky, 2003. *High Court Case Summaries* (5th edition), edited by D. Blatt and M. Stedman. Minnesota: West Group.

Zimmer, Lynn. 1986. *Women Guarding Men*. Chicago: University of Chicago Press.

Zupan, L. 1992. "The Progress of Women Correctional Officers in All Male Prisons." Pp. 323-340 in *The Changing Roles of Women in the Criminal Justice System: Offenders, Victims, and Professionals* (2nd edition), edited by I. Moyer. Prospect Heights: Waveland Press.

17. Instrumentalism as the Ideology of Discipline: The Impact of Technology on "Corrections"

Kevin R.E. McCormick and Livio A. Visano

1. Introduction: Technology and Social Thought

From the introduction of the papyrus in ancient Egypt to the current proliferation of global communication devices, technology has increasingly become an integral feature of the human condition (Roszak, 1986; Postman, 1992; Huxely, 1962). The 'technical" is an alternate frame of reference and mode of articulation adopted to further enhance what is perceived as "emancipatory". For example, the computer continues to be heralded in the popular culture as the "greatest invention since the wheel". This infatuation overshadows current theoretical debates regarding the impact of technology on social order. Despite the commonsensical belief that the computer liberates users from tedious tasks and increases the opportunities for leisure, this paper suggests that the computer scripts actions and mediates social interaction within a coercive technological order. This seemingly innocuous social electrification is essentially an exercise in control (Marcuse, 1964; Meyrowitz, 1985; Postman, 1992; Franklin, 1990). Specifically, the technological mediations (technopoly) are assessed in terms communicative systems and bureaucratic structures that discipline social relations. Further, this paper delves into the implications of techno – criminology especially in reference to the ubiquitous applications of technologicalization on the carceral process.

Technology designates linguistic, mechanical and conceptual contours within which prospective users must learn to develop and execute strategies of social interaction and articulation. It is the "power" of the device "...that reaches into the very grain of the individual, inserting itself directly into their actions, attitudes, discourses, learning processes and everyday lives" (Foucault, 1980: 39).A power dynamic between apparatus and user, mediates and defines human experiences in terms of technologically generated relationships that coerce the user to submit unconditionally to the language and definitions of the device. As a direct result of this technological intrusion, the user becomes a "servomechanism of the apparatus, substituting a language of codes of processed information for 'natural experience'" (McLuhan, 1967). To successfully utilize the device it is imperative that the above identity and role become internalized. In internalizing the apparatus users do not necessarily extend themselves technologically, but rather the device internalizes the individuals—becoming "an electronic extension of their central nervous system" (McLuhan, 1967). This technologically consuming relationship cements a "culture of compliance" (Franklin, 1990: 24) causing the user to surrender to a technological calculus that constructs and de-constructs individual and collective social realities.

Somnambulistic approaches towards an investigation of the impact of technology on social interaction were firmly premised in "the old 'hypodermic needle theory'. The 'hypodermic needle theory', popular in the 1920's postulated a direct and universal response to a message stimulus (Meyrowitz, 1985: 13). Based on the scientific model of stimulus and response, this normative approach suggests that there is a direct and calculable relationship between the device and the individual. Accordingly, all individuals using a certain technology are expected to receive the same stimulus from the interaction, a response that then could easily be generalized to all users of similar devices. These generic claims defy social diversity, assuming that all individuals act the same in all situations. These positivistic paradigms were direct extensions of the technically utilitarian structures of thought. By submitting to the normative agenda of the apparatus, both users and social researchers failed to respond analytically to the distinct dichotomy that exists between the manifest and latent repercussions of technology. While the computer may be observed as stimulating the individual by increasing his/her levels of communication, "there is a general tendency for scholars and researchers, to ignore or even deny the effects of invisible environments and the latent effects of technologies, simply because they are invisible" (Meyrowitz, 1985: 20).

In response to positivistic explanations, "technological determinism" posits that technology is a powerful and autonomous agent that dictates in some detail the patterns of human, social and cultural life" (Pfaffenberger, 1988: 18). "Technological determinists" contend that any apparatus sets upon its users' agendas, definitions and lexicons, - a "technological order" (Huxley, 1962: 123) which imprisons the user both technically and socially. This perspective, which was rooted in discourse of the Luddite movement in the early 19th century (Dinwiddy, 1989) argued that technologies are selected by users for reasons beyond the apparent convenience to the user so that the user is forced into the technological relationship. The computer is not merely selected by users, but imposed directly upon individuals and their respective methods of social interaction. While the contribution of determinists was to "break the spell" that apparatuses have on individuals, Meyrowitz (1985: 24) notes that "missing from it, was any real attempt to link an analysis of media characteristics with the structure and dynamics of everyday social interaction".

The determinist perspective has recently been reformulated by Postman (1992), who argues that there has been a "surrender of culture to technology" which constitutes a "technopoly" (Postman, 1992: 44). Technology transcends convenient functions and extends beyond the "global village" (McLuhan, 1964). Postman asserts:

> New technologies alter the structure of our interests: the things we think about. They alter the character of our symbols: the things we think with. And they alter the nature of community: the arena in which thoughts develop...For something has happened in America that is strange and dangerous, and there is only a dull and even stupid awareness of what it is - in part because it has no name. I call it Technopoly, (Postman, 1992: 20).

The control that the apparatus has over the user is powerful, monopolizing not only the time, work and leisure, but the very essence of social organization. As briefly illustrated, there is a resurgence in the deterministic paradigm, namely "Technopoly", which challenges the more positivistic perspectives that embrace euphorically each new technological device.Interestingly, a conceptual synthesis of these two distinct perspectives, somnambulism and determinism, was advanced by a more humanist orientation to the study of the effects of technologies. Most notably, McLuhan utilized a "technological humanist" perspective (Patterson, 1990; Kroker, 1984; McLuhan, 1964; McLuhan, 1967; McLuhan, 1969) which maintained that an apparatus imposed itself upon the user and that this relationship would result in an "*internalization of the technology*" (McLuhan, 1967). While realizing the power of technology to transcend the convenience function, McLuhan nevertheless celebrated the potential liberating consequences of implementing electronic technology. Highlighting the positive aspects of this affiliation, "McLuhan's project was to break the spell cast upon the human mind by electronic technologies -- which operate in the language of seduction and power" (Kroker, 1984: 54). By understanding the ways in which technologies dominate the user, individuals could develop successful strategies that capitalize on the emancipatory abilities of the technology. Once technically literate and circumspect of the "seductive language" of the device, the user could readily utilize and manipulate technology without becoming imprisoned.

The "humanist" perspective (Patterson, 1990; Kroker 1984) was a critical paradigm for examining the dynamic relationship between the power of a device and its social benefit. This approach also assumed naively that social researchers are all too willing to concede to the loss of control over the process and become a "servomechanism of the apparatus" (McLuhan, 1967: 16). It is precisely because of this reluctance to recognize their technological incarceration that few are willing or able to escape the disciplinary cadence of the techno-culture. Instead, practitioners continued to celebrate the emancipatory potential of the machine.

McLuhan articulates the ways in which various technologically enhanced mediums of communication have become not external to, but direct extensions of the individual. As a consequence of this relationship, "man in his normal use of technology (or his extended body) is perpetually modified by it and in turn finds new ways of modifying his technology" (McLuhan, 1964: 56). This conceptual framework implies a technology that is not an external apparatus utilized by an individual for the sake of increased convenience, but rather a direct extension of the individual, "part of their extended nervous system" (McLuhan, 1964: 57). Therefore, just as modes of physical perception are extended technologically, so too are the various social dramas altered by and through the social stages and scripts imposed on the situation by the specific device.

The introduction of such technologies establishes a new mode of communication, anchored in a structure of social presentation and expectation similar to the framework utilized in "face to face" and aural encounters. Within the context of social interactions and the presence of "others", "performance cues" such as physical and aural gestures, are transformed as visible extensions of the individual's perception of his or her audience's expectations.

The technological environment is mediated as in any other social circumstance, by the language, social practices and obligations unique to any culture or social performance. Interestingly this setting and the techniques employed for a successful performance of presentation are considerably different from face to face encounters, given the device's ability to incorporate external criteria into the encounter. In examining technologically enhanced social interaction, we note that the effects upon individuals are far greater than the increased convenience or entertainment levels of the users. Technologies have established a dynamic medium of communication and a technological culture, in which an individual's ability to manipulate is arbitrated by the specific characteristics of the device utilized. This in turn establishes the foundation upon which the articulation of social self may begin to be explored as constituting a 'technological self', directly extending the traditional perspectives associated with the dynamic process of societal presentation.

The concept of a 'technological self', defined as "social interaction mediated by the specific qualities of a certain device" (Meyrowitz, 1985) continues to be popular. To reiterate McLuhan's observation, technology is not a separate entity apart from the individual, but rather the device becomes a part of the user, a direct "extension of the users central nervous system", that is,

> "by means of an electronic media, we set up a dynamic by which all previous technologies become mere extensions of hands, feet, teeth and bodily controls - all such extensions of our bodies" (McLuhan, 1964: 68)

Performance of the technological self and its attendant constructed stages of social presentation is scripted according to a technically articulated and socially enforced contract. It is this techno-script which enforces the asymmetric power relationship between the individual and the apparatus, forcing users to unconditionally surrender themselves to the device and readily translate their modes of social presentation within the script dictated by the device. Further, this paradigm illustrated that within the "technological drama" (Pfaffenberger, 1988; Manning, 1992) users as social actors, utilize technologically mediated performance techniques in an attempt to interact according to the expectations of others - the community of similarly circumstanced device users, adjusting to the expectations and acceptance of respective audiences. When an individual enters the presence of others, he or she seeks to acquire information about them or to bring into play information about them already possessed" (Goffman, 1959)—expectations that are generated within a specific social context. As Meyrowitz (1985: 46) adds,

> While Goffman's model of 'back and front region' behaviour describes a static set of stages and is limited to face to face interaction, the principles implicit in it can be adapted to describe the changes in situations and behaviours brought about by a new media.

With electronic interaction, the actor via a technology performs and relates to the audience as does the personally intimate actor in small group encounters through electronic impulses, appropriate cultural etiquette and language of the technological culture. In order to 'succeed' socially the user must be accepted into the 'techno-cultural' environment. Demonstrated in this process must be a functional use of the technology as well as a basic level of the language fluency and general etiquette dictated by the device. This process of 'getting connected' (Visano, 1987) is a technological rite of passage no different than if the environment was face to face in nature because "when anyone enters into a social setting, they need to know and demonstrate something about the situation and other participants" (Meyrowitz, 1985: 28). By gaining initial access to the 'techno-culture' the device imprisons users by forcing them to be committed to a particular performance evaluated according to audience expectations, as defined and mediated by the lexicons and modes of social interaction dictated by the technology. Thus, the process of 'getting connected' to a specific device causes the user to perform on both a socially and technologically erected stage of interaction. This initial stage imposes conflicting expectational structures and performance difficulties wherein the "technological drama" (Pfaffenberger, 1988; Manning, 1992) presents itself to the actors as an omnisciently imposed social script which "infuse their activity with signs which dramatically highlight and portray confirmatory facts that might otherwise remain unapparent" (Goffman, 1959: 30). Demonstrating to the techno-audience an unwillingness or inability to accept the lexicons and ideologies scripted by the device causes the user to become alienated from the other users. To repeat, to indoctrinate the users into the techno-culture, many aspects of their performance are mystified by "accentuating certain matters and concealing others" (Goffman, 1959: 67); ambiguity and role confusion cause the new user to become even more dependent upon the agendas imposed by the technology. While performance techniques of the 'techno-actor' are similar to those employed in more intimate settings, "technological drama" highlights the specific language, definitions and modes of social interaction which *superficially* are presented as technically liberating. But upon closer scrutiny these practices are carceral physically and ideologically.

2. Technology as a Culture of Control

Thus, the implementation of technological innovations in countless social settings illustrates clearly the power of the device to script social relations. Through its electrification of the social order, computers have become the most powerful apparatus in the last twenty years to alter the fundamental nature of social interaction. Geographic, political, economic and communicative boundaries have shifted as a result of the computerization of social and political institutions (Roszak, 1986; Patterson, 1990; Pacey, 1983; Ackroyd et al., 1977).

The justice system and specifically its penal structures have experienced dramatic periods of challenge and change as a result of the implementation of various technological innovations (Manning, 1992; Harper, 1991; Marx, 1988; Bresnick, 1988; Colton, 1979). While these innovations are powerful in their impact on imprisonment, decarceration and rehabilitation strategies, they are firmly entrenched well within the wider neoliberal ideologies on the "rational" role of technology in society.

The criminal justice system subscribes unconditionally to a perspective that reflects 'technological somnambulism' (Pfaffenberger, 1988: 14); that is, in the "relationship between the electronic device and user" (Winner, 1986:5) the computer is considered a "tool" to be consciously manipulated for a specific "function". Missing from this voluntaristic perspective, however, is the realization that technologies 'work over the individual' without her/his consent. For example, how often are electronic files generated on individuals without their knowledge? To what extent are actors cognizant of the functions, manifest or latent?

Specifically, in the correctional system, the very precepts underlying care/control practices and policies have been transformed by the introduction of the computer into the carceral culture (Visano, 1994; Finkelstein, 1993; Hunt et al., 1993). Guards, parole officers, social workers and (x)offenders have recently experienced the transformation not only of procedures and policies in the correctional system as a result of computerization but also new communicative forces which establish new forms of control drawing individuals into a larger web of surveillance. Irrespective of convenience and speed, technology establishes new forms of social control, as Marcuse and Foucault state eloquently:

> The brute fact that the machine's physical (only physical?) power surpasses that of the individual and of any particular group of individuals, makes the machine the most effective political instrument in any society, (Marcuse, 1964: 33).

> The major effect of the Panopticon is to induce in the inmate a state of conscious and permanent visibility that assures the automatic functioning of power. So to arrange things that the surveillance is permanent in its effects, even if it is discontinuous in its action; that the perfection of power should tend to render its actual exercise unnecessary; that this architectural apparatus should be a machine for creating and sustaining a power relation independent of the person who exercises it; in short, that the inmates should be caught up in a power situation of which they are themselves the bearers. (Foucault, 1977: 201)

The proliferation of devices such as electronic inmate monitors and offender management computer systems serve to designate linguistic, mechanical and conceptual practices that electronically transform traditional penal techniques. As a cultural marker, technology mirrors a generic deference to authority, electronically translating care/control practices and management principles throughout all sectors of the penal system. Thus, technology has become the physical and ideological catalyst through which the penal agenda is transformed.

The purpose of this section is to provide a critical appreciation of the role of electronic technology within various contexts of the correctional system: prisons, parole and rehabilitative programmes. This techno-criminological investigation will detail clearly the extent to which the correctional process has become electrified, arguing that techniques of control have become increasingly dependent on electronic devices as physical and ideological instruments of imprisonment and rehabilitation. A careful examination of these intrusive processes demonstrates that technology is essentially an exercise in control despite the popular celebration of its liberating potential and increased citizenship.

The administration of punishment has been profoundly affected by various technological advancements that have expanded the traditional notions of the omniscient power of the penal system. These penal techniques establish a disciplinary cadence that readily transcends traditional mandates of the prison and rehabilitative programmes. From the advent of the panopticon (Foucault, 1977; Bentham, 1791) to the implementation of prison monitors and computer systems, (McCormick, 1997; Gomme, 1992; Renzema and Skelton, 1990; Rogers and Jolin, 1989; Schmidt, 1986), the ubiquitous institutions of the state require that all carceral actors become imprisoned within the gaze of the electrified eye of the penal system. The power of various methods of penal persuasion expands infinitely especially when cloaked in the pallium of invisibility. Indeed, those within the system are often unaware of the surveillance and control techniques enacted upon them daily by the state; as Foucault (1977: 187) elucidates:

> Disciplinary power is exercised through its invisibility; at the same time it imposes upon those whom it subjects a principle of visibility. In discipline, it is the subjects who have to be seen. Their visibility assures the hold of the power that is exercised over them. It is the fact of being constantly seen, that maintains the disciplined individual in his subjection.

Therefore, as techniques of control and punishment continue to be contextualized within the hegemonic (Gramsci, 1971) order and conceptualized within the liberal mantra of efficiency, cost effectiveness and instrumental rationality, the correctional system will continue to be dependent upon and susceptible to a plethora of technological innovations.

The prison, as an apparatus of social control and as a mechanism of moral regulation, establishes the "carceral network" (Foucault, 1977) through various ideologies of penal persuasion. Whether through the utilization of intensive institutional based programmes or the physical isolation of the offender, the methods of control have become just as crucial as the legal or moral foundations upon which this penology is premised. Interestingly, servitude to religious doctrines as a method of rehabilitation characteristic of penal practises centuries ago has been expanded considerably to include more secular notions of obedience, notably to the state and its functionaries. Notwithstanding the glaring contradictions inherent in such notions as control/punishment and care/rehabilitation, the penal system has succeeded in perpetuating common sense and consent as forms of penal persuasion. Although the methods and ideologies of various agencies may differ within the penal system, each clog in the penal machine is cemented within a set of interdependent institutional ideologies that structure control in terms of the sophisticated marketing of accountability and community input (Visano, 2004). For instance, the concept of a community has always been a convenient and yet seductive instrument of technological control. Since the 1970's we have witnessed a proliferation of programmes, strategies and policies ostensibly designed to encourage a greater degree of community participation. This notion of a community, as a juridic invention and a controlled social artifact, has invited a painstaking return to apparently parochial values as well as a more passionate rediscovery of viable alternatives to supplement extant more formal state controls.

Indeed, the concept of a community has been appropriated ideologically by the state to legitimate decisions, preserve privilege, and maintain authority relations. This shift towards community crime prevention, compensation, restitution, victimization and the simple return of the bad or the mad to the sacred community echo a lingering pastoral nostalgia, a return to more "basic" familiar values by providing a pervasive belief system that preserves social harmony, integrates and constrain deviance. Penal practices also appeal to prevailing logics of "rational" bureaucracies - expedience, and effectiveness.

Interestingly, although the penal system has adopted new and highly obtrusive technologies of surveillance, the fundamental effects of these devices on the entire correctional system (public and private) still remains under-investigated correctional administration and policy formation (Marx, 1988; Marx, 1985ab; Ackroyd, et al, 1977; Buchanan, 1962). These influences, however, ought to be assessed not solely in terms of intrinsic utilitarian criteria, but rather, it is instructive to inquire how repressive technologies were developed to help suppress the revolt of a partially subjugated caste (Ackroyd, et al., 1977).

Physical computer systems and their operating systems have become the centre point of all interactions within the correctional structure, ranging from imprisonment, decarceration, rehabilitation and dialogue with other institutions. Human experiences are organized according to the state agenda and translated through a socially articulated and highly coercive technological script (Pfaffenberger, 1988; Meyrowitz, 1985). Technological applications in the penal setting function to facilitate the performance of tasks and the division of labour within an economy of bureaucratic convenience. Further, the implementation of technologies in the correctional system establishes a "culture of compliance" (Franklin: 1990) among all the members of the "carceral culture" including inmates, guards, policy makers and social workers. It is this cultural context that establishes a mortgage between the device and the user,

> the mortgage means that we live in a culture of compliance, that we are ever more conditioned to accept orthodoxy as normal, and to accept that there is only one way of doing 'it', (Franklin,1990:24)

Equipped with the technology of computers, these organizational actors extend the scope of their own senses as well as enhance opportunities for their respective institutions. These sites of interaction are not physical settings, but are in effect "virtual communities" (Halal; 1992), cultures comprised of electronic impulses housed in technical casings. Agents of formal control present themselves electronically through the medium of the computer. Pursuing well defined organizational expectations, they perform before an electronically constructed and politically constituted audience.

Admittedly, extant technological power differentials are evident in all aspects of life. The negative impact of these devices, however, are more fully felt whenever they succeed as forms of social and technological incarceration. To illustrate, individuals first become imprisoned in "technological barriers" and later internalize the unique lexicons of the apparatus as methods of social articulation and definition. These processes of identity and communication are not temporally nor spatially restricted. That is, control is not only situationally - specific but rather it is a social context, condition and consequence of the relationship between the device and the user.

On the one hand, technologies readily assist the user in certain tasks. On the other hand, technologies readily transcend the "convenience function" by imposing on the user an electronically defined and mediated framework that comprehends and traverses immediate social environments. Users of devices have disregarded the carceral implications inherent in technology. Rationalizing technology as a mere cost-saving programme blatantly ignores "technology as a system of exploitation" (Buchanan, 1962: 535). In order to be "convenienced" by the device, the user suspends and brackets his/her personal experiences and modes of social presentation. Technology unconditionally submits the unsuspecting and at times euphoric user to a foreign dogma replete with rituals, a catechism of lexicons and a set of reconstructed societal values and beliefs (McCormick and Visano, 1992).

From the advent of radio communications, mainframe computer systems to the use of personal computers, the penal system has undergone a dramatic period of change over the last few decades. The proliferation of various electronic devices has transformed agents of the correctional system into technocrats, concerned with expediting justice through the most convenient and accessible apparatus.

Within the physical prison the individual's movements are observed within the parameters established by the prevailing political and economic sentiments of the state. The introduction of electronic devices such as penal techniques of punishment translates directly the physical manipulation and isolation of inmates into a technological sphere.

For years, electronic surveillance has retarded the actual nature of traditional work itself by injecting different and "more improved" neutralizations and vocabularies of motive. From the cumbersome ankle bracelets to powerful and miniature devices, "modern" penal administration has welcomed uncritically each new innovation. Interestingly, electronic monitors physically limit the offender and simultaneously serve as visible reminders to offenders of their deference to an omnipresent process of social control. Again, these apparatuses of penal servitude are technologically restricting and physically oppressive. We are witnessing, as Berry (1985) details, the technological translation of carceral conditions of the physical institution to the widespread generation of "electronic jails".

Electronic monitors physically limit the offender and simultaneously serve as visible reminders to offenders of their deference to an omnipresent process of social control. The monitor, as a new form of penal practice, extends the physical features of penal servitude to the reconstituted body of the released. Through a program of house arrest (Ball, 1988), a criminal is required to wear an electronic monitoring device around his or her ankle or wrist. The device transmits signals to a monitoring base where data are analyzed and recorded. That is, the monitor reports to a computer center that determines whether the individual is present or absent. Interestingly, the offender usually pays all, or most, of the electronic monitoring cost as a condition of release. Such goals as crime deterrence, efficiency, punishment, prison over-crowding, costs associated with incarceration are all shaping the use of electronic monitoring (Visano, 2001). For Pacey

(1983:6), electric monitoring has been employed, if not developed, as a result of a paradigm shift which places a great degree of emphasis on budget cutting and balancing, as well as an increased awareness of the need for rehabilitative models. In essence, electronic monitoring serves as a convenient tool in punishing criminals at a reduced cost. In this manner public confidence in community safety is also restored as a result of the belief that this device is "technically sound", built by qualified technicians, whose skill and knowledge are directed towards the personal safety concerns of the community and furthermore ensuring the personal safety of the community. The device details curfew violations and geographic movements. On the other hand one may argue that electronic monitoring provides a more humane punishment while enabling rehabilitation - rehabilitation which traditional facilities fail to produce. With house arrest - electronic monitoring initiatives, correctional officers remain in full control over minor offenders serving time in their homes through telephone check-ups around the clock, periodically dropping by, and of course through electronic monitoring. Offenders are permitted to remain with their loved ones, maintain their employment as well as perform community services. This transformation increases self-confidence, self-esteem and aids the rehabilitative process.

Deficit cutting, balanced budgets and downsizing of governments throughout the 1990s, have resulted in an increased interest in electronic monitoring. Issues of privacy and rehabilitation have been overshadowed by such central concerns as penal costs.

3. Panopticon as Hegemonic impulses

The introduction of electronic devices such as computers into the penal system has erected an invisible cyber-cell of imprisonment that constricts the actions of both the offender and correctional workers. The implementation of the computer in parole and probation has established an invisible electronic system of technological "decarceration" (Chan and Ericson, 1981; Scull, 1977) where the all-seeing eye of the state becomes directly internalized by offenders and consequently present in all aspects of their existence. Interestingly the carceral contexts that the computer constructs are systemically overlooked. As a result of this fixation with the "liberating" capabilities of the apparatus, Meyrowitz (1985: 20) argues:

> there is a general tendency for scholars and researchers, to ignore or even deny the effects of invisible environments and the latent effects of technologies, simply because they are invisible.

Computerization entraps the (x)inmate within an electronic cage of social articulation. This stage of presentation, though ambiguous in intent, causes offenders to rely upon formal organizations (Clegg and Wilson, 1991) to define the parameters of their social interactions. The role confusion established by the disproportionate power relationship incarcerates all social performances within an electronic file. Every aspect of their offender's human existence and not merely those acts that violate specific conditions of release are affected. Infusing itself directly into all actions of the inmate, the computer re-articulates the carceral experiences. Clearly, the constitution of an electronic control perpetuates the cultural values of penal institutions, including compliance with authority and a liberal sprinkling of participation in activities exposing the accredited values of the system. Subsequently, the computer has electronically extended the traditional model of the "Panopticon", (Lyon, 1993; Strub, 1989; Marx, 1988). The daily lives of offenders both within and outside of the institution are under the constant scrutiny of penal agendas, dictated and enforced by an all encompassing 'technological eye'.

Throughout discussions of electronic methods of surveillance and social control, the concept of the "Panopticon" (Bentham, 1791) serves as a point of theoretical departure. Bentham, an 18th century philosopher and penal reformer wrote the,

> Panopticon or Inspection House. In this work he described in detail how prison (or work house or factory) could be constructed on a circular plan, with a central observation point from which the jailer or superintendent could keep the whole establishment under continuous surveillance, (Dinwiddy, 1989: 7).

Bentham's prison design that incorporated morality directly into the physical design of the prison was a response indirectly to John Howard's ground breaking work *The State Of Prisons* (1777). This architectural design was firmly entrenched in the ability of the physical design of the prison to replicate the religious tenet that God was all seeing and knowing (Mill, 1974; Whewell, 1974). Given the unique structure of Bentham's moral architecture, the Panopticon provided a physical environment in which the offender's actions were continuously under the vision and scrutiny of the guard. Structurally, the cells of the prison were arranged in a circle shape with a guard tower in the centre. This design allowed the prison officials to view the offenders during their entire stay in the institution. This subjugation reinforces institutional expectations and identity. The rational herein maintained that once offenders left the prison they would continue to feel that they were being watched and the guard would be replaced by God, subsequently making the person a better member of the religiously based society.

The all encompassing architecture exposed by Bentham was never fully acted upon by officials of Britain. Other countries adopted these principles of punishment implicit in the panoptic design, including "Spain (1852) and in the 1880s three locations in Holland" (Johnston, 1973: 20). Further, other states, while not fully implementing the complete moral architecture of Bentham, mimicked the panoptic gaze in their respective prison design. These include the Kingston Penitentiary in Canada, the Illinois State Penitentiary and the Petite Roquette Prison in Paris.

Principles of moral growth through innovative prison design were driven by the technological innovations available to officials at the time, where:

> Considerable impetus was given to innovation by technology of the newly-evolving industrial and scientific revolutions...New developments in the central heating and ventilation of large buildings, and the use of plumbing were to find some of their first applications of the prison of this period, (Johnston, 1973: 18).

The evolution of the prison, from an institution of punishment and penance, such as the Workhouse, to the movement towards rehabilitative models of justice, has rested firmly on technological innovations as the impetus upon which to base the fundamental nature of correctional theory and practice. The Panopticon, as a prison was firmly based on the available technological discoveries of the time and reflected the prevailing ideological perspectives through the media of the current technologies and their scientific foundations. The Panopticon, therefore is a direct extension of the synthesis between the dominant ideology of the society and the availability of technological innovations with which to best carry out the desired form(s) of punishment. Thus, a critical analysis of the trajectory of penological practice and theory clearly articulates inextricable links between technology prevalent at the time and definitions of punishment and control manifestations of these scientific developments.

The Panopticon, as a physical prison design was also appropriated in theoretical discussion concerning social control and the philosophy of punishment. Foucault noted that the Panopticon was extremely powerful as a technology of control, because the physical design leaves: "each individual fixed in his space. And, if he moves, he does so at the risk of life, contagion or punishment" (Foucault, 1977: 195). The Panopticon expressed a powerful mode of social control that filtered into other aspects of daily life, where the power of the state to observe all actions is of paramount importance for the maintenance of 'law and order'. The panoptic gaze of Bentham's "moral architecture" (Lyon, 1991: 596) was intrusive through a high visible presence causing all within its view to submit unconditionally to the rules of order that it imposed. Foucault notes:

> Hence the major effect of the Panopticon: to induce in the inmate a state of conscious and permanent visibility that assures the automatic functioning of power... To achieve this, it is at once too much and too little that the prisoner should be constantly observed by an inspector: too little, for what matters is that he knows himself to be observed; too much, because he has no need in fact of being so, (Foucault, 1977: 201).

The ability of the Panopticon to impose on those within its view a feeling of omniscient presence allows the power of the state to become internalized and operationalized in daily practices.

For Foucault, punishment and the prison becomes the manifestation of the "corrective technologies at its disposal" (Foucault, 1977: 224) and that "this architectural apparatus (Panopticon) should be a machine for creating and sustaining a power relation independent of the person who exercises it" (Foucault, 1977: 201). Punishment and modes of control over those within penal institutions are organized according to the susceptibility of scientific discoveries to celebrate measures of justice and penance according to technological innovations that both define and expand the physical and ideological scope of the state's agenda of punishment and control. Thus, the Panopticon, as originally physically conceived by Bentham and philosophically examined by Foucault, stands as testament to the fact that the prison is not merely a vehicle for social control, but is also a very powerful manifestation of the process by which scientific discoveries and technological innovations script the actions of all within the penal system, including: (x)offenders, guards, policy makers and social workers.

Current correctional plans continue to incorporate directly into the administration of the penal system new and highly technical apparatuses. Eventually, the advent of electricity brought about the use of electronic lock-ups and electrified fences with which to contain the movements of the (x)offenders. Later, the introduction of audio and visual recording equipment enabled officials to observe the actions of the inmate and record this information for subsequent action against the individual. Recently, scholars have noted that with the advent of various electronic apparatuses, surveillance techniques utilized by the state are increasing greatly (Lyon, 1992; Lyon, 1991; Strub, 1989). There has been a movement from the Panopticon of the 1790s to a highly electrified system of surveillance:

> In the Panopticon we find physical expression of Bentham's utilitarian philosophy, which came to dominate Victorian capitalism. Today, the influential idea of the Panopticon lives on, but in a new context. Electronic technologies monitor everyday lives so intimately, it is said, that society itself is like a panoptic prison, (Lyon, 1991: 596)

Technology has become the driving impetus behind recent alterations within not only the prison system but within the entire justice system. Police (Manning, 1992; Harper, 1991; Wright, 1990; Marx, 1988; Marx, 1985ab; Colton and Herbert, 1979), criminal law (Gibbons, 1988; Bresnick, 1988; Calhoun and Copp, 1988; Henkel, 1973) and the penal system have become extensions of countless scientific discoveries and technological innovations. Specifically, the electrification of justice has expanded the scope of the state in new and highly obtrusive directions, reaching all aspects of a person's daily life, from work to the home. Many technological sociologists note that this power will make individuals highly amenable to the influence of the state creating a "maximum-security society" (Marx, 1988). Building on the tenets of the Panopticon, Marx notes:

> His (Bentham's) ideas helped give rise to the maximum-security prison, which today is characterized by perimeter security, thick walls with guard towers, spotlights, and a high degree of electronic surveillance. Many kinds of the controls found in prison are diffusing into the society at large. It is important to ask if recent developments in technology, culture and social organization are not pushing us toward becoming a maximum-security society, (Marx, 1988: 221).

As new and more powerful apparatuses come to the disposal of the state, control over societal interaction will increase exponentially, mimicking the maximum control exhibited in the Panoptic prison.

While Bentham noted that the prison was constructed of various components, including inspection galleries and the inspectors lodge, modern panoptic illustrations observe society - based surveillance as creating a typology of social control premised on electronic apparatuses. Marx notes that electronic technology has created a "maximum-security society" with various characteristics:

1. A Dossier Society, in which computerized records play a major role.
2. An Actuarial or Predictive Society, in which decisions are increasingly made on the basis of predictions about our future behaviour as a result of our membership in aggregate categories.

3. An Engineered Society, in which our choices are increasingly limited and determined by the physical and social environment.
4. A Transparent or Porous Society, in which the boundaries that traditionally protected privacy are weakened.
5. A Self-Monitored Society, in which auto- surveillance plays a prominent role (Marx, 1988: 221).

These categories are not static; instead they are active areas of interaction within technological settings, each highlighting the infinite control over social interaction occurring as a result of the increased use of electronic mechanisms of surveillance. When this typology of surveillance is applied directly to the justice system and specifically to Marx's analysis of police work:

> the new surveillance is relatively one-sided. That is, it is likely to increase the power of large organizations, but not necessarily that of small ones or individuals. There is hardly equal access to these means, even if most of them are theoretically available to all and do not remain the exclusive property of the state (as in totalitarian countries), (Marx, 1988: 224).

In his examination of police undercover work, Marx (1988) demonstrates compellingly that the police utilization of computers have expanded police powers. Marx applies Panoptic modes of surveillance into a police social setting, arguing that in environments specifically constructed for surveillance, such as the police, Bentham's model of control is a technological extension of a "maximum-security society" (Marx, 1988). As an analytic tool, the Panopticon facilitates a well-informed understanding of the intrusions that the computer generated "cult of information" (Roszak, 1986) will have on the visibility of individuals in an electrified social order, (Lyon, 1993). Thus, Bentham's morally based prison architecture continues to guide criminological discourse as a cry in the darkness echoing off of the prison walls and resonating to the guard tower at the centre.

As noted earlier, not only are the actions of (x)offenders manipulated by an electrified penal agenda, but so too are the actions of those who are charged with their care/control. Specifically, parole officers and guards are becoming directly accountable to various technological innovations within the correctional system. The use of computers in the prison serves to restrict the actions of the correctional workers through elaborate camera and pass code entry systems. While some would argue that this is merely a price paid for additional safety, countless other correctional workers notice an erosion of their independence. Increased accountability that goes beyond their job description is the result of the increased reliance on technological apparatuses. To elaborate, personal habits such as individual washroom breaks or more collective lunchroom activities are now becoming sites that penal administrators are investigating (McCormick and Visano, 1992). This enhanced surveillance represents an insidious infringement on fundamental human rights of various care/control officers. In response to this perceived workplace harassment, employees have sought remedies through their unions and associations.

The automatic application of devices into the correctional system also serves to further alienate correctional actors from their labour. Their meaningful input into their job is minimized. As skills become increasingly mechanical and as self-esteem becomes routinely marginalized, the phenomenon of work becomes stressed. In other words, the relevant actors or constituencies (inmates, correctional officers, classification officers, living unit officers, parole officers, after-care workers, etc) are all affected by the quality of life in the workplace. The introduction of electronic devices in community corrections has also influenced relations between diverse communities and corrections. Whitehead notes:

> The contemporary community corrections worker may be conducting curfew checks or collecting urine samples, whereas yesterday's officer was leading group counselling sessions or referring a troubled probationer to a community counselling agency. Today's officer possibly thinks of the job of community corrections as a job of surveillance whereas yesterday's officer often saw the job as one of service, (1992: 155, Studt, 1973).

The gradual attenuation of ties and the elimination of personal contacts ensure the failure of rehabilitation and related institutional programmes. Instead, penal progress is measured according to technological initiatives that are functional for control purposes.

4. Conclusions: Computing Carceral Consequences

The electrification of control has affected all stages of the penal process. The penal agenda has become a highly electrified site of punishment and control, from the physical design of the prison, methods of decarceration and rehabilitative practices and the very nature of the inmate culture in the prison. The state's intrusive eye has moved to a certain extent in the direction of Orwell's classic 1984 (1949), Huxley's Brave New World (1932) or the controlled justice of Clockwork Orange (Burgess, 1972). Through an in depth exploration of the impact of the computer on the penal agenda (technology of control) the electrification of the prison will demonstrate that the Panopticon constructed of stone is now constituted of impulses.

Specifically, this paper positions the concept of the panopticon (Bentham, 1791; Foucault, 1988) as a penological model and links this technology to the impact of computers on the penal system. Further this research will develop notions of surveillance in a technological society (Postman, 1992; Lyon, 1993; Lyon, 1992; Gomme, 1992) and in more generic settings of social control (Strub, 1989; Marx, 1988; Wilensky, 1967; Boguslaw, 1965) to illustrate the ways in which control in the penal structure has become electrified, altering dramatically the penal surveillance and punishment.

The subject matter of technology is a problematic discourse that defies simplistic interpretations. It was argued that the convenience of technology reproduces compliance. Seasoned users or technocrats have become the new philosophers concerned with the hegemonic moralities of convenience (Visano, 1994). But, the phenomenon of technology is about exclusion and resistance, and not just about accommodations contextualized within the normative culture of convenience. Technology is an extension of traditional modes of social control, designed to mirror a generic deference to authority. The dominant order with its emphasis on convenience, scripts technology as a commodity that is marketable and profitable for those who have a stake in the penal structure. What warrants further investigation is the extent to which technology itself is contextualized culturally, mediated politically and articulated economically. The user must challenge the myths, monologues, and recipes that mediate knowledge and encourage electronic colonialism. Users are not well-informed citizens; knowledge is not available but filtered through self-serving organizations demanding deference to technology. A carnival of illusions and images render the user a vulnerable target of manipulation. Lamentably, the user readily consents to his/her own incarceration and in turn, reproduces forms of incarceration in encounters with less privileged and yet technologically empowered populations.

References

Ackroyd, C., K. Margolis, J. Rosenhead and T. Shallice. 1977 *The Technology of Political Control*. London: Pluto Press.

Benedikt, Michael. 1991 "Introduction" in Michael Benedikt (Ed.) *Cyberspace: First Steps*. Massachusetts: The MIT Press.

Berry, B. 1985 "Electronic Jails: A New Criminal Justice Concern". *Justice Quarterly*. Vol. 2, pp. 1-24.

Bowring, John. (Ed.) 1962 *The Works of Jeremy Bentham* . New York: Russell & Russell, Inc..

Bresnick, David. 1988 "The Lawyer as Information Manager". *Legal Studies Forum*. Vol. 12, No. 3, pp. 275-284.

Buchanan, R.A. 1965. *Technology* and Social Progress. Oxford: Pergamon.

Campbell, Colin. March 1989. "Laptop Computers For Parole Officers," *Let's* Talk. Vol. 14, 2.

Calhoun, Craig and Martha Copp. 1988 "Computerization in Legal Work: How Much Does New Technology Change Professional Practice?". *Research in the Sociology of Work*. Vol. 4, pp. 233-259.

Chan, J.B.L. and *R.V. Ericson*. 1981. *Decarceration* and *the* Economy of Penal Reform.Toronto: Center of Criminology, University of Toronto.

Clear, T. and L. Hardyman. 1990 "The New Intensive Supervision Movement," *Crime and Delinquency*. 36: 42-60.

Clegg, Stewart and Fiona Wilson. 1991 "Power, Technology and Flexibility in Organizations," in Law, John (ed.), *A Sociology of Monsters*. London: Routledge.

Colton, Kenneth W. 1979 *Police Computer Technology*. Lexington: D.C. Heath. Colton,

Kenneth and Stephen Herbert. 1979 "Police Use and Acceptance of Advanced Development Techniques: Findings from Three Case Studies," in Colton, Kenneth W. (ed.), *Police Computer Technology*. Lexington: D.C. Heath.

Corbett, R. and G.T. Marx. 1991 "No Soul in the New Machine: Technofallacies in the Electronic Monitoring Movement". *Justice Quarterly*. Vol. 8, September, pp. 399-414.

Correctional Service-Canada. 1982. "C.S.C.'s Computer Revolution: Greater Management Controls The Watchword For 1982 Says Commissioner," *Let's Talk*. Vol. 7, No. 2.

Ellul, J. 1976 "The Technological Order," in *Technology as a Social and Political Phenomenon*. NY: John Wiley and Sons, Inc.

Foucault, M. 1986. *Power/Knowledge*. New York: Pantheon.

Foucault, Michel. 1977 *Discipline and Punish: The Birth of the Prison*. New York: Vintage Books.

Franklin, Ursula. 1990 *The Real World of Technology*. Toronto: House of Anansi Press.

Garland, D. 1996 The Limits of the Sovereign State: Strategies of Crime Control in Contemporary Society. *The British Journal of Criminology:* 36, 4, 445-471.

Garland, D. 1997 Governmentality and the Problem of Crime: Foucault, Criminology, Sociology, *Theoretical Criminology: An International Journal:* 1, 2:173-214.

Gerson, Elihu M. 1987 "Do We Sincerely Want To Be Programers?" *Qualitative Sociology*. Vol. 10, No. 4. Human Sciences Press.

Goffman, Erving 1959 Presentation of Self in Everyday Life New York: Anchor

Gomme, Ian M. 1992 "From Big House to Big Brother: Confinement in the Future," in McCormick, Kevin R.E. and Livy Visano (eds.), *Canadian Penology: Advanced Perspectives* and Research. Toronto: Canadian Scholars' Press.

Gooderham, Helen. November 1986 "Staff Microcomputers Revolutionize CSC's Way of Handling Information," *Let's Talk*. Vol. 11, No. 13.

Heise, David R. 1981 "Microcomputers And Social Research," *Sociological Methods and Research*. Vol. 9, pp. 395-536.

Huxley, Aldous. *Brave New World*. New York: Granada Publishing, 1932.

Jupp, Victor. 1989 *Methods of Criminological Research*. London: Unwin Hyman Ltd.

Kroker, Arthur 1984 *Technology and the Canadian Mind: Innis/ McLuhan/ Grant* Montreal: New World Perspectives.

Levin, M.L. 1986 "Technological Determinism In Social Data Analysis," *Computers and Social Sciences*. Vol. 2.

Makus, Anne. 1990 "Stuart Hall's Theory of Ideology: A Frame for Rhetorical Criticism" *Western Journal of Speech Communication*. Vol. 54, No. 4, Fall, pp. 495-514.

Manning, P.K. 1992 "Technological Dramas and the Police: Statement and Counterstatement in Organizational Analysis," *Criminology*. Vol. 30, No. 3.

Marcuse, Herbert. 1964 *One-Dimensional Man*. Boston: Beacon Press.

Marx, Gary T. 1985 "I'll Be Watching You: Reflections on the New Surveillance". *Dissent*. Winter, pp. 26-34.

McCormick, Kevin R.E. and Livy Visano (eds.) 1992 "Technology and Control: Generic Trends" in Canadian Penology: *Advanced Perspectives and Research Toronto*. Canadian Scholar's Press.

McLuhan, Marshall. 1967 The *Medium* is the Massage. New York: Random House. –

McLuhan, Marshall. 1964 *Understanding Media: The Extensions Of Man*. New York: Mentor Book.

Meyrowitz, Joshua. 1988 *No Sense of Place*. New York: Oxford University Press.

Murphy, C. 1988 "Community Problems, Problem Communities, and Community Policing in Toronto", *Journal of Research In Crime And Delinquency:* Vol. 25 No.4 November 392-410.

Olaniran, Bolanle A. 1994 "Group Performance in Computer-Mediated and Face-to-Face Communication Media". *Management Communication Quarterly*. Vol. 7, No. 3, February, pp. 256-281.

Orwell, George. 1948 *1984*. New York: Oxford University Press.

Pacey , Arnold. 1983 *The Culture of Technology*. Cambridge, Massachusetts: The MIT .

Pfaffenberger, Bryan. 1988 "Microcomputer Applications" in *Qualitative Research.* Sage.

Postman, Neil. 1992 *Technopoly: The Surrender of Culture to Technology*. New York: Alfred A. Knopf.

Roszak, Theodore. 1986 *The Cult of Information: The Folklore of Computers and the True Art of Thinking*. New York: Pantheon Books.

Scull, A. 1977 Decarceration. Englewood Cliffs: Prentice-Hall.

Stone, Allucquere Rosanne. 1991 "Will the Real Body Please Stand Up?: Boundary Stories about Virtual Cultures" in Michael Benedikt (Ed.) *Cyberspace: First Steps.* Massachusetts: The MIT Press.

Studt, E. 1973 *Surveillance and Service In Parole.* Washington: U.S. Department Of Justice.

Visano, L.A 1987 *This Idle Trade*. Concord: VitaSana Books.

Visano, L.A. 1994 "The Culture of Capital as Carceral: Conditions and Contradictions" In Kevin McCormick (Ed.), *Carceral Contexts: Readings In Control.* Toronto: Canadian Scholars' Press.

Visano, L.A 2001 "Community-Based Corrections". In J. Winterdyk (ed.) *Corrections in Canada: Social Reactions to Crime* Toronto: Prentice-Hall (pp 296-322).

Visano, L.A. 2004 "Degrees Of Freedom: The Applied Degree As The Pedagogy Of Praxis, Dialectics Of Discipline And The Primacy Of Partnerships" *College Quarterly*, Summer Volume 7 Number 3.

Whitehead, John. 1992. "Control And The Use of Technology in Community Supervision," in Benekos, P. and A. Merlo (eds.), *Corrections: Dilemmas and Directions.* Anderson Publishing Co.

Winner, L. 1986 *The Whale And The Reactor*. Chicago: University of Chicago Press.

Woolgar, Steve. 1991 "Configuring the User: The Case of Usability Trials," in Law, John (ed.), *A Sociology of Monsters.* London: Routledge.

18. The Impact of Colour in "Correcting" Youths: A Program of Action

Wesley Crichlow and Livio A. Visano

1. Introduction

Racism, the negation of identity, is a process of criminalization. The criminal justice system with its colour-crime connections (Visano, 1998) institutionalizes inequality. Rooted in wider hegemonic cultural controls, the criminal justice system promotes popular beliefs and common-sense notions about the colour of crime that saturate media discourses and current legal logic. Accordingly, at every stage of the justice system - from arrest, pre-trial hearing, conviction, sentencing, to classification and parole hearings, there is ample evidence of cultural annihilation. Of central concern to our discussion are the fundamental links between racism and youth in corrections as well as the institutional/administrative practices which contribute to a complex set of social meanings constantly shaped by both internal (local) and external processes (outside), pushing and pulling which contribute to alienation, powerlessness and exclusion of minority youths.

Racism is not an incidental element of the social order within institutions; rather, it is at the very heart of political, cultural and economic conditions experienced by minority youths. The prevailing institutional ideologies within correctional facilities incorporate strategies that compel youths to abandon distinctive ethno-cultural traits in favour of widely held dominant Anglo- American values. Racism is an ideology, not simply of differences, physical or cultural, but an ideology of superiority that denies the meaningful participation of Black youth, for example—it disarticulates and impoverishes human beings; in essence it is an act of violence. This central organizing principle prevents youths from fully developing their citizenship. This structured alienation contributes to low educational outcomes, high unemployment, low self-esteem, antisocial behavior, family turmoil and high recidivism. Instead of graduating from high school, entering college and university (Ruck and Wortley, 2002), and taking leadership roles in their respective communities, "minority" youths are assigned to prisons, wasting away and treated like societal refuse. Prisonization, the most coercive apparatus of the state, can never facilitate the development of critical thought and a positive sense of self. Angela Davis, in her autobiography describes jails as "thoughtless places, thoughtless in the sense that no thinking is done by their administrations; no problem solving or rational evaluation of any situation slightly different from the norm. The void created by this absence of thought is filled by rules and the fear of establishing a precedent" (Davis, 1988:290).

This paper investigates the experiences of Black youth in "correctional" facilities. Conceptually, the impact of colour in the control of youth requires an investigation of the differential treatment of youths, youth-staff relations, the delivery of services and specific issues relating to separation, racism, ghettoization and access. This study, part of a larger ongoing study on youth, employed a community development approach committed to involving participants in a variety of ways throughout the process of research (from data collection, analysis and final editing). Over a ten year period (from 1994 - 2004), both a cross sectional and longitudinal sample of two hundred youths were collected in Ontario and Quebec. Data were also gathered from fifty formally incarcerated youths who use drop-in facilities/services. Also included was information on institutions regarding race awareness training, policies, composition of minority staff and resident staff relations. In addition, twenty five interviews were held with institutional staff from six facilities and ten interviews with representatives of community based agencies. Both open ended (unfocussed) interviews and fixed item questions from survey instruments were incorporated. Group discussions and individual face to face interviews generated data on barriers to access, information and awareness, forms of psychological, emotional, and physical punishment, dominant cultural norms, administrative policies, racism and specific measures or strategies that organizations had taken to improve access.

2. Literature: "So what else is new? Tell us something we don't know?"

In North America the policing of Black communities reflects historical and colonial attitudes towards Blacks. The phenomenon of criminalization results in the over-representation of Blacks as both victims and offenders. High arrest rates are attributable to a racial inequality that creates discriminatory conditions. Police officers routinely stop and interrogate Black youth on the basis of unsupportable "suspicious" evidence. African Americans constitute a disproportionate representation of the prison populations. In 2004, 2,131,180 prisoners were held in US federal, state prisons and local facilities -- an increase of 2.3 per cent from midyear 2003, less than the average annual growth of 3.5 per cent since yearend 1995. At midyear 2004 there were 4,919 black male prison and jail inmates per 100,000 black males in the United States, compared to 1,717 Hispanic male inmates per 100,000 Hispanic males and 717 White male inmates per 100,000 white males (BJS, 2004). According to FBI and Department of Justice statistics studied by the Sentencing Project, a Washington-based non-profit lawyer financed group, 609,690 young Black men are under the control of the criminal justice system while 436,000 are in college (Washington Post, 27,02,1990 A3). One out of every two African American men is likely to be arrested during his lifetime; 1/4 Black men between the ages of 20 and 29 is incarcerated, on probation or on parole; a Black man is 7.5 times more likely to be arrested than a White man. In California, five black men are behind bars for each one in university; one out of every 20 Americans born this year will serve time in prison, according to a Justice Department study (Thornton, 1999). Black offenders are also overrepresented in Canada's prisons. Ontario data from the 1990s reveals a black prison admission rate of 3,686 per 100,000, an Aboriginal rate of 1,993 per 100,000, and a white rate of 705 per 100,000 (Tanovich, 2004: A21).

Stephen Lewis, author of Ontario's race relations report, explained: "Time and time again I was told of the disproportionate numbers of minority youth in detention centres, of the abuse gratuitously heaped upon them, of the woeful lack of 'rehabilitation' opportunities" (Department of Justice, 1993:4). According to Herbert, Afro-Caribbean youths make up 29 per cent of youth custody orders. Likewise, 31 per cent of all those receiving remands were for Blacks (ibid, 12). According to Correctional Services of Canada, 80 per cent of 14,500 male inmates were described as Caucasians, 11.9 per cent as Aboriginal and 4.7 per cent as Black (Mitchell and Abbate, 1994:A6). In Gordon's (1988:304) study of British inmates, Blacks made up 12 per cent of young offender population and yet represent only 6 per cent in the comparable age groups in the general population. In the case of under 21-year-old, the average sentence of White prisoners was nine months, but for those of West Indian/ African origin it was 12 months and for those of Asian origin it was 11 months. Not only are Blacks more likely to be arrested (Landau and Nathan, 1983), they are also discriminated against in probation reports (Herbert, 1986). Irrespective of the many state-sponsored commissions and studies in sentencing, guidelines continue to falter as judges act with impunity in enforcing the culture of white superiority. Bell and Lang (1985), Bishop and Frazier (1988), Pope and Feyerherm (1990), Lieber (1994) clearly indicate that African American youths receive more severe penalty outcomes than White youths. Stereotypes associated with drugs or alcohol, gang involvements, lower class standards, etc. influenced the decisions of judges. Judges also feel that African American youths may be poor subjects for rehabilitation. Leiber (1994) examined referrals to a district court in Iowa from 1980-1989 and discovered that White youths received less severe outcomes than African Americans and Aboriginal peoples.

Historically, the criminal justice system has always been ill responsive to young Black youths. The unequal treatment of minority youths is easily apparent by simply noticing how courtroom demographies of lawyers, judges, police, social workers and offenders influence sentencing practices, penal philosophies, and accountability. For instance, Black offenders are typically returned to detention facilities without knowing or understanding what had happened in the courtroom. Despite the1988 US Juvenile Justice Delinquency Prevention Act, (section 223a[23]) that requires each state to develop methods to reduce the disproportionate number of minority youths in secure facilities, Black youths continue to be over represented when one controls for the nature of crime and also when one examines the per capita basis representation.

3. Findings

3.1. The correctional experience: the voices of troubled youths and the denial of culture

Youths talked at great lengths about the lack of services available to them for any meaningful integration into society. Black/racial minority youths alluded to the bias and built-in racism of correctional workers (correctional and classification professionals) and support staff who do not refer them to treatment programmes and other meaningful services (day school, therapy, volunteer work, religious observances) which are intended to assist them in their re-integration into mainstream society. Basic services of support or community resources are not readily available to them. Thirty youths noted that they were reminded by correctional workers and support staff alike that the programmes and services would not rehabilitate them; that is they were incorrigible and *beyond reach* and that the only meaningful remedy is "hard time". It was the conviction of significant number of White youth care workers that the prison experience offers a plethora of opportunities for many Black youths. According to this distorted logic, youths were well served given that incarceration offered direction, three meals a day, television to watch and an opportunity to meet "their" friends. And yet, as a few youths reported: "They call us "ungrateful animals" as they placed "us in what they call the jungle unit or range." Many Black/racial minority youths, mostly those of Caribbean backgrounds, noted that they were punished for not speaking "properly", that is, for not speaking English, although English was their first and only language. Accented English was immediately labelled a deficit in the eyes of most White staff who would make no effort to understand the youths' cultural dialects and linguistic styles. White staff belittled these youths by trying to talk to them in Caribbean accents when they felt youths failed to listen to their commands. Approximately 65 per cent of youths admitted apologetically that they did not know how to speak properly. In addition, Vietnamese, Chinese, Hispanic, Somali and other youths who did not speak English as a first language were not only ridiculed but forced to speak English while in the institution. Youths, for instance, complained about being interrupted while on the telephone with their parents by staff who came up to them saying: `speak English; we need to know what you are saying, because you could be planning an escape'.

Imprisonment destroys the culture and memory of young people's history by denying them the opportunity to communicate and practice "their language". Youths felt that had to acquiesce to staff orders. In addition to language facility, White staff members often disparaged Rastafarian hair styles, colour of clothing, African medallions and various culinary tastes. Likewise, Native youths noted that their length of hair, sweet grass and other ceremonies were frequently ridiculed. Staff referred to Native youths as `wagon burners' and `car thieves.' Whenever some staff heard of stolen cars they would typically say to Native youths: `Are you sure the car is not on the reserve.' Similarly, staff made no apologies for their insensitive and ethnocentric biases regarding the Muslim faith. Four youths who observed pork free diets were told to eat the pork because `a little piece of pork would not hurt.' During the holy month of Ramadan no provisions were made for these youths to fast and pray.

Black youths routinely experienced official harassment. Officials would dictate an "appropriate" dress code; youths were punished for wearing their pants below their waist and for having their handkerchief hang out of their back pocket.

Staff explained that the attire symbolized aggression or violence; as one stated: "Caribbean youths are aggressive, rude, rebels against authority, they wear their pants -- ten times the size of their waist -- below their waist". In addition to what was perceived as "offensive appearance", staff berated youths for listening to "Black" music and for watching certain cultural TV programmes. The dominant culture of the prison institution defines what is considered appropriate music and film. Reggae, Calypso, Hip Hop and Rap were considered to be vulgar and pornographic by a large number of White staff who view this art form as dangerous – promoting sex, drugs, and violence. And yet rage rock, heavy metal or grunge video viewing by White inmates was acceptable.

Stereotypes and scapegoating are commonplace. According to seventy per cent of youths studied, staff members typically hurled racial slurs. Black youths are told to "play Buck wheat," address them as "nig" or "Hey Black boy". That is, youths are encouraged to engage in self hating racist stereotypes to entertain White staff in order to acquire a few privileges; Black youths act out stereotypes in prisons in order to survive. Many youths (45 per cent) reported that they were encouraged to abandon their respective communities and accept their new community, the prison. Staff constantly reminded these youths of the evils of their "ghetto" or "slum" communities -- Regent Park, Jane/Finch, James Town, Malvern, Rexdale, Bathurst Heights etc. areas which continue to be blamed for the city's violent crime rates.

But youths did not respond uniformly to this annihilation of self worth. Although a few youths internalize the imposed stereotypes, many others actively resist it. Resistance, however, invariably leads to anger, usually directed against correctional workers and support staff (i.e., psychologist, psychiatrist, social worker). White professionals uniformly failed to accept anger (or in their words, "the chip on their shoulders") as an appropriate emotional response to racial oppression. Eminent Black psychiatrists and psychologists Alexander Thomas, Samuel Sillen and W. Grier have all argued that the term anger has been labelled "a traditional feature of the racist syndrome, interpreting Black strength as primitive emotionalism".

Cultural annihilation in prison also incorporates intersecting stereotypes of race, sexuality and gender. A constant complaint heard from young racial minority women related to the insulting comments of staff about their babies. In addition, Black and Aboriginal women were routinely labelled promiscuous, immoral and sexually unstable by White correctional staff and child care professionals. Twelve young Black men also complained about staff assessment and behaviour reports which concluded they were sexual perverts and psychopaths because they walked around with their hands in their pants or were too close to one of their "brothers". Staff interpreted physical closeness solely in sexual terms. In one notable incident staff talked to residents about the media portrayals of a Black male rapist. During the course of watching a movie where there was a rape scene, staff shouted to one inmate, "Hey, is that you on the screen?" The message therein refers to the pernicious stereotype of a psychopathic Black rapist. An insidiously demoralizing message frequently communicated in staff banter or jokes concerns what staff members identify as the Black "bestial" appetite for White women. One youth indicated that he had filed a sexual harassment complaint against a staff member only to result with the police telling him he was lying, laughed at him and explained that he would never be able to win such a case. There is also the matter of Black volunteers who are not only suspected but also accused of engaging in sexual relationships with inmates. Visitors were berated for sexually arousing the inmates because they were "too touchy" and "too close". These visitors were reminded of the institution's policy against any form of touching. Hernton (1965, 1971) states that:

> Whether intentional or not the white world's definition of Negro sexuality has served to frustrate and arrest the political struggle of Black people throughout the years, especially in the South where oppression and racism have been most brutal. The sexualization of racism (or the racism of sex) as a political instrument to be used against the liberation of Black...Also, these youths described how front line male workers and clinical staff invaded their privacy with impunity. This abuse can only serve to further degrade minority women's existence.

3.2 Black skin as socialized trouble

Black/racial minority youths uniformly commented on the abuse of power by staff personnel. Youths felt that the abuse of power by mostly White staff was designed to keep inmates powerless and fearful -- in servitude. For such youths the powerlessness, the dehumanizing conditions of their incarceration, the alienation from their families and friends, boredom and a powerlessness that create considerable despair. For 80 per cent of Black youths, this hopelessness not only causes them to think irrationally, for example many of these youths accepted a generalized *blame worthiness*, accepting stereotypes holding them responsible for most of the crime. Youth workers refuse to counsel or treat Black youths who, in turn, adopt a generalized powerlessness. This hopelessness is manifested in forms of internalized oppression -- self hatred and conflict towards each other. This anger and hatred is often expressed in the form of but not limited to homicide which has become one of the leading causes of death among black youths between the ages of 15 and 24, both in Canada and the U.S. For youth workers, they are not "troubled kids" who are "in trouble" but rather "troublesome" and serious "trouble makers". The latter characterization led to a lack of staff trust; medical requests were often denied by staff who believed that youths were "faking". Staff suspicion of youth was institutionalized. The veracity of the accounts of Black youths was constantly verified and cross checked with various sources. Complaints were often dismissed by senior management, the police and correctional officers, a practice that soon discouraged any complaints. Moreover, staff threats of reprisal reduced the number of complaints; youths were reminded that their programming time would be cut and that they would do more "quiet time" (segregation) if they tried to "rock the boat".

Overall, the mental, psychological, emotional and physical forms of punishment usually silenced Black youths and provoke a few however into retaliatory action. Youths articulated a sense of uncertainty, powerlessness and distance. It was found that racist and cultural factors either inhibit youths from seeking services or programs ostensibly designed to serve them. Service providers, counsellors, correctional officers effectively negate the value of any assistance by failing to recognize any sense of self worth among youths, youths who by and large were simply dismissed as trouble.

3.3 Voices of authorities: Front line staff

3.3a Ghettoization

Staff members are professionally required to assist youths in their respective psycho-social development. Instead, as youths repeatedly indicated, staff manipulated institutional rules to justify their racist behaviour. We were overwhelmed by the large amount of complaints reported by youths that dealt with the staff practice of placing a Black youth in an all White unit or confine a White youth in an all Black unit. As fights erupted staff would align themselves with the White inmate(s) and use excessive force against Black youths ("taking down the punk"). According to six youths, when Blacks disagree and engage in a physical fight, staff for the most part would simply ignore the altercation and jokingly add, "Let them kill themselves." All Black disputants – victims and bullies usually ended up in solitary confinement and suffered excessive force by staff restraining them. Some recalled being dragged down stairs, handcuffed, thrown against the walls, and pinned to the floor. In the admitting and discharge area, staff members are responsible for the creation and maintenance of Black units, known in prison language as the "jungle range", Black range, or the "loud area". Several youths disclosed with great pain the stereotypes hurled at them by correctional staff, such as 'Monkey,' 'Dog', 'Beast', and 'Gorilla'. *Ghettoization* functions to foster solidarity (collective conformity) and justify exclusionary racist practices. A further and insidious "barbaric" justification for racial segregation in some youth facilities is the need to separate White youths from rural or even suburban areas from the urban Black youths primarily because the former have never had seen Blacks person and may fear them. Thus, race problems can be avoided by maintaining all white units and institutions. One staff member commented on the visible fear she saw in a White youth after he had seen a Black person for the first time in his life. It was reported that the White youth was "trembling and never came out of his room because he feared" the Blacks youths in the unit.

3.3b Inter-racial and Intra-racial Relationships

Despite the above situationally based race relations problems, there was a sense of unity among the majority of all youths in correctional facilities. They were more anxious about their charges, release dates, sentence computation, parole eligibility dates, etc. Second, they were very bothered by the social isolation, boredom and uncertainty in their lives. Consequently many youths strove to establish positive relationships with other inmates. Youths explained, for example, that they routinely asked staff to hold group discussions on conflict resolution and anti-racism but staff typically ignored such requests. Many correctional staff considered such requests beyond their responsibility and interest; they felt that the "bleeding heart" social workers should be more involved and yet they did little to inform case workers of the inmates' requests. In the prison occupational culture, the word social worker is one of the most condescending terms. The para-military structure of punishment rejects completely any semblance of a therapeutic or care giving role. In fact officers often blamed social workers, claiming that social workers were "screwing" up by getting too close to these "shit disturbers". In the execution of their daily routines correctional workers internalize racial segregation as necessary and expedient. Under these conditions, a youth will most likely want to be placed with their "own kind" in order to make their stay as safe as possible. Moreover, corrections staff members guarded their authority and uncompromisingly refused to be either questioned or challenged. Any correctional worker who deviated from this occupational norm was labelled a social worker who is "not one of us". Youths who deferred to this power relationship were rewarded by both by correctional officers and support clinical staff. As one seasoned described, "in all the facilities I have been in, White youths get better treatment than the Blacks, always". In fact another added that social workers, psychologists and psychiatrists spend more quality time with Whites than with Black/racial minority youths. They testified too that White inmates were encouraged by White staff to participate in racist jokes. A few Black youths would also be recruited and rewarded by White staff for engaging in racist banter. These co-opted youths also engaged in differentiating "Blacks" from "Gangstas" or "bangers". As one youth explained, the former inmates "speak okay, dress well, do not cause trouble, and are easy to get along with". The latter, however, he continued "would wear their pants four times the size below their waist, do not speak well, talk like 'Hey man,' wear lots of jewellery, and are always looking to outsmart whites." Black and White youths who accommodate to the staff viewed themselves as superior; they had accepted their prisonization, the process of acculturation in a white dominated society. Black youths made it quite clear that in their discussions with some staff, much of what is understood as "Black" originated from ignorant media portrayals that were all too ready to accept.

3.3c The Need for Racial Minority Staff

Thus far, our analysis has focused on the relationship between Black youths and white dominated prison institutions. But, what role do Black and other racial minority staff play in this process? Our data indicate that Blacks and other racial minority staff felt powerless in influencing meaningful changes. A few denied that racism exists and strictly blamed Black/racial minority youths for the high crime rate and for Black violence. The majority talked about not seeing race or colour as factors when caring for and treating Black/racial minority youths. Within this group some distanced themselves from Caribbean youths especially Jamaicans. We interviewed a number of Black/racial minority staff who proffered disturbing responses. One racial minority staff (CO4), for example, said: "Look at me. I am six foot plus and was born in Canada -- no one will `mess' with me, and besides there are no race problems in here." This worker added that because he does not speak with an accent like the Caribbean youths, he did not experience racism. For him racism was a problem associated only with those youths from the Caribbean who did not have a Canadian accent. He further noted that the Caribbean culture contributed to the many difficulties of prison adjustment. Another racial minority youth worker (YO4) stated that "the Black youths expect me to treat them better and give them extra points, only because they are Black." He considered this unfair since he had an obligation to treat all youths equally. "I do not see colour," he commented. Another racial minority worker (CO8) commented: "I can never understand these youths because I am not in jail and have all the privileges that go along with being a professional. I really treat them equally and do not see colour." Yet another (CO9) remarked: "Black youths are responsible for police stopping and shooting Black people, because they do cause the most trouble and commit the most crime."

Racism contributes to states of psychological damage and denial. Racism rendered Black/racial minority youth workers powerless -- they were reluctant to challenge the unfair care and treatment of Black/racial minority youths for fear of betraying their White colleagues or loosing their jobs. Some actually believed that racism was not a factor in the unequal treatment of youths. Like their inmate counterparts, Black/racial minority youth workers suffered from low self-esteem and racelessness. This on the job survival led to a state of denial. Our research indicated that the position of Black/racial minority staff was one of colour blindness -- reinforced by many of their White co-workers. This orientation is a form of occupational adaptation that encouraged the denial of institutionalized racism. Despite their "public" denials, Black/racial minority youth workers noted that they were told that they were hired or promoted because of their colour. A few complained about the way in which their assessment or behaviour reports were ignored by superiors while those of their White colleagues were respected and assigned greater credibility. A larger number complained about their lack of promotion despite their meritorious qualification. They claimed that they had trained many White junior staff only to see them promoted. Many more seasoned minority staff members indicated that White management officials and White correctional workers did not respect Black/racial minority professionals such as psychiatrists, psychologists and social workers. Staff viewed them as less clinically qualified than their White colleagues. Many Black/racial minority clinical support staff members usually hired on contact in youth care facilities were not given the positive support and encouragement.

Staff members referred too to the number of human rights complaints and union grievances that have been adjudicated in favour of management and their White counterparts. Staff—both Black and White—generally agree that there was a woeful lack of support for anti-racist training and cultural sensitivity; in fact, White staff viewed the employment of racial minorities as reverse discrimination especially in their view minority workers were less qualified. A number of Black workers also suggested that despite their promotion their authority was not respected. Much of the above indicate the prevalence of white normative measures or criteria of professionalism, deviation from which was viewed as inappropriate.

Many White dominated institutions hesitate to change the colour of their management boards as well as their traditional Anglo/ European "ways of doing things". From our interviews and visits to correctional facilities we discovered only two cases where Black /racial minorities were in positions of upper management despite the very large proportion of inmates who were Blacks and other racial minorities. Like their inmate counterparts Black/racial minority workers expressed powerlessness, alienation and hopelessness, a situation that vitiates their sense of authority and any hope in presenting themselves as role models. In general, management and staff claimed that their responses to youths were appropriate especially the refusal to provide some service requests. They alluded to "commonsensical" notions of firmness and discipline not leniency and inaction. As one staff member noted: "we are not running a Holiday Inn for youths". Drawing on their own experiences as youths, many White immigrant staff blamed recent immigrants and their children for failing to adjust to the "Canadian way of life". For them, Black youths exploited the government and expected "handouts when they have not contributed anything but crime". Staff also questioned extant race relations sensitivity programs. Accordingly, racism originated with inmates who refused to integrate in a multicultural society.

At one facility, administrators and front line staff chatted openly about the hypocrisy of youth offender legislation. On the one hand, they felt they were compelled to coddle inmates because of their age and colour; and, on the other hand, they were required to punish them. This frustration was expressed by one staff member who had introduced government representatives in the following words: "the corn bread eating cotton-picking people [were] here from Toronto to talk with us about racism". Teachers at these facilities also demonstrated considerable insensitivity. A youth also described a situation where he had asked his teacher permission to open the window because of the heat in the classroom. The teacher's retort: "it wasn't too hot in the cotton fields when you and your ancestors were picking cotton down South". When the youth complained to authorities about the incident, he was told to be less sensitive and reminded that the teacher was only joking. Interestingly, just in advance of our arrival at one institution a previously segregated unit was immediately "integrated". Youths informed us of this "staged" performance by staff and management. Even more disturbing was the behaviour of youth/ child advocate who refused our request to chat with the residents without his presence. When questioned about his interference, this advocate for youth rights sarcastically responded: "I feel like I am in the Spanish Inquisition". In brief, the majority of staff respondents agreed that:

a) racism is prevalent;
b) the service delivery system is frustrating;

c) administrative and bureaucratic rules are confusing; and,
d) penal institutions have done very little or nothing at all for the treatment of Black/racial minority youths.

Eighty per cent of the staff contextualized the above concerns in terms of the ongoing conflicts between the realities of the occupational culture and the unenforceable administrative rules. Overall, we found very limited evidence of any willingness on the part of service providers to consider, in any meaningful way, possible remedies to address a host of administrative barriers that negatively impact upon Black/racial minority youth. Similarly the issue of access to service is poorly understood by staff and administration. Clearly, both staff and administration failed to understand issues of diversity (culture, language, custom and tradition) and the nature of multicultural communities (role of the family, religion, recreation, work).

4. Institutional/Organizational Findings

It was found that correctional institutions/organizations devote little or no energy to effect change beyond the banal identification of barriers. While service providers express a limited appreciation of the problems inherent in discrimination, the results are disturbing in terms of the actual adoption of specific measures to reduce the many obstacles that impede equality in corrections. Serious gaps were revealed in the information base of staff regarding the cultural and racial characteristics of their clientele as well as their own workforce. Some institutions with a total staff composite of over two hundred employees had only one Black/racial minority worker. We also found that there is a great inconsistency in the delivery of services for youths in all of the institutions. The delivery of much needed basic services and treatment of Black youths was at best tentative and idiosyncratic. The following general conclusions, relevant in the delivery of services for Black/Racial Minority Youths in institutions, were drawn from the findings.

4.1 Institutional Barriers to Access

Institutions do not have nor are they willing to share, information or organizational data regarding the cultural and racial characteristics of their clientele, staff and volunteers. Most administrators conveniently argued that they do not know how to define a racial minority or simply added that they do not see colour among their staff or resident population. In institutions where there was a presence albeit token representation of racial minority employees, racial minority employees complained about the stress attendant with being burdened as the sole race relations educator. Few institutions recognize the existence of access barriers; staff members in correctional facilities were clueless about the role of the office of ombudsperson. Youths, for whom English was not their native language, frequently had to wait long hours for the arrival of any person on any shift to translate otherwise they had to be prepared to suffer the humiliation of not being able to communicate in English. No institution had an anti-racist policy or an effective mechanism for dealing with racism among residents and staff. Institutions experience difficulties in responding to barriers and are unable to devise strategies and programs to effectively address these barriers. Yet many Black / racial minority volunteer programmes that deliver culturally specific and supportive programmes are constantly harassed by management and correctional workers. In some cases these programmes were discontinued by management without informing the agencies involved or even giving reasonable explanations to the youths affected. Cost was always a factor cited by authorities. In our view costs must not be viewed as inhibiting effective intervention and innovation; rather increased costs must be considered in order to improve training, cultural sensitivity of staff and enhanced resources. Change efforts within individual units or programs are not sufficient to assure the necessary system improvements. Collective responses on the part of correctional services agencies, rather than isolated solutions, are required to achieve more equitable access for Black/racial minority youths. Correctional facilities do not effectively respond to their new multiracial realities. Instead, the onus for ensuring access falls on smaller, poorer funded and understaffed ethno-specific agencies, community volunteers or family members. Institutions operate as two solitudes in separate systems, distinguished by colour and culture, seldom taking into account their respective efforts to plan and deliver services without competing for scarce resources. Interviews confirmed that a majority of Black/racial minority youths experience considerable difficulties in adjusting to their respective incarceration. In some instances, Blacks and other racial minority youths were placed in youth facilities in total isolation from their families and friends thus making visits almost impossible. Isolation and alienation resulted in exorbitant telephone bills for relatives and extremely negative behaviour reports for Black /racial minority youths. The latter affects the prospects for early release (parole), temporary release passes and institutional privileges.

4.2 Information Barriers

As the data suggest, there is widespread discontent among Black youths about the staff and the services obtained. The most frequent criticism directed at staff relate to the failure to appreciate the predicament experienced by people of different races and cultures. Youths from visible racial and cultural groups encountered problems which are common to other residents, but are more acute for them because of their limited knowledge of rights and entitlements; limited language ability which renders it more difficult to secure services; and cultural differences which make them more susceptible to misconceptions and negative judgements. The following observations were identified by youth, staff and researchers:

1. Staff agreed that youths were ill-informed about available services, while a large number of staff agreed that information is available in English and French only.
2. Strategies to deal with information barriers were limited and did not specifically address the most pertinent barriers.
3. Only a minority of staff members have adopted strategies to deal with

information and communication barriers.

4. Some staff intentionally denied information to Black youths.
5. Some staff intentionally submitted negative behaviour reports about Black youths thus denying them privileges. These youths had little opportunity to counter these reports.

4.3 Cultural Barriers

All Black Youths agree that staff failed to act according to the role of helping professionals. All noted that the way in which services were delivered and that the kinds of services available were inappropriate for some cultures. For example, Muslim and other non Christian youths constantly complained about the lack of respect for their religious practices. They also noted that it was not a problem for Christians to secure their Bibles and attend regular services, but it took forever to get the Koran or ensure appropriate religious services. Many Muslim youths complained about staff touching the Koran and staff ridiculing certain religious observances. Respondents indicated that there were few specific programs/services directed to ethno-cultural groups. If and when services were provided, community agencies encountered numerous obstacles set by the administration and front-line workers. What is even more disturbing for Black youths were the privileges extended by management to mainstream agencies. These agencies offered token gestures or very limited programs, community outreach, and inter- community cooperation; they had no established multicultural or anti-racist policies, no minority representation as volunteers or professionals. Ethno-cultural agencies serving various Black, Aboriginal, South Asian, Latino, Chinese and other racial minority communities were rarely invited by these facilities. Where Black cultural programmes existed, staff discouraged youths from attending claiming that these "special programs" constituted reverse racism. Many Black youths also complained about being tested for drugs after family visits and returning from temporary releases (TR's) while White youths were seldom tested for drugs after their TR's. Black youths complained about staff sitting in on their family and friends visits, making it almost impossible for them and their families to express themselves freely, again extending a sense of powerlessness to the parents. If for example, a Black/racial minority youth yelled out at his/her visitor, staff intervened and would cut the visit short arguing that the youth is out of control and must be put back into the unit. Within different facilities youths were asked to perform various tasks (kitchen duty, maintenance, laundry duty and other chores) that assist in breaking the boredom and predictable daily routine of life in custody. Black youths, however were not assigned these responsibilities, opportunities which earned inmates extra privileges. Black youths were stereotyped as thieves and thus seen as unfit to work in these areas. Finally, there were the White non custodial care professionals who claimed to be working in the best interest of the youth. Typically, White professionals suffered from colour blindness, believing quite arrogantly that all youths have the same needs irrespective of race, class, and gender. This approach sought to detract Black/racial minorities from their history and current social conditions. In addition, there are White care professionals who ignored Black/racial minority youths and spent less quality time with them. The latter indicated that professionals reminded them that they lacked motivation and were too troublesome. Clearly, many professionals avoided working with Black/racial minority youths in an effort to avoid dealing with their own ignorance, fear, and discomforts with anti-racism. Some professionals also told us that they saw the Black/racial minority youth life tied to so much anger and racism that it was impossible to do anything.

5. A Programme of Action

A commitment to social justice requires solutions that are co-ordinated, comprehensive and strategic.

5.1 The issue of access

The interests of service providers and clients may not be in sync, despite the protestations of front-line workers and recipients. Robert Perlman (1975: 101) contends that service providers and clients have different orientations. The behaviour of providers is mainly bounded and shaped by the need to be economical in the use of available resources, and administrators and policy makers will seek maximum control of resources and programs. He adds:

> By contrast, consumers require services that are as accessible as possible on a geographic, psychological, or cultural basis and that afford them maximum choice. Their need is for accountability and effectiveness in meeting their problems. Consumers increasingly want to keep services and agencies responsive by having a strong voice in their planning and administration (ibid).

Acknowledging both that service systems seem to conspire against clients and that agencies as well as clients appear to have different interests, `equality seekers' must reconsider the issue of access if they are to ensure that people get the help they require.

Galper (1975: 61), for example, suggests that services are not meant to promote social change, and he sees the political function of the (correctional) services as merely being one of containing change:

> The general message to the client that is contained in the fact of underfinanced, inadequate, and inappropriate services is also a message to the worker. The worker is providing...services to people who have, for some reason, failed to contain within themselves the symptoms of our social crisis. The worker knows how poorly provided for these clients are. The message must necessarily be that if the worker does not remain properly at work and properly within the accepted standards of behaviour, he or she might someday be forced to accept the very kind of inadequate service being provided to present clients. The social worker knows better than anyone, save clients, that the social services are not what they claim to be

> and that making it on one's own in the market is the nearest one can come in our society to having security.

Access is located within the structure of inequality in the human service delivery system. "Mainstream services" refers to those programs which offer provisions to everyone in the institution who meet general eligibility criteria, not based on membership in a particular cultural or racial group while "ethno-specific" refers to the provision of services based on general criteria which emphasize membership in a particular cultural or racial group. The intention to provide access does not necessarily mean that the reality of access to available services exists. Availability refers to the existence or provision of a service while access deals with the actual delivery of a service to the client. Access involves two components: (a) client access, the extent to which young Black offenders are able to secure needed services; (b) organizational access, the extent to which members of diverse cultural and racial groups are represented meaningfully and/or participate in the planning, development, delivery and administration of those services. Organizational access is important since it relates very closely to the purposes and effectiveness of service organizations; they must both reflect the diversity of communities they serve and be culturally sensitive to consumers who seek their assistance.

5.2 Immediate, Intermediate and Long Term Remedies (from effectiveness to impact; latent and manifest; triangulated and multi-tiered)

5.2a Agentic Identities as Intrapsychic and Intersubjective

The solution rests with consciousness, knowing ourselves and our location (Jouve 1991:8). Critical self consciousness is not an illusion but a set of connections; it is created in "social" relationships which link levels of awareness. An awareness of being different and seeing differences inspires maneuvers that remove cultural closures and facilitate intersubjectivities. Whites are asked to situate themselves in the debates and struggles that characterize the dominant culture, to ground their perceptions, and to avoid self-incarceration by empowering themselves. As Whites come to terms with their whiteness, they will understand their privilege by confronting themselves and transforming their knowledge. But, understanding seems to be in short supply. Thus, character, courage and conviction are long overdue. It is not simply a matter of Whites "moving over" and making room but of genuine pressures from within White communities to challenge fundamental social inequalities. Quite simply, one must "connect" to oneself, each other and "those others" in order to become, in the Gramscian sense, an organic intellectual (Gramsci, 1971). The organic intellectual, is someone who is positioned to have experienced—and is experiencing—the particular consequences of living from a certain social position and has articulated a set of problems associated with one's life and other people's lives. As a result, one develops a relationship of familiarity with people and has the opportunity to think through issues, in order to effect change in the oppressive structures of dominance. For too long, the silence of the white culture has been deafening in its support for systemic inequalities. Struggle and the repositioning of identities are essential especially for Whites who have long enjoyed the benefits of racism and colonialism.

The second step for staff and residents is to connect with others. A strident movement, not just token gestures of state sponsored multiculturalism is required strategically. That is, Whites need to move outside their own programme of cultural incarceration to effect social emancipation in order to transform and authenticate their lived realities. Risks are inevitable. Given that whiteness is defined in terms of power propagated by institutions of the dominant culture, how and why would the white corporate structures surrender their privilege? The dominant culture of control challenges any social change that seeks to redress the wrongs of its white corporate interests (institutional and ideological).

A more critical interrogation of power warrants an examination of advocacy and empowerment in order to provide a conceptually more comprehensive appreciation of praxis. "Communities-in-action" not community inaction invites a commitment to immediate and meaningful action. The notion of "communities-in-action" does not suffer from the vagueness inherent in the currently fashionable neo liberal discourses of "civil society" nor is it vulnerable to corporate or state-sponsored "community" constructions. Changes in legislation, administrative rules and regulations albeit long overdue are limiting.

Vigilance on the part of genuine community groups is needed in reclaiming that which more appropriately belongs to them. Action- based initiatives assist in confronting numerous barriers that include, for example: the denial of a problem; the refusal to recognize the significance of community input; a self-arrogated sense of professionalism that fears change and remains suspicious of critical inquiry; a lack of commitment to change; a dysfunctional public accountability, and a displacement of responsibility. The following changes are warranted: the activist/researcher for instance, needs to - develop an understanding of community interests that moves beyond trite public statements; increase the flow of information; field questions from <u>all</u> community groups; encourage the proactive consultation; utilize community resources; invite participation in the programme planning and development stages; select informants from a cross-section of the community who will articulate issues of inequality, rampant in the criminal justice system. According to Warren (1977: 251), even when community based organizations are transformed, they may still remain as islands in a very hostile sea. Structural barriers such as the rigid bureaucratic framework, inadequate legislation, systemic bias against any challenge to authority and ineffective accountability prevail. Briefly, praxis is a collective movement that can easily handle the rancorous resistance of authorities denouncing the cacophony of ideologically biased protagonists. Mobilization of outside support, therefore, is necessary. But, efforts to mobilize a large number of people to bring about change (Stone, 1990; Visano, 1998) are determined by several contingencies. Mobilization is shaped by ideology, an able leadership, and channels of communication or networks of cooperative relationships (ibid). Ideology sustains participation by providing a litany of invaluable rationalizations. This set of inter-related values re-socializes volunteers or activists to become receptive to new competing definitions. Additionally, ideology is a reflexive process that is directed at the self and recasts present troubles through past experiences. Ideological challenges invite, as Lofland (1985) suggests, ongoing conversions in social and personal identities. A change in consciousness emerges as long as alternative visions are explored and a distance from official accounts is maintained. By moving beyond convenience and self-serving rationales, whites need to ideologically situate themselves as committed participants. The potential for mobilization is determined by the cohesiveness of the group, strengths of opposing control agents and the resources available. For Tilly (1978), mobilization is the process of creating commitments that generate a willingness to contribute in collaborative acts of resistance. Also, the process of coalition building with: community organizations for the socially disadvantaged; feminist organizations; anti-racist action groups; labour unions; aboriginal associations; media and civil liberty organizations, progressive opposition party members of the legislatures, and so forth constitutes a formidable force. Attempts by the state and white corporate privilege to promote inter- and intra- group conflicts in an effort to construct "the community" in its own image will falter. The influence of these corporate voices cannot be dismissed and the mobilization of non-economically privileged whites is essential. The divisive logic of privilege prioritizes oppressions. Clearly, the struggles against racism, misogyny, classism, ableism, ageism and heterosexism are linked to the interrogation of the power of privileged white male corporate structures. It is therefore critical and incumbent upon all of us to make the connections with historical trends, ideological closures, and the political economy of inequality. Since power does not negotiate its own demise, multi-tiered, long-term and immediate approaches are required which are oriented towards coalition building with local and more global movements. Incremental or sudden change is enhanced with the assistance of other more existing and newly created power blocs working within and outside extant structures. The following maneuvers are helpful: the labour movement, women's movement, the revolutionary spirit of various rights' movements, student, and community activists committed to social justice in confronting "white corporate privilege"; the political arena in forcing governmental changes in regulation; the use of the market to influence policies of corporations to affect their profits: attendance at share holder meetings, boycotting services and products to proverbially "hit them where it hurts-- the profits"; the practice of "shaming" the media, politicians, churches, education into action; and the exposure of the incestuous relationship between profit and law.

5.2b Institutional/ Organizational

1. There is need for services in languages other than English and French. We need to look at alternatives to incarceration, as well as more treatment and education programs. There is a need for an increased public consciousness, tolerance and respect of a new multicultural reality; at present there is no

shared vision to reflect equal and responsible entitlements.

2. There is a need for ethno-cultural communities to be better organized so that they can articulate their own needs and resources for the criminal justice system. Corrections need to identify community agencies and make full use of their resources in the delivery of services to youths. Community organizations need to be involved to ensure representativeness, two-way communications, and they need to work with other support staff to plan effective training. Volunteer ethno-specific organizations need to focus more on survival skills, conflict resolution and community re-integration rather than on political consciousness.
3. Governments need to invest more funding for programmes that are responsive to a broader range of diversity (religious, cultural, class, age). All institutions lacked reading materials for racial minorities; in some institutions there were no reading materials for racial minorities.
4. Youth with custody orders should be involved in the decision making of programmes and activities while in custody. Youths should also be involved in the plan of care and pre-release plan.
5. All youth serving facilities lack an agenda for anti-racism that is clear, consistent and reflective of the input from various constituencies. Likewise, we lack legislative commitments to support policy initiatives. Despite the rhetoric of entitlements for all youths to public services, Black and Racial Minority youths seldom experience the benefits of entitlement. There is a need to address specific barriers to equity and access in existing youth organizations.

5.2c Anti-racist Correctional Work Defined

Racism in correctional work practice must become a social political and ideological issue. It is about removing the conditions that oppress people; there is no neutral position. It is also about the conscientisation of care receivers about their oppressive conditions. Anti-racist work in essence seeks a redistribution of power and moves away from the practices of exclusion and towards principles of equity; away from the politics of superiority and towards an ethic of sharing; away from professional elitism and towards community accountability. Anti-racist education therefore, must become an integral part of correctional work education and in-service training. A commitment to anti-racism must become an integral part of criminal justice. Many human service providers tend to have very limited knowledge and understanding of the cultural place of Blacks and other marginalized populations in society. Consequently, the standards and values of the majority culture are generally used as the normative frame of reference, the discursive apparatus, for assessing development, coping strategies, and modes of interaction, while the culture of Black communities is frequently devalued and therefore greatly misunderstood. An understanding of various cultures includes *ab initio* the assumption that there is no one homogeneous minority culture. For example, the absence of Black produced information on Black cultures and experiences leads to inaccurate and incomplete assessments of individual, family and community functions. This ultimately affects the kinds of decisions made regarding appropriate intervention strategies, and teaching practices. It cannot be assumed that, human service practitioners/social workers, both professional and para-professionals, have received adequate preparation for work with Black, Native or Asian families. Extant curricula offer minimal coverage of how white privilege exists at the expense of "marginalized" groups. The goal, therefore, should be to encourage praxis in its fundamental sense of reflection and action. The academic and social change envisioned through transformation will not be painless. Program content should be organized along a systems perspective which includes information on power imbalances and characteristics of many excluded cultures. For instance, in service delivery Black identity continues to be defined by the White, male, Christian, heterosexual and western ethos replete with an unacknowledged sense of racism. Interestingly, spirituality or even the Black church as a viable source of hope, strength and resistance has always been a focal point of community life in Canada, the US and the UK. And yet it remains ignored by youth serving facilities. Likewise, the extended family has always been a source of identity, sustenance, celebration and cultural dynamics. And yet it too remains ignored in problem solving approaches. As former street youth workers we observed that there is a tendency to refer "othered" youths to ethno specific agencies. Regrettably, ethno specific agencies are underfinanced, overworked and marginalized in ways that make effective service delivery at times impossible. All mainstream institutions need to empower youths rather than "clientize" them by encouraging: mastery and competence; establishing and utilizing a support networks; identifying positive opportunities for performance; and, by assisting youths achieve/exercise self-determination.

Correctional Officers and Classification Officers must:

- be aware of anti-racist perspectives, that is, be able to understand the significance of cultural factors without laying the responsibility for everything that goes wrong at the doors of culture;
- overcome the use of value judgements presupposing the superiority of white cultural norms;
- become conscious of the impact of institutionalised racism, sexism and homophobia on their work and commit themselves to challenging it;
- explore the impact of white power and privileges in their relationships with "minority" communities;
- draw connections between racism, and the social control elements of social work;
- end the theoretical separation between corrections and other key elements of the state, especially, immigration, education, housing, health care, welfare, and the law and order apparatus;

- avoid totalizing "the" Black experience and recognize levels of consciousness;
- work collaboratively with all communities and their agencies;
- take responsibility for their actions;
- build on strengths rooted in cultural traditions, in survival of generations in spite of racial discrimination and the stresses of migration and sometimes prosecution;
- assist youth in the development of an operational knowledge of mediation, nonviolence, cultural differences, and the role of nonviolence in their lives;
- help restore a sense of security, safety, dignity and empowerment in lives of offenders and their communities;
- get young people to understand the underlying causes and the effects of those who have been harmed, and address the needs of the parties for healing and rebuilding of healthy lifelong relationships;
- encourage the whole community, (young people, community agencies, parents, business, labor) and other groups to support and use mediation as a violence prevention initiative and to play an active role in promoting violence free communities;
- reduce young people's crime through mediation as opposed too tougher sentences, booth camps, by addressing the social problems and providing community resources as alternatives to crime;
- address barriers between young people's and authority figures in both the adult and young people's lives whom both groups stereotype, resent and resist, without fact;
- direct education and advocacy on behalf of young people in the justice system, particularly on issues that disproportionately affect young people of colour such as conditions of over-imprisonment, from the punitive measures of the Schools Safe Act, youth on young people crime, Driving While Black and racial profiling; and,
- develop communication skills to provide an alternative to violence and anger.

As part of the mediation process, teams will also make attempts to begin on a small scale the assessment of the scope of the gang and gun problems.Corrections facilities are not known to offer real opportunities for a meaningful re-integration and social adjustment for incarcerated youths.

5.2c Structural/ systemic/ ideological

Racism is an ideology propagated by institutions of the criminal justice system and supported by the values dominant culture. Racist ideas are internalized and expressed as truths. Racist images find expression in state practices and policies. The war on crime, filtered through a culture of liberalism, rewards corporate power and privileges the ethos of possessive individualism. A punitive orientation destroys the dignity of those individuals, organizations and communities defined as the "others".

Moreover, the war on youth crime especially is constructed within a framework of sophisticated surveillance, characteristic of industrial and post industrial societies. This ubiquitous regulation is legitimated by institutions that promote a particular peace that protects privacy and property. Typically in our society, privacy and property are articulated within a well respected utilitarian framework of possessive individualism. In Canada, UK and the USA, the politics of profit and the protection of privacy are interconnected conceptual projects that define basic social relations. The fabric of order as envisioned by liberalism is woven together by a wide assortment of different fibres constituting a stratified quilt. The *war on crime* exacerbates extant inequalities. "Racialized" individuals, groups and communities are treated as commodities to be rented, sold and discarded. In brief, this war is nothing more than pathology of privilege. Privilege is not only normalized but its supremacy is taken for granted. How can we deconstruct codes of thinking and critically elaborate on the conditions and consequences of the war on drugs? The answer rests with consciousness, knowing ourselves and our location (Gramsci, 1971). Is self-knowledge an illusion? Is it not created in "social" relationships which link the conveniently bifurcated criminal and official worlds? Crime has become a discursively constituted institution that patterns and reproduces a particular form of servitude. Unfortunately, the race-drug nexus is seldom explicated or understood in relation to cultural debates that confront mythologies, illusions and hypocrisies. Cultural criticism, therefore, is essential in locating the marginalized "other" (Hooks, 1981; Kristeva, 1982) and in developing a liberating pedagogy. Hegemony is central to an analysis of identity and cultural practices and how differences emerge as responses to domination, as people live out the subject positions available to them (Horkheimer,1936).

The current "war on crime", "war on gangs" and the "war on drugs" must go beyond trite rhetoric that is manipulated in order to legitimate the control of "minority youths". The social construction of a public panic is presented as a moral crisis in promoting the violence of white power. Race has always been too easily exploited by the state and its private interests in criminalizing colour thereby obfuscating prevailing racist ideologies in the treatment of crime in Canada, UK and the USA. The above wars, replete with rituals, mythologies, and metaphors, are dangerous distractions from underlying social problems. This paper highlighted the cultural contradictions of state enterprises, fuelled by exorbitant funding, careerist aspirations and mystified cowardice that tend to satisfy the demands of self serving bureaucracies. Racism and crime are also contextualized within the ethos of politics and privilege. The current fascination with "gangs " for example subverts meaningful intervention and fails to unravel the contexts, conditions and consequences of this siege mentality. The war on drugs is an insidious convenience, an opportunistic accommodation to racist ideologies. Fundamentally, the "war on gangs" is about expressions of state injustices and cultural controls; the contagious talk of war valorises processes that criminalize, militarize and medicalize the drug phenomenon. Just like the currently popular "war on terrorism", images of danger, and cultural distance are exploited to muster support, mobilize resources and justify coercive operations. Morality plays are transformed into hostile declarations of power. This image of war sanitizes differences rather than sensitizes us to the complex social problems inherent in eradicating underlying inequalities by exploiting the credulities of the misinformed. The "war on drugs", "fighting crime", "clearing the streets" of drugs and the return to "family values" are inter-related vacuous and alarmist slogans designed to seduce and implicate an impressionable audience into supporting an insidious political agenda. The pragmatic interests of the powerful are buried in the language of fear and security, rehearsed routinely in public trials. In turn, public perceptions frame, inform and fan state intrusions. These crime waves and moral panics are generated by self-appointed guardians of public morality who attempt to identify the emergence of a problem and suggest action to be taken (Taylor, 1981:48-56).

6. From the Exclusion of Conclusions towards the Introductions of Inclusions

Problems in the justice system can never be resolved by liberal tinkering. Instead, new rules of conduct within cultures of accountability, equality and authentic communities are long warranted. These rules are informed by a series of interconnected issues. Accordingly, a number of questions need to be asked not only of criminal justice agencies but also of ourselves.

1. To what extent are we connected to a project of overcoming inequalities?
2. What do we individually and collectively want from and what can we contribute to change?
3. What kind of sacrifices, if any, are we prepared to make?

These questions are related to anti-racist plans of action which also invite us to ask:

1. What is our perception of the problem as we consider cultural elements, such as prevailing belief systems, customs, values, community involvement, self-concept, and the role of significant others?
2. How are our respective capacities for change defined and determined by our particular location vis a vis privilege?
3. What is the motivation for change? What elements of strength and sacrifice are to found in the everyday life situation?
4. What resistance to change can be identified? How are barriers to change internalized? What are the ways in which racism might be related to other forms of oppression? To what extent have we as a society developed and communicated the tools necessary for social justice?

As Martin Luther King Jr. suggested that the "ultimate measure of a man is not where he stands in moments of comfort and convenience, but where he stands at times of challenge and controversy" (1963:20).

References

Anand, Sanjeev S., 1999 *Preventing Youth Crime: What Works, What Doesn't and What It All Means for Canadian Juvenile Justice Policy*, 25 Queen's L.J.177-249; Quicklaw Version, 1-47.

Bell, D. and K. Lang. 1985. "The Intake Dispositions of Juvenile Offenders" *Journal of Research in Crime and Delinquency* 22(4):309-328.

Benac Nancy 2001 American justice is not blind when wielding death penalty: Area, race, education, age, gender play roles May. 8. A13 Toronto Star

Bishop,D. and C. Frazier. 1988. "The Influence of Race in Juvenile Justice Processing" *Journal of Research in Crime and Delinquency* 25(3):242-263.

BJS 2004 Prison Statistics June 30 2004. Bureau of Justice Statistics Online at http://www.ojp.usdoj.gov/bjs/prisons.htm (Accessed July 2005)

Bunyan, T. 1999 "The Cycle of UK Racism: Stop and Search and Imprisonment" 9 Statewatch 1.

Citron, Abraham 1972 *The Rightness Of Whiteness* Detroit: Wayne State University, Office of Urban Education, College of Education

Coelho, E. 1989 *Caribbean Students in Canadian Schools* Toronto: Carib-Can Publishers.

Crow, I. 1994 "Black People and Criminal Justice in the UK". In Baker, David (ed.) *Reading Racism and the Criminal Justice System.* Canadian Scholars Press, Toronto

Davis, Angela. 1988 *An Autobiography* International Publishers, New York.

Department of Justice. 1993 "Toward Safer Communities: Violent and Repeat Offending by Young People". Ottawa: Young Offenders Project, Department of Justice.

Fanon, Franz. 1976 *The Wretched of the Earth.* Grove, New York.

Gandy, John. 1992 Judicial Interim Release Hearings That Resulted in Detention Prior to Trial Of Youths Charged under the Young Offenders Act in Three Ontario Cities. Toronto: The Child, Youth and Family Policy Research Centre.

Galper,J. 1975 *The Politics of Social Services.* Englewood Cliffs, N.J.: Prentice-Hall

Gorden, P. 1988 "Black People and the Criminal Law: Rhetoric and Reality" *International Journal of Sociology of Law*

Gramsci, A. 1971 *Prison Notebooks: Selections* Translated By Q. Hoare and G. Smith New York: International Publishers.

Herbert, P, 1986 "The Colour of Justice", Law Union, UK, unpublished paper

Hernton, C.C. 1971 *Coming Together: Black Power, White Hatred and Sexual Hang-Ups*, New York: Random House.

hooks, b. 1981 *Aint I A Woman: Black Women and Feminism* Boston: South End Press.

Horkheimer, M. 1936 *Critical Theory: Selected Essays* NY: Continuum

Jouve, N.W. 1991 White Woman Speaks With Forked Tongue: Criticism as Autobiography London: Routledge

Kristeva, Julia. 1982 Powers of Horror: An Essay on Abjection New York: Columbia University Press.

Landau, W. and Nathan 1983 Selecting Delinquents for Cautioning in the London Metropolitan Area" *British Journal of Criminology* 23 (2).

Lee, J. and L. A. Visano. 1981 "Official Deviance in the Legal System" In H. Ross (ed.) *Law and Deviance* Beverly Hills: Sage.

Lewis, Stephen. 1992 "The Lewis Report". Office of the Premier of Ontario. Lewis, Stephen. Report to the Premier on Racism in Ontario (Summer)

Lieber, M. 1994 "A Comparison of Juvenile Court Outcomes for Native Americans, African Americans, and Whites" *Justice Quarterly* 11 (June) 2.

Mauer, M. 1999 *Race To Incarcerate* New York: The New Press, at 124-125.

Lorde, Audrey. 1984 *Sister Outsider* Freedom, Ca. The Crossing Press Freedom Series

Malcolm, X. 1970 *By Any Means Necessary* Pathfinders, New York.

Mitchell, A. and G. Abbate. 1994 "Crime-Race Data Laden With Hazards" *Toronto Star* (June 11) A1, A6, A7.

Newport, F. 1999 "Racial Profiling is Seen as Widespread, Particularly Among Young Black Men. Gallop Poll Releases, December 9. Online at www.gallup.com/poll/releases.

Perlman, R. 1975. *Consumers and Social Services* New York: J. Wiley and Sons.

Petrocelli, Matthew, Piquero, Alex R. & Smith, Michael R. 2003 "Conflict theory and racial profiling: An Empirical Analysis of Police Traffic Stop Data" (31) *Journal of Criminal Justice 1.*

Pope, C. and W. Feyerherm. 1990. "Minorities and the Juvenile Justice System". *Draft Report for the Office of Juvenile Justice and Delinquency*. US Department of Justice.

Report , 1996 *Racism Behind Bars, Final Report*: Queen's Printer, Toronto.

Ruck M.D and S. Wortley, 2002. "Racial and Ethnic Minority High School Perceptions of School Disciplinary Practices: A Look at Some Canadian Findings" 31(3) Journal of Youth and Adolescence 185 at 186, 194.

Solomos, J. 1988 *Black Youth, Racism and the State - the Politics of Ideology and Polity*. Cambridge University Press, Cambridge.

Statistics Canada. 2001 Children and Youth in Canada. Canadian Centre for Justice Statistics Profile Series: Ottawa.

Tanovich , D. 2004 Why race matters on sentencing. *Toronto Star* A21 Feb 25

Tanovich, D. 2002 "Using the Charter to Stop Racial Profiling: The Development of an Equality-based Conception of Arbitrary Detention" 40 Osgoode Hall L.J. 145 (QL).

Taylor, I. 1981 "Crime Waves in Post-War Britain" *Contemporary Crises* 5, 1:43-62.

Thornton, C. 1999 "Racism and the War on Drugs", The Second International Conference on Drug War Prisoners, *Toronto* March 20.

Toronto Star, 5 November 1994:1

Visano, L. 1988 "Equality and Multiculturalism" (with R. Doyle) *Journal of Law and Social Policy* vol. 3 (Jan.): 21-35.

Visano, L. 1998 *Crime and Culture*. Canadian Scholars Press, Toronto..

Visano, L. 1996 "War on Drugs: From The Politics of Punishment to the Prospects of Peacekeeping" *Addictions: An International Research Journal* vol. 1 (Fall): 81-95.

Visano, L. 2002 "The Impact of Whiteness on the Culture of Law: from theory to practice". In C. Levine-Rasky (ed.) *Working Through Whiteness* SUNY Press, pp 209-237.

Wortley, Scott. 1998 *Under Suspicion: Race and Criminal Justice Surveillance in Canada*, Toronto: Centre of Criminology, University of Toronto.

Washington Post, 27 February 1990 A3.

Youth Criminal Justice Act. Department of Justice Ottawa. 2003.

PART E

CRIMINOLOGICAL FRONTIERS

19. A Mood to Crime: A Critical Phenomenology of Youth

Paul Brienza

1. Introduction

This paper seeks to accomplish two interrelated tasks. First, the foundations of criminological theory in a rationalist action framework are questioned. The schema of pain, pleasure, and self-gratification, employed by such recent theorists as Hirschi, ignores the affectual bases of criminal action. If the 'deviant actor' is only understood within algorithms of means and ends, we miss a large motive of behaviour which is the non-rational or emotive. That is, criminal acts always occur within 'contexts of mood' that are given in particular settings and historical processes. These moods can give existential meaning to the acts that are performed, both in groups and in the individual psyche.

Second, we apply these gains in perspective and nuance and apply them to a critical analysis of youth crime. In this sense mood as well as spatial and temporal characteristics are of paramount importance. Boredom is a connecting mood that ties historicality with the immediacy of action. Youth are motivated by a 'waiting state' that often explodes into modes of action that are meant to break, through explosion, the banalities of a everyday 'waiting' for life to begin.

This approach is meant to critically question the structures of criminological thought and open its methodological approaches to inquiries that focus on immediate lived circumstances within a larger historical and cultural process. It is in this sense that we can speak, theoretically and methodologically, of a 'Phenomenology of Crime' as a unique and fruitful perspective within Criminology.

2. Method and Mood

2.1 *Crime and the Rationality of Action*

Studies of crime have tended to focus on the way that criminality, in terms of personality and/or environment, is determined in rational ways. The 'criminal' is seen to exist within a constellation of applicable models of action. From this context emerges the idea that purposiveness is a coherent part of the criminal event. The individual is aware of the consequences of his or her action in terms of a series of explicit steps that are geared towards a goal that is advantageous to the actor(s). Gain is a pre-determined rationale for the criminal event. This is not a new development by any means. Utilitarianism, as defined by either Bentham or Mill, is about this adequate planning that places risks, consequences, and tasks into a certain type of linearity. Hirschi and Gottfredson (1994:6) for example, claim in a traditional utilitarian frame that: "human action is oriented to the pursuit of pleasure and the avoidance of pain." The pursuit of pleasure, in a criminal frame, is the result of the drive towards gratification. The criminal is seen to have an inadequate adaptation to the determinants of pleasure or gratification in our type of society. They are unable to channel their desires for pleasures into legitimate or socially accepted venues such as status or success and, as a result, they are: "less likely to feel the restraining influence of the social and legal consequences of their behaviour" (ibid, 7).

A universal understanding of human action is the grounding of this perspective. There is a line of continuity between the 'average' or 'normal' individual and the criminal in that they both use rational techniques and thinking patterns in order to attain essentially the same goals. Humans are dominated by the linear attainment of pre-determined goods or pleasures. Criminals deviate from this linearity in their inability to choose appropriate means to their ends. They mistake their desire for pleasure with the spontaneity or impulsiveness that seems to be a part of their inherent personal disposition. If some wander into this lifestyle in an unsuspecting manner, then those who are able to break the cycle of recidivism, the reformed criminal, will be the ones who have adapted to the appropriate mechanisms of society and will leave their criminality behind. Those who do not, however, will remain in this perpetual cycle of immediacy without recognizing that gratification must be postponed; these are, according to restraint theory, the *real* criminals.

Restraint theories, like Classicism, Positivism, Functionalism, and many other theoretical perspectives, begin with the rationalism of human conduct as a primary grounding for their investigations. Rationality, and the logical pursuit of goals, is a given, an *a priori* of criminal conduct against which it is evaluated and judged. This remains an unquestioned assumption of criminological research; it is the starting point of inquiry from which theory construction builds upon. Even interactionists, who claim to examine the social psychological bases of human action, talk of the negotiations and problem-solving techniques of criminals that fit in, to a large extent, with this larger rationalist frame of reference. This frame pre-determines *interpretation*; it relies on the pre-given assumptions of a 'natural' scientist while ignoring those very *naturalized* settings in which crime, as an event, emerges from. Rationality, in individual conduct, is an assumption, a set interpretation of a given reality. This study seeks to break this rationalistic 'stranglehold' that limits the ability of criminological inquiry to see the phenomena and events that it so desperately wants to capture and understand.

2.2 *Mood and Alternate Forms of Inquiry*

When humans interact with their social and material contexts they do not necessarily evaluate these settings in an immediately rational way. Often the first response is what we would term as 'emotional'. Our approach is to see this as relating to the total constellation of action and its responses at the moment of the criminal event. This *momentarism* is not something that fades as the rational forms take over but is something that lingers over the entire context of past, present, and future law-breaking activity. Our attempt to grasp criminality as a human event means that we want to approach the total environment of the event, to encircle it with its specifically *naturalized* qualities. These qualities are expressed in terms of feeling and mood. These moods, which also have an important social grounding and context for their genesis, are the assumptions that lie behind much criminal as well as legitimate conduct. This means that we need to return to the 'experience' of crime to what Carlo Sini (1993:.100) refers as the "originary relations" of events. These originary relations are themselves the grounding for our objective or speculative knowledge of things. The human world of experience, with its moods and feelings, is what makes these objectifications of our sciences possible precisely because they are not simply about 'things' but about actors feeling their way through an often hostile or confusing environment. Few would argue with Sini when he claims that mood is a constant of our experience. If this is the case, then mood is an under-researched aspect of criminality. The reason for this is most likely to be found in the fact that mood-as-experience is difficult, if not impossible, to grasp as an object within the traditional philosophical *copula*. There is no clear and easy demarcation between subject and object because mood, and experience in general, is about the blurring of these methodological lines, which are considered essential to good social science. Mood is something which happens in mysterious ways. It often impacts the setting in more of an 'atmospheric' presence. It is equivalent to Merleau-Ponty's (1962) notion of *sens*. The French word expresses the way mood is both *directional*, that is leading to certain events, perceptions, interpretations, etc. and the way it engenders *meaning*. That is, mood's subjective meaning is not a possession or accomplishment of individual interpretation that is worked out by the subject. The setting, cultural, historical, interactional, economic, as well as all other social and psychological forms which impinge on the atmosphere of the situation, lead to the likelihood of particular responses in particular contexts, and lead to particular consequences. This *directionality* is always related to the interpretations that *can* be given to the material or phenomenological ecology as well as the cultural and psychic valuations that occur afterwards. The body, for example, leads to certain set material senses of meaning as well as allowing for great latitude in the very structure, discourse, and pragmatic creativity in the response to this materiality. Mood is such a phenomenological materiality. Invariably, we are 'thrown' into contexts of action that are inhabited by feeling states which we did not create. These moods are at the root of our responses and can, as many social scientists would agree, lead to more elaborate forms of conceptualization. However, as Sini (1993:100) argues: "Mood goes up and down, comes and goes, but in its own way is always there."

Mood, therefore, stands as the emotive, non-purposive, immediate backdrop to the further conceptualizations of a rational action model. Rational action emerges from this context and, as a result, imbues it with its own meanings and frames that can only be understood within a pre-assumptive grasping of the whole atmosphere. This backdrop emerges, in itself, through the vicissitudes of history and cultural formation. A time period or epoch is characterized by certain affective modalities of encountering the world which are determined, in their turn, by the immediacy of the ecology as well as the development of the human being's place in the world and his or her encounter with the totality of meaning that ensues. This is the immediate or 'radically empirical' confrontation with our social context; it provides us with the initial impetus for action and the qualities, colours, and tones of that engagement.

2.3 Nietzsche and the Affect(s) of Nihilism

In the late 19th century, philosophers and social theorists began to question the affective assumptions behind the contemporary or modern situation. Kierkegaard spoke of the dread and anxiety associated with the 'meaninglessness' of modern psychological conflict. On a larger scale, Nietzsche began to articulate the affective background to the heights of modernity and what 'mood' or 'state of mind' this placed the individual in. For Nietzsche, humans, in contemporaneity, were dealing with the breakdown of all the traditional sureties of previous ages. Particularly, the Enlightenment threw the existence of God into deep question and disoriented all prior meaning structures and hierarchies. This, for Nietzsche, was expressed through nihilism. Nihilism signifies the end of those concepts and beliefs that once oriented humans within a universe of meaning; in short, it is the end of *metaphysics*: "man has lost faith in his own value when no infinitely valuable whole works through him..."(Nietzsche, 1968:12). This means that humans can no longer interpret the world in terms of 'aim', 'unity' or 'truth'. Importantly, for Nietzsche, values become inverted and turn against the very life that they originally sought to strengthen; they no longer guide action but turn against it. Life, therefore, becomes difficult and problematic at a spiritual level as individuals begin to become unsure and confused about their world and what they believed lay behind it and bound it all together. Nietzsche makes a further distinction between *active* and *passive* nihilism. In terms of our analysis this will prove to be crucial. The active component of nihilism turns toward *anxiety* and in the will to destroy. In contrast, the passive aspect turns inward and seeks to not will or remove the responsibility and fate of its will from its world of action (Nietzsche 1968:17). The latter sense is best seen in forms of depression or *boredom*. The individual is repulsed by the space for his or her action and realizes that it cannot ground this action in anything cohesive. As a result, the actor *waits*, lingers, and is in-limbo. Modern individuals, according to the argument of this study, vacillate between these two poles of affectivity; one is *manic* while the other is *depressive*. In terms of mood, there is a psychic vibration and dance between the poles of *boredom* and *anxiety*. Flurries of activity are followed by decreased energy. The spaces we inhabit reflect and signify this vacillation in their ability to bring these moods into dialogue with our own engagement with any setting and context. We must begin from this historico-phenomenological assumption which grounds in real and concrete interaction with our environment. The affects of boredom and anxiety become materialities of our temporal and spatial existence that must be accounted for in terms of a "thick description" (Merleau-Ponty,1962). We turn, in order to get our journey underway, to Georg Simmel and an analysis of our metropolitan life that gets to some of the socio-logical roots of these moods or affects and their historicality.

2.4 Simmel and the Materiality of Boredom

Georg Simmel, the German social philosopher and, as many have claimed, one of the founders of sociological theory and inquiry, examined the affectual bases of modern life as it was experienced in the metropolis. The metropolis was one of the most extravagant and troublesome expressions of modernity. The large city, such as Simmel's Berlin, was inhabited by hundreds of thousands or millions of people and it was able to establish a type of harmony that was geared around the differences of the citizenry. The capitalist explosion and the correlative rise in productive capacities, allowed many individuals to live in the same space while at the same time taking part in diverse activities, labours, and idea-constellations. The metropolis was inhabited by artists, industrialists, politicians, and bureaucrats and each had the potential for different forms of individuality. For Simmel, the large city made the modern battle between individuality and society a question that all had to face because of the environment itself. The city, while composed of limitless diversities, also operated above or behind each individual as a type of "social-technological mechanism" (Simmel,1971:324).Parenthetically, it is important to remember that the other so-called 'founders' of sociology, Weber, Durkheim, and Marx, also approached an understanding of affectivity in the rise of modernity. Specifically, Weber, in his analysis of Puritanism/Protestantism and its effects on the rise of capitalism, recognized the pre-determinative importance of the affective or emotional reaction to the theological doctrine of 'predestination'. This doctrine made the believer unsure and uncertain about being able to discover 'signs' in this world that would indicate his or her salvation in the next life. This pre-disposed the Protestant to a certain excessive amount of anxiety-driven energy that was bound, according to Weber, to impact dramatically their interaction with others and the world. Unfortunately, Weber does not significantly theorize this insight in the same in-depth way that we find in Simmel. However, a study of this Weberian engagement with 'mood' and affectivity would, most likely, uncover many important aspects of our understanding of Weber. This machinery required human action and psychic energy in order for it to thrive. As a result, the human question, in the metropolis, became one of adaptation to a particular techno-environment. Therefore, Simmel (1971, 325) sought to uncover the personality: "in its adjustment to the forces that lie outside it." The metropolis is characterized by its frenzy, by its speed and rapidity of motion. Rapidity of motion meant, for Simmel, a rapidity of mood; that is, the individual was prone to be thrown into diverse and ever-changing alterations of affectivity as scenes, spaces, and times interacted quickly: "The psychological foundation, upon which metropolitan individuality is erected, is the intensification of emotional life due to the swift and continuous shift of external and internal stimuli…"(ibid). In contrast, small town life is characterized by a: "habitual, more smoothly flowing rhythm…"(ibid). In this environment, customs and hierarchies that are clear and direct maintain a set of adaptive parameters for the individual that have been tried and tested for generations. The metropolitan individual needs to survive and develop a daily flow with his or her setting. This flow means that the individual: "creates a protective organ for itself against the profound disruption with which the fluctuations and discontinuities of the external milieu threaten it" (Simmel, 1971, 326).Rationality, as a result, is a form of adaptation. Unlike many who followed, therefore, Simmel was able to see rational action as a type of adaptation that was coherent with a metropolitan scene. The ability to disguise emotions and to ignore the surface life of these moods was the ability of a personality that was looking for an appropriate way of surviving in the environment. The "depths of personality" were hidden and obscured in order to protect individuality from the churning machinery of the new life-world. Intellectualism and abstraction, as best exemplified by money, were defenses and are, as a result, not inherent motivations. Social relations, in order to be understood in their multiplicity and complexity, had to be viewed as something quantifiable and as developments of an "obligatory association"(ibid, 327). A historical form of repression emerges and comes to dominate the modern individual:

> Punctuality, calculability, and exactness, which are required by the complications and extensiveness of metropolitan life are not only most intimately connected with its capitalistic and intellectualistic character but also colour the context of life and are conducive to the exclusion of those irrational, instinctive, sovereign human traits and impulses which originally seek to determine the form of life from within...(ibid, 328-9).

The repression of elements that emerge 'from within' the individual lead to a type of "blasé attitude" that dominates the interactions that occur within the city and to an: "indifference toward the distinctions between things" (ibid 329). The meaning and value of differences and perspectives become impossible to deal with, because of their everyday rapidity, and, as a result, are increasingly experienced as meaning-less. Like Nietzsche, Simmel has led us to what would seem to be the ultimate dilemma of modern life. The body and mind respond to this chaos of modern life by: "renouncing the response to them" (ibid, 330). With this 'renunciation of response' and the devaluing of the 'objective world', the personality is itself dragged into the quagmire of distance and reserve, not only to the surroundings, but also to the experience of others. Other individuals are approached with reserve and suspicion as the individual is constantly trying to find stable ground for *any* type of sustained action. Antipathy and dissociation, according to Simmel, is a *naturalized* product of this blasé attitude. This is what we would refer to as, in general agreement with Heidegger, *boredom*. Over-stimulation leads to a defensive shutdown of the nervous and bodily faculties; the individual is prone to *renunciation* and *chronic repression* as an adaptive measure.

The individual feels the presence of the overbearing mechanisms of the techno-machine-like metropolis like no other time in history. In an almost paradoxical fashion, however, he or she is left to his or her own devices. This metropolitan individual is freer then any other and seeks to express his or her difference in more radical forms. In fact, the dominance of the techno-machine forces the individual into more extreme types of expression in order to genuinely feel the presence of his or her mark in the social. The individual explodes against the shutdown of his or her faculties with greater conflictual, dissociative, and charged ardour. *Boredom can only be overcome through greater feats driven by anxious energy*. This energy cannot compete with the accomplishments of objective culture since progress, cultivation, and spiritual advancement are now greatly distanced from the scope of individual action. Therefore, the individual is more likely to seek the boldness of action that, in many ways, moves away from values and drifts towards, what Nietzsche (1968: 12) would refer to as "the will that would rather will nothing then to not will at all". The subject is condemned to both *freedom* and *meaninglessness*.

Simmel provides us with a unique perspective on the development of modernity. Its ingenuity lies in its ability to combine "external" history with "internal history" (Simmel. 1971:339).Individuality and social, political, and economic conditions, are seen to be interrelated in the most profound ways. The modern psyche, its moods, feelings, emotions, and the very techniques of survival, have their historical structural linkages and determinants. At the same time, the internalizations and repressions of modern subjectivities have effects on the institutions of public society. A certain mentality is indicative of a society while that society has a representative psychological form. In other words, the subject and object of traditional epistemology fades into the opacity of relationality. Such an analysis reminds us that any serious and consistent attention to the behaviour of human beings throws us into a spiral of relationality between the multitudinous perspectives that are taken by all actors in every action context. Mood is a type of *methodological* tool that takes us to the space between subject and object. In Simmel we see how mood is experienced as a product of structural developments through time. It is not, therefore, a possession of individuality. It is the atmosphere, context, and space in which our actions unfold and signify the *immediacy of meaning* within these scenarios. We are 'thrown' or 'condemned' to these contexts and they are the places where meaning is gained and questioned. As a result, it is the place where crime attains its meaning and where we, along with the actors themselves, question its meaning.

3. Boredom and the Phenomenology of Youth Crime

The previous sections have sought to prove the methodological and theoretical importance of the study of mood. We have followed the development of our theory through the lineages of modern forms of questioning. In fact, coming to terms with mood as a key to experience is correlated to the questioning that intensifies in late modernity. In this section, we seek to apply these insights to an understanding of youth crime. Youth, therefore, are not seen as objects of inquiry but as creative actors engaging with a particular historical formation. Like Simmel's city-dweller, who becomes prone to a blasé attitude combined with more radical forms of expression, youth vacillate between moods of *boredom* and *anxiety*. In fact, the two moods are co-present and inform action at all points of the criminal event. Boredom, however, is an adaptive capacity that is present within the context of urban environments as an architectonic of the landscape. The streets, alleys, and suburbs, *provoke* and *encourage* reactions of withdrawal that throw participants into structural conditions of emotional hue. At this point, our question is: 'Why is boredom a significant factor *for*-youth in particular?' The answer to this question, we feel, is to be found in the unique *temporal* relations that youth are thrown into with the dawn of adolescence. In order to understand these temporal relations, we will briefly turn to Heidegger, who unlike many other thinkers, has placed the temporal dimension of human existence at the forefront of any depth analysis.

3.1 Heidegger and the Analytics of Boredom

Like Simmel and Nietzsche, Heidegger also identified the co-present vacillation of modern mood between anxiety and boredom. *Being and Time*, published in 1927, went into detail in its explication of the problem of anxiety and fear. No more then a year afterwards, Heidegger delivered a series of lectures, which have been preserved and published as *The Fundamental Concepts of Metaphysics*. These lectures contain a series of important analyses of the *attunement* of boredom; that is, Heidegger examines the throwness of this mood and how we can excavate its depth within an everyday context. Fundamentally, boredom is entwined with time; time moves through this mood as its primary method of orienting and creating meaning. The temporal nature of boredom is present, for Heidegger, within the very German word. *Langeweile* refers to 'a while' which extends or lingers. The 'while' represents a significant component of boredom since it expresses the temporal stretching or our feeling of being under the dominion of time. The first form of boredom refers to this 'waiting' which, for Heidegger, could be seen in our impatient desire to eliminate the space of time between the wait itself and the arrival that we so long for. A train that is late reminds us of our inability to control the flow of time; in this state we are bound by the desire for an arrival, an-*other* time which lies in the future and is beyond our control: "We fight *against* the progress of time which is slowing down and is *too* slow for us, and which in boredom *holds us in limbo*. We fight against this peculiar vacillating and dragging of time" (Heidegger, 1995:97). In this particular state we *fight against* this dragging of time by 'passing the time'. We 'pass the time' through *taking action* against this dragging and lingering. Our action in-itself is, therefore, unimportant since this is action that finds its meaning in *moving-against* a temporal relation to our environment.

The second form of boredom, according to Heidegger, transforms 'passing the time' into a *public* event. This state is particularly perplexing for the individual because we: "find *nothing that is boring*"(ibid, 114). That is, we are thrown back unto ourselves because we cannot identify the particular object, event, or person which is boring us; the boredom seems to reside at a deeper level. This type of boredom is insidious because it inhabits activity at an everyday level and is often present while something else is already going on. For example, as Heidegger claims, it could be found in an uneasy feeling at a social event that cannot be easily labeled or identified by us. We are bored at a party even though we are not necessarily *bored by* the surroundings or company present. The recognition of this form of boredom would take us to a fundamental questioning of ourselves and reveal much of our primary relation to the world. The final and third form of boredom is about this very recognition and the struggle with the attitude of indifference that emerges from such an understanding. The individual would have to ask about the emptiness of beings and of his or her relation to what is present-at-hand or the objects that entail meanings. Such an analysis, for Heidegger (ibid, 161) leads from the analysis of boredom, as a particular mood or *attunement*, to an "*essential questioning of Dasein itsel.*" In other words, the analysis of mood leads us to an important insight into our present relation to the world. It uncovers something essential to our environment and how we seek to establish a meeting ground between it and ourselves through quite everyday activities. What is essential to understanding our world, including the nature of criminality, is not to be sought in our structured methodologies and frames of view but in our searching for the places and points, in daily life, where the very meanings that we seek are creatively born.

3.2 A Phenomenology of Youth

Youth distinguish themselves, in their essential sense, in the way they inhabit our social spaces. If we apply a temporal analysis we find that youth occupy a space that is characterized by its *in-betweeness*. Youth, through our obvious and conscious cultural characterization of it, is a transitionary phase to adulthood; it is the place where adults emerge into our civil society. Adulthood is built upon the characteristic bruises of a previous battle. Age, in our culture, is signified as survival of a battle fought on a different day. The battle is not won, however, until the immature is dethroned from a position of dominance and the rational producer takes his or her place. Adolescence represents a place where the personality or character is undergoing a series of formative experiences that will allow for the development of the appropriate survival skills. The human adaptive systems, that is, the body, the organs, the psychic systems, are all learning how to adapt to this particular cultural, social, and economic environment. In childhood the contrast is the avoidance of confrontation witnessed in the usually protective parental attitude, which seeks to, in some sense, shelter the child from aspects of the world. The adolescent, on the other hand, is thrown into the need for preparation; *thoughts perceptibly turn towards the future*. Youth are told to 'think of their future' and to 'choose a career'. This experience seems to have universality in our culture since it seems to travel through social structures of inequality. That is, both working class and middle class youth are prone to the stresses of the transition to adulthood and both feel the need to turn their attention towards the future. The future, however, is undefined and it is shrouded in the veils of opacity; it seems as if its clarity is always beyond the reach of the probing young mind. Because of this inability to grasp the nature of one's own possibilities one is aptly prone to experience a *crisis of meaning*. This means that youth may be closer to the experience of nihilism because of their immediate and uncertain encounter with the nature of their own possibilities. The future orientation lacks the possible solidification of adulthood and exists within a space of uncertainty.

Boredom, in youth, is experienced as this lingering or waiting that is almost a 'waiting for life to begin'. Life is being formed in the cauldron of youth and yet the 'waiting' is a cause for constant anxiety. Beneath this immediacy of the 'being-bored-with-and-by', is the more profound sense of boredom and emptiness that Heidegger reminds us of. Therefore, we would likely find a series of distractions away from the emptiness and towards a form of expression that marks itself against the expanse of Simmel's techno-machine. Action *as action*, that is, action-in-itself, becomes a way of differentiating the identity of youth from all the formal quantifications of the social that surround him of her. The recognition of profound boredom is rare in a society that preaches work, and action in general, as a solution to these deep questions. Therefore, 'angst', boredom, and anxiety are disguised in modes of worldly behaviour even though the deepest nothing lingers underneath:

> The more we live, the more life
> is disgusting
>
> Life is black
> It is a black hole,
> Dirt, an impurity,
> A stain on polluted earth.
>
> I would like to disappear
> in a black hole
>   and come out
>   the other side
>   where all is beautiful.
>   No suicide.
>   No violence.
>   No pollution.
>   No war.
>   No black (Bibby and Postorski 1992:.78).

As this poem, written by a teenager, reveals, adolescence is characterized by this vacillation and questioning of one's surroundings and relations with others. The poem clearly identifies a 'hidden depth' to our social concerns which speak to the crisis of meaning. This poem by sixteen-year-old girl from Montreal is particularly noteworthy because of its self-conscious nihilism. Words like the 'black', and the 'hole' speak to the feeling of the nothing. This teenager, however, is fortunate because of her ability to self-consciously express this feeling in a creative way. The author consciously uses the metaphors of 'nothingness', desperation, and opacity. The world is, at the level of meaning that the poem aims at testifying to, chaotic, fragmented, and disjointed. A phenomenological analysis reveals to us that underlying these persistent problematics of meaning is a fundamental *experience of* time. Moods determine our first and primary understanding of time. Youth, like cultures and societies on a larger scale, are products of their *time within time;* that is, different historical epochs engender different perspectives on time. Our contemporary society is a particularly rapid one; as a result, an adolescent place within our time means that we are stretched between past, present, and future in certain ways. Youth, therefore, occupy a temporal 'no-man's' land between adulthood and childhood and this, in turn, adds a particular temporal dimension to their existence. Boredom, for example, reveals itself as a type of temporal location in a social world that uncovers, in a phenomenological sense, the plight of nihilism that speaks to the desire to deal with possibilities within a significant future orientation. Simultaneously, youth are 'thrown' into a range of choices and perspectives by their *history or past.* The present, on the other hand, is the 'space-between' past and future, between conditions, necessity, or history, and possibilities, hope, and freedom. However, possibilities and freedom, entail a direct encounter with our relation with nothingness; that is, we come to terms with our potentialities and limits. Fear emerges in this encounter with what we are unsure about, as Heidegger (1996: 174) claims: "The fact that what is threatening is *nowhere* characterizes what *angst* is about....it is already "there"-and yet nowhere." Boredom, as a primary mood, testifies to this encounter because of its temporal lingering and, for our purposes, because of its need to act against the emptiness revealed; in other words, boredom represents the *time that we seek to engulf and fill with action.*

3.3 Youth, Crime, and Boredom

Youth are *brought to* crime because of their creative attempts at dealing with their temporal location. Moods, not rational behaviour, are the primary orientation to this unarticulated experience. Crime, therefore, is a creative expression of the desire to solve these *problems of meaning.* Boredom reveals these problematics of temporality in their difference and vastness and demands a response that engenders a *filling-in* of this space of the 'in-between' with a proactive reaction against the very futility of symbolic action. Crime, for youth, 'fills in' the space with a creative response that is seen in the criminal event itself. Juvenile delinquency symbolizes this attempt at placing destiny within the purview of intentional conduct forcing it to reside in the context of an individual's or group's solution to an *affectual state.* Like the subcultural theorists, therefore, we see youth crime as a solution to environmental constraints and context (Cohen, 1971:51ff). Cohen (ibid, 25), for example, began to see this 'play of meaning' and was able to identify its non-rationalistic tendencies: "What we see when we look at the delinquent subculture....is that it is *non-utilitarian, malicious,* and *negativistic.*" However, he still sought to place it within a rational longing for status and recognition and did not seek to expose the affectual bases of this feeling. In contrast, our analysis has brought us to a deeper understanding of the *non-utilitarian, malicious,* and *negativistic* aspects of youth crime. Such an understanding is necessary to identifying the appropriate vacillations, responses, and creative expressions of crime within the mood-contexts of the *time of youth*.

References

Bibby, Reginald and Postorski, Donald C. 1992 *Teen Trends: A Nation in Motion*. Stoddart Publishing. Toronto.

Cohen, Albert K. 1971 *Delinquent Boys: The Culture of the Gang*. Free Press. New York.

Heidegger, Martin. 1995 *The Fundamental Concepts of Metaphysics*. Indiana University Press. Bloomington.

Heidegger Martin 1996 *Being and Time*. Joan Stambaugh (trans.), State University of New York Press, Albany.

Hirschi, Travis and Gottfredson, Michael.1994 *Contemporary Criminological Theory*. Francis T. Cullen and Velmer S. Burton Jr. (Eds.) New York University Press. New York.

Merleau-Ponty, Maurice. 1962 *Phenomenology of Perception*. Routledge. London.

Nietzsche, Friedrich. 1968 *The Will to Power*. Translated by Walter Kaufinan and R.J. Hollingdale. Vintage.

Simmel, Georg. 1971 "The Metropolis and Mental Life". *George Simmel: On Individuality and Social Forms*. Donald N. Levine (Ed.). University of Chicago Press. Chicago.

Sini Carlo. 1993 *Images of Truth: From Sign to Symbol,* Massimo Verdicchio (trans.), Humanities Press, New Jersey.

20. The Significance of Simmel's Stranger and Benjamin's Flaneur to Interpretive Criminology

Andreas Georgiou

"In the whole, as in each detailed part, theoretical study consists everywhere equally of unerring devotion to the actual, and of constantly renewed value-judgments". Max Horkheimer (cited in Stammer, 1971; 53)

1. Introduction

In modernity in general, and in the modern city in particular, there is an experience of remoteness different in quality from anything that went before. The socio-economic transformations, movin—to refer to Ferdinand Tönnies' categories—from "community" in the direction of "society", constitute a world in which life on the margins becomes a complex and difficult dialectic of distance and engagement. There are those who become friends with 'Haros' (death); there are those who live in melancholy and die of a broken heart. Those who have been most remote have suffered most, at least in consciousness. And yet some few of these manage as part of their life on the margins to articulate the experience of modernity that, in some ways, appears only from the perspective of their '*distant engagement*'. Two such individuals are Walter Benjamin and Georg Simmel, both of whom attempt to grasp and communicate a cultural-sociological understanding of the estranging modern world and of the individual living within it.

Both Benjamin and Simmel examined the affectual bases of modern life as it was experienced in the modern metropolis. The large city, such as Simmel's Berlin or Benjamin's Paris, was inhabited by hundreds of thousands or millions of people and it was able to establish a type of harmony that was geared around the *differences* of the citizenry. The capitalist explosion and the correlative rise in productive capacities, allowed many individuals to live in the same space while at the same time taking part in diverse activities, labours, and idea-constellations. The metropolis was inhabited by artists, writers, industrialists, politicians, and bureaucrats and each had the potential for different forms of individuality. For Simmel as well as Benjamin the large city made the modern battle between individuality and society a question that all had to face because of the environment itself. The city, while composed of limitless diversities, also operated above or behind each individual as a type of "social-technological mechanism (Wolff, 1950:409). As a result, the human question, in the metropolis, became one of adaptation to a particular techno-environment.

Thus, both Benjamin and Simmel provide us with unique perspectives on the development of the modern city, constructing their approaches from a praxis that contains both being and doing from the margins. They develop categories for expressing the site of the perspective of 'distant engagement', the "flaneur" in Benjamin's case and the "stranger" in the case of Simmel. Both of these categories have a lot in common with the perspective, also specifically modern, of the "sociologist/criminologist" per se.

The flaneur and the stranger are two images within early modernity of how one inhabits the city. Both types inscribe themselves within the city and the city incorporates itself into themselves through their distant gaze. The stranger comes from afar and brings that distance to the presence of his perspective. He/she comes and goes, but finally makes of him or herself a lawyer, a doctor a teacher, a writer, becoming in a way indispensable and settles. The stranger wants to be successful, to participate, to engage. The flaneur, on the other hand, is a "native" who comes, for ethnic or other reasons, from the outside to play in the space of the modern city:

> There was the pedestrian who wedged himself into the crowd, but there was also the *flaneur* who demanded elbowroom and was unwilling to forgo the life of the gentleman of leisure. His leisurely appearance as a personality is his protest against the division of labor, which makes people into specialists. It was also a protest against their industriousness. Around 1840 it was briefly fashionable to take turtles for a walk in the arcades; the *flaneur* liked to have the turtles set the pace for them (Benjamin, 1999:20).

An important difference, then, between the stranger and the flaneur is that the former comes to feel more at home; he comes to stay. Benjamin's flaneur, on the other hand, may or may not stay, but, in any case, the "*flaneur* acts in *flanerie*", a would-be artist, writer, actor, etc., who needs some one to buy him or her in order to survive; the question is who buys and how one is bought. The flaneur, then, exemplifies with his or her life the fetishization of the modern capitalist city, exemplifies, that is, the central fact of commodification as the actual milieu of the Denison of the modern metropolis:

> The crowd was the veil from behind which the familiar city as phantasmagoria beckoned to the *flaneur*. In it, the city was now landscape, now a room. And both of these went into the construction of the department store, which made use of *flaneurie* itself in order to sell goods. The department store was the *flaneur's* final coup. As *flaneurs*, the intelligensia came into the market place, as they thought, to observe it –but in reality it was already to find a buyer. In this intermediary stage ...they took the form of the *boheme*. To the uncertainty of their economic position corresponded the uncertainty of their political function (Ibid., 10).

In the end, both Simmel and Benjamin show how in modernity not only the native (flaneur) but also the stranger find dissatisfaction in the new metropolis where both are displaced. But their distance and the angle of vision it allows provides the potential for a uniquely inclusive perspective as participant observers. An inestimable advantage of the historical experience of the flaneur and stranger, then, is that the unique tensions of their particular efforts to find "elbow room" place with clarity both 'near' and 'far'. Both of these polarities exist within a dialectical tension. They allow the potentiality for the reciprocities of distant observation and close participation that are crucial to the space of the interpretive sociologist/criminologist. Embodied in the everyday life of modernity, yet critical of the world of "reality" constituted there, Benjamin's and Simmel's points of view pit the usual modern meaning of reality against a kind of being and doing that is grounded in everyday experiences where people actually live, eat, sleep and find their pleasures and pains.

Central to this essay is both an epistemological and methodological rejection of "passive detachment" and an insistence on a strategy of scientific distance in social research. As long as scientific social research rests on social disengagement the opposing view must be an '*engagement distance*'. This argument is premised on the conviction that social conditions do not determine social theory, and that all sociological theorizing and practicing has some roots in both the biographies and histories of its creators. Through Georg Simmel and Walter Benjamin this work illustrates how in modernity not only the "flaneur" (native) but also the "stranger" find dissatisfaction in the new metropolis where both are displaced and marginalized. But their distance and the angle of vision it allows provide the potential for a uniquely inclusive perspective as participant observers. An inestimable advantage of the historical experience of the flaneur and stranger, then, is that the unique tensions of their particular efforts to find "elbow room" place with clarity both 'near' and 'far'. Both of these polarities exist within a dialectical tension. They allow the potentiality for the reciprocities of distant observation and close participation that are crucial to the space of the interpretive sociologist or criminologist.

2. Walter Benjamin

Walter Benjamin, born on July 15, 1892, studied philosophy in Freiburg, Munich, Berlin, and Bern, earning his doctoral degree in 1919, with the work *The Concept of Criticism in German Romanticism*, but, like Simmel, he had the misfortune or fortune to fail in his efforts to become a university professor. His habilitationschift, *On the Origins of the German Trauerspiel*, was rejected by Frankfurt University. Already marginalized as a Jew in an ethnocentric and highly anti-Semitic society, he attempted to make a living as a free-lance writer, an experience that furthered his marginalization. In anomie, alienated first by prejudice and then by his unwillingness to accept the modern world as it was, Benjamin became a wanderer without a home.

Like the flanuer, Benjamin is nostalgic for an authenticity and originality that seemed to be lost in the modern world, or the age of mechanical reproduction. Subjectivity itself is reified in the modern forms of existence and, as such, is incapable of aesthetic creative life. The given, and rejected, world for Benjamin is characterized as a society by its instituting of an "anonymous individuality", a disconnected and unknown personhood, isolated in both the public and private spheres. Here, he stands in stark contrast to Emile Durkheim's "sui-generis" comprehension of societal development, his celebration of life in the collectivity and eternity of society, where life is breathed into society by the ideal it has of itself and needs for itself. For Durkheim, this society is naturalized, exaggerated, and becomes a reality in itself. That is, life brings into being life, which is external to it, so that it develops historically, and periodically to become life "par excellence", overshadowing the real live individuals who created it. Thus the creation becomes something larger, truer and more 'natural' than the creators (Durkhiem, 1995:424-425).

But, for Benjamin this characterization is nothing but a mythos that loosens one's connection to one's ethos and ends by further alienating the person from the society. Contra Durkheim and other such socially integrating perspectives, his project becomes that of debunking mythic theories of history. Benjamin's attack is against all myths of automatic historical progress. In this regard, he argues that historical materialism has every reason to distinguish itself sharply from bourgeois mental habits, because its basic principle is not progress but actualization. For Benjamin, as Hannah Arendt points out in *Illuminations*, the object should not be to become a useful actor in a humanly irrational world; he specifically singles out for criticism the "doctrine of natural selection [for] popularizing the notion that progress was automatic"(Buck-Morss, 1989:79). Benjamin wants to overcame "the ideology of progress in history which it acknowledges only progress in the mastery of nature, not the regression of society" (Ibid.: 80). For Benjamin the ideology of the progress of history is an experience that is the same over and over again, as in the exchange of consumption and commodity. Benjamin's sense of history is one of connectness (past, present, and future) influx constantly forming within social material. The subject in history is not the abstract empty individual of bourgeoisie, but subject in history made by people. The world is not mystical but material where the subjects inter-subjectively are making and remaking history.

The world rejected by Benjamin (and Simmel) is the rationalized, productive and allegedly inescapable one characterized by Max Weber. As a sociologist, Benjamin, like Simmel, attempts to develop a perspective that is external to the "iron cage" (Weber, 1958) with what will later be called its "possessive individualism" (MacPherson, 1979). This modernity is rejected with a critical sociology that is directed toward escaping the bourgeois "rational world" as the only possible reality. This is a world characterized by a fundamental differentiation of functional spheres (economic, political, cultural, etc.), each with its own functionally determined ethic, connected to other spheres if at all only in the contradictory tensions within the individual and his or her choices. This differentiation is only one of the larger effects of an overall direction in history toward "rationalization", the rendering of the world more calculable and the subjection of it to calculation. Weber refers to modernity as having become "disenchanted", that is, as having become a "causal mechanism" in which its various functioning parts (including its 'personnel') are understood to be susceptible to causal calculation.

In this analysis of capitalist modernity Weber argues that the causal efficacy of values can be rationally calculated because we live in a "rationalized' world, but that they cannot be judged good or bad, true or false on a social or cultural level. For Weber, values in modernity become simply an individual decision, which, from a social or cultural point of view are ultimately arbitrary: there is no rational way to choose among values within the functional reality of the "iron cage". Thus, in contrast to "traditional" societies, where religion and other cultural 'habits' integrated values, modernity leaves the individual in the position of having to (arbitrarily) select the values he or she will prioritize. Then, insofar as he or she is rational, these values will be 'rationalized' (rendered internally consistent) and the individual will move on from this "value rationality" to "purposive rationality" where the world, including values among all of the other possible causal influences, will be comprehended as a causal mechanism and the individual will attempt to manipulate the variables in such a way as to maximize the chances of producing the desired effect.

The modern world, as Weber depicts it, is very alienating. First, Protestant asceticism, entering the spirit of capitalism, rejects the legitimacy of sensuous pleasures alienating the individual from the body. Secondly, people are alienated from others through competition which determines the quality of survival within the causal mechanism. In the end, as Benjamin sees it, people become alienated from social and cultural life; whether marginalized or not, they effectively become "outsiders" to their own world because capitalist modernity forces them into conformity with a structure dominated by an exclusive trajectory of functionalist production. The thrust of Benjamin's project, then, is the utter rejection of this "rationalization" that becomes dominant in modernity where capitalism and feteshization lives.

3. Georg Simmel

Like Benjamin's experiences in the years prior to World War Two, Simmel suffered greatly from the anti-Jewish sentiments that flourished in Germany and Europe in the years leading up to World War One. Also, just as Benjamin, Simmel was an academic outsider, never having been accepted in the academy. When a recommendation on Simmel's behalf was sent to the Ministry of Culture in the state of Baden, the minister of education requested Professor Dietric Schaefer in Berlin to evaluate Simmel's candidacy. Schaefer reported that the candidate was quite unsuitable for professorship. He described Simmel as "a dyed-in the wool Israelite, in his outward appearance, in his bearing and in his manner of thinking" (cited in Ashley and Orenstein, 1995:306).

Thus marginalized not only by the "rational" modern society which forces one to "react with his/her head instead of her/his heart" (Wolff, 1950:410), Simmel is also marginalized by the irrational parts of modernity, the racism, anti-Semitism etc. But, unlike Benjamin, Simmel articulates a more ambivalent relationship to the modern, recognizing along with the losses entailed by the transformations positive developments in the dialectic of distance and engagement. The profound advance in the tensions of this dialectic that becomes clear to him from his position on the margins is that the tremendous, rationalized and bureaucratic formalism of the modern world allows anonymous participation in the central stream to an unprecedented degree. Thus, he, as well as others, can participate as the "stranger", the "sociologist"; existential space becomes available for the development of a critical interpretive sociology/criminology. As Orenstein (1995) states: " It has been suggested that Simmel based his understanding of the role of the stranger on his own position in academia. If this is true, he might have selected his social type quite deliberately. To some extent, the sociologist is always the stranger-always the outsider, never an organic part of human society" (Ibid.: 325). Orenstein, unless one takes "to some extent" very seriously, overstates here the position of the sociologist as Simmel conceives it. It would be more accurate to say that the sociologist is never (except for the sociological hacks working for major corporations and the like to improve the bottom line) just an organic part of human society, but the point that the sociologist (as opposed to the sociological hired gun) is always also a stranger still holds. Simmel sees a relationship-in-tension between the isolated, alienated or otherwise marginalized locations and the 'organic' mainstream of the 'iron cage".

For Simmel, then, what is characteristic of the stranger is a certain *distant engagement:* "the sociological form of the "stranger" presents the unity, as it were, of these two characteristics" (Wolff, 1950:402). The unity of nearness and remoteness involved in every human relation is organized, in the phenomenon of the stranger, in a way which may be most briefly formulated by saying that in the relationship to him, distance means that he who is close by, is far, and strangeness means that he, who also is far, is actually near. For, to be a stranger is naturally a very positive relation; it is a specific form of interaction (ibid.).

This recognition is what provides Simmel's sociology with its critical method; it is a recognition that the sociological 'stranger' is also a participant in that which he observes (and that, perhaps, the participants he or she observes is also to some extent a stranger). It is a recognition, in short, of the crucial fact of participation and thus of the necessity of engagement. For critical sociology the object is to recognize this engagement, the (wonderfully) inescapable elements of one's experiences, alienation, neuroses and so on and to include them in one's theory. Among other things, it is only in this way that one can recognize the effects of one's participation in one's observations and only in this way, whether recognized or not, can one understand the relationships between impinging forces and the participation in them of the 'objects' of analysis so that these relationships can be included in that analysis. The position of the interpretive sociologist here, and the consequent need for recognition of one's own participation (as well as the need for a wide range of sociologists) is exemplified in the problem of attributing value motivations to social actors as Weber (1978: 5-6) presents it in *Economy and Society*: "... many ultimate ends or values toward which experience shows that human action may be oriented, often cannot be understood completely, though sometimes we are able to grasp them intellectually. The more radically they differ from our own ultimate values, however, the more difficult it is for us to understand them empathetically. Depending upon the circumstances of the particular case we must be content either with a purely intellectual understanding of such values or when even that fails, sometimes we must simply accept them as given data".

In short, we have to include ouselves in the object of analysis. Our meanings and values are part of understanding the object and to remove them is to remove the possibility of reflexive knowledge.

On the other side of the coin, Simmel recognizes a positive side in the phenomena of the modern stranger with respect to the value of the distance itself. He notes that, historically, the European Jew as a trader achieved a settling down in the place of his activity, and later on the Jew, the "outsider", becomes useful to the group as a man of letters (ironically enough, not in his own case in academia), a lawyer, a doctor, etc. But, remaining also an 'outsider', he or she maintains a distance, a distance that is of great value to the 'objectivity' of the observer. The strangers "freedom" contributes to the objectivity of the interpretive locale, among other reasons, because her/his objectivity is bound by no commitments which could prejudice perception, understanding and evaluation of the given. Then too, the psychological distance of the stranger's social location does wonders for the critical eye.

4. Conclusion

Simmel's stranger, as Benjamin's flaneur, represents both an epistemological and a methodological rejection of "passive detachment"; it insists rather on "a kind of active limited participation" (Wolff,1950:402). Ignoring the lack of dialectical sensitivity in Wolff's formulation, it suggests that both Benjamin and Simmel are informed by Marx's conception of "active subjectivity". It is, of course, Marx (through Kant) who recognizes our situation as a dialectical tension between our subjection to conditions and our freedom to change conditions through our aesthetic production. This "active subjectivity" stands at the heart of Marx's epistemology. It ties the subject to the present, actual, everyday world where people live, experience and make their own history. He emphasizes that we do not make history as we choose, but under the actual conditions we find already given. For Benjamin and Simmel, as for Marx, history is not an abstraction standing outside and in front of us, but the whole of the internal and external environment, the subjective and objective reality which we experience as potentially free subjects. History finds it's meaning in the actual presence in which people spend their lives. For both of these marginalized thinkers it can truly be said with Marx that "Men make their own history, but they do not make it just as they please; they do not make it under circumstances chosen by themselves, but under circumstances directly encountered, given and transmitted from the past" (Marx,1845 cited in Tucker, 1978: 595).

For Simmel, the preservation of autonomy and individuality is problematic in modernity. So is engagement. The question he asks is not essentially different from the one that Benjamin is asking, "how the personality accommodates itself in the adjustments to external forces" (Wolff, 1950: 409). How does one find elbow room, a degree of 'freedom' to maneuver without "being leveled down and worn out" (ibid.). As with Benjamin in the "mechanical age of reproduction" the modern individual "resists being leveled down and worn out by the social-technological mechanism" (ibid.). One must, of course, ask here "at what price?". For many modern personalities perhaps it would help to have an understanding of their marginality and alienation in the modern metropolis, an understanding that the necessity of living in the tensions, the neuroses and the isolation is the price of life itself. As for the struggle against the cultural monopoly of the space of engagement that works against the participation of the marginalized: "The preconditions of a slackening of the cultural monopoly are above all economic and social. We can do no other than fight for the creation of these preconditions" (Hauser, 1962: 246).

References

Ashley, D. and D. M. Orenstein. 1969 *Sociological Theory: Classical Statements*, Boston: Allyn and Bacon.

Benjamin, W. 1969 *Illuminations*, (ed.). H. Arendt, New York: Schocken Books.

Benjamin, W. 1999 *The Arcades Project*, (ed.) R. Tiedemann, Cambridge, Mass.: Belknap Press.

Buck-Morss, Susan. 1989 *The Dialectics of Seeing: Walter Benjamin*, Cambridge, Mass.: MIT Press.

Durkheim, Emile. 1995 *The Elementary Forms of Religious Life* (ed) Karen E. Fields, New York: The Free Press.

Hauser, Arnold. 1962 *The Social History of Art V. IV*, London: Routledge.

MacPherson, C.B. 1979 *Democratic Thory:Essays in Retrevial*, London:Oxford University Press.

Simmel, Georg. 1950 *The Sociology of Georg Simmel*, (ed.) K. H. Wolff, New York: The FreePress.

Stammer, Otto (ed.). 1971 *Max Weber and Sociology Today*, New York: Harper and Row.

Teater, Keith (ed.). 1994 *The Flaneur*, London: Routledge.

Tucker, C. Robert (ed.). 1978 *The Marx- Engels Reader*, New York: W.W. Norton and Company.

Weber, Max. 1978 *Economy and Society* Volume 1. Berkeley: University of California Press.

Weber, Max. 1958 *The Protestant Ethic and the Spirit of Capitalism*. New York: Charles Scribner's Sons.

Wolin, Richard. 1982 *Walter Benjamin: An Aesthetic of Redemption*, New York: Columbia University Press.

21. The Prison Industrial Complex and Social Division in Market Societies: The Hyper-Security State, Crime and Expendable Populations

Claudio A. Colaguori

1. Introduction

In many respects the social and political reorganizations of the last decade have represented a de-civilising trend (Pratt 1998) in North American social and political life and indeed in many other parts of the globe as well. The widening of the gap between those who prosper in the economic arrangements of neo-liberalism and those who have had their life chances curtailed by the reconfiguration of economic and political power has transformed the cultural climate from one of civil justice to one of 'security'. People are becoming accustomed to living in a state of alert and the security mandate of post 9/11 state policy has taken on even greater hegemonic proportions than is generally associated with the social controls of the 'disciplinary society' (Foucault 1979, O'Neill 1986). Gone and forgotten is the self-assured post-communist political climate of the early 1990's and the corresponding triumphalist discourses which trumpeted the virtues of the emergent civil society and the expansion of a new prospects for global peace, democracy and justice. In stark contrast to this ideal the present time is marked by a rise in trends towards increased concern with conflict and defence, security and control. The new security scenario has given rise to particularly pernicious intensifications of state power: the fallout from the so-called 'war on terror' includes such concerns as numerous restrictions on civil freedoms and in the sphere of criminal justice phenomena such as mass incarceration have become the norm. The discourses of power which shape social policy and popular consciousness discursively define social life as being in an era of neo-crisis – one with drastic consequences for social life and where drastic measures of social control are seen to be required. The two dominant mandates of security and control are systematically related in that they call upon the values of *agonism* and *liberalism* in their ideological and economic justification for punishment.

The new political climate with its rationalizations of the state's power to punish is qualitatively a new modality of power, one that has entered into a mode of hyper-security, which is a more open form of the hegemonization of social life that takes its legitimacy and authority from the ongoing declaration of war – the war on crime, the war on drugs, the war on terror, economic-competitive warfare. A number of these occurrences along with the intensification of punishment as seen in the formation of the 'prison industrial complex' are part of the new trend in state sponsored order and its use of power in the name of security. The 'prison industrial complex', which is the primary object of analysis in this paper, is a response typical of the insecure order of the hyper-security state and its *spasm of power*. This response to problems of social order and legitimation is a reflection of the deep social contradiction contemporary society has inherited from early industrial capitalism which is tied to the historical problem of social order in urban modernity – a problem which involved the hegemonic maintenance of the system of liberal market expansion and the interminable fact of class inequality in the face of this expansion.

What we have seen developing in penal practices is a pronounced and disturbing rise in mass incarceration and the subsequent formation of the prison industrial complex as described by many authors including Garland ed. (2001), Davis (2002), Wacquant (2001), Herivel and Wright (2003), Mauer & Chesney-Lind eds. (2002) and Schlosser (1998). Ian Taylor (1999) remarks that there has been an 'explosion of penality in market societies'. The USA for example has upwards of two million people incarcerated at a time when the general crime rate has been stable or falling. And, the stimulus behind the new frenzy of punishment is to be found in the present day cultural climate of security – one which has intensified into the pursuit of security in the militarization of everyday life that has accompanied the 'war on terror' and within the realm of crime control. Barbara Hudson (2002) asks how it is that we can account for the dramatic increase in prisoners when by all indications criminologists had predicted – based on a strong economy and falling crime rates – that incarceration in the USA and Canada should have been in decline? Part of the answer is that there has been a change in criminal justice policy towards determinate sentencing, especially instruments such as the Three-Strikes law, but the societal conditions which enable such a law also has to be enquired into. The concept of the Prison Industrial Complex provides a useful means of entering into an understanding of the social forces that make possible such things as mass incarceration, the corporatization of prisons, and the ethnocide of an urban underclass in North America and the continuing role of the state in the maintenance of social inequality.

This paper will enquire into the relationship between hyper-security and the institutionalization of punishment. It will also raise questions such as: How has the hyper-security mandate created new forms of economic opportunism within the functioning of the institutions that make up what Althusser (1971) refers to as the 'repressive state apparatuses' – the military, the legal system, prisons and policing? How has this mandate contributed to a new era of social division resulting from systemic oppression? In particular this paper will focus on how punishment has become intensified in the context of hyper-security to such an extent that it has taken on new roles beyond the publicly stated aim of crime control. The regime of punishment now plays a role in the creation of *expendable populations* as a normal course of business and in the administration of social policy. Punishment has become reconfigured as a new type of institutional formation where administrative and bureaucratic spheres of social control have become normalized dimensions of contemporary social order and where individuals and corporations prosper at the expense of a growing underclass. Just as the 'military industrial complex' is tied to billions of dollars of revenue, so the prison industrial complex is becoming increasingly a key sector of the financial infrastructure of market society. As the military industrial complex is tied hegemonically to the imperialism of the state, so the prison industrial complex is tied to the state program of the internal colonization of its own domestic populations. Clearly then, there are numerous forces that combine in the 'overdetermined' formation that is the modern prison industrial complex – a disturbing phenomenon clearly in need of explanation.

This analysis is informed by the critical theory of the state (Davis and Stasz 1990, Nagengast 1994), where organized punishment is seen as the pathological symptom of a social system that has not been able to resolve its deep systemic contradictions. The lived results of social contradictions are manifested in growing social strain, poverty, crime and the normalization of state power as an exercise of force on its own citizens. Also of concern is whether established critical theories of penal practices are adequate to the study of the prison industrial complex. Do they still hold merit in the context of the contemporary social, political and economic change? Is punishment to be understood as something beyond the logic of class conflict and capital versus labour? Further, this paper will address the way punishment fits into liberal market society based on how such a society mediates social relations of survival, social relations of power, of economic production, and of hierarchical relations and moral authority and entrepreneurial opportunity. This analysis examines the phenomenon of the prison industrial complex at the level of 'system' and 'order' and thus on the macro-social patterns which occur many levels above the participating actors in a given society.

It is proposed here that the prison industrial complex can be understood as an institutional formation which serves the interests of and/or is supported by a constellation of factors including:

- the carceral state and its right of punishment, the legalization of state violence and the general use of repressive force in the preservation of state sovereignty and security including the use of such forms of power over its own citizens
- the market and its pursuit of the profit motive including both the corporatization of penality and the individual pursuit of economic self-interest in terms of prison industry jobs, security work etc, all of which correspond to shifting paradigms in business cycles and the increasing liberalization of the economic order of market society
- the popular cultural legitimation of punishment through ideologies of crime and crime control and the apparatus of the culture/entertainment industry which creates a public demand for authoritarian measures in response to the perceived threat of crime

The term 'complex' within the name – 'prison industrial complex' indicates the network of societal elements contained within this particular institutional formation.

'Complex' refers to being tied into macrosocial elements of society such as rulership, marketization and cultural signification. The prison industrial complex is also tied to the historical program of liberalism which links modern society with its political and economic precursor in the form of early industrial society.

According to the critical sociology of the carceral state punishment doesn't control crime, fight terror or increase security, rather the enforcement of law systematically produces a punishment response (Visano 1992, 1998, Taylor 1999, Foucault 1979). In addition, punishment institutions do not have an 'independent life' that is detached from the order of liberal modernity in some autonomous way, instead punishment is tied to the system of market liberalism in a way that is economically functional as well as is culturally meaningful. The history of punishment is based on the dual function of the state's inability to resolve deep social contradictions and then use the social fracture this creates as an opportunity for hegemonic repression. Punishment therefore is a symptom of internal decay which does not call attention to this contradiction as a prelude to its resolution but rather punishment becomes a means of dealing with marginalized members of society deemed 'surplus populations' and 'dangerous classes'. The liberal humanist philosophies of incarceration that arise as forms of the discursive legitimation of punishment only serve to reinforce the ideology that certain classes and types are the objective problem rather than the order of society which produces marginalization and subsequent punishment.

Punishment is seen to emerge from a historical trajectory in early urban industrial society where the problem of inequality and scarcity created the social fiction contained in the idea of 'surplus populations'. The concept of 'surplus populations' refers not just to people but to a situation – one where certain groups of people who could not be accommodated (enfranchised) into the new liberal market system and therefore became both symbolic and material representations of systemic inadequacies and were therefore designated as 'dangerous classes' precisely because of the contradiction their social presence raised. These groups were categorized into non-existence by being named 'surplus' – a euphemism for unnecessary. The legacy of this hostile categorization of vast groups of citizens lives on in today's liberalism in the concept of 'expendable populations' which is that mass of incarcerated peoples from the ranks of the jobless, the psychologically disfigured and other subjectivities of social strain and social repression caught in the web of law and punishment and whose presence continues to signify the systemic contradictions of advanced liberalism. These are institutionally incorporated into the mode of economic and cultural production as criminal commodities.

Present-day market society liberalism developed around the features of early industrial society and its problem of surplus populations and so retained and continued these primal contradictions in a way that was functional to the order of liberalism in the most rationalized manner, as industry (Christie, 1993). A social system which was unable to meet the basic social needs of members of society was a system with deep internal contradictions and economic incompatibilities – a problem which did not go unrecognized by classical economics. It therefore becomes necessary to define liberalism not only in its positive connotation as 'freeing' – to liberate, but also the liberalization of, or the enfreeing of both the progressive and regressive tendencies particular to the early order of urban industrial society including its repressions. Liberalism therefore is substantially defined by *punishment* just as liberalism must include the punishment values of justice as revenge in its set of social ideals. It must be argued therefore that punishment is a fundamental structural aspect of liberalism and not an aberration or a symptom of an 'incomplete project of modernity' (Habermas 1980) or even an element of corruption but a normal aspect of social functioning.

A number of the tendencies in the societal use of punishment mentioned here are identified in the work of Foucault (1979), Rusche and Kirchheimer (1968), and Garland (1990, 2001) – what is new about the prison industrial complex is the neo-liberal intensification of punishment, which is part of the intensified dialectic of social growth associated with the globalization of market society, the widening of class division and the corresponding extremes of wealth and poverty that exist within the culture of liberalism. Two main supra-forces of the historical dialectic are: production/progress and destruction/punishment. The program of punishment and security is part of the dialectic of liberalism and the growth of market society. The dialectic of liberalism repeats the original social dynamic and societal problematic of the early industrial capitalist state which involves the "explosive development of market society and the problem of social order itself" (Taylor 1999:7), and it is to the state and its liberalization of punishment to which we shall now turn.

2. The State and its Liberalism: The Forces of Social Contradiction and the Place of Crime and Punishment in Taylor's 'Critical Criminology of Market Societies'

How is it that with advances in so many areas of human endeavour as for example in the areas of culture and knowledge, including science, medicine, communications, technology and the explosion of critical scholarship in the human sciences we also have the simultaneous regression of the human condition across cultures and populations from socially constructed scarcity and inequality, to the rise of infectious diseases and the intensification of global conflict and war? How is it that progress and production seems always to be inextricably bound with repression, punishment and the degradation of life? What singular characteristic of the state accounts for this self-defining dialectic of production and destruction? An answer to this heightened antagonism can be seen in the practices of the political state and its liberalization of the forces and values which stimulate the pursuit of certain types of advancement and which simultaneously create corresponding forms of regress or social injustice. Historically this is seen to emerge from the liberalization of Enlightenment ideals organized around rational individualism and economico-political sovereignty but which get realized culturally as the competitive, aggressive, predatory social relations permeating the instrumentality between individuals in a hyper-competitive society. These social relations, Ian Taylor argues are, "in significant measure, a product of the competitive individualism that has been widely identified... as an essential feature of market society itself" (Taylor 1999:5). Taylor, following Currie (1990) argues that the advance of free-market society has been accompanied by 'a culture of Darwinian competition for status and resources in both the sphere of consumption and the struggle for position within the established order' (quoted in Taylor 1999:53), an order which is exemplified in the laissez-faire liberal state promotion of free (unbridled) competition and the emergence of corresponding forms of instrumental social interaction and social conflict. The promotion of ideologies of liberalism pertaining to economic self-interest are realized in their most aggressive manifestations as types of *agonistic* behaviour, which is what the market state encourages in its liberality. Liberalism and agonism are therefore dialectically related. Liberalism is characterized by its mandate to allow for 'free competition' in all aspects of political, economic and social life. In this way liberalism is seen as thriving on competition and conflict to generate societal growth. The values of agonism form the ideological foundations of the dialectic of production and destruction as the supra-systemic model of social order in advanced industrial society. In the culture of agonism, conflict is seen as the generator of social results, where competition and adversarialism are believed to be the highest virtues of liberal freedom (Colaguori 2002). Agonism defines the rationality that informs legal order and legal process from courtroom procedure all the way to the instrumentality of final punishment.

We can see how the prison industrial complex emerges as the logical extension of agonistic social forces of market liberalism. The prison industrial complex is not simply a reflection of dominant class repression but rather it is a form of *economically functional social division* based on social relations of predation or what Adorno and Horkheimer (1969) refer to as the "economic mechanism of selection". Therefore the social relations in market society come to mimic the Darwinistic relations of predator-prey relations – the survival of one depends on the destruction of the other. Surplus populations (which can be seen through the Darwinian metaphor as 'endangered peoples') result from being socially expelled by the pressure of competition for resources and a 'way of life' in a society of scarcity. Agonistic liberalism therefore mimics the laws of social Darwinism in its model of society except that natural selection is replaced by the aforementioned 'economic mechanism of selection' modeled after the predatorial natural order of beasts. This is the most anti-social aspect of liberalism's social dynamics: its naturalistic ideology of unbridled conflict. Thus we have in market societies types of class segregation without open class conflict. There is no class conflict as such – there are only institutionalized relationships of simultaneous domination and the pursuit of economic self-interest. These occur across all social groups and cannot be confined solely to the subject positions of dominant and subordinate classes, but include race, legitimate access to money, abilities, skills and education level all of which are significant forms of social status that create privilege and subsequent market opportunity along the lines of social capital. This form of status as market capital gives enfranchised people more power than others to pursue economic self-interest thus leaving other people out of the flows of capital (both legitimate and illegitimate capital opportunities).

The conflict model which theorizes domination as a function of class struggle or a conscious type of conflict between opposing social classes differs from the conception of 'economically functional class division' in significant ways. The difference is that the former implies a type of concerted consciousness along the lines of the dialectical model of social uprising theorized by Marx's conception of class-revolution based social change. Economically functional class division speaks of a continuation of the repressive mode of social inequality but one which is not based on the bifurcation of the population on the basis of their relation to the mode of production but rather on the basis of a survivalist individualism. Social division is maintained in part through a carceral bureaucracy which operates more along the lines of the competitive, opportunistic social ethics of classical liberalism rather than the class conflict Marxist model.

Taylor's analysis is useful in its broad consideration of the overdetermining factors that give rise to the problem of crime and punishment in market societies because it conceives of social domination as a multi-factorial dimension of the social system rather than giving primacy to capitalist relations. Taylor's (1999) critique of the state in relation to crime in 'market societies' involves the identification of the systemic social crises that give rise to various forms of social depravation that contextualize criminal behaviour. The state in its ultimate duty to uphold the forces of the free-market ends up engaging in its own politics of self-interest and promotes this ethic as a type of social norm realized in the cultural ideologies of individualism. Social relations in this context cannot be separated from sociological understandings of social deviance and the state's reinforcement of social control. The loss of a welfarist social policy structure and other forms of the negation of social responsibility that have occurred with the rise of neo-conservative economic order intensify a series of crisis axes long associated with liberal market order and through which many social problems emerge, such as:

- the crime crisis, which is a reflection of the central structural problem of social inequality and the danger it poses have increased to new heights of intensification in the globalization of market society to create a 'new poverty'.
- a system of law that is driven by mandates other than justice bolstered by mass cultural appeals for reifying and extremist criminal justice policies such as determinate sentencing which produce a mass population of prison inmates as fodder for the punishment industry
- the war on drugs and the repression this unleashes both in terms of crime control and in terms of how the drug problem multiplies a whole series of other problems stemming from it such as gun violence and individual

impairment, the breakdown of families and the seizing of children by the state.

- The state itself is complicit in criminal fraud through its participation in the legalized and financially rationalized rule breaking of the corporate sector which occurs at great cost to the fiscal wealth of the taxpaying citizenry. Related to this axis , but not developed by Taylor, is the underground economy created by overtaxation, the legal restrictions on trade and the ongoing incentive to 'break rules in order to get ahead'.
- the firearm and weapons economy which the state participates in at both an international and a domestic level
- the development or urban spaces that conform to consumerism and the architecture of inequality as zones of competing self-interest rather than as a space of social commons or community.
- the crisis of labour and the continual capitalist pressure to create a pool of exploitable labour forces both domestically and in the globalization of manufacturing and production abroad
- childhood poverty and the general problem of youth anomie, and the tampering with advancement opportunities in such proportions of magnitude that it can be seen as the despoliation of a generation

Social life within such a culture of crisis has "a profound effect of the life-chances and possibilities of individuals located in these specific positions" (Taylor 1999:12). The extent to which the state actually produces these social realities through policies that construct the hierarchical nature of social reality is what connects state order to the bulk of what is legally processed as criminality. The above list thus constitutes the axes of social marginalization from which the expendable populations may be drawn.

Taylor's broad context for an understanding of 'crime in market societies' presupposes a number of insights pertaining to the nature of the state as an institution which has historically engaged in various forms of social control as a means of establishing itself. These range from covert political hegemony (soft control) to overt tyranny (hard control) and have been elaborated by Althusser through a Marxist model of societal reproduction (Althusser 1971). The critical theory of punishment has traditionally been seen as an element of the state's attempt to preserve the power to punish in a strategy of social regulation that involves a more widespread and generalized system of control mechanisms that are seen as necessary to affirm the primacy of the state form itself as the highest priority of society (Foucault 1980). In this sense punishment serves to reinforce the antagonistic nature of social relations in a society based on inequality. This is why Foucault argues that prisons are not a failure as institutions – they serve to reproduce the basic power dynamics of the disciplinary society. We misunderstand the variegated role of the prison if it is looked upon solely as something used to control crime. For Foucault it is more historically valid to see the prison system as a 'punishment machine', one that is used to exact punishment in the name of whatever dominating discourse or philosophy of incarceration prevails at a given time in history. When a system of punishment is firmly institutionalized in place it gets used to make punishment happen whether for its stated purpose or otherwise to suit various power interests, so to institutionalize punishment entails leaving it in place for potential abuse, and this happens as a matter of course in the administration of 'justice'. The mechanization of punishment arising from its institutionalization is also why Foucault talks about systems and forces as 'social technologies'.

Foucault's critical theory demonstrates that one of the State's characteristic features is the right it maintains to punish its own citizens and that this measure absolutely diminishes the value of individual human life and places the preservation of the dominant state apparatus alone as the highest of all official priorities. Foucault knows the self-preserving nature of the state to be a threat to its citizenry by its very definition of its own sovereignty:

the sovereign exercised his right to kill, or by refraining from killing: he evidenced his power of life only through the death he was capable of requiring... the principle underlying the tactics of battle – that one has to be capable of killing in order to go on living – has become the principle that defines the strategy of states (1980:136-137).

And further,

> We must consequently see things not in terms of the substitution for a society of sovereignty by a disciplinary society and the subsequent replacement of a disciplinary society by a governmental one; in reality we have a triangle; sovereignty-discipline-government, which has as its primary target the population and its essential mechanism apparatuses of security (1979b 18-19).

The 'security' ideal contained in Foucault's insight is certainly relevant to the rise of the hyper-security state and the intensification of discipline and punishment but it can also be translated into a related economic ideal within liberalism – which is that the survival and support of the corporate marketplace takes precedence in the list of societal priorities of the state. If the institutional network that administers punishment can not be rationalized on the basis of controlling crime then it must be rationalized in other ways. Presently these ways are located in the constellation of forces that give rise to the prison industrial complex and its admixture of punishment and profit/opportunity and oppression.

The right to punish is therefore a significant dimension of state rule within liberal democracies and part of the state's normalization of violence. The prison is one of the social foundations that emerged from that original experiment in social control (through the construction of surplus populations) – prisons exist in the present order by filling other social functions, but their effect of segregation and the specific role of incarceration is but one function in an overdetermined system of what Foucault calls generalized systems of control. This is partly why Foucault dispenses with class analysis in the Marxist sense but still recognizes the hierarchies that create social division stemming from the effects of social power. The prison industrial complex as we have argued here is misunderstood as merely a product of instrumental class domination but rather makes more sense as the result of new market shifting of economic hierarchies that invites entrepreneurial opportunities in the prison industry and crime control industry. In the midst of economic scarcity this creates predation of the weakest and most easily criminalized segments of the population. The disenfranchised, the ghettoized, and the insane all become the fodder of the punishment industry thereby confirming Rothman's (1971) view of it as an "enduring institution".

Prisons came to be seen as a problem of liberal legitimation not because they were evidence of massive social inequality, injustice and inhumanity (social divide) but because they 'didn't work' at things like reducing crime and recidivism, rehabilitate or correct offenders. It was up to economic rationality to render punishment functional within the productive logic of agonistic society – one which translates the 'economic mechanism of selection' into a social order where interpersonal relations becomes relations of instrumental predation. The disfunctionality of prisons did not render them obsolete, they dialectically transformed into something new – the solution of the prison was not its abolition but how to rationalize it both culturally and economically in a new historical and discursive context – which became the present-day marketization of crime and crime control.

3. The Marketization of Crime: The Entwinement of Economic Opportunity and Over-Criminalization

Typically, analyses of the economic division of populations within market societies have been theorized on the basis of class power along the lines of the classical Marxian conflict model. Problems with that approach call upon us to reconstruct the sociology of class based power in different societal and historical contexts. Marx wrote at a time when class consciousness was at its peak, and at a time prior to the rise of the hegemonizing effects of mass communications on the deformation of class consciousness. Today we have a public consciousness fully absorbed by the ideology of upward mobility that is more interested in joining the ranks of the 'well to do' rather than overthrowing the economic order. And clearly the Marxist model of class conflict does not comply with the reality of the numerous manifestations of capitalism that operate in various nations worldwide. China for example is not a strictly capitalist society but it most certainly is a market society and economic opportunity is a highly pronounced social force in the Chinese rise to global consumerism. This is why it is proposed throughout this paper that the classical Marxian model of class conflict is inadequate to a critical theory of the prison industrial complex, and that the Weberian approach with its emphasis on status opportunities and pluralistic conflict, although requiring critical modification, is better suited. In the Weberian conception of pluralist conflict theory groups with differential status who have access to power-relevant resources compete for opportunities within an economic playing field afforded by the open liberal marketplace so that the opportunistic actions of individuals are realized as strikes against others unable to compete for legitimate forms of prosperity.

Institutionalization, rationalization and bureaucratic administration transform class based domination from one of open class conflict to a Weberian model which argues that power relations are realized in a pyramidal hierarchy of social status and the differential opportunities status provides. 'Status' thus denotes the unevenness of individuals' positions vis-à-vis different markets of 'opportunity' and 'threat' in 'market society' (Taylor 1999:225).

As Taylor indicates, the rise of market society has been accompanied by an intensification of self-interest activities and also, by a quite startling decline in the level of voluntary activity (and, indeed of any kind of shared public activities other than sport) in 'the community'(Taylor 1999:64). The very low number of social worker professionals who exist versus the large number of punishment professionals is an indication of the social ethics of agonistic liberalism and the labour opportunities it demands.

In the most macrosocial sense the punishment of disadvantaged and marginalized peoples is a reflection of overall class privilege, however the class conflict model doesn't ring true when we approach the problem of the prison industrial complex from the standpoint of how it is generated by the persons, groups and corporations involved with it. It is proposed here that both 'economic opportunity' and 'over-criminalization' operate as incentives for the participation in crime control industries. When people work within the staff of the prison industrial complex they do not necessarily do so as moral activists of law and order but as workers who gain status and economic sustenance from doing so. In the advanced capitalism of market society the entrepreneurial consciousness replaces class consciousness as the mode of individual salvation. Social control is nevertheless maintained (in terms of one's benefit is another's pain) but not as a type of direct conflict but rather as one which is mediated by institutional-bureaucratic forms of social regimentation.

As Edwards states,

> What distinguishes bureaucratic control from other control systems is that it contains incentives aimed at evoking the behaviour necessary to make bureaucratic control succeed. It is this *indirect* path to the intensification of work, through the mechanism of rewarding behaviour relevant to the control system, rather than simply to the work itself, that imposes the new behaviour requirements on workers. (Edwards 1979: 148-9)

Entrepreneurial opportunity and criminal opportunity are the dialectical relations of social action that allow bureaucratic forms of control to succeed. It should not be surprising that we can develop a critical sociology of punishment on the basis of entrepreneurial opportunities (individual incentives) afforded by institutional structures of various sorts since such opportunities are available even in the context of criminal sanction. Illegal drug smuggling and sales, human trafficking and sex trade are examples of entrepreneurial opportunity (albeit illegitimate forms) that are opened up precisely by attempts at their restriction under criminal law. So it stands to reason therefore that entrepreneurial opportunity is more easily facilitated when the pursuit of economic self-interest is not hampered by criminal sanction but is indeed entwined with it. Both events occur across varied strata of economically disempowered persons who must survive economically in the margins of society opened up by criminal opportunity. And thus both the grey economy and that which is considered to be the legitimate economy are enmeshed.

Job seekers in the field of justice and security work, court workers, prison workers, police officers, private security officers, judges, lawyers and prosecutors are social actors mostly unaware of the larger power dynamic within which they work and which gives them status and pay while at the same time feeds off of institutionalized social repression and to some extent demands that the reality of crime be produced and reproduced to satisfy the organizational demands of crime control and its punishment. To understand the life-world roles of the punishment personnel listed above on the basis of 'class domination' along the lines of the typical Marxist model would be misleading. Participation in relations of domination begins first and foremost as an aspect of the pursuit of self-interest. Self interest in the context of the penal apparatus gets mediated into institutionalized repression. This is partly why the structure of bureaucracy and the administration of penality is so important in understanding the ways in which institutions serve various roles of empowerment, employment alongside relations of domination, social exclusion and punishment.

As Garland (1990) indicates, penality gets coordinated w/other practices that may or may not be part of the institutional framework of repression – but are related or stem from the policies, administration and implementation of a 'crime control industry' (Christie 1993).

Punishment therefore does not continue only as the societal response to crime, or as a form of crime control but rather the institutionalization of punishment needs crime to propel its bureaucratic and administrative growth and it actively secures criminals to fulfill the needs of a system that is held in place by the vested interests of secondary *material realizers* such as: private security companies, private prisons, prison building contractors and their numerous suppliers, the small town unemployed who are all too pleased to find themselves in a new career in "corrections", the myriad of "colleges" that have sprung up to offer courses on security work, prison guardsmanship and police studies, and the politician careerists who have rallied around the cause of crime-fighting in the name of law and order. These are among the economic benefactors in the order of punishment. When this many interest groups have an investment in the production of a new type of reality then this reality comes to be, sociologically speaking this is *institutionalization*.

The function of punishment has been analyzed by Rusche and Kirchheimer (1968) in terms of how it fits into 'productive forces and relations' thereby indicating that punishment cannot be understood simply on the basis of crime control techniques or even as responses to historically changing philosophies of incarceration. This is not to say that in early industrial capitalism the punishment machine was not used as a mechanism of class control. Clearly the state criminalized those who were deemed a threat to bourgeois order and the punishment of marginalized populations existed in relation to the availability of the human pool of labour. When industry needed workers incarceration was less likely, thus the performance of the economy, then as today, has a relationship to the rate of crime and punishment. However the functioning of the punishment apparatus changes according to the dynamic needs for system maintenance, and include:

- the ideological legitimation of the need for punishment
- shifts in employment and unemployment
- shifts in the offset of state-run institutions to private industry

The privatization of formerly state run institutions created the shift that gave rise to the re-birthing of the criminal justice system as a profit system. The more the liberal state downloads social responsibility to the private sector the more marketization of social welfare programs will occur. This only corporatizes those forces of the state that are involved in the repressive state apparatuses and intensifies them because of profit motives that exist for those who stand to benefit economically thus practically replaces a 'justice' model with a 'market' model. Therefore the prison industrial complex can be seen to emerge in response to changes in the 'political business cycle' (Melossi 1985) in addition to the larger societal paradigm shifts in the regime of punishment.

The new cultural climate of security, alert and "culture of suspicion" (Visano 1998) has given new meaning to the pursuit of individualism where self preservation is not only tied to economic benefit (entrepreneurial interest) but also, social repression has to be understood as a dialectical transformation in the relation between the persecution of an underclass and the interests of class opportunities.

4. Popular Cultural Ideologies of Crime and Crime Control and the Public Demand for Punishment

In order for mass punishment to become a normalized part of the institutional structure of society public consent is required. In many respects mass incarceration is a direct expression of the public vengeance directed against what is believed to be "criminal evil". It seems as if the public sphere is most vehemently determined in matters involving crime and punishment and in this respect the public has a voice in policy matters in the criminal justice domain more than in virtually any other area. The public zeal for matters involving crime in the present era cannot be understood separately from the mass mediatization of crime. The role played by the portrayal of crime in the media is significant in reproducing and disseminating ideas concerning threat and danger as well as security and control. Crime control is one of the very few areas of social life in which the public feels compelled to act and empowered to have a voice. So it should not be surprising that the popular values about law and order correspond directly to the policies that give rise to the prison industrial complex.

Elements of public fear about crime become primary social concerns above most all other social problems since the fear of individual victimization is more captivating than fears about environmental degradation or economic downfalls and other social crises. Public fear is therefore easily mobilized by crime panics. However the crime crisis is more televisual fiction than real-life fact. James Carlson writes that 'prime time crime' is experiencing a 'crime wave' (Carlson 1985). Indeed the crime show genre, in its numerous manifestations from crime dramas like *Law and Order* to reality television shows such as *Cops* is arguably the largest genre on television. The ideological biases of prime time crime programming are supportive of a social system that sees fit to industrialize punishment on a mass scale. Punishment in this sense is the agonistic strike against crime in the so-called 'war on crime'. Carlson (1985) remarks on how 'prime time criminal justice' viewing fosters attitudes among viewers that favour authoritarian attitudes. This follows from observation that popular crime shows overwhelmingly support a 'crime control' or 'law and order' ideology rather than a 'due process' orientation. Authoritarianism is thus a basic ideology of prime time crime programming, however it would be misleading to understand this phenomenon as an expression of ruling class ideological dominance over a docile audience. Authoritarianism was a popular public sentiment long before mass media depictions of crime (as evidenced in the mass popularity of fascism in 20th Century Europe). Producers of crime shows in producing programs with authoritarian content are responding to an attitude which is already present in those who take pleasure in consuming shows that reinforce revenge, authoritarianism and agonistic conflict. Authoritarianism makes its presence known not only in the graphic depiction of the use of violent force in the "war against crime" but also in the ideological content of shows. Prime time crime shows create pleasure for the viewer on the basis of affirming the viewer's disappointment with the due process restrictions placed on police and courts having to follow proper legal procedures. In this way the show can create anger at 'the system' for being too weak on crime. However the more active dimension of viewers' pleasure is the pleasure of revenge – where the criminal is convicted and punished or shot dead. Prime time crime shows therefore function ideologically in promoting a tough justice, law and order mentality which becomes the basis for a *popular criminology* that is pro-punishment.

Ian Taylor also speaks of a 'common sense criminology' that seems to pervade the formation of public opinion about matters involving crime, justice and law. This common sense criminology is part of the popular pseudo-science of crime disseminated by the entertainment media and supported by positivist criminology (Taylor 1999:2). The perception of common sense criminology is one which stridently promotes the idea that criminality is a social fact and that criminals are a subspecies of pathological humans – this is an idea supported by positivist studies. Common sense criminology is supported academically by the discourse of biological and psychological positivism and popularized in the non-academic magazines that routinely publish the 'findings' of such scholars on social behaviour including crime to the almost total exclusion of input by real sociologists who are popularly replaced by the presumably more 'scientific' sociobiologists. Common sense criminology thus supports the ideal of a true criminal type that fits in well with the *animalization of the human* that corresponds ideologically to the value set of agonistic liberalism and its adherence to social Darwinistic principles.

The primary ideological dimension of common sense criminology is the public demand to get tough on crime. The demand for revenge against what is popularly seen as criminal injustice is formulated as a right of the public to exercise the power of penal sanctions against criminals. Popular crime programs, and most of the coverage of crime in the media, form part of the ideological justification of the *right to punish* as the cultural dimension that allows intensifications like the prison industrial complex to take place. Public vengeance against a visible enemy fits in well with the relentless and strident fetishization of repressive power that is a mainstay ideological system of thought in the consciousness of popular culture. Popular vengeance is part of what Stuart Hall et al (1978) refer to as an 'authoritarian consensus' which forms in response to crime-panic reporting.

One way of understanding the dominant influence that the valorization of repressive power is manifest in advanced-industrial-consumer societies is its relation to secondary (ideological subsystems) discourses of power: such as the discourse of competition, the discourse of predation, of imperialism, of championship, of history as victory – discourses that combine to form a culture that defines itself in relation to the values of agonism – all of which are tied ideologically and materially to the perpetuation of domination, punishment and the virtues of continuing a war on crime (Colaguori 2002). Public passions about crime and revenge therefore have serious implications beyond the realm of criminal justice and actually create an agonistic/authoritarian consensus that metes out its judgment in other areas of social life. The manner in which the public sees issues of crime and punishment serves to reinforce the formation of strong opinions of the public on other issues in society. Thus, the *cultural response to crime* (Visano 1998) forms the basis for public judgment in matters involving: welfare of the needy, the treatment of the other, the celebration of difference – all of which are compromised by the dominance of a zero-tolerance public attitude. Public passions and media presentations of prime time crime create strong convictions, and *people with convictions like to convict*. It is not surprising then that there is virtually no public outcry or concern for what is taking place in the name of extreme crime control. Matters dealing with criminality and concerns for inmate populations are among the lowest of public concerns and command virtually no sympathy despite the fact that what takes place in prisons in terms of aids, mental illness, captive labour and drug abuse has a direct effect on the larger society outside of the prison walls. Conscientious members of the public are not out lobbying and protesting against the minor atrocities of the prison industrial complex, when it comes to matters of crime they are on the couch having private fantasies of moral condemnation and sadistic indulgences while gripped by the agonistic drama of *Law and Order*. Most people do not raise serious questions about the role and practices of the criminal justice system – the issues of prisoner's rights is not a fashionable choice of social concerns even among the socially conscientious, in fact people who raise questions about the injustices of the justice system are themselves looked upon with suspicion. The vengeful pleasures experienced by the prime time crime enthusiast in the course of being entertained by law and order programming can be understood as part of the rituals of everyday violence and thus serve to extend the realities of authoritarianism into the private lives of individual viewers.

Popular culture and its dominant production and reproduction of power as a moral system of good and evil is also part of the popular legitimation of revenge. Good and evil is the basic formula at the foundation of crime drama and forms the basis for a mass appeal. Thousands of years of religious indoctrination have seen to it that people will come to judge the world through these simple categories for casting judgment, and being able to clearly decipher who is good from who is evil forms one of the participatory pleasures of crime viewing for many crime show fans. The measuring rod of good and evil is just imprecise enough to have a widespread usage for many people of different persuasions. Even non-religious types believe in the reality of good and evil. Evil functions as the supreme metaphor of the authoritarian power to label. It seems that for many good and evil is written into the very fabric of life. The public demand for criminal judgment and its punishment is thus historically rooted in traditional religious ideals. The rise of ideologies about good and evil constitute a neo-Manicheanism where the religious worldview of an everlasting soul and the morality of rewards and punishments is based on the correctness of one's behaviour. As a religious ideal it is maintained in the secular order as law and punishment. Religious sanctity [measurement by acts and deeds in life are rewarded in the afterlife on Judgment Day], gets replaced by secular rationalism [individual free will, risk/benefit rationality].

The 'authoritarian consensus' that forms part of popular public perception in this context bears a significant relation to the ideology of crime and criminal justice and the psycho-politics of revenge that 'prime time crime programming' fosters in the public consciousness. Clearly not all of the public sees justice and crime issues this way – I am referring to the mass public whose social perception has been constructed by the dominance of the televisual image and the aesthetics of domination stridently portrayed in prime time crime: This is an aesthetics characterized by the celebration of militarism and warriorism, by hyper-masculinity and by extreme forms of competitive vengeance – these are all informed by a set of values that are justified on the basis of the need for security and which contribute to the societal formation of authoritarian mass consciousness, one that is eager to support programs which seek to engage in the mass incarceration of those deemed to be a criminal threat.

5. Conclusion: Hyper-Security, Punishment and the Prison Industrial Complex

What do the condition discussed in this paper say about the changing nature of the state and its incapacity within a liberal market model to overcome its original systemic contradictions conceived of as a 'problem of populations' rather than a problem of political economy? How is it that the hyper-security mandate of the state has come to pose a threat for domestic populations? And, more specifically – what does the intensification of various forms of security and the focus on 'life at risk', say about the changing character or market society? It is becoming clear that the problems formerly associated with politics at a distance have spread directly into the life-world of market societies. The globalization of markets has created the localization of trouble.

The features of the hyper-security state include new intensifications of the political and legal technologies of control and have given rise to things such as the renewed use of torture as a tactic of penality, the unprecedented mass incarceration of prisoners, many of whom are used as a captive labour force, and an insidious complimentarity between penal practices of the state in partnership with the corporate sector. The prison industrial complex is possible because of the continuation of historical trends involving contradictions of inequality and social forces that affect life-chances within liberalism. These combine with market forces which turn criminality into corporate opportunity. The role of the state, its law and policy also forms part of the constellation of forces that have created intensifications of mass punishment.

Determinate sentencing policies create fiscal irresponsibility on the part of the state which becomes economically untenable in the long run and is therefore downloaded onto the private/corporate sector thereby cementing the punishment institution into a new type of efficient industry which continually depends on the production of criminal subjects. Thus market liberalism is involved in turning bad social policy into a good business opportunity. The huge fiscal cost of mass incarceration affects the state's ability to fund other social services that are essential to the well-being of the population such as education, health, child care and welfare. Ironically "cost cutting" in these areas actually creates the social conditions that stimulate criminal deviance. In addition, mass incarceration creates a sub-class of inmates, the majority of whom are not guilty of violent offences and whose lengthy incarceration deems them 'expendable' members of the population.

In this age of hyper-security punishment has taken on new meanings and new utility beyond mere deterrence. Punishment now extends beyond the traditional institutions of the military and corrections and into areas of social life formerly excluded from the overt use of repressive force. In the Canadian context of hyper-security the intensification and the open display of repression is seen in examples such as the treatment of journalists who investigate wrongdoings by the state who have met with police repression, lawyers who choose to defend those accused as terrorism have been targeted for threats, and the state has engaged in the deportation of persons deemed suspicious on the basis of hearsay. The suspension of due process and the selective expression of legal authority akin to martial law are the characteristics of a pre-fascist social order that is a significant dimension of the hyper-security mandate many states are following in the lead of the United States of America. Such extreme forms of social regulation have come along with ideological justifications so that the public has come to accept necessary suspensions of liberty as a trade-off for overall security. This cultural value shift has created a situation where similar attitudes of authoritarian necessity combine with moral fortitude to create a consensus where inhumane punishment and questionable incarceration practices are accepted in the sphere of the criminal justice system. There is a significant qualitative difference between how power is manifested in military practices and within the criminal justice system nevertheless the two institutional spheres are related insofar as they have both been pursuing a more openly laissez-faire set of repressive policies due to the legitimacy afforded them through the authority sanctioned by the US sponsored war on terror.

The prison industrial complex is thus part of a general trend towards catastrophic intensification and extremism we are seeing in many areas of social life and across nations – dialectical pressures are mounting as the deep contradictions of liberalism go unresolved.

References

Adorno, Theodore and Max Horkheimer. (1969 [1947]) *Dialectic of Enlightenment.* New York: Continuum.

Althusser, Louis. 1971. *Lenin and Philosophy and Other Essays.* New York: Monthly Review Press.

Colaguori, Claudio. 2002. "Agon Culture: The Ideology of Conflict and the Order of Domination." Ph.D. dissertation, Department of Sociology, York University, Toronto, Ontario.

Carlson, James M. 1985. *Prime Time Law Enforcement: Crime Show Viewing and Attitudes Toward the Criminal Justice System.* New York: Praeger Publishers

Christie, Nils. 1993. *Crime Control As Industry.* London: Routledge

Currie, Elliot. 1990. "Heavy with Human Tears: free market policy, inequality and social provision in the United States" in *The Social Effects of Free Market Policies.* Edited by Ian Taylor. Hemel Hempstead: Harvester Wheatsheaf

Davis, Angela. 2002. "Incarceration and the Imbalance of Power" in *Invisible Punishment: The Collateral Consequences of Mass Imprisonment.* Edited by Marc Mauer and Meda Chesney-Lind. New York: The New Press

Davis, N and Clarice Stasz 1990. *Social Control of Deviance.* Toronto: Mcgraw Hill.

Edwards, Richard. 1979. *Contested Terrain: The Transformation of the Workplace in the Twentieth Century.* New York: Basic Books

Foucault, Michel. 1979. *Discipline and Punish.* New York: Vintage Books

Foucault, Michel 1979b. "Governmentality." *Ideology and Consciousness.* 6: 5-21.

Foucault, Michel 1980. The History of Sexuality, Volume One: An Introduction. New York: Vintage Books

Garland, David. 1990. *Punishment and Modern Society: A Study in Social Theory.* Chicago: The University of Chicago Press.

Garland, David. (ed.) 2001. *Mass Imprisonment: Social Causes and Consequences.*London: Sage Publications

Habermas, Jurgen 1983. "Modernity: An Incomplete Project" in Hal Foster (ed.) *The Anti-Aesthetic*, New York:Bay Press

Hall, Stuart; John Clark, Chas Crichter, Tony Jefferson and John Clarke.1978. *Policing the Crisis: Mugging, the State and Law and Order.* London: Macmillan

Herivel, Tara and Paul Wright, editors. 2003. *Prison Nation: The Warehousing of America's Poor.* New York: Verso

Hudson, Barbara. 2002. "Punishment and Control" Pp. 233-263 in *The Oxford Handbook of Criminology, 3rd Edition.* Edited by Mike Maguire, R. Morgan, and R. Reiner. Oxford: Oxford University Press.

Mauer, Marc and Meda Chesney-Lind editors. 2002. *Invisible Punishment: The Collateral Consequences of Mass Imprisonment.* New York: The New Press

Melossi, Dario. 1985. "Punishment and Social Action: changing vocabularies of motive within a political business cycle." *Current Perspectives in Social Theory.* 6: 169-97.

Nagengast, Carole. 1994. Violence, Terror, and the Crisis of the State. *Annual Review of Anthropology* 23: 109-136.

O'Neill, John. 1986. "The Disciplinary Society: From Weber to Foucault." *The British Journal of Sociology.* 37: 42-60

Pratt, J. 1998. "Towards the 'Decivilizing' of Punishment'. *Social and Legal Studies.* 40: 127-45

Rothman, David. 1971. *The Discovery of the Asylum: Social Order and Disorder in the New Republic.* Toronto: Little, Brown & Company.

Rusche, Georg, and Otto Kirchheimer. 1968 [1939]. *Punishment and Social Structure.* New York: Russell and Russell.

Schlosser, Eric. 1998. "The Prison Industrial Complex". *Atlantic Monthly.* Dec. pp 51-57

Taylor, Ian. 1999. *Crime in Context: A Critical Criminology of Market Societies.* Boulder: Westview Press

Visano, Livy, and K. R. E. McCormick, editors. 1992. "Regulating an Urban Order: Policing Pathologies in the Carceral City." in *Understanding Policing.* Toronto: Canadian Scholars' Press

Visano, Livy.1998. *Crime and Culture: Refining the Traditions.* Toronto: Canadian Scholars' Press

Wacquant, Loic. 2001. "Deadly Symbiosis: When ghetto and prison meet and mesh." in *Mass Imprisonment: Social Causes and Consequences,* edited by D. Garland. London: Sage Publications

22. Two Views on the Problem[s] of Creating a Liberal-Democratic Political Culture

Claudius Alexander

1. Introduction

A political culture is formed by the practice of politics. This practice is the sum of dispositions created by the regular operation of the political system of a particular society. A political culture can encourage participation and involvement by the majority of citizens, as tends to be the case in democratic politics, especially the smaller ones (e.g. ancient Athens). In modern societies, there is a complex and sometimes *contradictory* relationship between the attitudes and values developed in formal political practice, and those formed by other institutions such as the law, criminal justice, education, religion, family and the media. What is learned and practiced in these normative institutions *confirms* the practices of the political system.

Over the past few centuries one of the recurrent themes in Western political discourse has been the difficulty in reconciling the Liberal mind with the Democratic pulse. Put otherwise, the difficulty for Western political theorists has been that of formulating a sufficiently coherent prototype of what might here be called an idyllic environment for the practical development of Liberal-Democratic 'political culture'. The reasons for this difficulty are today no doubt innumerable, and for many commentators the prospect of such an ideal coming to practical fruition remains, at best, the needless preoccupation of a utopian imagination. However while the failure of the last few centuries does seem to validate such pessimism, there are those who, if judging merely by their theoretical efforts, maintain that the search for an idyllic Liberal-Democratic 'political culture' cannot be abandoned. And this necessity is perhaps hardest felt by those theorists focusing on the US and Canada. Indeed, and particularly since WWII, a perceived steady decline in voter-participation rates of these two countries has given substance to the question of whether, and the extent to which, the ordinary citizen can actually influence the political culture of his or her society. (Here the term "ordinary citizen" refers to the individual of eligible status and thus the right to participate in his or her local politics, and the term "political culture" is meant the generally acceptable state of affairs produced by the determined exercise of this eligibility/right.)

In the brief analysis that follows I introduce a number of the concepts more frequently employed by post-World War II Western political theorists, especially as these concepts may apply to an understanding of US and Canadian political culture which in turn facilitate a deeper appreciation of law and criminal justice in terms of their concomitant responses to "crime". More accurately, the concepts are introduced via two varyingly influential theorists—the eminent German scholar Jurgen Habermas and the more recently recognized American detractor Cornell West—both of whom place lofty faith in the interpretive authority of these concepts to interrogate the Liberal-Democratic politico-cultural dilemma. And assuming a satisfactory degree of fidelity to these men's intentions, the analysis hopes to spotlight two things.

First, although Habermas and West each accept the exegetic capacity and importance of the selected concepts in conferring authority onto the other's theoretical position, they differ strikingly insofar as where within in the actual political culture-making process such authority is (potentially) best located. That is, while both scholars agree on the necessity for determined political action in the aim of building a distinctively Liberal-Democratic culture, they disagree on which stratum (the elite/middle class vs. the grassroots) of the politico-cultural hierarchy is better positioned to be the bearer of this responsibility. Second, while the question of the extent to which the ordinary citizen can or does impact his/her politico-cultural environment remains the main concern of the analysis, I would ask that one's reading of this environment not be corrupted by the usually more narrow interpretation of "political" reserved for explaining voter motivation[s] around election time. Instead, I would encourage the reader to follow along with the theorists in their efforts to identify such motivation[s] as only one instance of a much wider, increasingly unhealthy yet apparently unavoidable *subversion* of human capacity for action-oriented thinking, the implications of which are enormous for law and criminal justice.

2. Concept[ualizing] the Problem

German political theorist Jurgen Habermas offers a vision of the liberal-democratic state that hints of roots in ancient Greece, where the philosopher Plato and his contemporaries spent their days debating on the most practical way to order political society. Like the Platonists, Habermas' vision of the idyllic polity will be one sustained through an ongoing, rigorous dialogic process he calls communicative action. Theoretically, the process of communicative action, if conscientiously practiced, would promote an extent of argumentation that would see ideas continually challenged by involved parties as they search out the validity or legitimacy of these ideas, eventually arriving at their potential to remedying particular civic concerns. If validated—that is to say, a common understanding on the superior merits of a particular idea or course of action has been agreed upon—then this idea/action would become the operating standard.

Of course, this is not as simplistic a process as made to seem here; Habermas himself makes this clear when he instructs that "public discourse must keep alive both the meaning of an undistorted political public sphere...and the very goal of democratic will-formation". Today, this process of democratic will-formation is always and necessarily shrouded in what Habermas calls "the existential presuppositions of a nonorganizable practice"—nonorganizable because by its very own logic the communicative action-practice automatically and perpetually induces change upon itself. In other words, the communicative arena or public sphere—

where the individual motive or will of the political actors are existentially manipulated through incessant public debate—"reproduces itself self-referentially", making the goal of a well-ordered democratic state an ever-changing, ever-illusive pursuit.

Taken together, these premises—the need to maintain meaning throughout the will-formation process, the problem of reaching an actual existential harmony within the public sphere, and the consequent unavoidable replication of difficulties immanent in these two premises—may be regarded as the core components in Habermas' communicative action theory. The "deliberative" method behind the theory would more than likely have been the basis for perpetual argumentation between Plato and his contemporaries over two thousand years ago. But this would also be the extent to which the similarities between then and now can substantively go. Indeed, the fundamental ideas—e.g. citizenship, equality, liberty, etc.—that would constitute an "actually existing" democratic culture have over time reproduced themselves into "an intersubjectively dissolved" and incoherent idea of what democracy, or "popular sovereignty", means. Put differently, while the fundamental concepts of democracy are still hotly debated today, the actual political landscape that the Habermasian communicative action has to contend with is in every other way immeasurably more complex than that confronting the Platonists.

In formulating his theory of communicative action Habermas probes into the existential fusion of democratic principles/values with the aim of extracting from within whatever elements appear most conducive to operationalizing what he now redefines as "the proceduralist conception of deliberative politics". These elements identified, the theory in essence then attempts to re-fuse the useful normative extracts with the further aim of reintroducing them to their sources, which are also the two most popular forms of political practice in contemporary Western societies: liberalism and democracy. Habermas argues in effect that despite its obvious merits and past successes as a political system, the liberal-democratic form of governance has become exhausted; no longer can it adequately harmonize the complex of differences shaping most Western cultures today.

Habermas points to the liberal-democratic governance's emphasis on manufacturing a politico-cultural sphere wherein the state is understood as "an apparatus of public administration, and society [as] a system of market-structured interactions of private persons and their labour". The theorist points first to the fact that because liberals hold the rights of private, self-interested persons as superior to the aggregate interests of the collective, the democratic exercise insofar as the state is concerned becomes an increasingly diffuse and difficult act of mediating between these individual interests. However if, to paraphrase Habermas, these private interests became unified into a powerful enough politico-economic force, under the liberal schema this force is too often able to bring its collectivized concerns into direct conflict with the state—this potentially to the detriment of political society at large. What seems intended in Habermas' reasoning here is that, should the guardians of the liberal-democratic ideal allow such special-interest forces to continually reproduce themselves, the likely result is that whatever inequalities are present within modern multivocal societies are likewise prone to self-reproduction.

This yet sketchy state of affairs, though thus far intended to depict Canadian-style liberal-democracy, is also very true of American republicanism. For Habermas, the American republican interprets democracy in much the same way that the Canadian liberal does, as this interpretation also takes a market-centered approach to the organization of political society. Indeed here, more than anywhere else in the industrialized world today, can be witnessed the powerful influence of competing special interests (and capital), an influence which dominates the politico-cultural sphere and much to the exclusion of the general citizenry. Nevertheless Habermas recognizes in the republican model a superior capacity for concerted resistance to special interest power, a resistance which under the more liberal-inclined Canadian interpretation is either more easily thwarted or ignored outright owing to the latter model's more favourable disposition to the superiority of individual rights.

According to Habermas, with the republican model "politics is not exhausted by [the] mediating function", a mandate forced on the liberal model by the agglomerates of competing private/special interests. Instead, because the republican model is normatively "constitutive for the socialization process as a whole" it allows for all participants of "quasi-natural solidary communities [to] become aware of their dependence on one another". This quasi-communal awareness, premised as it is on shared pre-political values, opens the way for the further development of the aforehinted "existing relations of reciprocal recognition". This existential relationship built of common cause will, in theory, foster the environment for more effective union(s) among these "free and equal consociates". Habermas calls this eventual consociation the "autonomous...civil society", and which he sees already existing and operating as described but effectively practiced only by the special interests capable of bringing enough force to bear on the administration. What this says is that a similar challenge can be put forward by the usually excluded portions of society, who as individual citizens are as entitled to the rights of political practice under civil law as, say, a corporation. With a unified and deliberate voice, then, any agglomerate of these individuals (not just the powerful market interests) is theoretically capable of swaying the administration as long as such is exercised within the limits of civil law.

However, while this normative superiority of the republican model may allow for easier access to (and as such can exert more influence upon) the administration/state, it does not give one enough freedom to detach greatly from the alluring ideals of liberalism. In fact, Habermas takes great pain in instructing us that the legacy of the French Revolution is still with us in a big way, which is also to say that the liberal ideals of liberty, equality, fraternity, (and private property) are seemingly here to stay. Habermas tells us that these values born out of the 1789 revolution, along with the institutions (oligopolies, monopolies, etc.) enshrining them, have since "exploded worldwide", and further that this explosion has left but one compound question. That is, how do we "reconcile equality with liberty, unity with diversity, or the right of the majority with the right of the minority".

American social theorist Cornel West has also been grappling with this question of reconciliation. According to West, "the pervasive processes of objectification, rationalization and commodification [of civic life] throughout the world" has produced a state of affairs in American democratic practice tantamount to a "self-referential" crisis, one not dissimilar to the self-reproduction Habermas spoke of. West traces the roots of this crisis back to 1492 and Europe's first encounters with America. In outlining his view on the subtle interconnectedness of his three pervasive processes West, like Habermas, recognizes the lasting impact that such historical processes has had on today's western psyche, going on to propose a particular strategy for "substantially alleviating" the force of this yet largely unrecognized crisis.

In a 1993 essay titled 'The New Cultural Politics of Difference' West informs that the first process, objectification, "consists of transforming human beings into manipulable objects". The process "promotes the notion that people's actions have no impact on the world, that we are but spectators" and not at all capable of active participation in "making and remaking ourselves" in the holistic sense of a larger society. In short, since the late 15th century western societies have been lulled into believing that the advances made by capitalism, the individual rights provided under liberal law, and in general the comforts afforded by the idea of democracy together have served to eradicate any real urgent need to deal with the social inequities borne out of these advances, rights and comforts.

The second of West's processes, rationalization, "expands [the] bureaucratic hierarchy" and imposes "impersonal rules and regulations in order to increase efficiency", and which, ultimately, "leads to disenchantment with past mythologies". In interpreting West, the big concern with the process of rationalization is that the disenchantment created by the impersonal norms further marginalizes segments of American society. These norms serve to promote a "reflexive" detachment, a self-disenfranchisement if you will, from the rigorous scientism which has been used to rid ourselves of the "deadening, flat, banal ways of life" adhered to, suggestively, since Plato. Here too it might be inferred that scientism—that process of rationalization which has guided western societies' progress for the past four hundred years or so—has served magnificently to suppress the inner conflict perpetually brewing between and amongst these societies' peoples.

Finally West argues that the process of commodification "augments market forces in the form of oligopolies and monopolies that centralize resources and powers that promote cultures of consumption that view people as mere spectatorial consumers and passive citizens". In combining these now psychologically entrenched forces of objectification, rationalization and commodification West concludes that today "these processes cannot be eliminated", but he nonetheless remains convinced that with a certain diligence "their pernicious effects can be substantially alleviated".

Now whereas Habermas clearly understands West's "processes" and advocates a counter-project guided or regulated by normative standards, West sees the budding of a different kind of politics, an agitational kind that aims "to thrash the monolithic and homogeneous". This thrashing, to paraphrase West, calls for outright rejection of the "abstract, general and universal" principles that have so captivated American society and, indeed, western civilization on a whole. West's "new politics" aims to re-invent history—to re-contextualize progress—by closely reexamining the contingencies and variables that European scientism has so painstakingly and perfectly glossed over for the past four centuries. The new politics aims to emphasize and physically tackle the myriad cultural differences that constitute American society today. How does West see this happening?

In order to effectively address the "diversity, multiplicity and heterogeneity" of American society West advances a program of incessant agitation, a rigorous, direct, personal assault on the hegemonic institutional structures now fundamentally woven into western liberal-democratic politics. As West puts it, the new politics of difference

> [Embraces] the distinct articulations of talented...contributors to culture who desire to align themselves with demoralized, demobilized, depoliticized and disorganized people in order to empower and enable social action...to enlist collective insurgency for the expansion of freedom, democracy and individuality.

Explicit in this excerpt is a clamor for a forgotten belligerence, a strident call for an abrupt re-reawakening to the true repressive nature of European-style political development, which is deceptively latent in contemporary American [and Canadian?] political culture. And although West's essay focuses primarily on the plight of the American Blacks, he, like Habermas, acknowledges the intersubjective nature of the western life-world, the inextricable linkages formed amongst the innumerable nationalities and ethnicities now dissolved into a single pseudo-consciousness. Also like Habermas, West believes that this fact makes it all the more crucial that the new politician of difference—an agitator West labels the Critical Organic Catalyst—find and maintain effective ways to bring pressure to bear onto the state. The Critical Organic Catalyst (COC) will create this pressure by identifying and collectivizing the "concrete, specific and particular" needs and virtues of those persons continually forced to the margins of political activity. For West, however, his COC needs to do more than merely organize his followers for the communicative action/deliberative democracy supposedly afforded by the Habermasian public sphere. Here the artistic, articulate and avant-garde COC must be capable of convincing these followers of the never-ending needfulness of keeping "their bodies and lives" tuned for the occasional opportunities to accelerate their consciousness re-awakening.

Indeed, West's Critical Organic Catalyst will recognize that although many of the repressive relations that he/she confronts will remain rooted in systems designed to serve the capitalist elite, unlike yesterday today's politico-cultural agents are made more aware of the true meaning(s) behind concepts such as age, class, education, gender, nationhood, race, and a host of other concerns that are not of a specifically economic nature. What this means is that, whereas, say, the post-1789 pre-1950 western political culture was dominated by concerns of economic growth and stability, today's culture is more enamoured of the necessity to recognize cultural difference. This does not mean that the COC turns a blind eye to the fact that "the majority of inhabitants on the globe [are] smothered by international communication cartels and repressive postcolonial elites...or starved by austere World Bank and IMF politics that subordinate them." On the contrary, West sees these very institutions (oligopolies and monopolies) as "vital areas of analysis". As such, it is the job of the COC to infiltrate these institutions, bringing into them a new sociopolitical consciousness and apprising those in charge of "this new cultural terrain" that is the real life-world today.

Like West—who calls for a coming-to-terms with our historical upbringings—Habermas, as earlier noted, harks back to the ideals left us by the French Revolution for inspiration. In Habermas' mind, West's concerns regarding demoralized, demobilized, depoliticized and disorganized people, people whose progressive efforts are everywhere co-opted by "the systemic imperatives of differentiated economic and administrative systems" , are very real and hard-felt concerns. But unlike West, who clearly sees the propensity for these "systems" to remain perpetually "circumscribed by immoral patriarchal, imperial, jingoistic and xenophobic constraints", Habermas is of the belief that the integrated dynamics of these differentiated systems have "for the first time...created the conditions for a cultural activism stripped of all high-cultural privileges and stubbornly eluding administrative manipulation."

3. Actualizing the Problem

Now although not calling for the immediate and rigorous agitation advocated by West, Habermas nevertheless reminds us that the republican consciousness bequeathed by the French Revolution "is not a possession we simply accept as our fortunate inheritance from the past. Rather, it is a project we must carry forward in the consciousness of a revolution both permanent and quotidian". In other words, the masses of today's western societies must keep this revolutionary consciousness alive; the masses must not allow themselves to be lulled further into the false security of the customary, which, to interpret Habermas, might be that quietly felt "mourning over the failure of a project that nonetheless cannot be relinquished". However Habermas is somewhat ambiguous whether this new politics of cultural awareness reflects only the commercially and strategically "exploited power of the beautiful"', an ambiguity spawned by what he calls "a social intercourse characterized by both socially de-differentiated forms of expression and individualized lifestyles". This ambiguity is, of course, the direct progeny of the combined liberal and republican ideas of democracy, intermeshed as they are and manifest in West's earlier processes of objectification, rationalization, and commodification. Indeed, all one has to do (if I understand the two texts at all) is look around York University on a given day of the week to see this mass of individualized lifestyles, each imitating the other as they strive to become different from the other.

Also like West Habermas believes that it is up to the intellectuals—that coterie of capable and "usually privileged" souls around us—to lead the process of excavating ourselves out of our present flux. But where the two thinkers can be seen to differ is in this: whereas West calls upon the intellectuals (his COCs) still on the periphery, that is, those on-the-outside-looking-in, Habermas calls on those intellectuals on the inside, those in control of the processes but who are somehow unwilling or as yet unable to see out. Habermas calls on these insider-intellectuals to rethink their conservatism, to renounce their long-standing hegemony on the traditions of power, that is to say, to relinquish their hold on the means of cultural production, a production which subsumes and distorts both the liberal and republican sociopolitical public spheres. This rethinking will perhaps allow the intellectuals opportunity to expose their ethical consciousness long enough to recognize West's disempowered and disabled cultural mass. Habermas' ultimate aim is therefore to determine how "a resonant political culture"—that legacy of the French Revolution, which is (or can be) best understood by the intellectuals—might perhaps be made to meet the disenfranchised public multitude "half-way".

Speaking directly to "a leftist in the Federal Republic", Habermas emphasizes that "the principles of the Constitution will not take root in our souls until reason has assured itself of its orienting, future-directed contents. It is only as a historical project that constitutional democracy points beyond its legal character to a normative meaning—a force at once explosive and formative". Habermas informs us too that "the ideological struggles between democrats and liberals, between socialists and anarchists, between conservatives and progressives...display basic patterns of argumentation that are still instructive today". Here we do not have time to discuss precisely what Habermas says these ideological struggles entail that is "instructive", but their effects are as popular in his Europe as they are in West's America. You might recall that earlier we spoke of a distorted political public sphere, of existentially manipulated presuppositions in need of recognition, reversal, collectivization and actualization, and of a certain nonorganizable practice. We also spoke of a need to maintain meaning in political practice and of an unavoidable replication of difficulties. Habermas' deliberative democracy, via our normative accesses to the communicative sphere, hopes to address these concerns.

Habermas expounds also that, for contemporary Western societies, their governments' "integrative capabilities...continue to diminish under the pressure of regional movements, on the one hand, and worldwide corporations and transnational organizations, on the other". Nations today face what he calls a legitimation crisis, which is the result of a state's inability to effectively mediate between the interests of the commercial class and the needs of the masses. The pressure exerted on governments everywhere in the face of the alleged globalization phenomenon, according Habermas, is forcing together "into a single process", into an "abstract system of reference", all the indelible fragments we know today as constituting world history. Any "future-oriented action considered capable of uncoupling the present from the past", capable of de-differentiating differences long enough so as to recognize our intersubjective dependence, must therefore be initiated in the sphere of communicative action. This last is so because

> As the equal participation of all citizens in the political will-formation was laboriously institutionalized according to the rule of law, the contradictions built into the concept of popular sovereignty itself became manifest. The people from whom all governmental authority is supposed to derive does not compose a subject with will and consciousness. It only appears in the plural, and as a people it is capable of neither decision nor action as a whole. In complex societies, even the most earnest endeavors at political self-organization are defeated by resistant elements originating in the stubborn systemic logics of market and administrative power... Democratization now works to overcome not genuinely political forms of resistance but rather the systemic imperatives of differentiated economic and administrative systems.

In classical democratic theory, Habermas reminds us, it is assumed that the society can—by way of its "sovereign legislature"—influence itself. It was assumed that through popular participation the will of the people would be converted into laws, which in turn would "program the implementation and application" of these laws, leaving the administrative and juridical processes the reciprocal task of ensuring a more or less equal redistribution of the general benefit qua security supposedly embodied in these laws. Habermas calls this circumlocution the "action-upon-self" process—the same self-referential, reflexive process spoken of earlier, and which republican style democracy still (supposedly?) normatively allows for.

West, however, contraposes this by suggesting that the moral consciousness which once underpinned the Habermasian action-upon-self is today too heavily constrained by bureaucratic logic; no amount of internal deliberation could promise that this morality would permeate downward to the level where it should be best received—i.e., to those most reliant on that bureaucratic logic: the general civil society. West attempts to illustrate the practical difficulty in realizing the Habermasian view when he analyzes the logic of a scheme put forward by the mid-nineteenth century literary critic, Mathew Arnold, whose "discursive strategy"

> [W]ould be lodged in the educational...apparatuses of modern societies as they contained and incorporated the frightening threats of an arrogant aristocracy and especially of an "anarchic" working-class majority... [Ideals] of disinterested, dispassionate and objective inquiry would regulate this new secular cultural production, [and] justifications for the use of state power to quell any threats to the survival and security of this culture...widely accepted.

If we here accepted the Habermasian thesis that the effects of the French Revolution are still with us today, then we must be willing to accept—or at least be open to the possibility—that the "sensibilities of cautious reform and fear of anarchy" held by the period's arrogant aristocracy are also still alive. To be sure, the question can be propitiously raised here as to why this acceptance must be made, and to which an equally propitious reply might be the question: Whose sensibilities are responsible for determining "justifications for the use of state power" in America today? Is it not, for the most part, the very fear of an "anarchic working-class majority" which gives Habermas' republican America the peculiar stigma of being the society with the highest incarceration rate in the universe? One could argue "Yes!"; for the aristocratic fear of anarchy may indeed have become synonymous with the capitalist/liberal-democratic need for incarceration.

A significant difference between Mathew Arnold's life-world and ours, as suggested before, is that today the concentration of capitalist special-interest power has almost totally demobilized and depoliticized North American culture. This general degeneration of the meaning of civil society was gradually realized through "an interlocking affiliation among the emerging middle classes" over the course of the last few centuries. The "homogenizing of cultural discourse in the educational...networks, and a state advanced enough in its policing techniques to safeguard it" thus became the working mechanism of the Arnoldian scheme. West concludes here by saying that those most fit to carry out this "grand endeavor of cultural renewal" were to be the "detached individuals willing to shed their parochialism, provincialism and class-bound identities" in the broader interest of spreading Eurocentric maleness.

West admits that in today's world, where the Arnoldian dream is definitely alive—a world in which "most of the resources, wealth and power are centered in huge corporations and supportive political elites"—his cultural politics of difference may appear utopian, especially when considered in light of state-supported [neo]liberal retrenchment. Indeed, governments today are not afraid to or restrained in any way from attacking social service programs instituted in the early post-WWII years. This attack on civil society is of course fuelled by the heavy-handedness of transnational corporations who seem intent on pushing the liberal-oriented market ideology of legal rights to its limits. Beyond this West emphasizes the "growing disintegration and decomposition of civil society'", with families, schools and entire communities put on the chopping block, not to mention the "buildups of military budgets" to reinforce the perception of necessary protection against the resultant decrepit, anarchic citizenry.

To conclude, then, might the Habermasian vision of a communicative/deliberative democracy not now seem even more utopian than West's faith in the potentialities of his Critical Organic Catalyst? Can West's COC (and his/her associates) mobilize a society that is as politically dispassionate as the one he says exists in America, and the one I have said exists in Canada? How far, we might also ask, can West's COC agitate before it becomes necessary to bring bodies and lives to bear on the state?

For Habermas, this suggested necessity is a clearly already-dissipated likelihood. We will recall him saying, for example, that in complex societies such as America, "even the most earnest endeavors" at generating this kind of spontaneous force are thwarted by the "resistant elements originating in the stubborn systemic logics of market and administrative power". On this view the battle for real democracy is no longer waged with fists or guns, as the process "now works to overcome not genuinely political forms of resistance but rather the systemic imperatives of differentiated economic and administrative systems". It is clear that by genuinely political Habermas refers to the real forms of resistance used in 1789 France, which is to say fists, guns and stubborn ideology. Does it really matter, then, whether the method to realizing a democratic polity is Habermas' deliberate communicative action, or West's COC agitation? Perhaps it does matter! Why?

Despite that many today will likely consider as far-fetched West's reference to "ordinary people" putting their bodies and lives on the line, there are realities—many of them economic—capable of thwarting even the most rational and deliberative mind of its agentic capacity. While both Habermas and West recognize and accept the mystifying power of market-driven liberal ideology, neither seems ready to admit that the acute consumerist consciousness created by that ideology may prove a better unifying force than the sort of cultural harmonization that they both, in varying degree, argue for. Indeed, it is quite possible that the intersubjective dynamic mediating within western political societies today has already eradicated the possibility of any kind of organized, mass-scale physical confrontation such as that played out in 1789 France.

But then to accept this premise is also to deny Habermas' intellectuals the necessary reason to continue their search (assuming they are) for a more genuine, inclusive democracy. And by a more genuine, inclusive democracy is meant that bureaucratic, parasitic, unprincipled, exploitative, etc. body of persons reproducing itself within the comfortable confines of what West earlier referred to as a "monolithic and homogeneous" political culture. But then again, and keeping in mind all that has been said about the practical difficulties in identifying distinctly politico-cultural differences today, should it at all matter which of these intellectuals are at the forefront of the project of change that both Habermas and West demand? I suggest that it doesn't matter, since either way "the intellectuals" are today the ones best capable of engaging in the kind of sustained public-sphere activity that both theorists say is needed. And so I ask you: Where do we go from here?

References

Habermas, J. 2001 "Contributions to a discourse theory of law and democracy", in S. Seidman, and J.C. Alexander, *The New Social Theory Reader, Contemporary Debates.* London and New York: Routlege, pp. 31-38.

West, C. 1993 'The New Cultural Politics of Difference', in R. Ferguson, M. Gever, Trinh Minh-ha and C. West, *Out There: Marginalization and Contemporary Cultures*. Cambridge, MA: MIT Press